# The Global Economy

## CONNECTING THE ROOTS
## OF A HOLISTIC SYSTEM

DR. DENISE R. AMES

# Acknowledgments

This book had been evolving for many years prior to when I started to actually sit down and write about the global economy. I would first like to thank Frank Beurksens for introducing me to the topic back in the 1970s. He patiently described options and futures trading to me until I finally grasped a semblance of the topic. I found during a trip to the Soviet Union in 1989 with a group of agricultural economists that the global economy was not an exact science, and I could hold my own in a discussion of the topic with them.

I continued my exploration of the global economy in the 1990s as part of my research and teaching in world history. I discovered that the economy changed through time, like other cultural elements. Our current organization of the global economy is not at all etched in stone and is certainly subject to continuous change. Special thanks to my thesis and dissertation advisor and friend, Professor Joseph Grabill, for helping to guide and mentor me through this exploration.

My teaching, research and interest in the global economy continued through the 2000s as I conducted workshops, lectures, and classes for the lay public and educators on the subject. I extend a thank you to all those who listened to my ramblings and insights on the global economy and to those who offered suggestions for improvement.

I started to write this book on the global economy in 2010. It was a formidable journey that I was, nonetheless, happy to embark upon. In this process I especially want to thank my partner in the Center for Global Awareness, Nancy Harmon, for her encouragement, remarks, and crisp editing. Without her unfailing support this book would not have been completed. I would also like to thank Margaret Govoni for her editing and input and special thanks to our Program Director Sarah Wilkinson. Thanks to several readers who provided helpful comments, feedback, and editing: Cliff Wilke, Bob Riley, Sally Jacobsen, and Phil Fisk. Thanks to Daryl Fuller for his creative graphic design of the book and cover. And a final thanks to my husband, Jim Knutson, for his encouragement and listening.

# CONTENTS

# PREFACE

## *The Global Economy: Connecting the Roots of a Holistic System*

My first immersion into examining different economic systems took place on a trip to the Soviet Union in 1989 with a group of agricultural economists. I accompanied my husband who was in the grain marketing business and had a good grasp of economics. I was perplexed by the site of an immaculate modern subway system, complete with chandeliers, in Moscow, while in the countryside, horse-drawn wagons of elderly women with hoes in hand went out to work the fields, and tractors sat idly by in a state of disrepair in the rickety sheds. I was also stunned by the vibrant black market, where anything, even the coveted caviar, could be bought and sold at a reasonable price, while the state-owned grocers showcased empty shelves, displaying a prized cow-tongue when available. The beautiful production of the classic ballet Swan Lake showed the system worked in some ways, but in others, such as the shabby tractors, it failed miserably. The American economists were unable to explain this discrepancy very well, except for a standard statement about the virtues of the capitalist system.

I continued my fascination with the global economy in the 1990s when I was teaching undergraduate U.S. and world history and working towards my doctoral degree at Illinois State University in Normal, Illinois. Since my students overwhelmingly liked current issues, I wanted to include more up-to-date information about both the world and the U.S. Globalization was the buzzword of the day and frequently in the news, so it was a topic that I investigated with gusto. At first glance, most of what was written referred to globalization in glowing terms. The increasing integration of economies and people around the world promised a rosy future of increased prosperity, not only for Americans but for those around the world who embraced innovation, an entrepreneurial spirit, and the desire to make a better life. If people were more connected through transportation and communication networks, it stood to reason that the world would be a more peaceful place. Communism had collapsed in the Soviet Union and Eastern Europe in the early 1990s and, therefore, the capitalistic economic system and democratic political system appeared to be victorious over their communist Cold War rivals. It all sounded great! As proof of the victory, the newscasts of the day showed the newly-democratic Russians clamoring for American-style blue jeans and the rising middle class youth of China lining up for hours at McDonald's just to get a Big Mac. Globalization was often equated with the spreading of American style values and consumption habits. The closed system of communism had given way to open markets, free expression, and democratic ways.

Many in America thought that globalization meant that the rest of the world, especially the former communist world, had discovered the wonders of the American way of life and were eager to embrace it. Newscasts showed exuberant formerly communist youth dancing to western music in newly-formed night clubs, complete with strobe lights and pulsating rhythms. Others thought that the youth of China were willing to risk their lives for American-style democracy and freedom, as witnessed on cable television when a lone student demonstrator bravely faced a formidable Chinese military tank ready to crush him at any moment in the June 4, 1989, demonstration at Tiananmen Square in Beijing. The business section of any American book store in the 1990s portrayed globalization as a "win-win" proposition with untold profits for entrepreneurs to easily earn with a little initiative and little risk. New internet start-up companies, such as Netscape and Amazon, popped up almost daily and promised riches for the founders, as well as for those who invested in their companies. Bill Gates, who founded Microsoft in 1975, was the hero of the 1990s. He was the richest person in the world, and his entrepreneurial spirit and work ethic were the envy of all those who aspired to follow his path to fame and fortune. We were all exhorted to get on the globalization train, since it was an inevitable process that could not be held back by those fearful of change. It was an optimistic time.

As often happens with dazzling new trends, the globalization craze of the 1990s turned out to be too good to be true. I realize that many Americans and others were able to make a good living or even fortunes from high-tech start-ups and more expanded business opportunities. I acknowledge that the appeal of the "American way of life" is a dream many people around the world aspire to. But I knew that globalization meant more than that. To understand globalization, I needed to dig a little deeper than a CNN newscast or an article written in the pro-business *Fortune* magazine. After the initial euphoria melted away, another side to globalization that hadn't been told began to emerge. Although some people were profiting from globalization, on the other hand, it was already adversely affecting other people's lives. Many manufacturing workers in the U.S. were losing their well-paid, secure jobs that companies were outsourcing to Mexico or China. Small farmers in the rural heartland of America, where I lived at the time, were being swallowed up by large corporate farming operations that had better political connections and enormous economies of scale and were able to fatten their bottom profit line with exorbitant agricultural subsidies funded by American taxpayers. There were also dire effects on the environment that were a direct result (and some indirect) from economic globalization. Tax cuts and new economic rules made it easier for the wealthy to profit from the system, while stagnant wages and higher living costs were squeezing the middle and working classes. As I dug a little deeper into the topic of globalization, I found that it was much more complex than was simply communicated in the media.

Another viewpoint about globalization burst into public consciousness in November 1999, when 40,000 "anti-globalization" activists converged in Seattle, Washington to protest against the World Trade Organization (WTO) Ministerial Conference, in what became known as the "Battle in Seattle." The protesters ranged from labor unionists to students to religious-based groups to anarchists who wanted to overthrow the government. The media lumped the groups together under the umbrella of anti-globalization protesters, although what they were protesting and the tactics they used varied considerably. Unfortunately, a small percentage of the protesters turned violent, and the police responded with force to quell the disturbances. Many Americans were glued to their TV as angry young protesters randomly smashed store windows, damaged cars, and taunted police. The public linked all those who questioned globalization with violent acts. The media helped to create this distorted message by continuously showing the violent acts committed by angry young protesters; the peaceful protesters, some sporting gray hair and sensible shoes, were of secondary importance. But the protests, despite their violent component, had the effect of raising awareness about the other side of globalization, and I and others became interested in finding out more.

My research into the global economy in the 1990s helped me refine my model for teaching world history. What became apparent was that at the turn of the millennium, a new force was emerging on the world stage that was a noticeable break from the past. In my book *Waves of Global Change: A Holistic World History*, I identify this evident break as the Global Wave. According to my holistic world history model, there have been four other waves or major transformations in our human history, and the Global Wave represents a fifth wave. The other four waves – Communal, Agricultural, Urban and Modern – all represent major discontinuities in our human story. The Global Wave is such a significant transformation as to warrant the distinction of representing a fifth significant change. Thus, the global economy that was changing in the 1990s was morphing into a momentous force shaping many aspects of world society and defining the Global Wave. Therefore, the phenomenon widely known as globalization was more than just a mere business craze or a way to sell more hamburgers around the world; it was a multi-faceted process that continues to be in the making.

Many of you have possibly observed the changes that are presently occurring or have actually experienced the changes yourself. Perhaps you or someone in your family has lost a job as a result of the latest downturn in the economy, or perhaps your company has outsourced your job to India or China. If you are a student, perhaps your teachers have admonished you to study harder, since millions of well-educated Chinese students are your global competitors for future jobs. Or perhaps you realize that almost all the clothing you buy is made in China, Indonesia, India, or other places besides the U.S. Or your house has declined in value to the point that you owe more than it is worth, a phenomenon known as being "underwater." Or you realize that our dependence on oil to fuel the economy contributed to British Petroleum's (BP) horrendous oil spill in the Gulf of Mexico in 2010. Or perhaps you are a member of the global elite, and you have made a fortune by expanding your national business into a global business that has tripled its profits. These events are signs of major and disruptive changes that are occurring today. So, you may ask, how is the global economy related to all these changes that are taking place in the Global Wave? That is the very question we will be exploring in this book.

A study of the global economy will not be an easy task. It holds many contradictions and uneasy tensions that challenge our way of looking at the world. This book does not offer easy answers or solutions listed 1 through 10. Instead, I have designed this book to be an examination of the global economy today as it really works. If you are reading this book, you most likely have experienced the benefits that capitalism has brought to your life: an education, the latest technology, communication devices, constant entertainment, plentiful food, medical care to extend your life, and a social safety net to keep you out of total destitution. But just because capitalism has had successes in the past, and many in the present, it does not mean that all is well with the system. We will uncover many of the failures of the capitalist economic system along with its successes

Most of us know very little about the global economy. I certainly didn't until I started to concentrate on contemporary global issues in graduate school and my teaching career. Even then, it was hard to uncover the real workings of the global economy. It always seemed to be covered in a veneer of mistaken assumptions or by an intractable worldview that everyone seemed to accept as reality. But once I started to peel away the layers of veneer covering the real global economy, I was surprised to find that the reality was quite different from the commonly held assumptions. When President Clinton signed the North American Free Trade Association (NAFTA) in 1994, I thought free trade was good for everyone, just as our president claimed. We smugly laughed as a family when we headed to the malls in the mid-1990s to do our Christmas shopping, jokingly claiming that "we were helping the economy." When I first heard about global warming, I was confident that an engineer would invent a new technology to cut emissions, or that we would have cheap solar and wind energy by the time my children reached adulthood. I had some rethinking to do as I learned more about the global economy and uncovered some of the deep-seated assumptions that turned out to be untrue. I also learned that our worldview (see chapter 1) has a lot to do with how the global economy is structured. This rethinking has led me to question our whole global economic system.

As I contemplated writing a book about the global economy as part of the Global Awareness Program series (GAPs), I struggled with how to organize this massive topic. I wanted to simplify the information and put it into an order that readers could grasp. It seemed to me that when discussing the global economy, the general public used many vague terms and made false assumptions without basis. I thought people's perception of the global economy is like a wad of hard-as-a rock taffy, all stuck together and difficult to pull apart. So my goal in this book is to pull apart the taffy-like global economy so that we can see and identify some of the sticky strands. When I did this myself in order to write this book, I found that three dimensions to the global economy surfaced; each dimension is distinct but interconnected, as well. By organizing the global economy into these three dimensions – neoliberalism, economic globalization, and financialization – the wad of taffy is pulled wide apart.

I have found in my research that there are very few books that give a general, holistic overview of the global economy. They may concentrate on what is wrong with the economy or the disastrous financial crisis of 2008, but they do not give us a firm grasp of why this turmoil all started in the first place. Blaming it all on greedy bankers or clueless homeowners doesn't seem to get to the roots of the issue. This book attempts to give an overview of the global economy today. What are the different roots of the global economy and how do they connect? Once we have a better idea of how the global economy is organized then we are better equipped to critique it, see the fault lines, and propose solutions.

I like to think that I am a fitting person to write and teach about the global economy. What gives me this confidence? My illustrious career as an investment banker on Wall Street? My PhD in global economics from Harvard College? My tenure teaching in "third world" countries? My career in the Treasury Department advising the Secretary of the Treasury during times of economic crisis? Well, none of these remotely apply. Compared to many who are writing about the global economy, such as Nobel Laureate Paul Krugman, my credentials are modest. But, before you slam this book shut or turn off your Kindle, I do have unique reasons for writing about the global economy. I do have the degreed credentials, I have taught in the classroom for many years, I have conducted ample research about the topic, I have personally experienced many of the wrenching economic changes that have taken place since the end of World War II, and I am able to place the global economy into an understandable framework.

Since I have witnessed many of the changes that have taken place over the years, I will chronicle some of my experiences and reflections in this book to give you a personal account of the changes. I encourage you to do the same. Ask others you know about what they experienced during the high unemployment era of the 1970s or the economic changes they witnessed during the Reagan era of the 1980s or the difficulty of finding a well-paying job in the 2010s. You are bound to get interesting insights and a wide reaction to the events. Everyone has his or her own story.

I searched to find an apt metaphor for the subtitle of this book on the global economy. I came up with several different ones, such as a puzzle, a network, a tsunami, a stew, and even taffy. Even though I used some of them in explaining different topics in the book, none resonated with me as a subtitle. Then, in the fall of 2012, my husband and I visited a remote cabin in the mountains of Chama, New Mexico, for a few days of relaxation. We took long hikes along a mountain trail, and we felt a sense of awe and wonder as we gazed upon groves of majestic aspen trees clinging to the mountainous terrain, just about ready to turn to shimmering gold. It was then that it came to me in a flash; why not use the aspen trees as part of the cover and subtitle of the book. The roots, of course, are intertwined below the earth's surface, and the aspen roots are unique in that they are all connected. The global economy is like the aspen trees. The roots of the global economy form an interdependent system of connections below the surface, while supporting a maze of what looks like individual facets of the global economy above the surface. A global corporation, such as Bank of America, seems as though it is a separate entity, traded on the stock exchange with the symbol BAC as its identifying stock ticker. But below the surface, Bank of America is intricately connected to many parts of the global economy, such as money market funds, government regulations, foreign investments, debt, shareholders, CEO compensation, and so on. Thus, the subtitle of the book was born: Connecting the Roots of a Holistic System. Thinking of the global economy as an interconnected system is the purpose of this book.

So please join with me in the adventure of examining the global economy. I hope you will find this holistic approach to the global economy a journey that is challenging but worthwhile.

## FEATURES OF THE BOOK

Chapter 1, The Global Economy: An Overview, offers an introduction to the organization of the global economy along with a definition of important terms and concepts, such as state capitalism, core and periphery, West and modern, and others. It distinguishes between the various forms of capitalism, such as neoliberalism and managed capitalism. A brief overview of a systems thinking approach used in this book is given, along with a look at five worldviews – indigenous, modern, fundamentalist, globalized, and transformative.

Chapter 2, Historical Roots of the Global Economy, traces the roots of capitalism from 1500 onward. The first phase, commercial capitalism (1500-1750), evolves into industrial capitalism beginning in Britain around 1750. Capitalism expands and splinters in the tumultuous 20th century, yet survives. During the crisis of the 1970s, conservative business leaders steered capitalism to its neoliberal form. The various forms of capitalism are highlighted along with their repercussions on the world economy.

In chapter 3, The Neoliberal Stew: A Dozen Essential Ingredients, the turn to neoliberal restructuring that occurred in the U.S. in the 1970s is investigated by examining 12 essential ingredients in the "neoliberal stew." The 12 ingredients include free trade, privatization, deregulation, push for small government, supply side economics, lower taxes, deficit reduction, faith in markets, support of corporations and the financial sector, suppression of labor, celebration of individualism, and spread neoliberalism.

In chapter 4, The Impact of Neoliberalism in the United States: Ten Consequences, the effects of neoliberalism are examined. The 10 consequences are reduction of the local economy, unbridled economic growth, rampant consumerism, increased commodification, concentration of corporate power, rise of externalized costs, build-up of debt, emasculation of labor, widening social inequality, and ascension of dollar democracy.

Chapters 5, The Economic Globalization Puzzle: Ten Pieces, looks at economic globalization from an interacting systems perspective. The 10 interacting pieces are a reduction of local communities and self-reliance, economic growth, a promoting network, rules of economic globalization, privatization, commodification, concentration of power, specialization, the labor squeeze, and military hegemony.

In chapter 6, Evaluating the Impact of Economic Globalization, three criteria are used in the evaluation: the impact on the environment, the growing socio-economic gap, and human well-being. A comparison between two economically different nations – the Democratic Republic of the Congo and Bhutan – rounds out the chapter.

Chapter 7, The Financial Sector of the Global Economy, begins with a brief overview and then highlights the financial sector's 10 fatal flaws: too big to fail banks, unchecked deregulation, the federal reserve, the real estate bubble, a mountain of debt, dicey financial products, speculation, moral hazard and lack of transparency, deceptive rating agencies, and bloated compensation plans.

In chapter 8, The Financial Sector: Crisis and its Aftermath, it begins with a look at patterns found in financial crises and examines several different ones through history. Next, the chain of events of the financial crisis of 2007-2008 are studied. Finally the response to the financial crisis is looked at through five responses: revolt, restore, react, reform, and rebuild.

Accompanying the book are carefully designed supplemental resources for educators and students, for those using the book in a study group, or for whoever wishes to examine this topic more closely. Please visit the Center for Global Awareness website at *www.global-awareness.org/global economy* or email us at *info@global-awareness.org* for more information.

**CHAPTER ONE**

# An Overview of the Global Economy

*"Think not forever of yourselves, O Chiefs, nor of your own generation.*
*Think of continuing generations of our families, think of our grandchildren*
*and of those yet unborn, whose faces are coming from beneath the ground."*

*Peacemaker, founder of the Iroquois Confederacy (ca. 1000 AD)*

## THE GLOBAL ECONOMY

Our global economy represents a paradox. The spread of capitalism as the dominant economic system and culture at this point in time represents in many ways the most successful system ever developed in world history in terms of providing for large numbers of individuals in relative and absolute comfort and even luxury. It has solved the problems of feeding large numbers of people (but not all) in an efficient way. It has provided unprecedented advances in health and medicine (but not for all) which allow billions of people to live longer and more productive lives than in the past. It has promoted the development of amazingly complex technological instruments and fostered a level of global communication and transportation without precedent. In many ways it has united people in common cultural pursuits as has no other culture. It has opened up the mysteries of the universe through scientific research and astonishing discoveries. It has promoted the dignity and worth of every individual as a universal value system. It has unlocked educational opportunities to billions of people who desire to learn about the world.[1]

Here lies the paradox. It remains to be seen when the balance sheet is tallied whether capitalism, despite all its breathtaking accomplishments, represents the epitome of "progress" that has been claimed in its honor. It has been undeniably creative, but it has also been indisputably destructive. Its failures are beginning to creep into our awareness, jolting us into a fear that perhaps our accomplishments are turning against us in a kind of hushed revenge. The environment is groaning under our huge and growing population who are demanding more and more of the earth's resources to satisfy the consumer life-style of a modern world. The industrial machine that has belched out products to make our lives easier and more comfortable is torturing the earth with its excesses. The signals are clear: our way of life is not agreeing with the earth, and she has the last word.

Yet with all the technological advancements and increase in food supply, it is clear that the world's population does not share them in any equitable measure; this unequal divide and unequal distribution of the world's resources remain one of the global economy's visible failures. For the vast majority of the world's population, jobs are scarcer for those in both the poor and rich countries, as wages decline in response to global competition. Despite our material comforts and pleasurable activities, there is a deep gloominess that affects many who have made capitalism the centerpiece of their economy and culture. The rush to the cities by many of the world's poor has not resulted in a better way of life for many of them. Could it be that our sense of well-being and innate desire for social connection have diminished in our pursuit of capitalism's bounty?

The rethinking about the global economy that I explained in the preface has led me to question our whole economic system. I see an economic system that is set up for a different period of time. It is outdated and no longer able to deal with the realities of the global situation today. All of the economic systems that provide the foundation for our global economy today – from capitalism to communism – grew out of the 18th and 19th century modern ideologies. These economic ideologies have served their purpose: they have provided a comfortable standard of living for many around the world, medical breakthroughs that have extended our lives, educational achievements that have expanded our knowledge, and technological wonders that have entertained us and enhanced some of our lives. But I contend that these economic ideologies have reached their limits. We had already seen the collapse of Soviet-style communism in the former Soviet Union and its Eastern European satellites in the early 1990s. The mixed economies (socialism and capitalism) are encountering difficulties in Europe. In 2008, free market capitalism (neoliberalism) experienced its most serious financial crisis since the Great Depression. The state capitalist economy of China is experiencing high growth rates but a population of 1.4 billion people weighs it down, along with possible environmental calamity, and an authoritarian communist party. The repercussions of all these negatives are yet unknown. You might ask, what will replace these economic systems? My honest answer is "I don't know." I doubt that neoliberalism will collapse as quickly as Soviet-style communism did, since the governments of neoliberal countries, including the U.S., are fairly stable and have somewhat of a handle on the economic controls. But the signs of instability are everywhere. The debt ceiling debacle in the summer of 2011 was a clear signal that below the rhetorical surface is a teetering American and global economy which is fueling the hotly contentious political rancor in Washington D.C. Europe was reeling, in the summer of 2012, under strict austerity measures imposed by individual nations, the policies of the European Union, and the main European creditor nation: Germany. Different political parties have different ways in which they want to "fix" the economy, but in my opinion, just patching up the old economy with band aids used in the past is not a viable option any longer. Perhaps the band aids will stop the bleeding of a wounded economy temporarily, but it is not a long term solution.

An economic system is needed that takes into consideration environmental sustainability, the huge social inequalities around the world, resource depletion, the straining of the waste absorption capacity of the earth, our burgeoning population, the unequal distribution of goods and services, and the malaise associated with the current global economy. If there is criticism of the neoliberal economic system, as I will be doing in this book, the first assumption is that the critic is advocating communism or socialism. But just because people are critical of neoliberalism doesn't mean they are automatically for socialism. In an interview about his views on socialism, noted environmentalist Bill McKibben plainly states the issues that I think should be at the forefront of the debate about the global economy.

*Bill McKibben* ..."I'm definitely not a laissez-faire libertarian capitalist. Is anyone anymore? But I'm not much of a socialist either, because both those faiths seem to me rooted in an earlier moment – a moment when we had some [environmental] margin. A moment when the problem was growth and how best to make it happen and share its fruits. That's not our problem anymore. Our problem is how to deal with an [environmental] crisis that will define our world for the foreseeable future....That world is necessarily going to be tougher. We will have to focus on essentials, like food and energy, far harder than in the past. I think we need to find our livelihoods more locally, reducing the inherent vulnerabilities that go with a heavily globalized economy. At the moment less than 1 percent of America works on the farm – that's a number that must rise. ... The only way to endure the transition will be with a renewed sense of community. The real poison of the past few decades has been the hyper-individualism that we've let dominate our political life... In the end, that has damaged our society, our climate and our private lives. The first and final hope we have is a resurgence of a politics that calls on us to work together."[2]

Therefore, I do not think that the present economic systems operating around the world are able to adapt to the present global realities. There are too many flaws in the different systems to make this adjustment. I want to be clear, though: I **do not** advocate a revolution that overthrows the whole system. I imagine that to be a real catastrophe and I would be irresponsible to advocate such a proposal. However, I believe change is needed, and if we are aware of the problems, it will help us to frame an economic system that is more in keeping with real human needs and the needs of the earth. But you may ask at this point, "What is the old system you refer to?" That is the very question that this book attempts to answer. I will attempt to flesh out the complexity of the global economy in understandable terms, so that you can get a better handle on it. I will do so through the lens that the present day global economy has serious flaws and is no longer a viable economic foundation. What kind of economic system will evolve to displace our current global economy? Although I touch upon economic alternatives at the end of chapter 8, this fascinating topic is left for another book. Let me first describe further what this book is about and then what this book is not about.

In our classrooms and our everyday life, what is learned is usually divided into separated subject matter for more in-depth study. Educators often use a post-hole approach, which means that you take an isolated topic and bore down into that particular topic as far as possible. The purpose is to learn as much as possible about a separate topic. This approach to learning certainly has its place; after all, I want my heart surgeon to be an expert on every aspect of the heart! But my argument is that students taking introductory classes or the general public should not have to be a degreed economist to understand what is going on in the world today. There is a place for "a big picture" approach to a topic. We should be able to look at a topic without being overwhelmed by all the details. In other words, we should be able to see the forest, not just the trees. We can examine a subject from a systems approach, and see all the interconnections and how all parts of the system interact. The global economy needs to use an interdisciplinary (or a better term, transdisciplinary) approach to be fully understood, which means that other relevant subjects such as history, sociology, psychology, politics, and ecology are necessary to describe and understand this multi-faceted global process.

What this book is not is a "textbook" on the global economy. I will leave that to the economic experts. But a book about the realities of the global economy should be available for the typical student or lay person today. I will include in this book economic concepts that I think are necessary for a better understanding of the topic, but I will not overburden you with concepts that do not enhance this understanding. I will make it my mission to provide you only with information that relates to the global economy. The purpose is to understand this global economy as an interconnected system rather than as a specific, separate topic. Let's get started into understanding more about the global economy.

**SEE THE FOREST, NOT JUST THE TREES.**
PHOTO DENISE AMES

### Questions to Consider

1. Do you think our global economy is structured according to an era of the past? Explain.

## Key Features of Globalization

1.  Integration of humans across the globe, more so than at any time in the past. Instantaneous high-speed communication devices with sophisticated digital technologies have revolutionized our relations with each other by dissolving former barriers of time and distance and providing new connections between people.

2.  Global Capitalism is the dominant (but not the only) economic system in the world, with almost all nations pulled into its economic web. National and local economies, regulated and protected by national and local governments, have been largely subsumed or face the threat of being subsumed into a globalized economy where multinational corporations make many of the rules and conduct the business of the world marketplace.

3.  Environmental Pressures and the health of the planet are a primary concern for global citizens regardless of national identity. This is a global issue that knows no national boundaries; viable solutions have to be made at a cooperative international level. We have already overshot sustainability levels; to avert disastrous consequences, dramatic changes must be made.

4.  Nations are no longer the only defining political entity. The nation still exists as a workable political organization, but shares its former sovereignty with other world organizations such as the United Nations (UN) and the World Trade Organization (WTO); regional organizations such as the African Union (AU) and European Union (EU); regional trade alliances like the North American Free Trade Association (NAFTA); human rights agencies

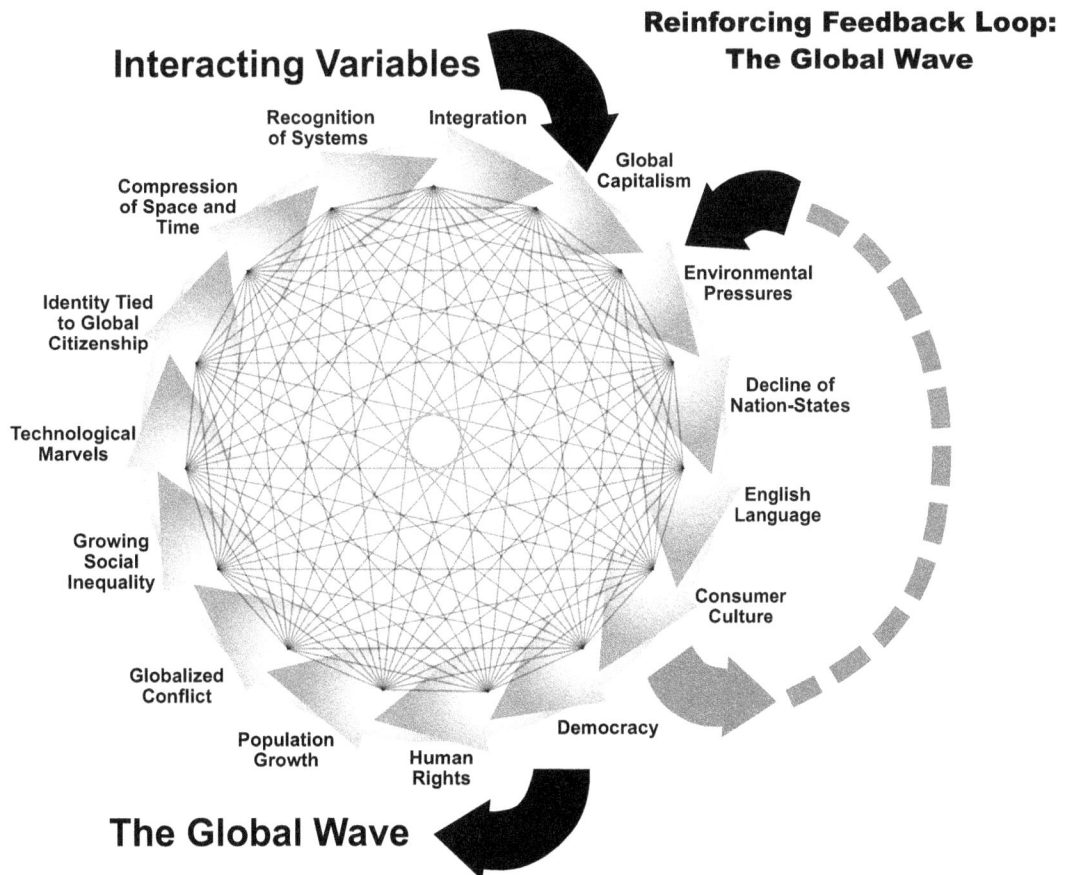

**Interacting Variables**

**Reinforcing Feedback Loop: The Global Wave**

Recognition of Systems
Integration
Global Capitalism
Compression of Space and Time
Environmental Pressures
Identity Tied to Global Citizenship
Decline of Nation-States
Technological Marvels
English Language
Growing Social Inequality
Consumer Culture
Globalized Conflict
Democracy
Population Growth
Human Rights

**The Global Wave**

## Key Features of Globalization (cont'd)

such as Amnesty International; and environmental watchdog groups like Greenpeace.

5. English is the language of business, commerce and education, and the unofficial language of global interaction. A common language acts as a unifying factor, and English is increasingly that universal language. The world's elites speak English in part because of the influence of the British in the 19th century and the hegemony of the U.S. in the 20th century.

6. Consumer Culture has become a dominant ideology. Led by the U.S., a vast entertainment and advertising sector has perpetuated and glamorized the notion of consumerism as a form of status and as a symbol of affiliation with modern culture. Consumerism promotes products as necessities that define individual identity. The automobile is a convenience and a symbol of personal freedom.

7. Democracy is promoted by the U.S. and others as a favored political structure in much of the world. Nations struggling to unify, stabilize, and participate in the world economy are encouraged to adopt democracy as a form of political organization.

8. Human Rights are being embraced by many nations across the globe as a universal cultural value. Although not the reality in about half the world, equality and justice for women, children, and non-elites, along with racial equality and protection from hate crimes, are becoming common moral, ethical standards to guide nations. The idea of social justice is increasingly accepted on a global level.

9. Population Growth in the 20th century has increased exponentially and is an urgent issue in the 21st century. Our current population and its consumption levels severely strain the carrying capacity of the earth. Will our earth be able to sustain 9 to 12 billion people, a number projected to occur around 2050?

10. Globalized Conflict is much different from the warfare between relatively equal nations in the Modern Wave. Conflict has become unpredictable, asymmetric, random, irrational, and volatile. Many different factors spark wars. Acts of violence directed towards the West are often called terrorism.

11. Social Inequality has increased between rich and poor within nations and among nations. This growing gap has concerned many around the world, but the causes and solutions are in dispute.

12. Technological Marvels have exploded since the 1990s. The positive effects of technological innovations have brought people around the world closer together, yet on the downside, technology has been dubbed the savior for all our social ills, a role that is bound to disappoint. The Internet, television, high-speed travel, cell phones, electronic social networks and other forms of sophisticated telecommunication devices link the world.

13. Identity Tied to Global Citizenship has resulted in a growing awareness of connections, commonalities, and differences among people of the world. Sometimes global citizens seek to sever that relationship, while at other times global citizens who relish connections across geographical and political boundaries wholeheartedly embrace it.

14. Compression of Space and Time extends across vast expanses of space and operates with reduced time constraints. As the time necessary to connect distinct geographical locations is reduced, distance or space undergoes compression. The speed of social activity alters the traditional notions of space and time, while also working to undermine the importance of local and national boundaries. High speed technology plays a pivotal role in the velocity governing human affairs.

15. Recognition of Systems means there is an increasing recognition that formerly autonomous events, actors, and institutions are all linked together as an interconnected system. No longer do separate and isolated solutions to problems work as well as viewing the whole process as a system.

## Globalization: A Definition

I have been using the term globalization freely in the opening pages; it is time to be more precise in its usage. Simply put, the term globalization describes the dramatic changes that are taking place today, but there are and have been many different definitions and interpretations of the term. It is a notoriously fuzzy concept, and has lots of interpretations and different meanings to different people. The term has been used in so many different ways it is difficult to come up with a useful definition. But here goes.

---

**Globalization** is a complex, dominant, multi-dimensional phenomenon that interconnects worldwide economic, political, cultural, social, environmental, and technological forces that transcend national boundaries. Greatly intensifying since the 1980s, it reflects the many ways in which people are being drawn together, not only by their own movements but also through the flow of goods, services, capital, labor, technology, ideas, and information. Globalization refers to the worldwide compression of space and time and the reduction of the state in importance. In globalization the world becomes a single place that serves as a frame of reference for everyone, and it influences the way billions of people around the world conduct their everyday lives.

---

## Economic Globalization

From the above list of features, it is clear that globalization has many different dimensions that are all integrated and interact together. In fact, my book *Waves of Global Change: A Holistic World History* describes in the last chapter – *The Global Wave* – the different dimensions of globalization. The dimension of globalization that we will be studying in this book is economic globalization. It is not only difficult but virtually impossible to separate out just the economics from this globalization process and study it alone and unconnected to the other dimensions. Instead, we will look at economic globalization as embedded within the system of globalization and one of the most important dimensions of this multi-faceted process. Thus, in this book economic globalization is studied as a system embedded within the larger system of globalization. We will examine economic globalization holistically, meaning that we will look at the relationship of the economy to society, politics, culture, the environment, technology, education, and other dimensions of globalization. All these dimensions interact and shape each other; hence, the approach is **holistic**.

When talking about the global economy, the term economic globalization is often used. It is a term that we hear all the time, but it means something different to almost every individual asked about it. It is one of those "**over-determined**" words. I tell people that I am writing about the global economy for students and they say that is a great idea because students need to know about economic globalization. I then ask them how they would define the term. Just about every person I ask gives me a different answer. The answers range from, "It is a way to make life better for people around the world" to "It is a conspiracy for corporations to get more money." Many say, "It is just the way the economy works today."

Let's next turn to a workable definition of economic globalization. Once again, like the term globalization, it has many different definitions that can often be conflicting and confusing. But I am offering "a" definition, not "the" definition, which means that it is just one of many.

### Questions to Consider

1. What does economic globalization mean to you? Before we go any further, it might be a good idea to jot down a few ideas about what you think economic globalization is all about.

---

**Economic globalization** refers to the increasing integration and expansion of the capitalist economy around the world. In this economic system, trade, investment, business, capital, financial flows, production, management, markets, movement of labor (although somewhat restricted), information, competition, and technology are carried out across local and national boundaries on a world stage, subsuming many national and local economies into one integrated economic system. There is a growing concentration of wealth and influence of multi-national corporations, huge financial institutions, and state-run enterprises.

---

Economic globalization, as already mentioned, is just one dimension of the globalization process. But when we describe the whole global economy there is more to it than just economic globalization. This can get confusing because economic globalization is often the term used to describe the whole global economy. But it is our job in this book to get to the roots of the global economy, which is composed of many different economic systems around the world that work together and apart. It is also composed of different trends, such as the increase of the financial sector that we will look at later. Let's first turn to a description of the different economic systems that exist today in the global economy.

## AN OVERVIEW OF ECONOMIC SYSTEMS

The definition of economic globalization mentions that the economic system is capitalist. But capitalism is not the only economic system in the world today. In fact, I would argue that it would be hard to find any two nations that have identical economic systems. There is great economic diversity. When you factor in the nations around the world that are at different economic stages of development, then you have increasing variability. But we cannot describe each individual nation's economic system; doing so would take thousands of pages and the project would certainly be beyond my abilities. Therefore, for simplicity's sake, once again, I have organized the economic systems of the world into two divisions: capitalism and socialism. Within these two divisions I differentiate neoliberal capitalism from managed capitalism, and within socialism I also describe its branch – communism. A fifth economic system has emerged in the first decade of the 21$^{st}$ century that combines elements of socialism and capitalism with authoritarian rule – state capitalism.

To explain the relationship of the five economic systems, I have placed them on a continuum. At one end are capitalist societies and at the other end of the continuum are communist or command economies and in the middle is state capitalism. In today's global economy, on the right end of the spectrum, are neoliberal economies, often called free trade or laissez-faire capitalism. Basically, these economies remove tariffs from imports and exports, and limit government regulation of the economy. Located somewhere in the middle right of the continuum are managed capitalism societies in which there is more government regulation of the economy, home industries are protected by tariffs, and a social safety net protects individuals who have fallen on hard times. Socialist societies, in which the government plays an active role in the economy and which have more of a social safety net to help individuals, would be located on the center left of the continuum. Communist societies would be on the left end of the continuum, where governments run the economies and there is no private enterprise or private property. In the middle are state capitalist societies that have part of their economy following capitalist principles, but the state governs the overall economy. Thinking of these types of economic systems on a continuum helps to recognize that diversity is the norm in the way that each nation creates and changes its economy.

STATE CAPITALISM

| COMMUNISM | SOCIALISM | MANAGED CAPITALISM | NEOLIBERALISM |

In Eastern Europe during the Cold War, this humorous popular graffiti plastered the walls of Communist capitals: "Capitalism is the exploitation of man by man. Communism is the opposite: the exploitation of man by man." This simple riddle, although stressing the negative aspects of both systems, echoes the common roots of the economic systems that operate in nations around the world today. Aside from the small, isolated, local, domestic economies that still dot the landscape in remote areas of the world, the vast majority of the world has an economic system rooted in the modern ideologies of the past 200 years. Paradoxically, communism and capitalism have the same ideological underpinnings.[3]

Capitalism and communism emerged out of the same 19th century modern worldview. The political ideologies of the era – liberalism, communism, and fascism – were also products of the modern worldview. Liberalism evolved during the 17th and 18th centuries in Britain and the Netherlands in response to the absolute rule of monarchs. The state acted as protector of an individual's basic rights of life, liberty, and property; an independent parliamentary branch controlled and limited the monarchs' powers. Communism and socialism grew out of the 19th century writings of Karl Marx. He wrote of a system of social organization in which a single and self-perpetuating political party in a totalitarian state controls and dominates all economic and social activity. Fascism is a political philosophy that views the nation above the individual and stands for a centralized despotic government headed by a dictatorial leader who imposes severe economic and social regimentation and forcible suppression of dissent. Generally, the political ideologies of liberalism and fascism embraced a capitalist economic system, and communism embraced a command economy.

Both capitalism and communism believed in the inevitability of continuous progress and continuous change, the ideology of modernism. Both elevated rights for interest groups, such as the corporation or the politburo (communist rulers), above freedom and responsibility for individuals and communities. Both favored the material over the spiritual – for example the Soviet Union outlawed religion. Both believed in *homo economicus*, economic man, in which the individual is subject to economic forces outside of his/her control. They both highly regarded the rational implementation of their economic principles by a rational bureaucratic structure – by the command economy or by rational corporate actors. In varying degrees, they scorned traditions and enduring values, disregarded the stability of the family, friendships and relationships, and derided or ignored spiritual aspirations. They both exalted constant change and ridiculed those hostile to change. They both disregard the environment as an externality, but instrumental to material progress.[4] In the name of progress, both economies have exploited the environment. Both economic practices sought to derail the domestic and local economy and bring it into either the communist or capitalist orb. They both embraced industrialization in the 19th and 20th centuries as the preferred method for production of goods and services, but they advocated different systems of ownership and distribution.

## Capitalism

**Questions to Consider**

1.  What is your reaction to the list of similarities of the communist and capitalist economic systems?

Capitalism is defined here as an economic system in which private parties make their goods and services available on a free market and seek to make a profit on their activities. Private parties, either individuals or companies, own the means of production – land, machinery, tools, equipment, buildings, workshops, and raw materials. Private parties decide what to produce. The centerpiece of the system is the market in which individuals or corporations compete, and the forces of supply and demand, not the government, determine the prices received for goods and services. Businesses may realize profits from their endeavors, reinvest the profits gained, or suffer losses.

Wages and profits earned from the capitalist system are used to buy goods and services from the market place with prices determined by supply and demand. The capitalist system rewards those who capture productivity, efficiency, initiative, and creativity, while the marketplace leaves those unable or unwilling to participate to their own means Although capitalism is sometimes referred to as a market economy, I distinguish between the two. The market economy operates according to capitalist principles but is smaller in scale and mostly locally based.

Capitalism is a multi-dimensional system that has diverse ways of functioning; there is no one standard way in which it operates. When we hear people talk about capitalism or hear about it in the media, it seems as if there is just one type of capitalism, but in reality there are different types. Capitalism as an economic system can operate with minimal government regulation or with government taking an active role in guiding and regulating the process. Under capitalism, the elites can devise laws and regulations that favor them in their accumulation of wealth or, on the other hand, laws and regulations can require that greater numbers of people allocate wealth in a more equitable way. A capitalist economy is not just associated with liberal forms of democracies such as in the U.S., but it can also operate in association with fascism, such as Adolph Hitler's Nazi Germany in the 1930s-40s. Even today, China is politically a communist country, but a portion of its economy operates according to the rules of global capitalism, while another part follows a command economy. Where the dividing line is between the two is anyone's guess. Some European countries are socialist, but in reality their economies are connected to global capitalism and operate according to capitalist principles. Parts of India are tied to the global economy, while parts of the rural areas continue with local methods of exchange or barter. There is no clear cut line drawn between the economic systems of different countries, and even within countries each one operates an economic system compatible with its particular interests. Thus, capitalism takes on different forms. Next, we will discuss neoliberalism and managed capitalism.

### 1. Neoliberalism

Neoliberalism has prevailed in the U.S. since the early 1980s. Other terms describe the same concept: free market capitalism, free trade capitalism, market capitalism, supply-side economics, laissez-faire capitalism, classical capitalism, corporate capitalism, or an Anglo-American version of capitalism (the UK and U.S.). Sometimes commentators will say capitalism but in reality mean neoliberalism and not make the distinction between the different versions. But it is of utmost importance to distinguish between the different types of capitalism since they vary considerably. I found it difficult to select a term to use consistently throughout the book. However, with some reservation I will use the term neoliberalism because it is more commonly used around the world and in academic circles, yet is not as familiar in everyday usage.

The neo in neoliberalism means new, since it is a newer version of the type of economic system found in the 19th and early 20th century which Great Britain promoted (see chapter 2). **Neoliberalism** is the modern politico-economic theory favoring free trade, privatization, minimal government intervention in business and reduced public expenditure on social services.[5] Free market capitalism is probably used more in the U.S. than neoliberalism, but I have problems with the term. The term "free market" implies that there is a free market. We will find out that, indeed, the market is not free. In the U.S. in particular we toss around the word free too freely (pun intended). If we want something to sound good, we just put a "free" in front of it: free choice, free elections, land of the free, or free trade. My favorite is food that is calorie free, a dieter's dream! Therefore, I think the term free-market is misleading and prefer to use it sparingly. However, if you prefer to use it in discussions with others about the global economy, since it is more commonly used, then please go ahead; it is the concept that is more important than the particular term.

Neoliberal supporters maintain that it is the best economic system around, especially since the collapse of communism was discredited and sent to the dustbin of history. Supporters give several reasons why they consider it the best economic system.

Neoliberalism as an economic philosophy got an infusion of energy in the early 1980s when two world leaders were enthusiastic cheerleaders of the neoliberal agenda: Margaret Thatcher, prime

### Reasons for the Advancement of Neoliberalism[6]

1. Self-interest motivates humans, which is expressed best through the pursuit of financial gains.

2. The actions that result in financial gains benefit society.

3. Competitive behavior is more rational than cooperation; hence, this motive should structure societies.

4. Progress is measured by increased materialistic consumption, which should be favored.

5. Free markets without government "interference" allow for the most efficient and best allocation of resources.

6. Governments should mostly protect property rights and contracts, and allocate money for defense.

7. Globalization leads to global poverty reduction.

### Ten Principles of Neoliberalism[7]

1. Free trade (remove protective tariffs).

2. Deregulate industries (remove government oversight).

3. Cut taxes for the wealthy who will invest in business.

4. Wealth will "trickle down" from the wealthy to the poor.

5. Government support for some infrastructure.

6. Privatize publicly held industries and services.

7. Continued economic growth is the way to prosperity.

8. Rapid commodification of every remaining aspect of life.

9. Wages tied to supply and demand, eliminate minimum wage and unions.

10. Economic globalization is beneficial to everyone.

minister of the United Kingdom (UK) and Ronald Reagan, president of the U.S. They were convinced the principles of neoliberalism were best for their countries and would help reinstate their nations' preeminence on the world economic stage. They favored the above principles of neoliberalism.

### 2. Managed Capitalism

Pushed by Great Britain, the economic powerhouse of the time, neoliberal capitalism generally prevailed in the West in the late 19th and early 20th centuries. World War I (1914-1918) interrupted neoliberalism, but it falteringly resumed during the 1920s. The future of neoliberal capitalism was in doubt with the start of the Great Depression that dominated the whole decade of the 1930s. Analysis of the Depression is shaped by one's economic persuasion. Marxists, on the left, argue that it was the most severe in a series of periodic economic crises to emanate from an unregulated and immoral capitalist system. Conservative neoliberals, on the right, regard the Depression as a temporary setback characteristic of capitalism; government interventions enacted as the "New Deal" in the U.S. smacked of socialism and should have been abandoned. Whatever the explanation, the great suffering inflicted by the Great Depression has been seen as instrumental to the rise of fascism in Europe.

With the crippling effects of the Great Depression affecting Western nations, many economists advocated that governments should take a more active and responsible role in planning national economies. To these economists, government intervention would soften the "boom and bust" cycles of unfettered, laissez-faire capitalism characteristic of the 19th century. These boom and bust cycles wreaked havoc on workers laid off from jobs during the bust cycles and had to fend for themselves. Business owners would also have to weather the bust cycles when demand for their business products collapsed. The British economist **John Maynard Keynes** (1883-1946) argued that the government must accept more responsibility for regulating capitalist economies. He advocated regulation through a number of controls: running government surpluses or deficits when necessary; creating public works projects for the unemployed during economic downturns; adjusting the flow of money and credit; and raising or lowering interest rates. The purpose of these interventions was to make capitalism work better through government planning. The U.S. implemented and accepted Keynes' ideas during the Depression, but Western nations more fully adopted his ideas after World War II. For example, during the Depression President Franklin Roosevelt initiated the New Deal to help stimulate the U.S. economy. Although these programs eased the situation for many working people, the New Deal did not officially end the Depression. An even larger government program, World War II, with its tremendous government spending and astronomically high tax rates on the wealthy, brought an end to the Great Depression.

In **managed capitalism** the government closely regulates the financial sector to prevent wild financial speculation and insure transparency of the system. Tariffs protect manufacturing jobs in the home country; therefore, wages and prices are set according to supply and demand at the national level rather than the global level. For the most part services such as education, health care, the military, and prisons are government run and paid for through taxes. The state sometimes owns large service providers such as utilities, airlines and transportation networks or closely regulates them. Private enterprise exists but is carefully regulated with high tax brackets for the wealthiest individuals, for example hovering as high as 90 percent during World War II and the 1950s. Corporations also pay a larger share of taxes than in the neoliberal model. Labor unions have a powerful say in wages and benefits, as long as their wages keep up with productivity and don't spark inflation. There is a more equal circulation of wealth with managed capitalism than with neoliberal capitalism, resulting in a vital middle and working class and less concentration of wealth in the hands of the elite and corporations.

The "Golden Age" of capitalism, as it is often referred to, was during the period 1947-1973 in the U.S. and later in other Western countries as well. During this heyday of managed capitalism, the U.S., in particular, experienced high growth, low unemployment, and low inflation; the real wages of the middle and working classes rose and prosperity was more widespread than ever before or since. However, the continuance of racial segregation and discrimination excluded many African Americans from this abundance and pockets of rural poverty, such as in Appalachia, were severe. The golden era ended in the mid-1970s. The U.S. and other nations, such as the UK, switched from managed capitalism to neoliberalism in the 1980s. Economic globalization accompanied this shift.

### Socialism and Communism
Economic alternatives to the prevailing private, laissez-faire capitalist system arose in 19th century Europe in response to labor's egregious working conditions in the newly industrialized factories. Wages and working conditions for workers in the early years of industrial capitalism were abysmal. Alternatives to capitalism – communism and socialism – arose during this time to remedy the suffering of industrial workers. Therefore, it is not surprising that the key supporters of socialism/communism were/are industrial workers. One of the leading critics of capitalism was **Karl Marx** (1818-1883), who, along with co-author Frederich Engels, proposed a socialist/communist alternative to capitalism in their short book, the *Communist Manifesto* in 1848.

**Socialism** advocates for collective or governmental ownership and administration of the means of production and distribution of goods and services. Socialism, ideally, is a way of organizing an economy in which the central tenets are that the society owns the means of production or they are placed into collective or common ownership and that, as far as possible, market exchange is replaced by other forms of distribution based on social needs. The fundamental feature of a socialist economy is that publicly owned, state or worker-run institutions produce goods and services in key segments of the economy. There is more emphasis on government planning by state officials than in capitalist societies, and less response to supply and demand pressures. Workers in state enterprises have little risk of unemployment and labor unions have more influence than in capitalist societies. As a political ideology, communism is a system of social organization based on the holding of all property in common, actual ownership ascribed to the community as a whole or to the state.

The ostensible purpose of a socialist or communist system is to eradicate abject poverty, reduce the degree of economic inequality, both inherent in neoliberal societies, and provide a comfortable safety net for those unable to par-

**Karl Marx in 1875**

ticipate in the workplace. Like capitalism, socialism encompasses a broad range of economic systems, from the centralized Soviet-style command economy to participatory planning via workplace democracy. Market socialism refers to various economic systems that involve either public ownership or management or worker cooperative ownership of the means of production, or a combination of both, while the market influences production and in what quantity.

With the collapse of the Soviet Union in 1991, there are few "pure" communist countries, if there ever were any. Arguably, North Korea and Cuba are the only hold-outs. In many countries today, the economies are a combination of some large state owned enterprises (socialism) with private capitalism. For example, today Canada's medical system is socialized in order to provide health care for all of its citizens at no charge to individuals. The government pays for this medical care through taxes from all citizens. There is no profit derived from this system, since the purpose is to provide good medical care, not enrich individual businesses or shareholders in private insurance companies. About half of the medical care in the U.S. is socialized: Medicare for its senior citizens (65 and over), veterans, Medicaid for the very poor, and some programs for children not covered by private insurance. Private medical insurance is available for purchase at a substantial cost by those unable to receive government medical programs. Some workplaces offer medical insurance to their employees, who most often must share in the cost. This leaves a vast number, approximately 52 million people in 2010, who "fall through the cracks" and do not have either type of insurance. They are left to their own means to find whatever medical care, if any, they can.[8] The U.S. has found that private insurance companies will not provide affordable insurance for these groups either because of high costs or the inability of the members of these groups to pay for the medical insurance.

## State Capitalism

The neoliberal version of capitalism prevailed in the 1990s, but that changed in the 2000s. The power of the state is back in the form of state capitalism. This economic system is not merely the re-emergence of socialist central planning in a 21st century package, but it is a form of state engineered capitalism particular to each government that practices it. Economist Ian Bremmer offers a good definition of **state capitalism**: "It is a system in which the state plays the role of leading economic actor and uses markets primarily for political gain."[9] The nations that support a state-capitalist system believe that public wealth, public investment and public enterprise offer the surest path toward politically sustainable economic development. These governments will micromanage entire sectors of their economies to promote national interests and to protect their domestic political standing. It is similar to the principles of mercantilism found in the past (see chapter 2).[10]

Over the past decade, the governments of several developing countries have worked to ensure that valuable national assets remain in state hands and governments maintain enough influence within their domestic economies to preserve their survival. In some cases, they have used state-owned energy companies to accumulate wealth or to secure access to the long-term supplies of oil and gas needed to fuel further growth. They have created **sovereign wealth funds** – a state-owned investment fund composed of financial assets such as stocks, bonds, property, precious metals or other financial instruments – that invest globally using pools of excess capital. Among the world's leading state capitalist countries are China, Russia, and Saudi Arabia, where there are close ties with institutions like the Chinese Communist Party, the Saudi royal family, or individuals associated with the powerful former Russian President Vladimir Putin.[11]

Over the past several years, lists of the world's largest companies published by business magazines such as *Forbes* and *Fortune* have begun to feature state-owned companies. Between 2004 and the start of 2008, 117 state-owned and public companies from Brazil, Russia, India, and China (BRIC countries) appeared for the first time on the *Forbes* Global 2000 list of the world's largest companies, measured by sales, profits, assets, and market value. A total of 239 U.S., Japanese, British, and German companies fell off the list; their market value dropped from 70 percent to 50 percent over those four years. The market value of the BRIC-based companies rose from 4 percent to 16 percent. The corporate failures and government bailouts of 2008-2009 accelerated the trend. *Bloomberg News*, a business news agency, reported in early 2009 that three of the world's four largest banks by market capitalization were state-owned Chinese firms – Industrial and Commercial Bank of China (ICBC), China Construction, and Bank of China. The 2009 *Forbes* Global 2000 listed ICBC, China Mobile, and Petro China among the world's five largest companies in the world

by market value. Energy giants like China National Petroleum Corporation, Petro China, Sinopec, Brazil's Petrobras, Mexico's Pemex, and Russia's Rosneft and Gazprom are among the world's richest companies.[12] State capitalism is a powerful economic system.

### Questions to Consder

1. From these brief descriptions of the various economic systems, which one do you prefer? Explain.

BANK OF CHINA HEADQUARTERS IN BEIJING, CHINA. FOUNDED IN 1927, IN 2010 IT HAD 389,827 EMPLOYEES AND $1.723 TRILLION IN ASSETS. ONCE 100% OWNED BY THE CHINESE STATE, NOW 26% IS PRIVATELY OWNED.

DRILLING PLATFORM OF THE BRAZILIAN OIL COMPANY PETROBAS. IN 2010 IT WAS THE 4TH LARGEST COMPANY IN THE WORLD MEASURED BY MARKET CAPITALIZATION. THE GOVERNMENT OWNS 64% OF THE COMPANY.

# THE GLOBAL ECONOMY:
# DEFINITIONS, TERMS, AND CONCEPTS

### Four Ways Wealth Grows and Accumulates

With a modern global economy wealth has grown through accumulation and reinvestment. I have identified four sectors of the global economy that contribute to wealth creation and accumulation: primary industries, secondary industries, service industries, and the financial sector.

During the early modern era (1500-1750), the main ingredient in capitalist wealth creation was the development of **primary industries** – mining, agriculture, forestry, trapping animals, and fishing – that changed natural resources into primary products. The manufacturing industries that amass, package, clean or process the raw materials close to the primary producers are generally considered part of this sector as well, especially if the raw material is unsuitable for sale in its raw form or difficult to transport long distances. For example, in boiling houses attached to sugar cane plantations in the 17th and 18th centuries, slaves boiled the raw cane into raw sugar for easier transport to markets in Europe. Another source of wealth creation, sad to say, was the capture, transport, and sale of African slaves. There was a great deal of wealth generated from this ghastly activity. Production and trade in these primary industries along with an increase in commercial agricultural productivity became the most dynamic sectors of the European economy during this time and spurred wealth creation. Thus, capitalism in the early modern era has often been called commercial capitalism.

A profound change in labor patterns accompanied industrialization. With industrialization some workers moved from primary industries which produced raw materials, into **secondary industries** – manufacturing and construction – that processed the raw materials into manufactured goods. Labor, expertise, and so on added value to the raw materials, these products generated even more wealth than primary industries. A by-product of industrialization was the decline in the proportion of workers who were self-employed, as workers increasingly moved to factory jobs.[13]

Along with the primary industries and the industrialized secondary industries another form of wealth creation expanded in the 20th century: tertiary or **service industries**. **Services** are intangible goods that workers provide for businesses and final consumers. Services may involve the transport, distribution and sale of goods from producer to consumer. Goods may be transformed in the process of providing a service, as happens in the restaurant industry. However, the focus is on serving the customer rather than transforming physical goods. The many examples of services include retail, police, fire protection, government, clerical work, insurance, tourism, banking, education, public utilities, entertainment, legal, medical, accounting, finance, and social services. Sociologists Gerhard and Jean Lenski note, "As industrialization proceeds, the initial rapid growth in secondary industries slows down considerably, and tertiary industries become the chief growth sector of the economy."[14]

The fourth level of capitalist wealth creation is financialization. This is where financial specialists create financial products, attach a certain monetary value, and then they are bought and sold on different exchanges, such as the stock exchange. Many factors contribute to the value of the financial products created, including supply and demand. There will be more on this subject in chapters 7 and 8.

## The Core and Periphery

In discussing the global economy it is readily apparent that economic discrepancies exist among individual nations, within individual nations, and even among people as well. Several different terms describe this reality, but which terms are the best ones to use? In the post-war era, the terms first, second, and third world were used; the first world was the U.S. and western Europe, while the second world was the Soviet Union and its satellites, and the remaining nations were lumped into the third world category. As you can imagine, this ranking was offensive to those in the third world category; therefore, other terms, which basically mean the same, are now used. Today terms such as "developed" and "developing," or even "less-developed" nations are more common. Sometimes critics pejoratively call the U.S. "over-developed." Terms such as "emerging" often refer to countries that are becoming more economically developed. Sometimes the terms industrialized or non-industrialized are used as well. Also, the more neutral but geographically inaccurate terms, "the global South" or "the global North" are used, but once again the meaning is the same – the South is the poor region, and North is the rich region. But I find that it gets confusing when referring to a country like Australia that is geographically in the south but is economically in the "global North." Is China in the global North or South? How about Brazil? Are you confused? To simplify this I am using the imperfect but more versatile terms "core" and "periphery."

In explaining the global economy, the core and periphery concepts illustrate the unequal relationship among nations and also the unequal status of people within nations.[15] Therefore, these versatile terms are fluid and can describe more than one phenomenon. **Core areas** are where intense and extensive modern developments in technology, military, politics, culture, and especially the economy have taken place. These areas are where wealth generation and accumulation are concentrated and also where the core devises and enforces the rules for the system. For example, England was a core area when it first industrialized around 1770. Detroit, Michigan, in the U.S. was a core area in the 1950s when it was a manufacturing center of automobile production; sadly, it is no longer a core area. New York City is a core financial city, along with London, Shanghai, China, and Singapore. Core areas draw the **periphery areas** into a dependent interaction with the core regions; commercial wealth is extracted from the periphery in the form of cheap raw materials produced with cheap labor – or, more recently, manufactured goods produced with cheap labor. Core areas siphon the wealth from this transaction to areas that are somewhere in the **middle** of the core and periphery I refer to as simply middle countries or areas. **External areas** remain outside modern developments and are not incorporated into the core-and-periphery world system. Core, middle, periphery, and external areas are not fixed but shift over time.

Inequality among nations and within nations characterizes the global economy. A core and periphery model helps explain the asymmetrical levels of participation and development in the global economy by different nations and people. Unequal wealth distribution and ownership of resources has characterized world history in most areas of the world since the beginning of civilizations over 5,000 years ago; today is no exception. Core areas continue to be the centers of wealth creation, management, experimentation, and concentration. These areas usually have an industrial past, sophisticated technology, a well-educated workforce, sacrosanct private property laws, and an entrenched ideology that emphasizes the value of wealth accumulation and advanced technology. Today the major core nations include the United States, the world's largest economy; parts of China, the world's second largest economy; individual nations of the European Economic Community (EEC) that have robust economies: Germany, France, and Netherlands; Japan, the third largest economy; United Kingdom (UK), Canada, Australia, and other smaller nations such as South Korea and Singapore.

Middle areas fall somewhere in-between core and periphery status and have characteristics of both. Nations such as Brazil, Russia, India, Argentina, Indonesia, Saudi Arabia, Turkey, China, and Union of South Africa, all members of the G-20 nations, aspire to core status, but many parts of these countries are mired in poverty. This group is sometimes referred to as the developing world or emerging economies.

Other nations and peoples live on the periphery of global developments, separated from core regions by a wide economic gap. The periphery nations supply core areas with cheap or relatively cheap raw materials such as oil, mineral resources, agricultural products, and timber, which have increased in price as supplies diminish. Many people within the periphery nations labor for minimum wages to extract, grow, and manufacture raw materials into finished goods that are then shipped to core areas as affordable consumer items for elite consumption. Many eke out a living growing crops for the global market. Today about 80 percent of the current world population either lives in periphery or middle areas or occupies periphery status in core nations.

Although the periphery areas remain poorer than core areas, elites and non-elites reside in both. In the periphery countries, the wealthy elites are large land and mine owners, business entrepreneurs, government officials, and other professional people. Usually their numbers are small, with an undersized middle class, while non-elites make up the vast majority of the periphery population. An elite class also resides in core countries with tax policies, superb education and laws that favor their retention and accumulation of wealth. Core nations usually host a larger middle class than periphery nations. Favorable tax policies, laws to support home ownership, and other legislation, such as outlays for education, help prop up those who hold middle class economic status in core nations. As these governmental policies erode in core nations, such as the U.S., there is a corresponding shrinkage of the middle class.

A significant percentage of periphery-status people live in core nations as well. For example, in the U.S. some estimate the periphery population or the underclass at 25 percent of the total U.S. citizenry. They are unemployed or labor for minimum wages, lack health insurance, do not own homes (or lost their home in foreclosure), live in blighted neighborhoods and are increasingly pushed to the margins of society. This group also includes undocumented workers from other countries who labor for minimum wages at low-skilled jobs.

There are various reasons for the periphery status of certain nations and regions. Some core nations encouraged or coerced leaders of periphery nations into following the path to modernize their countries. Periphery nations attempted to share in economic abundance that modernization promised to bring. Many periphery nations borrowed heavily from the World Bank and other financial institutions for infrastructure construction with the implicit understanding that this would lead them on the path to higher living standards and improved economic status. But now many periphery countries have discovered that it is much harder to reap benefits from the global marketplace than they originally thought. They have found the deck is stacked against them. Many of the reasons for failure are found in the way the structure of the world economic system itself is organized; it needs dependent periphery nations for the core to prosper. The core nations are able to profit from cheap labor and obtain resources for the benefit of elites who usually reside in core nations. Also, inept leadership and corruption among the leaders of periphery nations contribute to failure. In addition, they lack sophisticated technology, are paid low commodity prices for their raw materials, are ravaged by disease, and are mired in debt. The economic realities in the periphery and the economic policies of the core nations ensure that the global economy is not equitable for all participants.

The core and periphery concept can also be applied to what is happening within the United States and other nations. Core areas within the U.S. are the cities where information processing and information workers add value to goods and services. Core areas import finished products made by cheap labor from periphery areas and then adds value or information to these products. The added value may be in the form of a service such as accounting procedures, insurance, marketing and advertising, or political lobbying for favored legislation that helps them profit in the market place. For example, athletic shoes may be manufactured for as little as $5.00 in factories in China, and then shipped to the U.S. where value such as advertising by a well-known sports figure is added to each shoe. The shoes then command a much higher price, perhaps even $100, in the retail stores of shopping malls. Under the current system, the wealth added to these services is paid out in high salaries, bonuses and benefits for those who control the process, such as Chief Executive Officers (CEO), boards of directors, other corporate officials, or to a sports celebrity in the shoe example.

Those who add information or wealth to the cheaply produced goods and services or devise financial instruments for investment are the ones who create, generate, and control the process of wealth concentration and distribution in the global economy. These information workers are members of the upper middle class, or identified as the world's elite. Hence, the wealth creation of the elite class has shifted from manufacturing goods to adding information to goods manufactured elsewhere or creating financial instruments for investment. The global elite class consumes a disproportionate amount of the world's resources, siphoning wealth from the periphery areas of the world and from periphery workers in order to corner that wealth for themselves. Although the upper 50 percent of Americans are part of the global elite class according to income, education, and standard of living, all but the top 10-20 percent of Americans has witnessed stagnant or declining wages in the last 30 years.

Within wealthy core nations there are pockets of periphery-status people who, for varying reasons reside on the margins of economic development and political participation. For example, within the U.S. approximately 50 percent of the population is not considered part of the global elite and about 25 percent can be considered members of the underclass or economically disadvantaged, many of them children. One of the periphery pockets in the U.S. are ravaged inner cities dotting the urban landscape. Inner city residents who do find jobs are usually unskilled service workers or low-wage manufacturing employees toiling for minimum wages that barely provide for basic needs, let alone health care or other necessities. To add to their troubles, many workers must commute long distances from their blighted neighborhoods to service jobs in more affluent parts of the city. Having to rely on public transportation or an unreliable car, the costs of commuting add to work-related expenses and worries. Housing woes also plague many low-wage workers. Unable to afford to purchase a home, they often live in sub-standard housing with high rents. Or they may have purchased a home with a sub-prime mortgage in which the adjustable mortgage rate rose considerably after a few years, forcing them into foreclosure. The collapse of the housing bubble in late 2007 has led to a decline in home prices, subtracting net worth from a family's balance sheet. Compared to their wealthy fellow citizens, the poor endure inferior education, fewer governmental services, higher crime rates, sub-standard transportation services, limited choices of healthy foods, and often work at mind-numbing, dead-end jobs.

The unprecedented growth of mega-cities in periphery nations such as Mexico City, Sao Paulo, Brazil, Mumbai, India, and Cairo, Egypt has exacerbated inequality. As a result of population growth and the migration from rural villages to urban areas, urban residents face extreme poverty, few job opportunities, horrendous living conditions, crime, and hopelessness for a better life. The villages, once vibrant and full of life, are decimated, left with the elderly, children, and a handful of women who stay behind. This shift from village life to urban squalor is occurring for millions around the world.

A fundamental problem with uneven economic development, especially in the United States, is that wealth is concentrated in the hands of large corporations and their upper level CEOs and not circulated in a fair and equitable manner. I am not suggesting that money should just be handed out so everyone has an equal income. But one of the reasons that periphery regions and people are becoming poorer is that it is more difficult for local businesses to survive. The presence in a neighborhood of a goliath retailer like Wal-Mart forces smaller businesses to close shop because they cannot compete with its primary appeal, low prices. This means that profits end up in the pockets of corporate giants, instead of circulating in the local community where they might be re-invested locally. This scenario has contributed to the economic decline of many local economies, destabilizing these local communities that have long provided a sense of steadiness, identity, and meaning for their residents.

All these labels, including the core and periphery, project the attitude that the economic system is what should be the criteria for judging a nation. When economic development is used as the criteria to evaluate the status of different nations in the world, a nation's poverty or wealth becomes an implied value judgment of its success. Using this system of evaluation, the core areas are superior to that of the periphery areas. It further implies that in order to be taken seriously in the global economy the periphery must emulate and adopt the economic procedures and policies of the core areas lest they be "left behind." I think it would be more indicative of a nation's well-being to consider its environmental policy or social relations as the deciding factors for evaluation. Perhaps we should use a happiness index. In a recent happiness survey ranking nations according to such an index, Denmark ranked first, Switzerland came in second, Austria was third, and Iceland and the Bahamas rounded out the top five "happily developed" nations. The United States, which ranks 23rd on the index, would be "developing happiness"![16]

## Western and Modern

Two confusing terms – "Western" and "modern" – have imprecise meaning and are often interchanged. Europe has historically been divided into two sections: eastern and western. The imaginary line dividing these imaginary entities roughly splits Germany in two and runs north to south. The Western part of Europe is the region that led the way in the Modern Wave of history (beginning 1500). Western Europe earned its recognition during the Enlightenment era of the 18th century when ideas were formulated that define Western principles. Some of these **Western** ideas, often collectively referred to as **liberalism**, emerged from the Enlightenment era or were added later and include (or partially include) a representative government, division of government, individual rights and freedoms (speech and press), private property, scientific method, reason, individualism, freedom of religion or secularism, and later women's and gay rights and sexual freedoms. Most European countries and the U.S., Canada, and Australia have adopted these Western principles as part of their form of government and values system. When referring to the West today, the above areas are included in this rather fuzzy terminology.

**Modern** is somewhat different from Western; it applies to that which is near to or characteristic of the present in contrast to that of a former age or an age long past; hence the word sometimes has the connotation of up-to-date and thus, good, such as modern ideas.[17] In my world history book, *Waves of Global Change*, I start the Modern Wave around 1500 and is distinguished from other waves by the changes in technology, a shift to a capitalist economy, political liberalism, scientific ideas, and changes in social values. What is modern constantly shifts over time. For example, modern technology today is different than modern technology 25 years ago. For example, China, Brazil, Saudi Arabia, and others have modernized their economies without becoming Western.

Let's take Japan as an example to illustrate the difference between Western and modern. Tokyo, by any measure, is a modern city. It has tall skyscrapers, an efficient subway system, lots of cars and enough lights to blind you. As an Asian nation, Japan was one of the first countries in the 19th century to adopt, especially from Germany, many Western ideas about government, the economy, and unfortunately, a modern military. After its defeat in World War II, the U.S., as the victor nation, required Japan to adopt Western political and economic ideas. It did. Therefore, many observers would think that Japan had adopted Western ideas, and I would reply yes, many Western ideas, but not all of them. Japan has not adopted to the full extent the Western ideas of individualism or sexual freedom. Family obligations and social responsibility are very much part of Japanese culture.

Having freeways, good infrastructure and all the trappings of modernity does not mean that you have become Western. Acceptance of Western liberal values is certainly not universally recognized in many nations considered modern. For example, Dubai, a city and emirate in the United Arab Emirates (UAE), is a very modern city but it is not considered Western in its outlook or governance. Another example is the country of Saudi Arabia, where the cities have modern technology and infrastructure, yet the state does not allow women to drive, and they have an inherited monarchy; these are not Western political ideals. An example of a country adopting a Western value is South Africa, which recently accepted and legitimized gay marriage, still largely taboo in Sub-Saharan Africa. Therefore, modern and Western are two more of those nebulous terms that mean different things to different people and should be applied mindfully.

## Right and Left

We learned to distinguish right and left in elementary school. Some learned quicker than others. It took me awhile. But "left" and "right" are also political terms that designate political positions. This is important to our understanding of the way that the global economy is structured. The terms first appeared during the French Revolution of 1789 when members of the National Assembly divided into supporters for the king to the president's right and supporters of the revolution to his left. Traditionally, the left – progressives, social liberals, social democrats, socialists, secularists, communists and anarchists – believes in reason as a way to make social progress and implement social justice. The right – conservatives, reactionaries, laissez-faire capitalists, monarchists, supporters of established religion, nationalists, and fascists – supports the ideas of social cohesion and individualism.[18] In modern political discussion, those on the left typically support working people and accuse the right of supporting the interests of the wealthy, whereas those on the right usually support individualism and accuse the left of supporting collectivism. The debate between right and left in the U.S. has often morphed into ranting incidences, where common sense and meaningful dialogue are the causalities. As a result, the rancorous debate raises emotional prejudices rather than a meaningful dialogue about policy.[19]

## Eight Interest Groups

Since the time that capitalism started to develop in the early modern era (around 1500), there have been conflicting interest groups who have sought to benefit from the wealth creation of the capitalist economic system. Which interest groups have profited the most have fluctuated over time, depending upon the particular economic circumstances and which group has been able to shape governmental policies that benefit them the most. The interplay of these conflicting groups over the last 500 years has created untold dramas and sometimes outright armed conflict. The eight groups have been the main groups over the 500 year time span of modern capitalism. Sometimes the groups overlap; for example, a consumer can also be part of the middle class or a small business owner. The diagram below helps you to see what type of capitalism favors what particular group or groups.

Usually the government or state is the mediator and decides which group to favor through their policies. Keep this diagram in mind as you read the history section in the next chapter.

### Questions to Consider
1. What interest group(s) do you associate yourself with?

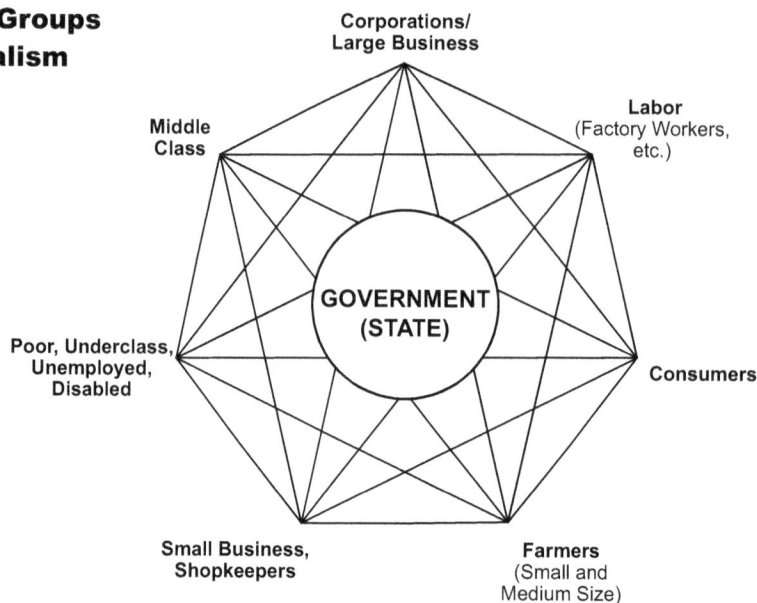

8 Interest Groups in Capitalism

36

# UNDERSTANDING THE GLOBAL ECONOMY: TWO APPROACHES

Tsunami waves are shifting events in our world today. We live in an increasingly interdependent world, and we are grappling with rapid changes that are dramatically affecting our lives. We are attempting to sort out what paths to follow today and into the future, while also trying to make sense of the momentous changes affecting our fragile planet. Global problems of tsunami proportion are battering us at such an alarming frequency that fear and inaction paralyze us. These global problems require a collective effort to solve, something that we have never had to undertake in the past and for which there is no template. The question begs, where to begin? Perhaps one way to better understand the enormity of the issues and the consequences of our actions is to draw upon different approaches to solving these problems. I would like to introduce two approaches that I will use in this book and hope you will use when thinking about and discussing the global economy.

## A Holistic Approach

"Holistic" is the name of an approach that I will use to understand and think about the global economy. **Holistic** in this context means that all a society's cultural traits – political, economic, technological, cultural, religious, social, arts, values, attitudes, and environmental – reinforce and support each other. A change in any cultural trait changes the others. This means that a society's economy reflects its political policies, its treatment of the environment reflects the values of its citizens, its technology reflects its economic characteristics, and so forth. For example, in the U.S. a brown smog from car emissions often hangs over a large city, such as Los Angeles, California. Obviously this brown smog is unhealthy, and if cars were outlawed, the hazardous smog would be gone. However, the entire U.S. economy is dependent upon fossil fuels to run its transportation system and, therefore, the smog is a necessary by-product of this system as it currently operates. It would be impossible to simply outlaw cars, since all parts of the economy are dependent upon cars as a means of transportation and as a cultural icon. The term holistic emphasizes the full range of

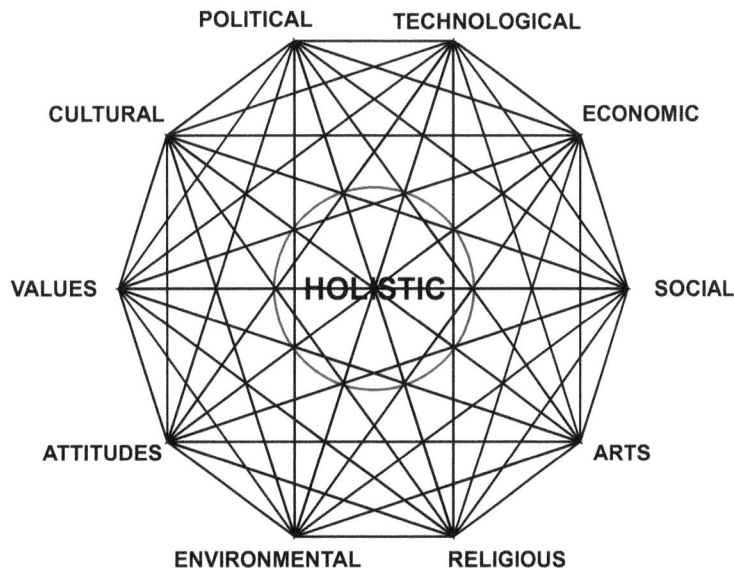

relations among the cultural traits of a system and the ways the operation of those parts helps to perpetuate the whole system.

This holistic approach offers a "big picture" vision of the global economy, drawing upon various disciplines – history, sociology, anthropology, political science, geography, economics, psychology, and the sciences. With this holistic approach, we connect seemingly disparate strands into a holistic process that provides an intelligible framework for understanding the global economy.

**A Systems Approach**

The increasing complexity and interdependence of the world today calls for a new perspective. Our global community faces a long list of problems – climate change, resource depletion, poverty, wars, terrorism, inequality, population pressures, political corruption, and many others. Although the list hasn't changed much over the past few decades, the problems have significantly accelerated and intensified and, obviously, have not been solved. The current mode of thinking, which looks at only parts of issues and problems in isolation, will not move us forward to create a more livable, stable, and hopeful future. Instead of looking at each isolated part of the global economy, we need to understand the whole economy as a system. In systems thinking, individual elements of the global economy are like roots that, when connected together, can give greater meaning to the whole panoramic picture. We will draw on the past to gather wisdom that will be useful in addressing and solving some of the critical economic issues that are begging for immediate attention. To understand systems thinking, let us next turn to a description of it.

Systems thinking informs the approach I will be using in this book. A **system** is something that maintains its existence and functions as a whole through the interaction of its parts. To put it another way, a system is a collection of parts that interact with each other to function as a whole and continually affect each other over time. A shared purpose logically organizes systems. For example, the human body is a system; each part of the body affects another. A school is a system. An aspen forest is a system in which its roots are all connected. Systems can be simple or complex.[20]

Business, the sciences, health, medicine, and other areas draw upon the field of systems thinking currently applied in this approach to the global economy. **Systems thinking** looks beyond what appears to be isolated and independent events to identify deeper structures within the system. The whole system and the interrelationship of the parts to the whole are the focus, not just the isolated basic building blocks. Seeing the connections between events is a basic principle of systems thinking, where connections and the larger context inform the subject. In other words, as the saying goes, "See the forest, not just the trees."

If systems thinking is so wonderful, why haven't we been using it all along? Good question. Changing the way we see the world or our worldview does not happen easily or quickly; conventional ways of thinking have deeply entrenched roots that resist change. When using **conventional thinking**, sometimes called traditional, linear or mechanistic thinking, people tend to see simple sequences of cause and effect that are limited in time and space, which as-

### In a system...

- Parts are interconnected and function as a whole.

- A complex web of relationships unifies the parts.

- The system is changed by addition or subtraction of the parts.

- Arrangement of the pieces is crucial.

- Behavior depends on the total structure; change the structure and the behavior changes.

sumes that cause and effect occur within a close time frame. But the causes and effects may be far apart in time and space. For example, industrial pollutants have accumulated over a 200 year time period since the beginning of the Industrial Revolution around 1800, but the effects are only beginning to be felt today in the phenomenon known as climate change or commonly referred to as global warming.

Conventional thinking segments issues, events, and even the economy into small divisible parts for careful analysis and scrutiny. The economy is seen as a collection of separate objects while the relationships are secondary. In a systems view, networks of relationships are nested into larger networks. An example of conventional thinking is when school officials administer standardized tests to students, who earn a score that ranks them with other students. This isolated score does not take into consideration the whole student: his/her relationship to other students, teachers, or parents, his/her contribution to the community, or even the student's ability to think about the subject beyond the questions in the test. The test score only represents one aspect of the student's ability, yet in classifying a student's abilities it has undue significance.

Conventional thinking continues to shape Western society in many ways. One example is the way that schools arrange desks in linear straight rows; this arrangement reflects linear or hierarchical thinking in which the teacher wields a position of authority at the front of the classroom. Medical treatment of a patient's isolated symptoms with medications or surgery without recognizing the impact on the entire body is an example of conventional thinking. The way the international political structure is organized into separate, autonomous nations exemplifies conventional ways of organizing the world. And even measurements such as Gross Domestic Product (GDP) or annual growth rates evaluate the world economy, which are often not a true indication of the actual economic performance, while the number of people starving is ignored all together. All of these examples in our daily lives represent the expression of conventional thinking. It is deeply rooted in Western ways of thinking that have prevailed over the last 500 years. This way of thinking is habitual, familiar, deeply embedded, and hard to change.

Our daily lives are dramatically changing, while our future at this point looks uncertain and unpredictable. Although many of us wish to hide our heads in the sand and pay no attention to our critical situation, the reality is that we urgently need to address crucial global issues, such as the global economy. But the complexity of the situation requires that a different way of learning, thinking, teaching, and communicating be used to even address, let alone solve, these urgent issues such as climate change and resource depletion. Although, according to some, conventional thinking served us fairly well for centuries, this type of thinking cannot cope with the monumental problem-solving challenges that face us in an interconnected world. Therefore, it behooves us to be aware of a systems thinking approach and consider it as a way to study the global economy.

Secondly, a detailed analysis of any specific problem or issue in isolation limits understanding of its complexity and ramifications. A look beyond individual issues towards a broader

---

### Conventional Thinking

- Separates and divides people, nations, events, cultures and actions.
- Sees simple sequences of cause and effect that are limited in time and space.
- Uses only causes and effects to explain historical events.
- Zeroes in to fault and blame an individual or group.

---

perspective is necessary. Studying something in isolation, separate from the context in which it exists, restricts understanding because it does not include the effect one part has on another, or on the whole. But when systems thinking is used any proposed adjustment or correction to the system takes into consideration how all aspects affect the whole situation. For example, when planning for the development and growth in cities and suburbs, consideration of the availability of fresh water should be given high priority.

Third, we can't solve any of the problems on our own because only one perspective is not enough to fully understand a problem; we need to be aware of as many different perspectives as possible. Therefore, it is useful to have people from diverse ethnic, racial, class, and gender perspectives working together on an issue, as well as people who have different worldviews. Those holding different perspectives provide unique angles for looking at problems and are instrumental in contributing to more effective solutions to problems.

Fourth, a systems thinking perspective enables us to understand why simply fault-finding is such a futile activity. Singling out the decisions or actions of participants to establish culpability for the cause of a problem is often limiting, as most blame is misdirected. A problem is usually not just one person's fault, for most people are usually doing the best they can working within the existing system. The structure of the system, not the effort of the people, has created most of the problems and determines the outcome. Just listen to a television or radio newscast and count how many times the interviewer asks someone, "And who is to blame for this or that failure?" Systems thinkers progress beyond simply seeing the events and mishaps in isolation to seeing patterns of interaction and the underlying structures or worldviews that are accountable for the problems. Systems thinking is always process thinking.

The global economy is a system. It might not be easy to think of it in systems terms, it might seem strange or unfamiliar at first, but as we practice this type of thinking and apply it, I hope you will recognize the benefits. There is nothing to lose and everything to gain from looking at the global economy from this different perspective.

### Benefits of Systems Thinking[21]

- Recognizes patterns that underlie events.
- Sees underlying structures that are responsible for the patterns.
- Learns from history by discerning patterns so that we are not doomed to repeat the same problem.
- Predicts events and prepares for them, rather than being helpless in their wake.
- Appreciates how our thinking is inseparable from the problems we encounter.
- Understands obvious explanations and majority views are not always right.
- Goes beyond blaming others or one's self.
- Challenges, probes, and clarifies our own habitual ways of thinking.
- Encourages long term thinking.
- Predicts unintended consequences.

### Questions to Consider

1. Do you think a systems thinking approach is a beneficial way to study the global economy? Explain.

### The Interacting Parts of a System

Systems are quite complex and contain many different interacting components. The stability of a system – whether it changes or remains steady – depends on many factors, including the size, number and variety of the subsystems within it and the type and degree of connectivity between them. A large complex system is not necessarily an unstable one. Many complex systems are remarkably stable and resist change. Overall, stability is positive, but it comes with a price – resistance to change.

When a stable system does change, it can change rapidly and quite drastically. There is a threshold beyond which a system will suddenly change or break down. If it is under a lot of pressure, a small trigger can cause collapse – the proverbial "straw that breaks the camel's back." Or, systems can change instead of collapsing. For example, with just the right combination of steps, smart leaders can sometimes initiate change with surprising ease. This is the principle of leverage. Leverage doesn't mean piling on the pressure, but knowing where to intervene so that a small effort can get a huge result. To apply leverage first ask what stops the change, and then look at the connections that are holding in place the part you want to change. Cut or weaken these connections and the change may be easy. Applying leverage to initiate change is a key principle of systems thinking.[22]

Feedback loops are integral components of a system. The parts in a **feedback** system are all interconnected directly or indirectly, and when change occurs in one part it ripples out to affect all the other parts. The new parts change, and the effect of this change ripples back to affect the original part. The original part then responds to the new influences, and the influences then come back or feed back to the original part in a modified way, making a loop, not a straight line.

**Reinforcing feedback** is when changes in the whole system feed back to amplify the original change. Change goes through the system, producing more change in the same direction as the initial change. Reinforcing feedback drives a system in the way it is going. Reinforcing feedback is more commonly referred to as positive feedback, but this can be confusing since not all feedback is positive or beneficial. Reinforcing feedback may lead to growth or decline, depending on the starting conditions. We use several reinforcing feedback metaphors in everyday conversation to help describe this process: we're on a roll, jump on the bandwagon, it's downhill all the way, spiraling into oblivion, the sky's the limit, a ticket to heaven, can do no wrong, on the way up, on the slippery slope, snowballing out of control, and nothing lasts forever.[23]

The second type of feedback, **balancing feedback**, limits, restricts, and impedes change and keeps the system stable. Although more commonly called negative feedback, it is neither good nor bad but merely means the system resists change. All systems have balancing feedback loops to stay

**THE STRAW THAT BROKE THE CAMEL'S BACK.**

**A Feedback Loop**

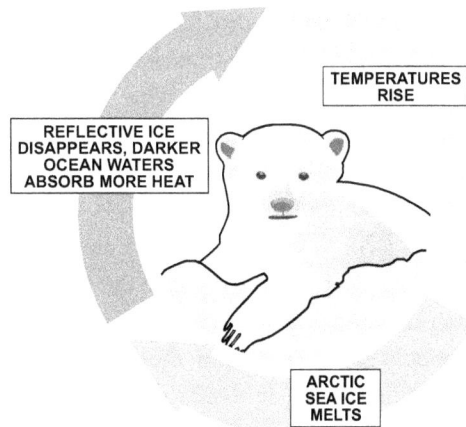

TEMPERATURES RISE

REFLECTIVE ICE DISAPPEARS, DARKER OCEAN WATERS ABSORB MORE HEAT

ARCTIC SEA ICE MELTS

stable because all systems have a goal, even if it is to remain as they are. Balancing feedback loops keep our environment steady, such as in a rainforest, prairie, coral reef, desert, or marsh. However, today climate change is disrupting the balancing feedback loops and creating change in the atmosphere. Other examples of balancing feedback are bodily healing, body temperature, air conditioning, a car's cruise control, predator and prey relationships, food and population balance, markets, supply and demand, and election cycles.

The more dynamically complex the system, the longer the feedback takes to travel around the network connection. When there is a time delay between cause and effect, we often assume there is no effect at all. This delay may fool us into adjusting too late or too much. Many scientists believe this is the case with climate change; what we are doing to correct climate change is too little too late. The feedback delays in signaling climate change have been too far apart in time for us to recognize that the main cause is industrial pollutants and the burning of fossil fuels. One hopes we can make the needed adjustments.

## WORLDVIEWS: THE WAY WE LOOK AT THE WORLD

Systems thinking is a viable method for solving the myriad problems that we face and an interesting way of looking at the global economy. But the question remains, if we all know what the problems are and we have known for decades, why haven't we been able to solve the problems? In fact, why have they gotten worse? Why isn't systems thinking within our radar screen as a problem solving approach? Quite simply, I would argue, because the ways we think, communicate, learn, and understand causes in large part these global problems! Our way of thinking or worldview heavily determines the kind of political, economic and social structures that we create, and those, in turn, create the episodes and events occurring in the world. You might respond and say that if we had a better president or more responsible corporations, the problems could be solved; or you might blame governmental and economic roadblocks for the impasse – after all, Congress moves at a snail's pace. However, the real roadblocks are not merely material but mental. Remember, one of the systems thinking principles states that placing blame on individuals does not solve the problem; it is the underlying structures that create the problems in the first place.

If the ways of thinking that got us to this point are inadequate for coping with the future, we need to purposely learn to explore new ways of thinking. Systems thinkers often use an iceberg as an analogy for looking at a problem. At the tip of the iceberg, the 10-20 percent seen above the surface represents events. These events are reported on the television news, headlined in the newspaper, or featured on the Internet. But looking beneath the surface level of the iceberg's events are the episodes. For example, we saw the event of Hurricane Katrina on the news, but the hurricane was not an isolated event; it is part of larger episodes of hurricanes and extreme weather that are wreaking havoc across the world. And if we look further below the surface of the iceberg's episodes, we see that the political, economic, technological, social, environmental, and cultural patterns (I call these patterns "currents" in my holistic world history) create these episodes. Many scientists attribute such violent and extreme weather conditions as Hurricane Katrina to climate change, which the burning of fossil fuels causes. The modern economic system, the pattern or current, is based on the burning of fossil fuels for energy consumption to drive our modern way of life, while the environmental impact of burning fossil fuels is an unfortunate but necessary byproduct.

Farther down towards the base of the iceberg lies what I call the worldview. This worldview, in turn, influences the underlying patterns (currents), episodes, and events.[24] Our worldview is fashioned around the idea that unlimited economic growth is the unquestioned path to prosperity and well-being. However, the environmental repercussions of this worldview are finally revealing the unintended consequences of this unquestioned belief in unlimited growth. Finally, at the very base of the iceberg are our human behaviors, the universal human commonalities that shape who we are as a species. If we want to change the events, episodes and patterns, we must change the underlying structures that create them; this means we need to modify the way we think, learn and communicate. In other words we must transform our behaviors or worldview.

## A Worldview

What is a worldview? A **worldview** is an overall perspective from which one sees and interprets the world, a set of simplifying suppositions about how the world works and what what one sees and does not see. It is an internal collection of assumptions an individual or a group holds and firmly believes to be self-evident truths. These assumptions shape an individual's beliefs, ideas, attitudes, and values, which, in turn, affect behaviors and actions. A worldview is a paradigm, a fundamental way of looking at reality which functions as a filter. It admits information that is consistent with our deeply held expectations about the world while guiding us to disregard information that challenges or disproves these expectations. When we look through a filter we usually see through it, rather than seeing it – so it is with worldviews. A worldview acts as a built-in "operating system," even though most people are unaware that their perceptions are filtered through it. We rarely bring our worldview out into the light of day, so people are not usually aware of them. Deep in our human consciousness hides our worldview, all the while quietly shaping our reactions to new ideas and information, guiding our decisions, and ordering expectations for the future. Every book read, policy statement enacted, vote cast, the way children are raised, the way solutions are made, the particular method of teaching, a religious sermon, and opinions about the global economy are shaped as much by our worldview as by any objective data or analysis.[25]

**An Iceberg**

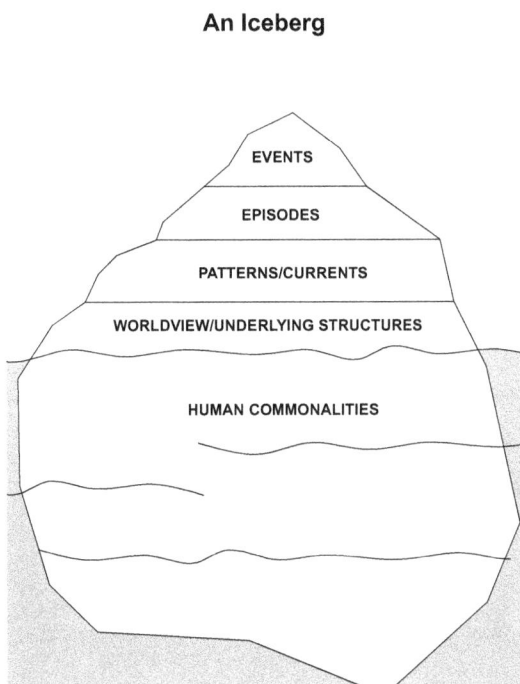

## Contemporary Worldviews

A unique period of human history is occurring at this time, a fifth turning – what I have called the **Global Wave** – that is transforming our human story as this new millennium dawns. Within the Global Wave there is not one all-pervasive, homogenous way of thinking and perceiving reality. Instead I have identified five often contentious and conflicting worldviews, with contradictory ways of knowing and understanding the world, each promoting dissimilar visions for the present and future. In the

43

United States and throughout the world, most people identify with one or a combination of these worldviews. The following is a brief summary of the five major worldviews: indigenous, modern, fundamentalist, globalized, and transformative.

## 1. A Indigenous Worldview

A few people today hold an indigenous worldview. **Indigenous** peoples are any ethnic group who share a similar ethnic identity and inhabit a geographic region with which they have the earliest known historical connection.[26] The adjective "indigenous" has the common meaning of "from" or "of the original origin." Therefore, in a sense, any given people, ethnic group or community may be described as being indigenous in reference to some particular region or location. Indigenous peoples are usually a politically underprivileged group, whose ethnic identity is different from the nation in power and who have been an ethnic entity in the locality before the present ruling nation took over power.[27] Other terms used to describe indigenous peoples are first people, native people, or aboriginal. However, the preferred term, "indigenous peoples," appears to be used by different international agencies such as the United Nations and will be used here.

Indigenous societies are found in every inhabited climate zone and continent of the world from small, farming villages in India and Africa, to Native American pueblos in the Southwestern United States, to farming and herding communities high in the Himalayas, to nomadic groups in the African savannah, and to remote groups in the far Arctic reaches of Canada and Alaska. Indigenous societies range from those who have been significantly exposed to modern influences such as the Maya peoples of Mexico and Central America, to those who as yet remain in comparative isolation from any external influence such as the Sentinelese and Jarawa of the Andaman Islands in the Bay of Bengal to the east of India.

The total world population of indigenous peoples is hard to estimate given the difficulties of identification and inadequate census data, but recent estimates range from 300 million to 350 million as of the start of the 21st century. This would be just under 5 percent of the total world population. This total number includes at least 5,000 distinct peoples in over 72 countries.[28]

Indigenous peoples today survive in populations ranging from only a few dozen to hundreds of thousands or more. Many groups have undergone a dramatic decline and some have even gone extinct, while others remain threatened. Some groups have also been assimilated by other, more modern populations, while in other cases indigenous populations are undergoing a recovery or expansion in numbers. Some indigenous societies no longer live on the land of their ancestors, because of migra-

INDIGENOUS PEOPLES, THE KUNG. THEIR VILLAGE IN NAMIBIA, AFRICA. THEY HAVE SURVIVED FOR OVER 50,000 YEARS AS HUNTER/GATHERERS IN THE KALAHARI DESERT.

tion, relocation, forced resettlement or having their land taken by others. In many cases, indigenous groups face ongoing changes that include permanent loss of language, loss of lands, intrusion onto traditional territories, pollution of traditional lands, and disruption in traditional ways of life.

In the past and even today, many indigenous peoples have been subject to intense discrimination by Europeans or other people holding a modern worldview. The modern societies which held superior warfare technology and medical ways to treat deadly diseases, derisively labeled indigenous people as primitive, inferior, savage, uncivilized, backward, undeveloped, ignorant, and other derogatory terms. Through education and greater awareness, these labels have been largely jettisoned and replaced with terms such as indigenous people, which do not hold an evaluative judgment of superior or inferior.

A characteristic among some indigenous people is that they reached a social and technological plateau in the past. Characteristics common across many indigenous groups is that they rely upon subsistence-based production based on pastoral (herding), horticultural (simple agriculture) and/or hunting and gathering techniques. They are also predominantly non-urbanized societies, although a small number live in urban settings. They may be either settled in a given locale or region or follow a nomadic lifestyle. Even though their numbers are small, and the modern perception of inferiority still continues among some, inclusion of their worldview is important in the Global Wave. Since they have successfully survived for thousands of years, compared to modern society that has continued for a mere 500 years, they have much wisdom to share with all of us.

## 2. A Modern Worldview

The **modern worldview** traces its historical origins back more than 500 years to the expansion of Western European power and its influence and/or ultimate dominance around the world. The modern worldview has been especially powerful over the last two centuries and has today expanded to the farthest reaches of the world. According to the modern worldview the world operates as a giant machine, often re-

**Modern Worldview**

extols scientific reasoning
exalts individualism
treats nature as a commodity
promotes liberal political traditions
separates church and state
promotes industrial production
places faith in technological solutions

ferred to as a Newtonian mechanistic view of the universe. A description of the economy according to the modern worldview has already been presented in section 3: An Overview of Economic Systems. Once again the five dominant economic systems that have developed out of a modern worldview are neoliberal capitalism, managed capitalism, socialism, communism, and state capitalism.

Many individuals continue to follow a modern worldview with its accompanying values of rampant consumerism, cut-throat competition, unlimited economic growth, faith in technological progress, use of force as a way to resolve problems, punishment as a way to correct behaviors, and the staunch defense of individualism. The modern way of understanding the world and solving problems continues today in countless ways. For example, I contend, a modern worldview shaped the decision to invade Iraq in 2003. Based on an optimistic scenario in which the people of Iraq would gladly welcome conquering American troops, Iraqi progress would be achieved through the introduction of democratic institutions and policies in a predictable, rational manner. The certainty that Iraqis would enthusiastically embrace American-style democracy and capitalism was detached from the reality of the situation.

Environmental catastrophe is also largely a result of seeing the environment through the modern worldview lens. Resources are extracted from what is seen as inanimate nature in a detached and mechanistic way. Nature is an object, separate and inferior to human extractors. Often environmental damage is not experienced immediately but at some time in the future, yet the unseen long-term consequences are conveniently ignored or postponed to a vague future date. Nature's purpose in this worldview is to provide the materials necessary for human beings to achieve "progress."

The modern worldview has ushered in a host of astonishing achievements such as the equality of women, medical breakthroughs, educational progress, a high material standard of living for some, and the advancement of human rights, as well as appalling failures such as values of rampant consumerism, cut-throat competition, unlimited economic growth, the use of punishment as a way to correct behaviors, and military force to resolve conflict. One of the challenges of the 21$^{st}$ century is how to draw on the achievements produced from a modern worldview and rethink or discard the darker elements.

---

**Questions to Consider**

1. What is the relationship between capitalism and a modern worldview? Communism/ Socialism?

---

### 3. A Fundamentalist Worldview

Fundamentalism is the term I will be using in this book to describe the people who embrace the third worldview. **Fundamentalism** refers to a belief in a strict adherence to a set of basic principles (often religious), sometimes as a reaction to perceived compromises with modern social, ideological and political life.[29] Many who hold to fundamentalist ideas wish to preserve what they see as traditional beliefs of the past and seek continuity with traditional religious ways. Fundamentalists follow religious traditions that were formed during the Urban Wave, a time when civilizations and universal religions emerged that continue today. However, those who follow a fundamentalist worldview are not following the exact traditions of the past, which would be impossible in a modern society; instead their ideas have grown out of a rejection of modern ideas coupled with a response to the disrupting influences of globalization. Fundamentalism is a rejection of and reaction to the modern concepts of secularism and humanism. They see their religion as true and others as false, which usually results in a denouncement of alternative religious practices and interpretations. There are fundamentalist sects in almost all of the world's major religions, including Christianity, Islam, Hinduism and Judaism. Across cultures, a cluster of common characteristics define fundamentalism, including a literal interpretation of scripture, a suspicion of outsiders, a sense of alienation from the secular culture, a distrust of liberal elites, and a belief in the historical accuracy of their own interpretation of their religious scriptures. Also, religious fundamentalists are often politically active, striving to shape the social order in line with their beliefs, and they may feel that the state should be administered according to religious principles.

Fundamentalism is a movement through which its followers attempt to rescue their religious identity from inclusion in modern, secular Western culture. They have thus created a separate identity based on their particular religious community and upon the fundamental or founding principles of their religion. This formation of a separate identity is deemed necessary as a defensive measure to stem the real and perceived assault from the modern world. Often they see the choices for the organization of their nation as limited to a modern society or a traditional society. Since they reject a modern society, the only other choice they see is the preservation of their traditional ways. Also many people in modern nations find that traditional values give resolute comfort and reassurance in a fluctuating and inexplicable world. Therefore, many people from the Middle East, to India, to the United States find that the familiar traditions of the past give meaning, identity, and steadfastness to their lives. Although the fundamentalist worldview is very diverse and not unchanged from the past, the essence of many of these beliefs continues today and is zealously held by millions, if not billions, of people throughout the world.

Although fundamentalism has largely retained its religious references, the term has more recently been generalized to mean strong obedience to any set of beliefs in the face of criticism or unpopularity. Some refer to any literal-minded philosophy with the pretense of being the sole source of objective truth as fundamentalist, regardless of whether it is called a religion. For example, some people hold the belief – called market fundamentalism – that market capitalism is best and can correct all of society's ills. Many have strong opinions about social and political values and voice their opinions in a forceful and sometimes violent manner. The application of the term fundamentalist to both a religious and social-political situations seems appropriate.

FUNDAMENTALIST WORLDVIEW
WOMEN IN TRADITIONAL DRESS BY MOSQUE IN IRAN.
PHOTO DENISE AMES

### 4. A Globalized Worldview

A third worldview, a **globalized worldview**, is sweeping the world today. One of the most important dimensions of globalization is economic globalization, both terms have been defined above. The globalized worldview has grown out of the modern worldview and has many of its attributes. But I have categorized it as a separate worldview since it differs from the modern worldview in that "time has speeded up," the pace of growth and development has intensified and spread to the farthest reaches of the earth, and a global consciousness is developing. At this point, the United States heavily influences a globalized worldview, the leading economic, cultural, political, and military power in the world today. However, the U.S. as the preeminent power in the world is waning; other nations, such as China and India, are challenging its number one status. A globalized worldview has taken hold in intensely industrialized areas of Canada, Europe, Japan, and Australia and reaches across the world into parts of China, India, Southeast Asia, Latin America, and parts of the Middle East and Africa as well. A globalized worldview affects all patterns of society.

Global capitalism is the dominant economic system in the world, with almost all nations pulled into its economic web. National and local economies, regulated and protected by nation-

al and local governments, have been largely folded into one integrated economic system governed by capitalist principles. Ignoring national boundaries, a global economic marketplace conducts business, exchanges currencies, and regulates trade policies. Global multinational corporations make many of the economic rules and conduct the business

### Descriptors of a Globalized Worldview
interconnections, blurring of boundaries, approximation, speed, demassification, networks, diversity, differentiation, specialization, productivity, consolidation, mergers, acquisitions, interdependence

of the world marketplace. They promote a consumer-focused economy and a powerful financial sector by extending their broad influence to the farthest reaches of the globe. The globalization process, and in particular economic globalization, has both negative and beneficial aspects.

Technological changes have ushered in faster and more sophisticated communication and transportation technologies that transcend national boundaries and more intricately connect the world than at any time in the past. These instantaneous high-speed communication devices with sophisticated computer technologies revolutionize our relations with each other. The Internet, television, high-speed travel, cell phones, social media, and other forms of telecommunications link the world by dissolving former barriers of time and distance and provide new connections between people.

Conflict and warfare are different in a globalized worldview from the modern worldview. Conflict has become unpredictable, random, irrational, and volatile. Wars can be sparked by many factors: scarce resources like water, food, fuel, or other basic necessities; religious differences and perspectives; different worldviews; exploitation of natural resources by elites; destabilized governments; and tensions and anxieties created by rapid social disruption with the accompanying loss of solidifying traditions and customs.

The issue of environmental pollution and the health of the planet is a primary concern for global citizens, regardless of their national identity. The well-being of the environment is a global issue that knows no national boundaries; viable solutions have to be made at a cooperative transnational level. Yet, as is often the case, those adhering to a globalized worldview place profits above all else, even the future well-being of our planet. The horrific pollution in China is a prime example of the Chinese government and people preferring high economic growth rates (about 9 percent a year in the 2000s) to the detriment of the environment. A globalized worldview contributes to the overshooting of sustainability levels of the planet by promoting unlimited growth. Humans began to **overshoot** the planet in the mid-1980s, which means that our species is taking more resources from the planet than can be replaced by natural processes in a given year.

The new "religion" promoted by multi-national corporations and their political allies is that of worldwide consumerism. Led by the U.S., a vast entertainment and advertising sector has perpetuated and glamorized the notion of consumerism as a form of status and as a symbol of affiliation with modern culture. Rampant consumerism has gone way beyond the basic products for a comfortable material life to the frenzied accumulation of items that purportedly bring an individual psychological well-being and status recognition. Advertisers promote consumer products like Coca-Cola, McDonalds, i-pods, blackberries, i-phones, travel destinations, and designer clothes as necessities that define individual identity. The automobile is a convenience and symbol of personal freedom. Many cultural expressions – music, dance, art, film, and dress – have been made into commodities for the world consumer market and follow a distinctive Western commercial bent.

Mainstream American thought reflects a globalized worldview in what I label the "consumer creed." The principles of the consumer creed are generally accepted by a vast majority of Americans, who have energetically exported it to others, such as India and China. But the consumer creed has left many people discontented, alienated, unfulfilled, and in a spiritual malaise, while leaving the planet environmentally ravaged.

Although a globalized worldview has "opened up" the world in many positive ways – communication networks, especially the internet, transportation linkages and travel opportunities, sophisticated technology, breakthrough medical discoveries, and comfortable living standards for some – there are many who challenge its corporate dominance, unbridled consumerism, expedient business climate, mistreated environment, and uncertain future.

## 5. A Transformative Worldview

At this point in time, diverse people are actively challenging the negative parameters of the four other worldviews. A different worldview, some say a different story, is urgently needed in order to assure the continuation of our human species and life as we know it on earth. Leaders from diverse fields – religious leaders, business entrepreneurs, international political leaders, indigenous farmers, political activists, environmentalists, entertainers, scientists, working people, artists, writers, academics, educators, economists, concerned citizens, and others – are contributing to the creation of what I call a **transformative worldview**. Those who adhere at least in part to this worldview assert that diverse paths are possible and attainable and that the globalized worldview is not an inevitable or desirable scenario of how the future will or should be played out. Millions of people around the

**MCDONALD'S MEGA BIG MAC AND COKE IN MALAYSIA.**
**EVERYTHING IS BIGGER ACCORDING TO THE**
**GLOBALIZED WORLDVIEW.**

### The Consumer Creed

1. The desire for a comfortable life-style with a profusion of consumer comforts.

2. A belief in progress, which blesses hard work with ample financial rewards.

3. A right to material abundance without concern for the environmental or social costs.

4. Competitive, ambitious, individualistic values.

5. An entrepreneurial career preference, where wealth is realized without regard for how it is obtained.

6. Faith in technological progress as the means to solve all problems.

7. A disconnect between a materialistic/consumer way of life and its effects upon the environment.

8. The attitude the consumer creed is the highest ideal, and should be shared with the rest of the world.

world are promoting alternative ideas and diverse options for a different worldview and voicing their convictions in a forceful, yet usually peaceful fashion.

Critics contend that none of the above worldviews seem sufficient to meet the complex, interrelated challenges of the 21st century, and each has glaring detriments with the potential to harm our planet and undermine our future life. For example, they contend that the rigid dogma of fundamentalism will not generate a more inclusive and culturally tolerant worldview in an increasingly interracial environment. Some people advocating a transformative worldview admire the sense of local place and the importance of the environment that many traditional people have connected with for millennia without losing a shared consciousness as global citizens. Some argue that we need to move beyond the mechanistic, segmented order of the modern worldview without sacrificing the value of scientific inquiry, public secularism and rational, logical thought. Many people advocating a transformative worldview admire the advances in technology, transportation and communication, while rejecting the despoiling of our planet through environmental exploitation. Transformative supporters draw upon the idea that we are all global citizens, heralded in the globalized worldview, yet we need to take steps to limit the dominance of the world's economy by giant, multinational and often self-serving corporations.

Elements in the formation of a transformative worldview come from diverse sources; some are positive aspects of the other worldviews. For example, highly regarded from the indigenous worldview is the wisdom of indigenous people who call upon the wise council of their elders, respect and connect with nature, and value the strong relationship with territorial place. From the fundamentalist worldview, many want to preserve the sense of shared meaning and universal values, such as compassion and love, that universal religions offer, as well as the importance of family connections. From the modern worldview the ideals of democracy, the advancement of scientific inquiry, medical improvements, beneficial technological innovations, public-supported, mass education, and the expansion of human rights to include women and people of color are all noteworthy accomplishments. The globalized worldview's stunning technological developments, especially high-speed, integrated computer networks and reasonably-priced, global transportation have provided instantaneous communication linking diverse people around the globe. Even some indigenous people in remote villages are linked to the Internet and use appropriate scientific knowledge for enhancing their goal of achieving self-reliance in food production. And some would say that the globalized worldview's vision of "opening up" the world to unfettered trade has benefited many people with a more materially comfortable standard of living than ever experienced before.

**WIND FARM IN UK REPRESENTS THE TRANSFORMATIVE WORLDVIEW**

**ROYD MOOR WINDFARM IN THE UNITED KINGDOM (UK)**

Yet the transformative worldview is in a process of evolution. Its many proponents offer alternatives to prevailing notions of cultural uniformity, corporate dominance, consumer-driven values, unchecked individualism, oligarchic concentration of wealth and power, and environmental destruction. Although this diverse array of thoughts, beliefs, ideas, theories, lifestyles, choices, and actions defies rigid categorization, these visionary conceptions share common characteristics that define the transformative worldview. Even though the modern and globalized worldviews are the dominant paradigms at this point in time, the transformative worldview is challenging their sway and offering viable options for a sustainable, more equitable future.

Which worldview or combination of worldviews will we as global citizens choose for our future? We all have a voice and a critical stake in the future outcome.

### Questions to Consider

1. Which worldview to you most closely identify with? Explain.

## CONCLUDING INSIGHTS: AN OVERVIEW OF THE GLOBAL ECONOMY

Now that we have gotten the introductory chapter under our belt, let's stop to ponder why you are taking the time to read this book about the global economy. Since you are reading this book, chances are you are puzzled by the workings of the global economy. Why are so many people unemployed? If they are employed, why are many of them looking for better jobs? Why are so many people angry and fearful and taking it out on their political representatives? In the U.S. we are still experiencing the effects of what has been termed the "Great Recession" starting in 2008. Why did so many people buy houses that they could not afford? Why did banks loan them the money to do this? Why didn't politicians step in to stop these abuses? Why did financial speculation bring untold riches to some and misery to others? When searching for answers to these questions, it soon becomes apparent that the very nature of our global economic system (especially as practiced in the U.S.) needs a complete examination, and ultimately, major changes.

The foundation of our global economy has historically profited from addictions. The early global economy profited from sugar, tobacco, and addictive caffeine drinks, such as coffee and tea; alcohol derived from either corn or sugar; and cotton to make a variety of consumer clothing. Today the addiction continues from compulsively playing video games, to fixated texting, to consumer shopping for goods that are beyond mere necessity, to prescription drugs, to eating addictive fast foods that have an inordinate portion of fats, salt and sugar, to social networks such as Facebook that are also obsessive. Is creating more addictions for consumers a good way to create wealth in a society?

Our global economy as currently structured: 1) has been leading to ever more movement of wealth from the middle class to the top income layers of our society over the past three decades; 2) is built upon endless growth with little regard for the natural environment which sustains all life on earth; 3) encourages overconsumption of both food and other items for the sake of profit (as opposed to human well-being); and 4) has bled periphery countries of natural resources, often with no real benefit to the people in those countries except for a very few.

It is imperative that we dig deeper to better understand the underlying forces driving the problems mentioned above. Only if we understand the driving forces will we be able to correct the situation. That is our job in this book, to understand the operating system of the global economy at work.

It is a holistic and complex set of political, economic, and social arrangements. It is my estimation that the political economy of today is, in fact, in crisis precisely because it cannot find reasonable solutions to its current dilemmas. The inability to contain ecological destruction is a major one, and overproduction, over-accumulation, population pressures, and inequality are others. The issue before us is how do we respond to the global economy crisis. Do we essentially remain the same, or do we have a revolution, enact reforms, or rebuild a somewhat different economic system? This is the central debate of the next 25-50 years.[30]

My approach in this book will be to question and critique the assumptions and foundations of our current global economy. I do not purport to have all the answers. But I do realize that something is amiss today, and I find it is of vital importance that we start to think about and discuss the predicament we are all in. I hope you will find this discussion stimulating, and I challenge you to keep up your study of the global economy in order that these intractable problems will have a solution beneficial to a majority of the people in the world and to the environment.

---

### Questions to Consider

1. Do you feel that the global economy needs transforming, or is fine that way it is? Explain.

---

# CHAPTER TWO

# Historical Roots of the Global Economy

*"Written into the long history of our planet, in one form or another, is the record of what is coming our way."*

*Julia Whitty writer and filmmaker*

Our global economy did not magically start overnight. It has a long history. To get a clear picture of the global economy today and the changing nature of capitalism, we need to travel back in time to around 1500, the beginning of what I have called the Modern Wave (see *Waves of Global Change: A Holistic World History*). This date signaled the beginning of profound modern transformations that would ultimately change the world; one of the most significant was the expansion of capitalism.

## THE WESTERN EUROPEAN ECONOMY PRIOR TO 1500

A market economy existed before 1500. Phoenicians, Greeks, Romans, and merchants in other ancient civilizations had a market economy to some extent. For example, ancient Greek farmers grew capital and labor-intensive olives for olive oil and grapes for wine as a profitable cash crop that they sold in the market place. Greeks, in turn, imported cheaper subsistence staples, such as wheat, from their numerous colonies. Gradually it became very expensive for small farmers to grow these cash crops, and wealthy landowners stepped in to quickly buy their land. With no other livelihood available, many small farmers made the exodus to the cities. Social upheaval ensued.

Western Europe after the collapse of the Roman Empire around 500 CE (Common Era) was composed of small competing, unstable, decentralized political units loosely connected by the Catholic Church. It was subject to repeated nomadic invasions and internal political squabbling. Western Europe became an unlikely future core area, since it remained on the periphery region of world history from 500 to 1500, commonly referred to as the European Middle Ages. Politically, warring feudal kings and land-owning lords replaced Roman imperial authority, resulting in fragmented, decentralized political structures and instability. Militarily, the centralized, well-oiled armies of the Roman Empire gave way to local feudal knights defending their enclaves from aggressive neighbors or launching offensive attacks. Socially, the vast majority of the European people were peasants, with a small, elite noble class and a very small merchant class. Economically, a self-sufficient, local, domestic economy and city guilds gradually replaced the highly centralized Roman imperial economy. The household was the basis of the economy in the European Middle Ages. Almost everyone lived in a household – family, servants, and apprentices – and everyone worked: men, women, and children. The market economy was on the fringes of society during the Middle Ages, but as cities grew in the later part of the Middle Ages, trade and commerce increased. The merchant class slowly began to fill a gap not covered by the local, domestic economy or guild system, although they still remained on the economic margins.

The urban economy, especially in the later part of the Middle Ages, was based on what was called a guild system. A **guild** is where artisans who had a common business or trade banded together to carefully control and regulate the production and distribution of their products. For example, bakers, blacksmiths, hat-makers and many others formed guilds. The guilds restricted membership, regulated standards of quality and price, discouraged competition, and resisted technological innovations. Guilds charged a just price, not a market price, for their products. A **just price** would cover the expenses of the guild member and a small, but not an exorbitant, profit. The guilds did not seek to realize profits as much as to protect markets and preserve their members' livelihoods and security. They did not follow capitalist principles.

Western Europe is recognized as the seedbed for the sprouting of capitalism. Changes were occurring in this region prior to 1500 that would provide the incubation for the capitalist economic system to take hold and expand. Beginning with the rise of cities in Europe in the 1200s, a capitalist economic system called **cottage industries** began to flourish alongside the domestic economy and guild system. Textile merchants seeking profits found the guild system restricted their efforts; therefore, they decided to sidestep the city-based guilds and move textile production to the countryside, away from the prying eyes of the city guilds. They set up shop in rural cottages, hence the name cottage industries. Instead of relying on an urban artisan in a guild to produce cloth, the merchants organized a "putting-out system" where they delivered unfinished materials like raw wool to rural households. Men and primarily women in their countryside cottages would take on the tasks of spinning the wool into yarn, weaving the yarn into cloth, cutting the cloth according to patterns, or assembling the pieces into garments. The merchants paid workers a piece work wage for their services, picked up the finished goods, and sold them in the market place for a profit. This system of textile production continued until industrialization in Britain started around 1750, when the factory began to replace the cottage as the place for textile production.

By 1400, Europe's unfavorable balance of trade with Asia verged on an economic crisis. Europeans imported valuable spices, silk, sugar, perfume, and jewels from the East, while they exported less valuable wool, tin, and copper. Faced with a need for new markets, Europeans embarked on a frenzied pursuit of trade and profit. For about two centuries Portugal and Spain forged the way in finding new trade routes and lands, and spreading Western ideas, values, and power across the world. But Britain, France, and the Netherlands impatiently snapped at their heels as they sought to overtake the leaders. In a fortuitous occurrence for Spain, the explorer Christopher Columbus blew into the Western hemisphere, which Europeans countries promptly claimed as their colonies and began the search for treasure. Capitalism did not emerge as a viable economic system until roughly the 1500 date. It was the chance "discovery" and conquest of the Western hemisphere that helped Western Europe create the capitalist economic system as we know it. To better understand the historical roots of the global economy, I will divide it into three sections: Commercial Capitalism in the Early Modern Era Economy (1500-1750), The Modern Industrial Economy (1750-1900) and The Twentieth Century Economy (1900-2000).

### Questions to Consider

1. Would the use of just price work in a capitalist economy? Explain.

# COMMERCIAL CAPITALISM IN THE EARLY MODERN ERA (1500-1750)

Capitalism burst onto the world stage around 1500 largely because Western Europe incorporated the riches from the Western hemisphere into its economic orb. As mentioned in chapter 1, there are many dimensions to capitalism; at this time mercantilism, a particular dimension, emerged. **Mercantilism** was the economic relationship between a European country, called the "mother country," and its colonies, which they established throughout the Western hemisphere and beyond. Following the economic precepts of the time, the colonial rulers strove to maintain a favorable balance of trade for their country by importing cheap raw materials from their colonies and in turn exporting back to them the more profitable manufactured goods that the mother country produced. With this economic policy, Western European commercial cities were the core areas and the colonies were the periphery. Many European colonial governments like the British and the Dutch encouraged mercantilism through legislation that made it legal and profitable to monopolize as much manufacturing as possible in the mother country.

Mercantilism depended upon a form of control called **colonialism**: the extension of a powerful country's control over a dependent, weaker country, territory, or people. Colonizers dominated the resources, labor, markets, and internal affairs of their colonies, and also imposed religious, socio-cultural, and linguistic structures on the native populations. The colonial periphery supplied natural resources to the colonial rulers: silver from Mexico, Bolivia, and Peru; furs and skins from North America and Siberia; sugar and cocoa from the West Indies and Brazil; tobacco, rice, and indigo, and later cotton from the American South; coffee and rubber from Southeast Asia; and jute and spices from India. Low-paid native laborers, indentured servants, or slaves extracted and processed the raw materials.

The former Spanish colonial city of Potosi in Bolivia, for example, purportedly the highest city in the world, lies in the shadows of the fabled "mountain of silver." To extract the prized ore, the Spanish from 1540 to 1640 forced local indigenous men to labor in the mines for weeks on end; some never saw the light of day. Indigenous miners died by the thousands due to exhaustion, horrible working conditions, and mercury poisoning from the mining method. The Spanish eventually replaced disease-ridden indigenous workers with slaves from Africa, who were called "human mules," since they replaced mules who could not survive the horrible conditions.

Wealth accumulated in the core Western European cities from this commercial process. Money poured into Western European treasuries and profits were reinvested in other enterprises. The additional infusion of money into the European economic system eventually flowed to British bankers and investors or to private shippers, financiers, merchants, and manufacturers.[1] This transfer of wealth spelled the eventual decline of Spain from core status and the rise of the Netherlands and Britain to that station. Because the economic wealth was derived from commerce, it is often called an era of commercial capitalism.

Agrarian changes also spurred the growth of commercial capitalism. European peasants for centuries practiced an **open field system**, a form of agricultural organization in which they farmed large tracks of land for elite landlords. Peasant farmers produced food for their own subsistence needs, and paid a required amount of the surplus as tribute (taxes) to the landowner. In this system efficiency and productivity were largely secondary, with the tribute payment to the landowner and the subsistence needs of the peasants as primary. But with the **enclosure process**, the open field system began to give way to farming according to capitalist principles, where efficiency and productivity became primary. Farms, as well as shared areas called "the commons," were first enclosed or converted to privately owned plots marked with

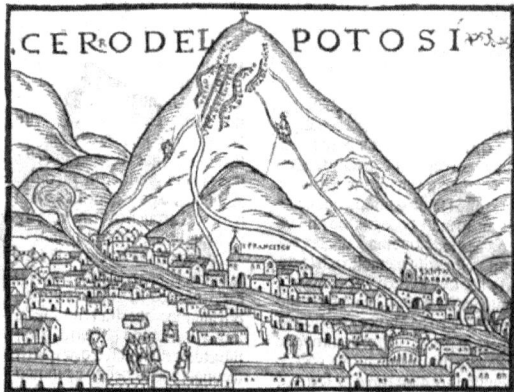

**FIRST IMAGE IN EUROPE OF THE MOUNTAIN OF SILVER IN POTOSI, BOLIVIA.**

clear boundaries and specific private ownership. Privatization and commodification first took off in England where landowners who benefited from this capitalist move, enthusiastically embraced it. Uprooted peasant farmers vainly protested their plight since they were the ones who lost the land they had farmed for centuries; this strictly financial process largely ignored their welfare.

Farmers applied scientific methods to newly enclosed fields to increase crop yields that were now capable of producing two crops yearly, while one-third lay fallow. Many landowners found these new agricultural methods generated sizable profits in expanding domestic markets. With these agricultural innovations, increased productivity, and favorable climate conditions, demographic growth ballooned. Europe in the 18th century continued to be predominately agricultural, but the function of this key sector changed from the general production of foodstuffs for the local population to a profitable business enterprise.

## Trade

With invigorated European exploration, the trade network shifted from Arab merchants concentrated along the Mediterranean Sea to northwestern European merchants centered on the Atlantic Ocean. Spices and tropical products formerly carried in Arab ships now traveled via European vessels; in return, European manufactured textile goods flowed to ports in Africa and Asia. For example, in the 18th century the **Triangle Trade** started between Africa, Europe, and the Americas. European ships carried guns, knives, metal ware, manufactured items, beads, colored cloth, and liquor to the West African coast to be exchanged with African chieftains who dealt in captured slaves. The captured slaves shipped to the Americas were exchanged for raw materials, such as sugar, tobacco, furs, precious metals, and raw cotton that were in turn transported to Europe to be made into finished goods that were either shipped back to the colonies or to Africa to begin the trading network again. The slave trade generated exorbitant profits, about one-third of English capital formation in the 17th century.[2]

Slavery was a common practice in earlier civilizations, but with the Modern Wave and the increasing expansion of the capitalist economic system, the buying and selling of slaves expanded and intensified. Along with their European counterparts, West African elites engaged in the slave trade to gain an economic advantage for themselves by trading captured slaves for European firearms and other manufactured items. The African slave traders used their additional firepower to raid neighboring tribes and villages to capture even more slaves for trade and profit. Slaving sparked conflict between local tribes as deadly competition increased. African slavers sold their human commodities to eager European buyers at port cities along the Atlantic seaboard who, in turn, transported their human cargo to slave dealers in the Western hemisphere. Misery, starvation, or early death awaited many of the captured victims; estimates show that on average 25 percent of the slaves apprehended and transported to the Western hemisphere in what was known as the Middle Passage suffered an agonizing death.[3]

The slave trade had a destructive effect by disrupting and contributing to the collapse of previously stable and prosperous African village societies. Using a systems approach to examine the slave trade, all the actors in the process – both African and European traders and slave buyers – were intricately connected in this lucrative line of work with little regard for the ethical considerations. The slave trade also pitted Africans against each other as they competed for captured slaves in the ghastly era of enslavement and genocide.

Indigenous people, along with slaves, provided the labor that aided the expansion of commercial capitalism. For example, the North American fur trade could not have provided the riches it did without their involvement. The fur trade tapped into the rich fur-producing regions of North America. Indigenous peoples trapped animals for Europeans and exchanged the pelts for manufactured goods, such as wool blankets, iron pots, firearms, and distilled spirits. The hides shipped to Europe supported a burgeoning demand for fashionable furs, such as beaver skin hats and fur clothing. Beaver populations declined so rapidly that trappers had to push further inland to obtain this valuable commodity. When trappers depleted the trapping grounds, they poached or invaded a neighboring tribe's territories. This encroachment frequently led to conflict or war. Therefore, it was necessary for the invaders and defenders to obtain more weaponry either to garner more furs or to defend their territory. This cycle of violence and exploitation, like the slave trade, perpetuated brutality and upheaval but contributed to the wealth of the European powers in the region.

With a capitalist economy came the creation of cartels or corporations, when the British and Dutch merchants formed joint stock companies in the 16th century. European monarchies granted royal charters to **joint-stock companies** for trade with their colonies. One advantage of these companies was that now one individual was not required to raise all the capital for entrepreneurial activities and, therefore, investors could pool their capital to lessen their possible losses from risky ventures. This form of organization was more advantageous for risky ventures where large investments were essential and capitalization needed a large pool of investors.[4] On the other hand, the main objective of joint stock companies, the forerunners of the modern corporation, was to make a handsome profit for their shareholders with little regard for the social, environmental, or moral consequences of their actions. The most famous – or infamous – joint stock company was the **British East India Company**, chartered in 1600 by England's Queen Elizabeth I. The company obtained monopoly trading privileges with India which expanded into virtual rule of the sub-continent until its dissolution in 1858.

Although the early modern era marks the emergence of Western Europe as a core area, aside from the Americas and a few other coastal areas, European influence had not yet reached world hegemony. It is not until industrialization began mid-18th century that industrialization and capitalism spread and engulfed new areas of the world and began to have a profound and lasting influence.

## Core Areas of Commercial Capitalism

By the 1540s, Spain was the world's most important political and economic force. The lure of easy money in the colonies undermined Spain's real economy, which was based on wool manufacturing and steel. The government did not strengthen its domestic industry; instead, incessant borrowing led to huge debt. Since elites were exempt, peasants, artisans, and merchants paid most of the taxes. Spain had come to be an extreme of rich and poor with a tiny middle class. In the early 17th century, wars drained Spanish coffers and led to its inevitable decline. Half of their population fled from the cities to the countryside.[5]

Independent Holland (United Provinces) started its climb to commercial leadership while Spain was still strong. The era from 1648 to 1670s was a period of economic openness and Dutch expansion. They had the world's largest merchant fleet in 1669, 6,000 ships, and large pools of investment capital accumulated from their advances in technology, textiles, shipbuilding, agriculture, and fishing. But by the 1700s another shift to a new core area took place – Britain. The basic reason for the decline of the Dutch free-trade system in the 1720s and 1730s was that the wave of mercantilism that swept the European continent did not favor the world's core economy. When trade barriers went up Dutch profits weakened. The fortunes of the Dutch Republic in the 18th century ebbed. By the late 1700s finance began to displace hands-on commerce. Two costly military conflicts were severely harmful to the Dutch economy. As in Spain, town populations fell, and food and tax riots were common in the 1760s and 1770s.

A harbinger of problems in the U.S. today, the Dutch upper classes were preoccupied with passive financial methods of creating wealth – holding bonds and securities – instead of producing real products or services. A transfer of Dutch capital abroad, mainly to Britain, spelled the decline of the Dutch core economy in the 18th century and a shift to British dominance.[6]

---

**Questions to Consider**

1. What lessons can be learned about capitalism from the Commercial Capitalism era 1500-1750?

2. What similar problems did Spain and the Netherlands face as they declined from their core status?

---

# INDUSTRIAL CAPITALISM IN THE MODERN ERA (1750-1914)

The expansion of capitalism continued unabated into the modern era that stretched from the end of the 18th century to 1914. A new source of wealth creation developed: industrialization. **Industrialization** is the process of change from an economy based on home production of goods to one based on large-scale, mechanized factory production with a wage-based labor force. The industrialization process, known as the **Industrial Revolution**, moved rapidly from Britain to neighboring countries, which, along with a change in technology, resulted in vast political, economic, social, and cultural implications. This transformation marks one of the turning points in world history, when humans fundamentally change the ways in which they live.[7]

Along with the primary industries – commerce, trade, and agriculture – the capitalistic economic system extended into a new area of wealth creation with the development of secondary industries – manufacturing and construction – which converted raw materials into finished, usable products. This required greater inputs of fossil fuel energy, primarily coal in this era. Profits from commercial enterprises poured into certain regions of Western Europe. As capital accumulated, enterprises plowed profits back into businesses that generated even more income if successful, making a profit for owners and investors.

## Early Industrialization in Britain

Britain was the first country to industrialize, and the first industry was cotton textiles. Through legislation, the British government aided the infant British textile industry by imposing tariffs to protect the domestic industry from cheaper and higher quality imports from their colony, India. **Tariffs**, an import tax, made India's imported textiles more expensive than domestic British cotton goods. Consumers chose the protected and cheaper domestic product, and, thus, the British textile industry flourished. At this time India, a private colony of the British East India Company, had a centuries-old textile industry that made high quality, hand-loomed goods. Britain essentially shut down the Indian textile industry and then forced them to import sub-quality textiles from Britain. This further enriched the British textile industry.

The events contributing to industrialization in Britain can be linked to the insatiable demand for cotton that helped spark the tumultuous conflict over slavery in the United States which led to the Civil War (1861-1865). High consumer demand for the popular cotton textiles spurred a rush of new technological innovations to process cotton more rapidly. For example, Eli Whitney, an American, invented the cotton gin in 1793, which quickly separated seeds from the raw cotton, a process which previously slaves performed in a time consuming manner. With this labor-saving invention the American South responded to increasing demand for raw cotton by growing more of the valuable raw commodity. The capitalist trade network and British textile production were intricately connected to the growth of large cotton plantations in the American South: slaves toiled longer hours to produce more cotton, cotton farming expanded into new U.S. territories, more slaves were needed as farm laborers, and the price of land, slaves, and cotton skyrocketed as demand for cotton swelled.

British textile entrepreneurs responded to the mounting demand for their product by creating a new method for producing greater quantities: the factory system. Before the 18th century, as noted, a guild member or cottage workers produced textiles at what we would consider today a leisurely pace. But a very different work environment existed in the new **factories**: numerous workers, sometimes hundreds, gathered under one roof, earned a standard wage, divided tasks into individual parts, and worked under the close supervision of the owner or manager. The small guild owners had to compete, eventually unsuccessfully, with this more cost effective production process. Although the factory-produced products were lower in price than guild products, workers merely performed routine and repetitive tasks in an impersonal, mass-production environment, most often under horrendous working conditions.

The factory method of production was economically successful as individual productivity increased substantially, but at the expense of worker autonomy and creativity. The more relaxed work styles typical in home production and small farming, and the varied work of the guilds, were abandoned for robotic, impersonal, and dangerous work in assembly-line factories. With the increase in the numbers of workers, factory organization shifted to an emphasis on greater specialization and subdivision of tasks, resulting in a tremendous increase in total factory output.[8] Even cotton planters in the American South organized slave labor into gangs of workers that replicated the mass-production factory system in Britain, performing repetitive tasks at a relentless pace closely supervised by an ever-watchful overseer.

### Free Trade Capitalism and Protectionism

Introduced in this era was a new form of capitalism, as opposed to mercantilism. Englishman **Adam Smith** championed a different form of capitalism that Britain promoted. In his seminal book *The Wealth of Nations* in 1776, Smith opposed mercantilism and instead argued that a free market or free trade economy was better. He said that natural laws govern the economy, especially the law of **supply and demand**. In his classical economic theory, the relation between these two

COTTONOPOLIS, EARLY PAINTING OF COTTON MILLS IN MANCHESTER, ENGLAND.

factors determines the price of a commodity. This relationship is the driving force in a free market. As demand for an item increases, prices rise. When manufacturers respond to the price increase by producing a larger supply of the item in question, this, theoretically, drives the price down.[9] In a free-market economy, competition will force producers to manufacture goods more efficiently so that they can sell lower cost goods than their competitors. Government laws and regulations that interfere with what Smith regarded as the natural laws of a self-governing economy – or, as he called it, the "invisible hand of the marketplace" – should be repealed. Smith disagreed with the mercantilists' regulations on trade and protective tariffs. He believed that the home industries should be left to freely compete in the marketplace. The term **laissez-faire** capitalism describes the principles of free trade and deregulation.

By the 1820s the Industrial Revolution was in full swing in Britain. It was the leading industrial economy of the world and its factories could undercut competitors in virtually every market. The British manufacturers viewed mercantilism as harmful to them and embraced free trade. If foreigners were allowed to sell their products, such as raw materials, to Britain tariff-free, then British manufacturers promised they could lower their costs even further. With cheaper imported food allowed into the country, factory owners reasoned that they could pay lower wages to their workers without reducing their living standards. Manufacturers reasoned that if foreigners could buy all the goods they needed from Britain, then foreigners would have less incentive to develop their own industries.[10]

Opponents of mercantilism in Britain focused on repealing the **Corn Laws**, the taxes imposed in the early 1800s on imports of grain, "corn," according to the British. The tariffs substantially increased the domestic price of grain. Of course, British farmers were eager to maintain restrictions on agricultural imports, since this meant less competition for them. They relied on the Corn Laws' very high tariffs on imported grain in order to protect their grain market, and rightly argued that repeal of the laws would doom British farming. Supporters of the laws argued that self-sufficiency in food was important to the security of the British people and the tradition of farming reflected a time-honored British way of life. Nonetheless, free traders won out, but only after a long and bitter struggle. In 1846-1847 Parliament repealed the Corn Laws, the last vestiges of British mercantile controls on foreign trade.[11]

The British industrialists were eager to promote the laissez-faire form of capitalism in the 19th century. At the time its industries were already well established and more efficient, and thus able to sell products at a lower price than their nearest competitors in the U.S. and France. The British lobbied for its competitors to remove any tariffs that protected their domestic industries. The U.S., which was industrializing in the early 19th century, wanted to protect its infant industries from cheaper British products and thus had protective tariffs. Although American consumers had to pay more for the tariff-protected products, the factories that made these products for U.S. consumers were able to flourish and grow. It was a trade-off policy that the U.S. continued through the 19th and well into the 20th century. The revenues from the tariffs went directly into the U.S. treasury, which produced enough of a budget surplus that an income tax was not needed until 1913.

U.S. manufacturers were much more protectionist than their German or Japanese counterparts – but almost all the industrializing countries protected their industries to some extent. Unconcerned about foreign competition, national manufacturers with protective tariffs could charge domestic prices well above world levels and earn very high profits. Russia imposed some of the highest tariffs in modern history, 84 percent on manufactured goods, which was nearly double the second highest tariffs in the world: an average of 44 percent in the U.S. One of the downsides of high tariffs is that they tended to establish monopolies. High trade barriers also contributed to foreign ownership, as European firms unable to export to the Russian market, for instance, "jumped" tariff walls and set up shop inside the country.[12]

Britain, the U.S., and most other industrializing countries have used aggressive **infant industry** promotion policies in the early stages of industrialization. This means that legislation is used to erect protective tariffs in order that industries just getting started are able to grow and prosper. Only after a country achieved industrial supremacy would it start practicing free trade policies. As economist Ha-Joon Chang explains, "Infant-industry promotion was a "ladder" that most countries have needed (and actively used) in order to climb up to the top – and which was eagerly "kicked away" when no longer necessary." Thus when mature industrialized nations try to prevent the periphery countries from using infant-industry protection, they are effectively "kicking away the ladder" that helps them industrialize, which critics accused Britain of doing in the mid-19th century.[13] Economic historian Jeffrey Frieden concludes that "the contribution of trade protection to rapid industrialization in the late 19th and early 20th centuries was controversial then, and the judgment of history remains ambiguous. Trade protection harmed consumers. Whether the costs outweighed the benefits for societies at large is an open question."[14]

## Corporations

With industrial capitalism many joint stock companies, small family businesses, and guilds gave way to the modern corporation. A **corporation** is a formal business association with a publicly registered charter recognizing it as a separate legal entity having its own privileges, and liabilities distinct from those of its members.[15] During this time, corporations extended their operations globally in order to gain cheap or hard-to-find raw materials and more markets. Commercial expansion required additional capital for investments in factories, ports, warehouses, and transportation networks. An expanding stock market, partnerships, financial institutions, speculation, and government programs raised considerable investment funds for corporate formation. A national banking system – established in Britain, the U.S., and other countries – regulated currencies and provided capital for further corporate enterprises. The bank's role in early industrial growth should not be overly emphasized, since bankers often considered loans to industrial enterprises as too risky.[16] Instead of corporations, often national governments took the greater financial risks and built infrastructure such as railroads, canals, harbors, roads, and dams. In 1914, the British invested three-fourths of their sizable investment funds in the U.S., Canada, Australia, South Africa, India, and Argentina. The British used

**Tariffs Illustration before Corporations***

| Sewing Machine (in $) | U.S. | Britain |
|---|---|---|
| Cost to manufacture | 10. | 5. |
| Profit | 2. | 2. |
| Cost to U.S. consumer | 12. | 7. |
| US tariff added | | + 6.** |
| New cost to U.S. consumer | 12. | 13. |

\* not historically accurate, for illustration purposes only
\*\* tariffs were deposited into the U.S. treasury

most of the money for railroads, ports, power plants, and other infrastructure projects instrumental in industrial development.[17]

A new class of entrepreneurs ably calculated risks, raised capital, and adapted new ideas and technology for profit. Although they came from varied backgrounds and rags-to-riches stories were not unknown, most industrialists came from an artisan or manufacturing background. Most entrepreneurs were able to recognize the potential of new technology, to seize opportunities for making a profit, and to adopt personal habits and beliefs that rationalized and justified their acquisitive, aggressive behaviors. A close symbiotic relationship existed between political leaders and entrepreneurs. Political leaders relied on entrepreneurs to provide a stable economic foundation for the nation; the government rewarded entrepreneurs with laws and policies that promoted a secure economic environment with limited risks for their financial undertakings.[18]

An increase in capital-intensive forms of production like machines, factories, transportation networks, and communication enterprises resulted in greater economic productivity. More enterprises reinvested the surplus wealth accumulated from increased economic productivity, which the industry circulated to a wider population, although certainly not to everyone. Greater economic surplus for the few translated into their more lavish standard of living.[19] An industrious, and in many cases exploited, work force labored long hours in capital-intensive industries for relatively low wages, while the productivity gains from low wage labor were diverted to the factory owning elite. It would not be until later into the 20th century that workers would be able to divert more of the productivity gains from their labor into their own pockets.

The industrial capitalist economy produced a dizzying range of manufactured goods and some services. In this era the government and private business built mechanized transportation networks, such as railroads, harbors, and roads; telecommunication systems, such as the telegraph and telephone; and military equipment such as huge naval squadrons. Other industries emerged, such as the chemical industry, energy production that included petroleum and coal-fired electricity, machines that made machines, the steel and the construction industry employing engineers, architects and carpenters. Although the manufacturing industry dominated during this era, the infant service industry provided education, medical care, consumer retail services (as in large department stores), entertainment, organized sporting events, leisure activities, publishing, and the news.

## Labor

Men, women and children entered the ranks of an emerging industrial work force. A large work force was on hand for factory employment due to a growing population, the dislocation of peasant farmers as a result of the enclosure movement, and the displacement of cottage industry workers. Workers faced limited options for earning their livelihood as they made their way into factories where their unskilled wage labor was in high demand. Factory workers arguably received slightly higher wages than agricultural laborers, domestic servants, or workers in the cottage industry, but they also became more dependent upon others for employment. With the mechanization of spinning, many rural women lost income from their cottage industries as factories absorbed their jobs. Artisans' standard of living declined, since the higher cost of their handcrafted items could not compete with lower-cost, mass-produced, machine-made goods. For example, linen weavers in Scotland experienced high unemployment and the eventual disintegration of their craft in favor of cheaper, machine-loomed linens. Ironically, one of those displaced workers was the father of Andrew Carnegie, who would go on to become one of the world's richest men and a leader in the mass production of steel.

Deplorable conditions and low wages generally marked the debasing experience of most industrial workers. Although the standard of living for the industrial working class improved minimally by fits and starts from 1750 to 1850 in Western Europe, the wages of the lowest paid workers improved only slightly in comparison to higher middle class incomes derived from salaries, rents, interest on investments, and profit from business. Historian Rondo Cameron adds, "The inequality of the distribution of income and wealth, which was already great in the pre-industrial economy, became even greater in the early stages of industrialization."[20] Early industrialization was built upon the backs of exploited cheap labor and the poor.

By the end of the 19th century, small groups of workers, disgruntled with their miserable working conditions and low wages, banded together to form unions, like the Knights of Labor in the United States, which formed in 1869 to demand better wages, reduced hours, and improved working conditions. Working-class organizations, friendly societies, trade unions, and cooperatives lobbied politicians for reforms: higher wages, accident insurance, unemployment benefits, reduced working hours, medical insurance, regulation of child labor, and improved working conditions.[21] Businesses countered labor's demands by encouraging immigration and internal rural migration to guarantee an ample labor supply, thereby keeping wages low. Even though the government did not regulate the boom and bust cycle inherent in unregulated capitalism, workers did gain slightly better wages and working conditions.

By the turn of the 20th century industrial workers were the largest occupational group in most industrialized societies. In many countries, such as Britain, labor unions and socialist parties strongly supported free trade, since more trade meant more work for them. Many in the labor movement backed socialism, since they would technically own the means of production and benefit economically. However, socialism was not a large scale movement in the 19th century. As the labor movement grew, it increasingly challenged the practice that prevailed at the time in which business relied on what was known as flexible wages – laying off workers or lowering their wages during bust cycles. Business also advocated for minimal government interference in industry, which clashed with the interests of labor that wanted government to implement their demands. Most workers needed a cushion against unemployment and the down times of the cycle. On the other hand, employers argued that the ease with which they could reduce wages gave them little reason to lay off workers, since unemployment was often of short duration. Therefore, business interests pressured the government not to intervene in the marketplace to soften the edges of capitalism's ups and downs.[22]

A massive labor migration from the countryside to cities and even across continents took place during the late 19th century as displaced workers moved to seek employment. Millions of

LABOR UNION DEMONSTRATORS HELD AT BAY BY SOLDIERS DURING THE 1912 LAWRENCE TEXTILE STRIKE IN MASSACHUSETTS, USA.

people from Europe and other nations sought work elsewhere. Escaping starvation, unemployment, and displacement, approximately 12 million people left their homelands in Europe to immigrate to the United States from 1870 to 1900. Peasants and artisans uprooted from their traditional occupations were forced to cope with the shock of starting a new livelihood in a factory town while living in crowded, unsanitary tenements, and while experiencing profound disruptions to their traditional family life.[23] Alcoholism, domestic violence, and rising family desertion rates all accompanied these wrenching social disruptions.

The flow of people from low-wage Europe and even lower-wage Asia depressed wages in high-wage North America and Australia. The result of an increased labor supply in industrializing nations was appreciably lower wages than would have prevailed without immigration: lower by one-third in Argentina, by one-fourth in Canada and Australia, and by one-eighth in the U.S. The depressing of wages drove labor movements in these countries toward favoring limits on immigration. There were many examples of immigration restrictions, yet in the global sense they were relatively rare. Labor was seldom strong enough to affect immigration policy and did so in only a few countries.[24]

### Questions to Consider

1. What problems did labor face during this time? Are they similar to issues today regarding labor?

## The Gold Standard

From 1815 to its decline at the end of the 19th century, Britain was the leading industrial economy of the world, and it championed the gold standard as the foundation for currencies and exchange. Centuries of tradition that used both gold and silver as currencies came to an abrupt end in the 1870s, when most major industrial countries joined the gold standard. When a country's government went on gold, it promised to exchange its own national currency for gold at a pre-established rate. The country's currency became equivalent to gold, interchangeable at a fixed rate with the money of any other gold standard country. In 1871 only Britain and some of its colonies and Portugal were on gold, but Germany went on gold in 1872, Scandinavia in 1873, Netherlands in 1875, Belgium, France, and Switzerland in 1878, and the U.S. in 1879. Gold was the common global money for all countries on the gold standard, but each individual country had its currency under different names – marks, francs, pounds, dollars, and so on. Unlike the situation recently, exchange rates did not move. The gold standard was predictable, and bankers and investors could be certain that borrowers would pay debt in gold equivalents or that profits would be paid in gold-backed currencies. It favored the investor but not the debtor or consumer. Although international investments soared, the economy did not evenly circulate the benefits.[25]

The benefits of the gold standard did not reach everyone because countries on gold were committed to making their national economy fit the currency. The most common way to trim an economy to keep its gold parity (exchange rate) was to push wages down. Since countries on gold were not able to **devalue** their currencies (make them worth less on the global market), they used wages as the variable with which to reduce prices on their goods, in order to stay in compliance with the gold standard. Employers were able to force wages down by paying their workers less; this in turn meant that an industrial employer could charge less for his product and, therefore, sell his product overseas at a competitive price. Wages served as the variable to lower prices under the gold standard, since there were no laws to protect labor from having their wages reduced at will; industry used this as a way to reduce prices. All this was essential to the functioning of the gold standard. If a country with a persistent **trade deficit** (imports more than it exports) needed to restore balance, it would increase exports by cutting wages and thus reducing prices. If national producers faced import competition or were priced out of foreign markets under the gold standard, wages would be forced down until the price of domestic products was competitive again.[26]

The burden of adjustment under the gold standard in the classical economic era was on labor. It would be difficult today to force prices to decline by 20, 30, or 50 percent and to force workers to accept such drastic wage reductions as in the past. But such reductions were common during the 19th century: indeed, they were essential under the operation of the gold standard and the classical world economy. If business conditions worsened, the solution was to cut wages. But profits also suffered and prices were usually cut as well, so a big drop in the wages earned might have only a slight impact on living standards since prices dropped too. But the adjustment required wage reductions. A growing labor movement voiced its dissatisfaction with the unfairness of stabilizing the economy on the backs of labor; they demanded change.[27]

---

### Questions to Consider

1. What do you think about the debate today to return the U.S. and other currencies to the gold standard?

2. What do you think about the fact that the gold standard economy was stabilized on the backs of labor? Do you think it is true today? .

---

## The Long Depression (1873-1896)

Not all welcomed economic integration and the gold standard. The **Long Depression of 1873-1896** contributed to great dissatisfaction with free trade and the gold standard. This was generally a period of deflation and low growth. The financial collapse of 1873 revealed the degree of global economic integration, and how economic events in one part of the globe could reverberate in others. Europe and the U.S. felt the depression most heavily, which had been experiencing strong economic growth fueled by what was referred to as the Second Industrial Revolution in the latter half of the 19th century and the conclusion of the American Civil War in 1865.

The Long Depression was hotly contested on the playing field of the United States. Two factions – free silver and gold stalwarts – battled each other over the direction of the U.S. economy for nearly a quarter of a century. There were winners and losers. The free silver camp, the losing side, included farmers, miners, and debtors primarily from the rural areas of the South and West, and they wanted the coinage of silver to inflate the money supply to drive up prices for their ag-

**Hypothetical Example of a Country Using Wages as the Variable in Adjusting Prices for Export.***

| Cost of Sewing Machine | U.S. | Germany |
|---|---|---|
| Fixed Costs (factory costs, etc. can't adjust) | $20. | $20. |
| Raw Materials (fixed can't adjust) | $10. | $10. |
| Labor (can adjust) | $20. | $20. $10. |
| Profit | $10. | $10. |
| Price of Sewing Machine | $60. | $50. |

*In this example, since the other costs are fixed, Germany adjusted the only variable it could – wages. Those on the gold standard cannot adjust their currency. If Germany is experiencing a trade imbalance and wants to sell more goods abroad it has to lower the wages of labor to make their good more desirable abroad.

ricultural products or mineral resources. North American farmers flooded the world market with overproduced grain, contributing to its very low price; as a result, many rural areas and farmers were devastated. New mass production factory techniques contributed to industry's overcapacity as well. Prices and earnings declined, but debt burdens remained constant.[28] Producers such as farmers, faced with declining prices and heavy debt, demanded that the U.S. return to a gold and silver standard and lift tariffs on imported manufactured items in order to drive down prices on national manufactured products that usually carried high prices. For example, the price of grain in 1894 was only a third what it had been in 1867,[29] and the price of cotton fell by nearly 50 percent in just the five years from 1872 to 1877,[30] imposing great hardship on farmers and planters. On the winning side were the manufacturers, industrial-

**Silver vs. Gold Conflict in the U.S. (1873-1896)**

| Free Silver | Gold Standard |
|---|---|
| Losers in the world economy | Winners in the world economy |
| Inflate the money supply | Deflate the money supply |
| Silver and gold standard | Gold standard |
| debtors | creditors |
| rural | cities |
| Free trade | Protective tariffs |
| Farmers, miners | Business, bankers |
| South and West | Northeast and cities of Midwest |

ists, bankers and creditors from the core cities who sought to hold onto the gold standard, fearing the inflationary pressure that silver coinage would bring. They also wished to retain tariff protection on imports, which benefitted their industries. The gold standard glue that held global capitalism together seemed to be weakening. As the political frenzy peaked, new gold discoveries brought more of the precious metal onto the market. Prices rose as the supply of gold grew. By 1896 the price of wheat was nearly 50 percent higher than it had been.[31]

**Debtors and Creditors/ Deflation and Inflation in Money Supply**

| Amount borrowed | Deflation 10% Money now worth | Who Benefits Who Does Not Benefit | Inflation 10% Money now worth | Who Benefits Who Does Not Benefit |
|---|---|---|---|---|
| $100. | $90 | Creditors benefit from deflation since money paid back in deflated dollars. Money paid back = $100 plus interest. | $110. | Creditors do not benefit from inflation since money paid back in dollars worth less than when loaned. Money paid back = $100 plus interest |
| $200 | $180. | Debtors do no benefit from deflation, must come up with more money to pay back loan. Money paid back = $200 plus interest. | $220. | Debtors benefit from inflation since money is paid back in dollars worth more than when borrowed. Money paid back = $200 plus interest |

The crisis temporarily eased. But the Long Depression revealed another problem with global capitalism and its drive for perpetual growth; it can continue only as long as there is a ready supply of raw materials and an increasing demand for goods, along with ways to invest profits and capital. Farmers overproduction of wheat on the Great Plains of the U.S. was one example of a greater problem – what to do with overcapacity and increasing global competition. Along with labor demands, increasing competition and overproduction were squeezing business profits. Given this situation, if you were an American or European investor after 1873, where would you look for economic expansion?

---

### Questions to Consider

1. How would you resolve the crisis at the turn of the last century? Who would benefit? Who would not? .

---

### Imperialism

Business' interests obvious answer to the question posed above was expansion overseas, particularly into external areas that remained relatively untouched by capitalism. From 1873 to 1914, the West embarked on a form of aggressive intervention in the non-Western world: imperialism. This period of imperialism is often referred to as "new imperialism," (neoimperialism ) which differentiates it from colonialism in the early modern era. The term **imperialism** describes political and economic control by a greater power over a less powerful territory or country. During this imperialist era much of Asia, the Pacific islands, the Middle East, and sub-Saharan Africa were the objects of an extensive land-grab by the more powerful nations of Europe – particularly Great Britain and France, and to lesser extent the Netherlands, Belgium, Russia, Portugal, Spain, and Germany – and the United States, Japan, and Australia.

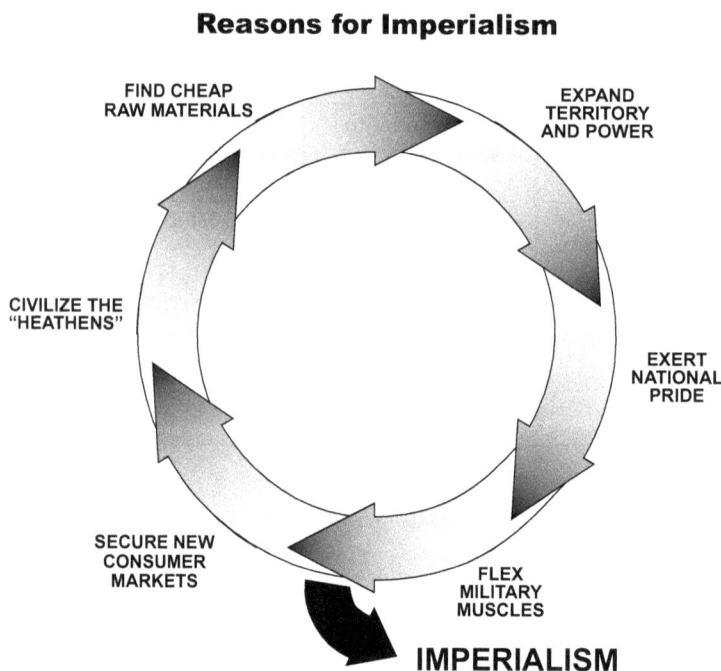

## Reasons for Imperialism

FIND CHEAP RAW MATERIALS

EXPAND TERRITORY AND POWER

CIVILIZE THE "HEATHENS"

EXERT NATIONAL PRIDE

SECURE NEW CONSUMER MARKETS

FLEX MILITARY MUSCLES

IMPERIALISM

The roots of imperialism can be found in the frantic search for markets by the core countries whose industries faced declining profits and increased competition. The old core nations – Britain, France, Netherlands, and Belgium – were facing increasing competition from newly industrialized core nations – the U.S., Germany, Japan, Russia, and parts of central Europe. This increasing competition drove prices down and ate into profit margins and, in addition, increasing demand for raw materials necessary for industrialization squeezed producers' profits. Investors sought profits in new areas other than their home country and envisioned bringing the world into the capitalist fold. These economic factors, along with political factors such as rivalry among the newly constituted core nations, spurred the frantic search and conquest of new colonies to infuse the life-blood of capitalist growth into the core economies. These rekindled colonial aspirations fed into other dormant political frictions among the great powers that eventually contributed to the outbreak of World War I.

From a systems perspective, several interconnected factors contributed to the burst of imperial expansion. First of all, Westerners assumed that a nation must expand its territory and power in order to retain respect among its peers. If a nation stood idly by as others joined in territorial seizure, then its prestige, economy, and power base suffered. Second, nations were intent on flexing their military muscles. A proliferation of oceangoing steamships in the 1860s carried huge cargoes long distances, and these needed bases for refueling. Controlling key foreign harbors as refueling stations enhanced a nation's military control over a far-flung colonial empire. Third, industrial output in the last half of the 19th century exceeded consumer demand, and stagnation ensued. Industrialized nations were frantic to secure new consumer markets to peddle their excess products in the periphery areas and obtain cheap raw materials for their insatiable industrial machines. Fourth, many misguided but well-meaning people firmly believed that Western culture, European people, and Christianity were superior to non-Western culture, people, and religion, and they thought it was their duty to "civilize the heathens." The philosophy of the **white man's burden**, satirized by Rudyard Kipling's poem of the same name, placed responsibility on Christians and Europeans to "civilize" those considered unfortunate enough to be non-Western. A combination of these factors provided an impetus and justification for core Western nations to brutally colonize periphery non-Western areas.[32]

The early form of colonialism, practiced in particular by Spain and Portugal, had become a recognized solution to the need to expand markets, increase opportunities for investors, and ensure the reliable supply of raw materials. It was a solution that 19th century powers quickly relearned.

---

**First stanza of the *White Man's Burden* by Rudyard Kipling in 1899**

*Take up the White man's burden --*
*Send forth the best ye breed --*
*Go bind your sons to exile*
*To serve your captives' need;*
*To wait in heavy harness*
*On fluttered folk and wild --*
*Your new-caught, sullen peoples,*
*Half devil and half child.*

---

During the late 19th century and early 20th centuries there was a 300 percent increase in the acquisition of colonies. In the 45 years after 1870, colonial powers took over an average of 240,000 square miles each year, compared to an average of 83,000 square miles a year for the first 75 years of the 19th century.[33]

An essential element of globalization is integration, and in the late 19th century the world was becoming more integrated than ever before. In 1815, Britain and France together controlled over one third of the earth's surface, and by 1878 they controlled over two thirds. By 1914, Britain, France and the United States together controlled 85 percent of the earth's surface. European and U.S. imperial ambitions profoundly shaped the world we inhabit today. As a result of their expansion the world generally became – and remains – a world economic system. The integration and expansion of capitalism landscaped the highly uneven terrain on which that game is played.[34]

Cecil Rhodes, one of the leading figures of Britain's colonization of Africa, recognized the importance, in his mind, of overseas expansion for maintaining peace at home.

---

In 1895 Rhodes said: "I was in the East End of London yesterday and attended a meeting of the unemployed. I listened to the wild speeches, which were just a cry for 'bread,' 'bread,' and on my way home I pondered over the scene and I became more than ever convinced of the importance of imperialism.... My cherished idea is a solution for the social problem, in order to save the 40,000,000 inhabitants of the United Kingdom from a bloody civil war, we colonial statesmen must acquire new lands for settling the surplus population, to provide new markets for the goods produced in the factories and mines. The Empire, as I have always said, is a bread and butter question. If you want to avoid civil war, you must become imperialist."[35]

---

During the 19th century, the colonies of the European powers in Africa, Southeast Asia, and elsewhere were incorporated from external status into an economically dependent periphery status. For example, small farmers and plantation owners in the periphery regions grew **cash crops** such as coffee, tea, fruits, tobacco, cotton, and sugar that were sold on the world market. Small farmers in the periphery increasingly relied on growing cash crops for the market economy in order to earn income to purchase necessities and pay taxes. As they were folded into the world capitalist economy, they grew fewer subsistence crops for their own needs. The price small farmers received for their cash crop on the world market depended on supply and demand, but at the time, prices were usually low since overproduction by large plantations kept the supply high and prices low. In addition, colonial authorities imposed taxes on small farmlands that had to be paid in cash; thus, the only ways to earn cash were to work on a plantation or in a mine owned by the colonists or grow cash crops. This further enveloped the farmer into the capitalist economic web and reduced small farmers to a dependency status. Because of recurring taxes and low prices for cash crops, many small farmers in the colonies were unable to make a living and sold their farms to large landowners eager to expand their holdings. As a result of the transition to market based agriculture, farmers in the colonies suffered the same consequences as their small farmer counterparts in Europe; they were unable to stay afloat financially when agriculture became part of the global economy.

Even though each region had its own reaction to colonization, their experiences had much in common: colonial powers brutally interacted with their colonies but contributed to modern developments as well. Tensions flared between those who held to a colony's traditional culture and those who embraced Western culture. A modern, consumer-driven way of life, along with Western law, liberalism, and culture, seduced many colonized people. Others violently resisted the West's domination and ways of life.[36]

Some imperial powers restricted trade in ways reminiscent of European mercantilism in the early modern era. Most 19th century imperial powers used mercantilist-style policies to force their trade and investments into their colonies. They insisted that their colonies participate in the international economy, because getting resources from the colonies to market usually required active local involvement. Integration of a colony into the world economy required political and legal conditions, especially secure property rights and judicial authority. Infrastructure, such as railroads, roads, and ports to get products to market, helped to facilitate economic activity. The imperial powers drew their colonies into the world market by emphasizing export-driven goods and encouraged traders to search the hinterlands for more producers and consumers.[37] Britain increasingly relied on its empire's markets for its country's products, which postponed its industrial modernization. The British had a dependable outlet for its goods, which did not necessitate expensive technological changes that competitive pressure would foster. Because of this and other reasons, the 1870s signaled the gradual decline of Britain as the leading core nation.[38] But others were eagerly waiting in the wings to take over that coveted status.

## The Golden Era of Global Capitalism

The years from 1896 to 1914 were the high point of international economic integration. It was the closest thing the world had ever seen to an open world market for goods, capital, and labor. For the first time since the depression of 1873-1896, prices began to rise. The local, domestic economy, on the other hand, was rapidly giving way to the capitalist economy. It would be a 100 years before the world returned to that level of globalization. [39]

Adam Smith made specialization – the division of labor – the centerpiece of his economic argument. In earlier eras countries had tried to be self-sufficient – producing all the goods they needed – but now they focused on producing and exporting what they specialized in and trading for the rest. Every country in the capitalist network had its specialized role. The industries of the core countries flooded the world with machinery and equipment to work farms and run mines and to build railroads and ports to get products to market. Resource-rich regions of the Western hemisphere, Asia, and Africa exported their agricultural and mineral bounty. Mass migration from central and eastern Europe and Asia sent surplus workers and farmers to help labor in the new mines, plantations, and mills. World trade doubled during this period.

Viewed from the standpoint of those who benefitted from this early form of economic globalization and specialization, the process worked beautifully. Those who were able to capture the comparative advantage of their country benefitted. Labor and capital moved around the world from where they produced less to where they produced more. Profits were astonishing. But, on the destructive side, this process remade economies and often destroyed traditional ways. For example, the pampas in Argentina and the prairies in the United States specialized in the production of grain, which flooded the world market. Unable to compete with the price of this grain, smaller European farmers were driven into crisis.[40]

The very poorest periphery countries also tended to favor free trade. They had little manufacturing to protect and exported only raw materials and agricultural goods. For example, the south and west regions in the U.S. supported free

WHEAT FARMING IN OKLAHOMA, EARLY 20TH CENTURY. FARMERS FAVORED FREE TRADE.

trade, since the South's main export was cotton, a raw material in demand by textile mills, and the West's main export was wheat, which was a staple around the world. These regions had little manufacturing, thus no jobs or industry to protect by tariffs. On the other hand, the North wished to protect its industries and the government continued to levy tariffs on imported manufactured goods.

Enthusiasm for the golden age was not universal. Not everyone benefited from global economic integration. Many traditional societies stagnated or fell apart. Imperialists ravaged many of their colonies. For example, the Belgians dreadfully exploited their colony in Africa – the Belgian Congo – by forcing the indigenous people to collect quotas of rubber from wild rubber plants. Estimates are that 10 million Africans died as a result of their coercive and disruptive tactics. Economic integration put enormous pressure on those whose goods were not able to compete with the new world leaders. Those on the losing side of specialization and economic integration included European grain farmers, Latin American moneylenders, Chinese artisans, and Indian textile weavers, to name just a few. These forces made whole industries, regions, and classes redundant, and the losers of specialization turned to the government to ease their suffering. Opening markets, paying back debts to foreigners, and following the gold standard all involved sacrifices, which the poor and weak paid for.[41]

### Questions to Consider

1. What is the relationship between imperialism and economic stagnation? Do you see this phenomenon today? Explain.

## A Shift in Core Areas

Fifty million visitors thronged the Paris International Exposition of 1900, a dazzling showcase of technological progress. They may have noticed the clues showing industrial leadership was slipping away from the British and its fellow early industrializers, France and Belgium, to the new titans – Germany, U.S., and surprising to fair-goers, the island nation of Japan. The homeland of the Industrial Revolution was being left behind. In 1870, Britain, Belgium, and France together produced nearly half of the world's industrial output, but by 1913, they were producing barely one-fifth. German industrial output exceeded Britain's, and America's was substantially more than double Britain's. The U.S. introduced revolutionary methods of mass production, while the Germans made advances in electrical engineering and chemicals. Japan's early industrial growth was tied to the silk trade.[42] A shift in core areas was underway.

The British had held their core status since a shift in the 1700s marked their ascendancy over Spain and the Netherlands. The British defeat of the French in the French and Indian War, also called the War of 1763, marked the shift. Britain's golden age stretched from 1846 into the 1870s. International trade jumped fivefold between 1840 and 1870. Even though the British position as core leader started to slip, they still led the world economy on six fronts: world trade and shipping, visible and invisible exports, banking and finance, colonial expansion, overseas investments, and promoting the ideology for free markets.[43] But, from 1870-1900 there was a decline in Britain's share of world manufacturing as the U.S. and Germany overtook the world leader. After 1900, the U.S. and Germany made exports from Britain more expensive by applying protective tariffs. The British decline in exports from 1899 to 1913 affected the wages of British workers, which dropped by about 10 percent. By 1914, women constituted 41 percent of the manufacturing workforce because families needed two incomes to make ends meet.[44]

As the British decline ensued, there was a stunning rise in the percentage of income and assets going to the top 1 percent and the percentage of income they derived from investments. The share of wealth in the hands of the top 1 percent of the British population peaked in 1911-1913 at 69 percent. The lifestyle of the upper class was a whirl of ostentatious consumption, as the elite purchased huge yachts, frequented pheasant shoots, and vacationed in luxury hotels. [45]

British policy after the 1890s relied on its earnings from overseas investments, London's financial services, exports to India, and extraction of wealth from its semi-colonies of Argentina, Chile and Uruguay. Economic historian Eric Hobsbawm summed up the process as the British "living off the remains of world monopoly" while opting "to retreat into her satellite world of formal and informal colonies," and to "export her immense accumulated historical advantages in the underdeveloped world, as the greatest commercial power, as the greatest source of international loan capital."[46]

While Britain imported more than it exported, it made up the trade deficit with financial exports such as shipping, banking, insurance, and earnings on investment overseas. Although declining as the number one core nation, Britain still controlled much of the world economy; by 1914 it still held 43 percent of all global investments. Similar to circumstances in the U.S. today, some British argued for a revival of manufacturing, but instead finance and the concentration of income and wealth proceeded unabated.[47]

Having to pay for two costly world wars, the British all but liquidated its overseas investments. Coupled with the postwar devaluation of the pound and collapse of British world economic leadership, the share of British wealth in the hands of the top 1 percent declined from 69 percent in 1914 to 33 percent in 1960.[48]

### Questions to Consider

1. Do you see any similarities between the decline of Britain as a core economy in the early 20th century and the situation in the U.S. today?

## THE EARLY TWENTIETH CENTURY ECONOMY (1914-1945)

Before 1914 the benefits of international economic growth were available only to some of the people some of the time. But almost everything from 1914 to 1945 was bad for almost all the people all the time. Frieden paraphrased succinctly the world's economic situation during the period 1914 to 1945. During this time the world staggered around a vicious circle in which global economic collapse caused national crises, and national hardships drove domestic groups to extremes.[49]

After a grisly four-year war, the World War I Allies (Britain, France, U.S., Italy, Russia, and Japan) ground out a victory against the Axis powers (Germany, Ottoman Empire, and Austria). As the warring factions battled in the trenches, the field was clear for much needed U.S. capital and manufactured exports to its allies. But the Allies, especially the British, had to pay for their overseas purchases, mainly from the U.S., by selling what they could: goods, gold, and eventually foreign investments. For example, in Latin America European interests had been dominant for centuries, while U.S. interest was limited, but after World War I the U.S. asserted its financial, industrial, and commercial authority over its southerly neighbors. As the U.S. took over Britain's premier economic position, it began to find that the gold standard and free trade looked much better.[50]

At the Treaty of Versailles in Paris in 1918, the negotiations between the victors and defeated took a vicious turn. The victors demanded that Germany admit guilt for causing the war and pay them enormous war reparations, which were intended to saddle the German economy with debt for decades. The intransigent victors refused to renegotiate the war debts, eventually contributing to the collapse of the fragile German democracy and the rise of the extreme politics of the Nazi Party and Adolph Hitler.

One of the notable turn of events during World War I was the German annihilation of the Russian army. The fragile and inept monarchy of Czar Nicolas II gave way to a communist uprising led by Vladimir Lenin in 1917. The communist sympathizers executed the czar and his family, and a brutal civil war ensued between the white Russians, sympathetic to the monarchy, and the Red communists supported by a small, urban working class movement. The Union of Soviet Socialist Republics (USSR) or Soviet Union formed by 1922. The Soviets championed a communist or command economy, which continued until its collapse in 1991. After its successful revolution, the country embarked on hasty industrialization and agricultural collectivization. The heavy boots of the communist elites stamped out the infant free market.

**The 1920s**

With the end of World War I, an uneasy peace settled upon Europe. Inflation spiraled out of control, while currency values and wages could not keep up with prices. This gave rise to frantic attempts to compensate for the economic turmoil by printing more money, resulting in runaway inflation. It was particularly acute in Germany. It was best to get paid in the afternoon instead of the morning because the morning pay would be worth less by afternoon. If the holder of paper money held on to it for more than a few hours it could cost the holder most of its value. It was common to see people pushing wheelbarrows full of cash just to buy a loaf of bread. Chaotic instability reined. This was hyper inflation at its worst, which wiped out the life savings and purchasing power of millions of people in central and Eastern Europe. By raising taxes and cutting spending, governments finally brought hyperinflation under control.[51] Despite difficulties and some setbacks, by 1924 Europe had essentially recovered from inflation and the destruction of World War I. European industrial production returned to its 1913 levels, although considerable differences existed within Europe.[52] By investing in real assets or taking their money abroad, the wealthy during the period of high inflation protected themselves as the national currency lost its value. But the middle classes often had no recourse and lost all their savings in the space of months. To the German middle class, the chaos of the early 1920s showed that the liberal elites were unfit to rule. A whole generation never forgot or forgave the weak German Republic for those humiliating years of inflation. In light of this background, Hitler's authoritarian message was especially appealing to them.[53]

The European middle class was squeezed again as large corporations came to dominate industrial economies and farming was modernized. Small businesses faced fierce competition from large corporations and cheaper imports if tariffs did not protect their industries, while small farmers confronted both cheap imports and the need

BERLIN 1931, THE ARMY FEEDING THE POOR. THE DEPRESSION WAS FELT SEVERELY IN GERMANY.

to invest in expensive farm machinery in order to compete in the world market. It is no wonder that almost every European extreme right wing or nationalist movement found its main base of support among small business people or small farmers, or both. The main opponents of large corporations were the socialists and communists, but small business or farm owners were rarely sympathetic to these labor-based movements. Fascism had a strong anti-corporate, anti-labor, and anti-foreign message. Farmers and businessmen in some nations, where there were many Jewish-owned businesses or small-town Jewish merchants, identified with the European extreme right wing anti-Semitic views, since they saw Jewish competitors, creditors, or middlemen as part of the problem.[54]

Wall Street in New York City took over London's claim as the world's international financial center, while U.S. corporations set up thousands of branch plants around the world. Before World War I there was almost no foreign investment in manufacturing; it was typically in raw materials and agriculture – copper mines, sugar or banana plantations, or oilfields – or in infrastructure investments such as utilities and railroads. But in the 1920s, corporations extended their interests into other markets. For example, U.S. investment in Latin America before 1914 was almost all in primary products, but in the 1920s American corporations expanded abroad, introducing the manufacturing multinational corporation.[55]

Even though the U.S. had become the world's largest economy, it refused to get involved in many international financial affairs. It continued its protectionist trade policy and became the world's premier creditor nation. Odd as it may seem today, American representatives to international monetary meetings were usually private bankers from J. P. Morgan and Company.[56] Today representatives would be government officials. Despite this detachment from world affairs, the U.S. economy, especially in the late 1920s, roared. One of the high profile industries was automobiles. The assembly line installed in Henry Ford's Highland Park, Michigan plant in 1913, reduced the time necessary to make a Model T chassis from over 12 man-hours to 90 minutes. Ford perfected the mass production assembly line, which in many parts of the world came to be known as **Fordism**.

Labor's strength grew as industry shifted toward very large corporations and factories. Frieden states, "Larger plants and firms were generally easier to unionize, both because the concentration of people made union organizing more effective and because large corporations could not maintain personalized ties with employees that small firms often cultivated."[57] The new large corporations were less hostile to unions than the older, smaller, firms. While labor was a much higher percentage of production costs in older, labor-intensive industries, in the larger factories labor was a smaller share. Instead, much of the cost of production was in machinery, research and development, and marketing. Also, tariff policies meant that prices would not face competition from imports, and therefore consumers absorbed labor costs in the form of higher prices. The growth of unions and large corporations went hand in hand.[58]

The 1929 financial crisis started with a gradual decline in growth outside North America. In 1928 farm conditions worsened, since production exceeded demand, while other investments waned. In 1928, much of Europe and Asia began to fall into recession, while the U.S. continued to boom. With fewer world-wide investment opportunities, capital from around the world flooded into the supposedly safe and surging U.S. stock market. With so much U.S. capital funneled into the stock market, it turned a mild world recession elsewhere into a full-fledged crisis. In response, European banks raised interest rates and imposed austerity measures supposedly to attract capital back to their economies, while austerity measures would hold down wages and profits in order to make the country's goods more competitive on world markets.[59] These measures didn't work; they only made matters worse.

The U.S. stock market quaked in the fall of 1929. High stock prices distorted the real value of companies, as a speculative fever swept anyone who could put a few dollars in the "safe bet" of the stock market. Finally, on black Tuesday, October 29, 1929, the U.S. stock market collapsed. It was a clear and ominous signal that the Great Depression was at hand.

## The Great Depression of the 1930s

The economic collapse of 1929-1934 was unparalleled in its depth, breadth, and severity. There had been financial crises before, most recently the Long Depression of 1873-1896, but never like this one. The industrialized world economies disintegrated for over five years, as output dropped by one-fifth and unemployment went above 25 percent almost everywhere. The prices of primary products declined faster than manufactured goods. For example, in the U.S. farm prices fell by 52 percent between 1928 and 1933. Commodity-producing nations were especially hard hit by price declines, the slump in American and European demand for their exports, and the cutoff of American credit. In response, conservatives in core countries argued that governments should do nothing; inaction, they argued, would eventually speed recovery. Don't just do something, they said to governments, stand there. The U.S. Congress passed the Smoot-Hawley Tariff Act in 1930, and within a few months other countries also began raising tariffs.[60]

Deflation was a major problem in the Great Depression. Commitment to the gold standard blocked attempts to halt deflation and raise prices, which meant deflation and inaction continued. Gold ruled. Countries on gold had to let prices take their course, for national prices were simply a local expression of world prices, and world prices were low, very low. Gold exacerbated the problems. The banking and currency crises so crippled credit markets that lending virtually ceased.[61] The British government, the purveyor of the gold standard, took its currency off gold in 1931, devaluing it for the first time in peacetime since Sir Isaac Newton established gold parity in 1717. President Franklin Roosevelt took the dollar off the gold standard when he came into office in 1933. As the dollar declined, prices of agricultural products and other primary commodities soared. With more money in circulation, prices rose continually, and the reversal of deflation was instrumental in helping the economy.[62]

The turmoil of the first few years after 1929 left its mark everywhere and it pointed away from free trade capitalism and toward forceful government involvement in the economy. In the beginning of the downturn, governments followed policies inherited from the classical era of global capitalism of the 19th and early 20th century, mainly adherence to the gold standard. The powerful supporters of gold – bankers, investors, industrialists, creditors and elites – now had to answer to the demands of the non-elites – labor, the middle class, farmers, and the poor. The Western countries had become more democratic since the classical era, and the latter group, who bore the burden of earlier policies to stabilize the economy, was no longer willing to make that sacrifice. Yet, governments, driven by faith in gold standard solutions, blindly soldiered on as conditions worsened.[63]

A worldwide depression had discredited laissez-faire capitalism, both domestically and globally. Among the factors that had deepened the Great Depression were bouts of competitive currency devaluation, defaults on international loans, and the collapse of trade. Laissez-faire principles made it more difficult to operate a managed form of capitalism at home, in several respects. A monetary system based on gold was deflationary, because discoveries of gold did not necessarily occur at the pace needed to expand the money supply to accompany economic growth.[64] Deflation gripped the whole global economic system. The depression did not abate.

## The Rise of Economic Nationalism

While Western democracies sought to rebuild international economic integration in the face of economic collapse, the fascists and much of the world looked to protect themselves from it through a policy of economic self-sufficiency. The West worked with organized labor, while the fascists destroyed their labor movements and ties to socialism. Adolph Hitler and his economic advisors took charge of the German economy in the late 1930s. They abandoned global capitalism after 1929 and proposed to separate from world markets, and instead vigorously intervened in the economy with massive public works. Their plans required a strong government for implementation, and the Nazis gladly engineered a turn away from weak governments inherent in classical, global laissez-faire capitalism.[65]

Many middle status, semi-industrial, debtor countries moved along an economic path that was often at odds with that of Western Europe and North America. They, like the fascists, embraced a new economic nationalism and rejected the gold standard, imposed high protective tariffs, tightly controlled foreign investment, and denounced foreign bankers and debts. They built thriving urban industries that produced for their domestic market, although not for export. Frieden points out a relevant fact to explain the divergent political and economic paths available to nations in the 1930s: "Every self-sufficient regime – fascist states in Europe, the Soviet Union, [middle status] governments in Latin America and Asia – ruled a net debtor nation. Every debtor country went the way of fascist or nationalist self-sufficiency; every creditor country remained democratic and committed to international economic integration.[66] As the debtor countries turned toward self-sufficiency during the 1930s, they rejected their foreign debts, dependence on world markets, and comparative advantage. Their previous areas of specialization, such as agriculture and primary commodities, were taxed to stimulate sectors of the economy that had been constrained by foreign competition, especially national industry.[67] For example, Argentina taxed its well-established agricultural industry to fund its infant national industrial growth policy.

By the early 1920s, mass movements on the left and right, such as the middle sectors of small businessmen, artisans, and small farmers, were battering at the gates of the traditional ruling class elites. They could not be ignored. Under Hitler, for example, unemployment ended within three years of his taking office by building a trade network in eastern and central Europe, the areas that they eventually annexed militarily. Their polices included placing high tariffs on manufactured goods, which forced farmers and miners to pay inflated prices to industry while delivering their food and raw materials at prices set on world markets. These policies turned the terms of trade in favor of industry; they raised the prices of goods that industry sold and lowered the price of goods that industry bought.[68]

The policies of national self-sufficiency favored industrial investment over agriculture and consumption. Again, Frieden explains, "Government directed resources out of the export-oriented primary producing sectors of the past and into the inward-oriented industrial sector of the future and out of the pockets of workers and farmers and into industrial investment. Expensive manufactured consumer goods and low wages translated into lower living standards for workers. This was true despite populist rhetoric."[69] Ironically, those who fervently supported Hitler, such as small farmers and small business, were hurt the most by his economic policies. Like Germany, Japan had established a fragile democracy and a generally open economy in the 1920s. Neither survived the Depression. By 1936 every country in southern, central, and eastern Europe and Japan – with the lone exception of Czechoslovakia – was a reactionary fascist regime. This group of authoritarian tyrants represented a clear alternative to liberalism, classical or laissez-faire capitalism, internationalism, and democracy.[70]

During the 1920s the Soviet Union promoted, despite its communist pledge, a hybrid economy that accepted the private farm and small business sectors. On the other hand, the government ran modern industry, finance, and utilities, which also controlled foreign trade and investment. But this brief lull in communist central control did not last long. After 1928, Joseph Stalin and his supporters seized and consolidated their power and began pushing the country toward rapid industrialization, the resources extracted from the agricultural sector and consumption. The Soviet regime forced peasants into government controlled collective farms. In 1928, 97 percent of the country's farmland was in private production; in 1933, 83 percent was in collectives. Farm production stagnated under this abrupt onslaught, dropping by more than half between 1928 and 1932 as the small to medium sized farmers (*kulaks*) resisted forced collectivization. Rather than surrender their animals to the collectives, farmers slaughtered their herds and ate or sold what they could.[71]

The Soviet government forced collective farmers to sell their crops to the government at artificially low prices, providing cheap food for workers and cheap raw materials for industry. High prices on consumer goods and their limited availability squeezed consumers. Although agricultural collectivization was a disaster, Soviet industrialization was a stunning success in many ways. But the government's base of support – urban workers, bureaucrats, Communist Party members – received most of the benefits of rapid industrialization, while farmers, the vast majority, inordinately suffered. Grain production plummeted and millions of peasants died in the famine years of 1932 and 1933.[72]

Economically cast adrift from the global economy from about 1929 to 1953 were Africa, Asia, and Latin America. In this period the more advanced periphery and middle nations broke from their open economy pasts to a model based on **import substitution industrialization** (ISI). ISI is a trade and economic policy based on the principle that a country should attempt to reduce its foreign dependency through the local production of industrialized products. Domestic production replaced goods that were previously imported. The term primarily refers to economic policies adopted in many Latin American countries from the 1930s until the late 1980s, and in some Asian

HARZBURGER FRONT OF 1931, A COALITION OF NATIONALIST CONSERVATIVES AND THE EXTREME RIGHT IN GERMANY.

and African countries from the 1950s onward. During the depression the export economies of Latin America and other middle countries, producing food and raw materials for export collapsed because of poor demand in the core countries and depressed prices. The middle nations shifted their attention from supplying primary products and absorbing manufactured goods of the core countries, to focusing their energies on national development. Urbanization and industrialization grew rapidly in areas of Latin America and the Middle East. For example, enterprising Egyptians, who had exported cotton to Britain for decades, began to use their own raw cotton to make clothing textiles, and soon a substantial, tariff-protected industry was in place.[73]

Even periphery countries historically oriented to farming and mining for export to foreign markets turned their economic structures around. They simply could not afford to import and had to produce more at home. Developmentalism and nationalism were the key policies. **Developmentalism** is an economic theory that means the best way for periphery countries to develop is through fostering a strong, diverse internal market and to impose high tariffs on imports. Profits would stay in national firms and thus circulate within the national economy, instead of flowing to foreign corporations. While the Depression's impact on periphery and middle countries was mixed, Latin America, the Middle East, Africa, and Asia found some aspects of the experience encouraging as their modern industries grew rapidly.[74]

### Building a Social Democracy

In the middle 1930s the Western democracies began to find a political alternative to elite-favoring policies of unfettered, laissez-faire capitalism: **social democracy**. The modern social democratic state was not truly in place until after World War II, but by the late 1930s its foundations were set in Western Europe and North America. At this point in history, it appears that in order to survive, modern democratic societies needed to shift to social democratic policies. Every industrial society developed social insurance plans whose similarities far outweighed their differences. Coalitions of workers and farmers demanded and got economic management, social insurance and social security, and labor rights. A clear alternative to fascism and communism was in place by the late 1930s. Countries with powerful labor movements and powerful Socialist parties turned more quickly to social democracy than the U.S. However, President Roosevelt and the New Deal illustrated the popular turn to social democracy in a country that boasted of rugged individualism as its core principle.[75] Social security for the aged, national pensions, and health insurance all helped respective nations as well as their direct beneficiaries. Private enterprise could not effectively offer these socially beneficial measures, nor could individual initiative alone obtain them. These benefits freed people from the severest worries of providing for adversity in a modern, capitalist society and cushioned the cruel booms and busts of the market place.

AN EXAMPLE OF AN ISI PROJECT. ARGENTINA, PRODUCTION LINE AT THE STATE MILITARY INDUSTRIES FACILITY, 1950; ON LINE SINCE 1927. POPULIST PRESIDENT JUAN PERÓN MODERNIZED AND EXPANDED THE COMPLEX.

Corporations in the social democracies of the 1930s largely backed the economic, social, and labor reform agenda. Known as **welfare capitalism**, many in the business community welcomed policies to stimulate their national economies, although some in the business quarter opposed reforms. The welfare capitalists quickly realized that their contributions to unemployment, pension programs, and social insurance did not affect their competitive conditions, since other Western nations were doing the same and there was limited global competition at this point. Especially during the 1930s many capitalists came to support, or at least drop, their opposition to social reform.

The cataclysm of the 1930s swept away the **classical economic order**, which was based on the gold standard, a limited government role in the economy, and the political influence of the business sector. The economist to have the biggest impact on shaping the transition from laissez-faire capitalism to the era of social democracy was the British economist **John Maynard Keynes** (1883-1946). His ideas have profoundly affected the theory and practice of modern macroeconomics, as well as the economic policies of governments. His ideas are the basis for the school of thought known as Keynesian economics, and its various offshoots. In the face of the economic disaster he abandoned his long-standing support for free trade and laissez-faire capitalism. Keynes spearheaded a revolution in economic thinking, challenging neoclassical economics that held free markets would automatically provide full employment as long as workers were flexible in their wages. Keynes instead argued that consumer **demand** for goods and services determined the overall level of economic activity, and that inadequate demand could lead to prolonged periods of high unemployment. He forcefully argued that governments should actively intervene in the economy to alleviate the boom and bust cycles of unfettered capitalism. Keynesian policies were influential in the social democracy movement of the 1930s and adopted by leading Western governments through the 1970s.

The economic systems of the world – social democratic capitalism, communism, and fascist style self-sufficiency – clashed on the global battlefield (1939-1945). The world had never witnessed a war of such global scope and horror. At the end of the devastation, the defeated fascist economies lay in ruins, while the Allied victors promoted their favored economic forms: communism and social democratic (managed) capitalism. As the world's leading economy at the end of the war, the U.S. was beginning to shift its economic vision to one that supported freer trade, although it continued to support social democratic principles as well. It was a popular, if not universally held, view that freer trade favored U.S. interests. But the Soviet Union was not about to submit to U.S. leadership. The world was in store for more tensions as the variations of capitalism and communism clashed in a Cold War of economic attrition.

### Questions to Consider

1. What were the alternatives to laissez-faire capitalism in the 1930s? Why did they emerge?

# THE POST WORLD WAR II ECONOMY (1945-1970s)

It was only after World War II, with its industrial supremacy unchallenged, that the U.S. started championing the cause of free trade. There were practical reasons for this conversion. As the war dragged on, it became obvious that the U.S. would not face much foreign competition from the devastated industrialized countries after the fighting ended. Free trade had traditionally been supported by export-based farmers, but now many protectionist industrialists changed their views once they saw that they had much to gain from trade liberalization.[76] However, economist Ha-Joon Chang states that the push for free-trade should not be overstated during this period. He notes "that the

United States never practiced free trade to the same degree as Britain did during its free-trade period (1860-1932). It never had a zero-tariff regime like [Britain's], and it was much more aggressive in using [certain] protectionist measures."[77] Economist Anup Shah states, "At that time, previously popular ideas became utterly foreign to the spirit of the time: that the market should be allowed to make major social and political decisions, that the government should voluntarily reduce its role in the economy, that corporations should be given total freedom, that trade unions should be curbed and that citizens should be given less social protection."[78]

Many nations, such as Europe, chose to continue their managed form of capitalism, social democracy, and mixed economies, where some state-owned enterprises, usually large public services such as electricity, coexisted with free markets. Some countries, such as Cuba, China, Vietnam, and North Korea, incorporated communist economic principles.

In the spirit of wanting to avoid another Great Depression and the devastation of another world war, the major economies of the world agreed to convene to discuss the post-war economic order. At the beginning of July 1944, nearly 1,000 delegates from more than 40 countries gathered at Mount Washington Hotel in the New Hampshire resort of Bretton Woods. Over the next three weeks, under the leadership of Keynes and Dexter White, (U.S. Secretary of the Treasury) the delegates finalized plans for a postwar monetary and financial order, simply called **Bretton Woods**.

Some delegates talked of a return to the pre-1914 gold standard, but many industrialists and organized labor were wary of this attempt. They did not like the inflexibility of gold, under which the government was unable to use monetary policy to stimulate the economy and devalue the national currency to improve industry's competitive position. Politically sensitive bankers were aware that a simple return to gold was unlikely and instead were willing to settle for a modified dollar standard. Fixed at $35 to an ounce of gold since 1934, many felt the dollar provided a reliable monetary anchor for international trade, finance, and investment. The delegates hammered out a compromise between the international stability of a gold-dollar standard and the national flexibility of managed currencies. Their plan balanced the objective of the American and British governments: currency stability with flexibility, gold backing without rigidity.[79] The ingenious compromise brought stability to the world economy for 25 years. It also meant that labor was a powerful force in shaping policies that benefitted them.

Lenders' reluctance to fund large infrastructure projects – railroads, dams and ports – was an obstacle to international investment, according to capitalists who saw these projects as crucial in providing transport of primary

BRETTON WOODS CONFERENCE, JOHN MAYNARD KEYNES (RIGHT) REPRESENTED THE UK AT THE CONFERENCE, AND HARRY DEXTER WHITE REPRESENTED THE U.S.

products from periphery countries to core countries. But infrastructure investments were enormous and risk-averse investors avoided them. Keynes and White proposed to solve this problem with an International Bank for Reconstruction and Development (World Bank), which would be backed by the core governments. The bank would borrow on private markets at low interest rates (because of its backers' guarantee) and relend for worthy projects in periphery countries.

The Bretton Woods system created long-lasting institutions. The International Monetary Fund (IMF) managed various nations' trade deficits so that there would be less of a possibility that nations would resort to devaluing their currencies. The IMF also embarked on setting up rules and procedures to keep a country from going too deeply into debt year after year. From 1949-1993, the General Agreement on Tariffs and Trade (GATT) regulated trade until the World Trade Organization (WTO) replaced it in 1995. GATT largely exempted periphery countries from its rules, and did not include farm products in its controversial free-trade rules. The Bretton Woods system was unique. There had never been an international agency like the IMF, to which member governments agreed to subject their decisions on important economic policies. Applied at the international level, the new post-war social democracies supported a managed type of capitalism.[80] The U.S., primarily, bankrolled the World Bank and IMF and provided them with headquarters in Washington D.C.

## The Golden Age: The Post-War Years

The post-war years turned out to be a golden age for nations across the globe. Prosperity increased for many and economic "progress" appeared to be limitless. Aside from an over-hanging shadow of nuclear self-destruction, it was generally a time of optimism and confidence in the future.

### 1. The Golden Age of Capitalism

The United States turned outward after 1945 because of changed conditions, not changed minds. Immediately after the war, Europe was in shambles. Europeans had sold off most of their foreign investments to pay for the war, losing the earnings from these investments and the ability to pay for imports. European empires were crumbling, which restricted their privileged access to the markets and raw materials of their former colonies. Meanwhile the U.S. and the rest of the Western hemisphere basked in prosperity.[81] In response to the devastation in Europe, the U.S. initiated the **Marshall Plan** from 1947–1951. Named for Secretary of State George Marshall, the wildly successful plan allocated millions of dollars for rebuilding and creating a strong economic foundation for the countries of Europe.

Until 1958 the world economy ran on dollars, since the currencies of Europe and Japan were too weak to return to full currency convertibility into gold or dollars. But in late 1958 most of European currencies were convertible, and were able to trade on open markets. From then until 1971 the international monetary system based on a U.S. dollar worth 1/35 of an ounce of gold linked currencies to the U.S. dollar at fixed exchange rates[82]

In 1961 the core democratic countries formalized their common economic and political bond by forming the **Organization for Economic Cooperation and Development (OECD)**. The system brought economic growth, low unemployment, and stable prices, although most of the growth favored multinational corporations (MNCs). Before the war, the typical foreign direct investment was in agriculture or mining in a periphery country or colony, but by the 1960s the typical investor was a corporation that built factories abroad in an already core country. Because many protective tariffs continued in many core countries, MNCs maneuvered to merely "jump the trade barriers" to set up their factories and gain a share of the country's market.[83]

In the classical era of global capitalism, the elite generally had little concern for social or moral issues but pushed the market as the way to solve social problems. In fact, they were often hostile to policies to ameliorate poverty. After the war an ethical shift occurred. The West's policies aimed to integrate market economies with equitable social policies in a new social democratic state.[84] Although imperfectly realized, this ethic prevailed until the 1980s, when a turn to a neoliberal philosophy took place; this shift marked a return to the free trade or laissez-faire ethic of the classical era.

This golden age of capitalism during the 1950s and 1960s was the result of the core countries in Western Europe and to a lesser extent the U.S. choosing managed capitalism. Some state-owned enterprises, usually large public services such as energy, electricity, and transportation, coexisted with small businesses and free markets. Friedan notes, "The new [economic] order combined …the market with social reform, prosperity with social stability and political democracy. It mixed pro-business policies with substantial government involvement in the economy, an extensive social safety net, and politically powerful labor movements. The result was a blend of active markets and aggressive governments, big business and organized labor, conservatives and socialists. The order oversaw the most rapid rates of economic growth and most enduring economic stability in modern history."[85] All prospered in this arrangement, but labor in particular made great strides. In contrast to the disorder and despair of the 1930s and 1940s, the heyday of the golden age was one of order and optimism.

## 2. The Golden Age of Communism and Socialism

The communist and socialist nations, on the other hand, argued that central planning needed to replace global and national markets. They maintained that integration with world markets would not help the needs of poor people or help poor countries achieve equity and a better standard of living. Instead it would be better to adopt a command economy. They had chosen equity and economic diversification at the expense of specialization and rapid growth, and the results impressed many dissatisfied with the glaring inequities of capitalism. For 25 years after 1948, the centrally planned economies did quite well. Greatly improved social services such as health care and education accompanied rapid growth. Illiteracy dropped. Medical care was free and plentiful, and many socialist countries had more doctors and hospital beds per person than did core capitalist nations. Infant mortality plummeted, often below that of wealthier countries. Communists and socialists ruled one-third of the planet and had millions of followers.[86]

## 3. The Golden Age for the Middle and Periphery Countries

While the core capitalist countries abandoned the inward orientation of the 1930s, for the most part, the middle and periphery world embraced it enthusiastically. Import Substitution Industrialization (ISI) could be inward-looking without significant links to world markets such as in Latin America or outward-looking in that it promoted exports such as in South Korea. The decision to adopt one or the other approach differed among countries.

The ISI countries largely closed themselves to foreign trade and either continued or rapidly industrialized. They met with general levels of success. The newly independent colonies, likewise, kept out foreign goods and often foreign capital to build up their independent national economies. Latin American countries continued the ISI policies of the 1930s, and India and some African countries restricted trade as well. Their principal aim was to make domestic manufacturing more profitable and provide subsidies and incentives to favorite industries in the form of tax breaks to investors and cheap credit from government banks. Local industrialists received preferential access to imported capital goods, parts, and raw materials. The ISI governments manipulated their currency to provide cheap dollars to manufacturers in order to buy foreign equipment and inputs. These policies resulted in remarkable industrial development. But industrialization was largely financed at the expense of the primary exporting sectors, such as farming and mining. Farmers and miners paid much more for the tariff-protected manufactured goods they consumed, but had to sell their own products without government assistance at world market prices, which were usually low. Taxes on the primary exporting sector, in effect, subsidized favored national industries. ISI policies shifted resources and people from farming and mining to manufacturing, from the countryside to the cities, in an effort to bolster the industrial sector. As a result, economic developments in Latin American, African and Asian industries were impressive.[87]

In the mid-1960s four East Asian countries, the so-called "Asian tigers" – South Korea, Taiwan, Singapore, and Hong Kong – tried a different version of ISI: they pushed exporting manufactured goods to core countries in a strategy called **Export-Oriented Industrialization** (EOI). The East Asians turned to EOI in part because they had few natural resources to export to pay for necessary imports, and the only way to earn foreign currency was to export manufactured goods. They specialized in labor-intensive goods for export, utilizing their hard-working and large pool of labor as their comparative advantage. To encourage exports their governments intervened heavily in the economy, giving subsidies and incentives to export industries. Plenty of jobs were created as industries devoured all the cheap labor they could get. Low wages kept exports cheap. Their exchange rates were also undervalued to make their exports more competitive on the world market, thus depressing consumers' purchasing power. The government at this time provided little in the way of social insurance.

The East Asian export-oriented model seemed to avoid some of the ISI's problems. The United States' strategy of building a containment belt of capitalist countries around China and other communist states in Asia also helped their economies, which involved the granting of incentives for

SOVIET UNION PREMIER NIKITA KHRUSHCHEV AND UNITED STATES VICE PRESIDENT RICHARD NIXON DEBATE THE MERITS OF COMMUNISM VERSUS CAPITALISM IN A MODEL AMERICAN KITCHEN AT THE AMERICAN NATIONAL EXHIBITION IN MOSCOW IN JULY 1959. UNLIKE THE SOVIET UNION, CONSUMERISM FUELED GROWTH IN U.S. CAPITALISM.

DESIGNED AND MANUFACTURED IN ARGENTINA, THE JUSTICIALIST WAS PART OF PRESIDENT JUAN PERÓN'S EFFORT TO DEVELOP A LOCAL AUTO INDUSTRY AS PART OF ISI POLICIES.

these countries to export to the U.S. In contrast, Latin American countries did not receive these incentives.

For capitalists, communists/socialists, and ISI nations, the early 1970s was the high-water mark of the postwar world economy. Almost all core industrialized nations, centrally planned economies rich and poor, middle-developing countries, and former colonies grew rapidly and consistently. Prosperity reigned.[88] But things were about to change.

---

**Questions to Consider**

1. Why did different economic models exist during the post-war years?
2. Why wasn't there a return to the classical era of laissez-faire capitalism?

---

# THE CRISIS OF THE 1970s

The 1970s, like the 1930s, 40 years earlier, proved to be a pivotal era in the world's economic history. Severe crises in the 1970s exposed serious defects in the post-war economic structure. The policies of the Bretton Woods post-war era lay in disarray. The question was, would the old Bretton Woods order be patched back into a workable system, or would the crisis result in the overturning of the old framework and the establishment of a new one? The answer in the turbulent 70s was not clear.

In the 1970s, the United States' position as the unchallenged superpower of the capitalist world was suddenly bombarded from multiple directions: rising international competition, production overcapacity, spiking energy prices, declining productivity and profitability, the end of the fixed-rate convertibility of the dollar for gold, soaring inflation, and high unemployment.[89] All the factors were significant, and it is hard to pin-point the most important one. They all combined to create a significant crisis of managed capitalism and other economic models of the post-war era.

### 1. The Dollar and Gold

Since 1944, the U.S. was committed to the Bretton Woods monetary order – the centerpiece of the post-war international economy. It was about to be undone. After 25 years of stability, the collapse of Bretton Woods unleashed a Pandora's Box of economic repercussions, most unbeknownst at the time. Because of rising U.S. inflation and other factors, confidence in the dollar waned. International holders of dollars demanded redemption of their dollars for gold, which led to the depletion of U.S. gold reserves. The dollar's fixed convertibility to gold ($1 = 1/35oz. of gold) needed to be undone and the dollar devalued. On August 15, 1971, U.S. President Richard Nixon made the dramatic decision to take the dollar off gold, meaning that no longer was the dollar exchangeable with gold. The dollar dropped compared to other currencies by about 10 percent and devalued again by 10 percent in 1973.[90]

### 2. International Financial Flows

When fixed exchange rates anchored by the U.S. dollar finally collapsed, currencies were allowed to **float**. When a nation's currency value fluctuates according to the foreign exchange market, it floats. Thus, it is a floating currency.[91] One side effect of floating currencies was the growth of currency speculation and the resurgence of international finance. International financial flows had remained dormant since the turmoil of the depression years; this dormancy had been one reason governments were able to manage their own domestic monetary policies. For example, if international financial markets had been active in the 1950s and 1960s, lower interest rates in France compared to Germany would have led investors to withdraw their money from their Paris invest-ments to invest in Frankfurt (Germany). But short-term money flows in the post-war era were practically absent, in part because governments imposed capital controls to prevent the speculative flows of money, which could cause economic instability. But in the 1970s, because of the collapse of the Bretton Woods order, short-term investors or speculators could move money around the world in response to differences in national monetary conditions and could possibly threaten the inde-pendence of a nation's economic policy.[92] Another side effect of floating currencies was increased short-term, often speculative lending to sovereign nations by private banks, surpassing the lending by public institutions such as the IMF and World Bank. Many developing countries were at the mercy of international creditors.[93]

### 3. Overcapacity

From the late 1940s to the early 1970s, the U.S., Europe and Japan derived mutual benefits from global expansion, largely because of massive outlays for the post-war reconstruction of Europe and East Asia. But by the mid-1970s, the key problem for the core economies was **overcapacity** or overproduction. This means that there is a tendency for capitalist economies to build up tremendous productive capacity to produce goods and services that outruns the population's capacity to con-sume. The overcapacity was a result of the productive capacity of not only the U.S., but Germany and Japan as well, which experienced rapid post-war industrialization and economies like Brazil, Taiwan, and South Korea added increased global competition. Yet, income inequality within coun-tries and between countries limited the growth of purchasing power and demand. Thus, overcapacity resulted in a steady decline in profitability. Core nations urgently sought to increase productivity and profitability, but achieving it had run into opposition from established monopolies, organized labor and powerful rival economies.[94]

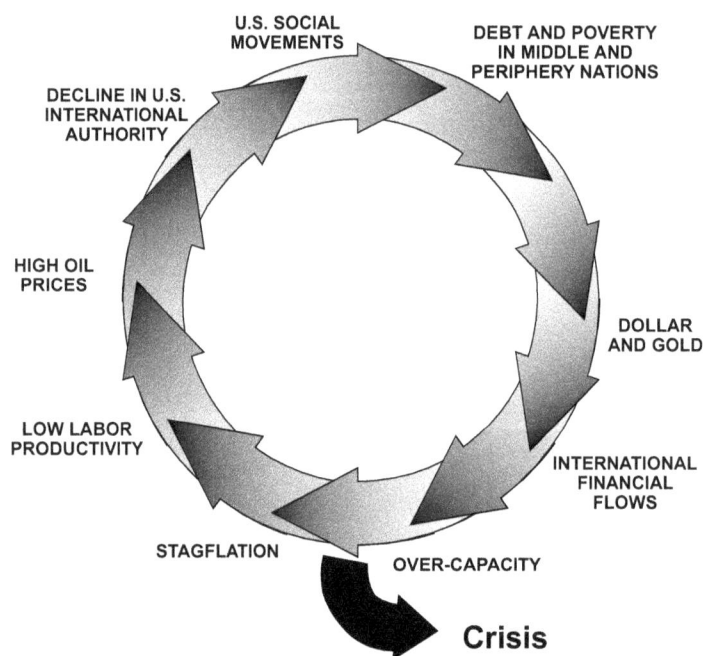

**U.S. SOCIAL MOVEMENTS**

**DEBT AND POVERTY IN MIDDLE AND PERIPHERY NATIONS**

**DECLINE IN U.S. INTERNATIONAL AUTHORITY**

**HIGH OIL PRICES**

**DOLLAR AND GOLD**

**LOW LABOR PRODUCTIVITY**

**INTERNATIONAL FINANCIAL FLOWS**

**STAGFLATION**

**OVER-CAPACITY**

**Crisis**

### 4. Stagflation

Inflation picked up in the U.S. in the late 1960s, ratcheting up from about 3 percent in 1966 to nearly 6 percent in 1971. These rates were high at the time, coming on the heels of a 7 year period in which the annual inflation rate never exceeded 1.6 percent. The annual inflation rate spiked to over 10 percent in 1974 and again in each of the three years from 1979 to 1981. Adding to the inflation woes, the annual unemployment rate topped 8 percent in 1975 and would reach nearly 10 percent in 1982. During the Vietnam War when the economy was overheating, both Presidents Johnson and Nixon failed to take the corrective steps to restrain an over-stimulated economy and price inflation – that is, raise taxes and reduce federal spending. The decade of economic stagnation that followed became a central factor in discrediting Keynesian managed economics.[95]

Growth in the core countries slowed to half its postwar rate for over a decade. Governments tried to stimulate their economies by lowering interest rates or increasing spending, but then inflation ensued with revenge.[96] The economy seemed trapped in the new, cleverly-termed nightmare of **"stagflation:"** a combination of low economic growth and high unemployment (stagnation) with high rates of inflation. Traditional Keynesian economic policy tools seemed powerless to deal with this new beast, since the theory stated that if the unemployment rate was high, then inflation was likely to be low, and vice versa. Thus, when policymakers faced a recession, they would lower interest rates, increase government spending, or lower taxes to stimulate demand and bring down the unemployment rate, at the cost of some increase in the inflation rate. But when dealing with inflation, they would raise interest rates, lower spending, or raise taxes to reduce demand and "cool off" the economy, at the cost of some increase in unemployment. When high rates of inflation and unemployment appeared simultaneously, the traditional policy did not work.[97] Policymakers seesawed back and forth between policies to solve high inflation and then policies to solve high employment. Nothing seemed to work.

### 5. Low Labor Productivity

Another problem that came to the fore in the 1970s was what economists called the "**full employment profit squeeze.**" Back in the 1960s there was very low unemployment, which, along with the cushion of unemployment benefits, resulted in a declining "cost of job-loss." This bolstered workers' confidence in demanding larger wage increases since there was little fear of being fired because employers realized there was a labor shortage. Business management sought to enforce a high pace of work in order to increase productivity and profits, but with a labor shortage their authority over their workers was reduced, and the rate of productivity growth declined as well. The combined effects of rising wages and declining productivity growth drove large increases in labor costs per unit of output. While unit labor costs were constant in the first half of the 1960s, they grew at nearly 2 percent per year from 1966 to 1967, and at over 6 percent per year from 1968 to 1969. These rising labor costs, in turn, ate into business profits. The "full employment profit squeeze" ended in the late 1970s with a return of high unemployment rates.[98]

### 6. Oil

The increase in the price of oil contributed to the economic instability, uncertainty, and inflation of the 1970s and early 1980s. However, some experts believe that the impact of the rise in oil prices on the economic distress of the decade has been overstated. Some estimates show that the increase in the price of oil only accounted for 25 percent of the inflationary surge of the period. To some, the world price of oil had lagged behind inflation for decades, and was merely "catching up" in the 1970s.[99] I remember paying only 25 cents a gallon to fill up my car in the late 1960s. My Mustang's mpg (miles per gallon) was not a concern to me since a couple of dollars would fill up the tank! But the situation changed in the mid-1970s when I had to wait in line to fill up my car. By the 1960s, the major oil producing nations – Iran, Iraq, Kuwait, Saudi Arabia, and Venezuela – had enough of supplying cheap oil to the core nations and decided to form a cartel called **OPEC (Organization of Oil Producing Countries)** that regulated the price and production of oil. Since oil supplied half to three-fourths of the energy of the industrial world and most industrial countries relied heavily on imports from OPEC, consumers were at their mercy.

### 7. The Decline of U.S. International Authority

The U.S. continued to be a major superpower in the world through the 1970s, although they no longer enjoyed the dominance they experienced in the post-war years. Even though the U.S. had financed the reconstruction of Western Europe and Japan, the revival of manufacturing in these countries also meant increased competition for U.S. firms in important industries like steel and automobiles. Also, the wavering U.S. dominance in the periphery regions undermined U.S. companies' easy access to cheap materials and energy resources. For example, the 1973 petroleum-producing countries' embargo of Western buyers and the following oil-price hike coincided with a low point in U.S. international power, just after its military defeat in Vietnam.[100]

### 8. Social Movements in the United States

The explosive mass social movements of the 1960s and 1970s – civil rights, women's liberation, anti-war, gay rights, anti-nuclear, consumer rights, Native American rights and environmental – were another factor that contributed to the crisis of the 1970s. The public's increased pressure for social reform gave rise to greater government regulation of private business. As economist Alexander Reuss explains, "Under the old economic regulation, government agencies had overseen specific industries such as railroads, trucking, telecommunications, utilities, or banks. In contrast, the new social regulations, including the environment, consumer-protection, occupational safety and health, and anti-discrimination laws, affected companies across all industries." Although corporations railed against the new regulations for imposing new "burdensome" costs of doing business, it was a way for the government to respond to increasing demands for reform without increasing government spending.[101]

### 9. Debt and Poverty in the Middle and Periphery Nations

With the restoration of international finance, for the first time since the 1920s the middle and periphery nations could borrow money from private international bankers. And borrow money they did. Tens of billions of dollars a year flowed from banks and bondholders in the core nations to the borrowing middle and

LINE AT A GAS STATION IN MARYLAND, USA, JUNE 15, 1979. THE OIL EMBARGOES IN THE 1970s CONTRIBUTED TO THE CRISIS OF THE 1970s

periphery nations. Inflation exploded. For example, Latin America borrowed $50 billion in 1981 alone, at which point the region owed $300 billion to foreigners. The periphery nations as a whole owed $750 billion abroad, 75 percent to private financiers.[102] Their future looked bleak as their debts mounted and interest payments appeared insurmountable.

Another problem in the middle and periphery ISI nations that contributed to the crisis of the 1970s was the policies dealing with the balance of trade and payments. ISI was supposed to reduce reliance on world trade by making a nation self-sufficient, but every nation needed to import something not available locally, such as raw materials, machinery, or spare parts. The more a country industrialized, the more it needed these vital imports. But countries needed to export products to earn money to buy imports, and ISI policies were strongly against encouraging exports. Therefore, the ISI nations were unable to export enough to buy the imports they needed. ISI countries also tended to run large budget deficits and had high inflation. The policies of ISI governments were to subsidize industrial investment by giving large tax breaks to politically connected industrial investors.[103] ISI national economies were breaking under the multitude of problems.

ISI nations favored industry at the expense of agriculture, which worsened rural poverty in countries that were heavily rural. Farmers migrated to the cities in droves to look for jobs in the new industries. But ISI growth was very capital-intensive, and, therefore, industrialists used lots of capital and not much labor. Poverty awaited farmers who flooded into the cities seeking non-existent jobs in industrial factories. Thus, ISI countries often ended up as "dual" economies." On one hand, skilled, well-organized workers earning relatively high wages worked in modern, capital-intensive industries, while on the other hand, a majority of struggling farmers and urban poor were frozen out of the modern economy and relegated to poverty. In Brazil, for example, ISI resulted in considerable successes but also created considerable problems. ISI appeared to have dire effects on poverty and income distribution. Although Brazil's income per person grew by one-third between 1960 and 1970, the conditions of the bottom four-fifths of the population barely improved, and those of the poorest third worsened. Brazil became the world's most unequal society: the richest 5 percent of the country earned as much as the poorest 80 percent, and twice as much as the poorest 60 percent.[104] It remains as one of the most unequal societies.

The socialist economies primarily relied on natural resources for export – petroleum, gold, timber, minerals– but these would not be enough to pay for necessary imports. Although the socialist countries were not in crisis in the 1970s, the warning signs indicated that problems lay ahead. Socialist reform programs had stalled, and the central planners struggled with poor living standards, lagging technology, and declining growth rates. The 1970s signaled that the glory days of socialism were over.[105]

SLUM OR FAVELA IN RIO DE JANEIRO, BRAZIL. MODERN FAVELAS APPEARED IN 1970s WHEN FARMERS LEFT RURAL AREAS FOR WORK IN THE CITIES.

## The Uncertainty of the 1970s

The postwar order (1948-1973) had achieved the goals of its architects. The advanced capitalist countries got economic integration, coupled with an expansion of the welfare state and a well-managed economy. Some of the middle status and periphery countries built their industrial bases, coupled with protection from foreign economic influence. The socialist countries got rapid industrial and economic growth, coupled with a somewhat equitable distribution of income. But in all three groups of countries the joint achievement of these goals had become more difficult by the 1970s. Global economic integration largely prevented a core nation's management of its own national economy, ISI nations experienced periodic crises and inequality, and central planning in the socialist nations slowed economic growth. The way forward in the 1970s was not clear.[106]

The late 1970s and early 1980s looked like the 1930s. Different interest groups fought over their preferred path to structuring national and global economies. There were the nationalists and globalists, free market advocates and those who pushed for managed capitalism, those on the political right and those on the left, there were leftists who pushed socialism and rightists who pushed for less government and more corporate power. Their political positions polarized and compromise appeared unattainable.

When the dust settled, it was the political right, the free-market advocates, who emerged as the group who had garnered political and popular support. It wasn't an over-night victory, they had been working on their agenda throughout the 1970s and even before, but the victory was decisive and shaped the economic and political landscape to the present day.

### Questions to Consider

1. Did you (or someone you know) experience any of the above problems during the crisis of the 1970s?

# THE SHIFT TO THE RIGHT

The crisis of the 1970s marked the end of the "Golden Age" framework and the ascendancy of neoliberal capitalism. It was also a part of a broader shift to the right in U.S. and UK politics. The neoliberal economic policy agenda advocated economic deregulation, an end to social welfare programs, and the dismantling of labor organizations. Reuss explains:

"The right drew on currents in U.S. political culture pining for an imagined past of individual independence and blaming government regulation, taxation, and social programs for the perceived economic and moral decay of society. It tapped into and fueled a backlash against the civil rights and women's liberation movements. Conservatives channeled this rage into attacks on social programs and affirmative action. It also drew on the power of nationalism, and the identification of many ordinary Americans with what they saw as the declining superpower status of the United States. Conservatives promised to reverse recent blows to the national self-image – the U.S. defeat in the Vietnam War, the rise of OPEC and the oil shocks, the Iranian Revolution and hostage crisis, the apparent loss of economic dominance to international competitors – and to restore the country to its rightful place of worldwide supremacy."[107]

These were pillars of populism that grew and were nurtured in the 1970s and 1980s, and to a great extent continue today. Even though conservatives were able to frame a populist appeal to the chain of events mentioned above, elites heartily supported the turn to the right in U.S. economic policy. Facing multiple threats from various sides during the crisis of the 1970s, some of the very largest corporations mobilized an effective campaign to ensure that the crisis was resolved in a way that was advantageous to their group. They had a three pronged campaign to ensure support for their agenda. First, they financed policy organizations or "think tanks" which helped develop the conservative economic policy agenda, like the Hoover Institution, the American Enterprise Institute, and later the Heritage Foundation. Second, they stepped up their lobbying efforts of government officials and channeled money into existing business organizations, such as the U.S. Chamber of Commerce, to support their agenda. During the late 1960s and early 1970s, large corporations had been on the defensive, facing a rising tide of environmental, occupational safety and health, and consumer-protection regulation, but by the late 1970s bills friendly to labor and consumers went down to defeat, largely due to business interests' mobilization against them. The business elites were turning the political tide to conservatism even before the watershed 1980 election. Third, they directed support to conservative candidates for public office. This support helped shift Congress in a pro-business direction. These mobilizations by the right during the 1970s played a big role in bringing about a sea change in economic policy, sometimes known as the "right turn," beginning late in the decade and continuing with the "Reagan Revolution" in the 1980s.[108]

It was in this conservative atmosphere that the beleaguered U.S. President Jimmy Carter appointed a new Chairman of the Federal Reserve in 1979: **Paul Volcker**. To curb inflation, the Federal Reserve under his direction pushed short-term interest rates up from about 10 percent to 15 percent and eventually above 20 percent. Volcker kept American interest rates at these extraordinarily high levels for almost three years, until late 1982. This drove the economy into two successive and deep recessions, reduced manufacturing output and median family income by 10 percent and raised unemployment to nearly 11 percent. But Volcker's massive shock to the economy got inflation below 4 percent, and it stayed low for the next 30 years.[109] This killed inflation and more broadly shifted the balance of power from the working and middle classes to investors and the financial sector. As we have seen, investors do not like inflation, while debtors like a modest increase in inflation each year, which effectively reduces their debts.

A new economic era dawned at the beginning of the 1980s. Conservative economic groups laid the groundwork and the timing was ripe for a turn to the right. The managed, social democratic form of capitalism followed for over four decades in the U.S. was replaced with an agenda reminiscent of the classical era of capitalism just under 100 years ago. The UK also moved to conservatism with the election of Prime Minister Margaret Thatcher, (1979-1990). Although Jimmy Carter, a Democrat, was advancing some neoliberal principles such as deregulation of the airlines, it would fall to his successor, Republican Ronald Reagan, to continue to forge a new economic agenda in the U.S. He was elected president in a decisive showing in November 1980; the new economic agenda had a new leader and a new name, "the Reagan Revolution."

# CONCLUDING INSIGHTS: HISTORICAL ROOTS OF THE GLOBAL ECONOMY

The crisis of the 1970s had been resolved in favor of a different version of capitalism than had preceded it. The neoliberal version was not a spontaneous creation of nature but a well-orchestrated plan to change the trajectory of U.S. capitalism to a system that benefitted specific groups of people. As we have seen in history, different groups of people have clashed with each other over who could grab the ear of government and structure policies and laws to benefit them. This time was no different. Beginning in the 1980s there was a significant shift in groups who had the ear of government. The golden era of post-war capitalism in the U.S. was a time when there was a balancing act among government, labor, the middle class, and business interests. Although not perfect, all groups generally profited from the cooperation. Yet, because of unions, regulation, and high taxes, many business groups felt they were limited in their capacity to make more profits. Even though neoliberalism was in the embryo stage during the 1970s crisis, business groups intent on creating a system that favored their interests was more organized and better funded to take the lead in shaping the future economic system. For them, their hard work and investments paid off handsomely.

The shocks of the 1970s' crisis discredited the postwar golden era of managed capitalism in the U.S. and much of the West. It had also discredited communism/socialism and the ISI model of economic development. During the 1970s crisis, business interests suffered along with everyone else; yet business leaders took the crisis as an opportunity to put forth a program – neoliberalism – that would benefit their interests more than managed capitalism. Neoliberalism drew on many of the principles found in the classical era of laissez-faire, free trade capitalism from 1896 to 1914. It was not an exact replica of the past, since the world had changed significantly since that time. However, the similarities are still striking.

The U.S. was not the only country to experience wrenching economic turmoil during the 1970s, but as the world's leading economy, the U.S. had a far more significant role in shaping the global economy than other countries. Three dimensions to the global economy emerged out of the bedlam of the 1970s – neoliberalism, economic globalization, and financialization. All three are interrelated and intricately connected. It will be our job in this book to pull apart, like taffy, these three economic dimensions and see how each one functions and what the repercussion are.

Let me briefly describe these three dimensions. Neoliberalism is the version of capitalism that has been in operation since 1980 in the U.S. (I will use this approximate date as the start of the process) and to a lesser extent in the UK. However, as the leading economic power at this time, the U.S. promotes this version of capitalism as the one which all other countries are encouraged to follow. As mentioned in chapter 1, there are different versions of capitalism which guide the way an economy is structured: what policies it promotes, what laws it passes, and what jobs it offers. Neoliberalism is just one of the ways in which the

**A LEADER OF THE CONSERVATIVE REVOLUTION WAS PRESIDENT RONALD REAGAN (1981-1989).**

capitalist system can be structured. As we saw in this chapter, there were many other versions of capitalism that have been in operation during its long 500-year history. Chapters 3 and 4 outline the 10 ingredients in what I have called the "neoliberal stew" or the 10 principles that distinguish neoliberalism from other versions of capitalism.

Simply put, globalization is the greater integration of the world into an interconnected process. When the integration is economic we call this process economic globalization. This process of economic globalization is pulling areas throughout the world that were not connected before 1980 into the capitalist web. The biggest capitalist "catch" – that is, the most important country to be brought into the capitalist web – is China, with India not far behind. When studying economic globalization in chapters 5 and 6, we will examine the roles of different countries around the world in the economic globalization process.

Financialization is a sector of the economy that specializes in creating financial products that have a certain value and can be traded in the market place. Some financial instruments are insurance, loans, real estate sales, stocks, bonds, and derivatives. In the U.S., since the 1980s, the trajectory has been to reduce support of the manufacturing sector of the economy or small businesses and farmers, but mainly to support large corporations and the financial sector as the way to create wealth in the economy.

The extensive agenda of creating a new economic order would be carried out in these three interrelated dimensions: neoliberalism, economic globalization, and financialization. These three dimensions will be the subject of rest of the book.

### Questions to Consider

1. What does it mean to you that we will be pulling apart, like taffy, the 3 dimensions of the global economy? Do you think this is a good idea? Explain.

# CHAPTER THREE

# The Neoliberal Stew:
# A Dozen Essential Ingredients

*Hear me, people: We have now to deal with another race – small and feeble when our fathers first met them, but now great and overbearing. Strangely enough they have a mind to till the soil and the love of possession is a disease with them. These people have made many rules that the rich may break but the poor may not. They take their tithes from the poor and weak to support the rich and those who rule.*

*… Chief Sitting Bull*

CHIEF SITTING BULL (1831-1885) WAS A
HUNKPAPA LAKOTA SIOUX HOLY MAN
WHO LED HIS PEOPLE AS A TRIBAL CHIEF
DURING YEARS OF RESISTANCE
TO UNITED STATES GOVERNMENT POLICIES.

Today is a perplexing time. We are often confused about the economy because different events such as the financial crisis in 2008 seem unconnected to economic globalization, the manufacturing boom in China seems unconnected to the financial crisis, and the hollowing out of the factories in the heartland of the U.S. seems unconnected to neoliberalism. But actually they are all intricately connected. The mainstream media is remiss in describing the big picture of the global economy and more interested in selling us products or filling us in on the latest celebrity mishap. But it is important to remember that all three dimensions of the global economy – neoliberalism, economic globalization, and financialization – are happening today and are part of an interconnected process.

Let's now turn to understanding the first dimension of the global economy – the neoliberal restructuring process – the subject of this chapter and the next. In this chapter I introduce the 12 essential ingredients that make up this version of capitalism, what I call the neoliberal stew. In these two chapters we will look at neoliberalism primarily in the U.S. Since the U.S. has been the dominant economic powerhouse in the 20th century, it has defined many of the ways and rules of the global economy.

## THE PHILOSOPHY OF NEOLIBERALISM

The first chapter defined neoliberalism but here is a refresher. Neoliberalism is a version of capitalism favoring free trade, privatization, deregulation, and reduced public expenditures on social services. The conservative political faction was hard at work during the 1970s drawing from events in the past and formulating new ideas about what neoliberalism would look like. They called their ideas the free market or free trade. Usually the term free is used as an adjective to make it more appealing to the American people who rightly identify closely with the word. The conservatives certainly don't call it neoliberalism, but since other countries use the term I will use the term since it is more of an academic term and less a jargon one. The first step in describing the neoliberal restructuring process is to describe the philosophy of the newly designated economic system.

Supporters of neoliberalism draw upon the works of free-market theorists such as Frederich Hayek and Milton Friedman. They had to take the abstract theories of these intellectuals and translate them into language that would convince millions of people in the U.S. that the old system of managed capitalism was broken and had to be discarded and that the new system of neoliberalism would ultimately benefit them. The backers of neoliberalism were extremely lucky to have the gifted communicator and affable personality of President Ronald Reagan to do the honors of explaining this new system in a manner the masses would understand. In the UK the dynamic and forceful Prime Minister Margaret Thatcher would convince many in her country and around the world that neoliberalism was the best possible economic system. Neoliberalism seemed a viable solution to the failed policies of the 1970s. As Reagan exclaimed, "It was morning again in America."

In the 1970s, neoliberals framed managed capitalism with its regulations of business and policy supports of the working and middle classes as an abject failure. Since nations did not specifically practice neoliberalism during the post-war years, it was hailed as an answer to the economic maelstrom of the 1970s. In contrast to the failure of other economies during the 1970s, supporters pitched neoliberalism as the solution to economic woes. Even though the track record of neoliberalism dated back to the classical era, alongside some of the moribund socialist enterprises in parts of Europe that were facing a decline in productivity and a rise in labor costs, it looked like a viable alternative.

The 1980s revealed the systemic weaknesses of the crumbling communist system in Eastern Europe and the Soviet Union. The Import Substitution Industrialization (ISI) economies of Latin America and elsewhere were not providing growth and prosperity for its citizens. And managed capitalism was facing a crisis in the 1970s. These three systems were in decline – socialism/communism, ISI, and managed capitalism – and neoliberals held up their system as much more efficient and democratic in allocating goods and services than the other systems, and the obvious choice.

But there needed to be more to neoliberalism than merely saying that the other economic systems didn't work anymore and here was the best alternative. Neoliberalism needed a founding theorist, like communism/socialism that drew on the works of Karl Marx and managed capitalism that drew on the works of John Maynard Keynes. The intellectual who provided this theoretical underpinning to neoliberalism was Milton Friedman, an economics professor at the University of Chicago. He and his followers who promoted and refined the neoliberal agenda were known far and wide as the "Chicago School." Let's turn next to Friedman and look at his contribution to the neoliberal agenda.

## Milton Friedman

Born in New York City, Milton Friedman (1912-2006) was the 20th century's most well-known advocate of what he called free markets. He distinguished himself in the academic field of economics, most notably as a professor at the University of Chicago (1946-1977) where he spearheaded the "Chicago School" of economics, known for its refutation of Keynesian ideas. In his influential 1962 book *Capitalism and Freedom,* Friedman made the case for free markets in a liberal society to a general audience. He argued for, among other things, a volunteer army, floating exchange rates, a negative income tax, and education vouchers. He promoted an alternative macroeconomic policy known as monetarism (see below) and theorized that there existed a "natural rate of unemployment." He predicted that Keynesian policies would cause high inflation and minimal growth, which later in the 1970s proved to be true. Keynes argued that monetary policy is ineffective during depression conditions and that fiscal policy – large-scale deficit spending by the government – is needed to decrease mass unemployment. Friedman refuted this prevailing assumption and claimed that monetary policy could have prevented the Great Depression and not government spending to boost demand. Although theoretically Friedman opposed the existence of the Federal Reserve, he thought that as long as the Fed was here to stay, the only wise policy was for it to assure a steady, small expansion of the money supply. In keeping with the 19th century classical era's economic principles, Friedman opposed many types of government regulation.

Friedman served as an adviser to President Richard Nixon and was president of the American Economic Association in 1967. In 1976 he was awarded the Nobel Prize in economics for his "achievements in the fields of consumption analysis, monetary history and theory and for his demonstration of the complexity of stabilization policy." After retiring from the University of Chicago in 1977, Friedman became a senior research fellow at the Hoover Institution at Stanford University in California. He served as an unofficial adviser to Ronald Reagan during his 1980 presidential campaign, and then served on his Economic Policy Advisory Board. His weekly columns for *Newsweek* magazine (1966–84) were well read and became increasingly influential among political and business people and the general public. Throughout the 1980s and 1990s, Friedman continued to write editorials and appear on television. Among other places, he made several visits to Eastern Europe, Chile, and to China, where he also advised their governments. He was a much admired and influential economist who was active in his profession until his death at the age of 94 in 2006.[1]

## Alan Greenspan and the Federal Reserve

An implementer of Friedman's theories was the chairman of the Federal Reserve and one of the most powerful financial men in America, from 1987-2006: Alan Greenspan. Greenspan enlisted the governing powers of the central bank in advancing the neoliberal agenda. The chairman thus became an important factor in achieving the profound neoliberal transformations that occurred during the last generation.

Alan Greenspan was born in New York City in 1926. He was an accomplished clarinet and saxophone player and had a brief fling as a professional jazz saxophonist before graduating New York University. He became head of an economics consulting firm in New York in 1954. Early in his life, Greenspan was a friend and follower of writer Ayn Rand, a noted free-market libertarian of the 1950s and 1960s. He described himself as a "lifelong libertarian Republican."[2] By the 1970s he was advising presidents Richard Nixon and Gerald Ford, and in 1987 President Reagan named him Chairman of the Federal Reserve. Greenspan held the post under presidents Ronald Reagan, George H.W. Bush, Bill Clinton and George W. Bush. As chairman, Greenspan was largely responsible for directing U.S. national monetary policy; he is often credited with keeping inflation at historically low levels, and is sometimes criticized for allowing the boom-and-bust nature of the economy in the so-called "dot-com" era of the 1990s. He stepped down from the post in January 2006, and Fed chairman Ben Bernanke succeeded him.

A brief history of the Federal Reserve at this point helps to show Greenspan's significant role as implementer of neoliberalism. Also, the neoliberal shift executed by the Greenspan Fed differs significantly from the time of managed capitalism during the New Deal years of the 1930s. A comparison of Greenspan's policies with a former Federal Reserve Chairman during the Depression, Marriner Eccles, illustrates this shift to neoliberalism from managed capitalism under Greenspan's watch.

The **Federal Reserve** (sometime called the Fed or central bank) is the central banking system of the United States. Created in 1913 under the administration of President Woodrow Wilson, it was a response to a series of financial panics, particularly a severe panic in 1907. The roles and responsibilities of the Federal Reserve System have expanded and its structure has evolved over time. Its duties today are to conduct the nation's monetary policy, supervise and regulate banking institutions, maintain the

ALAN GREENSPAN, 13TH CHAIRMAN OF THE FEDERAL RESERVE, A SUPPORTER OF NEOLIBERALISM.

stability of the financial system and provide financial services to depository institutions, the U.S. government, and foreign official institutions.[3] The Fed has in theory been an independent institution, staying above the political fray – its chairman is not a democratically elected position – making scientific decisions on money and credit, and acting like a regulator of economic growth for long-term stability.

Major events such as the Great Depression in the 1930s contributed to changes in the system. The Fed chairman at this time was Marriner Eccles (1890-1977), a Republican, Mormon banker from Utah. He attended Brigham Young College but did not graduate and then served a Latter-day Saint mission to Scotland. After the untimely death of his father, he took over the family's banking and industrial enterprises; he became a millionaire by age 22. In 1932 the newly elected President Franklin Roosevelt noted his business skills and appointed him to serve as Fed Chair between 1934 and 1948. He also actively participated in the post-World War II Bretton Woods negotiations.

Eccles was a leading architect of New Deal reforms, and collaborated closely with Roosevelt to reform the Fed and convert it to the economic understandings grounded in Keynesian principles. He took Keynes' formal theory and implemented it into the nation's economic policies: the Fed became the intervening balance wheel in a modern industrial economy – the stabilizing force that, when necessary, stimulated the economy to encourage faster growth and full employment, while at other times it puts the brakes on economic activity to avoid inflation. Eccles essentially invented the modern Federal Reserve, which had previously followed the inflexible doctrine of the gold standard during the 1920s.[4]

Eccles and Greenspan are like historic bookends on the gradual transition in economic thinking from managed capitalism to neoliberalism. Greenspan eliminated the vestiges of Eccles and FDR. In its place he resurrected the theory of the classical era: markets can run the economy better than the government. According to Greenspan, Keynesian demand-side stimulus for consumers produces no lasting effects for the economy, therefore wages and the consuming power of workers will be determined by the marketplace. The government should not intervene in the market, except to squelch price inflation.[5]

Greenspan chairmanship reflected the neoliberal tilt in economic policy. His monetary policy directly supported all of the various strands of the neoliberal ideology. He deliberately restrained economic growth for many years, effectively suppressing employment and wages. The economy, he argued, cannot grow faster than 2 to 2.5 percent without igniting price inflation, so the Fed was duty bound to prevent it. Capital gained in value as a result. Labor did not. Greenspan did not formally try to deregulate the banking system, but simply declined to use the Fed's regulatory powers to enforce order or discipline fraudulent behavior. In the name of greater efficiency he engineered legal approval for new megabanks like Citigroup even before Congress changed the law. According to economic journalist William Grieder, "Economic ideologies are often elaborate rationales to justify taking care of some folks and neglecting others. This was the era of business and other groups had to bow to them."[6]

### Questions to Consider

1. Which Fed Chair's economic philosophy do you most agree with? Explain.

## The Neoliberalism Stew: A Dozen Essential Ingredients

Milton Friedman was a prominent contributor and Alan Greenspan a notable implementer for the theory of what they called and popularized as free-market capitalism. However, I will continue to call the theory neoliberalism, even though it is often referred to as free-market capitalism, in order to keep the terms consistent throughout the book and keeping with its global context. In the section above, you may have gained a glimpse into what the principles of neoliberalism are all about. In order to think about these principles interacting together to form a neoliberal version of capitalism, I have explained them as separate ingredients that when all simmered and mixed together result in a stew – a neoliberal stew. I have listed a dozen ingredients in the table below with a short description. The rest of this chapter explains the 12 ingredients in more depth. Let's turn to this neoliberal stew and see if you think it is a tasty and satisfying stew or one that is a bland concoction that is no longer palatable to Americans today.

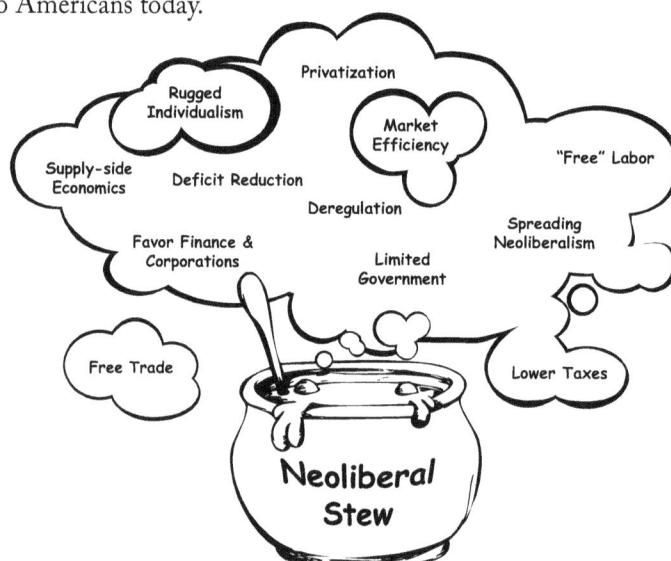

## The Neoliberal Stew: A Dozen Essential Ingredients

1. Free Trade – removal of so called "barriers" to trade such as tariffs, quotas, and subsidies.
2. Privatization – sale of state-owned enterprises, goods and services to private investors.
3. Deregulation – removal of many government regulations on enterprises.
4. Limited Government – scale down the size of government; let the market make decisions.
5. Supply Side Economics – when needed, stimulate supply side of economy instead of demand side.
6. Lower Taxes – especially for the wealthy, who will invest their surplus funds to create jobs.
7. Markets Know Best – efficient markets make better economic decisions than the government.
8. Reduce the Deficit – reduce budget deficits.
9. Support of Corporations and the Financial Sector – through government policy.
10. "Free" Labor – let the market determine wages and employment, destroy unions.
11. Rugged Individualism – is better than a shared community.
12. Spreading Neoliberalism – it is the best system, spread it around the world.

# INGREDIENT #1: FREE TRADE

Free trade is the first ingredient in the neoliberal stew and one of its cornerstone concepts. When we think of free trade we imagine that there are no restrictions to trade, and any country can decide who they want to trade with and who they may not. However, free trade really isn't free; it has rules and lots of them. But it is a term used most frequently in discussions these days, so despite my aversion to the overuse of the word "free" I will use it in this book. By **free trade**, supporters of neoliberalism mean the elimination of import and export quotas and tariffs that they consider to be "barriers to trade." A reminder, tariffs are duties or customs imposed by government on exports or imports. Free traders push to remove regulations on the flow of capital, which now moves from country to country at lightning speed. However, there is no free flow of labor, which the U.S. and most other countries control, unlike in the late 19th and early 20th centuries when migration among countries accelerated. Free traders argue that free trade will help everyone in the long run by encouraging countries to specialize in their comparative advantages, which will accelerate efficiency and economic growth. Because of the removal of checks on trade, business will be able to expand their markets and have access to resources around the world.

Supporters of free trade argue that with the removal of checks and tariffs on trade, each country will produce goods that are their specialty. A country that has plenty of capital will specialize in industrial goods because to set up a factory requires lots of money or capital, while a country that has abundant agricultural land will specialize in agricultural products. For example, today China is able to specialize in producing labor-intensive manufactured goods because they have an abundant supply of labor willing to work for low wages. When China embarked upon industrialization, they did not have enough capital to set up manufacturing plants themselves; therefore, they were successful in luring eager investors from the West to take advantage of their cheap labor and lack of regulations with the prospect of very high profits.

Since free trade and the tariff debate is an important concept in neoliberalism, it would help our understanding of the topic to briefly look at the debate in historical context. Even though we will primarily use the U.S. as our historical example, the concept of tariffs and free trade is a similar debate in other parts of the world as well, and it will be covered in chapter 5.

## A Brief History: Tariffs and Free Trade

The debate between free trade and tariffs has often been an acrimonious one in U.S. history. It might be hard for you to imagine that in the past different groups in the U.S. almost came to blows over the issue. Why has this been such a hot topic in the past, and who benefits under free trade and who benefits under tariff policies? This brief history will help to explain these questions.

As described in the previous chapter, the first form of modern capitalism was mercantilism, which was a restrictive form of trade in which the "mother country" or the colonial power would dictate the terms of trade with its colonial possessions. As designed, the mother country was the one to benefit from the arrangement, while the colonies were on the losing end. In colonial Boston in the early 1770s the confrontation involving mercantilist policies pitted the American colony against their British mother country. The colonists resented Britain's mercantilist control over their trade and revolted in the daring Boston Tea Party, which was a protest in part against British tea tariffs. On the eve of the American Revolution, one of the initial acts of the First Continental Congress was a vote to stop trading with England until it changed its policies.[7]

The leading economist at the time of the founding of the United States was the brilliant first Secretary of the Treasury, Alexander Hamilton (1789-1795). He argued that competition from abroad hampered the formation of new industries. Thus, in order to build up infant industries in the new country, the government needed to help protect home industries by leveling import duties on imported products that competed with national industries or, in rare cases, prohibition of certain imports. He pushed for high tariffs to protect the infant industries of the Northeast, which allowed the country to be less dependent on manufactured goods from Britain. Tariffs also provided a sizable source of income to the U.S. Treasury. Thomas Jefferson, whose supporters were mainly small farmers, opposed high tariffs and complained that the tariffs raised the price of manufactured goods for consumers like his farmer constituency.

A simple example will illustrate how tariffs protect home industries. We introduced this idea in chapter 2 but it is worth elaborating upon. Known as the infant industry argument, it states that tariffs, quotas, and other regulations benefit new industries because this protection allows industries to grow until they achieve an economy of scale that enables them to compete on an equal basis with foreign competitors. Let's use a historical example to illustrate the point. When the U.S. first started to industrialize in the early 1800s, Britain was ahead of the pack in the industrialization race and was therefore much more efficient in producing goods and already had the tools to keep costs low. Thus, Britain could produce industrial goods cheaper than the U.S. or, for that matter, anyone else in the world at the time. The U.S. wanted to protect its infant industries so they could grow and provide jobs for its citizens. The U.S. levied a tariff on imported goods from Britain. That tariff thus made Britain's goods more expensive, which would nudge U.S. consumers into purchasing American made products. Although it helped the U.S. manufacturers and provided jobs for industrial workers, consumers generally had to pay more for the tariff-protected products.

Since Britain was the world's leading economic power in the early 19th century, it advocated for free trade policies that would benefit its economy. By 1820 the British strongly pushed a free trade agenda but the U.S. was not ready to participate. But the British policy of free trade was not consistent: they continued to ban the import of superior products from some of their colonies, especially if they happened to threaten established British industries.[8] They supported free trade as long as it was in the interests of favored special groups. Although there was a round of British tariff reduction in 1833, the big change came in 1846, when the Corn Law was repealed and tariffs on many manufacturing goods were abolished. The British now wholeheartedly championed free trade, despite its protectionist past.

In the U.S., the dispute between free traders and protectionists carried over into the decades leading up to the Civil War (1861-1865). The debate pitted the increasingly industrialized North against small farmers in the West and the slave-holding plantation owners of the South. Essentially the free traders were attacking the tariffs on the grounds that they were in effect government subsidies, while the protectionists responded that by encouraging local manufacturing the tariffs were benefiting the country as a whole. Until the war with Britain in 1812, the average tariff level remained around 12.5 percent, in order to meet the increased wartime expense the government doubled tariffs in 1812. However, a significant shift in policy occurred in 1816, when a new law kept the tariffs close to the wartime level. Under the 1816 tariff law almost all manufactured goods were subject to tariffs of around 35 percent, which rose to around 40 percent in 1820.[9] In 1824, Congress enacted a still higher tariff. In 1828, the so-called Tariff of Abominations, with an average rate of 45 percent on almost all foreign goods, so infuriated Southerners that tariffs were reduced in another law that was passed in 1832. The Southerners, however, demanded an even lower tariff which led to the Nullification Crisis: the refusal by the state of South Carolina to accept the law. Passed in 1833, a compromise bill offered few immediate reductions but made a provision for gradual reduction over the next ten years to 20 percent for all goods. As soon as this 10-year reduction ended in 1842, a new tariff act raised duties back up to about the 1832 levels. Southerners applauded a reduction in import duties in the 1846 tariff law, and an even further reduction in 1857.[10]

The tension surrounding the tariff issue, as well as the slave issue, persisted between the North and the South. The tension finally culminated in the Civil War, which is commonly thought to have been fought solely over the issue of slavery, but in fact the tariff debate was another important issue. The importance of the tariff issue in causing the South's secession from the Union cannot be overemphasized.[11]

In 1862, during the depths of the Civil War, President Abraham Lincoln's administration supported a new tariff act. This raised the rates to their highest level in thirty years. In 1864, Congress raised tariffs still further to meet the war-time expenditures, and remained at those levels even after the war. In this way, the victory of the North in the Civil War ensured that the U.S. remained, at this point, the most protected economy in the world until World War I, with the notable exception of Russia in the early 20th century.[12]

With the second Industrial Revolution in high gear in the second half of 19th century, the U.S. was beginning to close Britain's technological lead, but it continued its policy of industrial promotion and protection. Trade policy continued to fracture the country, and the debate become more intense than ever. The Republican Party, which was becoming the party of business, was the party of protectionism, supporting the expansion of tariffs to shield American business from foreign competition. Meanwhile, farmers and miners remained intensely resentful of tariffs, and supported the Democratic Party. Since commodities prices collapsed from the 1870s onward, they wanted to export their products on the world market unimpeded by tariffs. As many small farmers faced economic ruin because of low prices, they were infuriated that the tariff policy favored the business circles and Northeast bankers. The resentment turned into anger contributing to the rise of the Populist Movement, which heartedly endorsed the policy of free trade.[13] However, the movement ebbed as the economic situation eased in the years 1896-1914, as new gold supplies were discovered that expanded the money supply and commodity prices went up. Tariffs became a less cantankerous issue as everyone prospered.

The Democratic President Woodrow Wilson supported the passage of the Underwood Tariff bill by Congress in 1913, resulting in a substantial drop in tariffs on manufactured goods from 44 percent to 25 percent. Since tariffs provided a large portion of the government's budget, the tariff law coincided with the passage of the 16th amendment permitting the implementation of a federal income tax. Republicans returned to office in 1921, after the interruption of World War I, and promptly passed tariff legislation in 1922 that raised tariffs again, although the tariffs did not return to their 1861-1913 high levels.[14]

Following the onset of the Great Depression, the Republican President Herbert Hoover pushed through the 1930 Smoot-Hawley tariff. Although the bad timing of the bill provoked an international tariff war, it was not a radical departure from the country's traditional high-tariff trade policy stance. Many in favor of free trade today have pointed to the Smoot-Hawley tariff as causing or extending the depression. As economist Ha-Joon Chang argues, "In fact, the Smoot-Hawley tariff only marginally (if at all) increased the degree of protectionism in the U.S. economy. The average tariff rate for manufactured goods that resulted from this bill was 48 percent, and it still falls within the range of the average rates that had prevailed in the United States since the Civil War, albeit in the upper region of this range." It was only in relation to the brief reduced tariff interlude of 1913-29 that the 1930 tariff bill could be interpreted as increasing protectionism, although even then it was not by very much. The average tariff rate on manufactured goods in 1925 was 37 percent and rose to 48 percent in 1931.[15]

By the end of World War II it was clear that free trade would be in America's best interest since the U.S. had unquestionably the world's strongest economy that accounted for an astonishing 50 percent of all world production. With production continuing to grow, the U.S. needed new markets for its goods. Since the U.S. essentially controlled the global marketplace, free trade would only assist them in maintaining their preeminence. The U.S. argument echoed Britain's free trade agenda in the 19th and early 20th centuries, when it was the world's economic powerhouse. [16] However, the value of the U.S. economy traded was only about 5 percent, and thus free trade didn't have as huge an impact on the economy as it would later.[17]

In the 1970s, the U.S. economy started to slip from its near century of economic dominance, when a combination of factors including an oil embargo, high inflation, stagnation, decrease in worker's productivity levels, and scrapping of the gold standard all contributed to the slide. In 1971, the U.S. registered its first trade deficit since 1893. The first mutterings that free trade might not be in the country's best interests came in the 1980s, when the ever-growing trade deficit led to concerns that the U.S. economy was in real decline. Some critics argued that as U.S. companies moved their factories outside its borders while continuing to sell here, the country lost in a double sense: It lost the jobs and local tax revenues from the runaway jobs, and it lost the tariff revenue when the products were brought back in for sale.[18] The tariffs on imports had dropped from a 1973 average of 12 percent to today's average of around 2 percent.[19]

Yet, on the other side of the debate, those promoting a neoliberal agenda were gaining ground and they argued that instead of less free trade, there needed to be more free trade. They promised a renewed emphasis on free trade would accelerate economic growth because business would have expanded access to resources and markets. Free traders point to two undesirable results of tariff protectionism. One argument is that tariffs effectively raise the prices on goods for consumers, and transfers money from them to producers. For example, a tariff on imported shoes makes shoes more expensive, which, in turn, benefits national shoe manufacturers because they can charge higher prices for their shoes. Yet, the shoe-wearing consumers will pay more. Second, tariffs make protected activities artificially profitable, which in some cases can divert resources to inefficient uses. In addition, historically tariffs were often associated with cartels, which were informal or formal monopolies among large corporations who benefitted from tariffs that protected their industries from outside competition.[20]

A systems approach that we learned in chapter 1 is useful in examining the tariff issue from a different perspective. The above shoe manufacture provides a good example for this system thinking exercise in deciding whether tariffs are beneficial or not. The free traders fail to measure the effect of tariff protection for the shoe manufacturing plant on the whole community in which the plant is located. Without the jobs for making shoes, many people in the community are unemployed, which adversely affects other businesses in the community, the tax base, and the vitality of the community. If the unemployed lived in the 21st century, many would draw on unemployment insurance financed through taxes and fees. Although the consumer would perhaps pay slightly more for the shoes being protected by tariffs (since the shoes would presumably be priced higher than a tariff-free import), what the above example shows is that the extra "tax" that the consumer pays for the shoes is off-set by other indirect taxes that citizens must pay as a result of the loss of well-paying jobs at the local manufacturing plant. Also, the U.S. and other countries have anti-trust laws to prevent the concentration of similar industries into monopolies. Therefore, after careful analysis according to a systems approach, tariffs on selected items may be advantageous to workers, the community, state, and nation, and to consumers in the long run. In addition, tariff duties are added to the federal treasury.

The purpose of this brief history illustrates the historic debate between free trade and protectionists and also sheds some light on the debate today. The different factions in the debate argue for their particular positions according to how the policies benefit them. For example, today labor unions often argue for tariff protection since the competing products from China and other low-wage, environmentally lax countries undercut their wages, which means that American consumers purchase the lower priced foreign-made product. In the 1950s and 1960s, though, unions favored free trade since they were eager to have their products sold on the world market, which would solidify their jobs and high wages. On the other hand, many business owners favor free trade since they have found it economically lucrative to pick up their established businesses in the U.S. and ship production overseas to take advantage of a foreign country's non-union, lower wages, fewer occupational safety and health requirements, and more lax environmental enforcement.[21] They are then able to import these foreign-made goods into the U.S. without tariffs. Consumers like the lower prices resulting from free trade, but if their jobs are eliminated because of free trade policies they might have a different opinion.

### North American Free Trade Association (NAFTA)

There are many free trade agreements between nations. I have selected one, NAFTA, as an example to show the impact of free trade in North America. The governments of Canada, Mexico, and the U.S. signed the **North American Free Trade Agreement (NAFTA)** on January 1, 1994 to create a trilateral trade bloc. Although President Bill Clinton signed the agreement, he also introduced clauses to protect American workers and required U.S. partners to adhere to environmental practices and regulations similar to those of its own. The goal of NAFTA was to eliminate tariffs and regulations on investments between the three countries. Implementation of the agreement brought the immediate elimination of tariffs on more than one half of U.S. imports from Mexico and more than one third of U.S. exports to Mexico. Within 10 years of the implementation of the agreement, all U.S.-Mexico tariffs would be eliminated except for some U.S. agricultural exports to Mexico that were to be phased out in 15 years. Trade laws between U.S. and Canada had already eliminated tariffs. As of January 1, 2008, the agreement created the world's largest free trade area, which links 454 million people producing over $17.2 trillion worth of goods and services in 2010. Total merchandise trade among the United States, Canada, and Mexico reached $944.6 billion in 2010, an increase of 218 percent since 1993. Canada and Mexico are the first and third largest merchandise trading partners, accounting for 32.3 percent of U.S. exports to the world in 2010.[22]

Critics of NAFTA say it has been beneficial to business owners and elites in all three countries, but has had negative impacts on farmers in Mexico, who saw crop prices fall because of cheap imports from the U.S., and a negative impact on U.S. workers in manufacturing and assembly industries, who have lost many jobs to factories across the border. Critics also argue that NAFTA has contributed to the rising levels of social inequality in both the U.S. and Mexico. Supporters of NAFTA, such as the conservative CATO Institute, argue that it has been positive for Mexico, which has seen its poverty rates fall and real income rise (in the form of lower prices, especially for food).[23]

From the earliest negotiations, agriculture was (and still remains) a controversial topic within NAFTA, as it has been in the World Trade Organization (WTO). The overall effect of the Mexico-U.S. agricultural agreement is a matter of dispute. In Mexico, over 38,000 small corn farmers lost their land when NAFTA simultaneously opened the gates to cheap, subsidized U.S. corn and took away Mexico's safety net – the system of domestic price supports and subsidies that once ensured a profit for small farmers. The U.S. Department of Agriculture (USDA) estimates that a quarter of all the corn consumed in Mexico now comes from the U.S. Although production of corn in Mexico has increased since the passage of NAFTA, internal corn demand has increased beyond Mexico's production capacity. Corn prices in Mexico, adjusted for international prices, have drastically decreased. The number of agricultural producers in Mexico declined substantially during the 1990s, although the Mexican corn sector still features a large number of small-scale producers.[24]

NAFTA rules have displaced over 2 million Mexican farmers from the countryside since its passage in 1994.[25] The farmers have fled to cities to try and obtain work or migrated either legally or mostly illegally to the U.S. for employment. In a 2007 trip to the farms and villages of Mexico, I repeatedly witnessed small villages ravaged by the effects of NAFTA. Larger farmers or corporations bought up small farms, while the displaced farmers looked for work elsewhere such as in the cities or U.S. Women, children, and the elderly often remained in the villages, while some men returned but many did not. Family and village cohesion bore the dire effects of these absences.

Under NAFTA, meat and poultry imports that do not meet U.S. safety standards can be imported and sold throughout the U.S. The increase of fruits and vegetables from Mexico under NAFTA actually coincided with severe cuts to Mexico's domestic food inspection budget. The safety of U.S. food is also being compromised because pesticides and agricultural chemicals banned in the U.S. are often marketed and sold to countries such as Mexico.

In Mexico in 2002, half of the people were living in poverty and 20 percent in extreme poverty, about the same level as before the passage of the North American Free Trade Association (NAFTA) in 1994.[26] One of the ostensible purposes of NAFTA was to reduce tariffs between Mexico, U.S., and Canada that would,

NAFTA SIGNING CEREMONY, OCTOBER 1992 IN MEXICO.

in turn, spur economic development in the three countries and reduce poverty in Mexico. It does not appear that NAFTA has accomplished this charge.

When we hear the term Chapter 11, bankruptcy often comes to mind. But NAFTA has its own controversial section called **Chapter 11**. Under this section corporations have the right to sue governments for any action that may decrease their company's future profits. For example, if a multinational health care company feels local labor laws curtails its operations it can sue the government for compensation. Likewise, if an oil exploration corporation believes local environmental protection laws are compromising its ability to drill for oil, the company will be able to sue the local government for lost profits. In other words, investors are allowed to demand compensation should the profit-making potential of a venture be injured by government decisions.

One of the first Chapter 11 cases illustrates the impact that NAFTA can have on government regulations. In 1997 the Canadian government voted to ban MMT, a chemical additive to gasoline linked to nervous system disorders. Canadian environmentalists hailed the vote as a win for air quality and public health. But the victory was put at risk when the Virginia based manufacturer of MMT, Ethyl Corporation, filed a NAFTA Chapter 11 suit demanding the Canadian government pay them $251 million in damages. Although the U.S. Environmental Protection Agency (EPA) had already banned MMT, Ethyl claimed that the Canadian government's action was against NAFTA's rules and had lowered its profits. Ethyl's challenge shocked those who didn't understand all the provisions in the new NAFTA law. They saw that a public interest law was under attack because it represented a so-called barrier to profit making by an individual company. The NAFTA court eventually ruled in favor of Ethyl's claim and awarded the company $17 million. The Canadian government repealed its ban on MMT.[27]

A strikingly similar case, with a different outcome, occurred in 1999: *Methanex Corporation vs. U.S.* A Canadian corporation, Methanex, used NAFTA's Chapter 11 to sue the U.S. government for $970 million because of a California phase-out of the gasoline additive MTBE. The phase-out was ordered because it had been shown that MTBE, a known toxin, was leaking into the state's ground water. Methanex claimed that the state's move caused a decline in its stock prices. Methanex based its $970 million claim on the profits the company said it lost over a 20-year period. The case was in arbitration for several years and finally in 2005, the NAFTA Tribunal dismissed all of the claims. The Tribunal also ordered Methanex to pay all the U.S. government's legal fees of approximately $4 million.[28]

Chapter 11 has been criticized by groups in the U.S., such as Public Citizen for a variety of reasons, including not taking into account important social and environmental considerations. In Canada, several groups, including the Council of Canadians, challenged the constitutionality of Chapter 11. They lost at the trial level and have subsequently appealed.[29] We will explore the effects of free trade on the American worker in the labor section.

## Questions to Consider

1. What policy do you favor, protectionism or free trade? What are the benefits and drawbacks of each one? Today, who benefits under protectionism? Under free trade?

# INGREDIENT #2: PRIVATIZATION

Have you ever gone to a state or national park and bought something to eat at one of their concession stands? Or have you driven down a major highway and suddenly realized that you had to pay a toll? Or have you noticed that the big garbage truck that picks up your garbage each week no longer has the name of your city on the door panel but a private enterprise? All of these examples have to do with our second ingredient in the neoliberal stew: privatization.

**Privatization** is a very broad term that is put most simply as the sale of state-owned enterprises, goods and services to private investors. Put another way, it is the transfer of assets or service delivery from the government to the private sector. This includes banks, key industries, railroads, toll highways, electricity, schools, hospitals, prison management, fresh water, and many other things. Although usually done in the name of greater efficiency, which is often needed, privatization has mainly had the effect of concentrating wealth even more in the investor class and making the public pay even more for its services and needs.[30]

This is a good time to introduce two different sectors of the economy: the **private sector,** which is businesses owned by individuals or corporations, and the **public sector,** where the government collectively holds ownership for the people. For example, all the people of a nation collectively own

---

## Privatization Configurations

1. Contracting Out. The government competitively contracts with a private organization, for-profit or non-profit, to provide a service or part of a service.

2. Management Contracts. The operation of a facility is contracted out to a private company; includes airports, wastewater plants, arenas, prisons and convention centers.

3. Franchise. The government gives a private firm exclusive right to provide a service within a certain geographical area.

4. Internal Markets. Departments are allowed to purchase support services such as printing, maintenance, computer repair and training from in-house providers or outside suppliers.

5. Vouchers. Government pays for the service and gives individuals a redeemable certificate to purchase the service on the open market. Vouchers subsidize the consumer of the service, but services are provided by the private sector. These include school, housing and other types of vouchers.

6. Self-Help. Community groups and non-profit neighborhood organizations take over a service or asset such as a local park, zoos, museums, fairs, remote parks and some recreational programs.

7. Volunteers. They provide all or part of a government service. Volunteer activities are conducted through a government volunteer program or through a non-profit organization.

8. Corporatization. Government organizations are reorganized along business lines. Typically they are required to pay taxes, raise capital on the market and operate according to commercial principles.

9. Asset Sale. Government sells its assets to private firms.

10. Long-Term Lease. Government sells an asset to a private firm then enters into a long-term lease for assets such as airports, gas utilities, real estate, or parking meters.

11. Employee Buyout. Existing public managers and employees take the public unit private, typically purchasing the company through an Employee Stock Ownership Plan (ESOP).

12. Private Infrastructure Development and Operation. The private sector builds, finances, and operates public infrastructure such as roads and airports, recovering costs through user charges.

---

national parks, while local parks are under the local government's jurisdiction. Privatization runs a very broad range, sometimes leaving very little government involvement, and at other times creating partnerships between government and the private sector. The textbox on the opposite page lists 12 different configurations that privatization may take.

## A Brief History of Privatization

Privatization accompanied the expansion of capitalism around the watershed 1500 date. Agriculture was one of the first sectors of the economy to undergo the privatization process, but in these early cases it wasn't a transfer of assets from the government to private hands but the privatization (a more accurate term "commodification") of large agricultural tracts of land loosely owned by elite land-owners which had been passed down over the generations from the king. For centuries in Europe peasant farmers practiced an open field system, a form of agricultural organization in which peasants farmed large tracts of land for elite landlords. They produced food for their own subsistence needs, and paid a required amount of the surplus as a tax to the landowner. In this system efficiency and productivity were largely secondary, with the tax payment to the landowner and the subsistence needs of the peasants as primary. But the open field system began to give way to farming according to capitalist principles with the enclosure process, where efficiency and productivity became primary. Farms, as well as shared areas called "the **commons**," were first enclosed or converted to privately owned plots marked with clear boundaries and legally-enforced private ownership. Enclosure first took off in Britain in the early modern era where landowners enthusiastically embraced it and benefited from the move to a capitalist economy. Although uprooted farmers vainly protested their plight, since they were the ones who lost the land they had farmed for centuries, this strictly financial process largely ignored their welfare.

John Locke (1632-1704), an English Enlightenment thinker, wrote about the primacy of property rights in his 1688 book *The Second Treatise of Government*. The book proved pivotal in the implementation of British and American property laws. One of the core ideas Locke espoused was that ownership was legitimate if men would convert "unproductive" land to "productive" land using their own labor.[31] Thus, the principle of private ownership became a central part of the Western tradition.

This concept of converting unproductive land to productive land by the sweat of one's own labor helped to justify the American conquest of lands held by indigenous peoples of North America. The American settlers claimed they were converting what they regarded as "unused waste land" into productive farm land, which they felt legitimated their ownership. An example of early privatization of Native Ameri-

A 1911 AD OFFERING "ALLOTTED INDIAN LAND" FOR SALE AS A RESULT OF THE DAWES ACT.

can land was the 1887 **Dawes Act** in Oklahoma. The act spelled out the division of commonly held tribal lands into individually-owned parcels, while settlers and the railroads opened up the remaining "surplus" lands. With its emphasis on individual land ownership, the Dawes Act proved to have a negative impact on the unity, self-government, and culture of Native peoples.

Fast forward to after World War II in 1945. At this time, many countries in Europe and some in the U.S. had public services, which the government provided for its citizens. Although they varied according to particular countries, they generally included such services as electricity, highways, public transportation, telephone, water, sanitation, broadcasting, fire protection, police, prisons, courts, military, research and development (R&D), education, health care, and social security. These public services constituted what economists called "natural monopolies." According to economist Susan George, "A **natural monopoly** exists when the minimum size to guarantee maximum economic efficiency is equal to the actual size of the market. In other words, a service company has to be a certain size to realize economies of scale and thus provide the best possible service at the lowest cost to the consumer." Public services also require an initial large capital investment – like railroad tracks, electric power grids, highway construction, sanitation facilities and others – which does not encourage private sector outlays or competition. That is why public monopolies proved to be the obvious best solution to provide services to as many people as possible in order to improve their standard of living at a reasonable cost.[32]

The 1980 date marked a sweep of neoliberal changes in the U.S., UK, and ultimately to other parts of the world. One of these significant changes was the privatization or attempt to privatize many of the public services that the government provided for its citizens. Neoliberals pressured nations with managed capitalist, communist, or socialist economies to privatize, or sell to private enterprises many of their large state-owned enterprises. Neoliberals framed government as too inefficient, corrupt, and inept at providing these valuable services, and promised the private sector would do a much better job and at a lower cost.

**Privatization: Beneficial or Detrimental?**
The reasons for this privatization movement depend on whom you talk to. Supporters of privatization cited that businesses would offer privatized services more efficiently and cost effectively. Customers would also have a choice in deciding for themselves which service provider to use. Those on the other side of the debate said that privatization was not more efficient or cost effective but was simply a scheme to transfer wealth from the public treasury to private hands. Which one is right? Both sides have legitimate arguments that will be explored in this section. However, in keeping with the message of this book, we will look at several alternative arguments that are critical of the privatization process.

Most of what we hear about privatizing public services carries the same simple message: privatizing is good. We often hear that refrain because it is assumed that only the private sector can deliver a quality product at the lowest possible price. The neoliberal message demonizes the government and labels it ineffective. For example, in the news in the fall of 2010, a debate raged about the tactics used by the Transportation Security Administration (TSA), a government agency charged with screening airline passengers for contraband that could cause harm. Apparently they have used procedures that many people found offensive, such as body pat-downs and full body screens. Instead of saying that the rules needed to be changed, one pro-privatization politician claimed that privatizing the agency would solve the problem. However, privatization is more complex. Whether to have certain public services and how to deliver them economically and efficiently has a profound impact on all of us. As the U.S. and the world move towards increased privatization, it's helpful to look at the other side of the issue. The following dispels some commonly held beliefs about privatizing public services.

## Assumptions about Privatization[33]

1. Governments are broke because public services and tax dollars have been mismanaged. Actually governments have lost major sources of revenue from lower tax rates, such as from wealthy individuals, an economic downturn, and increased spending on items such as wars, the military, and Medicare.

2. Privatizing would eliminate government incompetence, waste and fraud. This argument assumes that the private sector is free from these problems; waste and fraud will arise in the case of subcontracted public services. In fact, there are more chances for fraud since there is less oversight.

3. Market forces and competition ensure that the private sector delivers a higher quality service at a lower cost than the public sector. Simple math should tell us it's impossible for the private sector to deliver the same service for less and make a profit as well. Private companies must make a profit for their investors and this profit is subtracted from the money available to provide the service. Private service companies must be closely watched, especially when they have access to public money, information, and property. This oversight adds additional expense to delivering public services.

4. It's impossible to get rid of bad public employees that don't care about their jobs. There seems to be an assumption that public employees are bad workers. If public workers don't do their jobs, they can be fired. Although a few slip through the cracks, the public sector does not keep bad people in good jobs.

5. Private corporations are more efficient and eliminate waste. This view has become almost gospel. However, the rate of corporate bankruptcies is high and if bankruptcy occurs, the services will end. The corporation Enron that provided electricity in California was a supposedly efficient corporation. It employed illegal methods to milk its customers for exorbitant fees and then went bankrupt.

6. Money paid in taxes would make us all richer if spent in the private sector. This has been a popular belief since the 1980s. However, creating large numbers of low wage jobs with low job security often results in poor economic performance. The truth is we get a lot of services for our tax dollars; think of street cleaning, sanitation, police and fire protection, animal control, public parks and zoos. Public schools benefit all of us by educating the citizens of tomorrow. Every time we take an elevator, buy food, or eat a meal in a restaurant we can feel safer because we know that government experts have inspected what goes on behind the scenes. The state makes certain that people who provide important services, such as our car mechanics, are licensed and competent to do their jobs. We receive weather reports and know that disaster relief is available if needed. We have roads to drive on thanks to public services. Airplanes are guided by air traffic controllers. The list goes on.

7. All the studies show that privatization is better. Where do these studies come from? If you look below the surface, you'll see that a lot of what we know about privatization is mere puffery. Privatization supporters have spent a lot of time and money convincing the public that privatization is better. You see very few follow-up stories on what has really happened. Privatization failures are rarely publicized. Yet they exist. For instance, Waste Management, Inc. is an example of a disposal company convicted for financial improprieties. It is well known that organized crime has infiltrated the sanitation industry.

## Privatization of Water

I recently received in the mail a 15 page glossy brochure with the glaring headline: The Global Water Crisis & How You Can Profit from It. I was shocked! How can I profit from other people's misery? But there was a way. According to the marketing blast, water was considered to be one of the "fastest-growing markets on earth." It was also advertised as recession-proof. Global investors were poised to privatize water, which should be a right for everyone, into a profit-making opportunity. As the brochure stated, "where there is crisis, there's opportunity."

The consumer advocacy group Food & Water Watch found in a 2009 study that privatizing municipal water systems threatens jobs and negatively affects local economies. They found that while multinational corporations often claim to reduce operational costs, they do so by cutting corners, downsizing jobs and wages. Corporate utility takeovers lead to an average job loss of 35 percent and workers earn 7.4 percent less at private utilities and accrue fewer benefits than their public sector counterparts.[34]

### Questions to Consider

1. Would you support the privatization of your municipal water supply? Why or why not?
2. What are some examples of privatization of public services in your local community or state? What have been the results of the privatization?

# INGREDIENT #3: DEREGULATION

**Deregulation** is the removal or reduction of government rules and regulations that regulate the operation of market forces. The rationale for deregulation is that fewer and simpler regulations will lead to a raised level of competitiveness, therefore higher productivity, more efficiency and lower prices overall. Neoliberals are often hostile to the regulation of wages, working conditions, how business is conducted, and environmental protections. Indeed, legislation intended to protect workers, consumers, or the environment is often challenged as a barrier to trade. In the global marketplace, as in China, part of a country's competitive advantage is weak labor, consumer, or environmental standards.[35]

## A Brief History of Deregulation

Most of the stock market had gone haywire in the euphoric, laissez-faire days of the 1920s. Large investors repeatedly manipulated the unregulated stock market. It was a common occurrence for a large investor to put out favorable publicity about the profitability of a stock market darling such as Radio Corporation of America (RCA); after the stock invariably went up in price s/he sold and reaped enormous profits. Today, this would be fraud. Ordinary investors knew the shenanigans pulled by large investors such as Joseph P. Kennedy (father of President John F. Kennedy), but were not deterred because they too thought they could become rich if only they were on the right side

CROWD GATHERING ON WALL STREET DURING THE STOCK MARKET CRASH OF 1929.

of the market at the right time. After all, the stock market just kept going up in the late 1920s. Of course, we know today what goes up must come down, and down the stock market came with a thunderous collapse in the fall of 1929. The machinations of the stock market did not make for a sound economy, as evidenced by the Great Depression which followed in the 1930s.

Officials charged with bringing the U.S. out of the Great Depression had recognized the need for large-scale reform in the laws that governed those who managed the nation's money. They had witnessed the terrible consequences of banking abuses in the 1920s, and they consequently implemented a number of regulations to prevent repeated abuses. The government applied regulations most intensely to the heart of capitalism itself: the financial markets. The government regulated commercial and investment banks, brokerages, stock exchanges, and the accounting profession, as well as closely allied industries deemed to be natural monopolies, such as public utilities.[36]

The most significant of the Depression era regulations was the **Glass-Steagall Act** of 1933 that prohibited a single company from offering investment banking, commercial banking, and insurance services; the act set up a "firewall" that separated these services because of potential abuses and fraud. The **Securities Exchange Act** of 1934 aimed to maintain a stable economy through laws governing the trading of stocks and bonds. The reforms continued after World War II due to concerns that the banking industry was headed toward competition-reducing consolidations. The **Bank Holding Company Act,** passed under President Dwight Eisenhower in 1956, specified that the Federal Reserve Board of Governors had to approve the establishment of a bank holding company. In addition, it prohibited a bank holding company headquartered in one state from purchasing a bank in another state and it forbad banks from participating in most nonbanking activities.[37] These and other regulations helped to provide a stable economic foundation for the prosperous post-war years.

The deregulation craze of the 1980s sparked a series of acts carried out by neoliberals. When Democratic President Jimmy Carter deregulated the transportation industry in the 1970s, it marked the first infant steps to deregulation that were continued into the 1980s and onward. One notable banking deregulation act was the **Riegle-Neal Interstate Banking and Branching Efficiency Act** of 1994 that overturned the Bank Holding Act of 1956 and allowed interstate mergers between adequately capitalized and managed banks, subject to concentration limits and state laws.

Deregulation of the broadcasting market was the primary goal of the **Telecommunications Act**, passed under President Clinton in 1996. The act amended the Communications Act of 1934, which meant that media cross-ownership was now allowed. A radio station could now be owned by a television station or both could be owned by a newspaper or internet company. This deregulation act led to a wave of acquisitions and mergers, to a significant decline in the number of commercial radio stations, and to a substantial increase in the prices cable companies charged. Although purported to increase competition, this act actually decreased competition. The deregulation wave throughout the media sector has radically reduced the number of media companies. Fifty corporations controlled the vast majority of all news media in the U.S. in 1983; by 2004 this number had dropped to six: Time Warner, Disney (which owns ABC), Murdoch's News Corporation, Bertelsmann, Viacom (formerly CBS), and General Electric (NBC).[38]

One of the most significant deregulation acts, as we will find out in the financial chapters, was the Gramm-Leach-Bliley Act of 1999, which rescinded the long-standing Glass-Steagall Act. This act allowed commercial banks, investment banks, securities firms, and insurance companies to consolidate.

## Enron

The energy giant Enron provides a high profile example of the dire effects of deregulation. Formed in 1985, Enron grew in just 15 years from nothing to become America's 7th largest company, employing 21,000 personnel in more than 40 countries. The company started with the merger of two gas pipeline companies and diversified under the management of its CEO, Kenneth Lay, into an energy trading company offering various services. It bought the name of the Houston Astros' ballpark and Fortune magazine named it the most innovative company of the year for five consecutive years. The company peaked in the year 2000 with revenues of $100 billion and a share price of $90, its rapid growth attracting many investors.[39] In 2001, however, the public exposed Enron's success as a fraud. Behind the veneer of fleeting achievements, the firm's elaborate scam included lying about its profits, concealing debt, and conducting a range of shady deals.

Enron's management developed innovative ways to scam the public and deceive the weakened federal regulatory agencies. One of the most highly publicized scams was the special-purpose entity (SPE) it created. After the company's collapse, the public discovered that it had invented an illusion. The SPEs appeared profitable because they were specially designated, unregulated offshore business entities that avoided taxation and sold assets to each other at much higher prices than the market price. They also anonymously moved currencies about and hid the company losses in unofficial accounting balance sheets. Enron's officers carried out distorted financial transactions to show that billions in profits were being made, while in reality the company was hemorrhaging cash.

One of the most deceptive and costly of Enron's practices was the California electricity crisis, also known as the **Western U.S. Energy Crisis** of 2000 and 2001. This was a situation in which Enron, through market manipulations and illegal shutdowns of pipelines, caused the state to have a shortage of electricity and multiple large-scale blackouts. California had an installed electric generating capacity of 45GW, but at the time of the blackouts, demand was only at 28GW. Enron manipulated the demand supply gap to create an artificial shortage. Energy traders took power plants offline for maintenance in days of peak demand to increase the price of electricity.[40] They were thus able to sell power at premium prices, sometimes up to 20 times its normal value. This caused a whopping 800 percent increase in wholesale prices from April 2000 to December 2000. Because California had a cap on retail electricity charges, this market manipulation squeezed the industry's revenue margins, causing the bankruptcy of Pacific Gas and Electric Company (PG&E) and near bankruptcy of one of the state's largest energy companies, Southern California Edison, in early 2001.[41] The rolling blackouts hurt many businesses dependent upon a reliable supply of electricity and the economic fall-out greatly harmed the standing of California Governor Gray Davis. The uproar over the scandal resulted in the recall of Governor Davis and the subsequent election of Arnold Schwarzenegger as the new governor.

The Western U.S. Energy Crisis in California was possible in part because of deregulation legislation instituted in 1996. Enron took unscrupulous advantage of this deregulation. Ordinary taxpayers have had to pick up part of the tab in California, as a result of electricity deregulation. The crisis cost $40 to $45 billion.[42]

Enron's conniving deals finally surfaced and the company entered bankruptcy proceedings in December 2001. In 2002, its shares traded at 11 cents, a far cry from their $90 a share highs. On May 25, 2006, the courts convicted CEO Kenneth Lay on ten counts of securities fraud and related charges. Arthur Andersen, once considered one of the five largest and most respected accounting firms in the world, did not expose Enron's deceptive accounting practices, and as a result Andersen surrendered its license to practice as certified public accountants in the U.S. in 2002. The company's collapse destroyed thousands of dollars in investors' savings and thousands of lost jobs. [43]

---

**Questions to Consider**

1. Have you personally benefited from the passage of deregulation laws? Not benefitted.

---

# INGREDIENT #4: SMALL GOVERNMENT IS BEST

---

*"Government is not a solution to our problem, government is the problem."*

*President Ronald Reagan First Inaugural Address, January 20, 1981.*

---

This simple sentence by President Ronald Reagan sums up the neoliberal philosophy towards government. Neoliberals believed that the economic problems arising during the turbulent 1970s were a result of big government: forcing taxpayers to pay high taxes and regulating Americans to the point of strangulation. To them the solution to these problems was clear: downsize government, lower taxes, and deregulate.[44] Neoliberals strongly support limited government.

Neoliberals framed the debate about downsizing government as a way to "liberate" private enterprise from any bonds imposed by the government. They sought to reverse the federal government's growth and power and instead return that power to the states and the people. Although he denied any intention of doing away with government, in 1981 Reagan made it clear that "we are a nation that has a government – not the other way around." Grover Norquist, a neoliberal strategist, once famously said: "Our goal is to shrink government to the size where we can drown it in a bathtub."[45]

**PRESIDENT RONALD REAGAN DELIVERING HIS FIRST INAUGURAL ADDRESS JANUARY 1981.**

Some proponents of small government actually want to reduce government revenue. They have argued in favor of tax cuts in order to reduce government revenue, which will, in turn, force spending cuts to balance the budget. This strategy is known as "starve-the-beast."[46] Part of the neoliberal, small government agenda is to do away with or reduce social service programs that have been added over the 20th century, such as providing allowances for housing, health care, education, the safety net for the poor, disability, social security, Medicare, unemployment, and even provisions for new infrastructure such as high speed trains and maintenance of roads, bridges, and water supply – again in the name of reducing government's role in the economy.[47]

The intention is to turn over these public social services to the private sector. For example, the U.S. Transportation Department has in the planning stages a high-speed rail network connecting the Midwest's largest cities, with the intent of fostering commerce and revitalizing the hard-hit economy of the region. After the 2010 mid-term elections, I heard on the radio that Republican governors in Ohio and Wisconsin in the Midwest did not want a high-speed rail network and were refusing the federal funds attached to its construction. At first I was surprised to hear this, and then I thought that this is a part of the neoliberal agenda: limit the size and role of government.[48] Defense and security are among the very few government expenditures excluded from being reduced or eliminated, although neoliberals have privatized many military functions. Ironically, they generally don't oppose government subsidies and tax benefits or loopholes for business.

Despite Reagan's pledge to curb the government's size and influence, he was not successful. Neoliberals have not reduced the size or cost of government. In 1981, the year Reagan made his anti-government speech, the federal government spent $678 billion; in 2006, it spent $2,655 billion. Inflation-adjusted federal spending increased in every year but two over the past 26 years.[49]

The neoliberals have framed the debate as big government vs. small government. I don't think this is a very good way to discuss the role of government in our society. The question is what should the role of government be. When looking at the big picture of world history, strong, centralized governments have had both creative and destructive effects. Hitler governed a strong centralized state – I would call that a destructive role played by government. On the other hand, the Danish government has helped to provide its citizens with a very high standard of living. If done well, the government can target investments into specific areas that will pay off in the long run, such as the high speed rail corridor in the Midwest mentioned above. But if money is appropriated based solely on political expediency, as was the case in the $398 million "bridge to nowhere" in Alaska in 2005, then government is not doing a good job.[50]

One of the ways in which government supports the economy is in the areas of research and development (R&D). Much of the technology-based economy has rested on the Internet, which government-funded research created. A myriad of other advances in medicine and biology, just two examples, have been derived from basic research and biotechnology, which is reliant on government-funding. Between the 1950s and mid-1990s, U.S. federal government funding accounted for 50-70 percent of the country's total research and development funding. Lacking such investments, the U.S. would not have been able to maintain its technological edge over the years in key industries like computers, semiconductors, life sciences, the internet and aerospace.[51]

---

### Questions to Consider

1. What do you think should be the role of the government in the economy? Cite some examples.

---

## INGREDIENT #5: SUPPLY SIDE ECONOMICS

In 1981, the Reagan administration implemented a different approach to governmental economic policies than the long-standing Keynes approach: **supply side economics**. This school of macroeconomic theory emphasizes the importance of tax cuts and business favors in encouraging economic growth, in the belief that businesses and individuals will use their tax savings to create new and expand old businesses, which in turn will increase productivity, and employment and improve general prosperity.[52] This economic policy focuses on the total supply of goods and services rather than Keynesian policy, which states that in order for the economy to grow the demand for goods and services must be directly manipulated.

The supply siders maintain that the role of government is to create an atmosphere in which free enterprise and competition will flourish and that market forces will allocate the supply of resources most efficiently. The best government can do for the economy, neoliberals argue, is to boost the supply side – that is, favor wealth holders so they will have more capital to invest in new factories and production. This logic led to huge tax cuts for the wealthy and for business. To facilitate the supply side policies, they sought to privatize government assets, deregulate business, remove tariffs, foster competition, and contract out public sector services to the private sector. It also meant deregulating the financial markets.

Supply side policy aims to stimulate output, rather than to stimulate demand. For example, in 2010, neoliberals were against funding for unemployment insurance and government spending to stimulate the economy in a recession. They maintained that the government should not increase the supply of money into the economy through the demand side, which is what these two programs would do. Instead, they supported tax cuts for the wealthy, which they believed would stimulate the economy through business creation. Keynesians, on the other hand, believed that if there was a downturn in the economy, then the government should provide an economic stimulus by spending more to help create demand. Friedman believed that CEOs of private companies will serve the public interest better than government's civil servants, who neoliberals often derisively call government bureaucrats. Keynesian principles, Friedman argued, led to stagflation, (high inflation and low economic growth), the very economic conditions he predicted would happen in the 1970s. The solution to economic downturns, according to neoliberals, is to reduce taxes and annul regulations.[53]

Critics of supply side economics, such as Philippine economist Walden Bello, argue that a key problem with supply-side economics is that there is an over-supply of goods and services compared to the demand, especially since the 2008 recession. He believes that demand is not evenly distributed throughout the world, since many of the world's poor do not have enough money to purchase goods and services. Therefore, all the demand is concentrated in core countries, in which many people are heavily in debt for over-consuming relative to their income over the last three decades. Increasing an already overabundant supply of goods and services will not bring the U.S. out of recession, he and others argue.[54]

In the 1980s and 1990s, Milton Friedman advanced his macroeconomic policy known as **monetarism**. Monetarism aims to control inflation. Monetarists believe that the central bank should expand the money supply at a constant rate every year, equivalent to the rate of growth of the real GDP, and irrespective of business cycles. This policy works because the U.S. has the world's leading currency and the Federal Reserve could inject dollars into the economy through buying Treasury Bonds, to a degree that does not spark inflation.

### Questions to Consider

1. To end the recession, what policy makes more sense to you, stimulate demand or supply side? Explain.

## INGREDIENT #6: LOWER TAXES

A sixth ingredient in the neoliberal stew is the reduction of taxes. Neoliberal policies are specifically designed to give the wealthy more disposable income, particularly through tax cuts, pushing down workers' wages, and low inflation. Their ideological justification for such measures is that higher incomes for the wealthy and higher business profits (because of lower wages) will lead to more investment, better allocation of resources and therefore more jobs and welfare for everyone.

The big question is: Has this worked? Actually, in the 1950s and 1960s, when tax rates for the wealthy and corporations were much higher, there was more of an incentive to reinvest profits in a business to shelter that money from paying the high rate of taxes. This resulted in more reinvestment in business, more economic growth, and, indirectly, more jobs from this reinvestment. Today, lower tax rates have put more money in the pocketbooks of the wealthy, which, in many cases, instead of large scale reinvestments money has gone into consumer buying binges. Consumer spending on expensive luxury items like cars, jewelry, yachts, and second homes has increased among the wealthy in the last 30 years. According to economist Jospeh Stiglitz, "the myth that lower taxes would unleash huge increases in savings and work effort has proved remarkably resistant to evidence. Reagan lowered taxes markedly, but neither savings nor work effort increased, and indeed, productivity growth hardly budged. Clinton raised taxes on the rich, and dire consequences did not emerge."[55] Instead, he adds, moving money up the economic ladder has led to stock market bubbles, untold paper wealth for the few, and financial crises.

Lower taxes have resulted in a concentration of wealth among the top 10 percent of American households, and particularly the top 1 percent. Through the late 1930s and early 1940s, President Roosevelt put in place a top tax rate of 91 percent on incomes over $3.2 million in today's dollars. Part of the reason was to finance World War II. The income going to the top 1/10th of 1 percent (0.1 percent) of American wage earners had crashed, down almost two thirds to just over 3 percent by 1943. High tax rates continued into the 1950s; as a result the top 0.1 percent of American wage earners dropped further to just over 2 percent, where it stayed until around 1980 when Reagan slashed taxes on the very wealthy. By the late 1970s, the share of the nation's wealth owned by the top 1 percent

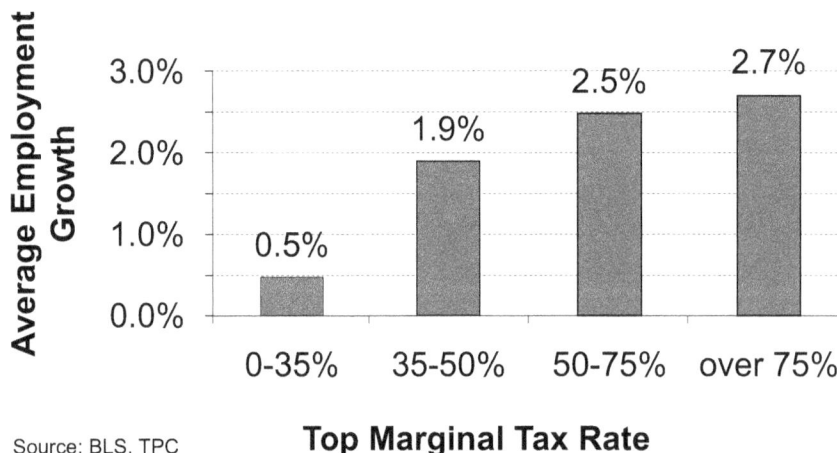

AVERAGE ANNUAL GROWTH IN U.S. EMPLOYMENT, BY TOP INCOME TAX BRACKET RATE, 1940-2011.
HTTP://EN.WIKIPEDIA.ORG/WIKI/SUPPLY-SIDE_ECONOMICS

of asset holders had fallen in the U.S. from almost 50 percent in 1929 to a low of around 25 percent. Instead of disappearing, the money lined the coffers of working and middle class families.[56]

In 2008, the U.S. had the highest number of billionaires in the world: 355; 45 percent of the world's total and altogether worth more than $1 trillion. According to the Government Accountability Office (GAO), nearly two thirds of the companies they own and manage do not pay any income taxes at all, despite their profitability and combined revenues of about $2.5 trillion. This fact is all too common among corporations today, reflecting the fact that the percentage of federal taxes they paid dropped from 40 percent of the total federal revenue in 1943 to 7 percent in 2003. In the 1960s, corporate tax receipts produced 16.1 percent of all federal revenue. Surprisingly, median income workers in 2006 paid a much higher combined rate in payroll taxes, income taxes, and sales taxes than they did in 1966.[57]

Though corporate profits are a higher fraction of GDP than ever, corporate tax revenues fell to 9.4 percent in the 1990s and around 7 percent today. Even though the highest corporate tax rate is 35 percent, worldwide the U.S. has one of the lowest effective tax rates (after deductions and loopholes) on corporate profits. However, business groups continue to demand tax "relief" and claim that low taxes are needed to be globally competitive. The more that global capital becomes portable, the easier it is for business to avoid higher tax rates. Yet, the Internal Revenue Service (IRS) continues to direct its resources away from audits of international corporations and the tax avoidance partnership schemes of wealthy individuals – and onto small taxpayers.[58]

Workers and consumers absorb more of the tax burden because of lower taxes on capital. This leaves ordinary people bearing a relatively higher tax burden in exchange for relatively fewer social services. In all of the advanced democracies, business taxes have steadily declined. Lower nominal tax rates on corporate profits and investment income and through deliberately weakened enforcement practices has reduced tax revenues.[59] Also, reduced tax revenues means an increase in the federal deficit, as has happened over the last 30 years. Because of the deficits, neoliberals call for cuts to social programs, which disproportionately hurt the poor.[60] Note, there is not a call to cut military spending or outlays for the wars.

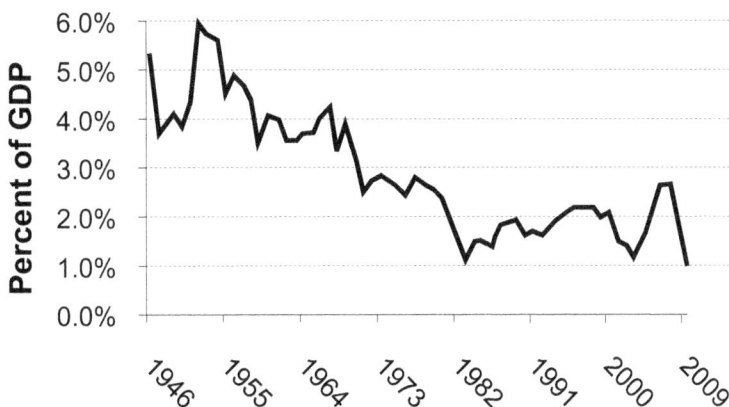

Source: Budget Office of the United States Government, Historical Tables, FY 2011
Based on Adam Carasso, "The Corporate Income Tax in the Post-War Era." Tax Facts Column, Tax Notes Magazine. March 03, 2003

**CORPORATE INCOME TAX AS A SHARE OF GDP, 1946-2009.**
HTTP://EN.WIKIPEDIA.ORG/WIKI/CORPORATE_TAX_IN_THE_UNITED_STATES

Warren Buffett, one of the richest people in the world and the chairman and CEO of the investment firm Berkshire Hathaway, caused quite a stir when he weighed in on low tax rates for the wealthy with an editorial on the Opinion Page of the New York Times on August 15, 2011.

## Stop Coddling the Super-Rich  by Warren Buffett[61]

"Our leaders have asked for 'shared sacrifice.' But when they did the asking, they spared me. I checked with my mega-rich friends to learn what pain they were expecting. They, too, were left untouched.

While the poor and middle class fight for us in Afghanistan, and while most Americans struggle to make ends meet, we mega-rich continue to get our extraordinary tax breaks. Some of us are investment managers who earn billions from our daily labors but are allowed to classify our income as "carried interest," thereby getting a bargain 15 percent tax rate. …These and other blessings are showered upon us by legislators in Washington who feel compelled to protect us, much as if we were spotted owls or some other endangered species. It's nice to have friends in high places.

Last year my federal tax bill was $6,938,744. That sounds like a lot of money. But what I paid was only 17.4 percent of my taxable income – and that's actually a lower percentage than was paid by any of the other 20 people in our office. Their tax burdens ranged from 33 percent to 41 percent and averaged 36 percent. If you make money with money, as some of my super-rich friends do, your percentage may be a bit lower than mine. But if you earn money from a job, your percentage will surely exceed mine.

To understand why, you need to examine the sources of government revenue. Last year about 80 percent of these revenues came from personal income taxes and payroll taxes. The mega-rich pay income taxes at a rate of 15 percent on most of their earnings but pay practically nothing in payroll taxes. It's a different story for the middle class: typically, they fall into the 15 percent and 25 percent income tax brackets, and then are hit with heavy payroll taxes to boot.

Back in the 1980s and 1990s, tax rates for the rich were far higher, and my percentage rate was in the middle of the pack. According to a theory I sometimes hear, I should have refused to invest because of the elevated tax rates on capital gains and dividends. I didn't refuse, nor did others. I have worked with investors for 60 years and I have yet to see anyone – not even when capital gains rates were 39.9 percent in 1976-77 – shy away from a sensible investment because of the tax rate on the potential gain. People invest to make money, and potential taxes have never scared them off. And to those who argue that higher rates hurt job creation, I would note that a net of nearly 40 million jobs were added between 1980 and 2000. You know what's happened since then: lower tax rates and far lower job creation.

Since 1992, the IRS has compiled data from the returns of the 400 Americans reporting the largest income. In 1992, the top 400 had aggregate taxable income of $16.9 billion and paid federal taxes of 29.2 percent on that sum. In 2008, the aggregate income of the highest 400 had soared to $90.9 billion – a staggering $227.4 million on average – but the rate paid had fallen to 21.5 percent. …In fact, 88 of the 400 in 2008 reported no wages at all, though every one of them reported capital gains.

I know well many of the mega-rich and, by and large, they are very decent people. They love America and appreciate the opportunity this country has given them. Many have joined the Giving Pledge, promising to give most of their wealth to philanthropy. Most wouldn't mind being told to pay more in taxes as well, particularly when so many of their fellow citizens are truly suffering. … My friends and I have been coddled long enough by a billionaire-friendly Congress. It's time for our government to get serious about shared sacrifice.

### Questions to Consider

1. What is your opinion about Warren Buffet's opinion letter in the New York Times? Do you agree or disagree with his position? Why?

# INGREDIENT #7: REDUCE THE DEFICIT

Deficit reduction was a hot topic in the 2010 mid-term elections. It seemed as if everyone was on the deficit-cutting bandwagon. The vote to raise the debt ceiling (authorization by Congress to increase U.S. debt) in the summer of 2011 brought the topic of the deficit to the political forefront. Republicans called for cuts in spending on social programs, but not cuts in the two wars or defense budget, and no tax increases. Democrats called for tax increases and spending cuts, but didn't mention the wars either.

First of all, what is a deficit? A **deficit** is simply an excess of expenditure over revenue. It can get confusing because the term "deficit" is often mixed up with the federal debt. Put simply, when the federal government raises less in taxes and other revenues than it spends, it must borrow the difference. Such annual borrowing is each year's deficit. The U.S. Treasury borrows that money by selling bonds, which are federal IOUs to the people that buy the bonds and in essence lend money to the government.[62] The annual (yearly) budget can be a deficit or surplus; lately it has been a deficit, a big deficit. But President Clinton balanced the annual budget back in 1998, and there was a surplus! The accumulation of annual deficits comprises the national debt, the total amount of outstanding U.S. treasury bonds. The national debt, or the federal or public debt, is the amount of outstanding debt of the U.S. through its history.

National debt is not necessarily a bad thing; Alexander Hamilton, the first Secretary of the U.S. Treasury, thought it would be good to have the government borrow from its wealthy citizens to ensure that they were invested in the government. But by most people's estimation, the federal debt has alarmingly ballooned in the 2000s. The national debt has increased by over $500 billion each year since 2003, with increases of $1 trillion in 2008, $1.9 trillion in 2009, and $1.7 trillion in 2010. As of September 9, 2011, the gross debt was $14.71 trillion, of which the public held $10.07 trillion and $4.64 trillion was intra-governmental holdings, a portion of which was the Social Security

## Total Federal Debt 2000 - 2010

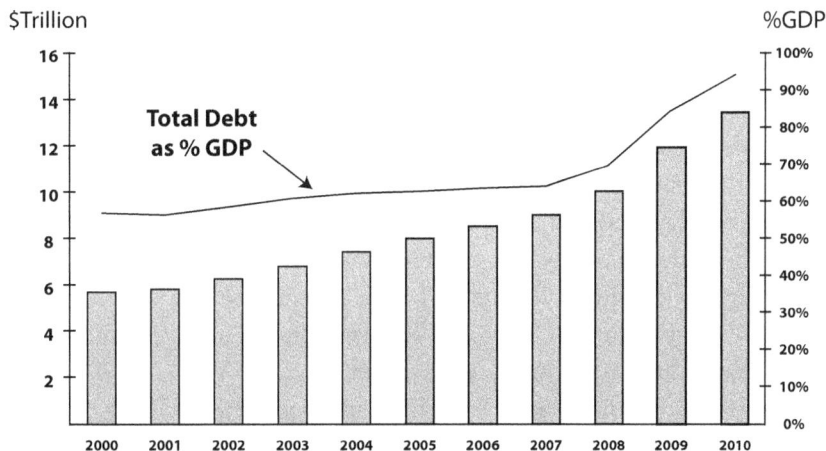

Source Data: BEA, CBO, Treasury Direct    **Total Debt Level $**

**2010 BUDGET: TOTAL DEBT $ AND % TO GDP 2000–2011**

Trust Fund ($2.2 trillion in 2007).[63] The annual gross domestic product (GDP) to the end of June 2011 was $15.003 trillion with gross debt at a ratio of 98 percent of GDP.[64] Now there are a lot of numbers for you to mull over.

The debt to GDP ratio is a number frequently bandied about. In 2011 in the U.S., that ratio is nearly 100 percent, which means our annual debt is equal to the amount that we make as a country. Greece, facing economic problems in 2011, had a debt to GDP ratio of 140 percent. France is at 99 percent, Italy at 119 percent, UK 94 percent, and Japan at a whopping 204 percent. What is too high? Well, of course it depends on who you talk to. Greece's ratio is considered too high, way too high, but Japan at 204 percent is not causing as much alarm, mainly because it has to deal with a little thing called a tsunami. The U.S. has a much larger economy than Greece, and the U.S. is able to manipulate its own currency; Greece is tied to the Euro, and thus cannot.[65]

Economists debate the level of debt relative to GDP that signals a dangerous percentage. Economist Kenneth Rogoff states that debt of 90 percent of GDP might indicate a danger level. He says high debt/GDP levels are associated with lower growth.[66] On the other hand, economist Paul Krugman disputes the existence of a danger level, arguing that low growth causes high debt rather than the other way around.[67] Economist Joseph Stiglitz reasons that if a country is in a recession and has large deficits, cutting those deficits will not bring back prosperity. It was tried during the Great Depression and failed. Many economists recommend an expansionary fiscal policy, fueled if necessary by larger deficits. In the short run, deficits may be absolutely essential for the recovery from a recession, and the economic and social costs of prolonging a recession are far greater than the costs associated with the increase in the deficit.[68]

The question remains, "How did we get here?" How did the U.S. accumulate so much debt? The New York Times analyzed Congressional Budget Office (CBO) reports going back almost a decade, with the aim of understanding how the federal government came to be far deeper in debt than it was in the years just after World War II. This analysis is also partially applicable to other Western countries and Japan.

The story of today's deficits in the U.S. starts in January 2001, as President Clinton was leaving office. Official estimates calculated that the government would run an average annual surplus of more than $800 billion a year from 2009 to 2012. Today, the government is expected to run a $1.2 trillion annual deficit in those years. You can think of that roughly $2 trillion swing as coming from four broad categories.[69]

The first category – the business cycle – accounts for 37 percent of the $2 trillion swing. It's a reflection of the fact that both the 2001 and 2008 recessions resulted in reduced tax revenues, and safety-net programs for those in need required more revenues. The two events changed economists' assumptions about how much in taxes the government would collect in future years.

The second category – President George W. Bush's policies – finds that about 33 percent of the swing stems from new legislation that he signed. That legislation, like his tax cuts and the Medicare prescription drug plan, continue to cost the government bundles.

In the third category are the policies from the Bush years that were to expire but President Obama extended. He extended the two wars, tax cuts for households making less than $250,000, and tax cuts for the wealthy. Together with the Wall Street bailout, account for 20 percent of the swing.

The fourth category – new policies proposed by President Obama – account for 7 percent of the swing. These come from the stimulus bill that he signed in February, 2009, while only 3 percent comes from his agenda on health care, education, energy and other areas.

If the analysis is extended further into the future, well beyond 2012, the Obama agenda accounts for only a slightly higher share of the projected deficits. Therefore, it is fair to criticize both political parties and presidents for the deficit problem. Economist Alan Auerbach weighs in on the dangers of the current deficits: "Bush behaved incredibly irresponsibly for eight years. On the one hand, it might seem unfair for people to blame Obama for not fixing it. On the other hand, he's not fixing it." "And," he added, "not fixing it is, in a sense, making it worse."[70]

The solution, though, is no mystery. It will involve some combination of tax increases and spending cuts and a re-evaluation of enormous war and military expenditures, as well as skyrocketing medical costs. And it won't be limited to pay-as-you-go rules, tax increases on somebody else, or a crackdown on waste, fraud and abuse. Taxes will probably go up, and some government programs will become less generous. That is the legacy of trillion-dollar deficits. Erasing them, or at least reining them in, will be one of the great political debates of the coming decade.

**Questions to Consider**

1. Do you think there is a debt problem? What do you think is the most sensible way to solve the deficit (debt) problem?

# INGREDIENT #8: MARKETS KNOW BEST

The eighth ingredient in the neoliberal stew is what is often called the **Efficient Market Theory**; in other words, markets rather than government are able by their very nature to be more efficient and accurate in pricing and allocating resources. Perhaps no idea has had more power than that of Adam Smith's metaphor of an invisible hand guiding the market to greater efficiency. He reasoned that unfettered markets lead, as if by an invisible hand, to efficient outcomes; that each individual, in pursuing his or her own interest, advances the general interests.

There is an unyielding belief among neoliberals that markets are rational. Unlike government that is not rational, as they see it, the markets are the most capable of directing the world of commerce in the most efficient manner. They firmly believe that the government should "liberate" markets and businesses from the bonds of government. Through greater openness to international trade and investment and the freedom of movement for capital, goods and services, the markets will bring prosperity to the greatest number of people. The markets, by their very nature, have the key to unlock human creativity and enterprise which will in turn spur economic growth, ultimately benefitting everyone.[71]

The Efficient Market Theory obviously has its critics. Anthropological research has long suggested that basic human nature does not conform to the narrow model of economic rationality that our society often assumes to be a self-evident truth. This model of human nature, which is the foundation of the neoliberal economic framework, is often referred to as *Homo Economicus* or Economic Man. The classical economic model, as developed by Smith and others, uses these underlying assumptions of rational human behavior as the basis for mathematical models to develop economic policy and shape social outcomes. The rational Economic Man thereby left the sphere of philosophy, and many policymakers saw it as scientific fact. This marked the advent of a neoliberal era based on assumptions of a highly individualistic and self-interested human being. Behavioral scientist Alexia

Eastwood, proposes that "If it can be proven once and for all that Economic Man is not an accurate representation of the essence of human nature, the entire economic system upon which it was based begins to seem less logical and certainly not natural or inevitable." She suggests an alternative. She concludes "that new findings in behavioral science also support a more cooperative basis of human nature. Recent experiments in behavioral and evolutionary psychology have found that human beings as social animals are generally inclined to share and cooperate, and that it is these principles that have given our species an evolutionary advantage rather than the more recent tendency toward competitive individualism."[72]

Human emotions are, according to some observers, more dominant in guiding human behavior then reason. Have you ever attended a divorce proceeding? Clearly, emotions rule the day rather than reason. Along with the rebuke of humans as rational robots, further evidence has concluded that markets are not rational either. According to Stiglitz, "Modern economics has shown the limitations of the invisible hand and unfettered markets." He found that in the 1990s and beyond, CEOs, in pursuing their own interests, did not strengthen the American economy – and even as they benefitted themselves, others often paid the price.[73] Economic journalist William Grieder states that "[Neoliberalism] was recklessly experimental, testing out its new theories in the human laboratory and ignoring any negative results. Who can still believe in efficient markets?"[74]

Even critics of neoliberalism commonly believe that markets do work well in a variety of sectors of the economy. I doubt if we would have the i-phone in a communist-run economy. But in some sectors the market does not perform well: health care; education from kindergarten through the university; security such as the military, police forces, fire protection, and prisons; Social Security including disability insurance; some forms of transportation such as mass transit and roads; regulation of the environment; unemployment insurance; public charities; safety net for the poor; public necessities like water and sanitation; research and development; the post office and mail delivery to all; and even the regulation of capitalism itself.[75] The market alone cannot address the above issues in the most socially acceptable and economically efficient manner. This means that government has a role to play in the economy. Contrary to neoliberal ideology, markets cannot solve all the problems of modern society.

---

**Questions to Consider**

1. What do you think of Eastwood's research that finds humans are more cooperative than competitive?
2. How is our modern society shaped by the notion that competition among humans is best for society?

---

# INGREDIENT #9: SUPPORT OF CORPORATIONS AND THE FINANCIAL SECTOR

The ninth ingredient in our neoliberal stew is the support of corporations and financial sector through government policies such as deregulation and favorable tax policies. A brief history of corporations can give us a context for the growth and power of corporations today.

## A Brief History of Corporations

In the 16th century, English and Dutch merchants formed joint stock companies, the first origins of cartels or corporations. As I introduced in chapter 2, European monarchies granted royal charters to joint-stock companies for trade with their colonies. One advantage of joint stock companies was that a group of investors could pool their capital to lessen their possible losses from risky ventures. The main objective of these forerunners of the modern corporation was to make a profit for their shareholders with little regard for the social, environmental, or moral consequences of their actions.

North America's first corporations in the 17th century were the Massachusetts Bay Company and the Hudson Bay Company that had a charter life of 20 years to accomplish their goals. These early corporations were temporary institutions serving the public interest. At the time the British government needed huge amounts of capital to develop North America, and to encourage such a risky enterprise they needed to insulate investors from legal and financial responsibility for their undertakings, beyond their initial investment. Although this undermined the English bedrock principles of individual responsibility, for the first time, business investors were privileged with limited liability.[76]

Colonial Americans feared these chartered corporations. Colonists fought against monopolistic corporations when they led the Boston Tea Party revolt against the East India Company in 1773. The Declaration of Independence in 1776 freed Americans not only from Britain but also from the control of British corporations, and for the 100 years after the document's signing Americans remained deeply suspicious of corporate power. Actually, the word "corporation" doesn't exist in the constitution; only states chartered corporations, so local citizens could keep a close eye on them. The founders were clear when they wrote the Bill of Rights that humans had rights, and when humans got together to form any sort of group – including corporations, churches, unions, fraternal organizations, and even governments themselves – those forms of human association had only privileges. Thus, by the year 1800, the government kept the 200 or so corporations operating in the U.S. on short leashes. They couldn't participate in the political process or buy stock in other corporations, and if one of them acted unacceptably, the consequences were harsh.[77]

Early state laws (and, later, federal anti-trust laws) forbade corporations from owning other corporations, particularly in the media. President Thomas Jefferson wrote in 1806, "Our liberty depends on the freedom of the press, and that cannot be limited without being lost." In fact, he and James Madison were so strongly opposed to this practice that, they proposed an 11th Amendment to the Constitution which would have banned commercial monopolies. Others, though, thought the amendment was unnecessary because state laws against corporate monopolies were already in place.[78]

By the middle of the 19th century, the nation's economy expanded along with corporations. They pushed for and gained extended privileges in their charters. During the U.S. Civil War (1861-1865), corporations bagged huge profits from government contracts, which they promptly used to further their advantage by buying the favor of judges, legislators, and even presidents. President Abraham Lincoln, wary of the rise of corporate power during the

HUDSON BAY COMPANY LOGO, FOUNDED IN 1670.

war, prophetically wrote, "I see in the near future a crisis approaching that unnerves me and causes me to tremble for the safety of my country. As a result of the war, corporations have been enthroned and an era of corruption in high places will follow, and the money power of the country will endeavor to prolong its reign by working upon the prejudices of the people until all wealth is aggregated in a few hands and the Republic is destroyed. I feel at this moment more anxiety than ever before, even in the midst of war. God grant that my suspicions may prove groundless."[79]

After the Civil War the wealthiest of the wealthy, the railroad barons, held great political power in their grip. To further consolidate their power, the railroad barons schemed to get the courts to regard corporations as humans, whereby corporations would have all the rights attributed to individuals. Citing the 14th amendment, they repeatedly attempted to get the court to declare they were persons. They finally got their chance in the famous 1886 Supreme Court case: ***Santa Clara County v. Southern Pacific Railroad***. Even though the Supreme Court strongly objected to the railroad's corporate claim to human rights, the court's reporter, who was in cahoots with the railroad barons, was able to secretly insert into the Court Reporter's headnotes in the case the rule that the railroad corporations were persons in the same category as humans. It held that, under the Constitution, a private corporation was a "natural person," entitled to all the rights and privileges of a human being. This single devious legal stroke fundamentally changed the U.S. and the nature of corporations. Thereafter, based on the court reporter's headnotes and ignoring the actual court ruling, subsequent courts have expanded the idea of corporate human rights.[80]

Courts expansion of the concept of human rights for corporations now includes the 1st Amendment human right of free speech, including corporate speech, the 4th Amendment human right to privacy, and the 14th Amendment right to live free of discrimination. Critics contend that now every corporation could compete directly against real people and demand equal treatment under the law. Journalist Kalle Lasn argues "Because of their vast financial resources, corporations were more powerful than people. The whole intent of the American Constitution – that all citizens have one vote and exercise an equal voice in public debates – had been undermined."[81] Interestingly, unions don't have these human rights. Neither do churches, smaller, unincorporated businesses, nor partnerships or civic groups. Nor, even, do governments, be they local, state, or federal. And, from the founding of the United States, neither did corporations. Rights were the exclusive province of humans, not institutions.[82]

Corporate abuses and consolidation of wealth and power reached a crescendo in the Gilded Age of the late 1800s. At the pinnacle of power and wealth was John D. Rockefeller, founder of Standard Oil Company. By 1890 he controlled 90 percent of the nation's oil refining capacity; 40 different companies were part of Standard Oil. The concentration of wealth and power was so widespread that the Progressive movement in the early 1900s emerged to curb their excessive control. The Theodore Roosevelt administration (1901-1908) passed numerous reforms such as the Pure Food and Drug Act, Meat Inspection Act, and regulation of the railroads. The government even forced Standard Oil to end its monopoly, breaking it up into smaller companies. More reforms followed, in particular the Clayton Anti-trust Act in 1914, which further broke up concentrated corporate monopolies.

From the 1920s onward, corporate power has grown and ebbed. The pro-business 1920s was followed by corporate reforms in the 1930s and 1940s. Many acts and laws passed under the umbrella of the New Deal that were designed to curb corporate power and corruption. Corporate reforms in the 1930s and 1940s followed the pro-business 1920s. Designed to curb corporate power and corruption, New Deal reforms passed with resounding support. A regulating system of checks and balances between three powerful U.S. institutions – labor unions, government, and corporations – marked the post-war years through the end of the 1970s. But by the 1980s corporate power had returned. Corporate mergers and consolidation proliferated, and emasculated unions limped along with a lessening of governments regulating powers. Neoliberalism reigned as the strategy of the day.

**Favoring the Financial Sector**

Many of the policies in the last three decades have helped financial markets make more money. Among America's heroes were the leaders of finance, who themselves became the most ardent missionaries for neoliberalism and the invisible hand of the marketplace. Finance was elevated to new heights. The financial purveyors thought they knew what was best for the economy, and if others paid heed to financial markets, growth and prosperity would reign.

Another indicator that the financial markets and big corporations have curried government favor is the repeated bailouts of financial institutions over the last three decades by governments in the U.S. and Europe. According to many critics, Chairman Greenspan favored the financial markets over the real economy. He applied rigorous discipline to the real economy; always ready to slow things down to block any price inflation in goods and services, especially in wages. He tipped the scales in favor of neoliberal policies that favored the financial markets and corporations, which produced very low price inflation. This boosted prices for financial assets such as stocks and bonds but also pumped up the financial bubble even further. Soaring stock prices encouraged fantasies that the good times would last forever.[83]

BANCROFT DAVIS, THE COURT REPORTER IN *THE SANTA CLARA COUNTY V. SOUTHERN PACIFIC RAILROAD* AND FORMER PRESIDENT OF NEWBURGH AND NEW YORK RAILWAY.

There have been a number of financial bailouts in the last 30 years. It is hard to pick just one as an example here. So let's pick one close to home: the 1994 Economic Crisis in Mexico. Critics, such as economist Robert Kuttner, argue that it was the direct consequence of NAFTA. Kuttner makes the case that the Clinton administration oversold NAFTA; thus American banks and other investors had visions of enormous profits from utilizing cheap labor and lax regulations. Far more money poured into Mexico than the Mexicans could prudently invest. The rapid inflow bid up the value of the peso (currency of Mexico) and financed a brief and unsustainable consumption boom. To attract money, Mexico offered high-yield bonds effectively denominated in dollars, so that U.S. investors would not face any risk of peso devaluation. But as the boom peaked and investors began to cash out, the peso started losing its value and bonds began trading at a discount. Mexico, which found it was unable to attract enough new money to pay off its bondholders, quickly ran short of reserves and faced the risk of default.

The Clinton administration arranged a $50 billion bailout comprised of various loans and guarantees. When Congress refused to go along, the Treasury department and Fed dipped into an emergency currency stabilization fund to lend to Mexico the necessary money to pay off the foreign investors who owned Mexico's bonds. The Mexican bailout attracted much criticism in Congress and the press.[84] The U.S. government came to the rescue by bailing out market excesses created by its own bad trade policy, which protected U.S. investors but left Mexico hobbled with even more debt. Critics cried that this was not market capitalism but a form of corporate socialism. The gains were privatized but the risks were socialized.[85]

Another way in which the financial sector is favored by the government is the outsized method of payment for top executives and traders on Wall Street. In 2010, compensation rose at 26 of 35 financial companies, which included banks, investment banks, hedge funds, money management companies and securities exchanges. According to the *Wall Street Journal*, financial companies paid out a record $144 billion in 2010. That was up 4 percent from 2009, faster than revenue rose.[86]

As you just read in the short excerpt by Warren Buffett, the wealthy have all of the advantages over the average wage-earner when it comes to reducing their tax responsibilities. Not only can financiers classify their investment income as capital gains, which are taxed at a lower rate than ordinary income, but their exorbitant compensation packages are deducted from corporate earnings, which results in a reduced amount of taxes that corporations pay into the federal treasury.

---

### Questions to Consider

1. Can you think of ways in which government policies favor corporations or the financial sector?
2. Do you think this is fair? What do you think would be a good solution to end this favoritism?

---

# INGREDIENT #10: LABOR AND NEOLIBERALISM

The tenth ingredient is how labor is folded into the neoliberal stew. **Labor** is defined as productive activity, especially for the sake of economic gain. It is also the body of persons engaged in such activity, especially those working for wages. This body of persons is considered as a separate class of people who are distinguished from management (employers, owners) and capital (those engaged in finance).[87] Traditionally, labor has referred to members of the working class who manufacturing firms employ. They often wore blue denim shirts, hence the term blue collar workers. In contrast, workers who were employed in management positions wore white shirts and were called white collar workers. In contrast, management position workers wore white shirts and were called white collar workers. However, in today's labor market the lines separating different classes of workers are increasingly blurred. Therefore, I will expand the term labor to include those traditionally in the working class, service workers, and members of the middle class.

## A Brief History of Labor in the United States

Labor has been an integral part of the capitalist system since early industrialization in the late 18th century. With industrialization many workers moved from primary industries into secondary industries – mills and factories – that processed the raw materials into manufactured goods. Tertiary or service industries employed more workers later in the 19th century. Men, women and children entered the ranks of an emerging industrial work force where their unskilled wage labor was in high demand.

Migration took place during the late 19th century as displaced workers moved to seek employment from the countryside to cities and even across continents. Huge numbers of people from Europe and elsewhere sought work in U.S. factories or in other countries in the Western hemisphere. Escaping starvation, unemployment, and displacement, approximately 12 million people left their homelands in Europe to immigrate to America from 1870 to 1900.[88]

Peasants and artisans uprooted from their traditional occupations coped with the shock of starting a new livelihood in a factory town while living in crowded, unsanitary tenements and experiencing profound disruptions to their traditional family life. Alcoholism and domestic violence accompanied these wrenching social disruptions. Although the standard of living for the industrial working class improved minimally by fits and starts from 1750 to 1850 in Western Europe, the wages of the lowest paid workers improved only slightly in comparison to higher middle class incomes. The unequal distribution of income and wealth, which was already great in the pre-industrial economy, became even greater in the early stages of industrialization."[89] Early industrialization, in other words, was built upon the backs of exploited cheap labor and the poor.

By the end of the 19th century, small groups of workers, disgruntled with their miserable working conditions and low wages, banded together to form unions, like the Knights of Labor in the United States in 1869. Working-class organizations, friendly societies, trade unions, and cooperatives lobbied politicians for reforms: higher wages, accident insurance, unemployment benefits, reduced working hours, medical insurance, regulation of child labor, and improved working conditions.[90] Business countered labor's demands by encouraging immigration and internal rural migration to guarantee an ample labor supply, thereby keeping wages low.

Labor made real progress in the 20th century. The Great Depression of the 1930s marked a shift in the dominant version of classical, laissez-faire capitalism throughout the Western world to a social democratic version that supported policies which more evenly circulated wealth. The adversarial antagonism between labor and business reached a shaky compromise in the 1930s and in the post-war years. The post-war "golden era of capitalism" from 1948 to 1973 linked the interests of business, labor, and government into a more balanced, reciprocal relationship than in the past. It was during this time that labor made its most significant gains in wages and benefits. In 1955, after a long estrangement, the American Federation of Labor (AFL) and the Congress of Industrial Organization (CIO) merged into the most powerful American union, representing nearly all unionized workers. Industrial labor peaked in the 1950s when 1 in 3 workers were union members, which significantly dropped in 2006 to 1 in 10. The heyday of manufacturing unions passed. In 2008 the AFL-CIO had 56 member unions; the largest was the one million member American Federation of State, County and Municipal Employees (AFSCME).

## Labor Under Neoliberalism

The progressive agenda of the last 100 years has been devoted to increasing the wages for the working and middle classes of America, while at the same time requiring the elite class to contribute their fair share of taxes to the economic pie. With the shift to neoliberalism around 1980, there has been a markedly different shift in economic priorities, actions, and policies regarding labor.

Neoliberals ostensible aim is to create low unemployment. They argue that unemployment exists primarily because labor markets do not follow the free movements of supply and demand. In a free market, they claim, an excess supply of labor (unemployment) would clear itself through a fall in the wages of labor. When trade unions or minimum wage laws prevent wages from falling, then unemployment continues. Thus, neoliberals strive to abolish unions and repeal minimum wage laws to have low unemployment rates. Hardship and poverty, they argue, are unfortunate but necessary in the short term if the market is to operate freely and bring about long-term prosperity. In addition, since wages are lower for labor, they believe there needs to be an increase in incentives to work. Lowering the rate of income tax would in effect increase workers' disposable income, which neoliberals see as an important way to incentivize work.

Full employment prevailed during the post-war golden years of capitalism. Although there were periodic rises in unemployment during a downturn in the economy, these increases in unemployment were generally short-lived. The full employment profit squeeze ended in the late 1970s with the Fed's policies aimed at taming "the wild beast of inflation," in which wages would take a hit. Companies continued to take a hard line on wages, even with the end of the inflationary spiral. The real wages of American workers, adjusted for inflation, did not begin rising for 10 years, in 1993, by which time they had fallen 15 percent below 1978 levels. By the late 1980s, the power of the labor movement had been waning for years, and corporations had adopted an increasingly aggressive negative stance toward labor.[91] As a result of the neoliberal version of capitalism, wages for labor have stagnated or declined over the last 30 years.

### Questions to Consider

1. What are your thoughts about neoliberals' actions towards labor? Have you or your friends been directly affected by neoliberal labor policies? Have you or someone you know seen labor changes in the last 30 or so years?

## The Rise and Fall of Union Membership in the U.S. 1930 - 2010

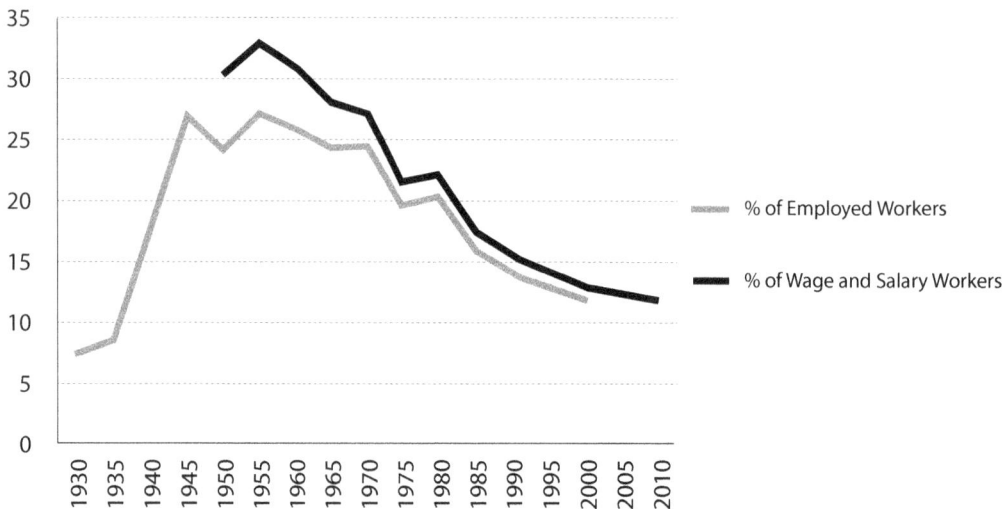

Legend: % of Employed Workers; % of Wage and Salary Workers

This labor section affects all of us directly and is a vital component of neoliberalism. Since it is so important, I will have a section in chapter 4 to explain further the neoliberal impact on labor.

# INGREDIENT #11: RUGGED INDIVIDUALISM

## Atlas Shrugged[92]  by Ayn Rand

The man at the top of the intellectual pyramid contributes the most to all those below him, but gets nothing except his material payment, receiving no intellectual bonus from others to add to the value of his time. The man at the bottom who, left to himself, would starve in his hopeless ineptitude, contributes nothing to those above him, but receives the bonus of all their brains. Such is the nature of the competition between the strong and the weak of the intellect. Such is the pattern of exploitation for which you have damned the strong.

The 11th ingredient combined into the neoliberal stew is rugged individualism. Many neoliberals, including Milton Friedman and Alan Greenspan, closely identified with the philosophy of the libertarian author quoted above, Ayn Rand (1905-1982). Born and educated in Russia, Rand immigrated to the U.S. in 1926. She gained fame for her two novels: the *Fountainhead* in 1943 followed by her best-known work, *Atlas Shrugged*, in 1957. Rand's political views emphasized individual rights (including property rights), neoliberal capitalism, and a constitutionally limited government; she considered reason to be the most important aspect of her philosophy. She held that humans are motivated by self-interest, greed, and survival of the fittest, which is expressed best through pursuit of financial gains.

Individualism has been a core American value since the founding of the country. But individualism has also been offset by values of compassion, volunteerism, altruism and concern for those less fortunate, especially during the period of social democracy from the 1930s to 1970s. But there was a shift in the winds in the 1980s. Neoliberals have elevated the individualist mindset to heights

HISTORICAL GRAPH OF REAL AVERAGE HOURLY WAGES IN THE US FROM 1964 TO 2005.

131

reminiscent of the late 19th century era of Social Darwinism and survival of the fittest. It was a significant shift in values.

Part of the individualist ethos is a widespread worship of business heroes. Successful businessmen (usually men) rise above adversity and mediocrity to create successful businesses and reap a fortune as well. The hero myth is dangerous in that it perpetuates the idea that anyone can make it big in the business world, with a little luck and perseverance. This often obfuscates the fact that making a success in business is very difficult and shifts attention away from the importance of policies.[93]

Bill Gates (b. 1955), founder and former CEO of Microsoft, was the poster child of the business community in the 1990s through the 2000s. Every word he uttered in the 1990s was gospel. He was the world's wealthiest person from 1995 to 2009, excluding his third place ranking in 2008. However, critics charge that his tactics are anti-competitive and monopolistic. Legendary investor Warren Buffet (b. 1930) is hailed as the "wizard of Omaha" for his market savvy and pithy words of wisdom. He is noted for his personal frugality despite his immense wealth. Along with Gates, Buffett is also a notable philanthropist, having pledged to give away 99 percent of his fortune to philanthropic causes, primarily via the Gates Foundation. Jack Welch (b. 1935) was Chairman and CEO of General Electric (GE) between 1981 and 2001. He pushed the managers of the businesses that made up GE to greater productivity by trimming inventories and dismantling the bureaucracy. He shut down factories, reduced payrolls and cut older products. Other CEOs across corporate America later adopted Welch's aggressive approach to bolstering the profit margins of their companies. The emphasis on individualism deemphasizes the concept of the public good and community and replaces it with individual responsibility. Placing blame on the poorest people in a society who are not able to find solutions to the lack of health care, education and good wages all by themselves is a way to scapegoat the real issue of policies that favor the wealthy over the poor. Instead the poor are labeled as "lazy" or lacking initiative or deserving of their situation. It makes rising inequality largely the individual worker's fault rather than a function of how the system is organized and for whose benefit.[94]

Neoliberals have weakened equalizing institutions such as education from pre-school to the university. Students must now pay more for their own education, with uncertainty as to whether they will be able to find employment after graduation. Many neoliberals and others claim that one of the reasons for many of the United States' ills is that students do not have appropriate skills and education for today's jobs and, therefore, a more rigorous curriculum that includes repeated testing is the answer. Neoliberals heap blame upon public school teachers for what they claim are their lethargic teaching practices. Teachers and other educators are the scapegoats for the real agenda of privatizing public schools via vouchers.

Rugged individualism is also linked to other values that are part of the national mindset: risk-taking, aggressiveness, rejection of limits, competition, conquest, and eschewing ethical standards. Although these are not the only values the nation shares, these deep-seeded values are threaded through the American psyche in ways that are not always readily apparent. Settlers held these values in the 19th century as they traveled West to conquer and claim lands held by Native peoples. It is the cowboy mentality – shoot and ask questions later – at its worst. This mindset also guided those on Wall Street and their cohorts who were swindling many U.S. homeowners and investors around the world to buy charlatan financial products. It meant millions for the swindlers but left the world economy ravaged in its wake. These values are an unsavory part of the American worldview, and they rear their ugly head when unleashed in particular circumstances and when proper limits from other institutions do not counter them.

The emphasis on competitive behavior further enhances the notion of humans as rational beings and deemphasizes cooperation, which is too sentimental. Eastwood suggests that it is perhaps time to "sit back and take stock, re-examine the truths we have taken for granted and think about the world we want to leave to our children. An inclusive 21st century society needs a new vision of and for humanity, and the renewed scientific interest in the essence of human nature may provide the building blocks for an alternative economic order built upon values of sharing and coopera-tion."[95] Eastwood's conclusions are similar to the ones I have found in my research of world history. The rational, competitive, individualistic behaviors that are extolled in our society today are, by far, not the values that humanity has held over our thousands of years of human history.

---

**Questions to Consider**

1. Do you think that rugged individualism is a worthwhile value for society to promote? What are its benefits? What are its drawbacks?

---

# INGREDIENT #12: SPREADING NEOLIBERALISM

The 12th and last of the ingredients blended into the neoliberal stew is the spreading of the neoliberal version of capitalism around the world. The demise of communism in the early 1990s brought about the myth of the triumph of capitalism to new heights. It reinvigorated a faith in American style capitalism and the free market economy. Neoliberals believed they had discovered the holy grail to the world's economic ills and pushed America's version of capitalism. There have always been a number of different flavors of capitalism; American-style capitalism is different from Japanese and European capitalism and in the 1990s and early 2000s, America's success relative to those other versions reinforced the belief that America's system was not just right for America but right for everyone else. It was American triumphalism at its peak; a one-size-fits-all state of mind. America preached a market fundamentalist version of capitalism.[96]

Although neoliberals continued to thrash away at the policies and protections that Americans had been assembling for decades, Americans themselves had essentially rejected much of the neoliberal agenda. Most Americans continue to believe that there is a role for government, not only in regulating large corporations but in providing essential services such as education, Social Security, health care, and Medicare. However, what Americans want and what they are getting are two different ball games.

## CONCLUDING INSIGHTS: THE NEOLIBERAL STEW

With this short description, we have the cursory information of some of the successes and failures of this neoliberal version of capitalism. Some critics contend that there are stunning flaws in neoliberalism and they significantly outweigh the benefits. They argue that managed capitalism was a practical success. Kuttner states, "Though few ordinary Americans understood this success [of the golden era] as the achievement of a managed form of capitalism, the idea was firmly implanted in the popular culture as a broadly shared premise about how the economy is supposed to work."[97]

However, the neoliberal agenda has gained widespread acceptance. I believe the overriding question at this critical turning point in world history is: How to organize capitalism, and for whose benefit? Various models of capitalism are possible, with very different distributive outcomes. None of this is inevitable.

**Questions to Consider**

1. From the short description of neoliberalism presented in this chapter, do you think it has many flaws in its theory and actual workings? What are they? Do you think the successes outweigh the flaws?

In the next chapter, we turn to the impact that the neoliberal agenda has had on the U.S. over the last 30 plus years.

CHAPTER FOUR

# The Impact of Neoliberalism in the United States: Ten Consequences

*Markets and money must again become the servants and not the masters of our vision and values.*

*Jakob von Uexkull*

This chapter continues to examine neoliberalism but shifts its focus to the effects of neoliberal policies over the last 30 years, particularly in the United States. When examining the effects of neoliberalism, I want to avoid the notion of a conspiracy theory, the idea that there are 10 neoliberals huddled in a room hatching out a diabolic plan to make their fortunes among unsuspecting, dull-witted American workers sounds like a good movie plot. Conspiracy theory aside, keep in mind that neoliberals have not necessarily planned the impact their policies have had in the U.S.; it is a matter of unintended consequences. I am certainly not labeling neoliberals as evil people, but their worldview and devotion to neoliberal principles have, in my estimation, blinded them to the consequences of their actions.

The consequences of neoliberal policies are organized into what I call 10 impacts. As you will notice in the list of 10 impacts of the neoliberal agenda, all of them are negative. You might surmise that I am just a gloomy pessimist. Actually, it is quite the opposite, I tend to be an optimist. But as far as the direction that the U.S. economy has taken in the last 30 years, I have seen a greater negative impact for the majority of American people than positive. One of the reasons that I have concentrated on the dire consequences of neoliberal policies is that I think it is important to have an alternative view of our economic policies and think about it from a different perspective. This chapter is purposely written from a different perspective than is typically found. Although I have evaluated these

### The Impact of Neoliberalism in the United States: Ten Consequences

1. Reduction of Self-Reliance and the Local Economy
2. Unbridled Economic Growth
3. Rampant Consumerism
4. Increased Commodification
5. Concentration of Corporate Power
6. Rise of External Costs
7. Build-Up of Debt
8. Emasculation of Labor
9. Widening Social Inequality
10. Ascension of Dollar Democracy

consequences as negative, I will point out what I consider some positive aspects of the consequences where I think it is appropriate. I am sure you might disagree with some of my assessments (or perhaps all of them). But an essential question to keep in mind when reading this chapter is "Have the neoliberal policies had a positive effect on the majority of Americans and the environment over the last 30 years, or have its policies had the opposite effect?" I think the best approach when learning about the global economy is to ask questions, lots of questions.

In this chapter we will look at 10 areas in which neoliberal policies have had a profound impact on American society.

## IMPACT #1: A REDUCTION OF SELF-RELIANCE AND THE LOCAL ECONOMY

The first consequence of neoliberalism is the undermining of small businesses and farms and local self-reliant economies and communities. A British economist of the 1970s, E.F. Schumacher, coined the phrase "small is beautiful," an alternative to the more popular phrase "big is better." Accompanying the rise of neoliberalism is the systematic reduction in small, local, self-reliant economies in favor of large, economies of scale dominated by large corporations that are intermeshed with the global economy. **Self-reliance** is trust in one's own capabilities, judgment, or resources; independence.[1] It is the opposite of dependence. The phrase self-reliant certainly does not mean that a community is completely self-sufficient – that would be practically impossible in today's modern world – but it does mean that small local businesses and farms can provide many locally produced goods and services for a large number of people. You might be thinking: "How do local economies undermine neoliberalism?" Local businesses owned by local people circulate money within the local economy benefitting the community, rather than dollars transferred to core elites and large corporations. Wal-Mart is a perfect example. Although wages paid to Wal-Mart workers and sales and property taxes stay in the local community, the profits generated through sales at the stores make their way into the bank accountants of the Walton family, the wealthiest family in the world. Think of the bonanza if just some of the profits stayed in the community where the store is located. This process benefits local people and does not create dependency on any one company in town as the main provider of jobs – which may move on a moment's notice.

Many of us are so accustomed to shopping in malls, on-line retailers and chain stores such as Wal-Mart and Target that we probably have no clue what a local business or self-reliance is all about. I definitely remember the local community and local businesses – especially since for eight years I was a local small business owner myself! I would like to tell a story to explain the local community in which I lived for a number of years.

## Self-Reliance and a Local Community: My Experience

In the late 1970s and early 1980s, my family and I lived in a small town in central Illinois near Champaign-Urbana. Since I wanted to care for my two young children at home, I did not have a wage-earning job at the time. Most of my shopping and contact was with small businesses. I shopped for groceries at a small, family-owned grocery store located in Fisher, Illinois. All the family members worked at the store, even the aging grandfather. If need be, they would offer you credit – you just had to pay them back by the end of the month. No interest was charged. For more variety I occasionally traveled about 15 miles to a larger grocery store in Champaign. Although it seemed large at the time, it was only a fraction of the size of the Wal-Mart Super Stores today. On occasion I would purchase soda drinks that were sold in returnable bottles that I took back to the grocery store and were rebottled and used again. My husband worked at a co-operative grain elevator, and we purchased a half side of beef from the local farmer that we had packaged at the local butcher shop. We froze the meat in our freezer and had more than enough for the year; in fact, I took the surplus to the soup kitchen in Champaign.

We planted a huge garden. It was easy to grow delicious and nutritious vegetables in the rich central Illinois soil. I canned or froze most of the produce from the garden for the coming winter, almost always having local produce at every meal. It was no problem to find the vegetables I did not grow, since locally produced fruits and vegetables were plentiful. I canned applesauce, peaches, pears, tomatoes, pickles, beets (my young daughter's favorite), beans, and other vegetables. I froze as many vegetables as our freezer would hold. I went to the local U-Pick field and picked a year's supply of strawberries and raspberries that I froze or made into jam. As you can imagine, we had very little waste from our foods.

There were few cheap, imported clothes made in China during this time, and since I was an average seamstress I made many of our own clothes. I mostly stuck to fairly simple things such as knit t-shirts for the kids but also ventured into clothes for myself and some shirts for my husband. For other clothing needs I loved to shop at two wonderful women's clothing stores that were located in nearby down-town Rantoul. Local women owned the stores and they offered stylish, high-quality clothes made in America.

Most of my other shopping was done at local businesses. There was a "Five and Dime" store that had just about everything in it; my son particularly loved to look at all the toys, located conveniently on the lower shelves. There were also men's stores, shoe stores that also repaired shoes, a drug store and pharmacy, and about anything else you could possibly want. There was no McDonald's at the time, but a Kentucky Fried Chicken was on the outskirts of town. We would go occasionally to a locally owned pizza parlor that had family specials that stuffed us all.

We were quite self-reliant housing-wise as well. As a young family, we were eager to move out of our cramped mobile home to a house with enough room for our expanding family. Since we did not have enough money saved up to buy a house and I was not employed at the time, we decided to build one ourselves. Since my father was a housing contractor and my husband was quite handy, we took on the challenge with gusto, or perhaps stupidity was more accurate. There was certainly a learning curve, but with the help of family and friends and some knowledgeable sub-contractors, we finished it in six months and moved in before winter. We did all the framing, roofing, electrical, plumbing, insulation, painting, trim work, and even poured the footings that support the foundation walls, a task I will always remember. Footings are concrete poured into 2-foot-wide trenches dug below the frost line, about 3 feet down in our case. I don't think I have ever been so exhausted in my life, wading through semi-solid concrete in rubber boots frantically trying to level it before it hardened. It's a wonder I wasn't cemented into the concrete for all eternity. Although building your own house seems a formidable task today, it wasn't that uncommon in farming communities. Farmers have always prided themselves in being self-reliant and ready to tackle problems that arise. In fact, we liked building the house so much we decided to tackle two more over the next few years and remodeled five more. Thankfully, I decided that pouring the concrete footings was a job I didn't want to tackle again.

We got all our lumber products for the house from the local, family-owned lumber yard in Fisher. They helped us figure out some of the intricacies of housing construction and had reasonably priced products; they even delivered free of charge. The small town of Fisher also supported a couple of hardware stores, a bank that boasted it had survived the Depression, many churches, and a couple of taverns. It was really a bustling place, but always closed on Sunday.

Does this sound like your life today? I imagine not. But it is far different from my life today as well. The point I would like to make in this short trip down memory lane is that small businesses were very much part of the landscape a generation or two ago, and self-reliance was something that was prized, especially in rural communities and small towns. We moved from that small community in the mid-1980s to a larger city, and when I returned a few years later I noticed that many things had changed. The Rantoul downtown was losing its small businesses; the clothing store I loved so much had shuttered its windows and many other businesses had been

DOWNTOWN RANTOUL, ILLINOIS

boarded up. They said they couldn't compete with the big box stores that were cropping up on the farmland just north of Champaign. Neoliberalism had arrived and displaced the small towns and local business owners with franchise stores owned by investors in larger cities, such as Chicago to the north. The prosperity of small town businesses and small farmers was beginning to disappear in the 1980s and this trend continues today.

### Questions to Consider
1. Are you or anyone you know self-reliant today? If so, in what ways?
2. Do you shop at any small, local businesses? What do they sell? Why do you shop there?

# IMPACT #2: UNBRIDLED ECONOMIC GROWTH

## Hamsters: Big Hamsters

Let's talk hamsters, big hamsters. Some of you may have a hamster for a pet; my kids did when they were young. Hamsters don't weigh very much. But let's imagine for a moment that from birth to puberty a hamster doubled its weight each week. Instead of leveling-off in maturity as animals do, the hamster continued this trend. How much do you think the hamster would weigh on its first birthday? We would be facing a nine billion metric ton hamster! If it kept eating at the same ratio of food to body weight, its daily food intake would be greater than the total, annual amount of corn (maize) produced worldwide! Hardly a sustainable pet.[2]

Nature knows when things should stop growing. I love to watch my spring flowers grow. My children grew up to be responsible adults. There are lots of different ways in which we use the word grow. Economist Herman Daly argues that growth's factual definition is to spring up and develop to maturity. Thus, growth includes some concept of maturity or sufficiency. In other words, development continues, but growth gives way to a steady-state balance in nature in which the rate of inputs is equal to the rate of outputs so the composition of the system is unchanging in time. For example, a bath would be in balance if water flowing into the tub from the tap then escaped down the drain at the same rate. The total amount of water in the bath does not change, despite being in a constant state of flux.[3]

From our simple examples above, we realize that growth cannot continue indefinitely. There are limitations to growth. These examples lead us to an investigation into impact #2: economic growth. **Economic growth** is the process by which wealth increases over time as the economy adds new market value to goods and services. Environmental economist James Speth notes growth is an essential component of capitalism, which must expand constantly to generate new wealth. Growth is inherent in capitalism; the two are inseparable. Capitalism is distinguished from other economic systems by its drive to accumulate and its built-in tendency to expand. Innovative activity – which in other types of economies is optional – becomes mandatory under capitalism, a life-and-death matter for businesses. Through history, the creation of new technology proceeded at an even-handed pace, often requiring decades or even centuries to develop, under capitalism time speeds up because, quite simply, time is money. The capitalist economy is a machine whose primary output is economic growth.[4]

The Western economy faithfully follows economic growth. Watch any newscast or read any news report about the economy, and I wager that they will mention the word growth. Economists constantly watch growth's movements, measure it to the decimal place, praise or criticize it, and judge it as weak or healthy. All levels – global, national, corporate, local, and academic – examine growth. I hope to grow my organization – the Center for Global Awareness – and sell lots of educational resources and books. Growth is assumed to be one of those good things in our lives that must be maintained. Promoting growth – achieving ever-greater economic wealth and prosperity – may be the most widely shared and forceful cause in the world today. It has been called the "secular religion" of the advanced industrial societies.[5]

Through much of human history having more comforts and surplus food has given humans easier lives. We all like easier, more secure lives. Hence, as populations have grown, so have the economies that housed, fed, clothed and kept them. Yet, the specific policy of economic growth has a rather short history. The reasons are partly to do with policy habits, partly political posturing, and partly because we have set our economic system up in such a way that it has become addicted to growth.[6] In fact, noted economist Paul Samuelson wrote in 1967 that "A growing nation is the greatest Ponzi game ever contrived."[7] Although I think that is a bit overstated, his point is well taken.

The pursuit of economic growth has been part of capitalism since its beginnings over 500 years ago, but it has especially come to be a central feature of U.S. economic policy since the end of World War II. The Council of Economic Advisors, established in 1946, advises the president on economic policy. It recommended in a 1949 report that growth should be elevated from an economic goal to a new organizing principle for the economy. The report distinguished "the new primary principle of growth …from the decidedly secondary aim of economic stability."[8] Not all signed on to the new policy; for example, some agrarian interests, especially in the South wished to maintain economic stability and preserve their way of life. Republican President Eisenhower questioned the wisdom of promoting economic growth over economic stability, but Democratic candidate John Kennedy, who championed the cause of economic growth in his campaign, severely chastised him and his administration for these views in the 1960 election. On the economic growth band-wagon were big business and organized labor, which both saw in growth policy an opportunity to further their own interests. Growth policies won the day and continue to be a central principle in economic policy for both parties.[9]

Economic growth meant that Americans would consume and produce more consumer goods, who would in turn make more wages in factories and businesses and thus spend this surplus on more consumer goods. Americans were eager to shed the austerity and hardship of the depression years and embark upon a new way of life based on plentitude and a seemingly endless supply of comforts. Economic growth and consumer spending went hand and hand. Also, the **Gross Domestic Product** (GDP) could scientifically measure growth. The GDP is an official measure of a country's overall economic output. It is the market value of all final goods and services made within the borders of a country in a year. Since Americans have an abiding faith in numbers, they widely consider the GDP to be an accurate measurement of a country's living standards. A high GDP is often a stand-in for measuring the standard of living. This measurement assumes that when the GDP is up the country's living standard also improves. A recession negatively describes the absence of growth. Prolonged recessions are called depressions. The joining of a consistent scientific number with rising living standards became entrenched in American and later global thinking.

The mainstream vision of unlimited growth made sense decades ago when the human population of the world was relatively low and natural resources for human consumption appeared to be endless. In this "empty world" money and human labor were the limiting factors, while natural resources were abundant. It made sense, in this context, not to worry too much about environmental destruction and social disruptions, since they were assumed to be relatively small and ultimately solvable. It made sense to focus on the growth of the economy as a primary means to improve human living standards. It also seemed reasonable to measure the economy in marketed goods and services and to measure the success of an economy by the number of goods and services produced and consumed.[10] But the world has changed dramatically and rapidly in the last 60 years. We now live in a world relatively full of humans and the infrastructure that we built. In this new world, human populations and labor supply are enormous, while the natural resources to support human life are limited. There is a dawning recognition that the growth model eagerly adopted by industrialized countries is no longer working for the world we know today.[11] Our model of growth is geared towards a time in the past that differs from the reality of today. All this is happening at the expense of our natural world, which is being battered by the demand to produce more for human consumption and absorb its wastes.

Perhaps a new measurement of economic well-being and a rethinking of economic growth is needed. Yet, the commitment to growth is so deeply engrained in our way of thinking that to question it is regarded as an affront to capitalism. My purpose in raising this issue is merely to examine and question the over-reliance on economic growth in our society and not to advocate for the overthrow of capitalism.

The fact is that a growing economy tells us nothing about the quality of economic activity that is happening within it. For example, when British Petroleum's (BP) oil leak spewed crude oil into the Gulf of Mexico beginning in April 2010, it actually contributed to an increase in the GDP! The number of dollars spent on cleaning up after disasters, such as the BP oil spill, Hurricane Katrina in 2005, pollution clean-up of Love Canal in New York in 1978, or cleaning up after Hurricane Sandy in 2012, all contribute to an increase in the GDP. Americans are experiencing "jobless growth" in the aftermath of the 2008 financial crisis, yet GDP rises modestly. New employment is not being generated, while environmentally destructive growth is created by liquidating irreplaceable natural assets. For example, those in the logging industry contribute to an increase in the GDP by cutting trees for lumber products, but if the forests that are cut are old-growth forests that take centuries to replace, it is actually harmful to our general well-being. Growth in GDP doesn't specify if the specific activity is good or bad. Spending on prisons, pollution and disasters pushes up GDP just as surely as spending on schools, hospitals and parks.[12]

**BP OIL SPILL ON THE DEEPWATER HORIZON.**

Oddly enough, history shows that in times of recession, life expectancy can rise, even as income decreases. This happens in rich countries, probably due to a number of circumstances: people become healthier by consuming less and exercising more, or by using cheaper, more active forms of transport such as walking and cycling. For example, in 2008 my son was laid off from his construction-related job in Phoenix, Arizona. Because of a decline in income, he and his wife ate out less, had more time for exercise, and began to cook healthier foods at home. As a result he lost 15 pounds and she lost 10 pounds!

Individuals support growth policies because they accept the commonly-held notion that growth will give them and the next generation a better standard of living. Governments seek growth as a remedy for just about every imaginable problem. Economists believe growth is essential for full employment, upward mobility, and technical achievements. Politicians encourage growth because it expands the economic pie, and they can postpone hard choices.[13] Growth, development, progress, advancement, gain, success, improvement, and prosperity are deeply embedded assumptions that are cause for celebration in today's economy. Systems thinkers refer to these qualities as structural reasons for the continuation of growth.

Mainstream economics is frozen in its one-eyed obsession with growth. But growth has a surprising drawback. The industrial world has come to expect its mature economies to grow by a certain percentage, usually 3 percent a year. That expectation evolved out of several centuries of experience with capital creating more capital. At this 3 per cent growth rate, the economy will double in just over 23 years. The 10 per cent growth rate of rapidly developing economies, such as China and India, will double the size of those economies in less than 7 years. This astonishing rate of growth is unsustainable.[14]

The concept of growth is seen differently using a systems approach rather than the conventional thinking that does not take the whole earth into consideration. As evident, growth can solve some problems but creates others. The earth is finite. Growth of anything physical, including the human population and its cars, houses and factories, cannot continue forever. There are limits to the rate at which humans can extract resources (crops, timber, fresh water, fish, etc.) and discharge wastes (greenhouse gases, toxic substances, and polluted water) without exceeding the carrying capacity of the earth. As is now readily apparent, the human economy cannot maintain present flows at their current rates for very much longer. The good news is that we can reduce our ecological footprint by lowering population growth, altering consumption, and implementing more resource-efficient technologies.

The challenge for those who take a holistic view of the converging crises of climate change, global poverty and inequality is how to confront the dogmatic belief that humanity's prosperity is dependent on the growth of GDP. But even a cursory analysis of economic growth reveals its dangerous shortcomings: growth pursued at all costs is ecologically unsustainable, socially unjust, and unnecessary.[15]

## Questions to Consider

1. Why do you think your nation wants to continually grow the economy? What are the dangers to this way of thinking? What are the benefits?
2. Why do people worry that it will be a disaster if the economy doesn't grow?

# IMPACT #3: RAMPANT CONSUMERISM

Impact #3 is rampant consumerism. Capitalism needs constant new sources of wealth in order to expand and grow. Manufacturing was the leading sector of the American economy in the post-war years, but since the 1980s, the expansion of consumerism has spurred the U.S. economy, which provides goods and services that satisfy consumers' artificial wants. Today 90 percent of the American work force is directly or indirectly in the business of producing consumer goods and services. Private consumption expenditures make up about 70 percent of GDP.

First used in the 1960s, the term "consumerism" means an emphasis on or preoccupation with the acquisition of consumer goods. **Consumerism** is a social and economic order that is based on the systematic creation and fostering of a desire to purchase goods or services in ever greater amounts. In economics, consumerism refers to economic policies placing emphasis on consumption. It involves a powerful, socially sanctioned commitment to ever-increasing purchase of goods and services. In this sense, it is similar to **materialism**, an approach to life and social well-being that elevates the material conditions of life over the spiritual and social dimensions. A **consumer society** acquires goods and services not only to satisfy common needs but also to secure identity and meaning. Consumption patterns are powerfully shaped by forces such as advertising, cultural norms, social pressures, and psychological associations.[16] Sociologist Madeline Levine criticized what she saw as a significant change in American culture in the post-war years – "a shift away from values of community, spirituality, and integrity, and toward competition, materialism and disconnection."[17]

Neoliberals have been successful in exporting a consumer ethos to the rest of the world. Many think of consumerism as the new religion of the world community, worshipping at the altar of the shopping mall or the on-line retailer, performing the ritual of purchasing dazzling products that are beyond that which makes for a comfortable life. On a summer 2011 trip to China with fellow educators, I was dismayed to see the proliferation of late model cars in the cities of Beijing and Shanghai. I was dismayed because the smog hung so thick in the cities that it stung my eyes and hindered my far-off vision. I found out that consumerism is indeed rampant in the two largest cities in China. The most desired consumer purchase is a late model car, preferably one with high status, such as the racy Audi sports car displayed at the airport in Xian, China. Who says the U.S. doesn't export anything? We have exported consumerism, and the rest of the world loves it.

Capitalism has been immensely successful at producing goods and services for about 20 percent of the world's population that can afford these products. They have enough goods for a comfortable life, yet the other 80 percent of the world's population do not. This is one of the many paradoxes of capitalism. Capitalism, which is supremely efficient at producing goods and services, is not proficient at distributing those goods and services to those in real need.

In fact, capitalism has been too successful in producing goods and services. Have you ever

AMUSEMENT PARK AT THE CENTER OF THE MALL OF AMERICA IN BLOOMINGTON, MINNESOTA, THE LARGEST SHOPPING MALL IN THE UNITED STATES.

been to a store that has racks and racks of clothes waiting for purchase and wondered who is going to buy all these items? Thus, producers have become inventive in seeking ways to induce consumers to buy more – more than they need. Enter the advertising industry. The single goal of this industry is to get customers to buy more things. The industry creates gimmicks and enticements to convince consumers that they need more and more. The advertising industry stimulates new needs and desires on the part of consumers whose only remedy for this malaise is to buy. The traditional values of the Protestant ethic that have shaped the American value system since the founding of this country include thrift, hard work and its rewards, long-term planning, rational behavior, stability, and adherence to rules and laws. The dilemma for advertisers is that a person with these values does not impulsively consume. The advertising industry figured out that it needed to change individual behaviors and values, and it launched a brazen campaign to change the entrenched Protestant and patriotic values that provided the foundation for American culture. The industry sought to transform the rational, logical, steadfast behaviors of mature adults into what journalist Benjamin Barber calls "infantilizing adult behaviors." The advertising industry encourages behaviors that are impulsive, irrational, self-centered, reckless and, in other words, infantile. Billions of dollars later, its efforts have proven to be worthy of its investment.

The advertising industry was not content to just transform adult behaviors but sought to change children's and teens' behaviors as well. Since children are young and have not fully developed rational, mature behaviors that we normally associate with adults, their impulsive, impetuous behaviors are perfect for consumption but needed to be refocused into desiring more profitable adult products. Advertisers, intent on luring even pre-consumer children as young as toddlers to identify with their brands, have found that this early brand identification will be embedded for the rest of their consuming lifetime. Teens, flush with cash from part-time jobs or indulgent parents, are prime advertising targets. With their impulsivity and need to vie for peer status, they must have the latest products, which adults typically bought in the past. They feverishly buy high end goods such as cars, technological gadgets, or a closet-busting wardrobe of the latest hip fashions.

Adults holding to a consumerist ethic are pawns to the advertising industry. The demands of the mobile global economy have severed their ties to traditional place, instead, their sense of belonging and identity has shifted to brands of consumer products. As Barber explains, "Consumerism has attached itself to a novel identity politics in which business itself plays a role in forging identities conducive to buying and selling. Identity has become reflective of 'lifestyles' that are closely associated with commercial brands and the products they label, as well as with attitudes and behaviors linked to where we shop, how we buy, and what we eat, wear, and consume."[18] The brands selected by an individual or family indicate their particular income, class, and place. These branded identities are superficial veneers replacing traditional ethnic, cultural, and national identity. Although it appears that we freely choose these identities, in reality they are reflective of the permeation of the ubiquitous commercial culture into every aspect of our lives. Advertisers happily promote this brand identification among consumers because it cuts across national and ethnic boundaries to mold a true globalization of identity.

The omnipresent impact of advertising on consumers actually homogenizes taste and narrows rather than expands variety and choices. Although there are many consumer choices, as evidenced by the multitude of cool clothing shops in any cookie-cutter mall across the world, the actual choices are not first order choices but actually second order choices. A first order choice might be to have a real option as far as public transportation is concerned, since we realize that automobiles contribute to climate change and foreign oil dependency, and they are expensive. The second order choice would be to select a particular make of automobile or model of a desired car manufacturer, since automobile transportation is the only choice available in many locales. Another first order choice would be the ability to pick from an assortment of high quality, nutritious food offered at a reasonable price in a convenient location; instead, we have a whole range of artery-clogging, pound-packing, second choice fast foods readily available for our immediate consumption.

Perhaps this would all be fine if the consumption of goods and services made us happier and healthier and resulted in loving relationships, something that advertising implicitly and explicitly promises. But we are not happier, and we are certainly not healthier. In fact, impulsive consumption actually leaves us more depressed and unsatisfied. Of course, this is exactly what advertisers have planned all along, since that unquenched desire is the catalyst for the consumption of more goods in an endless cycle of trying to achieve the pleasures that advertising assures us they will provide and that we innately crave. Fortunately, even though the consumer society may appear to be all-embracing, it is not totalitarian. Unlike citizens living under totalitarian regimes, we do have the choice to reject or participate in the consumerist society.

## Questions to Consider

1. Are you or someone you know avid consumers? What motivates you or your acquaintance to consume?

# IMPACT #4: INCREASED COMMODIFICATION

## A Cup of Coffee

Have you ever gone to a Starbuck's coffee house and purchased a coffee product that cost you $5 (US) or more? If you are a person earning minimum wage, you could easily spend an hour's pay on your coffee. My cousin's 10-year-old granddaughter recently purchased a grande latte at Starbucks with all the works, and it set her back her whole week's allowance! During the mid-1960s, I remember my father, a World War II veteran, going to a nearby diner's lunch counter and getting a cup of coffee for 10 cents, and it was refillable! In fact, the diner advertised that they had "Bottomless Coffee Cups." But he didn't have a choice of a latte or cappuccino; it was just regular coffee served in a ceramic cup and saucer. What happened? How did coffee become so expensive? Coffee has been commodified.

Commodification is a big word that is impact #4. Commodification comes from the word commodity, which in economics means an exchangeable unit of economic wealth, like a primary product or raw material. Although the term is a recent addition (1968) to our official language, I like to use the word because it signifies an essential process of capitalism that has magnified with neoliberal policies. Karl Marx, in his 19th century analysis of capitalism, referred to commodification as those processes through which social relations are reduced to an exchange relationship. He pointed out how commodification transformed the real, material activity of labor by individual workers into abstract labor. Labor was no longer a social exchange but just another cost in the production process measured in terms of hours, an abstract unit of time. With industrialization all inputs in the process needed to have a monetary value attached, human labor was no exception.

**Commodification** is used here to show the process of turning something with little or no economic value into a product or service that has a specific value or a higher monetary value. In the example above, the coffee is a commodity. Although coffee was a commodity in the 1960s, the commodification process has considerably enhanced its value today, so that it fetches a greater profit margin for the company producing the coffee: in the case above, Starbucks. Through clever advertising and promotion, Starbucks turned a commodity with relatively low value into a high value commodity. I include commodification

**Commodification
Since the 1980s**

domestic (maid) service, funerals, elder care, day care, child's play, children's birthday parties, weddings, family meals, medical services, beauty, dating, culture, art, performances, family reunions, high school prom, exercise, music, handyman repairs, retirement

as a consequence of the neoliberal push because the process has expanded into every conceivable nook and cranny of society. While consumerism is the wealth-generating process, commodification transforms products and services into marketable entities serving the appetite of voracious consumers.

Commodification is the process of developing things, concepts, activities, an article, services, events, ideas, products, relationships, labor, identities, and even people into products that are available in the marketplace; in other words, they are saleable. Ordinary efforts, pleasures, ideas are made into commodities that have a certain monetary value, and can be bought and sold. It even includes the transformation of relationships, formerly not commercial, into relationships that have an exchange value. For example, companies such as E-harmony have turned the dating experience into a commodity, which performs the service of connecting single people together for a fee. Since capitalism needs to constantly grow and expand, commodification is one way to create new products and services that have a certain monetary value or increased monetary value. Corporations and entrepreneurs are continually searching for goods, ideas, services and even individuals that they can turn into commodities.

Commodification has accelerated dramatically since the 1980s; nothing escapes its reach. The above list is just a few of the many arenas of commodification since the 1980s. Some of these are services that the family or neighbors used to provide for its members for free or very little money, but are now commodities. I am sure you can think of more.

One example of the commodification process listed above is weddings. Several decades ago most weddings were low budget affairs, with the reception held in a church basement, resplendent with cake and punch, mints if you were lucky. Today many weddings are extravagant affairs that even necessitate a costly wedding planner. Costs skyrocket upward into thousands of dollars. Or some couples choose a pre-packaged wedding in Las Vegas, Nevada, or on a Caribbean Island. My son and daughter-in-law chose to skip the hassle of a big wedding and instead, they and another couple wed through a Jamaican marriage/vacation package. They had a lot of fun, and it was relatively easy. But I missed not attending their wedding. My daughter and her husband, on the other hand, decided to have a medium-sized wedding, but to save money they did much of the planning and work themselves. It was a lot of work, but it did have a personal touch that made it uniquely their own. They were able to do it by making their family and friends work! A "crew" of us put together the wedding programs, arranged the flowers, shined the glasses, hauled supplies, cleaned up, and even set up tables. It was fun, though.

## Starbuck's Coffee: Get Those Creative Juices Flowing

Why would anyone want to purchase coffee that costs over $5.00 for a paper cup (although I admit it does taste good)? Well, aside from the good taste, advertising has carefully honed an image of a Starbuck's consumer as having sophisticated tastes, participating in a hip life-style, and partaking in a chic urban world. On the Starbuck's website, I viewed a commercial video that featured a coffee-loving, stylish looking, 30-something musician who expressed her passion for rock music and performance and was energized by her love for Starbuck's coffee. She cooed that she didn't know what ran more in her veins, plasma or Starbuck's coffee. When she wanted to kick-start her band, she would treat them all to a caffeinated fix that would "get those creative juices flowing." There were no scenes of a middle aged man, such as my father, hunched over his coffee cup at the local diner wearily sipping his generic coffee, but passionate rock musicians in full-playing mode energized by their daily infusion of coffee. Drinking a Starbucks not only satisfies the taste for coffee but also transforms the coffee sipper from a lethargic, uninspired average dim-wit to an impassioned creator of stirring music – a change we can all experience by the mere transformational act of purchasing a Starbucks coffee. I think I need one right now!

**STARBUCKS COFFEE IN SINGAPORE**

The king of advertising is arguably McDonald's. Its golden arches are more recognized around the world than any other symbol. It targets all age groups – from infants to the elderly. All of us have heard and seen the polished advertising message that eating at McDonald's is a socially rewarding experience. Here, advertising positions the commodity within non-commodified relations. For example, McDonald's ads often place commodities at the center of idyllic family relations. Just think of the McDonald's commercials over the years in which dad shares a moment of quality time with his son over a Happy Meal that most likely strategically places a plastic promo from the latest Disney movie by the soft drink. A caring moment between father and child replaces the mere act of having something to eat.

The majority of women just a generation or two ago – especially those with young children – were not in the full-time paid work force. Their labor was mainly at home taking care of family and home and perhaps taking in some part-time work here and there. In other words, their labor was not commodified.

The story (see inset) of my mother tells of women's typical non-commodified labor prior to the 1970s.

We find today that a full-time working woman is unable to carry out all these time-

### A Mother in the Post-War Years

My mother was a stay-at-home mom in the 1950s and 1960s, although she also did part-time accounting and other clerical tasks for my father's home construction business. She did all the cooking, washing, ironing, cleaning, gardening, shopping, caring for my sister and me, and helping with the care and transportation of elderly relatives. She was also involved in the school, the Parent Teacher's Association (PTA), Brownies, 4-H, League of Women Voters, and other activities. She was always busy and took pride in her endeavors. One of the most time consuming activities that my mother performed was making the meals and shopping for food. We rarely ate out at restaurants, nor did we have take-out meals; our meals were nutritious and home-cooked – most often three times a day.

consuming tasks as my mother did over two generations ago. Since the 1970s, women have increasingly been entering the paid work force, which means commodification has stepped in to fill the vacuum of women's unpaid labor services with comparable services that private business now performs for a market price. One is the family meal.

Food is a commodity unless you grow your own, but the labor at home to transform the food into meals is unpaid. Therefore, the food industry has found a way to commodify that labor of meal preparation. The food industry calls take-out meals or prepared meals at grocery stores "home-replacement meals." They state that what people seem to crave is the experience of the home-cooked dinner: the family gathered at its own table, the familiar smells and tastes, and the resemblance to a home cooked meal. Journalist Jerry Adler states that "increasingly the acres of Corian countertop in America's Versailles-quality kitchens are used not for chopping or whisking but for dumping take-out containers onto plates. For those who even bother with plates." According to researchers, the proportion of dinners that came from a takeout counter or a grocery freezer increased by 24 percent in the past decade – and by the time you are reading this they are likely to overtake home-made meals. At the Whole Foods Market chain, prepared foods have been the biggest growth category, while almost all the growth in the restaurant business has been in takeout.[19]

Another task that women (it was usually women) performed at home was the care of children and elderly parents or relatives. I felt I was lucky to be able to partially care for my children at home before they reached school age, although many times I needed day-care services and other family members helped out when I was teaching. Although parents still perform the vast bulk of childcare, there is a demand for day care for children either at home through the employment of nannies, through informal arrangements with relatives, neighbors or friends, or through for-profit day care corporations. For instance, in North America, Bright Horizons Family Solutions is one of the largest child day-care companies, with over 600 daycare centers. ABC Learning Centers is a publicly traded company running about 1,000 daycare centers in Australia and New Zealand and another 500 in the U.S.[20]

Funerals mark the end of life in much of Western society. I remember as a child attending the funerals of my elderly relatives in the home of the family members. Relatives would participate in what was called a wake, sitting around chatting and remembering the deceased for hours on end. Neighbors or church members brought in food to sustain the mourners. Although it was sad to say good-bye to a favorite great-aunt or uncle, there was always laughter when a funny story was told. Now our family funerals are held in the more modern way: in a funeral home.

Today the funeral home atmosphere is changing the way Americans see the end of life. Funerals were traditionally somber affairs with much weeping and consternation by family members. But funerals in some circles are no longer solemn but called "End of Life Celebrations." When it comes to spicing up the traditionally glum atmosphere surrounding death, Hollywood scriptwriter Lynn Isenberg has no shortage of clever ideas. For the lifelong golf enthusiast, she foresees an end-of-life celebration on the 9th hole, complete with glow-in-the-dark golf balls engraved with the name of the recently deceased. For the animal-rights activist, perhaps there could be arranged a soirée at the local zoo. Companies like Batesville Casket Company now offer caskets with customized interior panels of nature, religious, sporting and other motifs. Also, funeral directors around the country are offering a variety of commemorative video and slideshows. There is no one "cookie cutter approach."[21]

Water, which has traditionally been free, is becoming a for-profit commodity. Increasingly, private corporations are buying up and administering local water departments. Bottled water is also an example of the commodification of a previously free resource – clean, safe, drinkable water. Over the past decade, an increasing share of the bottled water sold in the United States is coming from municipal water supplies. Categorized as "purified" by the bottled water industry, bottling companies purchase municipal tap water, put it through a filtration process, bottle it and then sell it back to consumers for hundreds to thousands of times the cost. Between 2000 and 2009, the share of purified tap water bottled and sold in retail stores has increased by almost 50 percent.[22] The bottled water phenomenon in reality is a marketing gimmick that has duped consumers into believing that water parceled into little plastic bottles and priced 200 times higher than tap water is somehow healthier. Bottled water, however, can ruin local water sheds and drain aquifers, and it generates over 20 billion plastic bottles added to landfills annually. What is more, bottled water does not have to meet the same safety standards as public water systems. But communities are waking up. For example, McCloud, California, near Mt. Shasta, has won the first round of a battle to keep food giant Nestle from tapping their local springs for its bottled water business, which racks up more than $2.7 billion annually in sales.[23]

I am now part of the commodification craze. Even though we are a non-profit, the Center for Global Awareness now sells books and educational resources about world history, global issues, and cross cultural topics. I have commodified my ideas and put them into books that are in turn sold in the marketplace. None of us can escape commodification!

---

**Questions to Consider**
1. What forms of commodification do you encounter in your daily life? Are they beneficial or detrimental to your life?

---

# IMPACT #5: CONCENTRATION OF CORPORATE POWER

The fifth consequence of neoliberalism is the concentration of corporate power. If capitalism is a growth machine, corporations are doing the growing. In fact, as a result of deregulation and lax enforcement of anti-trust laws, corporations have merged, consolidated, and grown into megacorporations since the 1980s. Corporations can vary in size and complexity from small companies run by a few people to huge organizations that are larger than many nations, with lots of different sizes in between.

I once was the president of a corporation! Well, to be truthful, it wasn't a multinational corporation but rather a small sub-S corporation called the Willow Basket that consisted of my partner (my sister-in-law) and me, and about three part-time employees. We sold gifts, decorating items, furniture, rugs, and an assortment of other related products in a downtown location in Normal, Illinois. Since my partner and I both had young children at the time, we shared the work, and generally it was fun. However, I yearned to go back into the education field and after eight years sold the business for a small profit.

Our small, family-owned corporation was a far cry from the giant corporations that reach their tentacles around the world today and are the subject of this section. I am making a distinction between huge corporations that in many cases, in my opinion, should be broken up under anti-trust statutes and small to medium sized corporations that are the cornerstone of the American economy and way of life.

In 2000, of the 100 largest economies in the world, 53 were global corporations; only 44 were countries. In 2010 Wal-Mart was the largest publicly-traded corporation in the world with revenues of $408.2 billion and profits of $14.3 billion. The second largest were Royal Dutch Shell and Exxon Mobil.[24] However, it is no longer viable to just look at publicly-traded global corporations when many state-owned enterprises (SOE) or partially state-owned enterprises dwarf them in market value and profits. For example, Saudi Aramco, the state-owned oil company of Saudi Arabia, had an estimated market value of $781 billion to $7 trillion (US$), more than a dozen times the size of any corporations on the *Forbes* (a business magazine) list.[25]

Ownership of shares of stock in corporations is concentrated among the few. As recently as 1981, only 35.8 percent of stock income went to the wealthiest 1percent of Americans. By 2003, that concentration had increased to 57.5 percent, according to the Congressional Budget Office (CBO). Union and public employee pension funds together hold less than 5 percent of the total funds invested on Wall Street.[26]

Corporate CEOs have inordinately profited from a shift to neoliberal policies, which include reduced tax rates on upper income individuals. The total compensation for the average CEO of Standard and Poor's (S&P) 500 largest companies in 2006 was $14.8 million, and declined slightly to $10.8 million in 2010. In contrast, the pay for the average worker in 2010 was $33,121, up just 3.3 percent over the year before.[27] In 1970 the ratio of the compensation for a CEO of a corporation in the U.S. to that of an average worker was 45:1. It jumped in 2000 to 300:1 and then declined slightly in 2005 to 262:1 and 263:1 in 2009. Yet, despite the recession, it jumped to the highest ratio on record in 2010 to 325:1![28]

An Institute for Policy Studies (IPS) study found that 100 U.S. corporations that paid the most in CEO compensation in 2010, paid their chief executives more than they paid Uncle Sam in federal income taxes. The study analyzed the 25 companies' low tax bills – or large refunds – and found they could not be explained by low profit rates. Most of the 25 companies reported high profits in 2010. According to the study's authors, "The low IRS bills these companies faced reflected tax avoidance pure and simple." The lion's share of tax breaks was a result of accelerated depreciation, overcompensating their executives, and off-shoring their corporate activity to tax havens such as in the Cayman Islands and Bermuda. Corporations say these tax breaks are legal, but they still take advantage of government-funded services such as the transportation network, police protection, court system, and research and development programs. These tax avoidance behaviors are detrimental to society as a whole.[29]

SAM WALTON'S ORIGINAL WALTON'S FIVE AND DIME STORE IN BENTONVILLE, ARKANSAS, NOW SERVING AS THE WALMART VISITOR CENTER.

## Corporate Consolidation, Mergers, and Acquisitions

Industrialization and production expanded greatly during the post-war years from 1948-1973. The result of this productivity was that by the 1970s an oversupply of goods and services contributed to the crisis of the 1970s. In a feeding frenzy for markets, corporations faced fierce competition from each other, which usually resulted in a decline in their profit margins and market share. Corporations do not like competition and will do everything possible to limit or eliminate it for obvious reasons: it cuts into profits. To prevent corporations from forming monopolies that restrict competition, the U.S. has passed anti-trust laws such as the 1913 Clayton Anti-Trust Act. Enforcement of these laws is up to the interpretation of the courts, but since the 1980s, the courts have in many cases ruled in favor of large corporations. From the 1980s onward, corporations have been on a crusade to eliminate or severely reduce competition. Some of the tactics they have employed to reach this goal are consolidation, mergers, or acquisitions.

The 1980s was a time of "**hostile takeovers**" by "**corporate raiders**." These raiders bought up a company's stock when it was undervalued, which meant the company's assets were worth more than their stock. The raiders would sell off the assets of the raided company to make a profit, but as a result the companies raided were no longer operational. Some companies, in an effort to ward off the dreaded raiders, carried out what were called "**leveraged buyouts**," in which the soon-to-be raided companies would "go private" by buying up their own stock with borrowed funds to avoid the acquisition of their corporation by another. This was a very unproductive economic activity of the 1980s; the takeover added nothing of value to the economy. Financial acquisition specialists who engineered the deals were primarily the only ones to make money on the activity. In 1988 alone, corporations spent $500 billion on takeovers. The Safeway Supermarkets leveraged buyout exemplifies the 1980s corporate takeover culture.

## Safeway Supermarkets: A Corporate Takeover[30]

In 1986, Safeway Supermarkets owned 2,365 stores and employed 172,000 workers. Its motto to employees was "Safeway Offers Security." The company offered good job benefits and decent union wages. In 1985, the company reported record profits of $231 million. All changed in July 1986 after a hostile takeover bid by a group of corporate raiders. Alarmed, Safeway's management called in Kohlberg, Kravis, and Roberts & Co. (KKR), a leveraged buyout specialist, to help ward off the corporate raiders. KKR came up with a plan that that included $130 million of investors' equity, then borrowed more than $4.3 billion to buy up all the company's stock. In return, KKR received $60 million in consulting fees for the transaction; when added to fees received by investment bankers, junk bond financiers, lawyers, and accountants, more than $200 million went towards the Safeway buyout.

At this point the new private owners needed to come up with more than $500 million a year to pay off the interest and debt on the buyout. Taxpayers involuntarily kicked in their share; the company immediately stopped paying $122 million a year in taxes and even received a U.S. refund check for past taxes of $11 million. But that only paid for part of the debt. The rest had to come from liquidating stores, firing workers, and cutting people's pay. Eventually more than 1,200 stores were sold, putting 63,000 people out of work. In the Dallas area Safeway, for example, 60 percent of the former workers were fired. Those who were able to work for the bought out stores saw their hourly wages drop from $12 to $6.50. Although a small profit was being made in the Dallas stores, far more money could be made liquidating them and selling off their inventory and equipment. Safeway chairman stated, "There's so much debt in a leveraged buyout that you have to look at your assets in a cold and calculating way." Employees lost all their health benefits within two weeks and received a maximum severance pay of eight weeks. However, the chairman kept his million-dollars-a-year-job and wound up with options to buy shares of the company, which translated into a personal profit of $20 million.

A 1990 *Forbes* article proclaimed it was "The Buyout that Saved Safeway." It noted that profit margins were higher, largely because the leveraged buyout "freed" the company from "the albatross of surly unions and uncompetitive stores." Somehow *Forbes* thought that this undermining of the American workers, subsidized with an indirect tax subsidy which eventually exceeded $500 million, was good for the economy. No mention was made of the welfare, unemployment, and health benefits which the firings have cost all Americans, nor the loss of those hundreds of millions in taxes which tens of thousands of former Safeway workers no longer pay. Had the government insisted that existing labor contracts needed to be enforced and limited the tax deductions that corporations could take for their interest expense on debt to finance unproductive economic activity, the corporate takeover wave of the 1980s would never have happened.

### Questions to Consider

1. The 1986 corporate takeover of Safeway Supermarkets was widely regarded in business circles as the most successful leveraged buyouts of the 1980s. What do you think?

## Pacific Lumber Company [31]

The Pacific Lumber Company was founded in the heat of the Civil War in 1863. It flourished for decades on its substantial holdings of ancient redwood timber stands around the Scotia, California region. In 1931 Stanwood Murphy became president of the company. His foresight led to sweeping changes in practices from the industry standard of clear cutting to a "selective cut" system of logging. The company was highly regarded as a pioneer in the development of sustainable logging practices. By the 1950s, the company directed efforts to make Scotia a comfortable place to live and raise a family by providing affordable employee housing, stores, a school, a hospital, a skating rink, and a theatre. Under the direction of the Murphy family, the company implemented a fully funded employee pension plan, provided free life insurance, and maintained a no lay-offs policy during downturns in the timber market. By 1961, academic scholarships were available to children of company employees.

Pacific Lumber was a good corporate citizen in the local community. By the 1980s this huge lumber operation had absolutely no debt, which also made it a prime corporate takeover target. On September 30, 1985, the respected company, having maneuvered through more than a century of business peaks and valleys, was taken over as a result of stock purchases by outsiders. The Murphy family (the largest minority stock holders at the time) and other stockholders, mostly company employees, were bought out as a result of a hostile takeover by corporate raider Charles Hurwitz and his Maxxam Corporation of Texas. Maxxam immediately doubled the cutting rate of the company's holding of thousand-year-old trees, reaming a mile-and-a-half corridor into the middle of the forest that the company president jeeringly named "Our wildlife-biologist study trail." Maxxam then drained $55 million from the company's $93 million pension fund and invested the remaining $38 million in annuities with the Executive Life Insurance Company, which had financed the bonds used to make the purchase and subsequently failed. Turning reality on its head, corporate raiders refer to this process of pirating a firm's assets as "adding value." In January 2007 Maxxam filed for bankruptcy protection.

### Questions to Consider

1. What do you think is a good lesson to learn from the Pacific Lumber Company example?

If we look at corporate consolidation issue from a systems perspective, taxpayers have been subsidizing corporate takeovers. A study that reviewed the 302 mergers consummated between 1995 and 2001 found that the raided companies underperformed peer corporations by an average of 25 percent. Other studies showed that acquiring companies often overpaid for the companies purchased. Also, motivation for the acquisition was often to enhance the compensation and power of the CEO rather than to serve the shareholders.[32] Because of the interest deduction on debt, throughout the 1980s corporations paid $67.5 billion per year in taxes and avoided paying $92 billion a year. During the 1950s, corporations paid 39 percent share of all taxes collected in the U.S. During the 1980s that share dropped to 17 percent. In 1957, corporations provided 45 percent of local property tax revenue; by 1987, this number dropped to about 16 percent.[33] Fortunately, the 1980s takeover craze ebbed in the 1990s, but the precedent was set for corporate abuses in the 2000s that were largely unregulated by the government.

The decade of the 2000s proved to be an even more irresponsible era of corporate abuses. Of the 100 largest lobbying efforts in Washington between 1998 and 2004, 92 were by corporations and their trade associations. The U.S. Chamber of Commerce was the largest. In 1968 there were less than a 1,000 lobbyists in Washington. Today there is a discrepancy about the actual number of lobbyists; some estimates calculate around 35,000, while others, using different methodologies, say 11,500.[34] Either figure shows that it is a significant number that has had a definite influence on government policy.

# IMPACT #6: RISE OF EXTERNALIZED COSTS

A sixth impact of neoliberal policies is the increase in external costs or externalities over the last 30 years. It is probably an unfamiliar term, but it has a profound impact on our global economy.

A simple definition of **external costs** is the costs not paid by the producer but which are imposed on others. However, externalities can be costs or benefits, although we will primarily look at the costs portion of externalities in this section. Economists define external costs as follows: When some people bear costs that are not paid or compensated for, these costs are external costs or **externalities**.[35] The price of the goods and services we consume most often does not take into account the external costs.

---

## Categories of Externalized Costs[36]

1. Social Costs…paying less than a living wage, safety issues from poor working conditions.

2. Health Care Costs…government pays for the uninsured, increased private insurance premiums, increased Medicare and Medicaid costs.

3. Environmental Costs…such as toxic waste clean-up, air and water pollution, deforestation, over-harvesting resources such as fish, oil spills.

4. Military Costs… used to defend the nation, protect scarce resources, access natural resources.

5. Security Costs…such as for fire protection, police, border patrols, airline security, homeland security.

6. Subsidies… such as corporate welfare, direct grant payments, below-market insurance, direct loans, loan guarantees, trade protection, exemptions.

7. Tax Abatements/Deductions… tax loopholes, home mortgage interest exemptions, excessive executive salary deductions, bonuses, perks, and golden retirement parachutes deductions.

8. Infrastructure Development… payments for infrastructure that business disproportionately uses.

---

### Price

One way in which our global economy inefficiently operates is when corporations profit through the manipulation of price. Critics have often called today's corporations "externalizing machines," since they seek to keep the real costs of their activities external (that is, off their accounting books). Many corporations have distorted prices because they fail to account for external costs that they should be legally responsible for, and instead transfer the costs to the general public who picks up the tab through higher taxes or more debt. If corporations included these externalized costs when calculating the price of goods or services, prices would more accurately reflect their true value.

Economist James Speth states, "Basically the economic system does not work when it comes to protecting environmental resources, and the political system does not work when it comes to correcting the economic system."[37]

The price should reflect any activity that imposes a cost on society. For many goods and services, the market forces of supply and demand generate a market price that directs the efficient use of resources. But distorted prices occur in circumstances when costs are unknown. This is the case for many types of environmentally damaging activities such as driving cars, airplane travel, and burning coal for energy. The absence of a suitable price for certain scarce resources, such as clean air and water, leads to their excessive abuse. An example is the classic case of the factory that spews smoke over a nearby neighborhood. The factory imposes a real cost to society in the form of dirty air, but this cost is external to the company.[38] Or, if you are debating between a car that has great miles per gallon and one that does not, the gas-guzzler does not figure in a pollution cost in calculating the price of the car; therefore, you are not necessarily paying more for the car because of its mileage inefficiency.

Whenever a scarce resource comes free of charge, as is typically the case with our limited supply of clean air and water, it is almost always certain to be used to excess. Unfortunately, many of our environmental resources are unprotected by accurate prices that would help constrain their use. Thus, it is hardly surprising to find that inaccurate prices lead to environmental overuse and abuse. Government policies need to be passed to correct market failure and make the market work for the environment or society rather than against it. But powerful economic and political interests typically prevent lawmakers from making these corrections. For example, water could be used more efficiently if it were sold at its real market cost, which includes the estimated cost of the environmental damage caused by its overuse. Both politicians and farmers have an economic stake in keeping water prices low. Polluters should pay the full costs of their actions, in terms of both damages and cleanup. Although the capitalist economy is supposed to use price as a principal signal for guiding economic activity, the present market system basically doesn't allocate the use of environmental resources properly. When prices reflect environmental costs as poorly as today's price system does, the system is running without essential controls. The environment, of course, suffers as a result.[39]

The market externalizes environmental costs and health care costs as well, as we can see in the McDonald's example on the opposite page. Those who consume excessive sugar-laden or artery-blocking foods do not pay the real costs for these foods, since their inevitable and disproportionately higher health care costs may be sometime in the future as a result of their present-day unhealthy eating habits. The risks of higher health care costs, such as a triple by-pass heart surgery, are borne by either insurance companies, Medicare, Medicaid, or other tax-payer funded government programs. Critics have suggested that a "sugar tax" would help to stop these external costs but the soft drink companies and others have lobbied forcefully against such legislation.

For decades, the classic case for externalizing health care costs to the general public is the cigarette companies. The price paid for a pack of cigarettes does not accurately reflect the added health care costs to health insurance companies and public health programs that treat the chronic smoker. A study by Duke University economists estimated that if health related costs were added to a pack of cigarettes the actual costs of smoking would be nearly $40 per pack. That included roughly $33 for reduced life expectancy and tobacco-related disabilities; $5.44 for the costs of secondhand smoke, and $1.44 for pooled-risk programs like Medicare, Medicaid, group life insurance and sick

## A Big Mac at McDonald's

To see externalities and price distortions in action, let's look at the carbon footprint of a Big Mac. I bet most of you have had a Big Mac at some point in your lives but never knew the external costs associated with it. According to one estimate, the energy cost of the 550 million Big Macs sold in the U.S. every year is $297 million, producing a greenhouse gas footprint of 2.66 billion pounds of $CO_2$ equivalent. Add to that the broader environmental impact of both water use and soil degradation, together with the hidden health costs of treating diet-related illness such as diabetes and heart disease. If you added in all of these external costs to the price of a Big Mac, what do you think would be the cost? One estimate figured it would be about $200. It would be a big time sticker shock if you pulled up at the drive-through window and the McDonald's clerk said $400 for two Big Macs. That figure might seem off the charts, but it could be even higher if you factored in the cost of subsidized grain that is fed to the cattle butchered for their hamburger meat. For example, U.S. subsidies for corn topped $4.6 billion in 2006.[40]

**MCDONALD'S BIG MAC, INTRODUCED IN 1968.**

leave. Although the cost of cigarettes has increased over the years, it is far from reaching the $40 a pack price tag that reflects its real costs.[41]

Arguably, the all-time best poster child for externalizing costs to taxpayers is the world's largest retailer: Wal-Mart. The company offers the lowest overall prices in the retail industry and it has been very successful in this endeavor. Americans shop at Wal-Mart because of their slogan "everyday low prices." Yet Wal-Mart's low prices are the result of numerous hidden factors, and if we look at their low prices from a systems perspective, we can see that the price tagged to a particular item does not reflect the real cost of the item if externalized costs are added in. It is a given that Wal-Mart has certainly reduced costs through very efficient manufacturing and distribution networks and utilizing cheap Chinese labor to make most of their products, but a number of externalities are not factored into the price.

## Wal-Mart's Externalized Costs

1.  Health Care Costs ... their uninsured workers often must rely on state provided care.
2.  Low Wages ... many workers must rely on public services such as government food stamps.
3.  Overtime ... in some reported cases it fails to pay overtime to its employees.
4.  Loss of Local Tax Revenue ... local jobs and retailers have closed due to Wal-Mart competition.
5.  Subsidies and Tax Abatements ...offered by local, state, and national governments to entice Wal-Mart stores to their community.
6.  Infrastructure Subsidies ... for roads, sewers, and water, borne in part by local or state taxpayers.
7.  Loss of U.S. Manufacturing Jobs ... to low wage countries that supply Wal-Mart's products.

The Arkansas-based retailer has benefited from more than $1 billion in bricks-and-mortar subsidies that are given to them to build their stores in select communities. There are also costs – safety-net expenses – paid by taxpayers to help Wal-Mart workers and their families survive on everyday low wages. U.S. congressional staffs have estimated that each Wal-Mart store with 200 employees costs federal taxpayers $420,750 a year! That is because external costs for programs such as State Children's Health Insurance Program, Section 8 housing assistance, free or reduced-price school lunches, the Earned Income Tax Credit, and low-income energy assistance are added in.[42]

If the company paid the above external costs instead of the taxpayer, Wal-Mart's prices would be much higher. As it is, Wal-Mart's inaccurately promoted low prices give them an unfair advantage in the marketplace. If Wal-Mart did not enjoy government subsidies and bore all the true costs of their business, many locally-owned retail establishments would be able to hold their own and compete against "big box" stores such as Wal-Mart. Imagine the economic boost to local economies if the profits siphoned to the Walton family – the richest family in the world – were instead circulated in local communities and directed to local businesses.

## Subsidies

Subsidies are one of the most common forms of external costs. Although there are many different forms of subsidies, we will look at subsidies that go to corporations, which, in my opinion, are the most egregious and unjust. After all, according to neoliberal principles, corporations should operate in the marketplace without government assistance.

In order to reduce their costs and increase their profits, corporations are committed to finding government subsidies, tax breaks, and regulatory loopholes. A **subsidy** is a form of financial assistance paid to a business or a particular economic sector. Ostensibly, the government gives most subsidies to producers or distributors in an industry to prevent the decline of that industry. Making domestic goods and services artificially competitive against imports, subsidies are a form of protectionism or a trade obstruction. For example, the U.S. heavily subsidizes farm products such as corn, soybeans, wheat, and cotton, which drives down the cost of these commodities  for consumers. But when exported to countries that grow these crops, these farmers cannot compete with these subsidized low prices.[43] Subsidies, therefore, distort markets. For example, Mexican farmers have grown corn for centuries, yet with the passage of NAFTA in 1994, they must now compete with subsidized corn grown in the U.S. and imported into Mexico. Even though the Mexican government subsidizes their corn farmers, the price of Mexican corn is still much higher than U.S. corn. This means that many Mexican farmers have been economically unable to continue their livelihoods. Forced to feed their families and desperate for work, many of the ex-farmers have migrated to the U.S. or to the teeming cities of Mexico for jobs.

In the book *Perverse Subsidies*, Norman Myers and Jennifer Kent estimate that governments worldwide have established environmentally damaging subsidies that amount to about $850 billion annually. For example, subsides for agriculture, can lead to crop overproduction contributing to erosion and compaction of topsoil, pollution from synthetic fertilizers and pesticides, and the release of greenhouse gases. Subsidies for road transportation lead to overloading of road networks and promote the overuse of cars and trucks for hauling. Subsidies for fisheries foster overharvesting of already depleted fish stocks. Subsidies for forestry encourage overexploitation at a time when many forests have been reduced by excessive logging, acid rain, and agricultural encroachment.[44]

Some corporations claim that they need taxpayer subsidies to provide jobs. Almost every big company has gotten them. In fact, the average U.S. state has more than 30 economic development subsidies, many of which are locally granted by cities and counties. These subsidies include property tax abatements, corporate income tax credits, sales and excise tax exemptions, tax increment financing, low-interest loans and loan guarantees, free land, training grants, infrastructure aid, and just all out cash grants.[45]

Tampa, Florida-based Sykes Enterprises, for example, operates call centers in the United States and abroad. The company has a widespread history of receiving subsidies, typically in small cities or rural areas desperate for jobs. Indeed, a company vice president once said: "Every one of our locations is a result of some incentive plan. If a community is inviting Sykes to build a call center, they are expected to deed the land for two call centers to us, and give incentives of at least $2.5 million." One of their centers was located in Manhattan, Kansas, where the city and the state offered Sykes a subsidy package of about $6.2 million in 1998, based on its promise to create an estimated 432 jobs. From the city came a $2.6 million cash grant, free land, $500,000 for site improvements, and property tax reductions for five years. The state provided $550,000 from an Economic Opportunity fund, enterprise zone tax breaks worth nearly $1.8 million, and a project and training grant of $800,000. In June 2004, the remaining 256 workers lost their jobs when Sykes moved their work to Asia and Latin America. Conveniently, the Manhattan plant closed only six months after the enterprise zone tax breaks expired.[46]

Wal-Mart leads the pack in attracting subsidies. For example, in 2003 they collected $10 million in Denver, Colorado; $500,000 in Dallas, Texas; $36.7 million in Scottsdale, Arizona, (as part of a shopping center that includes Lowe's); $9 million in Bartlesville, Oklahoma; and $17 million in Lewiston, Maine.[47] A study by Good Jobs First found that 90 percent of Wal-Mart distribution centers received tax breaks and other subsidies, valued at an average of $7.4 million per distribution center. Wal-Mart sought and received subsidies averaging about $2.8 million at 1,100 of their locations, about one-third of its U.S. stores.[48] Local officials argue these big stores warrant subsidies

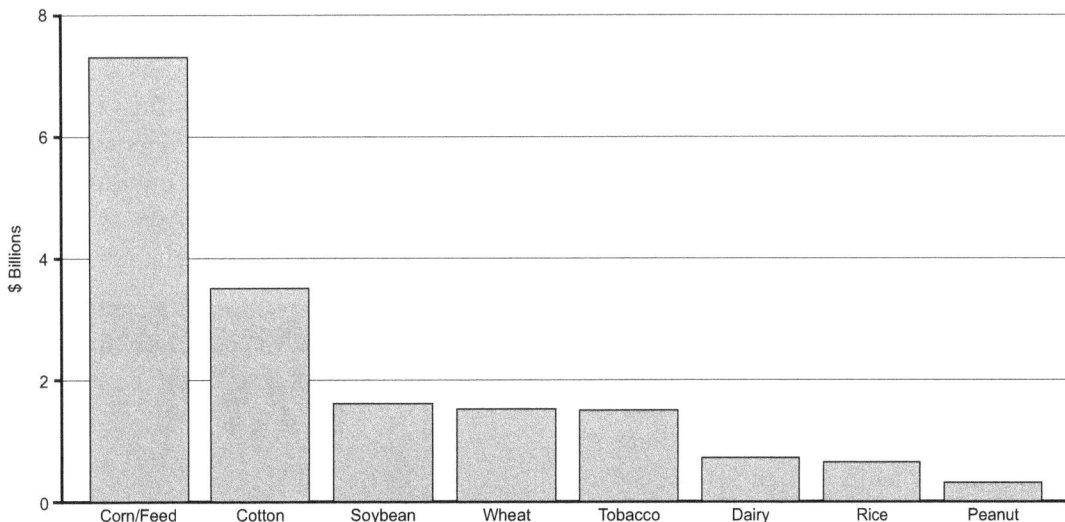

**FARM SUBSIDIES IN 2005, FROM A CONGRESSIONAL BUDGET OFFICE REPORT.**

because of the jobs and tax revenue they generate. But in most cases the big boxes do more harm than good. When big box stores move to town, other businesses shrink or close completely with hundreds of jobs lost, many of which provide higher wages and better benefits than Wal-Mart or other big box chains.

While the producer internalizes revenue and profits from certain products, society and the environment absorbs externalized costs. The externalizing of costs may make the consumer price low, but we all pay for it eventually through taxes, adverse health effects, and reduced quality of life. In this way, externalized costs equate to a subsidy.

# IMPACT #7: BUILD-UP OF DEBT

Have you ever been or are you currently in debt? Are your debts more than your assets? For many of you the answer may be yes! Debt is more a fact of life today for young people than when I grew up. Some of my peers had student loans, but they usually paid them off in a couple of years. They had no credit card debt because no one I knew had a credit card! In fact, I remember getting rejected when I applied for my first credit card – and I was a teacher at the time and didn't have any debt!

Today the words debt and deficits are on the lips of everyone – from the homeowner, to the credit card holder, to the student, to the retiree, to local and state governments, to the national government – many people, institutions, and governments are awash in debt. Big time

---

**Questions to Consider**
1. What are some examples of externalities that you encounter in your daily life?
2. What are some examples of subsidies that you encounter in your daily life?

---

debt. You may be wondering, how did we get to this point? The simple answer is we have spent beyond our means. Yes, that is true, but, as you can imagine by now, it is also a lot more complicated than that. In this section we will examine five kinds of debt: consumer debt, student loan debt, mortgage debt, national debt, and trade deficits.

## 1. Consumer Debt

In the post-war years, American families borrowed for consumer purchases, but usually it was not excessive and kept pace with the growth in their incomes. But the consistent rise in incomes in the post-war years gave way to stagnate incomes for the majority of Americans from the 1980s onward. Yet since the 1980s, American families have kept spending as if their incomes were keeping pace with overall economic growth. And their spending has, in turn, fueled continued growth. How did families manage this trick? First, women streamed into the paid work force. By the late 1990s, more than 60 percent of mothers with young children worked outside the home, while in 1966, only 24 percent did. Second, everyone put in more hours at work. By the mid-2000s, the typical male worker was putting in roughly 100 more hours each year than two decades before, and the typical female worker about 200 more hours. When American families couldn't squeeze any more income out of these two coping mechanisms, they embarked on a third: go-

VISA

ONE OF THE FORMER VISA LOGOS, USED FROM 1970 TO 2006. VISA IS THE LARGEST CREDIT CARD COMPANY.

ing deeper into debt. Their homes served as their personal ATM. House prices soared from 2002 to 2007, and through refinancing American households extracted $2.3 trillion from their homes. Eventually, the debt bubble burst – and with it, the last coping mechanism.[49]

**Consumer debt** is simply debts that are owed as a result of purchasing goods that are consumable and/or do not appreciate. For example, a house is not consumer debt, since the asset you are purchasing has traditionally appreciated in value, although it hasn't since 2008. Buying a designer purse or a computer game is a consumer item and once out of the store it loses its value. Consumer spending drives 70 percent of the economy. Consumer society pressures buyers to spend, and they have complied. Total U.S. consumer debt as of May 2011 was $2.43 trillion. About 50.2 million households carry credit-card debt, which averages out to about $15,799 per household. There were 176.8 million credit cardholders in 2008.[50]

In 2011, the ratio of household debt to personal income (wages and salaries only) was a staggering 154 percent. This means some people owe a lot more money than they are bringing in. Here lies the paradox: in order for the economy to recover from the recession, consumers need to consume more, which entails running up more consumer debt. And it seems as though consumers are willing to be the sacrificial lambs again. After steering clear of credit cards for awhile, consumers are racking up debt again at an alarming pace. They accumulated $18.4 billion in credit card debt in the second quarter of 2011. That's 66 percent more debt accumulated than in the same quarter a year ago, and a whopping 368 percent more than in the second quarter of 2009.[51]

## 2. Student Loan Debt

Do you have student loan debt? As in the housing bubble, could there now be a student loan debt bubble? The younger generation appears to have mortgaged its future earnings in the form of student loan debt. In 2012, total student loan debt in the U.S. reached over $1 trillion. In 2008, 62 percent of students from public universities obtained student loans, 72 percent from nonprofit private universities, and a whopping 96 percent from for-profit schools. The neoliberal agenda, which presses to decrease funds for public education, indirectly pushes more students into private institutions. Enrollments at for-profit colleges have increased in the last ten years by 225 percent, far outpacing public institution increases.[52] From 1994 to 2008, average debt levels for graduating seniors more than doubled to $23,200, according to The Student Loan Project, a nonprofit research and policy organization. Loans now saddle more than 10 percent of those completing their bachelor's degree with over $40,000 in debt. Of the $1 trillion in outstanding federal and private student-loan debt, students are actively repaying only about 40 percent of that debt. The rest is in default or in deferment (when a student requests temporary postponement of payment because of economic hardship). When the loans go into default, taxpayers are required to pick up the tab, since the federal government backs just about all loans extended before July 2010. Two out of every five students enrolled at for-profit schools are in default on their education loans 15 years after the loans were issued. There is no screening to receive these loans. A credit score is not required for federal loan eligibility. Neither is information regarding income, assets, or employment.[53]

The two largest holders of student loans are SLM Corp (SLM) and Student Loan Corp (STU), a subsidiary of Citigroup. SLM – Sallie Mae – started as a Government Sponsored Enterprise (GSE) in 1972. The idea was to prime it for eventual privatization, which occurred in 2004. The company, even before its privatization, jumped onto the securitization bandwagon, lumping together and repackaging a large portion of its loans and selling them as bonds to investors. SLM created and marketed its own brand of asset-backed securitized student loans, Student Loan Asset Backed Securities (SLABS). Financial firms packaged many of the students loans into the same securities that helped trigger the financial crisis. SLM's incurred minimal risk as long as the federal government guaranteed its loans, but starting in July 2010, federally subsidized education loans were no longer available to private lenders. Bankruptcy laws discharge credit card and even gambling debts but non-repayment of a student loan is virtually impossible. While a college degree tends to correlate with higher incomes, during the last 8 to 10 years the median income of highly educated Americans has been declining. Also, a college education has been producing diminishing returns, especially at non-select colleges.[54]

---

**Questions to Consider**

1. Do you, your friends, your children, or anyone you know have student debt? Do they think it was worthwhile to incur the debt? Are they having difficulty paying it back?

---

### 3. Mortgage Debt

Simply, a **mortgage** is a loan secured by real property through the use of a mortgage note. If you own a house, you probably have a mortgage loan, unless you pay cash for the house or the mortgage loan on the house has been fully paid. Up until the mid-2000s, the price of homes reflected what people could afford. But recently, all that changed. In 1980 the average priced home sold for $64,600, by 2006 that figure increased to $246,500. Because interest rates were very low and money was easy to come by during the 2000s, the price of homes skyrocketed to unprecedented levels. It was also easy for people to refinance their home at a lower interest rate and take that money to buy consumer items.[55] With the collapse of the housing bubble, many homes are now worth less than they were at the pre-bubble high. As a result, as of June 2011, roughly 1.6 million homeowners in the U.S. were either delinquent on mortgages or in some stage of the foreclosure process. Real estate data shows that 10.9 million, or 22.5 percent of homeowners are underwater on their mortgage – meaning the value of their homes has fallen so much it is now below the value of their original loan. That figure, which peaked at 11.3 million in the fourth quarter of 2009, has declined slightly not because home prices were appreciating but because houses entered foreclosure.[56] Total residential mortgage debt was $14.5 trillion in 2007, $11.7 trillion in 2009, $12 trillion in 2008, and in the second quarter of 2011, there was about $13.7 trillion in total U.S. outstanding mortgage debt. Compare these figures with the figure of $58 billion in mortgage debt in 1952.[57]

### 4. National Debt

In 1980 the national debt stood at $1 trillion. Over the prior 204 years, the nation paid for the Revolutionary War, the Civil War, the First World War, the Great Depression, the Second World War, Korea, Vietnam, and the better part of the Cold War, and, through all that, still only borrowed $1 trillion. Over the

HOUSE IN SALINAS, CALIFORNIA UNDER FORECLOSURE, FOLLOWING THE POPPING OF THE U.S. REAL ESTATE BUBBLE.

## The National Debt is Not Like Your Credit Card Debt[59]
### by Tim Koechlin, *Dollars&Sense*

The U.S. government borrows money by issuing bonds that are denominated in its currency that it has the power to create, and it is recognized around the world as a reliable currency. Unlike a household or business, the government does not need to worry about default. The U.S. Treasury can borrow from a long line of willing lenders, who are happy to lend to them because there is so little risk. At this moment in time, borrowing is especially easy and cheap because there are lots of potential investors sitting on big piles of cash, and in a depressed economy there are relatively few risk-free alternatives.

Unlike households and businesses, the U.S. government has no problem finding lenders because it has the authority to tax and it has the authority to create money. When investors have lots of other lending alternatives, the U.S. Treasury will likely have to pay a higher interest rate on its debt. But, again, they can always find a lender. And further, about half of the U.S. debt is owed to the Federal Reserve, which buys government bonds, in other words lends to the government, with money that it creates. The Fed does not literally print money, but it does create it – essentially out of thin air. Many people have a notion that "printing money" leads to high inflation. Deficits can indeed cause inflation, and overly exuberant money creation will surely make inflation more likely. But thankfully, the Fed understands this, and so it uses its power to create money with caution. Over the past 30 years – during which time large deficits have been common – the Fed has routinely used its power to create money and kept inflation low and stable, for example in 2010, the inflation rate was 1.6 percent. This may be a little hard to accept, but in the U.S. case – and for most of the world's rich countries such as Japan – it has not been a problem. In fact, it has played a key role in facilitating prosperity and growth.

next 12 years of relative peace and prosperity, the national debt quadrupled to $4 trillion. In the 1990s, as taxes on the wealthy increased and government spending declined, the national debt stabilized. In 2000, President Clinton produced a $140 billion surplus, the first budget surpluses since 1969. The deficit-producing policies of neoliberalism returned in the 2000s. The government lowered taxes on the wealthy to the tune of $1.6 trillion, in which 50 percent of the gains went to the top 1 percent of income earners. Two wars and a $600 billion prescription drug plan for seniors exploded spending to 20 percent of GDP. In 2000, the national debt stood at $5.6 trillion; at the end of 2011 the national debt was almost $15 trillion. Bring in less income while spending more money and the result is debt. Mountains of it.[58]

Understandably, there is a great deal of confusion about where our money comes from. Does it really fall from trees or is it really created out of thin air? Well, almost. The U.S. has been off the gold standard since 1972. So what backs up our currency now? Well, really nothing! It is merely the full faith and trust in the U.S. government. Since the U.S. has never defaulted on its currency, that is about as good as it will get. The above short except is one of the most succinct that I have come across on this confusing topic of how money is created.

### 5. The Trade Deficit

Another type of debt is the trade deficit. A **trade deficit** is simply the fact that imports exceed exports, which is the opposite of a trade surplus, where exports exceed imports. Since the 1980s, the U.S. had had a persistent trade deficit, a stunning total of $7.2 trillion. According to the Bureau of Economic Analysis, 65 percent of this amount was accumulated during the period 2000-2008. China now accounts for about 60 percent of America's current trade deficit in manufactured goods, a staggering $277 billion in 2008, largely because of what many consider an undervalued currency and massive subsidies to its manufacturers.[60] Oil is one of our biggest imports, while coffee comes in a distant second – energy for our cars and energy for us. The trade deficit set a record high of $828 billion in 2006, with second place in 2008, $816.2 billion. The number dropped as a result of the recession in 2009 with a trade deficit of $503 billion. However, it was inching its way back up to $427.7 billion as of July 31, 2011.[61]

**Questions to Consider**

1. Another interesting figure is the current accounts deficits. It is a bit complicated to explain here, but some of you may find it interesting to do additional research on this topic.

## IMPACT #8: EMASCULATION OF LABOR

As of this writing, one of the most important debates in our political arena is about jobs, which leads us to the eighth impact of neoliberalism: labor. Unemployment since 2009 has hovered around 8 to 10 percent, with little indication that it will substantially decrease in the near future. The heyday of fewer than 5 percent unemployment rates during the periods of the roaring 1990s and the 2000s appear to be reminiscent of a bygone era. You probably know someone close to you who is unemployed. As I mentioned earlier, my son was unemployed in Phoenix, Arizona, an epicenter of the housing boom and bust, for several months in 2009 and 2010. Two of my cousins have been unemployed in Rockford, Illinois, my former home-town, for over two years now. One of the vibrant manufacturing centers during the 1950s and 1960s, Rockford has profoundly experienced the transfer of well-paying, manufacturing jobs to low-wage countries like China. The current recession has taken its toll on this former factory town.

I will be discussing two aspects of labor in this book. One is the impact of neoliberal policies on the workforce, primarily in the U.S. The second part of the labor topic will be discussed in the globalization chapters, in which the impact of economic globalization on workers around the world will be examined.

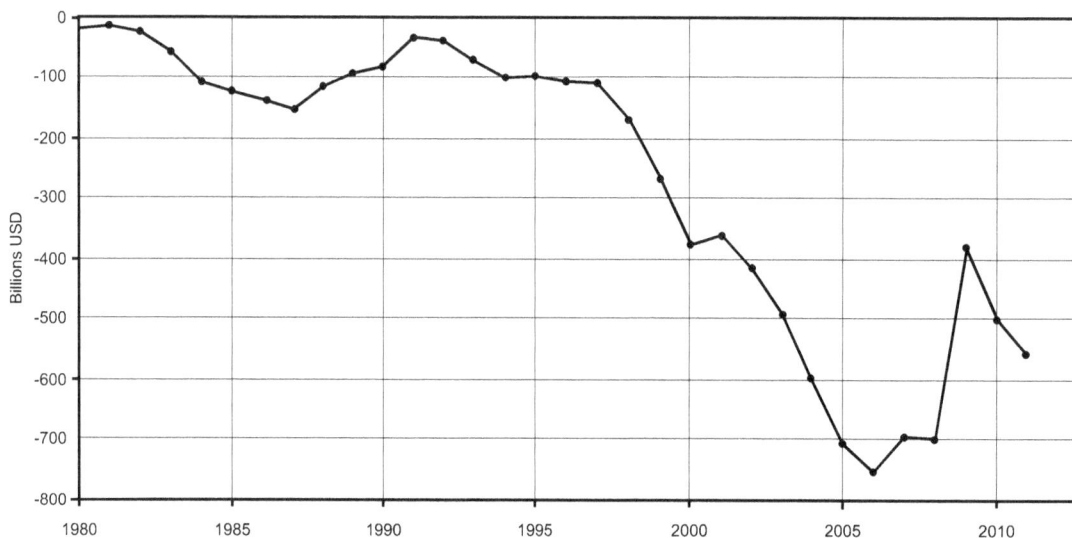

UNITED STATES BALANCE OF TRADE (1980–2011), WITH NEGATIVE NUMBERS DENOTING A TRADE DEFICIT.

Since neoliberals believe that unions and the minimum wage restrict the supply and demand of labor, eliminating or diminishing the impact of unions and abolishing minimum wage laws are part of their overall strategy. One of the first acts that illustrates this strategy was a stand-off between President Ronald Reagan and the air-traffic controllers, whose union voted to strike in 1982.

## PATCO vs. Reagan

Most unions strongly opposed the Republican candidate, Ronald Reagan, in the 1980 presidential election; ironically the Professional Air Traffic Controllers Organization (PATCO) union had supported him. In August 1981, the union rejected the federal government's pay raise offer and sent its 16,000 members out on strike to shut down the nation's commercial airlines. They demanded a reduction in the workweek from 40 hours to 32 hours, a doubling of wages, a $10,000 bonus and early retirement. Federal law forbade such a strike, and the Transportation Department implemented a backup plan to keep the system running. The strikers were given 48 hours to return to work; if not, they would be fired and banned from ever working in a federal job. One-fourth of the strikers came back to work, but 13,000 did not. The strike collapsed, PATCO vanished, and the union movement as a whole suffered a major reversal, which accelerated the decline of membership across the board in the private sector.[62]

### Questions to Consider

1. What do you think, was Reagan justified in his show-down with the union?

The decline of unions accelerated after Reagan broke the air-traffic controllers' strike in 1982. Strikes also dropped off dramatically. Total union membership in 2010 was 11.9 percent, down from 12.3 percent a year earlier. In 1983, the union membership rate was 20.1 percent, and there were 17.7 million union workers.[63] The year 1953 marked the height of union strength when 32.5 percent of the U.S. labor force was unionized. Today the unionized percentage of private-sector workers is 6.9 percent.[64] In the U.S. manufacturing sector in 1979, there were 21.2 million manufacturing jobs. By 1992, there were only 16.7 million such jobs. This was due in part to increasing automation, increasing productivity per worker, and the outsourcing of manufacturing jobs to low-wage countries.[65]

One of the dire effects of the drop in union membership is that workers' wages have not kept up with rising productivity levels. In principle, wages rise with productivity. **Labor productivity** is the amount a worker produces in a unit of time, usually per hour. But whether wages actually rise with productivity in practice depends on the relative bargaining power of workers and their employers. In the early 1950s, the **Treaty of Detroit** was an understanding between capital and labor, wherein employers accepted the idea that compensation would grow at the rate that productivity increased. This understanding continued in the 1960s until the crisis of the 1970s, when labor compensation exceeded productivity and it contributed to inflation. This agreement ensured that workers would share in the fruits of future economic growth. However, this agreement has been broken under neoliberalism.

Economist James Cypher has carefully analyzed productivity data. He found that "in 2009, stock owners, bankers, brokers, hedge-fund wizards, highly paid corporate executives, corporations, and mid-ranking managers pocketed – as either income, benefits, or perks such as corporate jets – an estimated $1.91 trillion that over the past 40 years ago would have collectively gone to non-supervisory and production workers in the form of higher wages and benefits. These are the 88 million workers in the private sector who are closely tied to production processes and/or are not responsible for the supervision, planning, or direction of other workers." If workers had been paid the value of their annual productivity increases, as they had been prior to the early 1970s, they would have received an average of $35.98 per hour in compensation in 2009 instead of the $23.14 they actually earned. The difference is $12.84. On an annual basis each worker lost an average of $22,701. From 1972 through 2009, non-supervisory workers transferred productivity gains to managers and owners. This upward redistribution of $1.91 trillion has remained hidden. It has taken various forms – bonuses, excessive salaries, large stock options, padded consulting fees, outsized compensation to boards of directors, expensive conferences, lavish offices, large staffs, private corporate dining rooms, and generous retirement agreements. Some would appear as profit, some as interest, some as dividends, realized capital gains, pension programs, retained earnings, or owners' income, with the remainder deeply buried as "costs of doing business."[66]

The total increase in the wages paid to all 124 million non-supervisory workers was less than $200 million in six years – a raise of $1.60 per worker – not per hour but a grand total of $1.60 in higher wages per worker over nearly six years. Compare this $200 million for workers to the $38 billion paid in bonuses by the top five Wall Street firms during the same period.[67] For example, during the 1990s, the reported pay of senior corporate executives increased almost fivefold. If worker's median pay had grown at the same rate as CEO's pay, their salary would be over $200,000 a year.[68]

Today three Americans in four pay more in regressive Social Security taxes than they do in progressive personal income taxes. **Regressive tax rates** decrease as the amount subject to taxation increases, which means those who have a higher income pay less of their total income on taxed items. While **progressive tax rates** increase as the taxable base amount increases, which means those who have a higher income pay more of their total income in taxes. Employees and employers each pay a Social Security tax rate of 6.2 percent but in 2012 the rules capped an employee' pay at a yearly income of $110,100. A worker paid a minimum wage pays 6.2 percent of earnings in Social Security

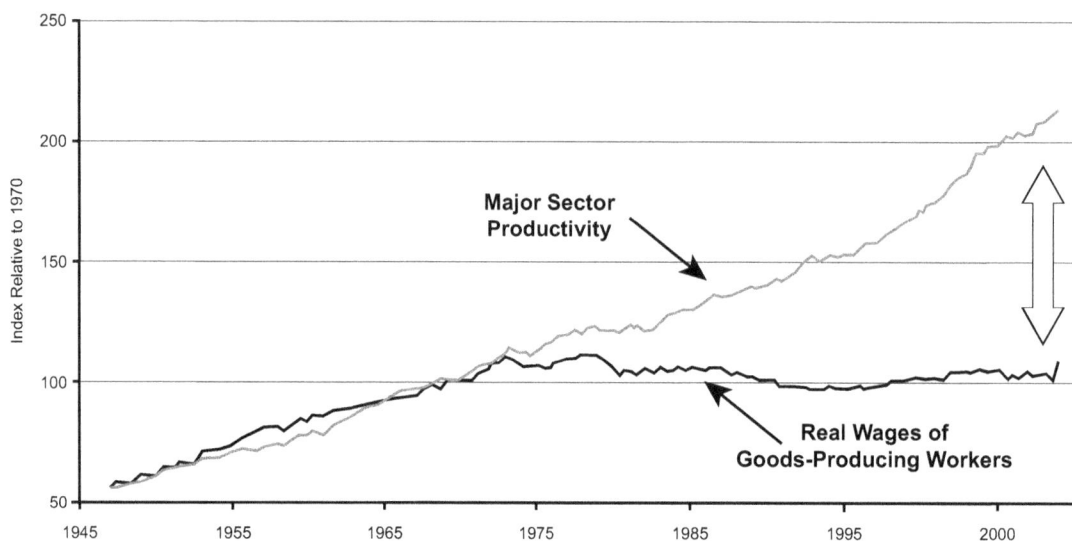

**U.S. LABOR PRODUCTIVITY AND AVERAGE REAL EARNINGS, 1947-2008.**

taxes and 1.45 percent in Medicare, while a person earning $2 million pays about 1/3 of 1 percent.[69] Hence, it is a regressive tax.

Neoliberals attack the federal minimum wage, which when adjusted for inflation is at a 50 year low. The wages paid to the low end of the service sector are generally decided by federally directed minimum wage laws and input by the business community, who generally fiercely resist efforts to increase the minimum wage. The minimum wage in 2007 was $5.15, an hourly rate that had remained the same since 1997. However, the actual value of the minimum wage has eroded since 1997; factoring for inflation, the $5.15 minimum wage was actually worth only $4.15 in 2006. Congress passed a law in 2007 to raise the minimum wage to $5.85 an hour; it increased to $6.55 an hour in 2008 and $7.25 an hour in 2009 where it remains in 2012.[70]

Hourly wages of people with jobs have been dropping over the last 30 years. Adjusted for inflation, weekly paychecks are down at an annualized rate of 4.5 percent. Americans are keeping their jobs or finding new ones only by accepting lower wages. My son, who was unemployed in Phoenix, Arizona, for about 8 months altogether, luckily found another job in 2010 that required more technical skills than his previous job. But, he also took about a 25 percent cut in pay. America's median wage, adjusted for inflation, has barely budged for decades. Between 2000 and 2007 it actually dropped.[71]

Unemployment compensation now covers relatively fewer workers and replaces a lower percentage of wages than at any time since the Franklin Roosevelt administration.[72] In 2011, there were nearly 14 million unemployed workers, and that was not counting those who have given up looking or those who are employed part-time but are looking for full-time work. Meanwhile there are a little more than 3 million job openings. The economy must produce 150,000 jobs each month just to absorb population growth.[73] Among the 18-25 year old group, the unemployment rate is around 20 percent, and in some locations, and among some socio-demographic groups, twice that rate.[74]

The question today is, "Is unemployment cyclical or structural?" Recessions cause **cyclical unemployment**. An increase in demand can be a cure for cyclical unemployment. As demand increases, employers may decide to increase output, and this may motivate them to start hiring again. Structural unemployment is different and more complicated. Structural unemployment, a part of the problem in the U.S., is a mismatch between workers' skills and the skills employers are seeking. An obvious response is to help workers gain new skills, such as through publicly supported job retraining and educational programs or even public hiring and on-the-job training.[75]

The postwar limits on trade and on immigration had protected American workers from pressures to cut wages. Government laws tightly capped immigration in the postwar years until President Johnson signed the Immigration Act of 1967.[76] In the 2000s, officials looked the other way as a flood of illegal immigrants crossed the borders into the U.S. to work in jobs most Americans did not want. As a result, there was a downward pressure on wages at the lower income and skill level.

Another impact on labor has been the neoliberal free trade policies, especially with a low-wage country like China. According to an Economic Policy Institute (EPI) report, the U.S.- China trade deficit has eliminated or displaced nearly 2.8 million U.S. jobs or 2 percent of total U.S. employment between 2001 and 2010. The trade deficit with China grew from $84 billion in 2001to $278 billion in 2010. Of the nearly 2.8 million jobs lost or displaced, 1.9 million of them were in manufacturing. These jobs represent nearly half of all U.S. manufacturing jobs lost between 2001 and

2010. According to economist Robert Scott, "Increases in U.S. exports tend to create jobs in the United States, and increases in imports tend to lead to job loss. Thus, a growing trade deficit signi-fies growing job loss." Scott goes on to say that "competition with China and countries like it has resulted in lower wages and less bargaining power for U.S. workers in manufacturing and for all workers with less than a four-year college degree."[77]

**Questions to Consider**
1. If you have a job, have your received a raise in the last four years? Do you know someone whose job has been outsourced?

# IMPACT #9: WIDENING SOCIAL INEQUALITY

The bottom line is that people who work for a living are getting a smaller and smaller slice of the nation's economic pie. The #9 impact of neoliberalism is the growing gap between rich and poor in the U.S. and worldwide. We will concentrate on the U.S. in this section and explore global inequality in chapter 6.

The neoliberal solution to poverty is to grow the economy. As President Reagan announced, "A rising tide will lift all boats." But a rising tide has not lifted all boats; some critics claim the rising tide has only lifted the yachts. In fact, real (adjusted for inflation) per capita GDP increased more than 80 percent between 1975 and 2005. In the ten years before the recession, it increased at an average rate of 1.8 percent per year. According to economist Robert Cramer, "That means that if the benefits of economic growth were equally spread throughout our society, everyone should have been almost 20 percent better off (with compounding) in 2008 than they were in 1998."[78] This has obviously not happened. The assumption that continuing growth would close the social gap has not materialized; in fact, it has gotten worse. Growth, will not reduce social inequality. Only changing the structure of the economic system will do that.

Structures in place contribute to widening the gap between the rich and the poor even in the presence of enormous economic growth over the last three decades. One structure is the social ar-rangement that rewards the privileged with the power and resources to acquire even more privilege. This includes ethnic and racial discrimination, tax loopholes for the wealthy, inferior schooling for children of the poor, use of money to gain political access (even in democracies), low or no inheri-tance taxes, and privileged access to superior education for the elite. In systems terms these struc-tures are called "success to the successful" feedback loops. They reward the successful with the means to succeed and tend to be prevalent in any society that does not knowingly implement offsetting structures to level the playing field. For example, offsetting structures would include passing and ex-ecuting anti-discrimination laws, more progressive tax rates, affordable higher education, universal access to health care, safety nets to support those who fall on hard times, higher taxes on wealth such as capital gains, taxes on inherited wealth, and democratic processes that separate policies from the influence of money. The poverty-perpetuating structures arise from the fact that it is easier for rich populations to save, invest, and multiply their capital than it is for poor ones to do so. The elite have built up a large stock of capital that multiplies itself. [79]

## A Brief History of Inequality

Seldom in American history has prosperity been more narrowly concentrated. The U.S. has been in this state twice before – the Gilded Age (late 1800s) and the Roaring Twenties. In each case, the concentration of wealth in the upper 1 percent was the result of rapid technological change, global integration, laissez-faire policies, and the spread of novel financial products.[80] In 1928, the richest 1 percent of Americans received 23.9 percent of the nation's total income. After that, their share steadily declined, but by 2011, the elite 1 percent were back to their 1928 level – with 24 percent of the total. A second parallel links 1929 with 2008. When earnings accumulate at the top, the elite invest their wealth in assets that are most likely to attract other big investors. This causes the prices of certain assets to become wildly inflated. Such speculative bubbles eventually burst, leaving behind mountains of near-worthless collateral.[81]

The domestic social compact of the postwar era (1948-1973) was built on a three legged stool: one leg was aggregate demand at high levels; one leg was state regulation, to give labor more equal bargaining power with business; and one leg was social insurance. Wages do not spontaneously rise with increased productivity and increased global commerce. But they do rise as a result of labor's bargaining power.[82]

The postwar years ushered in such programs as the GI Bill, an expansion of public higher education, civil and voting rights laws, and the Great Society programs, which further reduced economic inequality and helped expand the circle of prosperity. Marginal income tax rates of 70 percent to 90 percent on the highest incomes paid for most of these social programs. Real wages for workers in manufacturing rose 67 percent and real wages overall rose 81 percent. Income of the richest 1 percent also rose 38 percent. This period marked the birth of the American middle class. Two major forces drove these trends – unionization of major manufacturing sectors, and the public policies carried over from the New Deal. As America's middle class shared more of the economy's gains, they were able to buy more of the goods and services the economy produced. Those in the middle and at the bottom of the economic ladder made careers in stable corporations and were paid according to their productivity levels. Growth was widely shared, and income inequality continued

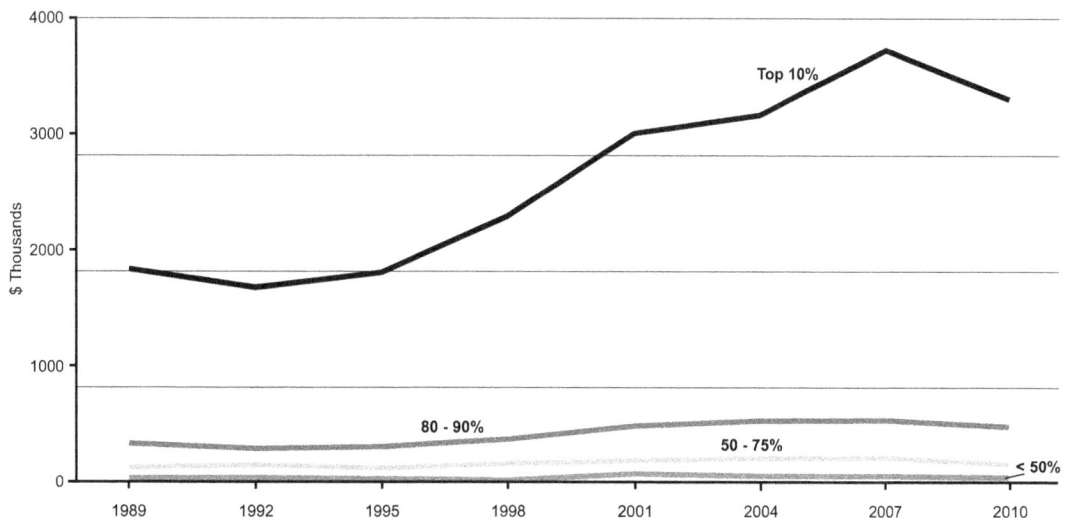

**FAMILY DISTRIBUTION OF WEALTH  - U.S. MEAN FAMILY NET WORTH BY PERCENTILE OF NET WORTH (1989–2010).**

to drop. By the late 1970s the top 1 percent raked in only 8 to 9 percent of America's total annual income. [83] The result: rapid growth and more jobs.

Another reason for prosperity during this era was regulatory policies constrained finance to playing its traditional role: providing capital to the main street part of the economy that produced goods and services. At that time, investment bankers feverishly pitching mergers and acquisitions made little economic sense except as sources of exorbitant fees.

During the crisis of the 1970s everyone lost ground. Real wages fell 3 percent and income for the richest 1 percent fell 4 percent. Then beginning in 1980, the tax policies of the Reagan administration unraveled the shared prosperity of the postwar years. Between 1980 and 2004, real wages in manufacturing fell 1 percent, while real income of the richest one percent skyrocketed to 135 percent.[84]

### Income Inequality by Percentages

When looking at inequality it helps to look at the levels of income and wealth distribution. Where to start? Let's start at the top, since that is where all the economic benefits over the last 30 years have gone.

### 1. The Top 1%

Where have all the economic gains gone? To the very top. Their lot in life has improved considerably. In 1979, the top 1 percent had 9.3 percent of all income in the U.S.; by 1985, it had climbed to 12 percent; by 2000, the share was 17.8 percent; and in 2011, it stood at 24 percent. In terms of wealth rather than income, the top 1 percent had 33.4 percent of the total net worth in 2001, while in 2011, that climbed to 40 percent. These figures are the highest since 1928, just before the Great Depression.[85] Astonishingly, the richest 1 percent of households earned as much each year as the bottom 60 percent put together; they possessed as much wealth as the bottom 90 percent.[86] The top .01 percent has made even greater gains. Between 2001 and 2007, the 400 richest individuals in the U.S., virtually all associated with multinational corporations, saw their wealth increase from $1 trillion to $1.6 trillion – an increase of $600 billion.[87]

Numbers show that CEO pay in 2010 skyrocketed by a whopping 23 percent. In 2011, the top earning CEO was Gregory Maffei of Liberty Media Corporation, who was compensated $87,493,565 for his services. That's about $42,064 per hour. In 2009, the country's top 25 hedge-fund managers in the financial sector earned $25 billion among them – more than they had made in 2007, before the 2008 crash.[88] Hedge fund manager John Paulson, for example, made $5 billion in 2010. That's $2.4 million dollars an hour – or $40,064 per minute. So Mr. Paulson made as much as a minimum wage worker in a year every 23 seconds. He and

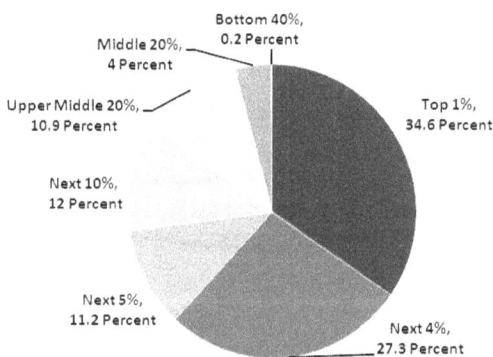

**U.S. Distribution of Wealth, 2007**

Bottom 40%, 0.2 Percent
Middle 20%, 4 Percent
Upper Middle 20%, 10.9 Percent
Next 10%, 12 Percent
Next 5%, 11.2 Percent
Top 1%, 34.6 Percent
Next 4%, 27.3 Percent

Edward N. Wolff, 2010

THE DISTRIBUTION OF NET WEALTH IN THE UNITED STATES, 2007. THE NET WEALTH OF MANY PEOPLE IN THE LOWEST 20% IS NEGATIVE BECAUSE OF DEBT.

HTTP://EN.WIKIPEDIA.ORG/WIKI/VOODOO_ECONOMICS

all hedge fund managers paid federal taxes of 15 percent instead of the current 35 percent (highest tax bracket) due to a special tax break for capital gains earnings. Compare this income to the average Social Security benefit for retirees, a sum of $14,160 per year – $38.79 per day (for all 365 days per year).[89]

### 2. The Top 10-20%

A tiny 1 percent elite continues to float up and away from everyone else. Below it, suspended, sits what might be thought of as the professional middle class – an upper tier of college graduates and postgraduates for whom the economy points progressively upward, but not spectacularly so. The professional middle class represents a second cleavage in American society – the one between college graduates and everyone else. Affluence for this group begins at about the top 20 percent. Annual family earnings of about $113,000 in 2009 would have been the 80th income percentile nationally. [90]

College graduates make up only about 30 percent of the population, and throughout the 2000s, their incomes barely budged. A college degree may be losing some of its luster. As more Americans have gone to college, the quality of college education has become arguably more inconsistent, and the value of a degree from a nonselective school has perhaps diminished. There is a marked difference for the prospects of unexceptional college graduates for whom the arrow of fortune points mostly sideways and those from selective colleges which points mostly up. A college degree is not the kind of protection against job loss or wage loss that it was in the past.[91]

### 3. The 80-90% and Below

Arguably, the most important economic trend in the United States over the past couple of generations has been the ever more distinct sorting of Americans into winners and losers and the slow hollowing-out of the middle class. The incomes of the bottom 90 percent of Americans have been stagnant for almost three decades. Between 2000 and 2010, median income for working-age households fell from $61,574 to $55,276, a decline of roughly $6,300, which is more than 10 per-

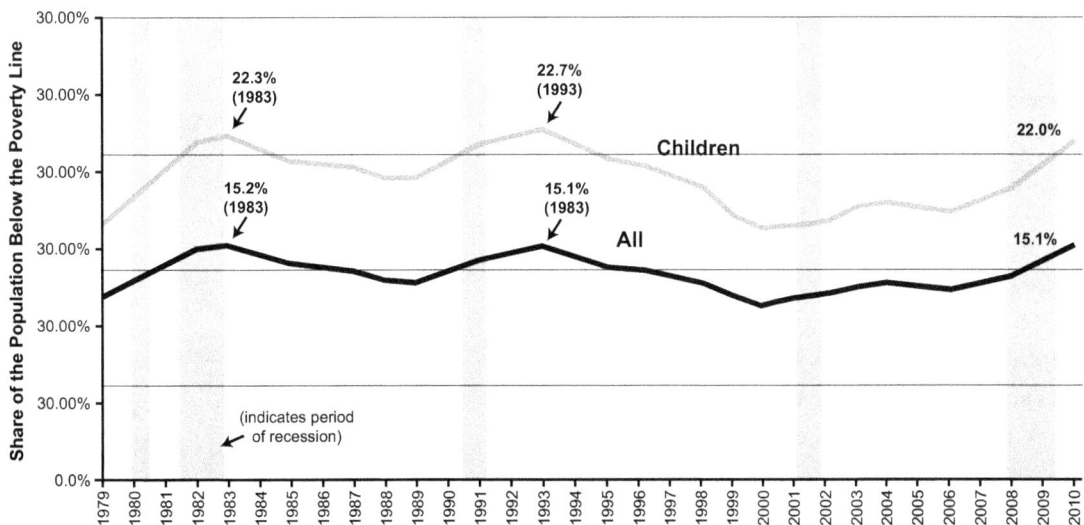

**CHILDREN AND POVERTY RATES.**

cent. For most of the 2000s, the housing bubble masked that trend, which allowed working-class and middle-class families to raise their standard of living despite income stagnation. But that fig leaf has since blown away.[92]

The true center of American society has always been its nonprofessionals – high-school graduates make up 58 percent of the adult population. And as manufacturing jobs and semiskilled office positions disappear, much of this vast, nonprofessional middle class is drifting downward.[93] For young adults without family wealth to help them in the task of accumulating wealth, trying to join the upper economic echelons is like running after a departing bus. Were it not for the fact that the average family was working at least 500 more hours a year in 2000 than in the 1970s, mainly because women's mass entry into the paid labor force, incomes for the vast middle would have fallen even farther behind.[94]

Many of the non-professionals in this group have been in manufacturing jobs. Since 2000, U.S. manufacturing has shed about a third of its jobs, many to China. Still, industry isn't about to vanish from the U.S., any more than agriculture did as the number of farm workers plummeted during the 20th century. As of 2010, the U.S. was the second-largest manufacturer in the world, and the number three agricultural nation. But as a result of mechanization, only about 2 percent of American workers make a living as farmers. American manufacturing looks to be heading down the same path. Meanwhile, another phase of the economy's transformation – one involving the white-collar workers – is just beginning.[95]

The bottom 30 percent of Americans – 100 million people – have an average net worth (total of all assets minus liabilities) of $10,000 or less. And, more than 50 million Americans have negative net worth – they owe more than they own. The bottom 80 percent owns just 5.8 percent of the value of all common stocks held outside pension funds, and including pension savings, the bottom 80 percent owns just 10.7 percent of the total. Only 14.6 percent of Americans have direct holdings valued at $5,000 or more.[96]

### 4. Poverty, the 15% and Below

Increasing poverty is one result of rising inequality. The combined impact of high unemployment and declining wages has resulted in a national poverty rate, as determined by the Census Bureau in 2010, of 15.1 percent. This was up from 14.3 percent in 2009. State-wide, poverty rates range from 8.3 percent in New Hampshire to 22.4 percent in Mississippi. Since 2010, poverty has expanded by an additional 2.6 million people, bringing the total number of Americans in poverty to 46.2 million. The poverty rate for children was 22.0 percent in 2010, representing 16.4 million kids living in poverty. In 2010, more than one-third (35.5 percent) of all people living in poverty were children.[97]

Fifty million people or 17.4 million families couldn't buy sufficient food in 2009. About one million children from more than a third of these households missed meals regularly. A to-

BLUE COLOR WORKING MEN IN THE MINING INDUSTRY.

tal of 1.6 million people used emergency shelters or transitional housing during 2007 – 2008, suggesting that 1 in every 50 Americans used shelters at some point. About 170,000 families lived in homeless shelters.[98]

## Men and Neoliberal Policies

As a woman, the women's movement of the late 1960s and early 1970s clearly had an impact on me. I thought it was about time to end discrimination against women and open up economic opportunities for us. I never dreamed I would be writing in 2012 that many men are suffering – economically and emotionally – from the consequences of neoliberalism. But, indeed, that is the case.

You may question this section, since you look at the bankers, economists, and business leaders in charge of the financial mess and you see a sea of male faces. Yes, those at the pinnacle of power and wealth are still men, but, consistently, men without higher education have been the biggest losers in the neoliberal economy. For men with only high-school degrees, the decline in income and status has been precipitous – 12 percent in the last quarter century alone. Real median wages of men have fallen by 32 percent since their peak in 1973, once you account for the men who have washed out of the workforce altogether. During the 2000s, construction provided an outlet for the young men who would have gone into manufacturing a generation ago, but those jobs have dried up with the recession. In 1967, 97 percent of 30-to-50-year-old American men with only a high-school diploma were working; in 2010, just 76 percent were. Declining male employment is not unique to the U.S.; it's been happening in almost all rich nations, as they've pushed the industrial age behind them.[99]

The loss of manufacturing jobs from inner cities in the 1970s – and the resulting economic struggles of inner-city African American men – is now happening to white men in many rural areas and lower-income fringe suburbs. Accompanying job loss are the social ills that crop up afterward, as evident among inner-city men. These social ills eventually became self-reinforcing, passing from one generation to the next. In less privileged parts of the country, a larger, predominantly male underclass may now be forming, and with it, more-widespread social problems.[100]

## Insights: Inequality and Neoliberalism

The neoliberal policies of the last 30 years and the double whammy hit of economic globalization have rendered a knockout blow to the bottom 80 percent of the U.S. population. On all counts, the more laissez-faire an economy, the more unequal it tends to be. Economic history tends to agree on this point. Critics, such as economist Susan George, argue that if you are in the top 20 percent of the income scale, you are likely to gain something from neoliberalism, and the higher you are up the ladder, the more you gain. Conversely, the bottom 80 percent all lose, and the lower you are on the ladder, the more you lose proportionally.[101] The changes in income distribution are not the result of "natural laws," they are the result of systems set up by human beings to benefit certain groups in the society. One of the most significant features of severe downturns is that they tend to accelerate and accentuate deep economic shifts that are already under way.

Many neoliberals do not believe their policies have contributed to greater social inequality. They counter that those whose wages have stagnated should improve their skills by getting further education. Yet, the weakening of all the equalizing institutions mentioned above contributes far more to the new inequality than changes in demand for skills. Blaming the economic plight on the individual is a handy escape hatch for politicians, economists, and commentators to avoid discussing the more politically loaded factors, such as how the system is organized and for whose benefit. Moreover, focusing on education conveniently blames the government and public school teachers for the problems. Neoliberals have a ready solution to education shortfalls: school vouchers and privatization of education.[102]

Economists long ago tried to justify the vast inequalities that seemed so troubling in the mid-19th century. The justification they came up with was called "**marginal-productivity theory**." In a nutshell, this theory rationalized that those with higher incomes would generate higher productivity and, thus, they would make greater contributions to society than their lower income fellow citizens. It is a theory that the rich feel justifies their status. Evidence for its validity, however, remains thin. For example, the corporate executives who helped bring on the recession – whose contribution to our society, and to their own companies, has been massively negative – went on to receive large bonuses.[103]

The more divided a society becomes in terms of wealth, the more reluctant the wealthy want to spend money on common needs. Sitglitz notes, "The rich don't need to rely on government for parks or education or medical care or personal security – they can buy all these things for themselves. In the process, they become more distant from ordinary people, losing whatever empathy they may once have had. They also worry about strong government – one that could use its powers to adjust the balance, take some of their wealth, and invest it for the common good. The top 1 percent may complain about the kind of government we have in America, but in truth they like it just fine: too gridlocked to re-distribute, too divided to do anything but lower taxes." The top 1 percent have the best of everything, but there is one thing that money doesn't buy: an understanding that their fate is bound up with how the other 99 percent live. Throughout history, this is something that the top 1 percent eventually learn, but learn too late.[104]

### Questions to Consider

1. Do you think the emphasis on social inequality should be a major concern for Americans today?

# IMPACT #10: ASCENSION OF DOLLAR DEMOCRACY

Neoliberal policies have influenced the U.S. political system and vice versa. In this section, impact #10, the ascension of dollar democracy, we will examine how the U.S. political process itself has changed because of neoliberal policies. Both the Republican and Democratic Parties support these policies, although it would be fair to say the Republicans have accepted them more enthusiastically. Neoliberals channel this influx of money into the political system to candidates who support those who give the money. This vicious cycle of influence and pay-offs has compromised our democracy, made our country more unequal, and threatened the long-term economic viability of a once very wealthy nation. This cannot go on indefinitely, since the interests of the wealthy elite are not necessarily in the best interest of the whole nation.

Two contending segments divide the political structure in the U.S. into what I call elite democracy and participatory democracy. **Elite democracy** can be defined as democracy in which elites manipulate the democratic process for their own self-interest and control. They exert their influence by channeling huge sums of campaign donations to buy the allegiance of supportive politicians. The way our election process in the U.S. has evolved is that politicians desperately need large sums of money to mount expensive campaigns for offices ranging from city council to president. Money pours into the advertising media where candidates portray their carefully honed message as benign and good for the public interest but in reality it serves the interest of the elites providing large campaign donations. The politicians then promote the elites' particular self-serving agenda such as privatization of community-owned assets, economic growth without regard for the environment, and military power to exert dominance throughout the world. Virtually all members of Congress and executive-branch policymakers are members of the top 1 percent when they arrive, are kept in office by money from the top 1 percent, and know that if they serve the top 1 percent well they will be aptly rewarded when they leave office.[105]

In contrast to elite democracy, **participatory democracy** attempts to check the abuses of elite democracy and corporate and political power with regulatory legislation and careful oversight of the whole process. Increasingly, participatory democracy takes the form of involvement by citizen groups who are playing a "watchdog" role over giant corporations in an effort to curb their financial excesses and detrimental corporate policies.

The citizens of the U.S. are proud of their democratic institutions and traditions, their open society, and their freedoms. We have the freedom to choose our elected representatives, participate in the political process, and voice our concerns in non-violent protests. Many of these freedoms are the envy of the world. Yet, our economic system – neoliberal capitalism – is not an open system. I once worked for Xerox as a temporary employee, but I was not able to vote for the CEO, nor could I partake in the organizational meetings to give my input. Although Xerox treated me well, it was still a closed system. Economist Peter Barnes explains: "The reason capitalism distorts democracy is simple. Democracy is an open system, and economic power can easily infect it. By contrast, capitalism is a gated system; the masses cannot easily access its bastions. Capital's primacy thus isn't an accident. It's what happens when capitalism inhabits democracy." For example, Congress and the executive branch have allowed the regulatory agencies to be co-opted by the industries they were intended to regulate.[106]

Interestingly, capitalism has taken on the trimmings of democracy, at least superficially. What the founding fathers considered vital first amendment rights for individuals corporations have now appropriated. As in the 1886 Supreme Court Case – *Santa Clara County vs. Southern Pacific Railroad* – the maneuverers of a clerk awarded corporations personhood status. A recent ruling in 2009 further extended the First Amendment rights of corporations. In *Citizens United v. Federal Election Commission*, No. 08-205 – a bitterly divided Supreme Court ruled in a 5-4 decision that the government may not ban political spend-

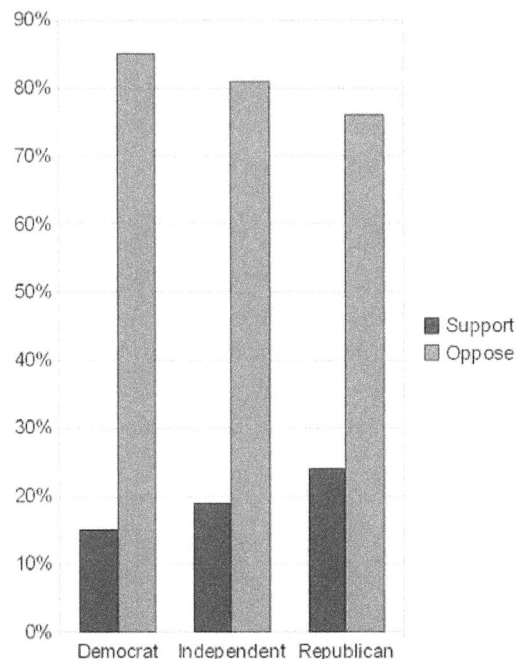

**FEDERAL ELECTION COMMISSION/ABC-WASHINGTON POST POLL RESULTS OF PEOPLE'S REACTION TO CITIZENS UNITED COURT RULING.**

ing by corporations in elections. The Supreme Court's majority said of the First Amendment: the government has no business regulating political speech. The dissenting justices argued that allowing corporate money to flood the political marketplace would corrupt democracy. The case has enshrined the right of corporations to buy government, by removing limitations on campaign spending. The ruling overturned several Congressional laws that sought to regulate corporate and union campaign contributions; this ruling represented a sharp doctrinal shift, and it has (and will have) major political and practical consequences in the way elections are conducted.[107]

### Questions to Consider

1. In what ways do you see "dollar democracy" being played out on the political stage?

## CONCLUDING INSIGHTS: THE TEN CONSEQUENCES OF NEOLIBERALISM

I have included in this chapter the 10 consequences or impacts of neoliberalism that I think are the most significant and destructive. You may ask, "Didn't anything good come out of neoliberal policies?" What about the internet, the technological achievements, and the amazing drugs we now have to save people's lives? I would agree that the above three examples are truly noteworthy and have had a positive impact on my life and many others I am sure. But government funding created the internet at one of the state-supported research universities, the University of Illinois. Also, the government funds much of the research for new life-saving medical drugs at research institutions. Philosophically, neoliberal policies do not support government sponsored research and development (R & D).

Although neoliberal policies have profoundly shaped government policy since 1980, the vestiges of managed capitalism have not been displaced altogether. There are still public schools, government funding for research, public parks, regulations, and many other aspects of managed capitalism. But neoliberal policies have been whittling away at managed capitalism for decades. Neoliberal principles were not set in place overnight; even though their supporters have made major headway in implementing their agenda, they have not had smooth sailing – there has been resistance on many fronts.

The U.S. at the time of this writing is in a ferocious gridlock. The forces supporting neoliberalism are locked in a heated war to preserve as much of their agenda as possible, such as the Bush era tax cuts for the elite, and to push their agenda even more, such as the elimination of bargaining by public sector state unions. Will the neoliberal agenda prevail? The cards are stacked in their favor.

### Questions to Consider

1. Do you think the 10 impacts of neoliberalism on American society are justified? Explain your answer.

# CHAPTER FIVE

# The Economic Globalization Puzzle: Ten Pieces

"We have a tug-of-war, really, between a domestic economy and a global economy."

*Bill Gross, founder and investor PIMCO Bond Investments*

## Is Economic Globalization Good or Bad?
## It Depends on Your Point of View.

Think of economic globalization as a train, a fast moving train. If you are lucky and can catch the train and take a good seat, then economic globalization seems like a great idea. But if you are on the tracks trying to catch the train, and it is not stopping to pick you up, then economic globalization is not all it's cracked up to be. If you own stock in a publicly traded company, then you cheer for economic globalization when the stock market goes up and your stock is worth more than yesterday. But if you work for that publicly-traded company and the stock jumped because you and your co-workers didn't get a raise, which meant there was more money on the profit bottom line but less money in your pocket, then you might not cheer for economic globalization. If you have a business that imports washing machines made in China for a good price that you can turn-around and sell to U.S. consumers for a sizable profit, then you might cheer economic globalization. But if you are a worker in the U.S. factory that made the washing machines that is now closed down because the jobs went to China, then you won't cheer for economic globalization. If you are a farmer in a periphery country that relies on free irrigation water to grow your crops, and then the water rights are bought up by a multinational corporation (MNC), which means that you now have to pay for water, then you would curse economic globalization. But if you are an investor in the multinational water company and you are making good returns on your investment, then you might praise economic globalization. In other words, your opinion of economic globalization depends on your point of view. Ask different people from different walks of life, and you are bound to get different answers.

# AN INTRODUCTION TO ECONOMIC GLOBALIZATION

Promoters of economic globalization often say that it is the result of economic forces that evolved and progressed over centuries to the present form, as if they were forces of nature destined to occur. Promoters cry that you can't go back, you must go forward. They persuaded nations, some say duped, into playing the economic globalization game, with the threat that if they do not participate in the global marketplace, they will be left behind and their countries will be mired in poverty. The metaphor of the train leaving the station illustrated in the story above is used to describe this phenomenon. If your nation is not on the economic globalization train, then you will be left behind at the station. Therefore, you must jump on board the globalization express for the fast ride to economic riches.

We have seen economic globalization played out during the 1896-1914 classical era of capitalism. The world operated according to classical economic principles, held in place by the gold standard, and directed by the maestro of the orchestra: Great Britain. Although Britain pushed other countries to follow free trade principles and remove tariffs, the system continued to operate despite such rebellious tariff-protected countries as the U.S. However, the economic integration of the world during that period of history pales in comparison to today. While classical economic principles have existed since the 19th century, economic globalization today is not an exact replica of the past. It has emerged from a set of institutions, rules, philosophy, and practices that supporters have purposely honed for the goal of spreading economic globalization to as many parts of the world as possible.

During the crisis of the 1970s there were three responses to the economic turmoil in the U.S.: neoliberalism, economic globalization, and financialization. While the previous two chapters focused on the formation of neoliberalism in the U.S. and its subsequent impact on American society, and chapters 7 and 8 deal with financialization, this chapter and the next looks at economic globalization.

Economic globalization refers to the increasing integration and expansion of the capitalist economy around the world. In this system, trade, investment, business, capital, financial flows, production, management, markets, movement of labor (although somewhat restricted), information, competition, and technology are carried out across local and national boundaries on a world stage, subsuming many national and local economies into an integrated economic system. There is also a growing concentration of wealth and influence of multi-national corporations, huge financial institutions, and state-run enterprises. Economic globalization operates according to capitalist principles, but there are different versions of capitalism. Indeed, neoliberalism is just one version. I introduced in chapter 1 a version of capitalism called state capitalism. Again, state capitalism is a system in which the state plays the role of leading economic actor and uses markets primarily for political gain and public wealth. These governments micromanage entire sectors of their economies to promote their national interests and to protect their domestic political standing.

Economic globalization incorporates different national economies into its economic web. The U.S. and Europe (to a lesser extent) promote neoliberalism as the favored economic system but, for example, China, Russia, Brazil, and India favor a more state-capitalist model. National economies follow their own version of capitalism, which may range from participating very little in the capitalist economy to full emersion of their national economy into the world economy. For example, Cuba is a socialist country yet exports sugar on the world market. Venezuela has prided itself in repudiating the U.S. and its policies of neoliberalism but gladly sells its oil to the U.S. on the world market.

Many nations differ in their national and cultural interpretations of how capitalism should operate. For example, some nations with long histories of mercantile activity and trade wish to maintain their traditional market economy. For example, in Iran the *bazaaris* or merchants that sell goods at the *souk* or marketplace have followed this market economy tradition for hundreds of years. If Iran would "open up" to competitive, economic globalization and neoliberal restructuring, the *bazaaris* and *souks* would give way to big-box chain stores that would offer more "choices" of consumer items but would ultimately drive the *bazaaris* out of business. For the time being, Iranian politicians have favored supporting the *bazaaris*. However, the Iranian economy is in dire straits with high unemployment that ranged from 11 to 16 percent through the 2000s.[1]

Certain factors are necessary for economic globalization to function. I have organized these factors into 10 puzzle pieces that when pieced together make up an economic globalization puzzle. All of the puzzle pieces are necessary for the full picture of economic globalization to emerge. Take away any one of the pieces and you don't have a complete picture or the system does not operate smoothly. Using a systems approach, let's look at each of these separate pieces of the whole picture.

ONE OF THE GATES TO THE GRAND BAZAAR IN TEHRAN, IRAN. ALTHOUGH ITS ECONOMIC INFLUENCE HAS DIMINISHED SOMEWHAT IN RECENT YEARS, IT REMAINS THE LARGEST MARKET OF ITS KIND IN THE WORLD.

When I first started to write and teach about economic globalization, it was easy to differentiate between the core and periphery. The core countries – the United States, the European Union countries (EU), Japan, Canada, and Australia – had all the economic pieces in place to give them an advantage. They, along with MNCs, made the rules of economic globalization to favor them. The big players on the economic stage were MNCs who took advantage of the middle and periphery countries' cheap labor and access to their raw materials. During the 1990s and 2000s the mantra was economic globalization would be good for the core countries. There might be a period of transition to endure, but all looked rosy in the future. Although many manufacturing and low-skilled jobs would be lost, the government would retrain these workers as high-skilled service workers and reap the benefits of economic globalization. This has not been the case. In fact, I argue that economic globalization has hurt the core countries, except for the top 10 percent.

## Ten Pieces of the Economic Globalization Puzzle

1. Reduce the Local and Self Reliance
2. Economic Growth
3. Promoting Network
4. Rules
5. Free Trade
6. Privatization and Commodification
7. Corporate and State Enterprise Concentration
8. Specialization
9. Squeeze Labor
10. Military Hegemony

Some middle and periphery nations have manipulated economic globalization to seize an economic advantage for themselves. Even though some middle and periphery countries are profiting from economic globalization, there are vast differences in prosperity among its citizens. On the other hand, many of the core countries are reeling with high unemployment rates and excessive debt. This is not how economic globalization enthusiasts in the core countries envisioned the outcome.

The rest of this chapter will examine the economic globalization puzzle pieces more closely. You may be surprised to find that many of the puzzle pieces are similar to the dozen ingredients in the neoliberal stew. As mentioned in chapter 3, one of the purposes of neoliberals is to spread their version of capitalism to as many parts of the world as possible. They have been successful in many countries, but still many areas have adopted state capitalist principles or have a more managed capitalist

**The Economic Globalization Puzzle**

economy. For example, Europe continues with many principles of managed capitalism or social democracy in which sectors of the economy, such as education and health care, are either socialized or heavily managed by the government. Many also provide a safety net for those who are unemployed or fall on hard times. Even in the U.S. some political factions, such as progressive Democrats, have fought against the neoliberal agenda. Cuba, a long-time socialist country, is now planning to shed inefficient, state-run enterprises and is introducing changes into its economy. Economic globalization does not neatly package the world into just a neoliberal version, which makes studying this subject challenging but also fascinating. Join with me now in investigating these 10 puzzle pieces that make up economic globalization.

---

**Questions to Consider**

1. Have you benefitted or not benefitted from economic globalization?

---

## PUZZLE PIECE #1: A REDUCTION OF LOCAL COMMUNITIES AND SELF-RELIANCE

In the first piece of the economic globalization puzzle, there is a push is to reduce local, community, and national self-reliance and replace it with integration into and dependence upon the global economy. Self-reliance, introduced in chapter 3, is reliance on an individual's own efforts and abilities, which also refers to communities and nations. I prefer to use the word self-reliance rather than self-sufficient, which are those who are not dependent upon outside areas for their livelihood, food or other essential items. Very few areas of the world are totally self-sufficient; a way of life that is fast disappearing. Reducing self-reliance means replacing small, local businesses with large mega-stores owned by those outside the community and replaces small, local, agriculture with industrial-scale agriculture owned by large corporate holdings. I also include in this section the reduction in the importance of the sovereign nation.

Large corporations do not profit from self-reliant communities. Therefore, one of the first targets of those promoting economic globalization is to integrate local, self-sufficient agriculture into the world economic system. Until recently, most of the world's people were farmers; today only one in eight people in the world is a farmer.[2] Economic globalization pushes farmers to abandon their land and community and engage in some way in the capitalist, urban economy. If farmers remain on the land, they are pressured into giving up subsistence agriculture and work as laborers on large monocrop plantations geared to export-oriented production. The plantations specialize in particular cash crops that the owners sell on the world market. For example, in China there has been a policy shift from supporting agriculture in the countryside to favoring industry in the urban centers. Hence, poverty has increased in rural areas resulting in a mass exodus of farmers to the cities to find work in construction or factories.

Local or regional self-reliance undermines economic globalization. Global corporations make no money when local economies care for or feed themselves. It is much more lucrative for corporations to have each country ship a massive volume of commodities across miles of oceans and receive goods on ships that pass each other in the night. During the 1980s and 1990s, the World Bank and the International Monetary Fund applied tremendous pressure to countries to abandon their practices of self-reliance and to instead specialize in producing a number of commodities for export.

The following historical example illustrates how the transition from self-reliance to integration into the global economy took place in Africa during the heyday of imperialism 1870-1914.

Most Africans neither joined nor fought Europeans colonizers; they tried to continue living as they had been for centuries. But they found this increasingly difficult to do; colonial rule disrupted every aspect of their traditional society. Colonial rulers handled access to land use, commercial transactions, and legal disputes very differently from the way they had been in the past, and traditional rulers lost all authority, except where Europeans used them as local administrators. Changes in landholding were especially disruptive, since most Africans were farmers or herders for whom access to land was a necessity of life. In places with a high population density, such as Egypt and West Africa, the colonial rulers left peasants in place but encouraged them to grow cash crops and then collected taxes on the product of their labor. Elsewhere, the new rulers declared any land that Africans did not farm to be "waste" or "vacant" land and gave it to private concession companies or to European planters and ranchers. Thus, Africans found themselves squatters, sharecroppers, or ranch hands on land where they had grown crops or raised animals for generations. In the worst cases, as in South Africa, colonial rulers forced Africans off their lands and onto "reserves," like Native Americans in the U.S.

While the colonial rulers harbored designs on the land, they were also interested in African labor. But they did not want to pay wages high enough to attract workers voluntarily. Instead, they imposed various taxes, such as the hut tax or the head tax, which Africans had to pay, regardless of their economic situation. To find the money to pay the tax, Africans had little choice but to accept whatever wage-paying work the Europeans offered, no matter how poorly paid. Colonizers recruited Africans to work on plantations, railroads, and other modern enterprises at exceedingly low pay. In South African mines, mine owners paid African on average one-tenth as much as European miners.

Despite the low wages, many Africans left their rural villages for cities and mining camps. Many migrated great distances and stayed away for years at a time. Most migrant workers were men who left their wives and children behind in villages or on reserves. In some cases, the authorities did not allow them to bring their families and settle permanently in the towns. This caused great hardship for African women, who had to grow food for their families during the men's absences. On the whole, African women suffered more than men from the economic changes. Almost all the jobs that were open to Africans, even those considered "women's work" in Europe such as nursing or domestic service, were reserved for men. Colonial rulers also replaced traditional African communal property rights with the modern concept of private property. They assigned property rights to the head of the household: men. Colonizers duped many men into selling their private property to pay taxes or get a little extra money.

Traditionally Africans consumed their own locally produced crops. But with integration into the global economy, there was an effort to shift farm production from local consumption to specialized crops for export. Since the marketplace paid small farmers the world price for their specialized cash crops, in effect the small African farmer was competing with other farmers around the world. Many small farmers could not make a living doing this and either sold their farm land to large landowners and moved to cities or became a hired hand on their former land.

This scenario is not particular to Africa in the late 19th century, but has been repeated untold times through modern history. Former colonies depended upon on a few export crops or raw materials to wealthy core countries. Even after former colonies became independent nations, many were encouraged to continue with the same economic system as under years of colonial rule. Today, the economies of the world's periphery nations remain in a deteriorated state.

Economic globalization has ushered in a global transfer of economic and political power away from national governments and into the hands of global corporations. The same can be said in state capitalist countries where the power of state enterprises is expanding. The modern nation state traces its roots back to the British Glorious Revolution (1688), the American Revolution (1776-1783) and the French Revolution (1789-1815). Modern institutions such as elected representatives, a separate judicial system, and an executive branch are all derived from these momentous events.

Economic globalization presents difficult challenges of governance to nations. The political organization of sovereign (independent) nations seems well intact in the first decade of the 21st century, but national boundaries alone no longer confine its economies. Nations participating in the global economy must follow its rules and regulations, such as the WTO rules, that supersede national law. For example, according to European Union rules, economically struggling nations such as Greece and Ireland must adhere to the Euro as their currency, not their own local currencies. Economic globalization undercuts managed capitalism and a nation's efforts to legislate equalizing mechanisms. By undermining national institutions that counter economic globalization, the owners of capital have been able to move the economic system back more than a century to an era when property rights were paramount and offsetting social rights nonexistent.[3]

---

**Questions to Consider**

1. Why are large corporations and state enterprises targeting local, self-reliant and independent national economies with managed capitalism for integration into the world economy? Are they successful?

---

# PUZZLE PIECE #2: ECONOMIC GROWTH

One impact of neoliberalism in the U.S. has been an obsession with economic growth, puzzle piece #2. Economic globalization supporters have latched onto the growth mantra as a way to measure the "progress" of the world's economy and as a way to "lift" the world out of poverty and into the middle class. In a 2010 interview, former U.S. Treasury Secretary, Timothy Geithner, discussed the health of the U.S. economy. But it was impossible for him to limit his discussion to just the national economy, he also had to include the world economy, since the two are inextricably linked, he stated. He was clearly relying on growth as a way to pull the U.S. out of its recession and to stimulate the world economy as well. At 50 I lost track of the number of times he mentioned the word "growth" in the hour long interview. One could not miss what he considered to be the best approach to solving

PRESIDENT OF AN AGRICULTURAL COOPERATIVE IN GUINEA, AFRICA IN AN ONION FIELD. PRACTICING SUBSISTENCE AGRICULTURE.

economic problems. I could not help but question his over-emphasis on growth as an answer to all economic difficulties.[4]

Why such an emphasis on growth? The purpose of growth is supposedly to ensure that more people are able to have a comfortable standard of living because an expanding economy will include more people under its wings of prosperity. However, I find that there are three important outcomes of growth that are rarely discussed in mainstream circles: growth and inequality, the impact of growth on the environment, and growth and well-being. I will cover all of these topics in chapter 6.

# PUZZLE PIECE #3: THE PROMOTING NETWORK

The fourth piece of the economic globalization puzzle is what I call the promoting network. It consists of three different entities that promote economic globalization: consumerism and advertising, media, and education. This interlocking promoting network has a message that economic globalization is good for everyone, and helps promote the existing system of growth.

## 1. Consumerism and Advertising

Consumerism has become a dominant ideology today, in fact, a new world religion. A key requirement for economic globalization to exist and expand is a well-entrenched consumer society. The world's consumers must continue to buy things, and the marketplaces needs to add new consumer products every year for the economy, as it is structured, to continue to grow. The act of consuming material goods and services instills certain behaviors and values in those who participate in this experience. Advertising agencies, whose job it is to encourage people to consume certain products, create and reinforce consumer behaviors. Critics argue that consumer-focused values promote instant gratification, perpetual discontentment, individualism, selfishness, and acquisitiveness. Consumers have a need for constant stimulation, exhibit restlessness, experience mood ups and downs, and think of outward appearance as most important. Consumers are always looking for something new and throwing away what is old. However, these values and behaviors transcend just consuming inanimate objects and carry over into how relationships are conducted, how our political process is carried out, and how our cultural and social traditions are played out. If the consumer isn't pleased, the product is disposable.

Most of us, including myself, want to enjoy a comfortable living standard and modern conveniences that makes our lives easier and more enjoyable. But the wobbly line between what enhances our well-being and what is too much is not easily determined. It varies with each one of us. I am not here to tell you where that line is, even if I could. In fact, that line has wavered throughout my life. As mentioned in the story I told you in the last chapter, for many years I was very satisfied living a simple life. Then in 1983, I started my own gift and decorating business. Twice a year my business partner and I went to gift shows to purchase merchandise for the next season. Suddenly all the merchandise at the gift shows glittered like gold and my personal con-

**AUDI SPORTS CAR SHOWCASED AT THE AIRPORT IN XIAN, CHINA.**
PHOTO DENISE AMES

sumption significantly increased. I not only consumed the merchandise myself, I bought consumer items for others to consume! Truly, it was a consumers' delight. At first I was happy decorating my house and making it stylish and comfortable for my family. I also enjoyed showcasing our business purchases at our small retail shop. But then I found that the glitter of consumption began to tarnish after a few years. I experienced the constant discontent that often accompanies the overly active consumer – no consumer items gave me fulfillment anymore. I had already decorated my house and my closets were full. What next? I yearned again for a simpler life, and I wanted to pursue what I considered more meaningful work. I sold my business and decided to return to the education field after a 12 year absence. I enrolled at Illinois State University to pursue my graduate degrees and taught there as well. My dalliance with passionate consumerism is a story often repeated in the U.S., as well as in some places throughout the world. It reminds us that we, including myself, need to be aware of the psychological pull of consumerism and how it can affect our lives.

The world is consuming goods and services at an unsustainable pace with serious consequences for the well-being of people and the planet. Around 1.7 billion people worldwide – more than a quarter of humanity – have entered the consumer class, adopting the diets, transportation systems, and lifestyles that were limited to the rich nations of Europe, North America, and Japan during most of the last century. In China alone, 240 million people have joined the consumer ranks.[5]

### 2. The Media

The world media system inculcates the consumerist ideology. The systematic blurring of the lines between information, entertainment, and promotion of products lies at the heart of the media. The dominant ideology indoctrinates audiences from an early age onward, creating the consumer demand necessary for the survival of capitalism. The public mass media has transformed their content into opportunities to sell ideas, values, and products.[6] Powerful corporations are major influences on the media. In many markets, major MNCs own media stations and outlets, while ownership is becoming ever more concentrated as mega-mergers take hold. An effect of this concentration is a reduction in diversity and depth of content for the public, while increasing the corporate message. Ownership interests may affect what is and is not covered. Stories can end up being biased or omitted so as not to offend advertisers or owners. As we all know, an informed population is a crucial element to a well-functioning democracy, but now corporate media concentration threatens that democracy.

Many of the large media company owners are entertainment companies and have vertical integration across various industries, such as distribution networks, toys and clothing manufacture, and retailing. Vertical integration gives the big players even more avenues to cross-sell and cross-market their products.

While this means that it is good for their business, the diversity of opinions and issues

### World's Largest Media Conglomerates
*(Fortune 500, 2010)*

| Company | Revenues in $ million | Profits in $ million |
|---|---|---|
| Walt Disney | $38,063 | $3,963 |
| News Corp | $32,778 | $2,539 |
| Time Warner | $26,888 | $2,578 |
| CBS | $14,059 | $ 724 |
| Viacom | $13,497 | $1,548 |

discussed suffers. For example, one cannot expect Disney to report on sweatshop labor when it is accused of being involved in such things itself.[7]

### 3. Education

I am including education as the third factor in the promoting network. You may find this a bit odd that I am making the argument that our educational system today promotes economic globalization. Since many of you may be students or educators you may find this a controversial assertion. I would like to make two points in making my case: 1. Education is increasingly focusing on training for specialized jobs in a highly competitive globalized society and 2. Corporations are having a greater influence as our educational system is becoming increasingly privatized.

First, you may assert that it is the mission of educators to train students to find a specialized job in a highly competitive global economy. I don't disagree, but I might add that the primary focus on specialized training has left a yawning gap in students' understanding of the world in which they live. Instead, some educators train students to be mere robots in a globalized economy, competing for the scraps thrown to them by the corporate world. The message of competition, individualism, and consumption is ubiquitous and drummed in with every billboard or 30 second commercial message on television. What is to counter this constant drumbeat? Not much, especially if educators renege on their job of fostering critical and creative thinking and promoting global awareness.

Second, corporations are exerting a greater influence on our educational system. For example, the creation of partnering university/industrial research centers during the past 25 years and the prominent place of businesspeople on university boards of directors shows corporate influence. At the university level, corporations now fund university chairs, departments, and research. Research support gradually shapes the curriculum and hiring of faculty. For example, in 2007 global energy giant British Petroleum (BP) selected the University of California, Berkeley and the University of Illinois, to lead an unprecedented $500 million research effort to develop new sources of energy and reduce the impact of energy consumption on the environment.[8]

The right to free, public education is also being eroded in countries around the world. Colleges and universities have become increasingly obvious channels for corporate training, recruitment and ideological penetration. Textbooks are using corporate logos in their exercises, and corporations provide free materials for student use. The idea reigns that students are "customers" who come to schools and colleges looking to purchase a commodity and expect the grades to reflect their financial investment.

## PUZZLE PIECE #4: MAKING THE RULES OF ECONOMIC GLOBALIZATION: THE WORLD BANK AND THE INTERNATIONAL MONETARY FUND (IMF)

Our national economy needs rules to run smoothly. But today our economic boundaries have expanded beyond the national economy to envelop the world. You may be surprised to learn that often the rules that guide a national economy are at odds with the rules that direct a global economy. But the big question is: "Who makes these rules?"

If you think that it is difficult for economic rules to be instituted at the national level, think about the how complicated it is at the global level. All kinds of diverse groups want the economy to benefit them! My argument is that the global economy should operate fairly, justly and sustainably, and bring prosperity and well-being to as many people as possible. Therefore, when I examine the global economy, I look for ways in which it accomplishes these ideals. If it fails, I am critical of it. So who makes the rules for the global economy and what are these rules? These are the very two questions that we will address next.

Close to the end of World War II, the main victors – U.S., Great Britain, Soviet Union and France – wanted to take proactive steps to avoid another catastrophic war and to ensure the depression would not return. U.S. and Britain wanted capitalism to be the dominant economic system on the global stage and not Soviet-style communism. The leaders held several strategic meetings during the war to establish a peaceful and prosperous postwar order. The meetings culminated at Bretton Woods, New Hampshire.

The rules for the global economy have a birth date, July 1944, and a birth place, Bretton Woods resort. The 730 delegates from all 44 Allied nations were the world's leading economists, politicians, bankers and corporate figures, all gathered together to forge a new economic order. Of all the participating nations, only the U.S. emerged economically stronger at the end of the war than before; therefore, they were able to direct the terms of the post-war rules. Led by the well-regarded British economist John Maynard Keynes and his U.S. counterpart, Harry Dexter White, they decided that a new centralized global economic system was required to accelerate worldwide economic development. And that the best way to implement this plan would be to create new institutions and rules. The new institutions were the World Bank, the International Monetary Fund (IMF), and soon after (1948), the General Agreement on Tariff and Trade (GATT), which would evolve into the World Trade Organization (WTO) in 1995. The purpose of the World Bank is to loan money to economically developing countries who must repay with interest. The IMF regulates monetary flows around the world to insure stability. From 1948 on, the rules of GATT regulated global trade, but it was mainly limited to manufactured goods.

The World Bank and the IMF were the brainchild of U.S. economist Harry Dexter White, who led the negotiations on post-war economic reconstruction. Since the U.S. was the world's leading creditor at the time, he insisted that the new institutions would place the burden of stabilizing the world economy on the countries suffering from debt and trade deficits rather than on the creditors. He insisted that the more money you put in, the more votes you have and that the U.S. should have enough votes to block any decision. Both the undemocratic voting arrangement and the U.S. veto remain to this day. White also insisted that national debts be redeemable for gold, and that gold would be convertible into dollars; thus, all exchange rates would be fixed against the dollar.[9] White also decided that both the IMF and the World Bank would be located in Washington D.C.

Because of the scale of its contribution, the United States has always had a dominant voice and has exercised an effective veto even though national economies were free to pursue their own strategies of development, whether state-led or private. At the time, all the major Western governments – center left or center right – were committed to domestic policies anchored in a managed version of capitalism to balance market goals with social goals.[10] The President of the World Bank is by tradition an American, and the IMF President is a European. Periphery countries have relatively little power within the institutions, while core countries decided what programs and policies to finance. The rest of this section examines the World Bank and IMF, while the next section will look into the WTO.

## The World Bank

The **World Bank** provides loans to developing countries for capital programs with the stated goal of reducing poverty. By law, a commitment to promote foreign investment and international trade, and assist in capital investment guides its decisions.[11] In the postwar years, the World Bank underwrote reconstruction loans in Europe, so that redevelopment did not depend on the whim of short-term private financing and, thus, Europe was steered in the direction of capitalism instead of communism. After an initial focus on Western Europe, the World Bank shifted its lending toward the periphery countries. Now its primary focus was to help middle and periphery countries develop their natural resources, obtain clean water, escape poverty and enter the modern economy. The World Bank projects undertaken – dams, harbors, and highways – helped them become fully enfolded into the global economy but required so much capital that private enterprise shied away from the investment.

From 1968 to 1980, the size and number of loans to borrowing nations greatly increased. The customary loans for infrastructure expanded into loans for social services and other sectors. Robert McNamara, appointed World Bank president in 1968 by U.S. President Lyndon Johnson, ushered in these changes. McNamara shifted bank policy toward measures such as building schools and hospitals, improving literacy and reforming agriculture. In addition to core nations' banks as the source of funding, McNamara added the global bond market as a new source of funding to increase the capital available for lending. However, this increase in lending was contributing to the rapid rise of debt among periphery nations. From 1976 to 1980 their world debt rose at an average annual rate of 20 percent.[12]

In the 1970s, the World Bank and other world financial institutions loaned fistfuls of money to periphery nations, especially in Africa and Latin America; these loans added little to their economic development and saddled these nations with a huge debt burden to repay in the 1980s and beyond. This debt proved difficult to repay because of rising interest rates and a general slowdown in the world economy. Lending to service third world debt marked the period of 1980-1989.

The World Bank's lending intentions appeared to be commendable; however, the reality of its lending is another matter. The focus has mostly been to loan governments money to build infrastructure – railroads, highways, electric power plants, airports, bridges, ports, dams, communication networks – and parts of the economy that are not profitable for private companies to build. Largely ignored are smaller-scale, less-expensive, and locally-appropriate alternatives. Since many of these projects require large-scale contractors and equipment to do the work, the loan recipients almost always require the materials and technical expertise of large corporate contractors from the core countries. Keep in mind that investors in the core countries largely finance the World Bank by selling bonds, and the World Bank in turn must collect interest and principle from the public sector, the taxpayers of the countries

**WORLD BANK HEADQUARTERS**
**IN WASHINGTON D.C., USA**

who are receiving the loans. Thus, the World Bank tends to finance bigger, more expensive projects which support large corporations in the core countries and multinational investors. It also contributed to the debt peonage of the periphery. The U.S. Treasury Department calculates that for every $1 contributed to international development banks, U.S. exporters win back more than $2 in bank-financed procurement contracts.[13]

### The International Monetary Fund (IMF)

The **International Monetary Fund** is one of the world's most powerful institutions – yet few know how it really works. The IMF is the "manager" of the international credit system. The IMF was established with the mandate to regulate an international monetary system based on convertible currencies (currencies were pegged to the US dollar), to use its reserve of funds to lend to countries experiencing temporary balance of payment problems, and to facilitate global trade while leaving sovereign governments in charge of their own monetary, fiscal, and international investment policies. Leaders of the IMF reasoned that its policies would benefit all trading nations.[14]

The Bretton Woods agreement in the post-war years designed the IMF to encourage economic growth rather than deflation. Governments pegged and managed exchange rates so that national economies were not at the mercy of private speculative capital movements. Unlike today, with fixed exchange rates there were no speculative markets in international currencies because no profits could be extracted from currency exchanges. The IMF helped nations that fell into temporary balance-of-payments problems; therefore, they didn't have to deflate their currencies in order to balance their economies, a drag on the entire system. The IMF puts pressure on surplus, creditor nations to expand their economies, rather than on deficit countries to contract their economies.[15]

Like the World Bank, the IMF is not a democracy where each member country has an equal vote. The amount of money each country pays into the IMF's quota system determines its voting power; thus, the core countries direct decision-making. It's a system of one dollar, one vote. The U.S. is the largest shareholder with a quota of 18 percent. Germany, Japan, France, Great Britain, and the U.S. combined control about 38 percent. The lopsided power held by wealthy countries typically means that the interests of bankers, investors and corporations from core countries are put above the periphery countries.[16] The IMF gets its budget from assessments of member governments, and interest it receives from loans.[17]

In the 1980s, the IMF morphed from the Bretton Woods goal of creating an institution intended to anchor growth and mixed market systems into one that served mainly private creditors' interests. According to critics such as Robert Kuttner, "The IMF began promoting a model based on financial speculation, seeking to impose a single brand of neoliberal capitalism on all nations." Kuttner goes on to claim that the "approved IMF model included low taxes, especially on capital; low social outlay; conservative fiscal policies; and a strategy of financial market opening that placed the interests of private finance far above the interests of small nations."[18] Neoliberalism influences IMF policies.

The IMF formula was known as the **Washington Consensus**, named for the three institutions that shaped its policies, all located in downtown Washington D.C.: IMF, World Bank, and the U.S. Treasury. Any nation that got into balance-of-payments difficulties in the 1980s or 1990s had to agree to a program of "market opening," especially their financial markets, as well as budgetary austerity, in order to qualify for an IMF bailout. The IMF seal, in turn, certified the debtor nation as worthy of taking on additional private debt. The IMF recipe did nothing for long-term development and resulted in extreme debt for the debtor nations. In fact, the middle and periphery nations that thrived in the 1980s and early 1990s were those of East Asia, with managed financial markets that had rejected the Washington Consensus prescriptions.[19]

Since the debt crisis of the 1980s, the IMF has assumed the role of bailing out countries during financial crises, which have been caused in large part by currency speculation that became rampant after 1980. The IMF has issued emergency loan packages tied to certain conditions, referred to as a **Structural Adjust Policy** (SAP). However, only after the recipients of the funds have agreed to economic policy reforms are the loans made available – in short, to implement a structural adjustment program (SAP). Part of the SAP is that the IMF decides how much debtor countries can spend on education, health care, and environmental protection, which most often is a reduced amount from their previous budgets.

If the indebted nations are unable to pay back the loans (must be paid back in US dollars) they were encouraged to borrow, they are subject to what critics of the SAP tellingly call a "**golden straight-jacket**." The SAP rules – the straight-jacket – mandate indebted nations to open their markets to development, thus inviting foreign corporations to participate in their national economies, and they must sell their natural resources at world market prices to anyone who wishes to purchase them. The IMF also expects them to cut government funded social programs, which usually means medical care and education. Money generated from these efforts is used for repayment of the debt to the World Bank or IMF. For two decades the IMF prescribed the same standardized medicine for troubled middle and periphery nations.

What are the consequences of standard IMF policy? The SAPs have provided core nations with cheap goods and resources, but for the vast majority of the periphery's people, these policies have been a disaster. An IMF paper found that countries following the standard IMF prescriptions for economic health tend to experience a "collapse in growth rates and significant financial crises." Another paper,

IN KEEPING WITH THE TRADITION, A EUROPEAN, CHRISTINE LAGARDE FROM FRANCE, WAS NAMED MANAGING DIRECTOR OF THE IMF ON JUNE 28, 2011, THE FIRST WOMAN DIRECTOR OF THE AGENCY.

### The Golden Straight Jacket [20]

1. Monetary Austerity. Tighten the money supply by raising interest rates to stabilize the local currency.

2. Fiscal Austerity. Increase tax collections and dramatically reduce government spending.

3. Privatization. Sell off public enterprises to the private sector.

4. Financial Liberalization. Remove restrictions on the inflow and outflow of international capital as well as restrictions on what foreign businesses and banks are allowed to buy, own, and operate.

Only when governments sign the SAP does the IMF agree to:

5. Lend Money, enough to prevent default on international loans that are about to come due.

6. Restructure the Debt among private international lenders, including a pledge of new loans.

produced by the United Nations, found that the 47 poorest countries in the world, which are most often fed IMF prescriptions, are poorer now than they were when the fund was founded in 1944.[21]

The predictable consequences for most residents of the countries that took out the loans have always been dismal. **Fiscal austerity** – raising taxes and reducing government spending – depresses demand, leading to reductions in output and increases in unemployment. Tight monetary policy and skyrocketing interest rates stop long-term productive investment in its tracks. It prevents many businesses from getting the kind of month to month loans needed to continue even ordinary operations. Job layoffs accompany the privatization of public utilities, transport, and banks. In its haste to reduce public sector budgets, the IMF has seldom taken the time to try and distinguish between poorly run and well run public enterprises. Surprisingly, there is little disagreement about the above effects. But the IMF claims that in the long run these policies will rebound to the benefit of the national economy and its residents. That prediction is based on the assumption that once the nation has gone through the necessary austerity steps to right its sunken economy, then revived exports, new international investments, and increased productivity will trickle down to everyone.[22]

The dirty little secret that no one wants to talk about is that the creators of IMF policy did not design it to help the majority of the people in troubled economies; it helps international creditors in the short run, and increases returns on global capital in the long run. When the IMF intervenes in a crisis, SAP policies are not sufficient to pay back all the creditors – particularly the ones whose loans are coming due immediately. That is where the second part of the IMF agreement comes in. The IMF loans the debtor country enough money to pay off the outstanding loans coming due in order to avoid default. Supposedly debtor countries will repay these loans once the beneficial effects of the SAP measures kick in.[23] IMF bailouts are not bailouts of debtor countries and their economies at all. That's just a popular misconception. International investors are actually the ones bailed out, because that is who gets the money in the end.

In recent years, the IMF has pulled back from its recipe of enforced austerity and mandatory market opening. After the East Asian collapse in the late 1990s, many governments vowed never again to work with the IMF. In the early 2000s, there was a quiet financial revolution in South America as Argentina and Brazil paid off the last of their debts to the IMF, and most Latin American countries have stopped doing business with the fund, whose outstanding loans are now a fraction of what they were at their peak.[24]

At the beginning of this section I asked the question, "Who makes the rules for the global economy." On this global playing field, MNCs have maneuvered to define the rules of international institutions like the World Bank, the IMF and World Trade Organization (WTO). Because rules made by these institutions take precedence over national laws, national enterprises are obliged to comply with them or risk economic ruin. Thus these three institutions have largely usurped national governmental oversight of global corporations. Let's turn to the next global rule making institution: the World Trade Organization (WTO).

## Questions to Consider

1. How have the World Bank and IMF policies hurt middle and periphery countries? How have they helped these countries? Which one outweighs the other?

## PUZZLE PIECE #5: FREE TRADE AND THE WORLD TRADE ORGANIZATION (WTO)

The ideological heart of economic globalization is #5 in our puzzle – free trade – or trade liberalization. Free traders demand that national governments eliminate regulations, laws, or tariffs that restrict trade across national borders. The goal of free trade is noble – global integration through trade in order to achieve a higher standard of living for all the world's people. Who can argue with that? However, in this section we will explore more than just the rosy surface of the global free trade debate.

When we think of free trade we usually think of goods imported and exported across national boundaries so that consumers can enjoy inexpensive clothes made in China, savor specialty cheese from France, pump cheap gasoline into our cars from Saudi Arabia, and take pleasure in movies from Hollywood. Free trade also involves trade in such services as insurance, accounting, legal, and sales. It includes patents that are used to protect inventors of medicines, music, books, and even seeds. Today free trade applies to capital – currency, stocks, bonds, and U.S. treasury bills – which is now traded at a higher volume than global trade in goods and services. Modern technology has made it possible to shift large sums of money instantaneously across borders anywhere in the world at the strike of a computer key.

In the historical debate between protective tariffs and free trade, several patterns have emerged. As we have seen in earlier chapters, one pattern is that a country that is just beginning to industrialize erects tariffs to protect their infant-industries in order for these industries to get off to a good start and not be crushed by competition. Britain and the U.S. are just two countries that have followed this policy in their early industrial stages.[25] For example, in 1699, the Wool Act in Britain prohibited the export of woolen products from its colonies; as a result the policy killed off the superior Irish wool industry because the British refused to import their products. In 1700, the British also banned the import of better-quality Indian cotton textiles (calicoes), devastating its efficient cotton-manufacturing sector.[26]

A second historic pattern to emerge is that the world's leading economy pushes for free trade, since it is able to produce the cheapest goods and services and it wants to sell its goods unimpeded across national borders. In the early 17th century, the Netherlands had the most advanced economy, and supported free trade. The British, after they had protected their infant-industries, were free trade cheerleaders in the 18th and 19th centuries. And the U.S., which was extremely protectionist throughout its history until recently, supported free trade policies, in varying degrees, in the post-war years and especially in the last 30 years.

A third pattern is that countries who specialize in a better and cheaper product than anywhere else usually favor free trade. For example, in the American South when "cotton was king" prior to the Civil War (1861-1865), Southerners fiercely shouted for free trade, since there

MAN CONTROLLING TRADE IN WASHINGTON D.C.

would be no export duties on their specialized export crop – cotton. As consumers, they would then be able to purchase tariff-free manufactured goods from Britain at a lower price than comparable U.S. goods.

A fourth pattern that has emerged in this free trade debate is that periphery and middle nations who would like to promote their infant industries using tariff protection, much like the U.S. did throughout most of its history, are unable to do so. With today's free trade rules it is difficult if not impossible for the periphery and middle countries to promote their infant industries.[27] Even the U.S. is unable to protect many of its established industries against cheaper imports from abroad. Steel is just one example. This is an important point since a close look at the historical record, shows that when today's core countries were developing their economies they used very few of the policies and institutions that they recommend to today's periphery countries. While it is often portrayed that the economic success of the U.S. and Britain is living proof of the superiority of free trade policies, in fact, they were often the most devoted users of protectionist trade and industrial policy measures in their early stages of development.[28]

Today the rules of the global marketplace are enforced by three major institutions: the World Bank and IMF, that we have already examined in the last section, and the third was established in 1995 to govern the global rules of free trade: the World Trade Organization (WTO).

## The World Trade Organization (WTO)

In the 1994 debate about the WTO in the U.S. Congress, consumer advocate Ralph Nader started asking whether members of Congress really knew about the world trade pact they were considering to vote on. Concerned that elected representatives had not read the agreement, Nader announced he would contribute $10,000 to the favorite charity of the first member of Congress who correctly answered 10 simple questions, in person, about the content of the WTO agreement and sign an affidavit that he or she had read it. He had one response – Republican Senator Hank Brown of Colorado, a free-trade advocate. Senator Brown correctly answered the questions posed to him, but after reading the whole document he had a change of heart. He stated that the anti-democratic provisions in the document so appalled him he decided to vote against the WTO agreement and urged everyone else to do so as well. What was in the document that caused such concern by a free-trade advocate who actually read it?

The General Agreement on Tariffs and Trade (GATT) was the precursor to the WTO. The Bretton Woods convention outlined the system in 1944 and 23 countries signed the agreement in 1948. Bretton Woods designed GATT to reduce and conform tariff rates among the major industrialized countries, but it mainly limited its rules to manufactured goods. Before Bretton Woods there was trade among nations, but most countries conducted trade through **bilateral trade deals**, which were one-on-one, country-to-country agreements.[29]

After Bretton Woods there was a more concerted global effort, led by private enterprises, to expand trade throughout the world. In response to this request, GATT hosted multi-year trade negotiations called rounds; the first six GATT rounds were limited to this objective. The seventh round in the 1970s, held in Tokyo, showed how the agreement's scope was expanding. At this time there was a push by corporations based in core countries for access to more unregulated and non-union labor, more consumer markets, and easier access to obtain cheap natural resources. Also, corporations pressured lawmakers to extend trade rules pertaining to manufactured goods to include regulating investments, services, copyright laws, patents, antidumping restrictions, and subsidies. The trend to expand the purview of GATT continued in another round of negotiations in Uruguay, known as the Uruguay Round, from 1986-1993. Along with a continuation of talks about the issues outlined above, trade officials had discussions concerning agricultural products, an area that had previously been considered "hands-off." They also started working to establish a permanent international body that would have the power to enforce GATT rules using monetary penalties. Trade officials would also delve into the service sector of the economy and tackle the thorny issue of intellectual property rights. Unbeknownst to most of the world's citizens, the formation of the WTO was being laid out.[30]

The WTO was born on January 1, 1995. It was originally an agreement among 125 countries, which has since expanded to 153 countries and now regulates 97 percent of world trade. Over 625 people staff the WTO headquartered in Geneva, Switzerland. The **World Trade Organization** deals with regulation of trade between participating countries; it provides a framework for negotiating and formalizing trade agreements, and a dispute resolution process aimed at enforcing participants' adherence to WTO agreements. The stated aims of the WTO are to promote free trade and stimulate economic growth.[31] The WTO operates on a one country, one vote system, but actual votes have never been taken. Decision making is generally done by consensus, and relative market size is the primary source of bargaining power. Therefore, the U.S. and EU have a powerful voice in WTO decision making.

Multinational banks and corporations were closely involved in writing the rules of the WTO and ensuring its passage in 1995. According to economic and political commentator Kevin Phillips, the U.S. fought for the formation of the WTO because, "The bottom line, from the standpoint of American multinational banks and corporations, was that the U.S. market had lost its old importance. Investment opportunities, production facilities, workers, and markets also had to be sought elsewhere, which would require the creation of a protective international legal and regulatory framework, one able to secure investment by overriding contrary local parochialism and procedures."[32]

The WTO's **Dispute Settlement Body** (DSB) is the official judicial branch of the organization. This body is comprised of panels of corporate and trade lawyers and officials who preside in secret hearings as final judges and arbiters of disputes among members. Unlike other international bodies, including the United Nations, the WTO has been granted sweeping enforcement powers. Under the DSB, any member nation can challenge any other member country's laws, if they view these laws as an impediment to free trade under WTO rules. The WTO does not make exception for a country's environmental, food safety, health or other laws that protect its citizen. If these protective laws violate free trade, then they must be eliminated, or the offending country must pay perpetual fines or face severe retaliatory trade sanctions.

WTO rulings by their arbitration panels are so powerful that they take precedence over all other international agreements, including labor agreements and environmental agreements such as the Kyoto Climate Change Accord. If there is disagreement, its rulings also override laws at every level of domestic governance, whether federal, state, regional, or local. It doesn't matter whether the domestic law has been in effect for decades.[33] When WTO standards rule that governments are non-compliant, then, economic and trade sanctions may result. Governments find it unwise to challenge WTO rules.

The WTO has such strong legislative authority that it is surprising that member nations should have granted such powers to an unelected, secretive global body. Critics such as Kevin Danaher argue that if the media had fully informed the public and the legislative bodies in the U.S. and other countries about the power global corporations and their bureaucracies were grabbing, there would be little chance that the WTO would be anything like its current form.[34]

One of the most controversial sections of the WTO is Article III, which prohibits countries from discriminating against goods based on "process and production methods." Critics say this provision denies countries the right to ban the import of products produced in an environmentally harmful manner. The bias in favor of commercial interests seems to bear out in one of the first cases brought before the WTO to test its rulings. In September 1997, a WTO panel ruled that the EU was giving preferential access to bananas produced by its former colonies in the Caribbean under the Lome Treaty negotiated in 1975. The U.S., which does not produce any bananas, had brought a lawsuit against the EU on behalf of the U.S.-based Chiquita Corporation, formerly known as United Fruit. Chiquita produces bananas in Latin America on huge plantations employing low-wage farm laborers. In the Caribbean, banana producers tended to be small-scale farmers who owned and worked their own land (an average of three acres), usually incurring higher production costs. Threats and sanctions were bandied about between the U.S. and the EU, nearly setting off a trade war. The EU eventually capitulated and said that it would comply with the WTO rules and not give preferential treatment to Caribbean producers. The small scale farmers would thus have to compete against large-scale corporate plantations.[35]

## Trade-Related Aspects of Intellectual Property Rights (TRIPS)

The WTO is not limited strictly to trade in goods. The institution took authority over so-called non-trade-related activity, such as foreign investment rules, intellectual property rights, and domestic regulatory mechanisms and including local laws, services such as insurance and transport, farm policy, and food and environmental standards. The TRIPS agreement introduced intellectual property law into the international trading system for the first time. It is an international agreement under the purview of the WTO that sets minimum standards for many forms of intellectual property regulations. **Intellectual property (IP)** is a term referring to a number of distinct types of creations of the mind for which property rights are recognized under the law. Under intellectual property law, these laws grant certain exclusive rights to a variety of intangible assets, such as musical, literary, and artistic works; discoveries and inventions; and words, phrases, symbols, and designs.[36] Common types of intellectual property include copyrights, trademarks, patents, industrial design rights and trade secrets. The objective of TRIPS' enforcement of all intellectual property rights is to contribute to the promotion of technological innovation and to the transfer and dissemination of technology. The U.S. made the case for TRIPS by arguing that nations who expected to benefit from exports should respect the intellectual property rights of its trading partner.

CAVENDISH BANANAS ARE THE MOST COMMON BANANA TYPE SOLD IN THE WORLD MARKET.

A major criticism of TRIPS is that in its current form, intellectual property rights serve to stifle competition and protect corporate investments and profits in what some consider an unfair way. Politics and powerful corporate influence have affected how patent processes work and who can or cannot get a patent. For poor nations it makes developing their own independent industries more costly, if it is possible at all.[37] For example, the WTO and TRIPS do not take public health needs into account. The patent protection period is 20 years, including medicines, which has the effect of denying periphery countries from developing generic medicines that would foster competition and result in better prices for drugs and other products.

Critics argue that TRIPS exacerbates the wide technological gap between rich and poor countries. Although periphery countries are rich in informal knowledge, they are net importers of the kinds of high-tech goods and know-how protected by TRIPS. Core countries, on the other hand, account for 90 per cent of global research and development (R&D) spending and an even higher share of patents.[38] Critics also contend that TRIPS further skew R&D towards rich-consumer markets rather than the basic needs of the poor, especially in the area of medicines and agriculture. Less than 10 percent of global spending on health research addresses 90 percent of the global disease burden. Similarly, much agricultural research aims to improve the appearance and taste of produce for consumers in rich markets, rather than to support the sustainable farming of staple foods such as sorghum and cassava, important to many poor farmers.

A source of tension among farmers in periphery countries is that TRIPS agreements undermine access to and distribution of seeds. TRIPS do not prevent corporations from collecting and patenting seed varieties held by indigenous peoples. Indigenous agricultural knowledge has been around for eons, yet, MNCs such as Monsanto have maneuvered to patent indigenous people's seeds, in most cases without consent or prior knowledge from them. As a result, many local farmers must now pay annual fees and/or sign agreements that limit their use of the seeds that they have used for generations. Subsistence farmers cannot afford the cost of purchasing new seeds each year, or some find that they have to buy back the seeds that they had already known and used freely. Because it is almost exclusively MNCs that patent seeds, there is no potential for poor countries or farmers to benefit from this patenting of life.

Another area that TRIPS has affected is the U.S. Human Genome Project, which is mostly taxpayer-funded. Private industry has filed thousands of patent claims on more than a hundred thousand gene sequences. Research depends on having a large information commons, in which broad knowledge is shared in the public domain. In the past, scientists have been forceful defenders of free, rather than proprietary, information. When Jonas Salk was asked why he hadn't patented his newly invented polio vaccine, he replied, "Could you patent the sun?"[39]

### Critics of Free Trade

Critics of the WTO contend that it has far greater powers than have ever been granted to any international body. They argue that small countries in the WTO wield very little influence, and the politicians representing the most influential nations in the WTO focus on the commercial interests of profit-making companies rather than the interests of all. As we have seen, the world's dominant economic power with the most competitive industries wants free trade. The core countries extol the virtues of free trade when it benefits them. It is my contention that as the U.S. continues to be battered by the loss of its industries under free trade policies, and as China becomes a more dominant

## The WTO: Is it Beneficial?

If there was the WTO in 1933, we might not have one of the world's largest corporations in the world today. In 1933 an Asian clothing manufacturing company decided to branch out into the manufacture of automobiles. They had everything going against them – they did not have any natural resources to make automobiles and the company had no experience with the product, plus other nations (particularly the U.S. and Great Britain) were already making vehicles that had captured most of the global markets. But the company caught the imagination of its country's leadership, and the Ministry of Trade decided to help it along. Government subsidies helped the company develop its first car. Decades of high import tariffs protected it from foreign competition as it grew into a serious contender. Domestic laws required that the company use parts made within the country, which guaranteed that domestic companies supportive of an auto industry – from tires to plastic components to precision machine tools and electronics – would create jobs. In 1939 both GM and Ford were expelled, forbidding them from making sales within the country. The struggling textile manufacturer was even bailed out by the government as it moved relentlessly forward in the development of an automobile.

The company was originally known as the Toyoda Automatic Loom Company. Today it is known as Toyota and is the world's largest automobile manufacturer.[40] The example of the founding and growth of the Toyota Corporation illustrates the fact that free trade is not usually beneficial to a country that is developing its infant industries. Of course, ironically, now Toyota chafes at any tariffs or trade policies that restrict the sale of its automobiles.

economic power, the U.S. government will ease its free trade mantra to a policy more beneficial to its economic situation.

Critics such as commentator Thom Hartmann contend that every time, without exception, when a periphery nation is forced (usually by the IMF, WTO, and/or World Bank) to throw open its doors to free trade, the result is a disaster. Foreign behemoths either wipe out or buy out and shut down local industries still in their developmental stages. Wages collapse. The middle class becomes the working poor. This has happened in Argentina, Chile, Mexico, and is happening now in the U.S. In the process, the largest corporations and wealthiest individuals in the world become larger, stronger, and wealthier.[41] Hartmann continues to argue that free trade policies do not benefit the bottom 90 percent of Americans. He claims that...

"In the 1980s, for the first time in its history, our (U.S.) country's smaller and medium size industries stood essentially naked and defenseless against those of other fully developed nations, most of which were still holding in place tariffs, generous research and development funding, and support of the common infrastructure, including subsidized higher education and health care. While today both China and India have import tariffs that run as high as 20 to 30 percent on manufactured goods (to protect their domestic industries and markets), we've dropped our tariffs from a 1973 average of 12 percent to today's average of around 2 percent. The result was just what the first U.S. Secretary of the Treasury Alexander Hamilton feared: "the rapid unraveling of the American middle class as the nation bled its industrial base into the gutter of cheap-labor countries."[42]

Instead of free trade, Hartmann argues that somewhat managed, regional trade between economically similar nations would be beneficial to all involved. Free trade in its current form between economically unequal nations continues inequality.

## Insights: Free Trade

Perhaps the most stunning irony of the free trade debate is that the nations of East Asia, including China, have danced around America's preferred recipe of free trade and have now become America's prime creditors. China, Japan, and South Korea have favored an export-oriented trade policy and have accumulated lots of U.S. dollars in the process. With their managed economies, huge export earnings, and high domestic savings, they have more than enough capital for their own development needs.[44]

---

### Is Free Trade Good for America? *Commentary by Robert Kuttner* [43]

Robert Kuttner succinctly summarizes the effects of free trade on a core country such as the United States... What are the appropriate policies for economic development? Free trade – operating across national borders – is a key ingredient of neoliberal capitalism. But if neoliberalism is not the optimal form of capitalism domestically, it is not the best brand of capitalism internationally. The rosy story of free trade is at odds with the way capitalism actually works. In practice, the pursuit of free trade causes the U.S. government to sacrifice the national interest for the self-interest of economic elites.

In American politics today, there is almost no serious discussion of how to reconcile the goals of cross-border commerce and periphery development with that of maintaining high and democratic living standards in the U.S. and other countries with similar social compacts. Our democratically elected national government needs to demand more reciprocal rules of trade and to find ways to bring the instruments of managed capitalism to the global economy. We need to align the interests of corporations once again with the interests of the citizens. Over the past century, managed capitalism has proven to be superior to laissez-faire capitalism, more efficient and more equitable, and it should not be sacrificed on the altar of utopian free markets, global or otherwise.

---

One way in which economies go from being periphery nation to more self-sustaining and competitive is that the government first determines which industries are worth growing and which are not. It was important in my home-town of Rockford, Illinois, in the 1960s to have a strong machine-tool industry that created well-paying jobs, and it was in the nation's strategic interest, as well. Machine tools are necessary for virtually every other form of heavy manufacturing. Once the government identifies strategic industries, it encourages and protects their domestic growth in a variety of ways. These include subsidies, legal protections (such as patent laws), import tariffs to guard against foreign competition, strong industry regulation to ensure quality, and development of infrastructure to ease manufacture, distribution, sales, and use of the product.[45] But MNCs have twisted this logic of protecting the home-front to the false slogan of "free trade will benefit us all."

A DIE FOR AUTOMOTIVE BUSHINGS AT ROCKFORD TOOLCRAFT, INC. ROCKFORD, ILLINOIS A TOOL AND DIE MANUFACTURER.

### Questions to Consider

1. Could the statements by Hartmann and Kuttner be true? Could the policies of free trade promoted by politicians and the mass media actually hurt the vast majority of Americans? How could this happen?

# PUZZLE PIECE #6:
# PRIVATIZATION AND COMMODIFICATION

An important piece, #6, of the economic globalization puzzle is the increasing privatization and commodification that is occurring on a worldwide scale. I introduced the two terms in chapter 3; therefore, in this section I will give a few examples of how the process is expanding globally. This includes privatizing "the commons," and commodifying elements of life that have so far been outside the trading system: culture, fresh water, seeds, and even the genetic structures of life.

## Schmeiser v. Monsanto

For over 60 years, Percy Schmeiser and his wife of over 55 years, Louise, farmed their fifth-generation family farm in Bruno, Saskatchewan, Canada. In addition to farming, he operated a farm equipment dealership in Bruno. Schmeiser considered retiring around 1995, but Louise expressed concerns about what he would do with his spare time, so he decided to keep farming for a while longer. What to do with his spare time was decided for him in 1998, when the agri-business corporation Monsanto sued Schmeiser for patent infringement. Monsanto charged that it had found GMO (genetically modified organisms) canola seed in Schmeiser's field, and that he had to pay a $15 an acre fee for using its patented GMO seed.

Monsanto, headquartered outside St. Louis, Missouri, is the world's leading producer of genetically engineered (GE) seeds, providing the technology for 90 percent of the world's GE seeds. GE seeds are genetically altered to have certain characteristics that boost productivity, in Monsanto's case the seeds can be used with their herbicide (weed killer) marketed as Roundup, of which Monsanto is also the world's leading producer. Monsanto is very determined to defend its patented GE seed business, in which each year farmers in their program must buy their expensive seeds. By 2003, Monsanto had built a whole department to enforce its lucrative seed patents and licensing agreements with 75 employees and an annual budget of $10 million.[46]

Schmeiser had developed his own drought-tolerant seed and never purchased seed from Monsanto. According to Schmeiser, Monsanto's GMO canola seed had contaminated his farm from the wind blowing pollen or seed onto his land. Genetically engineered corn, soybeans, cotton and canola are widely used, and evidence suggests that their pollen spreads to conventional crops. This means that any farmer whose neighbors grow engineered varieties could find himself in the same situation as Schmeiser – especially farmers of easily windblown canola and corn pollen.[47]

Schmeiser never had anything to do with Monsanto. But Schmeiser and an estimated 400 farmers have received threats of legal action from Monsanto over alleged patent infringement. Few of these cases ever get to court because most farmers don't have the financial resources to outlast Monsanto's deep pockets and simply give in. A clause in Monsanto's licensing agreement allows the company to hear such cases in the U.S. before Monsanto-friendly courts in Missouri, which can add thousands of dollars to a farmer's legal bills, especially those who live many miles away. Several of the cases that have gone to court are enough to scare farmers into surrendering to Monsanto's demands. For example, Mississippi farmer Homan McFarling was fined $780,000 for growing Roundup Ready soybeans without paying Monsanto's licensing fee. Tennessee farmer Ken Ralph was fined $1.7 million and sentenced to eight months in jail for a variety of offenses against Monsanto.[48]

PERCY SCHMEISER A FARMER FROM
BRUNO, SASKATCHEWAN, CANADA

In the Schmeiser case, the judge and appellate court ruled in Monsanto's favor. A Monsanto spokeswoman in Winnipeg, Manitoba, said "that the decision will help protect the intellectual property rights of the company and of thousands of farmers who pay for its technology." The court decision prohibits Schmeiser from using his seed again and requires him to pay Monsanto about $10,000 for its user fees and up to $75,000 in profits from his 1998 crop. The Schmeisers' appealed their case to the Canadian Supreme Court, which issued their decision in May 2004. The Court determined that Monsanto's patent is valid, but Schmeiser was not forced to pay Monsanto anything as he did not profit from the GE canola in his fields. The verdict was somewhat a vindication for the family. In the fight against Monsanto they received overwhelming support around the world for their efforts. Despite this support, the financial toll has been extreme. Because of the high legal costs, they faced losing their funds for retirement and their family farm. They realized that it was nearly impossible for an individual to stand up to a large corporation such as Monsanto. They felt that there is no justice for an average citizen in such a fight. Their legal fees alone in fighting against Monsanto exceeded $400,000.[49]

## Privatization

When Western economic consultants and World Bank advisors consult with periphery country officials about how to participate in the world economy, one of the first steps they recommend is to privatize their commonly held land. They recommend that if land is transferred from collective ownership and cut-up into individual parcels of land, the owner of the land will hold a legal deed that signifies individual ownership. The land can then be bought and sold in the market place and through the process of supply and demand have a monetary value attached to it. The individual owner of the land has an asset which s/he can use as collateral to borrow money from a bank to either fund a small business or buy more land.

This privatization process seems very logical and efficient to Westerners, since the law of property ownership has been in place for centuries. For example, I own my own house and I have a deed to prove my ownership of a specified tract of land and the house built upon that land. But to some people who live in collective communities, such as villages or tribes, individual ownership is an unfamiliar concept. For many, their land has been in their collective possession for untold generations. They may farm a small plot of that land and call it their own, but they do not have individual legal ownership. If they go ahead with the privatization process, they may use the land as collateral to borrow money from the bank for an enterprise. However, if they fail in their enterprise, they risk losing their land that has been used as collateral for the loan. The failed entrepreneur may have to forfeit the land that had been part of the community for generations to a bank or money lender for the repayment of the debt. Hence, the family land is lost forever. Also, the dismemberment of community land into individual plots further destabilizes the close-knit community.

The WTO seeks to privatize essential public services such as education, health care, energy and water. This means the selling off of public assets, such as radio airwaves or schools, to private (usually foreign) corporations that are run for profit rather than as a public service. It includes a list of about 160 threatened public services including elder and child care, sewage, garbage pick-up, park maintenance, banking, telecommunications, construction, insurance, transportation, shipping, postal services, and tourism.

In most countries, privatization is already well underway. The following is a brief description of three successful privatization efforts around the world.

## 1. The Privatization of the Coal Industry in the United Kingdom

Prime Minister Margaret Thatcher of the UK was an early leader in the implementation of neoliberal policies in the 1980s. One of her first acts was to privatize the state owned coal industry. After World War II, the government nationalized the coal industry in Britain, and it remained under public ownership until the 1980s. As expected, Thatcher's privatization of what was known as British Coal was carried out amidst great resistance by labor, which resulted in the massive UK miners' strike of 1984-1985. Nonetheless, the government privatized the industry by selling off a large number of coal pits to private concerns through the mid-1990s. Today the UK coal mining industry has disappeared almost completely.

### 2. The Privatization of Gazprom in Russia

After the break-up of the former Soviet Union in 1991, the government privatized in part the natural gas and oil industries in the new state of Russia. A cut-throat scramble to pick up Russia's immense reserves of natural resources at bargain-basement prices took place among aspiring Russian entrepreneurs. Although private interests latched on to the natural gas industry, currently the Russian government holds a controlling stake in what was the world's third largest corporation in 2009: Gazprom. It is the largest extractor of natural gas in the world and Russia's largest company. Gazprom's activities accounted for 10 percent of Russia's gross domestic product in 2008. To exemplify the close connection between government and corporations in state-capitalist Russia, Demitry Medvedev, elected president of the Russian federation in March 2008, had served as Gazprom's former Chairman of the Board of Directors.

### 3. The Privatization of Telemex in Mexico

The world's richest person in 2009-2010 was the Mexican billionaire Carlos "Slim" Helu. He is worth $53.5 billion, just edging out the American Microsoft founder Bill Gates who held assets worth $53 billion.[50] Slim owns many enterprises but amassed a fortune with the purchase of 50 percent of the stock in Telemex in 1990. Telemex is Mexico's profitable state owned telephone company, which the government was pressured to sell to comply with official policies of privatization imposed by the IMF in the 1980s. Service to customers has had mixed results but has contributed to the concentration of wealth in the hands of a very few well-connected business people.[51]

## Privatization of Water

The privatization of water is a volatile issue that we talked about in the U.S. in chapter 4. Privatization of water involves transferring some or all of the assets or operations of public water systems into private hands. The combination of increasing demand and shrinking supply has attracted the interest of global corporations who want to sell water for a profit. Some national governments have invited private companies to take over the management, operation, and sometimes even the ownership of public water systems. The World Bank touts the privatization of water as a potential trillion-dollar industry. Water has become the "blue gold" of the 21st century. Proponents hail the cost saving potential of private ownership for consumers. Ironically, local communities are concerned that privatization will lead to higher costs for water and water services. The actual record is mixed – both results have occurred.[52]

The commercial trade in bottled water has boomed. Some people in developing countries are increasingly turning to bottled water to meet their daily needs. World consumption is growing at 7 percent a year, with the largest increases in the Asia Pacific region.[53] In many of the periphery nations, municipal water systems often serve only cities or primarily upper-and-middle class residents. Usually, the only free-of-charge water available to the poor is found in festering pools or contaminated wells, which often contain killer diseases such as cholera. For example, many families in Ghana spend 10 to 20 percent of their meager income on water. Also, since many countries lack the infrastructure to recycle used water bottles, the plastic containers end up further polluting the local water sources.[54]

Leading the charge for privatization are three big transnational corporations based in Europe: Vivendi, Suez, and RWE. All three have systematically bought out smaller rivals to become the dominant global water businesses. These companies planned to take over the public water systems in periphery countries. Instead, a series of private-sector fiascoes in the periphery have derailed their plans.[55]

One of the most interesting and well-known examples in the battle over privatization of water took place in Cochabamba, the third largest city located in the Latin American country of Bolivia. The Cochabamba protests of 2000, also known as the "**Cochabamba Water Wars**," were a series of protests that took place due to the privatization of the municipal water supply.

Bolivia experienced hyper-inflation and political turmoil throughout the 1980s. To quell the disturbances, the Bolivian government turned to the World Bank for loans. As a requirement for lending the funds, the World Bank demanded that Bolivia privatize its railways, telephone system, national airlines, and hydrocarbon industry. In 2000, the World Bank also required that Bolivia privatize its water industry as a precondition for loan renewal.[56] The Bolivian government agreed to the terms of its sole bidder, *Aguas del Tunari,* a consortium of companies that included Bechtel Corporation (U.S.), and signed a $2.5 billion, 40-year concession. Within the terms of the contract the government guaranteed the consortium a minimum 15 percent annual return on its investment.[57] Upon taking control, the consortium raised water rates an average of 35 percent to about $20 a month, which was an excessive amount since their customers only earned about $100 a month, and $20 was more than they spent on food. Among the poor, protests erupted. Middle-class homeowners and large business owners joined in the protests when they saw their own water bills shoot up. When the massive protests grew larger and more intense, the Bolivian government declared martial law. As the protests turned violent, the authorities killed one teenage boy and more than 100 people wounded. But the protesters were persistent, and five years later they successfully ousted the consortium from the country.[58] The people of Bolivia did not choose to privatize their public water systems. The World Bank forced privatization on them, as it has been in many poor nations around the world, when the World Bank made privatization an explicit condition of aid in the mid-1990s.[59]

The big water companies are now changing their strategy and concentrating their operations and their investment on more secure markets in North America and Europe. Eighty-five percent of all water services in the U.S. are still in public hands, but that's a tempting target for water conglomerates such as Vivendi, Suez, and RWE. They have bought up the leading U.S. water companies – U.S. Filter, United Water, and American Water Works – intent on privatizing water in the United States and beyond.[60]

COCHABAMBA DEMONSTRATORS DEMAND REMOVAL OF CONSORTIUM AND END OF PRIVATIZATION OF WATER WORKS IN 2000.

## Questions to Consider

1. Who owns the water in your locality? If your water is not privatized, are there any plans to do so?

# PUZZLE PIECE #7: CONCENTRATION OF POWER: MULTINATIONAL CORPORATIONS & STATE ENTERPRISES

A **multinational corporation (MNC)** is an enterprise that manages production or delivers services in more than one country. Since the 1980s, the driving forces behind economic globalization have been several hundred global corporations and banks that have increasingly woven webs of production, consumption, finance, and culture across national and regional borders. Corporations are engineering a power shift of stunning proportions, moving real economic and political power away from national, state, and local governments and communities toward unprecedented centralization of power by global corporations, bankers, and global bureaucracies. The rise of the global corporation and economic globalization have both increased corporate power and weakened the capacity of governments to regulate it. With their vast resources and technical capabilities and without the responsibilities of nationhood, the corporation can move quickly when challenge or opportunity strikes.[61]

Corporations in and of themselves are not necessarily bad. There are many responsible corporations that are excellent employers and care about the planet and people. But, generally speaking, the power of huge MNCs has become excessive: their ownership has become more concentrated, their influence on governmental policy has been unchecked, and the systems of checks and balances on their power at the national level have virtually disappeared, while checks on their power at a global level are virtually nonexistent. Critics such as Speth are "clear that the corporation must be the main object of transformative change. We must dramatically change the publicly traded, limited liability global corporation, just as previous generations set out to eliminate or control the monarchy."[62]

MNCs span every sector of the global economy – from raw materials, to finance, to manufacturing. In 2007 there were 63,000 MNCs, increasing from 60,000 in 2000; in 1990, there were roughly half that number. Some estimates figure that just 500 of the largest MNCs account for at least 25 percent of world production and 70 percent of world trade, while their sales are equivalent to almost 50 percent of world GDP. In 2002, the top 200 corporations had combined sales equivalent to 28 percent of world GDP. But these 200 corporations only employed 0.82 percent of the global work force. In the U.S., 98 percent of all companies account for only 25 percent of business activity; the remaining two percent account for nearly 75 percent of the remaining activity. The top 500 industrial corporations, which represent only one-tenth of one percent of all U.S. companies, control over two-thirds of the business resources in the U.S. and collect over 70 percent of all U.S. profits. Despite employing less than one percent of the global work force, 200 of the largest multinational corporations have sales equal to 30 percent of the world's GDP.[63]

Corporate growth is around four times as high as global economic growth. *Forbes*, a business magazine, did a Global 2000 study to highlight the growth of the 2,000 largest public companies on the planet (there are also private corporations worth billions). The Forbes Global 2000 are public companies with the top composite scores based on their rankings for sales, profits, assets and market value. In the 2008 total, the Global 2000 companies accounted for $30 trillion in revenues, $2.4 trillion in profits, $119 trillion in assets and $39 trillion in market value. Around the world, just 72 million people, an astonishingly low number, work for these companies.[64]

### Questions to Consider

1. If we want more jobs in the global economy, is turning to MNCs the answer? Explain.

## The Influence of Corporations

Far from just supplying public demand, corporations actively direct cultural habits and create consumer demand by influencing the public through a sophisticated and well-funded combination of research, marketing, advertising and media manipulation. The result is the subtle alignment of public and corporate interest. Media corporations well understand the sophistication and effectiveness of their advertising and marketing methods. The ubiquity of television and the increasing number of hours it is watched, especially by children, is particularly disturbing to critics. In the U.S., watching TV is the third most time-consuming pastime after sleeping and working. And in the U.S., the 100 largest corporations pay for 75 percent of commercial television time and 50 percent of public TV.[65]

Corporations use the same aggressive marketing tactics in periphery countries as in core countries. The Nestle corporation in the 1980s conducted a notorious marketing campaign in periphery countries in which they claimed that their infant milk formula was superior to breast feeding. It led to disastrous results in infant health. Because of this practice, Nestle is still one of the most boycotted corporations in the world. In recent years, as public awareness about the dire health consequences of smoking tobacco have come to light in core nations, tobacco corporations have shifted their marketing focus to increasing demand in periphery countries. The World Health Organization (WHO) has reported that 84 percent of an estimated 1.3 billion smokers live in periphery countries.[66]

In light of the environmental crisis, many major corporations, particularly those which have the greatest negative impact upon the environment, have repackaged themselves as having "green" credentials. For example, the oil giant British Petroleum (BP) has claimed itself to be beyond petroleum and adopted a new green, flower-like logo. Before the catastrophic oil spill in the Gulf of Mexico in 2010, BP had successfully managed to shift public focus away from the fact that it is one of the world's foremost polluters of the environment and often ranks as one of the world's top 10 worst corporate citizens.[67]

The corporate sector wields its considerable political and economic power to restrain and shape governmental action. In many ways MNCs have become de facto governments, and the ethic that dominates corporations has come to dominate society. The U.S. and EU have 80 percent of all corporations. Over 30,000 corporate lobbyists are based in Washington D.C. and Brussels, headquarters of the EU, vastly outnumbering the U.S. Congress and European Commission staff that they lobby. These interest groups lobby for lower tax rates and advantageous tax loopholes that benefit their corporate clients. Although the U.S. corporate tax rate is 35 percent, among the highest of core countries, the number of corporations who pay this rate is very low. A study by the Government Accountability Office (GAO), the investigative arm of the U.S. Congress, found that two out of three U.S. corporations paid no federal income taxes on revenues from 1998 to 2005. The study covered 1.3 million corporations of all sizes, most of them small, with a collective $2.5 trillion in sales. It included foreign corporations that do business in the United States, which had a slightly higher percentage, 68 percent, that did not pay taxes during the period covered.[68] They also found that 95 percent of corporations paid less than 5 percent of their income in taxes. The corporate share of taxes paid fell from 33 percent in the 1940s to 15 percent in the 1990s. On the other hand, the individual's share of taxes has risen from 44 to 73 percent.[69]

Corporate influence on the global economy is measurable. MNCs have been re-locating their production facilities to periphery countries for years now, where taxes, labor costs, and environmental restrictions are negligible. This has contributed to large-scale unemployment in the core countries. MNCs argue that this is a necessary corporate decision in order to secure economic growth and opportunity in the core countries, but as we have experienced in this recession the manufacturing jobs are not coming back to core countries. It has also resulted in a glut of periphery laborers working in inhumane factories for comparatively low wages. These exploited workers often give up their families and rural lives to migrate en masse to overcrowded cities, inadvertently buying into an economic state of affairs which promotes unsustainable over-consumption in already wealthy countries.

One of the ways in which corporations can obtain lower tax rates and enforcement practices is playing one nation against another to their advantage. This practice has succeeded in drastically reducing the level of corporate taxation in the core nations. For example, the British government lowered its tax rate to 28 percent, and Germany lowered its rate from 39 percent to 30 percent, and raised taxes on workers and consumers to make up for revenue loss. Slovakia has passed very low tax rates to lure companies from nearby Germany. In the 10 years between 1995 and 2005, the government cut average corporate tax rates in EU nations by 8.1 percent among older EU members, and 10.8 percent among newer members in east and central Europe. Governments do this in the name of competing for foreign investment.[70] What gets lost in this new dynamic is that the original purpose of corporations was to serve the public good.

**Questions to Consider**
1. Can you think of ways to curb the influence and power of global corporations?

# PUZZLE PIECE #8: SPECIALIZATION

An eighth piece of the economic globalization puzzle is specialization. In today's global economy, the economic concept of specialization helps companies, nations, and workers answer a key question: what goods and services to produce? With **specialization** economic actors concentrate their skills on tasks they are the most skilled in. Specialized individuals and organizations focus on the limited range of production tasks they perform best. The key is efficiency. This specialization requires workers to give up performing other tasks at which they are not as skilled, leaving those jobs to others who are better suited for them. An example of specialization is an assembly line, where individual workers perform specific tasks in the production process. Countries also specialize in products they produce best. For example, corn is grown in the Midwest in the U.S. and bananas in Central America. The Congo in central Africa specializes in minerals, in which it is abundant. China specializes in low-wage manufacturing, because it has an abundant supply of labor. The list goes on.

Specialization relates to the concept of comparative advantage. Without getting too complicated, the theory of **comparative advantage** suggests that countries should specialize in the goods they produce most efficiently, rather than trying to be self-sufficient. It strongly favors free international trade.[71] Comparative advantage was at play in the global economy of the classical era of capitalism 1870-1914. The 18th century economist Adam Smith wrote about the concept of specialization and division of labor. He described how each worker in a pin factory performed a single specialized task: One worker measured wire, another cut it, one pointed it, others made the head and so on. Through this specialization process, workers produced thousands more pins than if each worker made each pin separately. Thus, specialization increases output. While Smith saw the advantages of specialization and division of labor, he saw its downside as well: monotony for the worker.

Two Swedish economists Eli Heckscher and Bertil Ohlin, published in 1933 a mathematical model of international trade. The basic idea is simple: A country will export goods that make intensive use of the resources it has in abundance. Countries with lots of fertile land will specialize in producing farm goods. Countries rich in capital will focus on capital-intensive products, especially sophisticated manufacturers. Regions with abundant labor will produce labor-intensive goods or crops. This pattern of specialization will lead to corresponding trade patterns: land-rich but capital-poor countries will export land-intensive agricultural products and import capital-intensive manufactured products. The insights of the two economists apply to movements of capital and people as well as trade. They theorized that countries rich in capital would export capital, and countries rich in labor would export labor.[72]

Specialization can be profitable for the companies, but it also can be repetitive and monotonous for the workers. Just ask any assembly line worker who performs a single task throughout the day sapping their creativity and spirit.[73] I know, I was one of them!

---

## A Summer Job in a Potato Chip Factory

I remember my assembly line summer factory job in a potato chip factory in Rockford, Illinois. I was an unskilled, but specialized worker. The potato chips traveled on a three-foot-wide, ceiling-level conveyer belt along one end of the factory. Along that belt were strategically placed sloping metal chutes in which the potato chips slid at specific intervals, every few seconds or so. I stood at the end of the metal chute holding a packaging bag, labeled with the particular potato chip brand, which I placed over the end of the chute and into which the potato chips dropped. Once the bag was full, I would then send the bag through a sealing-machine and then the sealed package of potato chips fell unto another conveyor belt bound for the packing room. I was bored after 10 minutes on the job! But I had to stay alert, because if I lost concentration and missed packaging the surging potato chips from the chute, I would end up with a pile of unbagged, salty potato chips at my feet. As you can imagine, it was hard to concentrate on such a mundane task for hours on end. After every two-hour shift I had to step out of the mound of potato chips encircling my legs and crunch my way to safety. Sometimes specialized "sweepers" would come by and clean up the pile that accumulated around the "chute workers." Since management knew that the workers got bored quickly from the repetitive tasks, they switched us to different but equally monotonous jobs. My favorite job was packing the potato chip bags into cardboard cartons to be shipped to supermarkets and discount stores. My least favorite specialized task was when I had to pick out bad potatoes from a sea of potatoes coursing down an ever-rolling, noisy conveyor belt. They came fast and furious. Since there were just a few of us on this task, I worried that many bad potatoes slipped by my ever watchful gaze and nimble fingers and ended up sliced into bad potato chips on someone's plate, but management didn't seem to be as worried as I was. Although the repetitive work was boring, my co-workers were nice and the pay was pretty good, especially with lots of overtime. I was able to last the summer. Since university tuition was very inexpensive during this time, my savings from my summer job were just enough to get me through a year of college tuition, books, and living expenses.

---

In the 1980s, a shift to increasing global specialization took place, reminiscent of the classical era of capitalism during which specialization was paramount. Within a short generation, a switch from generalization to specialization had taken place. Specialization even carried over into academic circles. I remember when I was in graduate school trying to decide my area of specialization in history. Would it be U.S. women's history or Middle East political history? I decided to ignore all the well-meaning advice from my professors and declared my "specialization" in world history. My advisers said it was too broad a topic, or it couldn't be done. I was undeterred – I knew that I wanted to learn about and teach world history; it was my real passion. I wanted to be a generalist, not necessarily a specialist. Luckily I found a professor who shared my passion for world history, and I successfully worked with him on both my master's and doctoral degrees. I even persuaded the history chair to let me teach world history!

Specialization is a vital part of economic globalization and a key buzzword. The generalist is someone in the past. To show the change over time, from generalization to specialization, I will tell another story about my experience with a non-specialized farm family of the 1960s. Since I grew up in the Midwest, the region will serve as an example of how specialization has destroyed economic livelihoods of the past and as of yet, not created many new economic opportunities.

## Farming in the Midwest in the 1960s

Farming is an example of how specialization has affected the way of life of farmers. Many Americans have a romantic notion of farming. I probably, do as well. I remember as a youngster, my family had good friends who lived down the road a mile or so and farmed a couple hundred acres. I often visited their family and stayed with them on numerous occasions. They also had dairy cattle – about 50 – and milked them precisely at 6 in the morning and 6 at night, seven days a week. It was physically demanding work, since they carried pails of milk to the gleaming steel pasteurizer in their barn, cleaned the barn, hauled in feed for the dairy cows, and handled hundreds of other daily chores. It was especially uncomfortable in the cold winters of northern Illinois, when the cattle had to be herded from their daytime pastures to the barn where they stayed at night. They had a number of chickens who roamed the pasture outside the white picket fence that enclosed their yard. When visiting, I helped collect the eggs from the chicken coop. They had a small herd of sheep which were sheared every spring and their wool bundled and sold. They had a few pigs, for their own consumption and a large garden in the summer. Corn and hay were grown on their land, which was mainly used for animal feed but still had to be bailed and stored in the hay maw above the barn. They also had a couple of horses that we could ride around the farm or out into the countryside.

The men were always working outside, and the women were always working in the kitchen or in the garden during the summer. To the six people living and working on the farm, it may not have been an ideal life, but I thought it was. As a youngster being in the fresh air and around animals was my idea of heaven. But I did not have to do it every day, 365 days a year. The farm came to an end when the father suddenly died of a heart attack at around age 45. The four children decided to go into other lines of work besides farming. The farm was eventually sold, and when I visit Rockford I am amazed that the farm on the hill overlooking a peaceful valley is now a shopping center circled by a busy four lane highway with cars whizzing by.

**DAIRY BARN SIMILAR TO MY FRIEND'S FARM IN THE 1960S.**

## Food and Specialization in the Midwest

Farms are not like they were in the 1960s. Few of them exist anymore. Generalist farms, such as the one I visited that grew crops and raised different animals have given way to specialist farms. Today's farmers – both the very big ones and the very small ones – are specialists. Since I am from the Midwest and lived there for many years, I witnessed how specialization has changed the factories and farms that contributed to the region's economic prosperity for over a century.

One specialist farmer, Melvin Stucke, operates an egg farm in western Ohio. He specializes in eggs – lots of eggs. Two mammoth henhouses, each longer than a football field, house 180,000 chickens. Each henhouse is 450 feet long and divided by six narrow aisles. Four stacks of cages line each aisle – each cage is 16x20 inches. Six 3-pound hens are crammed into just one cage, an animal rights nightmare. Each hen lays on average of 5-6 eggs a week. The cages are slightly tilted so that the eggs can roll down a conveyor belt running the length of the henhouse to the packers. Collectively, each day these chickens lay 165,000 eggs, which are packed into 460 giant cases. The cases are shipped to an enormous cracking plant, where the eggs are cracked and poured into huge vats of liquid eggs and shipped to a vast numbr of fast food restaurants. Once the hens are too old for laying eggs, they don't end up as someone's dinner; that would be the specialty of farms that breed roasters or fryers with lots of white breast meat that Americans love. Instead these spent-out laying hens end their productive years in the slaughter house, ground up as the main ingredient in dog food.[74]

How many times did I mention giant, fast, mega? Everything I mentioned was gigantic. This is in keeping with specialization. Stucke is a mega-farmer, which makes him typical of farming today. In an era of globalized agriculture, farmers must specialize in one branch of farming, such as egg production, hogs, dairy cattle, corn or soybeans, cotton, or plantation crops. This is not only in the U.S. but worldwide. Each farm encompasses thousands of acres and deals with such giant global agricultural corporations as ADM, Bunge, and Cargill, who dictate to the farmer not only price but almost every stage of the growing process. During the 1980s many farmers, unable to make the transition to specialization, ended up selling their family farms to larger farmers or corporations. Some of the large agri-business processors even own the farms and hire the former landowners as employees. Some farmers still own their own land, but, as in the case of many chicken producers, contract with large chicken processors such as Tyson, to whom they sell their products. Although the farmers may still own their own land, in essence they work for corporations. In other words, ownership may be personal, but control is corporate. Corporations may not choose to own the farm but they can own the farmer.[75]

Farming is specialized from state to state across the Midwest. Iowa grows more hogs, Minnesota grows more turkeys, Wisconsin and Indiana milk more cows, and Illinois grows more corn. In a mechanized and globalized world, efficiency rules and sheer size pays off. Farming has changed from my idealized vision in the 1960s. Farms have become factories, and farmers have increasingly become little more than employees of the big agribusiness corporations, which in turn sell to giant supermarket chains. Economic globalization is transforming farming according to the same pattern that changed manufacturing. It pits farmers who till high-priced land and expect a good standard of living against large farmers in Brazil who farm less expensive virgin land and hire low-wage laborers who have no expectations of a standard of living like an American farmer.[76]

We somehow think that farming is different from manufacturing – corn is different from

CHICKENS IN BATTERY CAGES, PART OF FACTORY OR INDUSTRIAL FARMING.

cars, hogs different from TV sets, eggs different from computer chips – and does not follow a mass production system of churning out undifferentiated products. But it isn't. Economic globalization treats both the same. Manufacturing workers must compete with Chinese workers, while core country farmers are competing with middle and periphery farmers in Brazil, Ukraine, and China. Core country farmers can't compete unless they become highly efficient and highly mechanized. This means huge multi-million dollar investments in equipment and vast tracts of land. Small farmers cannot afford these economies-of-scale and are selling out to those who have the capital to make their mega-farms even bigger.[77]

There were 3 million American farms in 1970; now there are about 2.15 million, possibly fewer. About 500,000 are located in the Midwest, half as many as 40 years ago. It seems like a lot of farms, but 1.8 million of the 2.15 million bring in less than $100,000 a year in total sales, with an average income of only $20,000. That is not much money for lots of work. Another 200,000 farms are intermediate farms, with total sales between $100,000 and $250,000; they average about $40,000 per year in net income. These are the endangered farmers who are unable to compete in the global market and are quickly disappearing. At the top end are the mega-commercial farms that till thousands of acres and average annual sales of at least $250,000 and usually more. The average big commercial farmer has income from sales at nearly $700,000 a year and annual profits of $200,000 or more. There are about 146,000 of these commercial farms which account for only 8 percent of all farms, 11 percent in the Midwest, but they produce about 68 percent of all U.S. farm output.[78]

If Brazil can produce soybeans more cheaply than the U.S., how can the U.S. compete with these farmers? We know what happened to manufacturers who were undercut by low-wage Chinese workers and costs, the manufacturers simply pulled up stakes and moved to China. If there are so many similarities between manufacturers and farmers, as I mentioned earlier, you may ask why are there still farmers in the U.S. There are two reasons for this: 1) the federal farm-subsidy program and 2) the growth of global corporations. Since we talked about subsidies in chapter 3, let's look at the second reason.

Some of the biggest global corporations are in the food business, such as Cargill, Nestle and ADM. It is like an hourglass with big corporations as both ends – big commercial farms producing the food, and big corporations processing and distributing the food. Mega-farms need huge amounts of equipment, seeds, feed, fertilizers, and other supplies. The big firms, such as Monsanto, can supply them quickly and cheaper than middle man distributors. Therefore, no mega-farm buys locally anymore. And the processors by-and-large don't buy from small farmers. Those days are also gone. As we saw in the corporations section, large corporations dominate in a globalized world, and the agriculture sector is no exception. Since we all need to eat, they have a powerful impact on the kinds of food we eat and the price we pay. Many of these corporations are headquartered in the U.S. but are truly MNCs with influence in almost every agricultural-producing country in the world. They dominate in meat products and grain. Among the largest are Cargill, Archer Daniels Midland (ADM), ConAgra, Tyson, Swift, Smithfield, Hormel, Perdue, Bunge, Monsanto, Pilgrim's Pride, and DuPont.[79]

The farms' produce travels from farm to plate – on average 1500 miles – mostly via one of the giant supermarkets, and Wal-Mart is the world's largest supermarket by a sizable margin in the U.S. and by a whopping margin in the world. Of the 250 largest retail chains in the world, 64 are supermarkets.[80] Along with Wal-Mart, Kroger, Safeway, and Albertsons serve U.S. consumers, Carrefour and Tesco, serve Europe, Edeka serves Germany, Jusco, serves Japan and Wellcome serves China. A chain of supermarkets owned by Australians, Spar, is the world's largest independent food retail chain and has recently opened stores in Nigeria and Hyderabad, India.[81]

The mammoth food processors, such as Cargill, ADM and Tyson, are, not surprisingly, the major suppliers to these giant supermarkets. Unbeknownst to most shoppers, some 50 to 75 percent of the supermarket's net profits come not from food sales but from retailer fees, which supermarkets charge food companies just to put their products on their shelves. Few small processors can afford these charges.[82]

The U.S. and Europe long dominated global agriculture, but now new areas of the world – China, Ukraine, and Brazil – are emerging as global agriculture powerhouses. They resent the heavy subsidies that both Europe and the U.S. lavish on their farmers. In a globalized world, size conquers. About 175,000 U.S. farms already produce most of the food for Americans but many experts predict that there will only be 25,000 to 30,000 farms in the not too distant future. Although niche markets in the food chain exist for farmers who raise locally-produced and organic food, the majority of shoppers will not abandon low-priced Wal-Mart, and other mega supermarkets. So both farms and the corporations will get bigger, and highly-advertised brands will be more dominant.[83]

---

**Questions to Consider**

1. List some areas of specialization that you see around you today? Is this area of specialization new?

---

# PUZZLE PIECE #9: SQUEEZE LABOR

Let's start this section on labor – #9 of the puzzle pieces – with a theorem: the Stolper-Samuelson theorem. This is a basic theorem in the Heckscher–Ohlin trade theory that I briefly explained in the previous section. Although this theorem dates back to 1941, I and others think this one is worth looking at. For our purposes, the **Stolper-Samuelson theorem** basically says that the effect of trade between a core nation and a periphery nation is that the wages for the unskilled labor force in the core nation will be lower because they are competing globally with the unskilled workers in a periphery nation.[84]

This theorem is being played out in the U.S. today. For example, when the global economy added two billion low-wage workers, you would expect that wages would fall across the board. When a core, capital-abundant country (such as the US) trades with a labor-abundant country (such as China), wages in the rich country fall and corporate profits go up. The theorem's economic logic is simple. Free trade is tantamount to a massive increase in the core country's labor supply, since the products made by periphery country workers can now be imported. Additionally, demand for workers in the core country falls as the corporations shift labor-intensive production to the periphery country. The net result is an increase in labor supply and a decrease in labor demand in the core country, and wages fall.[85]

Is the theorem actually depicting what is really happening in our global economy? Economist Thomas Palley makes the argument that "For the last three decades, U.S. policy makers, from both major political parties, have worked assiduously to create a global market place in which goods and capital are free to move. Over the same period, two and a half billion people in China, India, Eastern Europe and the former Soviet Union have discarded economic isolationism and joined the global economy. Now, these two tectonic shifts are coming together in the form of a 'super-sized' Stolper-Samuelson effect, and they stand to have depressing consequences for American workers."[86] Adding two billion people from low-wage countries to the global labor market is an unprecedented event in history. Stolper and Samuelson showed that owners of abundant resources gain from trade, while those with scarce resources lose. For example, those with capital are able to invest in products that return a high value in trade. Those without capital suffer. To see this relationship, consider a tangible resource like oil. In a country rich in oil, oil is cheap, and opening up to trade is good for oil producers because it allows them to sell oil to foreigners. Just think of the wealth in Saudi Arabia. In a country poor in oil, where oil is expensive, opening to trade is bad for oil producers because it leads to oil imports that push the domestic price of oil down. Even if the resource in question is more general – land, labor, and capital – the logic holds; protection helps owners of a nationally scarce resource; trade helps owners of a nationally abundant resource.[87]

In an era of rapid growth and free trade there is a debate about whether free trade policy is best for labor and for the country as a whole. The fact is that there are both winners and losers from free trade who fight for policies to benefit themselves. It can get very complicated. With the emergence of China, India and Eastern Europe, the dam of socialism that held back two billion workers from the global economic workforce has been removed. It is as if two swimming pools are joined, the water level will eventually equalize. A threat to labor is competition. Manufacturing workers in core countries are already competing with labor from periphery countries, with dire consequences for manufacturing workers in the core countries.[88]

Samuelson questioned the benefits of economic globalization for labor. He claimed "that since U.S. labor has lost its old monopoly on American advanced know-how and capital, free trade could indeed lower the share of wages in the U.S. GDP and increase overall inequality." He pointed to the drastic change in mean U.S. incomes and in inequalities among different classes and suggested that this may be the consequence of free trade. The outsourcing of jobs to foreign countries is tantamount to importing labor from those countries into the U.S., with similar consequences of depressing wages. The ability to import low cost consumer items is a poor consolation to the jobless.[89]

CHINESE WORKERS PERFORM FINAL TESTING BEFORE SENDING DRIVES OFF TO CUSTOMERS ON ITS 2.5-INCH NOTEBOOK LINES. WITH FREE TRADE, PRODUCTS MADE IN CHINA WITH LOW-WAGE LABOR ARE EXPORTED TARIFF FREE TO WESTERN COUNTRIES.

Economists examining long-range data find that the globalization of the American economy has helped to freeze or lower middle-class incomes, further widening the gap between the very rich and the middle class. While America's rich are enjoying the fruits of globalization, America's middle class and lower class are swallowing the bitter pill of economic globalization.[90]

**Outsourcing** is an imprecise term but involves the contracting out of a business function to an external provider, usually to a low-wage country. One of the reasons for the rapid decline in manufacturing jobs in core countries is the outsourcing of jobs to low-wage periphery countries, such as China, Mexico, Indonesia, India, and Vietnam. For example, many Mexican farmers left their villages to seek employment in Mexico's *maquilladores,* which were factory cities built along the border with the U.S. in the 1980s and 1990s. One of these cities, Juarez, Mexico, employed thousands of Mexican workers in factories that churned out television sets to auto parts, most of which were shipped to the U.S. However, many of these factories have now closed down in order to seek even lower-wage workers in China. Juarez is now left with high unemployment and a staggering crime rate.

The same is happening for professional and higher-paid knowledge workers in core countries with similar effects. Outsourcing is not just the province of the manufacturing sector. McKinsey Global Institute in 2005 predicated that from software to banking, insurance, pharmaceuticals, and engineering, between 13 and 50 percent of jobs could be sent offshore. Therefore, in core countries most of the new jobs are in domestic services and low-paying retail work.[91]

## PUZZLE PIECE #10: MILITARY HEGEMONY

You may be wondering what this big word that is hard to pronounce has to do with the #10 piece of the economic globalization puzzle. My answer: a lot. First of all let me define the term. **Hegemony** is the political, economic, ideological or cultural power exerted by a dominant group over other groups, regardless of the explicit consent of the latter. The term is often mistakenly used to suggest brute power or dominance, when it is better defined as emphasizing how control is achieved through consensus not force.[92] It is not solely about macho militarism, although that can be part of it as well. Hegemony is about economic efficiency, making possible the creation of a world order on terms that will guarantee a smooth-running world-system in which the hegemonic power becomes the core of an unbalanced share of capital accumulation.[93] The United States was the unquestioned hegemonic power from 1945 to the early 1970s but has been losing that overwhelming advantage ever since. Although the U.S. possesses the world's most powerful military, and holds the top spot as the world's largest economy, its unchallenged hegemonic economic power has been in decline as other nations, especially China, have surged forward.

Core nations use hegemony to make sure they have access to cheap natural resources and to ensure they have entrance to markets for their goods. One of the problems inherent in capitalist economies is stagnation, which was one of the reasons for the economic globalization push in the late 1970s. It occurs when there is an over-capacity in the production of goods and services and not enough demand to absorb the over-capacity. There was over-capacity in the 1970s as there is today. The export-oriented economies, such as China, Japan, and the "Asian tigers," have the capacity to efficiently churn out goods at an accelerating rate. Most of the goods are bound for the U.S., whose consumers have reached a saturation point of accumulation and burdensome debt, especially since the recession. This scenario is not new to capitalist economies, as we will see in this brief examination of the link between capitalism and the search for markets and natural resources.

### A Brief History of Colonialism, Imperialism, Development and Hegemony

1. **Colonialism** describes the first phase of capitalist expansion (1500-1750). Around the 1500 date European feudalistic society and the economy stagnated as Europeans were importing more goods from Asia, particularly China, than they exported. Thus, wealth was leaving Europe and an imbalance in trade ensued. The remedy to this dilemma was an outward thrust by European explorers to find new trade routes. An even better opportunity for Europeans occurred when they used the Western hemisphere as their private source for cheap raw materials, produced by cheap or slave labor that helped to develop a capitalist economy. Spain and Portugal were the earliest colonial conquerors but France, Netherlands, and Britain closely followed. Around 1700, the Western hemisphere, India, and some coastal cities in Asia and Africa were under European colonial rule. These European nations were able to extract commodity wealth such as sugar, furs, silver, gold, tea, spices, and tobacco from their colonial holdings. This wealth helped to fuel the industrial revolution in Britain in the last half of the 18th century.

2. **Imperialism**, the second phase, asserted itself after the initial burst of colonialism had quieted by the 18th century. During the heyday of imperialism, 1870-1914, there was a 300 percent increase in the acquisition of colonies, with an average of 240,000 square miles taken over each year. Compare this figure to 83,000 square miles per year, the amount land taken over by colonial powers in the first 75 years of the 19th century. The cast of characters taking up the imperialism gauntlet were the early colonial powers plus a few new converts: Germany, Belgium, Russia, U.S., Italy and later Japan. By the time of imperialism, the industrial revolution was in full swing. Intense competition among the imperialist nations heated up for markets and resources. Economic stagnation precedes imperialism as internal markets are reduced, consumption ebbs, profit margins narrow, and labor costs rise. In response to the crisis, imperialist nations search for new markets, investments, and consumers. There is no escape from capitalism's inner logic, which is to grow and expand. Since there is over-capacity of production in relation to consumption in the core countries, there is a drive to encompass more areas into the capitalist web that were heretofore external to the process. The further pace of capitalist growth depends on new products, new inventions, and large populations for nations to conquer or convert.

#### Reasons for Imperialism
1. Industrialization needed raw materials.
2. Control access to raw materials.
3. Profit margins were squeezed.
4. Intense nationalism, a colony was proof of a nation's prowess.
5. Moral justification, the "White Man's Burden" was used to justify the "unselfish task of civilizing and Christianizing the savages."

Although 1896-1914 is often called the "golden age of capitalism," underneath this golden surface was the abuse and suffering inflicted by European imperialists who exploited their colonial subjects and inflicted untold death and misery upon millions of indigenous peoples.

3. **Development 1945-1990** was the third phase in the drive for more markets and natural resources, which was more cleverly disguised than blatant colonialism and imperialism. Development is usually sold as helpful to the recipient countries, and in some cases it is. **Economic development** is the process of increasing the standard of living in a nation's population through sustained economic growth that requires a transition from a simple economy to a modern, complex economy.

This process includes the change in policies by which a nation "improves" the economic, political, and social well-being of its people from a local, national, and somewhat self-sufficient economy to a modern and interdependent economy.

The dates 1945-1990 describe the development policies spearheaded by the U.S. and the Soviet Union, who were locked in a cold war battle. Each nation thought its particular modern economic model of development was superior and rushed to convert as many newly formed nations emerging from colonialism to their particular economic brand – communism or capitalism. They were both eager to convert as many fledgling economies to their economic model for both pride and practical reasons. If they had an economic alliance with one of their allies, they could either trade or extract needed resources from them. Therefore, developers focused on countries which harbored rich natural resources needed by the two superpowers. For example, the U.S. was particularly close to Iran, until its revolution in 1979, since it supplied abundant and cheap oil to run the U.S. oil-dependent economic machine, and Iran was an eager purchaser of America's expensive, advanced weaponry.

Let's ponder economic development a moment; after all I put it in the same category as colonialism and imperialism. I must have a good reason, and I do. I see economic development as a code word for further incorporating as much of the world as possible into the capitalist economic web. The Soviet Union was doing the same thing during this time – just a communist economic web. But since communism virtually died out around 1990, let's mainly focus on the U.S. and capitalism. As David Korten, a dedicated development worker for 30 years explains "I have come to see the extent to which the Western development enterprise has been about separating people from their traditional means of livelihood and breaking down the bonds of security provided by family and community to create dependence on the jobs and products that modern corporations produce." He sees the modern development process as a continuation of colonialism and imperialism, except under a friendlier guise. The process replaced locally controlled systems of agriculture, governance, health care, education, and mutual self-help with systems that outsiders more centrally controlled.[94] Thus, development was based on the assumption that all societies should go through a process of national evolution from simple to complex: simple meant primitive and a low standard of living and complex meant capitalist and a high standard of living. If followed, the steps to modernization would result in a high standard of living and a modern society.

Americans had such faith in the superiority of its capitalist economic system (most still do) that it blindingly thought that others would embrace the system with a ground swell of appreciation. This did happen in many instances. Some leaders of former colonial nations eagerly embraced modernization and gladly accepted development assistance checks from the U.S. They embarked upon a restructuring of their nations, eager to emerge from the "underdeveloped" category. However, adjustments were painful, and many leaders felt duped by the promises from the West. Many countries in Africa, for example, actually sank into greater poverty after signing on to development than when they followed their traditional way of life. Many periphery countries thought that the pledge from U.S. leaders to help them modernize was in reality a ruse to cheaply extract their natural resources.[95]

The U.S. often posited development as a code term for supporting capitalism instead of communism. Since the U.S. assumed that its modern economic and political systems were superior to local, national, or communist societies, it was eager to spread its "economic truth" to as many willing converts as possible. If the converts weren't willing, there were other persuasive techniques used, including assassination and coups, to bring the errant into the capitalist fold. The U.S., through the Central Intelligence Agency (CIA), had a hand either directly or indirectly in the assassination or overthrow in a coup of uncooperative leaders. The following are a few of the deposed: Mohammed Mossadegh of Iran (coup, 1953), Jacobo Arbenz of Guatemala (coup, 1954), Achmed Sukarno of Indonesia (coup, 1965), Patrice Lumumba of the Congo (assassination, 1960), Salvador Allende of Chile (coup, 1973), Jaime Roldos of Ecuador (assassination, plane crash, 1981), Joao Goulart of Brazil (coup, 1964), Omar Torrijos of Panama (assassination, plane crash, 1981) and in 1979 when the Soviet Union invaded Afghanistan, the U.S. funded the anti-Soviet Mujahaddin rebels in Pakistan.[96]

4. **Hegemony 1990-Present**. After the fall of the Soviet Union and its satellite communist countries, the United States reigned as the world's leading economic, military, technological, cultural and political power. In the 1990s, there were no rivals. The U.S. did not shrink from its role as world leader. In fact, many Americans heralded the collapse of communism as the final verdict on the superiority of capitalism. American triumphalism reigned. The U.S. took the fall of communism as an indicator to expand its mighty reaches into lands previously under Soviet control and even beyond.

Under the George W. Bush administration (2001-2009), the U.S. called for the expansion of democratic institutions to authoritarian countries around the world. But in contradiction to these stated ideals, the U.S. often thwarted the democratic decisions of the people when they did not conform to America's "national interests." The U.S. announced human rights as a central tenet of its foreign policy, but it often does not practice this ideal. For example, the U.S. is critical of China's human rights record but is also dependent on its purchases of U.S. treasury bonds to finance its mounting debt. Therefore, it is often silent about crucial Chinese human rights abuses because of its monetary predicament. While espousing democratic ideals and promoting economic globalization, the U.S. often acts as the self-appointed world police. For example, the nation defied a resolution passed by the United Nations condemning its plan to invade Iraq in 2003. Instead, along with a sparse "coalition of the willing," it barreled ahead into a lengthy and deadly war. At the time of this writing, the U.S. is winding down its interventionist war in Afghanistan, which many critics regard as a colossal and very expensive mistake.

Despite U.S. aggression and meddling in many parts of the world, paradoxically, many global citizens still respect America's democratic ideals and open society. Although realized in a variety of forms, many nations emulate its political and economic institutions. Today, 118 nations – containing over 55 percent of the world's population – govern with some form of democratic organization, an accomplishment that the U.S. had a hand in attaining.

## Hegemonic Military Power in the United States

You would expect that the world's largest economy would have the world's largest military. After all, skilled diplomacy alone is not enough to keep all the hegemonic power's national interests in line. Indeed, the U.S. has the world's largest military, the biggest by a long shot. Of the planet's total military expenditures, the U.S. spends almost half of that total. Adding up the entire defense spending in the public sector in 2009, the U.S. government alone plowed over $1 trillion into its military (this figure includes defense related expenditures from all departments). Figures from just the Department of Defense (DOD) were $663 billion. This figure was significantly more than second place China, which increased its military budget 15 percent but still clocked in lower at $99 billion. The UK came in 3rd with $69 billion, only slightly more than France that closed in on 4th place with $67 billion. Russia rounded out the top 5 with $61 billion. India which upped its military budget 34 percent was in 10th place with $36.6 billion.[97]

The United State's hegemonic power is illustrated in concrete form in the sheer number and location of its military bases. They are today's version of colonies. In a 2008 inventory, there were 761 military bases encircling the planet. These bases in 151 different countries stationed 510,927 service personnel: troops, spies, contractors, dependents, and others.[98] Military expert Chalmers Johnson noted, that "if there were an honest count of the actual size of our military empire it would probably top 1,000 different bases in other people's countries, but no one knows the exact number for sure. Even though these numbers are astronomical, during the Cold War in 1967 the number was 1,014 military bases.[99]

Neoliberals affect the military by pushing to privatize functions that the government formerly provided. Johnson makes the claim that the "government [has been] hollowed out in terms of military and intelligence functions." The KBR Corporation, for example, supplied food, laundry, and other personal services to troops in Iraq and Afghanistan, based on lucrative no-bid contracts, while Blackwater Worldwide, (now operating under the name Xe because of repeated scandals) supplied security and analytical services to the CIA and the State Department in Baghdad. According to Johnson the costs of privatization – both financial and the number of personnel – in the armed services and the intelligence community far exceeded any alleged savings, and some of the consequences for democratic governance may prove irreparable.[100] Former Defense Secretary Robert M. Gates repeatedly warned that the U.S. has turned over far too many functions to the military because of the hollowing out of the Department of State since 1990. He believes, instead, we are witnessing a "creeping militarization" of foreign policy.[101]

The inevitable day of reckoning long predicted by Pentagon critics has, I believe, finally arrived. Our problems are those of a very rich country that has become accustomed over the years to defense budgets that are actually jobs programs and also a major source of pork for use by politicians in their re-election campaigns. Hegemonic powers do not last forever, and ultimately fail because of fate and folly. The U.S. appears to be following that path.

---

**Questions to Consider**

1. Do you think our military is outsized and needs to be reduced? Explain.

---

CAMP BONDSTEEL IN KOSOVO. AS AN EXAMPLE OF PRIVATIZATION, THE CORPORATION KELLOGG, BROWN, AND ROOT (KBR) IS THE PRIME CONTRACTOR FOR THE OPERATION OF THE CAMP.

## CONCLUDING INSIGHTS: ECONOMIC GLOBALIZATION

I started this chapter with the statement that our individual opinion about economic globalization was dependent upon our particular circumstances. Hopefully this chapter has helped you form a more complete picture of economic globalization than whether it just benefits you or not. One of the criticisms that I have with the way we make decisions as a nation is that at the bottom line the deciding factor is "does this help me or not." Our ideas and actions are cocooned into a myopic vision of our individual needs, while the fate of global humanity lies in peril. Turning to a way of thinking that is more inclusive and more global in scope can help inform the monumental decisions we need to make as a society.

Let's turn to the next chapter and look at the consequences that economic globalization has had on humanity and the environment.

# CHAPTER SIX

# The Impact of Economic Globalization

*"Socialism collapsed because it did not allow the market to tell the economic truth. Capitalism may collapse because it does not allow the market to tell the ecological truth."*

*Oystein Dahle, former Vice-President, Exxon, for Norway and the North Sea*

# EVALUATING THE IMPACT OF ECONOMIC GLOBALIZATION

Economic globalization has transformed the world. The impact is not felt just in the core countries, such as the U.S., but in periphery countries, as well. So, how are we going to go about analyzing the impact of economic globalization? Has it been beneficial or detrimental? This is a hard question that is broad and vague. Of course, once again, it depends upon your point of view. If you are a highly educated stock analyst in Tokyo, you might think that economic globalization is a great thing, since you are now able to provide your financial analysis to a wide group of consumers throughout the world. If you are a middle-aged, male automobile assembly line worker in one of the industrial cities of the American Midwest with a high school diploma, you might lament the outsourcing and automation of your job and the fact that you must return to a community college to retrain for a different type of economy – an economy that doesn't reward the skills you have. If you are a cotton farmer in the poorest country in the world, Mali, on the poorest continent, Africa, you might not like economic globalization because the cotton you produce for export must now compete on the world market with subsidized cotton from the U.S. The poor cotton farmer gets less for his crop because U.S. subsidies cause market distortions, but the farmer has few other options for eking out a living in such a poor country. If you are a well-educated, middle-class man who formerly lived in a rural Chinese village and now manages a Western-owned factory in a large Chinese city, you are happy that economic globalization has helped you achieve a higher standard of living. If you are a small farmer in India, you might not like economic globalization because you now have few choices but to purchase the Monsanto Corporation's patented seeds sold at world market prices, rather than to use your own heritage seeds that that your family has used for generations to grow grain crops.

All these stories make up a mosaic of perspectives of economic globalization, and, therefore, it is very difficult to simply answer the question, "Are you for or against economic globalization?" I would like to reframe the question by using certain criteria to evaluate whether it is beneficial or detrimental as a strategy for directing the world economy. I have decided to pick criteria that I think are the most essential issues of our day: the environment, social inequality, and human well-being. Now, there are many other criteria that are important as well, and you may disagree with my three selections. You could make the case that the criteria should center on the important issues of education, jobs, economic growth, national debt, consumer choices, first-rate medical care, an entrepreneurial spirit, financial opportunities, military might, individual rights, safe food, human rights, terrorism, religious freedom, ethical standards, and the list goes on. As an educator I debated about including education in my top three, but I am still sticking with my selections. Why have I selected these issues as a basis for evaluating economic globalization?

Landing in the top spot as the number one criterion for evaluating economic globalization is none other than the health of the earth itself. In my estimation it is by far the most important criterion for judging any program, policy, or theory. When thinking about the next generations, this clearly has to be at the top of the list. I know there are many who deny that global warming is caused by human activities and claim it is merely a change in climate patterns. Although I do think the scientific evidence overwhelmingly supports the conclusion that climate change (global warming) is driven in large part by human activities, if you don't, that is ok. There are many other important environmental stresses that are undeniably human driven: depletion of fresh water and air, water pollution, top soil erosion, ocean acidity, desertification, species extinctions, population growth, and the list goes on. We tend to fixate on one issue, such as climate change, and not see the whole picture of environmental deterioration. The polarizing debate between believers and non-believers of climate change is a distraction from all the dire environmental issues that are being ignored.

Earning the second spot in the criterion for evaluating economic globalization is the growing social and economic inequality found throughout the world. Economic globalization has not eased global inequality – the gap between rich and poor – in fact, it has exacerbated it. When discussing the issue of socioeconomic inequality, some politically expedient groups have often negatively framed it to mean redistributing wealth so that everyone has the same amount, as in the failed system of communism. I want to clarify that there is a difference between closing the wide socio-economic gap, which I favor, and the untenable idea that everyone should have the same income, which I do not favor. There are other ways to close the inequality gap than by simply taking from the rich and handing it to the poor.

The third criterion asks the question: Does economic globalization provide an acceptable standard of well-being for the global community? Now that is a tall order! You may think this is a rigged question, since obviously economic globalization is going to fail on this count. It would be virtually impossible for all the people on earth to have a standard of living equal to a middle class American, complete with two cars, a house, and all the consumer comforts. For one, the earth could not ecologically support such a population. But I ask if economic globalization provides an acceptable standard of well-being, not a standard of living. There is a big difference. It might be surprising to find what really makes people happy, instead of what advertisers tell us will make us happy.

In addition to the three criteria that I will use in this economic globalization evaluation process, I will be looking at how economic globalization has affected a periphery country, the Democratic Republic of the Congo in central Africa, and a middle country, Bhutan, located high in the Himalaya Mountains northeast of India. But let's first turn to the environmental impact of economic globalization.

### Questions to Consider

1. What do you think are the top three most important criteria for evaluating the benefits of economic globalization? Top five? What is your top pick?

## THE ENVIRONMENT

Most mainstream analysis of economic globalization discounts or ignores environmental costs. Today it is a vital factor in the debate about economic globalization and should be front and center in any discussion about its benefits and detriments. The Western world is ambivalent about our relationship with the earth; some people treat it in contradictory ways. We know that the resources of the earth are necessary for us to survive, but we treat the earth as if it is able to indefinitely churn out these "free" resources for us without any fuss. The earth doesn't work that way. The earth is beginning to make a fuss, and it behooves us to listen to its distress signals. The earth's signals say to us, "It is time you start treating me with respect and place limits on the ways that you plunder my resources or I may not provide the resources that you so desperately need to survive."

As the economic globalization agenda is played out on the world stage, these services are increasingly being compromised. Instead, the environment is regarded in three ways:

1. A Commodity. A supplier of natural resources such as good top-soil for our crops, fresh water to drink, minerals to fuel industries, oil and coal to run machinery, fish to eat from our oceans, and so on.

2. A Sink. A dumping ground for our refuse, our pollutants, and our toxic chemicals.

3. External Nature. It is a place to go for renewal, away from hectic everyday lives. We want "to get back to nature," as if nature was something we left behind. We don't live within nature, we live outside of it.

Some critics think we need a change in consciousness or awareness about the earth. Instead of the earth as a separate, non-living entity and treated as such, it should be an interdependent part of us and our daily lives. Nature is not away from us, but part of us. This change in consciousness is not only imperative for us and our survival, but also for the survival of earth's other species as well.

Today we are confronted with a very complex and fragile relationship with nature. One of nature's species – ours – has exceeded the limits of sustainability, threatening future generations with possible extinction. This dire prospect reminds me of a story about goats.

## The Earth's Free Ecosystem Services

1. Purification of air and water.

2. Water absorption and storage which helps mitigate droughts and floods.

3. Decomposition, detoxification, and sequestering of wastes.

4. Regeneration of soil nutrients; buildup of soil structure.

5. Pollination, seed and nutrient dispersal.

6. Pest control.

7. Moderation of wind and temperature extremes.

8. A variety of agricultural, medicinal, and industrial products.

9. Biodiversity that performs all of the above tasks.

10. Aesthetic, spiritual, and intellectual uplift.

## The Earth is an Island

During the days of sailing ships, sailors would leave goats on islands to guarantee that on their return trips they would have an abundance of fresh meat. But with no natural predators, the goats bred faster than the sailors could eat them. Lacking natural limits, the goats ultimately devoured all the island's vegetation and over-taxed the environment to such a degree that native species could no longer grow. The multiplying population of goats, in due course, starved to death. The lessons of this tale are applicable today. Our "island," the earth, has suffered the consequences of our goat-like instincts to consume everything in sight without regard for the future. With no natural predators or self-imposed limits we are in peril of suffering the same fate. The more aware we become of our impact on the planet, the greater is the likelihood that we will be able to arrive at solutions and remedy our voracious habit of abusing the environment.

The interdependent environmental issues we face today are immense and urgent. Population growth and the demand for a rising standard of living by more people mean that the environment is under increasing stress. Although climate change has received the most attention, other issues are also vitally important: desertification, deforestation, shortages of fresh water, climate change, rising sea levels, soil depletion, population escalation, rampant extinction of wild plants and animals, air and water pollution, and the carrying capacity of our earth. I try to walk a fine line between sounding too alarmist and presenting a scenario so pessimistic that you are reduced to a depressive stupor of inaction, or being Pollyanna-optimistic and suggesting that all we need to do is change our light bulbs and climate change will be solved. These issues won't go away and it will take collective effort and collective persistence.

In the following sections, I summarize some of the significant effects that economic globalization is having on the environment. Although it can be argued that economic globalization is not directly the cause of many of these problems, I will counter with the argument that the roots of environmental degradation are deep, but economic globalization has directly and indirectly exacerbated environmental problems because of its policies and actions. Using the systems thinking skills introduced in chapter 1 is helpful when looking at these monumental issues.

## 1. Desertification

Advancing deserts and expanding sea levels are squeezing our global community. These forces are significantly altering the physical geography of our planet. Expanding deserts, a process known as **desertification**, are mainly the consequence of deforested land and also overstocked and overgrazed grasslands. The problem of desertification is worldwide, but it is especially acute in China, where the loss of productive land is occurring at an accelerating rate. From 1950 to 1975 an average of 600 square miles of land succumbed to the desert each year, but by 2000 over 1,400 square miles were yielding to desert encroachment annually. Massive forest rings around the city of Beijing are the Chinese government's attempt to keep the prowling deserts at bay. Chinese officials report that within the last 50 years residents deserted over 24,000 villages in northern and western China as drifting sand silently buried the settlements. China's Environmental Protection Agency reports that from 1994 to 1999, the Gobi Desert grew by 20,240 square miles, an area half the size of Pennsylvania. With the advancing Gobi now within 150 miles of Beijing, China's leaders are beginning to sense the gravity of the situation.[1]

The Sahara Desert in North Africa is wreaking mayhem on people's lives. It is pushing the people of Morocco, Tunisia, and Algeria northward toward the Mediterranean Sea. In countries like Senegal and Mauritania in the west, to Sudan, Ethiopia, and Somalia in the east, the demands of growing numbers of people and animals, along with the effects of climate change, are switching arable land to desert at an alarming rate. Nigeria is surrendering 1,355 square miles to desertification each year. Its human population swelled from 33 million in 1950 to 134 million in 2006, and likewise its livestock numbers grew from 6 million to 66 million. Nigeria's population is being compressed into an ever-smaller marginal area of land.

THE ENCROACHING DESERT, ANTI-SAND SHIELDS IN NORTH SAHARA, TUNISIA.

In Mexico, the United States' southern neighbor, about 70 percent of its land is vulnerable to desertification. Cropland degradation forces some 700,000 to 900,000 Mexicans off the land each year. Most flee from the arid and semi-arid regions of Mexico, where the desertification process yearly impairs 1,000 square miles and causes the abandonment of another 400 square miles of farmland. Desperate former farmers direct their search for jobs to nearby cities or immigrate, either legally or illegally, to the United States.[2]

## 2. Deforestation

A wide belt of forests of immense diversity and significance to our earth's ecosystem stretches out from the equator. But this is changing. Large-scale forest clearance is dramatically altering tropical rainforests. Loggers are systematically reducing these ancient forests at the rate of about 100 acres per minute as humans harvest timber and clear the natural landscape to make room for farms and pasture. More than half the loss of the world's natural forest has occurred since 1950. If the clearing rate stays constant, the unprotected primary forest will be gone in 95 years. The tropics suffered most of the loss.[3] Although tropical forests cover only about 7 percent of the earth's dry land, they harbor an estimated half of all earth's species. Many species can be found in only small areas; their specialization makes them especially vulnerable to extinction. Forests take in and hold a great stock of carbon, which helps balance the stock of carbon dioxide in the atmosphere, reducing the greenhouse effect and global warming.

The reasons for tropical forest loss includes multinational timber and paper companies seeking higher sales; governments increasing exports to pay external debts; ranchers and farmers converting forest to agricultural or grazing land for profit; and landless people scrambling for firewood or a patch of land on which to grow food. A single old-growth tree can be worth $10,000 or more. That value sets up enormous temptations. Another problem with deforestation of tropical areas is that tropical soils appear very fertile but are actually very thin and poor in nutrients. When exposed to the tropic's high temperatures and torrential rains, the underlying rock weathers rapidly and this process leaches most of the minerals from the soil. Nearly all the nutrient composition of a tropical forest is in the living plants and the decomposing debris on the forest floor. When farmers deforest an area for cultivation, they cut down or burn trees and vegetation – slash-and-burn agriculture – to create a fertilizing deposit of ash for the crops. But after a few harvests, the forest loses its nutrient reservoir while flooding and erosion further deplete the soil of nutrients. The farmer abandons the site and moves to another location to start the destructive process once again.

Water evaporates from soils and vegetation, condenses into clouds, and falls again as rain in a perpetual cycle. Up to 30 percent of the rain in tropical forests has been recycled into the atmosphere. When vegetation cover is scalped from the earth's surface, then solar energy is reflected from the ground rather than absorbed by trees; hence, temperatures rise, soils dry, and dust accumulates in the atmosphere, hindering rain cloud formation. Pockets of disastrous drought are the result. Replacing tropical forests with pasture and crops creates a drier, hotter climate in the tropics and will disrupt rainfall patterns far outside the tropics, reaching as far as China, northern Mexico, and south-central United States.[4]

Forests take in great stores of carbon dioxide, helping to balance the stock of it in the atmosphere and ameliorating the greenhouse effect. In the Amazon alone, scientists estimate that the trees hold more carbon than 10 years' worth of human-produced greenhouse gases. And when people strip the forest, usually with

DEFORESTATION FOR OIL PALM PLANTATION. THE LAST BATCH OF SAWWOOD FROM THE PEAT FOREST IN SUMATRA, INDONESIA.

fire, carbon stored in the wood returns to the atmosphere, exacerbating the greenhouse effect and climate change. Once the forest is cleared, the soil can become a source of carbon emissions instead of carbon sequestering.

People have been deforesting the earth for thousands of years, but recently this has been done to meet global demands, not just local and national needs. Because of swelling populations, the single biggest direct cause of tropical deforestation is the conversion of forests to cropland and pasture for growing crops or raising livestock to meet the daily needs of burgeoning populations and selling for export. Commercial logging also takes its divvy from the forest. In Indonesia, for example, the conversion of tropical forest to commercial palm tree plantations to produce bio-fuels for export is a major cause of deforestation on the islands of Borneo and Sumatra.[5] The policies of the national government encourage economic development, such as road building and forest clearing, with tax breaks for related businesses, agricultural subsidies for farmers, and concessions for timber companies. Also, the accumulated foreign debt of developing countries means that they are often forced to sell off their natural resources on the world market in order to repay their loans to institutions such as the World Bank. These valuable lumber products are in high demand in core countries, where most of their forests have already been cut.

### 3. Fresh Water

Most people still think of water as abundant and renewable. It isn't. The amount of fresh water available to us is finite, and the world is quickly running out of it. The limited supply of fresh water is a grave environmental problem that will become an increasingly volatile issue in the future. Only 2 percent of the earth's water is considered to be fresh water fit for human consumption, and two-thirds of this amount is trapped in ice caps, glaciers, and underground aquifers too deep or remote to tap. Only 0.01 percent (one-hundredth of one percent) of the planet's water is accessible for human use. If the entire world's water was contained in 26 gallons (100 liters) then what is readily available to us would amount to one-half teaspoon.[6] While the world's population explodes, the fresh water supply necessary for human life is severely diminishing in many areas.

Compounding the fresh water shortfall is the fact that per capita water consumption is rising twice as fast as the world's population. Sophisticated technology and wasteful sanitation systems, particularly those in core nations, have encouraged people to use far more water than they need. Yet even with this increase in personal water use, households and municipalities account for only 10 percent of water use. Industry claims 20-25 percent of world fresh water supplies, and its demands are increasing considerably. Many of the world's fastest growing industries are water intensive. For example, the computer industry alone uses almost 400 billion gallons of water each year.[7]

Irrigation is the real water hog, claiming 65 percent to 70 percent of all the water used by humans. It takes some 500 gallons a day to produce the food each one of us consumes. Water-intensive commercial farming claims increasing amounts of irrigation, which often employs wasteful practices. Generally governments and their taxpayers subsidize water use, while farming operations don't have to pay the real costs of their water. This creates a strong disincentive for farmers to employ more conservation practices and to install more water-saving drip irrigation systems.[8]

Greater water usage accompanies rising standards of living. For example, diets of the affluent usually contain less grain and more meat. It takes approximately 1,000 tons of water to produce a ton of grain and 3,000 tons of water to produce a ton of rice; if grain is fed to animals for human consumption, the amount of water needed for our diets increases significantly. Consider that it takes 16 pounds of grain to produce one pound of beef – and no less than 2,500 gallons of water! With an increase in more Western style heavy meat diets by more affluent Chinese and Indians, you can imagine that this increase in water usage will become unsustainable.

Irrigation for food production depends heavily on aquifers that farmers are depleting at an unprecedented rate. China produces over 70 percent of its food with irrigation. Water tables on the fertile North China Plain dropped more than 12 feet in a recent three-year period, and the number of cities in China with water shortages represents about half the country's urban areas. India, with a population of over 1.1 billion, uses irrigation to produce 50 percent of its food, and the rate of groundwater withdrawal is twice that of the recharge rate, a deficit higher than any other country.[9] The U.S. produces 20 percent of its food with irrigation and is witnessing falling water tables as well. The enormous Ogallala Aquifer providing ground water throughout most of the Great Plains and in the American Southwest is dropping precipitously. Ominous droughts in the American Southwest have put greater demand on the region's rivers, including the Colorado and Rio Grande, which provide water for much of the Southwest. They are unable to keep up with growing demand.

Climate change and pollution are making it difficult for developing countries to provide food for themselves. Africa has 9 percent of the planet's water resources but uses only 3.8 percent because of distribution problems. Many of its water sources are also dwindling. Lake Victoria (Victoria Nyanza), for example, Africa's largest freshwater reserve, fell two meters below normal in 2005.[10] In central Asia, Iran, a country of 70 million people, is facing an acute water shortage, especially in the fertile Chenaran Plain in the northeastern part. The water table fell by 2.8 meters a year in the late 1990s. Vulnerable Iran must now import more wheat than Japan, the world's leading importer in the recent past.[11]

Historically, water shortages have been local, but in an increasingly globalized world, water scarcity crosses national boundaries to play out on the world stage. Countries facing water shortages need to accommodate the water requirements of their cities and industry as well as agriculture. They often do this by diverting water to their cities and then importing grain to offset the loss in agriculture production. Since a ton of grain equals 1,000 tons of water, importing grain is an efficient way to import water. But this precarious scenario depends on other countries, mainly the U.S., to continue to export plentiful grain at cheap prices and to extract their diminishing reserves of fresh water. Also, the explosive use of grain for ethanol production drives up grain prices and adds to already strained food budgets for the poor.

### 4. Climate Change

**Climate change** takes place when the climate is altered during two different periods of time, with changes in average weather conditions, as well as how much the weather varies around these averages. The cause may be volcanic eruptions, variations in the sun's intensity, or very slow changes in ocean circulation that occur over long time periods. But humans also cause climates to change by releasing green-

IRRIGATION OF LAND IN PUNJAB, PAKISTAN.

house gases and aerosols into the atmosphere. We often hear the popular term **global warming** to describe general shifts in climate. But actually global warming refers specifically to any change in the global average surface temperature. The world will not warm uniformly, even though the term implies that it will; some areas warm more than others, such as the North and South poles. Some areas will even become cooler. I will primarily use the term climate change in this book.

Triggering climate changes are **greenhouse gases**. These gases are a natural system that regulates the temperature on earth, just as glass in a greenhouse keeps heat in. Sunlight passes through the atmosphere to warm our earth, but the warmed earth also emits heat energy back to the atmosphere, thus keeping the earth's energy budget in balance. Clouds and greenhouses gases in the lower atmosphere absorb most of it. Next, a process of absorption and re-emission is repeated until finally the energy escapes from the atmosphere to space. However, because of the increase in greenhouse gases in the atmosphere, much of the energy is recycled downward, causing surface temperatures to become warmer than in the past. This natural process is known as the greenhouse effect.

The earth's climate has gone through countless cycles of warming and cooling in its long history. However, over the past 10,000 years the amount of greenhouse gases in the atmosphere has been relatively stable. But around 1800, the concentrations began to increase due to increasing industrialization, rising population, and changing land use. This change has resulted in excessive greenhouse gases that have turned from life enhancing to life threatening.

A major human contribution to greenhouse gases is the release of carbon dioxide from the burning of fossil fuels, which has increased astronomically during the 200-plus years of industrialization. For example, current coal consumption has jumped to 100 times more than it was in 1800, and current oil consumption has escalated more than 200-fold in the 20th century. Deforestation also contributes to climate change, since fewer plants and trees are around to absorb carbon dioxide during photosynthesis. The second major component of greenhouse gases is methane. The increasing number of rice paddy fields to feed Asia's growing population release volumes of methane gas from wet and decaying vegetation. Animal waste also injects methane into the atmosphere by the staggering number of domesticated animals raised for meat consumption by the world's affluent class. Chlorofluorocarbons (CFCs), a third source of greenhouse gases, were formerly used as refrigerants and cleaning solvents but have been banned by the Montreal Protocol in 1987 because of their effects on the ozone layer.

An international scientific consensus has emerged that our world is getting warmer, and humans are significantly contributing to the warming. Scientists predicted that hotter temperatures and rises in sea levels will continue for centuries no matter how much is done now to control pollution. This and other strong conclusions have been issued, making it virtually impossible to say natural forces are to blame.[12] Skeptics and disbelievers are finally beginning to change their position. The evidence is irrefutable. Alpine glaciers have been retreating, sea levels have risen, and climatic zones are shifting. The 1980s and 1990s were the warmest decades on record. The 10 warmest years in global meteorological history have all happened in the past 15 years.[13]

Climate change is more than a warming trend, which is why global warming is an imprecise term to describe the phenomenon. Increasing temperatures are leading to changes in wind patterns, the amount and type of precipitation, and types and frequency of severe weather events. These climate changes could have far-reaching and unpredictable environmental, social and economic consequences. The U.S. has five percent of the world's population but accounts for nearly 25 percent of global greenhouse emissions. It is crucial that the U.S. participates and actively provides leadership in efforts to address climate change and protect the livability of our planet for future generations to come.

## 5. Sea Levels

The melting of the polar ice caps is a result of planetary warming, which is raising sea levels and adding increasing levels of radiation into the atmosphere. Holes hovering over the north and south poles deplete the atmosphere's protective ozone shield at an astonishing rate of about one percent per year. With this rise in levels of ultraviolet radiation, the number of skin cancer cases each year goes up. During the 20th century sea levels rose by 6 inches but during the 21st century, it is estimated that seas may rise by 4 to 35 inches. Since 2001, record-breaking high temperatures have accelerated ice melting dramatically. If the Greenland ice sheet, a mile-thick in some places, melted entirely, sea levels would climb by 23 feet or 7 meters. A one-meter rise would deluge many rice-growing deltas and floodplains of Thailand, Viet Nam, China, Indonesia, and India. Forecasts predict that a one-meter rise in sea level would displace 30 million Bangladeshis. London, Bangkok, Shanghai, New York, and Washington D. C., along with hundreds of other cities, would be at least partially inundated.[14]

## 6. Soil Depletion

Soil depletion is another pressing and related environmental issue. It has occurred as a result of erosion, reduction in fertility, and desertification. One analysis of global soil depletion estimates that, depending on the region, topsoil is currently being lost 16 to 300 times faster than it can be replaced. The UN Environment Program estimated in 1986 that over the past 1000 years humans have turned about 2 billion hectares of productive farmland into wasteland. That is more than the total area farmed today. About 100 million hectares of irrigated land has been lost to salinization.

Between 1950 and 2000, world grain production more than tripled. From 1950 to 1975, grain output increased by an average of 3.3 percent per year, faster than the 1.0 percent per year rate of population growth. Yet during the past few decades, the rate of grain production increase has slowed until it has fallen below the population growth rate. Per capita grain production peaked in about 1985, and it has been falling slowly ever since. Still there is presumably enough food, at least in theory, to feed everyone adequately. The total grain produced in the world around the year 2000 could keep eight billion people alive at a subsistence level, if it were evenly distributed – not fed to animals and not lost to pests or allowed to rot between harvest and consumption.[15] Yet, in 2008, food riots in poor countries such as Haiti, Egypt, and Bangladesh point to the difficulty of providing food for everyone. Ethanol production uses valuable grain supplies, but it is apparent that grain production cannot supply enough ethanol to meet the needs of motorists and enough food for the world's poor at the same time.

HURRICANE SANDY, LATE OCTOBER 2012. DAMAGE TO CASINO PIER IN SEASIDE HEIGHTS, NEW JERSEY, U.S.

The methods of commercial agriculture that produced abundance for several of the past decades are unsustainable and show signs of exhaustion in many areas of the world. Efforts to conserve and enhance worn out soil using methods that have been successful for centuries are underway. Agricultural methods such as terracing, composting, cover-cropping, polyculture (as opposed to monoculture), crop rotation, and contour plowing do not have to use synthetic fertilizers and pesticides. This type of farming is not primitive or inefficient but actually produces crop yields equivalent to conventional methods; it also can improve soil fertility and has few environmental side effects. A demonstration model of these farming methods has been successfully accomplished in a small Mexican village called Vincente Guerrero in the state of Tlaxaca that I visited in the summer of 2007. Drought, soil depletion, North American Free Trade Agreement (NAFTA) policies, and migration had ravaged the area's farming community. Yet this small village is staging a dramatic comeback. Farmers are intent on becoming sustainable and organic in their local food production. Through terracing, crop rotation, organic methods, and lots of hard work, the soils are slowly recovering. These dedicated efforts signal hope that farmers can reverse devastating soil depletion and small agricultural villages can continue to be sustainable throughout the world.

## 7. Carrying Capacity

Earth's resources are being devoured faster than they can be replaced by her most rapacious species, us! We have overshot our earth's carrying capacity, which means we are taking from the earth more than it can replace through natural systems. **Overshoot** means to go too far, to go beyond limits accidentally or on purpose, and without consideration for the consequences. A useful tool for understanding this concept is called the "ecological footprint." Our **ecological footprint** is derived by calculating the amount of land required to supply needed resources, such as grain, food, water, and wood, and absorb the resulting wastes such as carbon dioxide and pollutants. Our footprint has become as large as Bigfoot's! According to the data, since the late 1980s, humans have been using more of the planet's resources each year than are regenerated. In other words, the ecological footprint of our global society has overshot the earth's capacity to provide.[16] Some experts conclude that we are about 20 percent above the earth's carrying capacity; others maintain that in 2003 it was 25 percent larger than the planet's carrying capacity, while some dire estimates project that it will be an astonishing 100 percent by 2050. In other words, by 2050 humans will demand twice the resources than the planet can provide.[17] While this imbalance can possibly continue for awhile, continued overshooting will ultimately lead to liquidation of the planet's ecological assets and the depletion of earth's resources, unless something is done to halt the devastating trajectory.

Some estimates calculate that the earth has the carrying capacity for somewhere in the range of 4 to 5 billion people, yet in 2012 there are 7 billion people on earth. The fear is that even if we could slow population growth markedly, that might not curb greenhouse gas production sufficiently, especially if more people adopt Western lifestyles and consumption habits. India and China are developing rapidly and have affected climate change. For example, China is opening one coal-fired power plant a week to meet its population's insatiable demand for electricity.

How many people can the earth sustain? It depends. If all the people on earth consumed at the level of high-income countries, such as the U.S. and EU, the planet could support only 1.8 billion people, much less than our actual population. For example, because each American consumes a heavy meat diet, farm animals need to consume 1,760 pounds of grain annually.. Grain consumption in the U.S. is far greater than in India where each person annually consumes about 440 pounds of grain. If everyone else in the world ate the same amount as the people of India, the world's grain production could support about 10 billion people.[18] The average American consumes 20 times as much in natural resources for food and consumer items as the average African. At current consumption levels, some estimates show that the U.S. has the resources to sustain less than half of its current population of over 300 million. While the average American ecological footprint is about 22 acres, the average citizen of India has a footprint 1/16th that size. Although not a very appealing scenario for Americans, the reality is if 7 billion people were to share the world's resources equally, we would have to reduce consumption by 80 percent for each of us to have a sustainable ecological footprint of about 4.4 acres.[19] This would mean a drastic reduction in energy use, meat consumption, transportation, and housing.

Our use of the world's resources has reached such a level that it can only be sustained on a planet 25 percent larger. In the early stages of overshoot, which is where we are now, the signals from the environment are not yet strong enough to force an end to growth and the overuse of resources. In systems thinking terms it is called a **delay in feedback**. In other words, we are not yet in a situation where the stresses on the earth have sent strong enough signals to force us to shrink our ecological footprint. Overshoot is possible because we can draw down on accumulated resource stocks. For example, you can spend more money each month than you earn, at least for awhile, if you have saved funds in a bank account. You can remove timber from a forest at a rate exceeding its annual growth rate as long as you start with a standing stock of wood that has grown and accumulated over many decades. The larger the initial stock, the higher and longer the overshoot. If a society takes its signals from the available stocks of resources rather than from their rates of replenishment, it will overshoot. This is what we are doing to our earth's resources.[20]

Any population, economy, or environment that has feedback delays and slow physical responses to the signals of overshoot and yet keeps on growing is literally out of control. If a society constantly tries to accelerate its growth, eventually it will overshoot.[21] No matter how fabulous its technologies, no matter how efficient its economy, no matter how wise its leaders, it can't ignore the consequences forever.

A period of overshoot does not necessarily lead to collapse. But it does require fast and determined action if collapse is to be avoided. We must quickly protect our resource base and sharply reduce the drains on it. It is necessary to reduce both population and living standards for humanity to lower its ecological footprint. If we believe that the size of the human footprint is a serious problem then the issue of population management must be addressed. It is a bombshell of a topic, with profound and emotional issues of ethics, morality, equity and practicality. The good news is there is so much waste and inefficiency in the current global economy that a tremendous potential exists for reducing our footprint.[22]

EASTER ISLAND (1600-1799) EXPERIENCED SEVERE EROSION DUE TO DEFORESTATION AND UNSUSTAINABLE AGRICULTURE. TOPSOIL LOSS LED TO ECOLOGICAL COLLAPSE, CAUSING MASS STARVATION AND CIVILIZATIONAL DISINTEGRATION.

## 8. Human Population

For most of the 2.5 million years of human history, the human population was less than one quarter million. Yet, in 2012 it has surpassed the 7 billion mark and is climbing rapidly. Every year the world adds approximately 80 million people to its total number. In fact, population time clocks on the Internet tick away the number of people added to our planet every few seconds![23] The overall growth rate hit a peak of about 2 percent in the late 1960s and the good news is it has recently fallen to 1.3 percent.

A 2007 United Nations forecast predicts that world population will rise to 9.2 billion by 2050, a 50 percent increase. This, however, depends on fertility in less developed countries dropping to 2.05 in the time period 2045-2050, it was 2.75 children per woman in years 2005-2010. If, on the other hand, fertility remains at 2000-2005 levels, world population in 2050 would reach nearly 12 billion. The increase in population will take place mostly in the periphery nations. The more developed regions expect population numbers to remain unchanged at 1.2 billion. This number would decline but for migration from the periphery to core countries, which is expected to average 2.3 million annually. An increase in ageing populations will continue into the future. Between 2005 and 2050, half the increase in the world's population will be in the number of people 60 and over, whereas the populations under 15 will decline slightly. Core nations expect their population over 60 to nearly double, while the population under 60 will probably decrease.[24]

World food production has dramatically increased since 1945. One of the problems is that increased food production that accompanied the Green Revolution of the 1950-1960s was made possible by the massive use of life-threatening chemical fertilizers and pesticides. Although these inputs initially increased production rates about 2.5 times, increasing population levels consumed the surplus production. Even though population numbers continue to rise, recently worldwide agriculture production levels have stabilized and declined in many areas. This shows the long-term negative consequences of chemical inputs on soil fertility and productivity, desertification, and dropping water tables.[25]

The population of the United States is over 300 million people; it is projected to reach 400 million by 2043 and will climb to 420 million by mid-century. The U.S. population grows by almost 1.8 million people each year or 0.6 percent; each day the U.S. adds about 8,000 more people. Another person joins the nation every 11 seconds! This contrasts with Europe and Japan where populations are either stable or declining slightly.

Of the largest populated nations in the world, the United States ranks third behind China which is the most populous with 1.3 billion people, and India a close second with 1.1 billion people. But taken as a whole, the 27-member European Union (EU) would rank third with a population of almost 500 million. Ranked fourth in population after the U.S. is Indonesia with a population of 231 million; Brazil, with its population of 187 million people, stands at fifth. Rounding out the top ten are Pakistan, Bangladesh, Nigeria, Russia, and Japan.

There are several reasons for the stunning population increases in the last two centuries, especially the last half of the 20th century. One reason has been the shift to carbon-based fuels in which the burning of coal, gas, and oil has produced energy to fuel the large scale machinery that mass produces agricultural products to feed a mushrooming population. Other contributing factors – clean water, sewage treatment, antibiotics, and medical breakthroughs – have resulted in lower mortality rates and increased life-expectancy. Paradoxically, the creative forces that have made it possible for many of us to live longer and healthier lives has the destructive flip side of increasing our capacity to multiply our numbers and consume more resources, placing our planet in peril. The present rates of population growth are unsustainable unless forms of population control are agreed upon and enacted in all countries.

## 9. Natural Populations

Another environmental challenge facing us today is the ongoing loss of biodiversity through species extinction. Although extinction is a natural process – the basis of evolution is the appearance of some species and the disappearance of others – this extinction is different: humans are almost wholly responsible. Fifty percent of the plants and animals on earth – cattle, hogs, chickens, corn, soybeans, wheat – are for exclusive human use. Since these species consume scarce resources, this disparity puts considerable stress on the survivability of species not contributing to human consumption, as well as the world's ecosystem as a whole.

This alarming extinction of species is sometimes referred to as the **sixth extinction**, following upon the five previous known extinctions in the Ordovician, Devonian, Permian, Triassic and Cretaceous periods. Some experts estimate the rapid loss of species to be between 100 and 1,000 times higher than the background or expected natural extinction rate. However, some studies suggest this estimate may be too conservative; current extinction rates could be as high as 1,000 to 11,000 times the background extinction rates. Habitat loss and degradation affect 86 percent of all threatened birds, 86 percent of threatened mammals, and 88 percent of threatened amphibians.[26]

Why should we care? Although the moral and ethical dimensions of contributing to the obliteration of our fellow species are important, there are also practical reasons to try to halt this destruction. Living organisms keep the planet habitable. Plants and bacteria carry out photosynthesis, which produces oxygen, while trees absorb carbon dioxide, which helps combat global warming. This complex, interdependent process is necessary for the natural food chain to produce enough for human consumption. The monetary value of goods and services carried out by natural ecosystems is estimated to be about 33 trillion dollars per year. But the monetary value means little to us if we create a world that is uninhabitable for us and our fellow species.[27]

## The Environment and Growth

I maintain that the principle of growth with its influence on escalating population numbers and the global economy has been the chief force driving our global society past its ecological limits. Growth forever isn't possible. Sooner or later we will hit the earth's buffers. This happens for one of two reasons: either a natural resource, such as fresh water, becomes over-exploited to the point of exhaustion, or because more waste is dumped into an ecosystem than can be safely

THE SIBERIAN TIGER IS A SUBSPECIES OF TIGER THAT IS CRITICALLY ENDANGERED; THREE SUBSPECIES OF TIGER ARE ALREADY EXTINCT.

absorbed, leading to malfunction or collapse. Science now seems to be telling us that both are happening, and sooner, rather than later.

Our global ecological footprint is growing, further overshooting what the earth can provide and absorb. The 2009 set of Global Footprint Accounts reveals that the human population is demanding nature's services, using resources and generating $CO_2$ emissions, at a rate that is 44 per cent faster than what nature can replace and reabsorb. In other words, it takes the earth almost 18 months to produce the ecological services that humanity uses in one year. For example, very conservatively, for the whole world to consume and produce waste at the level of an average person in the United Kingdom (UK), we would need the equivalent of at least 3.4 planets like earth. Most worrying, there are signs that the capacity of the earth to absorb waste is actually being reduced, worn out by current levels of overuse, setting up a negative spiral of overconsumption and weakening capacity for the earth to provide for human life. [28]

Once the ecological footprint has grown beyond the sustainable level, as it already has, it must eventually come down – either through a managed process or through the work of nature. There is no question about whether an enlarging ecological footprint will stop at some point; the only questions are when and by what means. Population growth will essentially cease because of a decline in the food supply and conflict over scarce resources. Birth rates will fall farther and deaths will begin to rise unless human's respond to this dire challenge.[29]

**Insights: The Environment**

One's particular worldview contributes to how these ominous environmental problems are addressed. Some people place an economic value on natural resources based upon the current standards of supply and demand and do not take into account their disappearing supplies. They generally hold that natural resources should be utilized for economic production, while environmental restrictions limit economic growth and result in job loss. Many Americans and others fear that instituting environmental limits will trigger a decline in our standard of living and threaten our livelihoods. Many think of immediate financial considerations instead of the long-term consequences of our present environmental practices.

Some people wish to treat the environment not just as an economic commodity; they see that the earth must be healthy to sustain humans and our fellow species. This ecological view represents a shift in attitude that has been gaining momentum throughout the world. Events such as Earth Day in 1970, the Rio Environmental Conference in 1992, the Kyoto Treaty in 2001, and the Copenhagen Climate Conference in 2009 address the importance of a safe, healthy environment for sustainable human life. A growing number of people think it is of utmost importance to save the planet from the ravages of climate change, melting glaciers, dropping water tables, and desertification.

A growing number of ecologists see the earth as an interconnected organism that can reawaken our sacred relationship with nature and in a positive sense support our psychic well-being. This shift of consciousness can revive an ancient mystical accord with nature that has sustained humans for millions of years. A modern, mechanistic view of life has contributed to a destructive relationship with the earth. Instead, some feel that a more benign connection with the earth would improve human health and mental well-being, as well as prevent the extinction of non human species that add to the diversity of life needed for a sustainable future.

After reading and reflecting upon this brief summary of the state of our environment, many of you may feel a sense of depression and hopelessness. I felt the same way when I was researching and writing this summary. But depression and hopelessness are the easy way out. Even though we are overshooting our earth's carrying capacity, it is not too late to make alterations. Our human capacity for thinking long-term, globally, and holistically does not have a proven track record, yet it is not beyond our capabilities. We can change, and it is my belief that we must do so. Adjusting our thinking to view the long-term consequences of our actions is paramount. In my humble opinion, growth needs to be reconsidered as the mantra of our society; instead, practicing and acting within the limits of our earth's capacity holds the key to our future well-being and survival.

This brief overview of environmental issues is a way each one of us can be more aware of how the issues interact together and affect us all. Much of the environmental destruction is due to human influence, but on the bright side modifications to our actions and policies can temper it. There are many organizations advocating specific ways to be actively involved in the effort to prevent our environmental suicide. Through our individual and collective actions we can turn around these devastating trends or risk being overwhelmed by them. Hopefully, we will feel empowered to act in constructive ways to prevent further environmental devastation and usher in positive changes.

**Questions to Consider**

1. What do you think is the most pressing environmental issue of our times? What can we do about it?

## THE GROWING SOCIOECONOMIC GAP BETWEEN RICH AND POOR

When I visited London, UK in summer 2000, I traveled on its very efficient subway system throughout the city. As the doors of the subway cars opened, a computerized female voice warned passengers to "mind the gap." The gap was the narrow space between the subway car and the landing platform, which would have been virtually impossible for anyone's foot to lodge into. But someone with a cane or a person wearing high-heeled shoes could have possibly wedged a cane or heel into the gap, and suffered a fall. Therefore, I heeded "her" warnings, and it would ring in my mind every time the doors opened. I think this is a warning that we as a global society should heed as well: "mind the gap." By the gap I mean the socioeconomic gap that is widening, not only among Americans but across the world, as well.

In evaluating the impact of economic globalization, I have selected as my second criterion: Does this economic approach bring greater prosperity to a majority of the world's people than other forms of economic policy? We constantly hear in the media that millions of Chinese have been "lifted out" of poverty from their meager existence in rural villages to middle class consumers in the cities. The implied goal of economic globalization is to increase the standard of living for global citizens. But, to me, nagging questions about the process of economic globalization remain. Is everyone who wants a job able to find one in a globalized world? What kinds of jobs are being created? What happens to just under half of the world's population who are farmers? Should farmers leave their villages and land to venture to the cities to find work? Should industrial agriculture and automation grow our food? What are the social implications of these changes? There are many questions to ask about the growing global gap between rich and poor and examine whether the process of economic globalization contributes to this gap.

What do I mean by a **socioeconomic gap**? I will use my own definition in this case since I am combining two concepts into one for the purposes of this book. The **social gap** refers to a situation in which individuals in a society do not have equal access to the social programs provided by the government for its citizens. These include voting rights, freedom of speech and assembly, legal rights, security, and access to quality education, health care, job training, and other social goods. The **economic gap** refers to the disparities in the allocation of economic resources to society. Governmental rules tilt policies in determining the allocation of resources to favor those with more capital than those with less. It also ensures the continuation of the concentration of wealth through policies, such as a low inheritance tax and a low capital gains rate, which perpetuate the concentration of wealth.

## What Causes Inequality?

I use the term **inequality** in this book to mean the disparity between rich and poor. But what causes inequality? A common response is that greed, power, corruption, and money creates inequality, which is true, but that is only part of the story. Even in societies where governments are well-intentioned, policy choices and individual actions or inactions can add to inequality. In core nations, the political left usually makes the argument that inequality is a moral responsibility or a social justice issue which worsens social unity and weakens the fabric of society. On the other hand, the political right in core nations makes the case that there is equality of opportunity and individuals should be responsible for their own situation. Both viewpoints have some merit, individual initiative is very important, but inequalities are built into the system that is governed by those with wealth, power and influence.

Using a systems approach, the neoliberal economic and political policies today perpetuate inequality, contribute to population growth, and exacerbate the tendency to overshoot the earth's limits. The poverty-perpetuating structures arise from the fact that it is easier for elite populations to save, invest, and multiply their capital than it is for poor people to do so. The elite have built up a large stock of capital that multiplies itself. The poor have not. In poor countries, capital growth has a hard time keeping up with population growth. Output that might be reinvested is more likely to be required to provide schools and hospitals and fulfill subsistence needs. Because immediate requirements leave little output for industrial investment, the economy grows only slowly. When women see no attractive alternatives to childbearing, children are one of the few safety nets available; thus, population grows without growing richer. As the saying goes: "The rich get richer and the poor get children."[30] All parts of this reinforcing feedback loop have a strong influence on the behavior of populations in poorer areas. They form a "system trap," a "less success to the already unsuccessful" loop that keeps the poor people poor and the population growing. Although food production in the periphery has increased greatly over the past 20 years, because of rapid population growth food production per person has barely improved, and in Africa it has steadily decreased.[31]

One school of thought makes the point that economic globalization results in growing income between all the sectors of society, and even low-income groups have emerged as winners. The second school of thought says that economic globalization may increase total incomes but the advantages are not equally distributed among the national population, resulting in clear losers The research data suggests that income inequality has increased across nations over the last 20 years, and at the same time the average real incomes of the weaker sectors of society has stagnated. This shows that growing economic globalization has had equal and opposite effects on income distribution patterns. The factor which is connected with higher inequality is associated with growing economic openness.[32]

Economic globalization has resulted in a change from a class structure that was formerly nation based to one that is now globally based. For more than 30 years, the American economy has been in the midst of a sea change, shifting from industry to services and information technology, and integrating itself far more tightly into a single, global market for goods, labor, and capital. China, India, and other developing countries have fully emerged as economic competitors, capable of producing large volumes of high-value goods and services at a low price. This transformation has been underway since the 1980s, but the pace of the change has quickened since the turn of the millennium, and even more so since the 2008 financial crisis.[33] The hollowing out of the American middle class has taken place, amidst a surge in the formation of a middle class in Brazil, Russia, India, China (BRIC), and other countries. Since the economy is global in scope, the class structure is, as well. Although in the U.S. government and charity programs for food, shelter, and health care subsidize the very poor somewhat, the BRIC nations have no such safety net. Neoliberals are anxious to shred some of the existing threads of the social safety net, as in the BRIC nations, such as a minimum wage, Social Security, and government programs for the poor.

The extreme gap between the global rich and poor is due in part to economic globalization. Although technology contributes to growing inequality, I will primarily focus on economic globalization. Economist Joseph Stiglitz makes the point, "There is growing inequality in most countries of the world, and globalization is one of the factors that has contributed to this global pattern."[34] Economist Nouriel Roubini adds, "Globalization and innovation are not without risk. Take the daunting challenge of adding billions of people to the global labor supply. Globalization has also been associated with growing inequalities of income and wealth in advanced economies and emerging-market economies alike."[35]

For those of us who despair over the bad news about growing worldwide inequality, the

FAVELA (SLUM) IN SAO PAULO, BRAZIL.

## Reasons for Global Social and Economic Inequality[36]

Financial liberalization

Financial instability

Debt (the developing nations together owe $2.3 trillion to foreign creditors)

High interest rates

Trade liberalization

Agricultural liberalization

Business liberalization

Flexibility of labor market

Intellectual property enforcement

Privatization of public wealth to private assets

Diseases

Revolution in information technology

Financial deregulation

Upper income tax bracket cuts (particular in the U.S.)

Human Development Index (HDI) interpretation of data provides some modest good news. This HDI fact reflects the fact that world income and greater inequality have both risen. The report cites that in some basic respects, the world is a much better place today than it was in 1990 – or in 1970. Over the past 20 years, many people around the world have experienced improvements in key aspects of their lives. Overall, they are healthier, more educated and wealthier and have more power to appoint and hold their leaders accountable than ever before. Combining information on life expectancy, schooling and income, the world's average HDI has increased 18 percent since 1990 and 41 percent since 1970. This increase reflects improvements in life expectancy, school enrollment, literacy and income. But there has also been considerable variability and much volatility. Of 135 countries in the HDI sample for 1970-2010, with 92 percent of the world's people, only 3 – the Democratic Republic of the Congo, Zambia and Zimbabwe – have a lower HDI today than in 1970. The countries that have made the greatest progress in improving their HDI score include China, Indonesia and South Korea. But progress has been made in the non-income dimensions of human development in such countries as Nepal, Oman and Tunisia.[37]

## Three Socioeconomic Classes

Our study of socioeconomic inequality continues with an examination of the following classes in the world: the elite, the middle class, and the poor.

### 1. The World's Elite Class

You might think the world's most expensive home belongs to the Bill Gates' family; after all he has topped the list of the richest people in the world for many years and lives in the richest country: the United States. No need to fear, Gates does have a very large home. His family home is a large earth-sheltered mansion built into the side of a hill overlooking Lake Washington near Seattle, Washington. It is 66,000 square feet in size (the average American home is 2,349 square feet) and it is noted for its sophisticated design and technology. In 2009, property taxes were reported to be $1.063 million on a total assessed value of $147.5 million. Yet, the Gates family home pales in comparison to the world's most expensive home which is in India – with a never-before-seen $1 billion price tag. Mukesh Ambani, India's richest man and the fourth-richest man in the world, owns the 27-floor, 570-foot-tall home located in Mumbai, India, one of the most unequal cities in the world. The home features such amenities as a health club with a gym and dance studio, at

ANTILIA IS A 27-FLOOR PERSONAL HOME IN SOUTH MUMBAI, INDIA BELONGING TO BUSINESSMAN MUKESH AMBANI. A FULL-TIME STAFF OF 600 MAINTAINS THE RESIDENCE.

least one swimming pool, a 50-seat movie theater, a ballroom, three helipads and an underground parking lot that holds 160 vehicles.[38]

Gates and Ambani are among the elites of the world, both billionaires and symbolic of the growing gap between rich and poor. While Gates is more well-known as founder and CEO of Microsoft, Ambani, born in 1957, is a rising Indian entrepreneur, and for a time in 2010 the richest man in the world. He is the managing director of Reliance Industries, the largest private sector enterprise in India, and a Fortune 500 company. His share of the company is 48 percent. Ambani took over Reliance Industries from his father, who founded the company in 1966 and entrusted leadership to his two sons – Mukesh and his brother Anil. The two brothers had business disagreements, which led to the splitting up of the company. Both have achieved billionaire status. Though Reliance Industries' oil-related operations form the core of its business, it has diversified operations to include financial products introduced to the Indian stock markets.

In a world where the 400 highest income earners from the United States earn as much money annually as the total population of 20 African countries, inequality seems out of bounds.[39] At the very top of the wealth pyramid, there are over 1,000 billionaires globally, of which 245 are in Asia Pacific, 230 are in Europe and 500 are in North America. Moving down the wealth pyramid, there are 80,000 ultra-wealthy individuals with worth over $50 million each. Added into this wealthy summit is another 24 million adults with worth between $1 million and $50 million – just over 800,000 live in China, around 170,000 live in India and over four million are in the rest of the Asia Pacific. Below this, more than 330 million individuals have average wealth per adult of $100,000 to $1 million. The world's richest 1 percent – adults who have at least $588,000 to call their own – hold 43 percent of the world's wealth. No other nation holds as much total wealth as the United States. With only 5.2 percent of the world's population, the U.S. boasts 23 percent of the world's adults worth at least $100,000 and an even greater proportion, 41 percent, of the world's millionaires.[40]

Switzerland and Norway have emerged as the richest nations in the world in terms of average wealth per adult, which stands at $372,692 and $326,530 respectively. They are followed by Australia, which is in third place with average wealth per adult of $320,909 and Singapore with average wealth per adult of $255,488. Figures for Australia and Singapore have both doubled in the last decade.[41] The U.S. itself also has the largest inequality gap between rich and poor compared to all the other industrialized nations.[42]

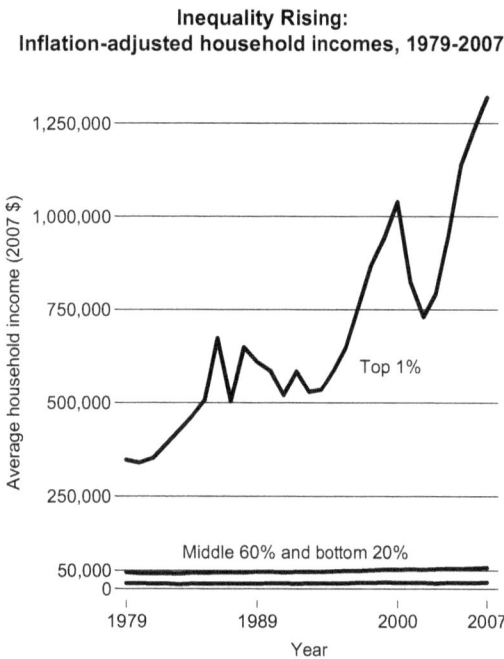

**Inequality Rising:**
**Inflation-adjusted household incomes, 1979-2007**

Note: Inflation-adjusted posttransfer-posttax incomes. The data are averages within each group. Incomes in 1979 and 2007: $15,500 and $17,500 for the bottom 20%; $44,000 for the top 1%. The years listed on the horizontal axis are business-cycle peaks.

GRAPH SHOWING CHANGES IN REAL US INCOMES IN TOP 1%, MIDDLE 60%, AND BOTTOM 20% FROM 1979 THROUGH 2007

Total global wealth fell from $104.7 trillion in 2007, to $92.4 trillion in 2008 – a decline of 11.7 percent. *Forbes* magazine lamented the drop in wealth saying 'The world's wealthy are getting poorer and poorer at an alarming rate." According to *Forbes*, "The rich seem to have joined the middle class on the metaphorical bread line, which is not good news for developed economies that are counting on consumer spending to help drive GDP growth rebounds. The wealthy may buy different goods and services than the middle class do, but their share of overall purchasing power is tremendous."[43] I am not exuding sympathy for the millionaires and billionaires who have joined the "middle class." They have enough to eat, and still enough wealth to carry them through what they consider "hard times." I am distressed to read that a reason cited for *Forbes'* alarm in the declining wealth of the elite class is that it will harm consumer spending. There is no mention of the fact that a decline in wealth among the elite could cause a reduction in their companies' ability to create jobs for those who really are in the bread line, not just the metaphorical one. I am suspicious of the reasons cited for cutting taxes for the wealthy: it will help stimulate the economy by creating jobs. According to *Forbes*, it looks as though a decline in their wealth means that they won't be able to buy luxury goods at Tiffany's or high end cars such as Bentleys.

I could churn out more facts about the world's elite class that could make your eyes glaze over. But I think a description of the world's very wealthy elite is more interesting and instructive in how they are fashioning their way of life. The following is an excerpt from an article in the *Atlantic Magazine*.

---

## The Rich Today    *by Chrystia Freeland* [44]

The rich of today are different from the rich of yesterday. Our light-speed, globally connected economy has led to the rise of a new super-elite that consists, to a notable degree, of first- and second-generation wealth. Its members are hardworking, highly educated, jet-setting meritocrats who feel they are the deserving winners of a tough, worldwide economic competition – and many of them, as a result, have an ambivalent attitude toward those of us who didn't succeed so spectacularly. Perhaps most noteworthy, they are becoming a trans-global community of peers who have more in common with one another than

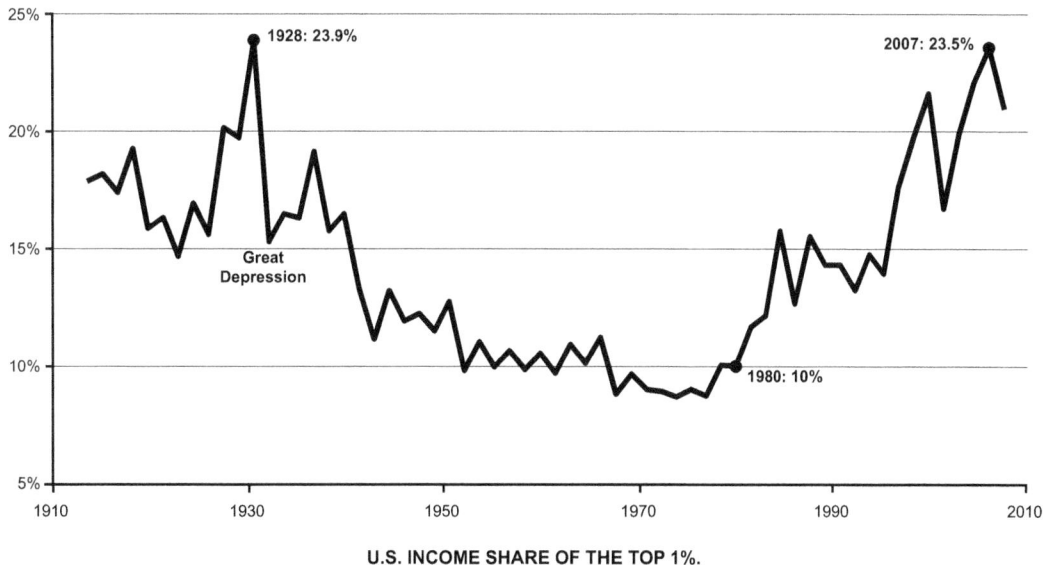

**U.S. INCOME SHARE OF THE TOP 1%.**

with their countrymen back home. Whether they maintain primary residences in New York or Hong Kong, Moscow or Mumbai, today's super-rich are increasingly a nation unto themselves.

Income inequality has also increased in developing markets, such as India and Russia, and across much of the industrialized West, from the relatively laissez-faire United States to the comfy social democracies of Canada and Scandinavia. The global market and its associated technologies have enabled the creation of a class of international business megastars. But the biggest winners have been individuals, not institutions. While their excesses seem familiar, even archaic, today's plutocrats represent a new phenomenon. The wealthy of F. Scott Fitzgerald's era were shaped, he wrote, by the fact that they had been "born rich." They knew what it was to "possess and enjoy early." In 1916, the richest 1 percent of Americans received only one-fifth of their income from paid work; in 2004, that figure had risen threefold, to 60 percent. They are not aristocrats, by and large, but rather economic meritocrats, preoccupied not merely with consuming wealth but with creating it. The debutante balls and hunts and regattas of yesteryear may not be quite obsolete, but they are headed in that direction. The real community life of the 21st century plutocracy occurs on the international conference circuit. The best-known of these events is the World Economic Forum's annual meeting in Davos, Switzerland, invitation to which marks an aspiring plutocrat's arrival on the international scene.[45]

The super-wealthy have long recognized that philanthropy, in addition to its moral rewards, can also serve as a pathway to social acceptance and even immortality: Andrew "The Man Who Dies Rich Dies Disgraced" Carnegie transformed himself from robber baron to secular saint with his hospitals, concert halls, libraries, and university; Alfred Nobel ensured that he would be remembered for something other than the invention of dynamite. What is notable about today's plutocrats is that they tend to bestow their fortunes in much the same way they made them: entrepreneurially. Rather than merely donate to worthy charities or endow existing institutions, they are using their wealth to test new ways to solve big problems. George Soros is a pioneer and role model for the socially engaged billionaire. Arguably the most successful investor of the post-war era, he is nonetheless proudest of his Open Society Foundations, through which he has spent billions of dollars on issues as diverse as marijuana legalization, civil society in central and eastern Europe, and rethinking economic assumptions in the wake of the financial crisis. A measure of the importance of public engagement for today's super-rich is the zeal with which even emerging-market plutocrats are developing their own foundations and think tanks. One of the most determined is the Ukrainian entrepreneur Victor Pinchuk, whose business empire ranges from pipe manufacturing to TV stations. With a net worth of $3 billion, Pinchuk is no longer content merely to acquire modern art: in 2009, he began a global competition for young artists, run by his art center in Kiev and conceived a way of bringing Ukraine into the international cultural mainstream. A defining characteristic of today's plutocrats is they are forming a global community, and their ties to one another are increasingly closer than their ties back home. Circles are defined by "interests" and "activities" rather than "geography." The elite of Beijing have more in common with fellow elites in New York, London, or Mumbai than Chinese citizens in smaller cities.

The good news – and the bad news – for America is that the nation's own super-elite is rapidly adjusting to this more global perspective. The U.S.- based CEO of one of the world's largest hedge funds said his firm's investment committee often discusses the question of who wins and who loses in today's economy. In a recent internal debate, he said, one of his senior colleagues had argued that the hollowing-out of the American middle class didn't really matter. "His point was that if the transformation of the world economy lifts four people in China and India out of poverty and into the middle class, and meanwhile means one American drops out of the middle class, that's not such a bad trade," the CEO recalled. I heard a similar sentiment from the Taiwanese-born, 30-something CFO of a U.S. internet company. An unpretentious man who went from public school to Harvard, he's nonetheless not terribly sympathetic to the complaints of the American middle class. "We demand a higher paycheck than the rest of the world," he told me. "So if you're going to demand 10 times the paycheck, you need to deliver 10 times the value. It sounds harsh, but maybe people in the middle class need to decide to take a pay cut."

Many of America's business elites appear removed from the continuing travails of the U.S. workforce and economy: the global "nation" in which they increasingly live and work is doing fine – indeed, it's thriving. For the super-elite, a sense of meritocratic achievement can inspire high self-regard, and that self-regard – especially when compounded by their isolation among like-minded peers – can lead to obliviousness and indifference to the suffering of others.

Many American plutocrats suggest that the trials faced by the working and middle classes are generally their own fault. This plutocratic fantasy is, of course, just that: no matter how smart and innovative and industrious the super-elite may be, they can't exist without the wider community. When the business elite view themselves increasingly as a global community, distinguished by their unique talents and above such parochial concerns as national identity, or devoting "their" taxes to paying down "our" budget deficit, they appear to be isolating themselves ideologically. The real threat facing the super-elite, at home and abroad, isn't modestly higher taxes, but rather the possibility that inchoate public rage could cohere into a more concrete populist agenda. The lesson of history is that, in the long run, super-elites have two ways to survive: by suppressing dissent or by sharing their wealth.

## 2. The World's Middle Class

The world's middle class is essentially a tale between two middle class groups: one is the old middle class of the core nations and the other is a newly emerging middle class of the middle and periphery countries. The old middle class is seeing the erosion of the established standards for what their countries defined as a middle class way of life, and the new middle class is developing its own standards for its way of life. The prospects for both of them are tied to economic globalization.

The period of 1948-1973 in the United States was a time when the American middle class made real headway. The wealthy made strides as well, but the middle class gained the most. It was a time when the working class, in "blue collar" jobs, also gained income and were able to attain a middle class standard of living. Although partially a result of America's unique status after the war, it was also a result of a set of governmental policies enacted to support the growth and prosperity of an expanding middle class. As I mentioned in chapter 1, the government is largely the arbitrator who determines what group reaps the most economic spoils. During the post-war years, governmental policy was firmly in the middle class camp.

The middle class way of life has changed since the 1980s for the core nations, with the double-edged onslaught of two policies that favor the wealthy: neoliberalism and economic globalization. The wealthy designed the rules of economic globalization to benefit them; they encourage competition among countries for business, which drives down taxes on corporations, weakens health and environmental protections, and undermines what was considered core labor rights, including the right to collective bargaining.[46] On the other hand, policies that favor the middle class – higher incomes tax rates on the wealthy, ample funding for education, low-interest loans for education, research and development that encourages job creation, a significant inheritance tax rate, tax deductions for home ownership, a safety net for economic hardships, and pensions for retirement – have all been eroding in the last 30 years. While income differences have widened in Britain and the U.S., social mobility, which favors the middle class, has slowed. Bigger income differences may make it harder to achieve equality of opportunity because they increase social class differentiation.[47]

Governmental policies in Europe favor the middle class, although this is eroding in some European countries. Denmark, Finland, the Netherlands and Slovenia ranked as the most equal countries, while Greece, the UK and Spain were among the most unequal in Europe. Canada, in North America, follows the European model. The wealth of the typical Canadian family in 2010 was $94,700; that is about double the $47,771 U.S. median net worth.[48] Studies have found that once nations are industrialized, more equal societies almost always do better in terms of health, well-being and social cohesion. Large income inequalities within societies destroy the social fabric and quality of life.

The policies of economic globalization favor the wealthy, but this does not mean that the middle class has disappeared. After all, during the highly unequal time of slavery in the American South, there was a professional middle class to provide services for the elite. A global phenomenon today is the emergence of one billion individuals situated in the middle segment of the wealth pyramid. This is the global middle class. The middle class has average wealth per adult of $10,000 to $100,000 and owns one-sixth of global wealth. Almost 60 percent or 587 million individuals in the middle segment are located in Asia Pacific, the fastest-growing economies of the world. The middle class of this region is expected to replace the indebted U.S. middle class households as the global growth locomotive.[49]

## The American Middle Class Way of Life

job security, retirement pensions, disposable income, home ownership, 2 cars, free highway transportation, free, quality public education in grades k-12, low-cost higher education, the chance for upward mobility, leisure time, low-cost medical care, low-cost material comforts, cultural stimulations, honest institutions, personal security, safe and low-cost food, low taxes, array of social services

How did the middle class expand in Asia Pacific countries and shrink in many core and other periphery countries, such as the United States? Mostly countries simply stopped making things and started buying them from the Asian Pacific countries. Since 2000, the U.S. has lost 3 million manufacturing jobs; Brazil has lost 2 million since 1998, and South Africa has lost nearly 1 million. In the past, Argentina assembled televisions; now it purchases most of them from abroad. Mozambique in Africa packaged its cashew crop 15 years ago; today the country ships its raw nuts overseas for others to bottle and can. Zambians made their own clothes in the 1980s; now they sort through bundles of clothes shipped from the U.S. and Europe. The Hunters Point neighborhood in San Francisco used to manufacture the ships that delivered American-made goods to the world; now the ships docked in the Bay Area's ports are mostly from East Asia, unloading foreign-made products for U.S. consumers.[50]

## 3. The World's Poor

Global inequalities exist at astounding levels. But before we go on, I would like to distinguish between inequality and poverty. Inequality – the disparity between rich and poor – is a broader concept than poverty in that it is defined over the entire population, not just for the portion of the population below a certain poverty line. **Poverty**, on the other hand, is the state of being poor: the state of not having enough money to take care of basic needs such as food, clothing, and housing.[51]

MIDDLE CLASS IN BEIJING, CHINA.
PHOTO DENISE AMES

The world's poor make up at least 80 percent of humanity. They live on less than $10 a day, which does not include populations living on less than $10 a day from industrialized nations.[52] Data from the IMF finds the earnings of 10 percent of the richest global population is 117 times higher than the poorest 10 percent. This is a considerable increase from the percentage in 1980, when the earnings of the 10 percent of the richest population was around 79 times greater than 10 percent of the poorest population.[53]

At other end of the global economic spectrum are parked three billion people – more than two thirds of the world's adults – whose wealth averages less than $10,000. About 1.1 billion of them have a net worth of less than $1,000 and of that number 307 million are in India. Half the people on earth who are 20 and older hold under $4,000 in net worth (subtract debts from assets). They hold less than 2 percent of global wealth.[54] There are now 1.3 billion people who live on the equivalent of less than $1 per day.[55]

Income inequality in Latin America has increased in the 2000s. For example, per capita income in Latin America increased by 82 percent between 1960 and 1980 and only by 13 percent from 1990 to 2005. The richest 10 percent of the Latin population earns 48 percent of its total income, while the poorest 10 percent earns only 1.6 percent. In 2010, the Inter Press Service (IPS) reported that 10 of the 15 most unequal countries in the world are in Latin America: Bolivia, followed by Haiti, Brazil, Ecuador, and Chile, which is tied in fifth place with Colombia, Guatemala, Honduras, Panama and Paraguay.[56]

What is the reason for this rising inequality? Critics such as Jeter forcefully argue that "The global economy has ripped a hole through the earth, city by city, block by block, house by house. Globalization has widened inequality, corrupted politicians, estranged neighbors from one another, unraveled families, rerouted rivers, emptied ports of ships, and flooded streets with protesters. It has created poverty where it did not exist and deepened poverty for women, people of color, and indigenous people."[57] For example, policies associated with economic globalization have been blindly

## World Bank Data Showing Poverty Decline

| Region | $1 per day | | | | $1.25 per day | |
|---|---|---|---|---|---|---|
| | 1990 | 2002 | 2004 | | 1981 | 2008 |
| East Asia and Pacific | 15.40% | 12.33% | 9.07% | | 77.2% | 14.3% |
| Europe and Central Asia | 3.60% | 1.28% | 0.95% | | 1.9% | 0.5% |
| Latin America and the Caribbean | 9.62% | 9.08% | 8.64% | | 11.9% | 6.5% |
| Middle East and North Africa | 2.08% | 1.69% | 1.47% | | 9.6% | 2.7% |
| South Asia | 35.04% | 33.44% | 30.84% | | 61.1% | 36% |
| Sub-Saharan Africa | 46.07% | 42.63% | 41.09% | | 51.5% | 47.5% |
| World | | | | | 52.2% | 22.4% |

prescribed to poor countries to open up their economies. The idea is that opening markets for foreign investment will also help improve exports and contribute to economic growth. Cutting back on social spending, such as health and education, is seen as a way to help pay back loans and debts. Periphery nations lose their ability to develop their own policies and local businesses end up competing with well-established multinationals. For example, world income has increased by nearly $1 trillion since 1990 while sub-Saharan Africa's per capita income has fallen by 20 percent in that same time. Black South Africa vanquished apartheid only to confront unemployment rates approaching 40 percent and whole city blocks plunged into darkness because no one can afford the rising costs of electricity charged by the newly privatized utility companies.[58]

The enduring gap between rich and poor, both within and between countries, is a crisis that lies at the heart of our political and economic problems. Supporters of economic globalization firmly maintain that it is the only path leading to global poverty reduction, while the causes of enduring

## Inequality Facts[59]

- Over 3 billion people live on less than $2.50 a day.
- At least 80% of humanity lives on less than $10 a day.
- The poorest 40% of the world's population accounts for 5% of global income.
- The richest 20% accounts for 75% of world income.
- According to UNICEF, 22,000 children die each day due to poverty.
- Around 27-28% of all children in periphery countries are underweight or stunted.
- The two poorest regions of the world are South Asia and sub-Saharan Africa.
- Nearly a billion people entered the 21st century unable to read a book or sign their names.
- Every year there are 350–500 million cases of malaria, with 1 million fatalities.
- Worldwide, Africa accounts for 90% of malarial deaths and African children account for over 80%.
- 1.1 billion people in the periphery have poor access to water and 2.6 billion lack basic sanitation.
- Of the 2.2 billion children in the world, 1 billion live in poverty – every second child.
- 10.6 million children died in 2003 before they reached the age of 5.
- In the periphery 2.5 billion people rely on fuelwood for cooking, such as charcoal and animal dung.
- World consumption: poorest 10% accounted for 0.5% and the wealthiest 10% accounted for 59%.
- 1.6 billion people live without electricity.
- 12% of the world's core population uses 85% of its water.
- 1 billion people in 2009 were hungry.
- At least 1.4 billion people live in extreme poverty.
- One out of every five people does not have access to clean drinking water.
- More than a billion people lack access to basic health care services.
- Over a billion people – the majority of them women – lack a basic education.
- Every week, more than 115,000 people move into a slum in Africa, Asia or Latin America.
- For decades, 20% of the world population has controlled 80% of the economy and resources.
- By 2008, more than half of the world's assets were owned by the richest 2% of adults.
- By 2008, the bottom half of the world adult population owned only 1% of the world's assets.

inequality are to be located principally in the failure of countries to integrate fast enough or deep enough into the world economy. They argue more, rather than less, globalization is the principal remedy for eradicating global poverty. And the way that economic globalization works to end poverty is an increase in economic growth. Many sincerely believe that the pursuit of growth will end world poverty. They cite the number of middle class Chinese and Indians as testimony to the growth strategy for ending poverty. They argue that wealth from growth will trickle down to the poor.

But growth will not abolish poverty. In fact, current modes of growth actually perpetuate poverty and amplify the gap between the rich and the poor. In 1998 more than 45 percent of the world's people had to survive on incomes averaging $2 a day or less. There were many more poor people than eight years earlier, despite astounding income gains. The 14-fold boost in world industrial output since 1930 has made some people very wealthy, but it has not ended poverty. Another 14-fold increase (even if that were possible within our earthly limits) would not end poverty, unless the global system was restructured to direct growth to those who need it most. In the current system economic growth generally takes place in the already-rich countries and flows disproportionately to the richest people within those countries.[60]

Despite the evidence, supporters of growth argue that it is still the best way to secure a prosperous future for the 3 billion people who continue to live on less than $2.50 a day. The fact that decades of economic growth have not made a significant dent in global poverty is enough evidence that the proceeds of growth are not sufficiently "trickling down" to those most in need. In fact, any trickle there may have been is rapidly drying up despite any increases in the size of the economic pie; in the 1980's, 2.2 percent of global growth went to the poor, compared to only 0.6 percent in the 1990s. The consequence of this skewed distribution of growth is, unsurprisingly, that the world is increasingly unequal, with the richest 10 percent having accumulated 3,000 times more wealth than the poorest 10 percent.[61]

The following interesting fact further supports the questioning of growth as a solution to reduce world poverty. Between 1990 and 2001, for every $100 worth of growth in the world's income per person, just $0.60, down from $2.20 the previous decade, found its target and contributed to reducing poverty below the $1-a-day line. Another statistic reinforces the dismantling of the growth solution to world poverty: A single dollar of poverty reduction took $166 of additional global production and consumption, with all its associated environmental impacts. It created the paradox that ever smaller amounts of poverty reduction amongst the poorest people of the world required ever larger amounts of consumption by the richest people.[62] In other words, the world's richest people cannot reduce world poverty by just consuming more!

URBAN POOR IN THIS SLUM IN JAKARTA, INDONESIA.

## Inequality in Cities Around the World

The United Nations Habitat's State of the World's Cities 2008/2009 report has found that disparities within cities and between cities and regions within the same country are growing. In cities that have high levels of inequality the

243

chance of more disparities increases with economic growth. This is because high levels of urban inequality have a dampening effect on economic growth and contribute to a less favorable environment for investment. For example, the report adds that in many developing cities, wealthier citizens live in private spaces and avoid visiting or walking around in city centers. As a result, they do not care much about city's parks or public schools but may be more interested in better roads.[63]

Within burgeoning cities are **slums**, densely populated, squalid, sections of the cities inhabited by poor people. The reasons cited for the rise in slums is migration from the countryside, changes towards neoliberal economic ideology, corruption, globalization factors and so on. The problem is so immense that, according to UN Habitat report, approximately 1 billion people live in slums – approximately 1 in every 6 people on the planet. While there have been some successes in reducing the number of people living in such areas in recent years by about a tenth (mostly in China and India), numerous problems persist. In developing countries about 1 in 3 people living in cities are living in slum areas.[64]

## Insights: The Socioeconomic Gap

My argument is that neoliberal policies that have shaped economic globalization have largely contributed to the growing socio-economic gap between the rich and poor and squeezed the middle class in core countries. The assumption that the ever-expanding path of growth

### Some findings of the 2008/2009 UN Habitat Report[65]

Half of all humanity lives in urban areas.

3 million people per week are added to the cities of the developing world.

The most unequal cities were in South Africa, Namibia and Latin America.

New York is the 9th most unequal city in the world while Atlanta, New Orleans, Washington, and Miami had similar inequality levels to those of Nairobi, Kenya and Abidjan, Ivory Coast.

Beijing is the world's most egalitarian city, just ahead of Jakarta, Indonesia and Dire Dawa, Ethiopia.

Generally rural areas exhibit more poverty than urban areas.

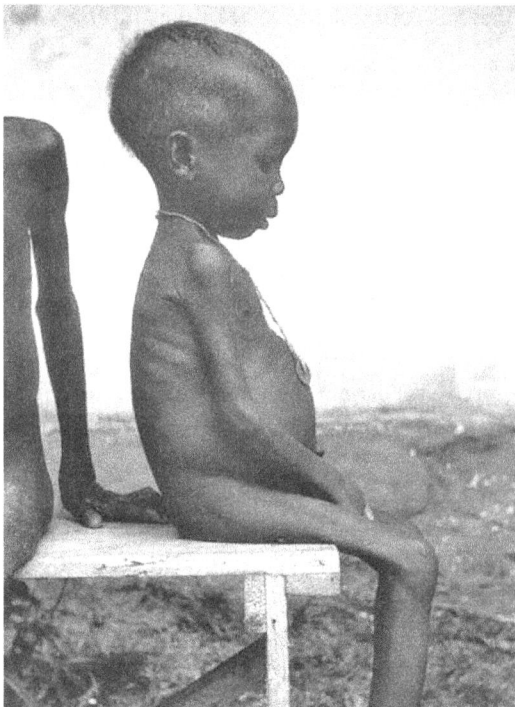

STARVED GIRL IN AFRICA.

STREET CHILD IN BANGLADESH.

and consumption is the answer to reduce social inequality is questionable. It does, however, allow us to skirt around the bigger issue relating to work-and-spend lifestyles that core nations have become accustomed to, and which we unquestioningly assume to be the correct and best development models for periphery nations to follow.[66]

---

### Questions About Growth[67]

1. Growth of what?
2. Growth for whom?
3. Who pays for growth?
4. At what cost is growth?
5. What is the real need?
6. What is the most direct and efficient way for those who have that need to be able to satisfy it?
7. How much is enough?
8. What are the obligations to share?

---

Yet, for decades, it has been a heresy for economists or politicians to question conventional ideas of economic growth. Therefore, it makes no sense to talk about growth with either unquestioning approval or unquestioning disapproval. Instead, we need to rethink growth and ask politicians and ourselves the eight vital questions on the left.

---

### Questions to Consider

1. How would you and your friends or colleagues answer the questions about growth?

---

# WELL-BEING

---

### Human Development Report from the United Nations

Human development is about much more than the rise or fall of national incomes. It is about creating an environment in which people can develop their full potential and lead productive, creative lives in accord with their needs and interests. People are the real wealth of nations. Development is thus about expanding the choices people have to lead lives that they value. This way of looking at development, often forgotten in the immediate concern with accumulating commodities and financial wealth, is not new. Philosophers, economists and political leaders have long emphasized human well-being as the purpose of development. As Aristotle said in ancient Greece, "Wealth is evidently not the good we are seeking, for it is merely useful for the sake of something else." Yet, for a variety of reasons, these "full rights" are not available in many segments of various societies from the richest to the poorest. When political agendas deprive these possibilities in some nations, how can a nation develop? Is this progress?

---

The UN Human Development Report is a good lead in to the final criteria I am using for evaluating economic globalization: Has economic globalization contributed to the well-being of the world's citizens? Now that is a vague question sure to elicit millions of different responses. First of all, I should define well-being. I think of **well-being** as a kind of contentment, happiness, or a state of life-satisfaction. One definition says it is the state of being happy, healthy, or prosperous. Another source says well-being is a good or satisfactory condition of existence; a state characterized by health, happiness, and prosperity; welfare.[68] Often well-being is associated with health, but philosophically it is broader than just health-related. A closely related term is welfare, which covers how a person is faring as a whole, or happiness, which I see as the balance between good and bad things in a person's life. In this context happiness is a feeling of contentment or life-satisfaction. However, I prefer to use the term well-being. Many years ago, my mother-in-law gave me a cherished gift – a round pewter plate with the inscription "health, wealth, and happiness, and the time to enjoy them." I think that sums it up.

The field of life-satisfaction and well-being critique the doctrine of economic growth. Studies have found that in core countries patterns of work and rising consumption are promoted and pursued but repeatedly fail to deliver the expected gains in life satisfaction. Despite high and sustained levels of economic growth in the West over a period of 50 years – growth that has seen average real incomes increase several times over – the mass of people are no more satisfied with their lives now than they were in the 1950s! At the same time, these patterns of work potentially erode current well-being by undermining family relationships and the time needed for personal development.[69]

The New Economic Foundation studies show that once people have enough to meet their basic needs and are able to survive with reasonable comfort, higher levels of consumption do not correspond to higher levels of well-being. Instead, people tend to adapt relatively quickly to improvements in their material standard of living, and soon return to their prior level of life satisfaction. But the consumer culture promotes the idea of "keeping up with the Joneses," in which ever higher levels of consumption are linked to the belief that this will lead to a better life. This treadmill effect means that higher expectations leave people "running faster" to consume more in order to be happier instead of merely standing still.[70]

Life satisfaction figures stay stubbornly flat once a fairly low level of GDP per capita is reached. For example, in the U.S., people in the 1950s scored higher than today on life satisfaction surveys, even though their standard of living was considered lower than today's.[71] We wonder how they could be happier without cell phones, internet, and facebook! If growth is intended to give us better lives, and this is its primary purpose, it has not lived up to its promises.

Some critics of the current Gross Domestic Product (GDP) method of economic measurement – measures national spending without regard to economic, environmental, or social well-being – suggest replacing GDP with a **Genuine Progress Indicator** (GPI). The GPI, created by the organization Redefining Progress in 1995, measures the general economic and social well-being of all citizens. For example, if a business degrades the environment in some way, such as an oil spill, the costs associated with the clean-up effort contribute to an increase in the GDP, since the total dollars spent in the clean-up add to national revenues and actually grow the economy according to this measurement. But this calculation ignores the environmental damage inflicted upon the earth that has a negative, long-lasting cost, impacting not only the economy but human health as

**SMILING GIRL, !KUNG, BUSHMEN IN SOUTHWEST AFRICA.**
PHOTO IZLA BARDAVID

well. In calculating the GPI, the costs associated with the oil spill would be subtracted from the national economy, since it damages the environment over the long-term. Interestingly, if using the GPI calculations, the U.S. economy has been stagnant from 1970 to 2004.[72]

---

**Questions to Consider**

1. What do you consider the components of well-being should be?

---

# TWO NATIONS AND ECONOMIC GLOBALIZATION

From many accounts the periphery has suffered under economic globalization. When the U.N. General Assembly decided in 1971 to create a new category of Least Developed Countries (LDCs), it labeled only 25 countries as the poorest of the world's poor. Currently, there are 48 LDCs – 33 in Africa, 14 in Asia and one in the Caribbean – which include over 800 million people. Botswana was the first LDC to buck the trend and graduate to the developing world back in 1994, and since then only two other countries have graduated: Cape Verde and the Maldives. The rest, however, have been going mostly downhill, say LDC leaders who complain of rising debts, declining development aid, poor commodity prices and increased Western tariff barriers for third world products.[73] The study says that 80 percent of the world's 20 poorest countries have suffered a major civil war in the past 15 years. These countries include Afghanistan, Angola, Cambodia, the Democratic Republic of Congo, Eritrea, Ethiopia, Haiti, Liberia, Mozambique, Rwanda, Sierra Leone and Somalia – all of them LDCs.[74]

I would argue that the continent that has suffered the most under economic globalization is Africa. The tremendous profitability of the current economic arrangement, not just a lack of political will, is one reason that keeps Africa poor. Sub-Saharan Africa, the poorest place on earth, is also the most profitable investment destination. It offers, according to a World Bank report, "the highest returns on foreign direct investment of any region in the world." Africa is poor because its investors and its creditors are so rich.[75] To illustrate why Sub-Saharan Africa is so poor and how economic globalization has contributed to its woes, I would like to focus on one particular country in the region, the largest and most mineral-rich and yet the most tragic: The Democratic Republic of Congo (DRC) or Congo. After reading this, you will get a better idea of why the region is so poor and the prospects of improvement so bleak.

Yet, each nation has somewhat of a choice in deciding its own future. I don't want to end on a note of despair. In contrast to the Congo, is the small Himalayan nation of Bhutan which is shaping its own destiny. It is fashioning its own future by weaving the benefits of economic globalization into its future plans while casting off the detrimental aspects. The two nations are a study in contrasts.

## The Tragedy of the Congo

The Democratic Republic of the Congo is a huge country located in Central Africa with an ethnically-diverse population of just over 66 million people. Ranking as the 11th largest land-area country in the world, it measures about one-fourth the size of the United States. Straddling the equator, the Congo has the second largest rain forest in the world. The capital and largest city is Kinshasa and the official language is French. It is often confused with its similarly-named neighbor the Republic of Congo. Through its modern history, it has been known as Zaire, the Congo Free State, and the Belgian Congo.[76] The Congo is one of those unfortunate countries that is resource rich, yet its people are poor.

Congo's modern exploitation started with European colonization from the 1870s until the 1920s. The famous British explorer and missionary, Sir Henry Morton Stanley, undertook exploration of the region under the sponsorship of King Leopold II of Belgium. Wanting to keep up with the British and French, who made earlier inroads into colonizing Africa, Leopold had designs on colonizing a huge swath of land in central Africa. He was able to formally acquire rights to the territory at the Conference of Berlin in 1885, the infamous conference in which the European colonial powers carved out claims for African colonies. Leopold made the land his private property. He ruled until 1908.

After 1889, the exploitation of the Congo began in earnest with the take-off of the ivory and rubber trades. The booming demand for rubber and its soaring prices sealed the fate of the Congo people. It took Leopold's government years to complete various infrastructure projects, such as construction of a railway that ran from the coast to the capital of Leopoldville (now Kinshasa). His purpose in creating these projects was to increase the investment returns from the colony. Leopold even used the Congo as his personal jewelry box, extracting precious gems worth a fortune. Under his rule, he subjected the Congo to the worst excesses and exploitation of modern European colonialism.

The colonists brutalized the local people to produce rubber. Used primarily in the manufacture of bicycle and automobile tires, rubber was originally derived from the milky latex sap found in rubber trees that grew wild in the Congo River basin. Although the plant was plentiful, the problem was how to harvest it cheaply. Since slavery was outlawed, a system to coerce indigenous people to work to collect rubber was needed. No African in his right mind wanted to work long, difficult hours under harsh conditions just so the Belgians would have an ample rubber supply, so the plan had to be brutally and rigidly enforced. And it was. The plan was to impose a general tax on the Congo people. To pay taxes one needs to have money. Most of the people of the Congo were subsistence farmers who lived in self-sufficient villages. They had no need for money. Since they lacked the Belgian money to pay the taxes, they had to pay the taxes in the form of labor collecting rubber. The Belgian government also conscripted their labor for special infrastructure projects, such as roads and harbors. Often these taxes were levied on chiefs or village headmen who then supplied slaves (although supposedly illegal) to the Belgian state. Once the plan for a steady supply of labor was set in place, rubber harvesting began in earnest.

Those in the rubber industry devised ways to acquire even more rubber. The industry hired agents to set collection quotas for villages. The agents rounded up workers and transported them to rubber vine regions, where they collected huge quantities of latex. As latex supplies dwindled from reckless over-harvesting, enforcement agents resorted to even harsher methods to meet their unattainable quotas. Agents forced men to bring their wives and children to work alongside them. Women and children were also kidnapped and held hostage, forcing men to work without pay as rubber-harvesters. The agents would not release their captives until the husbands brought back the required rubber quota. Even more common was a whipping with the fearsome *chicotte*, a thick whip fashioned into a corkscrew shape with edges as hard as wood and as sharp as knives. The agents implemented even harsher techniques to get more rubber. The most ghastly practices were limb amputations – cutting off hands and feet. Failure to meet the quota meant flogging, jail, or, in extreme cases, execution.

The Congolese population declined appreciably during Leopold's rule. Estimates vary, but some put it at 60 percent or more in certain areas. An astounding number of people died, approximately 10 million, more than the horrific Holocaust during World War II. Death was attributed to famine, pestilence, disease, crop destruction, overwork, hunger, and living in unsanitary work compounds. Leopold's rule unleashed a nightmarish deterioration in the conditions of daily life, contributing to the death of millions. The English author, Joseph Conrad, wrote *The Heart of Darkness* in 1902 about conditions in central Africa. Under King Leopold, the Congo became the heart of imperial darkness. Despite initial reluctance, the Belgian parliament in 1908 finally responded to international pressure, to end the atrocities under the rule of King Leopold II. It ook over the area and from then on, it was called the Belgian Congo and was under the rule of the elected Belgian government.

During the wave of post-World War II national independence movements in Africa, the Belgian Congo declared its independence on June 30, 1960. Patrice Lumumba led the independence movement and became the first Prime Minister. Shortly after he was sworn into office, rebels overthrew the popular Lumumba in a military coup in 1961, and he was subsequently kidnapped and executed. The U.S. and Belgium both supported the coup. The Congo has vast mineral wealth, in particular copper and diamonds, and both countries wanted a hand in gaining as much mineral wealth from the country as possible. Also, at the time, the U.S. supported very questionable world leaders, usually unelected military dictatorships, who took an anti-Communist stand.

For five tumultuous years, leadership changed hands in The Congo until Joseph Mobutu strong-armed his way to power in a bloodless military coup in 1965. Because of his staunch anti-Communist stance, Mobutu had U.S. support for his 31½ year reign. In 1971 he renamed the country the Republic of Zaire. While in office, he formed a totalitarian regime and regularly tortured or murdered rivals challenging his power. He notoriously mismanaged the country's economy and diverted money from the sale of vast natural resources to his supporters and for his own personal enrichment.

Mobutu almost single-handedly destroyed his country's economy, which had been one of Africa's best in the early 1960s. He presided over three decades of diverting revenue from the state's mining monopoly to his own personal piggy bank. Estimates showed that in 1984 Mobutu's personal fortune amounted to $5 billion, stashed away in safe Swiss bank accounts. While the nation's roads crumbled and people starved, he traveled between his numerous palaces in his personal fleet of Mercedes-Benz cars. His impoverished citizens looked

AMPUTEES IN THE CONGO AS A RESULT OF NOT MEETING RUBBER QUOTAS.

on as he bragged to a *60 Minutes* (a U.S. news program) reporter in 1984 that he was the world's second-richest man. Two years later, at the White House, President Reagan praised Mobutu, who the president considered to be a useful Cold War ally, as "a voice of good sense and goodwill." Many Congolese will never forget those words. During his reign, Mobutu had U.S. support, but relations noticeably cooled after the collapse of the Soviet Union in 1991. Through the 1990s, a cry for democratic reform swept the country. Although Mobutu promised reform and free elections, he failed to carry his promises through. By 1996, Mobutu's rule was weakening and tension with his numerous neighbors was mounting.

What followed is often referred to as the First Congo War (1996-1997). Although the war got little news coverage it claimed more than 200,000 causalities, mostly civilians. It ended when rebel forces backed by neighboring powers such as Uganda and Rwanda overthrew President Mobutu. Rebel leader Laurent-Désiré Kabila declared himself president and changed the name of the nation back to Democratic Republic of the Congo. However, Kabila failed to carry out democratic reforms, and charges of corruption against him were allegedly comparable to those committed by Mobutu. Democratic reformers turned against him, and they assassinated him in 2001. His son, Joseph Kabila, became president ten days later and continues to preside over the country at the time of this writing.

The more deadly Second Congo War (1998-2003) quickly followed. The war devastated the country, involved seven foreign armies and is sometimes referred to as the "African World War" or the "Great War of Africa." The war was the largest in modern African history and directly involved eight African nations – Rwanda, Zimbabwe, Uganda, Burundi, Angola, Chad, Sudan, Namibia, and about 25 armed militia groups – all vying for control of the country's rich natural resources. A 2003 peace agreement led to the formation of a transitional government in the Congo, and multi-party elections were held in 2006, President Joseph Kabila won. By 2008, the war and its aftermath had killed 5.4 million people, mostly from disease and starvation, making the Second Congo War the deadliest conflict worldwide since World War II. The conflict displaced millions of people from their homes, and they sought asylum in neighboring countries. Despite the peace accord, fighting continues in eastern Congo.

What has caused this horrible crisis that most people in the Western world know very little, if anything, about? The most obvious answer is corruption, graft, and greedy repressive dictators. Going below the surface to see why these ills have continued for so many decades, we see the Congo holds a treasure trove of valuable minerals that are the country's greatest blessing and most lasting curse. The Congo should be one of the world's richest countries, if the government honestly accounted for all the mineral wealth and distributed it evenly to its citizens. The Congo houses about a thousand mineral varieties: 10 percent of the planet's known copper; 30 percent of its cobalt; and 80 percent of its coltan. Between 1998 and 2001, coltan was the most desired mineral in the warring Congo, and the U.S. was the world's number one importer, until China took the top spot in 2002. Coltan is used in everything from PlayStations and iPods to magnets, cutting tools, and jet engines. The country also has untold quantities of bauxite and zinc, cadmium and uranium, gold and diamonds. The electronics and computer industries use cassiterite, a derivative of tin, and it has become the most coveted Congolese mineral (its use, ironically, makes devices more eco-friendly). Minerals in high demand by the modern electronics industry include tin, tantalum and tungsten, which are used in cell phones, iPods and digital cameras. Tin, produced from cassiterite, is used to solder circuit boards in cell phones and laptops. Tantalum, derived from coltan, is used to manufacture the batteries in cell phones, videogame consoles and laptops. Tungsten, from wolframite, creates the vibrations in cell phones.

The problem is that various factions in the Congo and in neighboring countries, along with rogue companies in the West and China are fighting over the mineral wealth. Since the Congolese government is so weak after decades of exploitation and war, the central government is unable or unwilling to stop the fighting and mistreatment of its people. When reformers forced Mobutu to resign, the network of graft he left behind easily shifted into a minerals-based war economy run by its own army, invaders, rebels, warlords, and mineral-seeking companies. Neighboring nations were willingly used as shipment points for the illegal minerals. Rebels have occupied two entire eastern provinces, where the bulk of the valuable minerals are mined. Congo's national army has become a partner in treachery and cooperates in the illegal trade. The army and rebels force workers, at the point of a gun, to extract the valuable minerals. Estimates show there are 1.5 million "diggers" in the Congo, who currently produce about 75 percent of the minerals exported from the Congo, mostly by clawing for nuggets with pickaxes or their bare hands. The mineral concentrate is typically smuggled to China on cargo ships or sent to Western or other Asian buyers.

This trade in minerals is fueling the conflict in eastern Congo. Armed groups control many of the mines and force individual miners to pay "taxes" on the minerals they mine. The money made by illegal mining funds militias who purchase weapons used to kill, loot and rape innocent civilians across the eastern Congo. Ongoing smuggling and corruption continues at all stages of the mining process. Without a strong central government or professional army, neighbors and trade partners have treated Congo's riches as an all-you-can-eat buffet.

Following the model of the "blood diamonds" campaign in Sierra Leone, there is a movement underway to make people who are buying these natural resources more thoughtful about their origin. A Congolese representative pointed out that while "blood diamonds" might be better known, there was also "blood copper," "blood gold," "blood coltan," and "blood cobalt." If the government honestly sourced and monitored all such exports, corporations would not buy "blood minerals," and there would

NORTHEAST PART OF THE DR CONGO IS HOME TO ONE OF THE WORLD'S RICHEST GOLDFIELDS, BUT ITS PEOPLE LIVE IN POVERTY, SCRAPING A LIVING FROM SMALL-SCALE GOLD MINING.

be no reason for militias to go to war to acquire them. Human rights activists are encouraging Congress to take action on "conflict minerals" as a way to stem the bloodshed.[77]

The long and brutal conflict has caused massive suffering for civilians. Along with millions dead either directly or indirectly as a result of the fighting, there are frequent reports of weapon bearers killing civilians, destroying property, committing widespread sexual violence, causing hundreds of thousands of people to flee their homes or otherwise breaching humanitarian and human rights law. Even though the UN continues to support a 17,000-strong peacekeeping mission, it is spread very thin across the vast territory. In 2009 people in the Congo were still dying at a rate of an estimated 45,000 per month, and 2,700,000 people have died since 2004. The death toll is due to widespread disease and famine. Children under the age of five are the hardest hit, accounting for nearly half of all deaths despite making up 19 percent of the population. They are especially susceptible to diseases like malaria, measles, dysentery, and typhoid, which can kill when medicine is not available.

Rape has been a tool of war throughout human history, but rarely in modern times have its practitioners been so brutal and random. Victims, as young as 3 and as old as 67, are turning up in clinics to seek medical treatment from vicious sexual assaults. Doctors say girls and boys have survived appalling violence, attacks that will affect them for the rest of their lives. The damage done to the victims is far more than physical. As is often the case, the victim is blamed in rape cases. Many Congolese men shun their wives for being raped, saying they must send them away because the women have been "unfaithful." Many rape victims are afraid to return to their villages for fear of being shunned or sent away, a near death sentence in a culture where family is of central importance. Although no one knows for sure how many women are rape victims, the United Nations estimates that 200,000 women have been raped in the past decade and that 40 are raped each day just in the eastern region of the Congo.

The aftermath of the war has gutted the country. Paradoxically, over a century of exploitation of the natural resources of this mineral-rich country has left the Congolese people one of the poorest people in the world. Of Congo's 66 million inhabitants, 80 percent live on 50 cents a day. The gross domestic product per capita is about $300, or less than a dollar a day. The Congo remains a humanitarian tragedy and a place of gross human rights violations.

## The Hope of Bhutan

Although the problems in the Congo appear unsolvable, there is a glimmer of light forming in the tiny nation of Bhutan. My partner in the Center for Global Awareness, Nancy Harmon, has traveled to the country several times with her tour guide husband, Roger Harmon. The following observations are her experiences traveling to the country.

In the fall of 2010, my husband and I fulfilled a dream by visiting the independent kingdom of Bhutan for the first time. We've now been there several times, leading tours for globally-aware travelers. We have been enchanted by Bhutan's beauty and charmed by its people. A predominantly Buddhist country, its colorful traditional culture is alive and well. Perhaps most interesting of all, this tiny country is in the vanguard of a new way of looking at economics and its relationship to well-being and happiness – the Index of Gross National Happiness (GNH).

Bhutan is a tiny country nestled in the beautiful valleys and on the slopes of the towering Himalaya Mountains between two giant nations, India and China. Its rugged geography and lack of roads kept it isolated from the rest of the world for centuries. Most people lived under a feudal system, working the land of wealthy landowners in exchange for food and protection. In the 1950s, the third in the dynasty of Wangchuckkings, King JigmeDorjiWangchuck, recognized Bhutan's need to modernize. China's invasion of Tibet around that time added urgency. Amazingly, this wise king was able to promulgate a non-violent land reform which abolished the feudal system and redistributed land, including that of the king's family, to peasants. As a result, most Bhutanese villagers ended up owning some land without a violent revolution! The National Assembly was also established, the first step toward democratic government, also a High Court, and an army and police force.

JigmeSingyeWangchuck, the fourth of the Wangchuck kings, vowed to continue modernization efforts after the death of his father in 1974. Although he was still a teenager, he understood from his father that accompanying the adoption of modern technology and higher living standards came devastating losses: environmental destruction, urban nightmares, family breakdown, loss of traditional values, and community dysfunction. Recognizing that Bhutan was in a unique position to prevent the mistakes of modernization, he instituted the Index of **Gross National Happiness (GNH)** as the core of Bhutan's development plan. The plan based GNP on the principle that wealth alone does not lead to happiness. Under the GNH plan, economic growth and modernization would not be allowed to jeopardize the peoples' quality of life, their traditional values or the environment, and all regions and segments of society would have to benefit equally from development through education, health care and a voice in a democratic government.

As we traveled through the country, we enjoyed the gorgeous scenery, the festivals and the friendly people, but we were most curious about GNH. What did it look like and how did people know if it was working? We learned that GNH was not just an interesting idea, but that it was being carefully described in ways that could be measured. Bhutanese leaders, consulting with respected scholars throughout the world, such as Ed Diener in the United States, worked to define happiness and use research on happiness to create, implement and evaluate their plan. Planners divide GNP into nine domains with indicators that break the domain into measureable parts.

What follows is a brief description of the nine domains contributing to gross national happiness with measureable indicators that have been assigned so that researchers can collect statistics to assess their progress. Included within each domain is what we witnessed as travelers, as well as what research on happiness says about the importance of each domain.

**1. Psychological Well-Being**: Indicators include life satisfaction, positive and negative emotion, and spirituality. Research on what creates happiness finds that people with a spiritual practice have more positive feelings than those without. We saw many indications of the importance of spirituality throughout our journey in Bhutan – prayer wheels turned by rushing rivers, prayer flags draped over mountain passes and bridges where they can more quickly send prayers throughout the universe, religious festivals attended by thousands, whole families making pilgrimages to holy places. Many schools begin the day with a few minutes of quiet meditation during morning assembly. These spiritual symbols and activities, so prominent throughout the country, seeped into our being as we traveled, and coupled with the kindness in the way people treated us, created the sense that there is compassion for all in this land. A common prayer/chant is, "May all beings be at peace."

**2. Health**: Indicators include physical and mental health. There is a school of traditional healing in Thimpu, as well as a hospital of Western medicine. The government subsidizes both and they were busy the day we visited. Health care is free to all, including travelers. The UN has deemed Bhutan a biodiversity "hotspot," and they use many of the plants in the high Himalayas in traditional healing. Life expectancy has increased from 44 to 65 in one generation thanks to local health clinics, vaccinations, and health education. Tobacco is illegal, and foreigners have to pay a fee in order to bring in their own supply. However, betel nut, a mild narcotic that when chewed turns the mouth red and rots the teeth, is still very common. Also, imported junk food is beginning to appear in packages, but fast food restaurants are still unheard of.

**3. Education**: indicators include literacy, schooling, knowledge and value given to education by the people. Happiness research indicates that people with at least a primary education are happier, but higher education does not seem to make a big difference. Education is free for all through the 10th grade and through post- secondary for those who pass a qualifying exam after 10th grade. We visited several schools and the courtesy and enthusiasm of the students impressed us. Information about GNH was posted around the schools, and several had banned plastic bags and junk food. All classes except the national language are taught in English, and students everywhere eagerly welcomed conversations in English with us. Although only 60 percent of men and 34 percent of women are considered literate, continuing education programs in the evening are helping adults, especially women, become literate. However, many in Bhutan are worried that as more people become well educated, traditional values will disappear, and young people will flock to the city rather than stay in villages. This has already begun to happen and is one of Bhutan's greatest challenges. Unemployment among young people is very high. There is acute awareness that the government must create an economic base that will provide opportunities for youth in rural areas.

TESCHU DANCERS AT A FESTIVAL IN BHUTAN.

**4. Cultural Diversity and Resilience**: Indicators include language, artisan skills, cultural participation, and a code of etiquette and conduct. Bhutan has a rich and colorful cultural tradition that, on the surface at least, seems to be alive and well. We visited several festivals attended by all ages, sitting in family groups. The whole community appeared to be involved, dressed in the colorful national dress. Folk songs and dances are taught in schools and performed by young people at these festivals. Schools also present their own cultural performances at the time of these festivals, and we were impressed by the way even the teenage boys participated enthusiastically in the dancing and singing. The Bhutanese government supports a school of traditional arts, where it provides young people from all over the country with scholarships to spend at least four years learning traditional arts such as painting, wood carving, sculpture, and embroidery. Bhutan's most skilled artisans teach there. While everyone now learns English in school, Dzongka, the national language, is also taught and spoken in everyday life, as well as 18 other languages. However, there is awareness that some of those languages are endangered.

**5. Time Use**: As travelers this is hard to assess, but the concern about time use is interesting. Life seems to move at a slower pace in Bhutan and the passage of seasons still governs life in the rural areas. The government only introduced TV in 1999 because leaders feared the cultural changes and materialism it would bring. Already, a respected Bhutanese author has found that the traditional stories are disappearing as people spend more time watching TV. There is a new organization that educates Bhutanese about the effects of media in their lives.

**6. Good Governance**: indicators include political participation, services, government performance and fundamental rights. Happiness studies have found that a sense of well-being correlates with greater "direct democracy" and government that is effective and trustworthy. In 2006, the king transferred governmental power to a democratically elected parliament. At first people were apathetic about it, but there is evidence that democracy has taken hold now. Signs in cities and along the road encourage people, especially women, to vote and run for office. The new constitution states that "the state shall strive to promote those conditions that will enable the successful pursuit of GNH." An open discussion of issues in the English press seems robust as the second round of elections approaches. Enthusiastic support for the monarchy remains strong, though. We were there at the time of the royal wedding in 2011; photographs of the king and his new bride were everywhere, and the wedding was an elaborate affair. The people still greatly respect the king's opinions and initiatives.

**7. Ecological Diversity and Resilience**: Indicators include wildlife damage, urban issues such as traffic and congestion, and responsibility towards the environment. The Bhutanese know that the beauty and pristine quality of their environment are national treasures and have government policies to protect them. More than 50 percent of all land in Bhutan is in parks or refuges, and by law, 60 percent of the land must always be covered by forest. Tourism is a growing source of income, but the government carefully controls the number of visas it issues – only 23,000 tourists visited in 2011, a very good number considering the narrow twisting roads and lack of infrastructure in outlying areas. Tourism can leave a big ecological footprint. Fishing and hunting are illegal, and biologists expect that as surrounding countries develop and destroy more and more of their habitat, Bhutan will become a refuge for tigers and other wild animals. Hydropower, mostly sold to India, will soon provide nearly 95 percent of Bhutan's GDP, but generating plants are being built underground to limit environmental impact. Modernization is taking its toll, however. In the capital city, many people are shocked by how quickly urban sprawl is happening. Although traffic in Thimpu is still controlled without a traffic light, the night before the king's wedding, we got caught in one of the very first traffic jams in Thimpu! Litter is also a concern as more plastic bottles and junk food packaging are imported from India.

**8. Community Vitality**: Indicators include safety, community relationships, family, and donation of time and money. Happiness research shows that people who feel a strong sense of community and have social connections are happier than those who are more isolated. Young and old from miles around attended the festivals we visited. Children roamed around the edges of the dancing but were well-behaved without parental intervention. Although these festivals were very crowded, we never witnessed an altercation. People were friendly and curious about us, and they offered food, places to sit, and explanations of what was going on if they spoke English. The elaborate costumes and the number of acts involved in school performances during festival time suggested a lot of community participation to pull off such shows. In the fall, harvesting is still a communal event, as is the building of traditional houses.

**9. Standard of living**: Finally, the domain that has to do with money! Indicators include household income, assets and housing. Of course, people's income has something to do with their sense of well-being, but happiness research shows that once basic needs (shelter, food and safety) are met, more money does not lead to more happiness. As we traveled through the country, we didn't see evidence of grinding poverty, such as malnutrition, although 23 percent of the people still live below the poverty line. This could be due to isolation, since there are still quite a few villages that are not accessible by road. In the city, many people live in apartment buildings that have running water and electricity, but most people still live in rural areas and survive by subsistence farming, which requires hard physical labor. Some houses in rural areas look small, cold and dark, but others seem sturdy and large and are beautifully decorated. We saw a lot of road construction on the national highway, and the goal is for every village to have electricity by 2014. Markets are busy and full of a large variety of vegetables, grains and yak meat. The main concerns in this domain seem to be high youth unemployment and the spread of materialism because of TV advertising.

While Bhutan faces many challenges, a recent survey revealed that more than 40 percent of its people qualify as happy in 6 of the 9 domains. Another 35 percent are ranked happy in 5 of 9 domains. Only 3 percent were considered unhappy. Almost all of what we experienced supported the claim that Bhutan is walking its talk and gross national happiness is, indeed, taken seriously. Bhutan's leaders do seem to be well aware of what its greatest challenges are, yet they are optimistic, and as one said, "Bhutan still has the luxury of ethical choices."

One day we climbed to the Tiger's Nest, a temple 9,000 feet up, clinging to the side of a cliff. A monk sat inside near a small window and began to chant. We sat quietly and as the mist swirled around the soft syllables of the chant, it was easy to believe the story that a tigress had flown a guru to this lovely place to meditate. And I knew that, indeed, there was happiness in this peaceful place and that I would carry some of it away with me.

### Questions to Consider

1. What do you think are the biggest challenges the Bhutanese people face as they implement the GNH principles?

# CONCLUDING INSIGHTS: THE IMPACT OF ECONOMIC GLOBALIZATION

As with any type of change, with the spread of economic globalization, certain tensions arise from the process. These tensions have played out on a local, national, regional, and global level, and even within families. The following is a list of tensions that have disrupted individuals' lives.

1. Local/National Authority or Global Authority. Local and national authorities are having difficulty countering the pull of economic globalization.

2. Neoliberalism v. Managed Capitalism. Economic globalization is able to rip apart national, managed markets and make them behave according to free market principles. Europe, a long-time managed capitalist economy, is experiencing difficulty keeping the free market forces in check.

3. State Capitalism v. Neoliberalism. The rise of state capitalist economies is more powerful than free market economies. Because of state support, they have the economic clout to infiltrate and manipulate neoliberal economies to their advantage. For example, China, with an endless source of state capital, has replaced the U.S. as the largest investor in Africa, building infrastructure and arranging deals to extract their precious minerals for China's industries.

4. Deruralization of the World. The huge migration and immigration from rural areas to cities has not only overwhelmed cities, but has contributed to the decline of the world's rural areas. Coupled with environmental woes, eking out a living on small plots of land is no longer tenable. Economic globalization has also neutered the local, domestic economy and crippled the strong, village social structures.

## Questions to Consider
1. What tension do you think is the most significant?
2. Can you think of other tensions resulting from the economic globalization process?

**TIGER'S NEST TEMPLE, BHUTAN**

## CHAPTER SEVEN

# The Financial Sector: Ten Fatal Flaws

*"When the capital development of a country becomes a by-product of the activities of a casino, the job is likely to be ill-done."*

*John Maynard Keynes*

Charles Ponzi, a dapper, five-foot-two-inch rogue, emigrated from Italy to the United States in 1903. Born in 1882, in Lugo, Italy, he allegedly came from a well-to-do family. He was a postal worker in his early years and later attended the University of Rome, which he considered to be a four-year vacation, enjoying the nightlife and opera rather than academic studies. He decided to try his luck in America. According to his own story, Ponzi had $2.50 in his pocket, having gambled away the rest of his life savings during the voyage. "I landed in this country with $2.50 in cash and $1 million in hopes, and those hopes never left me," he later told The New York Times.[1] He quickly learned English and spent the next few years doing odd jobs along the east coast, eventually taking a job as a dishwasher in a restaurant, where he slept on the floor at night. He managed to work his way up to the position of waiter but was fired for theft and shortchanging the customers. Next, Ponzi suckered naïve investors into a supposedly lucrative scheme to buy international postal-reply coupons. Money poured in, until an investigation by the Boston Police revealed that his business was a fake, and the company collapsed owing $4 million to naïve investors.[2] His next big scheme was nothing more than the age-old game: "Borrow from Peter to pay Paul." But it would lure gullible investors with visions of easy riches.

Ponzi devised a scam that would bear his name for decades: the Ponzi scheme. For their money Ponzi's investors received 50 percent interest in 90 days and later were promised 50 percent interest in 45 days. The money rolled in. Ponzi trained sales agents, who received 10 percent commissions for investments that they brought in to him. Many of these sales agents recruited subagents who received 5 percent commissions for new investors. Word of the financial "wizard" on School Street in Boston spread like wildfire when Ponzi paid off his first round of investors. Many people simply reinvested their profits with Ponzi, thereby relieving him of actually having to pay out interest as he promised. At its height around 40,000 people joined the feeding frenzy operated out of offices from Maine to New Jersey.

The Ponzi scam needed a constant supply of new investors to provide cash to pay returns to existing investors. The smooth-talking con-man raked in an estimated $15 million in eight months by persuading tens of thousands of trusting Bostonians that he had unlocked the secret to easy wealth. They believed him, at least for awhile. Ponzi's meteoric success at swindling was so remarkable that his name became attached to his simple but devious method.

### Questions to Consider

1. What lessons can we learn from the Ponzi scheme?

CHARLES PONZI CIRCA 1920

# THE FINANCIAL SECTOR: AN OVERVIEW

You may think it is odd for me to start out this chapter describing a scam. I seem to imply that the financial sector is a scam! In fact, I am making a point that, indeed, parts of the financial sector are scams and that we need to be aware of them. With that said, there are many parts of the financial sector that are legitimate and run by reputable people. But when the scam part of the financial sector gets out of hand, as it did with the financial crisis of 2008 – it can have a devastating effect on millions of people. These last two chapters will focus on the scam part of the financial sector, since that is an area that has created such economic misery for so many. Neoliberal changes ushered in governmental policies that supported the rise and dominance of the financial sector over other sectors, such as manufacturing and farming. My argument is that the rise of and concentration of wealth in a virtually unregulated financial sector has contributed to the instability and inequality found in the U.S. today, as well as the entire world. After a brief overview of the financial sector, this chapter will describe its 10 fatal flaws.

The financial sector of the economy isn't just banks; it encompasses a broad range of businesses and institutions that deal with the management of money. Among these organizations are banks (commercial and investment), credit card companies, insurance companies, consumer finance companies, stock brokerages, investment funds, foreign exchange services, real estate, bank holding companies, and some government sponsored enterprises (GSEs). One of the global epicenters of the financial sector is Wall Street, located in lower Manhattan, New York City. As a physical place, Wall Street houses some of the biggest powerhouses in the financial industry, including the New York Stock Exchange and numerous multi-billion dollar firms. Wall Street is often discussed as an entity, and a metaphor

---

**Five Sectors of the Global Economy**

1. Primary Sector
2. Secondary Industry Sector
3. Service (Tertiary) Sector
4. Information (Quaternary) Sector
5. Nonprofit (Quinary) Sector

---

for the financial sector as a whole. Let's first briefly look at the sectors of the global economy to see how the financial sector fits into the overall economy.

First, the primary sector involves changing natural resources into primary products. Most products from this sector are considered raw materials for other industries associated with the primary sector, including agriculture, mining, forestry, farming, grazing, hunting, gathering, fishing, and quarrying. The packaging and processing of the raw material close to the primary producers is part of this sector.[3] This sector is larger in periphery countries than in core countries.

Second, the secondary sector of the economy manufactures finished goods. Processing and construction lie within the secondary sector, as well. This sector takes the raw material output from the primary sector and transforms them into manufactured finished goods using machinery and labor to complete the process. The secondary sector includes metal working, smelting, automobile production, textile production, chemical industries, engineering expertise, aerospace manufacturing, energy utilities, breweries and bottlers, construction, and shipbuilding. Manufacturing promotes economic growth and development. Nations which export manufactured products tend to generate high GDP (Gross Domestic Product), which supports higher incomes and tax revenues needed to fund quality of life initiatives, such as health care and building infrastructure. In core countries this sector is a source of high paying jobs, facilitates greater

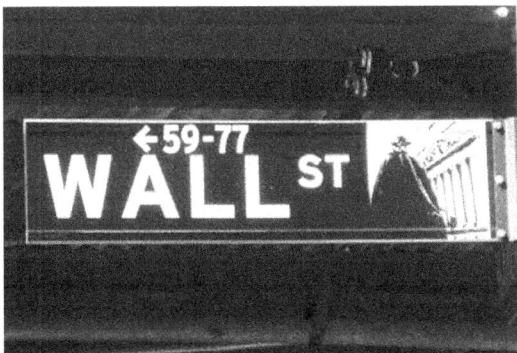

**WALL STREET**
PHOTO DENISE AMES

social mobility for workers to achieve middle class status, and contributes to greater wealth for successive generations.[4]

Third, the **tertiary sector** of the economy is the service industry, which provides services to the general population and to businesses. **Services** are defined as intangible goods. Activities associated with this sector include retail and wholesale sales, transportation and distribution, entertainment (movies, television, radio, music, theater, YouTube) restaurants, clerical services, media, tourism, insurance, finance, banking, healthcare, and law. The focus is on people interacting with others and serving customers. In most core and middle countries, a growing proportion of workers is included in the tertiary sector. In the U.S., tertiary workers comprise more than 80 percent of the labor force.

Fourth, the **quaternary sector** of the economy consists of informational and intellectual activities. Services associated with this sector include government, culture, libraries, scientific research and development, education, consultation, and information technology. In developed core countries, this sector is highly evolved and requires an educated workforce with advanced degrees. The government and business invest money in the quaternary sector in order to ensure further economic expansion and profits.

Fifth, the quinary sector, consists of **nonprofit** organizations, an organization that uses surplus revenues to achieve its goals rather than distributing them as profit or dividends. While not-for-profit organizations are permitted to generate surplus revenues, they must be retained by the organization for its self-preservation, expansion, or future plans.[5] This sector includes education, culture, research, science, healthcare, media, police, fire service, and government organizations not intended to make a profit. Our organization, the Center for Global Awareness, fits into this non-profit category!

## The Rise of the Financial Sector

The financial sector is part of the tertiary or service sector. Yet, there are other sectors that contribute to the national and global economy, as well. For example, the structure of the U.S. economy has changed, as it has moved from manufacturing (20 percent of the economy in 1980, to 11.5 percent today) to services.[6] But a problem has developed since the 1980s – the financial sector has grown to outsized proportions. One marker of the super-profitability of the financial sector is the fact that it accounts for 40 percent of the total profits of U.S. corporations, up from 10 percent during the postwar era (1948-1973). Today, 7.7 percent of U.S. GDP consists of the financial sector, which has soared from 2.5 percent in 1947 to 4.4 percent in 1977 to 7.7 percent in 2005.[7]

The U.S. has experienced a massive shift of investment funds from manufacturing into the financial sector. Because returns on stocks declined while those from loans skyrocketed, the economy flip-flopped from production to paper shuffling, from capital investment to debt financing. The business of mergers, acquisitions, derivatives, and hedge funds rose, while the auto, steel, and other industries declined.[8] Yet, the problem with many financial sector operations is that they are equivalent to squeezing value out of already created value. It may create profit, yes, but it does not create new value – only industry, agricultural, trade, and services create new value. Because profit is not based on value that is created, investment operations become very volatile and prices of stocks, bonds, and other forms of investment can depart very radically from their real value. For example, a stock, land, or other assets can keep on rising, driven mainly by upwardly spiraling speculative valuations, then suddenly crash. Thus, profits depend on taking advantage of upward price departures from the value of the asset and selling before reality enforces a correction, which is a crash back to real values. The radical rise of prices of an asset far beyond real values is what is a **bubble**.[9]

The outsized and excessive growth of the financial system did little to create any "added value" for investors. High flying financial managers often got higher returns because they charged higher fees for their supposedly indispensible services. Even more startling, the combined income of the nation's top 25 hedge fund managers in 2005 exceeded the compensation of the combined income of the Chief Executive Officers (CEO) of all companies listed in the S&P 500 (Standard & Poors). In 2008, no less than one in every $13 in compensation in the U.S. went to people working in finance. By contrast, in the postwar years a mere one in $40 in compensation went to finance workers.[10] Since 1980, innovation and creativity fled from manufacturing and other old-fashioned industries to Wall Street. Finance has attracted an ever-growing number of intelligent, highly educated workers. Among Harvard seniors surveyed in 2007, a whopping 58 percent of the men joining the workforce were bound for jobs not in medicine or public service but in finance or consulting.[11]

It is important in a stable economy to maintain a balance between the different economic sectors so that one does not come to dominate, because a downturn or collapse of the dominant sector can trigger adverse reactions in the other sectors. For example, the financial crisis of 2008 triggered a near collapse of the automobile industry in the U.S. Without government intervention and loans to the industry there would be no more General Motors or Chrysler. Another example is that at the time of the crisis approximately 34 percent of all the assets of major banks in the U.S. were real-estate related; the figure for smaller banks was even higher, roughly 44 percent.[12] This proportion was too heavily laden in just one economic sector. A problem arising since 1980 is that the financial sector has come to exert undue influence and power in the U.S. economy and even the global economy.

You may wonder at this point how the financial sector mushroomed into such a powerhouse. In order to more clearly understand this process, it is helpful to recall the events of the 1970s. The crisis of the 1970s had been resolved in favor of a different economic landscape than before. The U.S. was not the only country to experience wrenching economic turmoil during the 1970s, but as the world's leading economy, it had a far more significant role in shaping the future global economy during the crisis than other countries. Three interrelated dimensions to the global economy emerged out of the bedlam of the 1970s – neoliberalism, economic globalization, and financialization. Since we have already discussed neoliberalism and economic globalization, we will cover financialization in these last two chapters.

**Financialization** is a sector of the economy that specializes in creating financial products that have a certain value and can be traded in the market place. Some financial products are insurance, lending money, real estate sales, stocks, bonds, derivatives, and many others.

**THE HOUSING BUBBLE**

Since the 1980s, the American government has shifted its taxation and political policies from supporting the manufacturing sector, small businesses and agriculture to policies that support large corporations and the financial sector. They have viewed these two sectors of the economy as the engines for creating wealth and growth in the economy. In the last three decades, there has been a decline in the profitability derived from agriculture and industry as a result of over-capacity and competition. Since money in a capitalist system seeks the highest return on investment, there has been a shift from industries where profits were largely stagnant or low-yielding to the financial sector that channels capital towards financial products that have a higher degree of risk but also have higher returns.[13] Thus, the financial sector has come to be a dominant part of the U.S. economy.

Financialization took off after the crisis of the 1970s because of governmental policies, as already mentioned, and also because of technological advancements that made it easier and more efficient to devise new financial products. The take-off was also dependent upon the proliferation of novel, sophisticated speculative instruments that escaped regulation. Instability in the financial sector ultimately derived from the fact that speculative finance boiled down to an effort to squeeze more value out of already created value instead of creating new value, since there was overproduction in the real economy.

By the late 1990s, the indicators of overproduction in the real economy were stark. The U.S. computer industry's capacity was rising at 40 percent annually, far above projected increases in demand. The world auto industry was selling just 74 percent of the 70.1 million cars it built each year. So much investment took place in global telecommunications infrastructure that traffic carried over fiber-optic networks was reported to be only 2.5 percent of capacity. Retailers suffered as well, with giants like K-Mart and Wal-Mart hit with a tremendous surfeit of floor capacity. There was an oversupply of nearly everything.[14]

The result of these changes is an increased split between a hyperactive financial economy and a sluggish real economy. A disconnect exists between the real economy collectively known as **Main Street** and the financial economy known as Wall Street; they are operating on two different premis-

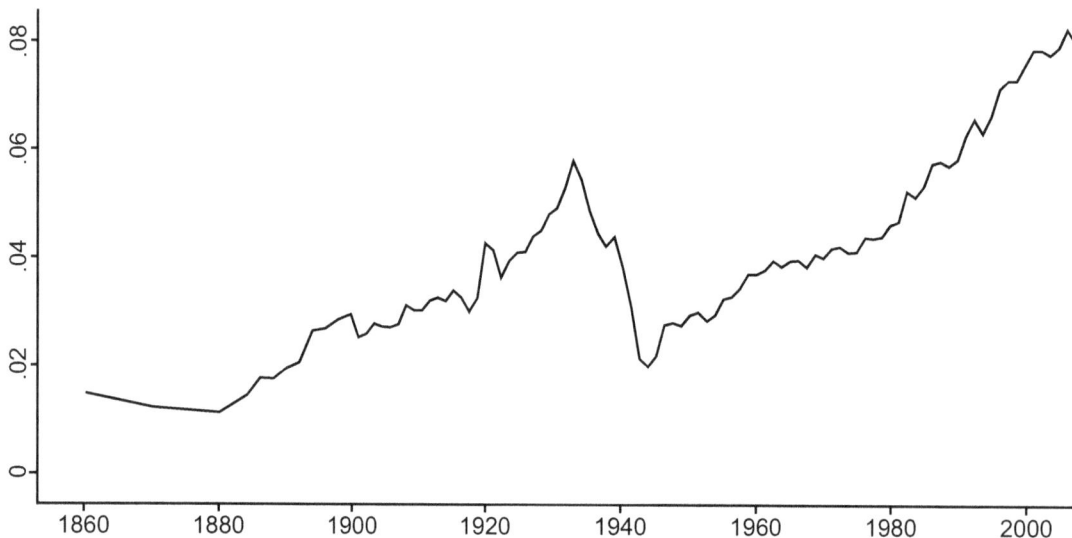

**SHARE IN GDP OF US FINANCIAL SECTOR SINCE 1860.**

es. **Wall Street** is operating according to what economist David Korten calls a "phantom economy," and Main Street operates according to the "real economy." This is not an accidental development, the financial economy exploded to make up for the stagnation owing to overproduction of the real economy.[15]

## Recklessness: The Master Narrative

I live in New Mexico. About 10 percent of the population is composed of native peoples. In the last few decades they have built casinos on their land as a source of revenue. Even though New Mexico is the fifth largest state in area, it seems as though there are casinos everywhere. In fact, New Mexico has 20 of them, which ranks us 15th among all 46 states that have casinos, even though our population is less than 2 million! Albuquerque, where I live, boasts 4 casinos. That means a lot of gambling. I wonder how our very poor state can support so many casinos; the parking lots are always full. But as I understand, many tourists and New Mexicans find that gambling is enjoyable.

This gambling observation leads to a point I want to make about the financial crisis. Ever since the financial crisis of 2008, I have been thinking and rethinking the catastrophic chain of events that wreaked havoc on our economy and society. I will be looking at 10 fatal flaws in the financial sector that contributed to the crisis, but I keep coming back to the nagging question, "Why did the financial sector take such crazy risks in the first place?" What made them literally gamble away their own and other people's money with a clear conscience? When asked what caused the financial crisis, many people without hesitation answer greed, pure and simple. I don't disagree with the answer, but I think there is more to it than simple greed. After all, greed is part of the human condition and has been for eons.

Greed during the lead-up to the financial crisis seemed to be a different sort of greed than just a sordid behavior; in this case, society embedded greed within acceptable societal and cultural values and behaviors. This is a far more harmful type of greed because it is largely an acceptable and encouraged behavior in society at large. When reporters asked some of the Wall Street tycoons why they acted with such duplicitous behaviors, they replied that everyone else was doing it; it is part of the Wall Street culture. This reasoning leads me to the question: "What is it in the U.S. that fosters an ethic of extreme risk-taking, greed, and other avarice behaviors?" What is the underlying story or master narrative that helped shape this crisis?

Whether we know it or not, our national ethic or story shapes many of our views and behaviors, what I will call here the master narrative. Since I have taught U.S. history for many years, I see the narrative unfold starting before the founding of the nation. It certainly helped shape the thinking of the financial crisis. What is this narrative? Many Americans follow a "frontier mentality." There is always an unknown to discover, conquer, control, and

AMERICAN PROGRESS (1872) BY JOHN GAST. REPRESENTS THE MODERNIZATION OF THE NEW WEST. COLUMBIA LEADS CIVILIZATION WESTWARD WITH AMERICAN SETTLERS.

eventually rule. Settlers built the country by expanding westward, conquering new territories, eliminating the native peoples, and growing a new country. Pioneers led the way, fearless of danger and ready to risk everything for new opportunities. It was the Manifest Destiny of the American nation to conquer. The cowboy archetype, taming the lawless West, has always been near and dear to the American psyche. Cowboys were intrepid, took inordinate risks, gambled with their lives, and expanded into a territory with seemingly unlimited bounty. The narrative continued after World War II, as the nation emerged as the overwhelming superpower of the age. Americans boasted they were the nation with the highest standard of living, the first to reach the moon, and had the best political and economic system. President Johnson was intent on conquering poverty, as well as the moon and the North Vietnamese people. The narrative continued with President Reagan, complete with donned cowboy hat, the ultimate rugged individual ready to conquer a new enemy: the government itself. Even President George W. Bush displayed manly hubris as he cloaked himself in aviator gear and descended from a hovering helicopter onto a floating battleship, swaggering before the cameras and proclaiming "mission accomplished." He was referring to the assumption that the mighty American military machine had subdued Iraq.

The heady days of the 1990s through the mid-2000s, except for the 9/11 tragedy, were a time of great triumphal optimism. The Soviet Union had collapsed. George H.W. Bush crowed it was his administration that brought the mighty Soviet Union to its knees, ignoring the fact that perhaps the Soviet Empire could fall on its own accord, since it was rife with corruption, inefficiencies, stagnation, and a demoralized population. Neoliberal capitalism reigned supreme. The markets were the new "god," bestowing their wisdom onto a holy grail of the efficient market hypothesis. Overconfident financial wizards were the new "chosen ones," ready to impart their financial miracles for the masses. These privileged men were told they were "born to rule" the marketplace, with limitless fame and fortune their destiny. Hubris, according to the ancient Greeks, often leads to the downfall of man. Hubris, unfortunately, was in ample supply during this giddy time.

Risk-taking is part of the American story. But understanding the other side of risk is not part of it. There is no back-up plan if risk-taking goes awry. There is never a thought that the frontier may have limits, or technology might not save us from all our problems, or markets may not be right in all cases. If there is a mess up, so the story goes, something or someone will come along as the savior. We tell ourselves, it will always be so. American movies are rife with saviors coming to the rescue of those in distress. In the case of the 2008 financial crisis, it was the government that rode to the rescue.

Too many Americans don't want to understand that the national story they have been telling themselves is a lie. Nothing is limitless, we must remember that with risks come consequences, Mother Nature always wins, what goes around comes around, with hubris comes humility, and with every action there is a reaction. These sayings balance risk with the notion that failure can result from risk-taking as well as success. And if failure does occur, there better be a back-up plan.

If the narrative is not changed, the same type of financial crisis will happen again. As I listen to the politicians and financial experts, I don't hear a different narrative. In fact, the narrative has gone into hyper-drive instead of stall mode. Our story of endless growth, risky "opportunities," and high stakes gambling with Mother Nature has gone ballistic. The markets tarnished our faith in them, but only slightly so. Our faith in technology is still sound; in some quarters technology has even emerged as the new god, rivaling the fallen market god. In fact, the narrative has shifted to one that government didn't ride to the rescue after the financial crisis, but government caused the problem in the first place. We are slamming our foot on the accelerator of unfettered markets, just when we should be putting on the brakes.

Excessive risk-taking, without regard for the consequences, is the master narrative of the financial crisis. It is apparent everywhere. If we understand the narrative as part of the American national character, instead of merely a personality defect among a few "bad apples" on Wall Street, we can more easily change it. We need to replace the tired stories of limitless abundance and perpetual growth, not only to avoid future financial crises, but to curb our voracious appetite for nature's limited resources. I hope you will join with me in stitching together a new national narrative, one that does not follow a reckless path, but one more in keeping with our place in the larger human and natural community and with the well-being of the next generations in mind.

---

**Questions to Consider**

1. How would your master narrative or story of the U.S. read? Explain.

---

# 10 FATAL FLAWS IN THE FINANCIAL SECTOR

According to my estimation, there are fundamental flaws in today's financial system. The 2008 financial crisis and Great Recession revealed that in a big way. Too many people think of the reason for the crisis as simply excessive greed exhibited by bankers. They did act greedily, but be wary of overly simplistic explanations for the crisis. They acted greedily because they had incentives and opportunities to do so. Some neoliberals say the crisis was a mere blip on the trajectory of continuous world economic growth. In fact, many now argue that the crisis was a result of too much government interference in the economy instead of not enough. Single answer explanations, although they make good headline news, are not going to get us to the understanding we need about the complicated financial crisis.

The 2008 financial crisis was different from others in the last 30 plus years – it was in the U.S. Most Americans like to think of their country as one of the engines of global economic growth, an exporter of sound economic policies – not recessions and bailouts.[16] Yet, that is exactly what happened. There are multiple reasons why the financial system has performed so badly since the 1980s and in the 2000s in particular. I have organized these reasons into what I call 10 fatal flaws in the financial sector. Once again, these flaws are all interconnected and hard to separate out for analysis. However, it is much easier to look at these flaws separately with the understanding that they all are

---

**Ten Fatal Flaws in the Financial Sector**

| | |
|---|---|
| Fatal Flaw #1. | Too Big to Fail Banks (TBTF) |
| Fatal Flaw #2. | Unchecked Deregulation |
| Fatal Flaw #3. | A "Markets Know Best" Federal Reserve |
| Fatal Flaw #4. | A Real Estate Bubble and Out of Control Lending |
| Fatal Flaw #5. | Mountains of Debt |
| Fatal Flaw #6. | Dicey Financial Products |
| Fatal Flaw #7. | Financial Speculative Mania |
| Fatal Flaw #8. | Moral Hazard and Lack of Transparency |
| Fatal Flaw #9. | Deceptive Rating Agencies |
| Fatal Flaw #10. | Bloated Compensation Plans |

---

part of a system – the financial system. We need to look at these flaws in depth if solutions are to be constructed.

I see these 10 fatal flaws in the financial sector as the most egregious and have a negative impact on 90 percent of all Americans, and also the world. These are not all the flaws, but organizing them into these categories should give us a basic understanding of what conditions contributed to the 2008 financial crisis and are still around today. I will be using the United States as the platform for how these 10 fatal flaws have played out. However, readers from other countries should be mindful that these flaws are also present in many countries, especially those ascribing to neoliberal principles, including Europe.

**Questions to Consider**

1. Would you add or remove any of the fatal flaws from the list?

# FATAL FLAW #1: TOO BIG TO FAIL BANKS (TBTF)

I would bet that almost 100 percent of you have some type of bank account. It seems a necessity in our high-tech cashless society. We have our non-profit organization's checking account at a credit union in Albuquerque, New Mexico. I like the idea that they are a non-profit credit union that helps its members with loans and low-cost checking. But it is big and has many branches. No one knows my name, and they always ask for my identification when I make a transaction. In the late 1970s through the 1980s, I banked at Dewey State Bank, in Illinois. It was a small, "no-frills" bank in a farming community, aptly adjoining the local grain elevator. Everyone knew everyone else. When I did business at the bank, the president would come out of his office to say hello and personally give a treat to my toddler daughter. His wife, whose family started the bank in the early 20<sup>th</sup> century, was my son's English teacher. Their claim to fame was they survived the Great Depression. They have even survived the banking mergers of the last 30 years and recently celebrated their 100<sup>th</sup> anniversary. But Dewey State Bank is far from typical of the banking industry today.

At the heart of it banking is a simple business. Before the arrival of modern innovations in finance, lenders lived in a straightforward world. There was a running joke in the past that tells a lot about how banks operated: it was according to the 3-6-3 rule. Bankers paid their depositors 3 percent interest, lent it out at 6 percent, and lined up to tee off at the golf course by 3 p.m. Customers deposited money in a bank in return for interest; the bank lent that money to other people at a higher rate of interest. It wasn't glamorous, but it was a guaranteed way of making steady money and creating credit in the economy. However, the bankers had to be careful to whom they lent money. The quality of the loans was crucial because those loans were the bank's earning assets. Bankers and banking were boring. That's exactly what the people who entrusted their money to them wanted. Ordinary banking customers didn't want someone to take their money and gamble with it. They didn't want the bank's CEO to have a yacht and five lavish houses around the world.[17] They wanted them to serve the needs of the community.

At the core of it, banking is essentially creating more money by loaning it out. If you have a bank and your clients deposit $100 with you, the money supply can be doubled simply by loaning it to someone else. Maybe the person who borrowed it spends part of it and leaves the rest in his/her own bank account, which someone else then loans out and so the process goes. An initial sum of currency can be "grown" into a much bigger money supply. The banking system takes money in excess of their reserve requirements and creates new money by loaning it out.[18] Banks take in deposits and invest the money in a variety of assets, from ordinary loans to complex derivative deals. They make their money on the **spreads** or the difference in what interest they pay depositors and the interest they charge borrowers for loans.

There are basically two types of banks: investment banks and commercial banks. **Investment banks** issue bonds and shares of stock, issue other complex financial instruments, trade on capital markets, and put together mergers and acquisitions. **Commercial banks** lend out the money deposited in them. The two types of banks have cleverly been called the piggy bank and the casino; the piggy banks are the commercial banks and the investment banks are the casinos. Investment banks issue stocks, and if a company whose stock they have issued needs cash, it becomes very tempting to make a loan, which can create a problem. If the casino activities of the investment banks get out of hand, it could endanger the piggy bank deposits of the general public. This is just what happened during the 1920s and contributed to the stock market crash of 1929 and the ensuing Great Depression. This catastrophe resulted in the passage of the Glass-Steagall Act at the depths of the Great Depression in 1933, which forced retail banks to split from investment banks. This act successfully regulated the banking system for almost 70 years.[19]

As part of the Glass-Steagall Act, the government set up **the Federal Deposit Insurance Corporation** (FDIC) to insure deposits. During the Depression, depositors were fearful that banks would close and all their hard-earned savings would be lost. With the FDIC people would feel that their money was protected, even if there were rumors that a bank was facing difficulties. Once the government provided this insurance, it had to make sure that banks did not take undue risks with depositors' savings. To make sure that the banks didn't speculate in the marketplace and lose money, knowing the government would then have to pick up the tab, the government regulated the banks from taking excessive risks.

Several procedures and polices monitored banks for excessive risk-taking in several ways. For example in the post-war years, banks required homebuyers to have a 20 percent down payment before they could purchase a house. The bank would then loan borrowers 80 percent of the value of the house they were purchasing. An independent appraiser hired by the bank provided an evaluation of the house's value by comparing it to similar houses that recently sold in the neighborhood. The likelihood that an 80 percent mortgage would wind up exceeding the value of the house was very small – prices would have to drop by 20 percent, which was highly unlikely (until recently). Bankers understood rightly that a mortgage that was underwater (a mortgage that is more than the house is worth) had a large risk of nonpayment. The system worked pretty well. The reality that homeowners usually had to put up 20 percent of a home's value to get a loan dampened their home ownership aspirations.

Previously, regulated banking provided an important check on U.S. corporate activity. By carefully monitoring a corporation's loan portfolio, banks helped prevent bankruptcies and

SENATORS CARTER GLASS AND HENRY B. STEAGALL, THE CO-SPONSORS OF THE GLASS–STEAGALL ACT IN 1933.

excesses in the business world.[20] Accountants, rating agencies, and other agencies also had a system of checks and balances, much like our three branches of government – in which each monitored the others' activities and reduced risk. Things began to change in the 1980s when neoliberal policies were phased in. Wanting to earn higher profits, some in the banking industry had been complaining that they were feeling constrained by what they perceived were excessive regulations of their industry. The Reagan administration in the 1980s enthusiastically responded by removing regulations on banking operations. The pro-bank forces also came up with a nontraditional area for international trade: financial services. The idea was that banks should be given free rein globally, and that foreign-owned banks operating outside their home countries should enjoy exactly the same rights and privileges as domestic ones. This was part of the broader agenda of what is called "**liberalizing**" the international financial sector from all kinds of national regulations.[21]

As the government loosened regulations and the culture of banking changed, bankers began to look for new ways to generate profits. They found the answer in a simple word: fees. For example, when consumers make purchases with credit cards, approximately two cents of each dollar go to the credit card companies that run the payment network, and the banks which supply the credit for the cards. The 2 percent charge comes to about $31,000 for a typical convenience store, just below the average per-store yearly profit of $36,000. The U.S. has the highest interchange fees in the world. The Wall Street Journal's description was that "these fees...have been paradoxically trending upward in recent years when the industry's costs due to technology and economies of scale have been falling."[22]

Since the early 2000s, the market share of the five largest banks grew from 8 percent in 1995 to 30 percent in 2008.[23] Exemplifying the concentration of wealth and power in a few banks is the trade in derivatives (more on derivatives later). There are 1030 commercial banks in the U.S. that trade derivatives, but 5 banks – JP Morgan Chase, Citigroup, Goldman Sachs, Bank of America and Wells Fargo – control 97 percent of all the derivative trades. These 5 banks hold assets of more than 60 percent of U.S. gross domestic product (GDP): $8.6 trillion.[24]

"Shadow" banks are another dimension of the banking industry. **Shadow banks** are organizations that lend money to people just like traditional banks do. The difference between the two is that in a traditional bank money comes from depositors, while in a shadow banking system the money comes from investors, who want to earn a return on their money. The government regulates traditional banks, and it does not regulate the shadow banking system. The investors in shadow banking are corporations, investment banks, and money market funds, and the borrowers are financial firms. Shadow banking comes in all shapes and sizes: nonbank mortgage lenders, structured investment vehicles (SIVs), commercial paper, hedge funds, money market funds, private equity funds, and others.[25] Shadow banking has emerged in American and European markets between 2000 and 2008 and plays an important role in providing credit for the global financial system. The volume of transactions in the shadow banking system grew dramatically after the year 2000. By late 2007, the size of shadow banking in the U.S. exceeded $10 trillion. By late 2009, as a result of the financial crisis, the number had shrunk to under $6 trillion.[26]

The shadow banking system was at the heart of the financial crisis. One of the reasons for this was that traditional banks are subject to government regulation and can, therefore, if need be, borrow from the Federal Reserve as a "**lender of last resort**." Shadow banks do not have access to what is called the Fed's "discount window" or the authority to borrow from the government. Therefore, when the financial crisis hit and the lending and borrowing conducted in the shadow banking system froze, the demand for money exceeded the supply. For example, the investment bank Lehman Brothers in September 2008, was unable to borrow enough money from the shadow banking system to meet its short-term needs. Since the government didn't step in to save Lehman Brothers with emergency loans, it went bankrupt.

It should come as no surprise that the financial sector is among the highest-contributing industries to U.S. political candidates. They use their deep pockets to fund electoral campaigns and congressional lobbying in order to influence public policies that benefit them. They receive many favors from the government representatives; since many personnel from the financial industry go on to serve in key governmental posts. For example, one of the most powerful investment banks, Goldman Sachs, has had two of their former CEOS serve as Secretary of the Treasury: Robert Rubin (1993-1999, Bill Clinton) and Henry "Hank" Paulson (2006-2009, George Bush). This underlying reality is why influential Senator Dick Durbin from Illinois said of Congress, "The banks own the place."[27]

**Questions to Consider**
1. Describe the place where you bank. Where do they make most of their money?

## FATAL FLAW #2: UNCHECKED DEREGULATION

Deregulation is the removal or simplification of government rules and regulations that manage market forces. It does not mean elimination of laws against fraud, but eliminating or reducing government regulations on how business is conducted. According to neoliberals, the rationale for deregulation is that fewer and simpler regulations will lead to a higher level of competitiveness and productivity, more efficiency, lower overall prices, and increased growth rates. Supporters of managed capitalism claim deregulation is necessary to rein in the excesses of market forces that cause disproportionate concentration of wealth and less prosperity for the vast majority of a nation's citizens. Since the 1980s, neoliberals have carried out a well-orchestrated deregulation campaign; however, in this section I will only mention a few of the many acts passed by the federal government to deregulate the financial sector.

Before the 1980s, American commercial banking was a small-scale affair. State laws prohibited state and nationally chartered banks from running branches outside their home state, or sometimes even outside their home county. In 1975, Maine and other states began passing legislation allowing some interstate banking. The passage in 1994 of the Riegle-Neal Act capped the trend; the act removed the remaining restrictions on interstate banking

GOLDMAN SACHS TOWER, AT 30 HUDSON STREET, IN JERSEY CITY, NEW JERSEY.

and allowed interstate banking mergers. Since "the regulatory light was green," a single banking company could now operate across the U.S. market.[28]

In the 1990s, the efforts of the banking lobby to further deregulate the financial sector were finally beginning to pay off for them. Banks saw the potential for earning huge profits. Drawing upon the philosophy of free market competition, bank lobbyists made the case that the barriers keeping American banks, investment banks, and insurance companies from merging – as their European counterparts were able to do – had to be removed. They argued that too much regulation had kept the U.S. banking system from reaching its full, globally-competitive potential. President Clinton's Treasury Secretary, Robert Rubin, led the refrain for the repeal of the Glass-Steagall Act. He pleaded that without its repeal, the U.S. was destined to lose out in the global marketplace. He stoked an already illusory fear that if the U.S. banking industry didn't have the same opportunities and structure as existed abroad, banks would move their most profitable businesses across the ocean.[29] The banks won.

The banking landscape was fast becoming a competitive game between a handful of very large banks. Among the teams in the financial big leagues were Citigroup, JPMorgan Chase, Bank of America, Washington Mutual, and Wachovia.[30] In 1998, the Glass-Steagall Act was put to the test when Citibank orchestrated a merger with Travelers Insurance, Primerica, a financial products firm, and the investment banking giant Salomon Smith Barney. The merger was openly illegal according to the Glass-Steagall Act, but it had the implicit backing of Fed Chairman Alan Greenspan and Rubin. According to journalist Matt Taibbi, it was a "dangerous concentration of capital in the hands of a single mega-company."[31] But the financial sector saw it as a blessing.

November 12, 1999 marked the final death blow to the 66 year-old Glass-Steagall Act, which contributed to banking stability and economic prosperity for decades. The new act, the **Gramm, Leach, Biley Act** or the **Financial Services Modernization Act**, was the culmination of the banking and financial-services industries' years-long massive lobbying campaign to reduce regulation in their sector. Banks could now offer investment, commercial banking, and insurance services all under one roof. The result was the infusion of the investment bank speculative culture into the staid world of commercial banking. The bill also kept risky derivative transactions free of government regulation. With the repeal of Glass-Steagall, the conditions were ripe for banks to invest monies from checking and savings accounts into high-flying financial instruments, such as mortgage-backed securities. These investment gambles led many banks to ruin and rocked the financial markets in 2008. The consequences of the repeal of Glass-Steagall would come to light a few short years later as corporate and banking scandals emerged.[32] Yet another bill to further deregulate the financial sector was just around the corner.

The passage of the Commodity Future's Modernization Act of 2000 financial sector granted another blessing to the financial sector. The high angel of dispensing blessings to the financial sector was Senator Phil Gramm from Texas. As chairman of the U.S. Senate Committee on Banking (1995 – 2000), Senator Gramm was not content with just the passage of his landmark Gramm-Leach-Bliley Act in 1999. The following eerie scenario about the passage of the act was told by a director in the Commodity Futures Trading Commission to author David Faber in an interview.

The **Commodities Futures Modernization Act** of 2000 officially marked the deregulation of financial products known as over-the-counter derivatives. These derivatives would be at the heart of the financial crisis of 2008. The bill was not without its critics. One in particular stands out as a future seer of the problems that an unregulated derivative market could unleash: Brooksley

## Financial Services Modernization Act

It was Friday night, December 15, 2000. The Presidential and Congressional elections had taken place. Congress was going home for the Christmas recess and ending their Congressional session. They had before them an 11,000-page Omnibus Appropriation Bill to fund the entire federal government for fiscal year 2001. Senator Gramm walks to the floor that night and puts a floor rider (addition) on it, a 262-page bill called The Commodity Futures Modernization Act of 2000. This Act further deregulates the market. I don't believe anyone in Congress besides Senator Gramm, and sometimes I wonder whether even Senator Gramm, understood what they were doing. This was a piece of legislation that was not written by any hand in Congress. It was written by Wall Street. And six ways from Sunday, it deregulated these markets, not only from federal oversight, but from state oversight as well. The controversial act had important consequences but was quietly signed into law by President Clinton on December 21, 2000.[33]

Borne. From 1996-1999, she headed the Commodity Futures Trading Commission (CFTC) under President Clinton. She sought to exert regulatory control over the unregulated market. But her efforts were quashed by fierce opposition from Treasury Secretary Robert Rubin and Fed Chair Alan Greenspan, who aggressively pushed for a more deregulatory approach. With Borne out of the way, the scene was now set for the use of financial derivatives in many types of financial products (see flaw #6).[34] The act prevented the federal government from regulating risky financial products and it even prevented the states from regulating them using gaming laws – since so many of the new financial wagers were indistinguishable from racetrack bets.[35]

When deregulation allowed investment and commercial banks to merge together, the investment banking culture came out on top. There was a demand for the kind of high returns that could be gained only through high leverage and big risk-taking deals. Also, ever larger banks dominated a more concentrated and less competitive banking system. One of the hallmarks of the America's banking system in the past had been the high level of competition, with a myriad of banks serving different communities and different niches in the market. This is no longer the case.

In 1975, the Securities and Exchange Commission (SEC) passed a rule requiring investment banks to maintain a debt to-net capital ratio of 15 to 1 or less. In simple terms, this meant that for every $15 borrowed, the bank had to have $1 in deposits to cover potential losses. This limited the amount of borrowed money the investment banks could use to lend out or for investments. In 2004, amidst the deregulation frenzy, the SEC succumbed to a push from the big investment banks – led by Goldman Sachs, and its then-CEO, Hank

BROOKSLEY BORNE  WARNED ABOUT THE DANGERS OF THE DERIVATIVES MARKET.

273

Paulson – and allowed investment banks to develop net capital requirements based on their own risk assessment models. With this new autonomy, as expected, investment banks pushed ratios to as high as 40 to 1. This meant that a bank only had to have $1 in bank reserves for every $40 they borrowed. This high debt to capital ratio employed by many investment banks made them more vulnerable when the housing bubble finally popped. It also enabled the banks to borrow funds that helped create a more tangled mess of derivative investments, adding fuel to the financial meltdown.[36] Deregulation was the watchword of the day.

Wall Street's capacity to turn out more and more sophisticated financial instruments ran ahead of the government's regulatory will. This was not because government was incapable of regulating, but the dominant neoliberal deregulatory ideology blinded the government from regulatory action. The idea that deregulation of the marketplace was the best way and only way to create wealth was golden. Many believed that the marketplace would regulate itself; outside governmental agencies were a hindrance and merely got in the way.[37] As the pattern of speculation, systemic risk, and costly bailouts kept repeating itself in the late 1990s and 2000s, it might seem as though regulators and legislators would have learned a valuable lesson: deregulation was not working. But so much money was at stake that the political elite either cheered on the whole affair or looked the other way.[38]

---

**Questions to Consider**

1. Do you think regulation has a place in the banking industry? Explain.

---

## FATAL FLAW #3:
## A "MARKETS KNOW BEST" FEDERAL RESERVE

We like to think of money as something tangible; a fist full of dollars means you've got money to spend. It seems strange to think of money in the U.S. as simply debts of the Federal Reserve that are in circulation, and checks written represent debts of banking institutions. The Federal Reserve (the Fed) is the central bank of the U.S. and is made up of a Board of Governors and 12 Federal Reserve Banks spread around the country. Although all 12 banks are supposedly equal, the New York Fed carries more clout. It's the Fed's job to oversee the American banking system and manage the money supply with the goal of promoting full employment, steady, healthy economic growth, and stable prices.[39] Since the U.S. is the world's largest and most influential economy, the Fed's policies and actions have worldwide impact. In the past, it was common for national economies to back up their currency with something of market value, most commonly gold or silver. Those days are gone. Today governments have to manage their money according to the level of economic activity they engage in at home and abroad, and that can be tricky.[40]

When I was a child I loved to play the game Monopoly. I coerced my grandmother to play the game with me for hours on end. I thought I was so smart, since I would usually win. But looking back, I am sure my grandmother was not as determined to win as I was, so she let me win most of the time. I just hope I am as patient and noncompetitive with my grandchildren as she was with me. I always imagined the monopoly money as real money. I would wheel and deal until all the play money ended up in my stack. But the money actually had no intrinsic value, just as our currency today has no intrinsic value.

If our currency has no intrinsic value, what makes it more valuable than the Monopoly money I played with as a child? A combination of three things gives value to money: its status as legal tender, its acceptability, and its scarcity. It is very tempting to politicians to try to slide more money into circulation in an attempt to increase wealth and alleviate political problems. When the government expands the money supply in a haphazard way, the value of money decreases and inflation may occur. **Inflation** is when price levels rise and the value of money drops. When it occurs, more money is needed than before to buy the same amount of goods and services. Moderate inflation isn't a real problem if incomes rise faster as well. In most of the world's economies, economists assume that there will be some inflation. Indeed, inflation of 2 to 3 percent is usually considered well within an acceptable rate.[41] If inflation spirals out of control, it can wreak havoc on a nation's economy.

I traveled to Brazil in 1987, amidst one of its infamous inflationary spirals. Upon arriving we had time to browse through the airport gift stores. In one of the stores, I spotted several moderately priced but unusual pieces of jewelry I thought would be ideal gifts to give to family and friends. I wanted to purchase them right away but decided against it since we hadn't even started our trip yet. I thought, "I will keep these in mind if I don't see anything better on the tour." Back at the airport after the tour, I decided to go back to the same store to pick up some of the jewelry items I liked so well two weeks earlier. To my surprise, the jewelry had practically doubled in price! Inflation was out of control. Resentful that prices had spiraled upward so fast, I decided to forgo my purchases. I thought of the hardship inflation imposed upon the citizens of Brazil as they bought necessities such as food and shelter.

There are tools with which the government can calibrate the American economy. Congress and the president focus on **fiscal policy**, which relates to decisions on spending and taxes, while the Fed enacts **monetary policy**, influencing the flow or availability of money and credit. "**Fine-tuning**" the economy is how people typically refer to the Fed's actions in raising or lowering interest rates. The Fed's principle tool is "printing" money, which actually isn't really printing money but a process in which the Fed attempts to expand the economy by making cash available for lending by buying bank securities such as bonds.[42] At the time of this writing, the Fed does not seem worried about inflation, but it is worried that the economy is in an extended recession. In response, the Fed has set a low interest rate, at the time of this writing hovering around 0 percent, and has flooded the economy with money. Where does it get the money? It creates it out of thin air. (Money does grow on trees if it is the Fed tree!) For example, the Fed effectively writes a check for $10 billion and gives it to the sellers of government debt. These sellers deposit the money they've received from the Fed in various banks. Now these banks can use it to make loans worth several times that amount. Money is suddenly more available and as a consequence, credit is easier to obtain. Also, the net effect of adding money to the economy is that interest rates will fall.[43]

On the other hand, if the Fed is worried about inflation and wants to keep the economy from over-expanding, often called overheating, it sells, for example, $10 billion worth of government debt. By doing so, it effectively removes money from the banking system because the purchasers of the debt have to write checks to the Fed drawn on their respective banks, which the Fed then cashes and keeps the checks. The banking system and the larger economy are now out that $10 billion. Because banks use every dollar on deposit to create many more dollars' worth of loans, the real hit to the banking system – and by extension, the money supply – is something approaching $25 billion or $30 billion because of the way in which banks loan out money. In this way, the Fed has tightened the money supply and made credit harder to obtain; it has effectively raised the cost of borrowing. Money, like any other commodity, responds to the laws of supply and demand, and now that the supply is lower, borrowing money costs more. Interest rates go up because lenders can now command a higher rate.[44]

At this point, you may think that the Federal Reserve is a good institution and wonder why I would consider it one of the fatal flaws in the financial sector. I think it is a good institution as well. But the reason I list it as a flaw is because of the actions and philosophy of the Federal Reserve Chairman from 1987 to 2006, Alan Greenspan. He articulated a libertarian ideology, in which he was loath to use the powers of the government to regulate the market place. Instead, he thought the market knew best, better than the government or highly trained individuals. Therefore, Greenspan directed the Fed to follow the market knows best philosophy. From the beginning of his term he was ambivalent about government's role in regulating the financial industry, the very task he was appointed to do.

Greenspan seemed to have had little interest in long-standing central banking thinking that considered it best for the Fed to step in to prevent bubbles from forming in the first place. Cleverly summarizing this action, former Fed chairman William McChesney Martin once said that the job of the central bank was "to take away the punch bowl just as the party gets going." Greenspan was unwilling to take away the punch bowl. In 1996, as the stock market spiraled into a giddy bubble focused on tech and Internet stocks, he warned of "irrational exuberance," then did next to nothing to stop the bubble from inflating. When the dot-com bubble finally popped in 2000, Greenspan poured plenty more alcohol into the proverbial punch bowl, channeling more money into the economy which ratcheted up the formation of the next bubble – the housing bubble.[45]

The markets believed that the Fed would always ride to the rescue of reckless traders who were ruined after a bubble collapsed. According to economist Nouriel Roubini, "It created moral hazard on a grand scale, and Greenspan deserves blame for it. For example, in 1994 Congress passed the Home Ownership and Equity Protection Act in order to crack down on predatory lending practices. Under its terms, Greenspan could have regulated subprime lending, but he refused to do so."[46] The kinds of speculative activities that got the banks into trouble after the 1980s were prohibited in earlier postwar decades. For example, there was no such thing as currency speculation in an era of fixed exchange rates and capital controls. There was no savings and loan speculation, given that they were charted to make only locally-based mortgage loans.[47]

In 2001 the economy was on the verge of serious recession. The dot-com bubble had burst and 9/11 had spooked markets, resulting in their steep decline. Greenspan, who had encouraged deficit reduction under the Clinton administration, suddenly changed course. To him, deficits didn't seem to matter anymore. The Fed took a "lose money" policy and supported

THE MARRINER S. ECCLES FEDERAL RESERVE BOARD BUILDING IN WASHINGTON D.C.

a stimulative budget based on large deficits. The need for cheap money was required to recapitalize banks still recovering from earlier bouts of speculative excess. Coupled with the willingness of foreign central banks to keep lending to the U.S., the American economy was awash in money.[48] It was ripe for another speculative bubble.

The administration of George W. Bush used the short recession following the collapse of the dot-com bubble as a reason to push its agenda of tax cuts, especially favoring the wealthy. Congress did not design the tax cuts to stimulate the economy and did so only to a limited extent. The burden of restoring the economy to full employment shifted from the federal government to the Fed's "lose money" monetary policy. Accordingly, Greenspan lowered interest rates to flood the market with **liquidity** (money). With so much excess money in the economy, not surprisingly the lower interest rates did not lead to more investment in plants and equipment. Since money is always looking for higher rates of return, the housing bubble replaced the tech bubble. A consumption and real-estate boom followed.[49]

Chairman Greenspan and the Fed held on to their markets know best philosophy despite warning signs of an impending crisis. But the financial sector doesn't really want to accept the consequences when the markets know best policy plays out. They hate regulation, but depend on bailouts after the fact. The key player in this financial drama was the Federal Reserve.[50]

## FATAL FLAW #4:
## A REAL ESTATE BUBBLE AND OUT OF CONTROL LENDING

As we can see from the three previous fatal flaws, the ingredients for some type of bubble were mixing together to form a noxious bubbling stew. Do you or your parents own a house? It is considered to be the American Dream to own your own home. But not just any old house, a house with all the latest gadgets and decorating style. I recently watched a show on the HGTV channel where home buyers were searching for an upgraded house to buy. As the youngish, affluent couple toured a spacious home overlooking a golf course, they were constantly pointing out the slightly dated decorating appointments. When they reached the kitchen the woman impatiently tapped on the kitchen countertop and insisted, "These have got to go!" The real estate agent meekly protested that they were just installed a few years ago. She quickly turned to confront him and admonished him for his outdated taste in countertop design. He deftly retracted his previous comments, and murmured that indeed she was the one in the know as far as countertops were concerned. The couple ended up buying the house, agreeing with each other that a substantial amount needed to be set aside for a "cosmetic house face-lift."

I tell this story because it reflects the attitude that was indispensable in creating the housing bubble. Americans love home ownership; it serves as a primary individual status symbol, as well as their largest financial investment. Americans were willing participants in buying and selling real estate that contributed to the bubble. Yet for many decades, the public purchased homes according to the rigid lending standards set by mortgage lenders described in the banking section. I remember when my family built our first home. I was taken in, like the couple on HGTV, with all the latest home appointments. I wanted them all. I especially had my sights set on the brushed nickel bathroom faucets, instead of just the plain polished nickel. They looked so elegant in the showroom. Yet, our budget would not allow another upgrade. I already went over budget with my decision to get the raised-panel oak cabinets built by the Amish in central Illinois, instead of the plain-faced cabinets they offered for the budget-minded shopper. Restraint was now in order. I grudgingly consented to the polished nickel faucets. After a few weeks in the house I forgot about the texture of the bathroom faucets. Nor did my family or guests ever comment on their pedestrian look. In hindsight, I wondered why I had been so obsessed with wanting them.

The real estate bubble, however, was not built solely on buyers purchasing homes that were beyond their means. Many politicians attributed the high foreclosure rates to individuals simply buying too much house for their income, or in many cases, no income at all. In my case, even if I wasn't able to finally exhibit some self-restraint in the cost of my first home, the lender would not approve a loan that was more than our income would allow. But during the housing bubble years, checks and balances on the system were out the window; the government had removed and regulators ignored most regulations. It was a time of deregulation, and the market was supposed to restrain over exuberance.

If it wasn't just individuals going house wild, what really made this housing bubble the worst in recorded memory? Using a systems approach, there were many interconnected factors contributing to the housing bubble. Hopefully, this section will help sort out the run-up of house prices and the subsequent crash that contributed to the financial crisis and economic woes since 2008.

Several decades ago banks that made home loans followed the "**originate and hold**" model. A prospective homeowner would apply for a mortgage, and the bank would lend the money, then sit back and collect payments on the principal and interest. The bank that originated the mortgage held the mortgage; it was strictly a transaction between the homeowner and the bank.[51]

To understand real estate lending even further, let's look at Fannie Mae and Freddie Mac. In 1938, during the Great Depression, President Franklin Roosevelt and Congress created **Fannie Mae (Federal National Mortgage Association)** and gave it a mandate to buy mortgages from lenders, thereby freeing up capital in order that those lenders could extend more mortgages. With an initial budget of one billion dollars, Fannie Mae modestly started to buy up mortgages. Since it was a government entity, it eventually sold bonds to investors in order to raise more capital and buy more mortgages. The bonds were an easy sell to investors because people were sure they would be paid back, since Fannie Mae was a government-sponsored entity (GSE). By 1982, Fannie Mae was funding one out of every seven mortgages made in the U.S.[52] By then it had company, a little brother. **Freddie Mac (Federal Home Loan Mortgage Corporation)** was launched in 1970 to expand the secondary mortgage market. Well into the 1980s, Fannie Mae and Freddie Mac retained most of the mortgages they bought. Fannie and Freddie had strict rules about who could be lent money and under what terms. Mortgages which conformed to their rules were known as "conforming loans." The mortgage lenders, sandwiched in between Fannie and Freddie and the general borrowing public, had even more rules. There were restrictions based on a borrower's credit history, on the appraisal of the house, and so on. But this originate and hold model was beginning to change in the 1970s with a new scheme. Another GSE institution, a sister with a cute name, in the mortgage lending business was being born.

**The Government National Mortgage Association (Ginnie Mae)** put together the first mortgage-backed securities. Ginnie Mae bought mortgages on the secondary market, pooled the mortgages it had originated, issued them as bonds, and then sold these pools of bonds as a mortgage-backed security to investors on the open market. Rather than waiting 30 years to make back the proceeds from a mortgage, Ginnie Mae received a lump sum up front from the purchasers of the bonds. Investors buying these new bonds received a certain portion of the revenue stream from the thousands of homeowners paying off their mortgages. This secondary mortgage market seemed like a win-win situation for everyone – it increased the supply of money available for home-mortgage lending and it was a sound choice for investors.[53]

This ground-breaking new process was dubbed **securitization**. Now **illiquid assets** – not easily or quickly converted into money, like mortgages – could be pooled and transformed into **liquid assets** – easily and quickly converted into money – that were tradable on the open market. These new financial instruments were called **mortgage-backed securities**, since the collateral backing the loans were home mortgages. Investment banks and others jumped on the securitization band wagon to gobble up profitable pools of the growing numbers of home mortgage bonds. Investors around the world snapped them up with the comforting knowledge that home prices never went down in the U.S. Though mortgage-backed securities became increasingly popular in the 1980s, it was not until the 1990s that they really took off. Now the mortgage model was "**originate and distribute**" rather than "originate and hold."[54]

The securitization method was a sound economic principle as long as the buyers of the securities could accurately assess the risk. But according to Roubini, there lurked a fundamental flaw in the process. He states, "If you're a bank selling off newly minted mortgages via the securitization pipeline, your primary objective is to unload as many mortgages as quickly as possible. Each sale gives you more money with which to make more loans. Unfortunately, because the bank no longer faces the consequences of making bad loans, it has much less incentive to properly monitor the underlying risk of the mortgages it originates." A bad mortgage is more likely to be passed along down the line like a hot potato.[55]

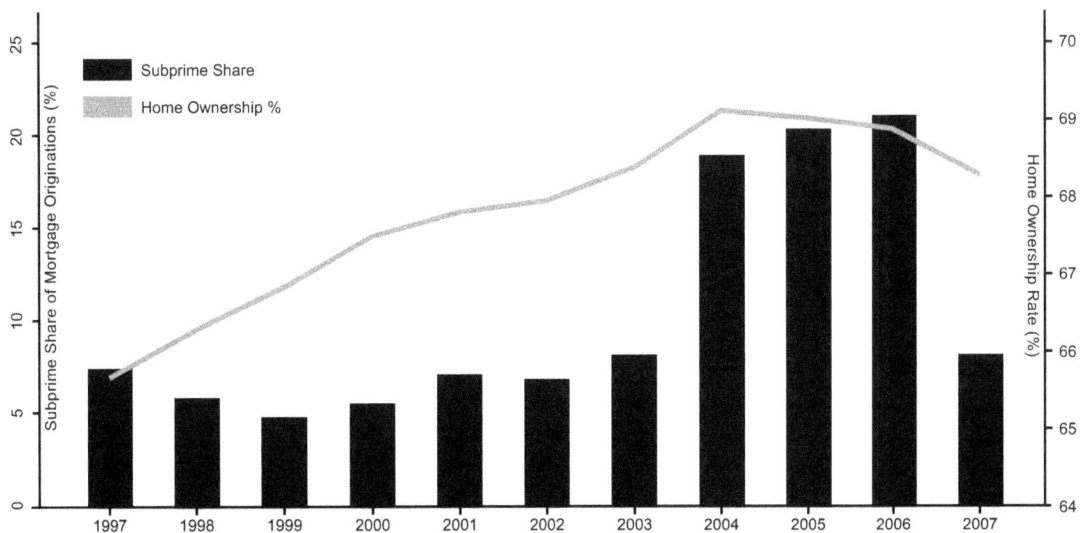

**U.S. SUBPRIME LENDING EXPANDED SIGNIFICANTLY 2004 - 2006**

Those "nonconforming" loan customers that Fannie Mae shunned were another thorny issue in the real estate industry; they had no place to go for lending. This changed too. It started with the **Community Reinvestment Act** in 1977, which was designed to encourage banks and savings associations to help meet the needs of all borrowers, including those in low-and moderate-income neighborhoods. A huge new market in nonconforming mortgages, which didn't fit Fannie and Freddie's strict borrowing criteria, grew. Mortgage lending to "underserved" communities was a principled government policy in which lenders gave lower-income, higher-risk groups, mostly minorities, a chance to get mortgages. Although they still had to meet certain qualifications to get loans, the lending policy seemed to work. Mortgage lenders quickly realized that there was a new market in riskier but more profitable lending to be found among less creditworthy borrowers. First cautiously, and then with increasing enthusiasm, lenders began extending mortgages – known as "**subprime**" mortgages – to this new group of creditors. From 2002 to 2006, subprime loan originations went from 8.6 percent of all mortgages to 20.1 percent.[56]

As securitization became more commonplace in the 2000s lenders no longer carefully scrutinized potential borrowers. Many different types of mortgages were available to both subprime and conventional borrowers. One was the 100 percent mortgage, in which banks would lend 100 percent or more of the value of the house. With no money down, homeowners were irresistibly tempted to buy houses more expensive than what they could afford. They were posed to make a killing in the booming real estate market – at least they thought they were. Like the sophisticated financial experts, they too thought that house prices would never go down. And because bankers and mortgage originators collected fees regardless of the outcome, they had little incentive to curb this recklessness.[57] Among the strangest of the new loan products were the so-called "liar loans." To get one of these loans, individuals were not required to prove their income, and in many cases borrowers lied about their income or failed to provide written confirmation of their salary. Most infamous of all were the "NINJA loans" for which a borrower had "No Income, No Job, and no Assets." In many cases, borrowers were encouraged by loan officers to overstate their income. In other cases, the loan officers did the overstating, and the borrower only discovered the "mistake" at the closing. This was all in the service of a simple refrain: the larger the house, the larger the loan, the greater the fees.[58] Lending practices had gone wild.

Low interest rates and lax regulation fed the housing bubble. Lower rates meant that it was cheaper for banks to borrow more money from the Fed and from one another. Lenders also had more funds to lend out. Since conventional loan rates were low and not earning much profit for lenders, they extended riskier, subprime loans at higher rates to sketchier borrowers. If some loans didn't go well, it wouldn't matter. If banks had to foreclose, lenders bet that they could either sell the mortgaged homes for a higher price, which would more than cover

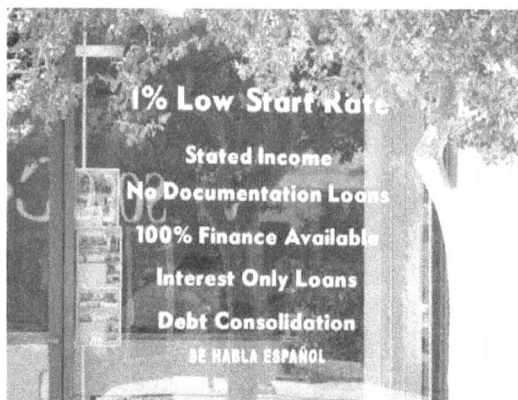

A MORTGAGE BROKERAGE COMPANY IN THE US ADVERTISING SUBPRIME MORTGAGES ON THEIR DOOR IN JULY 2008.

the defaulted loans, or convince borrowers to take out home equity loans backed by their homes' presumably rising value.[59]

As housing prices soared, homeowners could take money out of their houses in the form of **home equity loans** or by refinancing. Mortgage lenders encouraged borrowers to refinance their mortgages and withdraw their excess equity. **Equity** is the difference between the market value and unpaid mortgage balance on a home. Although some people chose to keep their mortgages the same size and simply lower their monthly payments, many others saw an opportunity to capture equity that had built up in their homes by increasing the size of their mortgages. Because their interest rate would be lower than before, their monthly payment might not rise at all, while they would find themselves with a pile of cash they could spend on whatever they desired.[60] These home equity withdrawals, which in one year hit $975 billion, 7 percent of GDP, allowed borrowers to make a down payment on a new car and still have some money left over for retirement.[61] Homeowners had their own ATM machine with seemingly no limit: their home.

Low interest rates and lax lending standards meant it was cheaper than ever for a family to buy a first home. In response, mortgage companies introduced new products: adjustable rate mortgages (ARMs), interest only mortgages (only interest on the loan was paid), and promotional "teaser rates" that would have a low introductory rate and then go up in the next few years. With all this credit readily available and demand skyrocketing, prices began to go up.[62] This encouraged speculation in housing units. House prices started to rise by double digit rates. Real estate prices rose by 50 per cent in real terms, with the run-ups close to 80 per cent in the key bubble areas of the West Coast (particularly Phoenix and Las Vegas), the East Coast, north of Washington, D.C., and Florida. Economist Dean Baker estimated that the run-up in house prices created more than $5 trillion in real estate wealth compared to a scenario where house prices follow their normal growth rate.[63] All this served to reinforce speculation, and the rise in house prices made the owners feel rich; the result was a consumption boom that fueled growth in the economy in the mid-2000s.

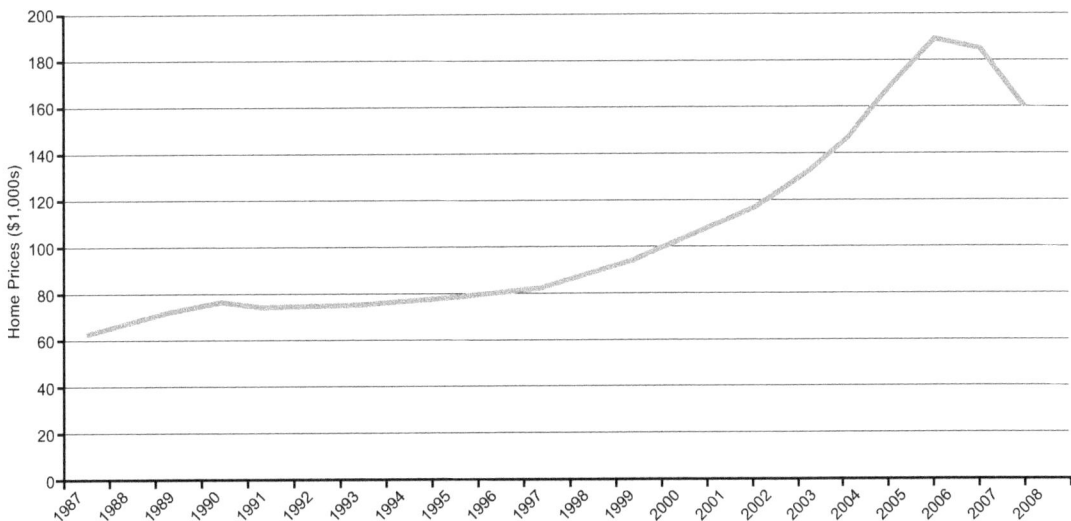

**HOUSE PRICE TREND (1998-2008) AS MEASURED BY THE CASE-SHILLER INDEX.**

These so-called "innovative" mortgages had several flaws. First, lenders assumed it would be easy to refinance these loans because house prices would continue to rise at the same rapid rate. However, the real income adjusted for inflation of most Americans has been stagnating since the 1980s; the median household income in 2005 was nearly 3 percent lower than in 1999. Meanwhile, home prices had been rising far faster than inflation or real income. To confirm the widespread expectation that home prices would continue to rise, from 1999 to 2005 home prices increased by 42 percent.[64] Yet, these trends were not sustainable. Stiglitz noted, "The economy was out of kilter: two-thirds to three-fourths of the economy was housing related: constructing new houses or buying contents to fill them, or borrowing against old houses to finance consumption. It was unsustainable – and it wasn't sustained. The breaking of the bubble at first affected the worst mortgages, but soon affected all residential real estate."[65]

Real estate offered a seemingly risk-free path to fortune. Eager buyers saw the opportunity to make a quick buck in real estate, mortgage lenders got rich on fees, and investment bankers clamored for more mortgage-backed securities to sell to investors. They were all giddy from the proverbial punch bowl that served up a seemingly continuous supply of addictive intoxicants. But when the Fed finally raised interest rates on many of the loans and supply exceeded demand, the party was officially over. We are still cleaning up the confetti and streamers celebrating the big bash. Years later, the repercussions are still being felt.

---

### Questions to Consider

1. How did real estate prices spiral out of control? Who do you blame for this occurrence?
2. Do you know someone whose house in "underwater?" What are they doing about it?

---

## FATAL FLAW #5: MOUNTAINS OF DEBT

What is debt? **Debt** is simply something that is owed or that one is bound to pay to or perform for another. There are different forms of debt, some of which we covered in chapter 4. In this section we will cover financial sector debt. Debt is an important component in a dynamic, modern economy. But on the down side, debt may also spiral out of control.

During and after World War II, the Fed had a large national debt and low interest rates, but the debt financed a war and later investment in productive assets, such as real homes, factories, and farms. Since the 2000s, as we have seen, low interest rates and a deregulated financial economy financed a speculative bubble of unproductive toxic assets. From the late 1990s until the credit crunch of 2007, as a result of trade imbalances, surplus funds from China, South Korea, and other developing countries poured into this country in the form of loans. These countries lent funds to the government, U.S. consumers, corporations, and banks that kept piling on the debt and inflating the latest bubble in the stock market or housing.[66]

This cycle of debt and bubbles is not new in world history. The basic message is simple, according to economists Carmen Reinhart and Kenneth Rogoff, "We have been here before." They state that no matter how different the latest financial frenzy or crisis always appears to be, there are usually remarkable similarities with past experience from other countries and from history. They go on to state, "Recognizing these analogies and precedents is an essential step toward improving our global financial system, both to reduce the risk of future crisis and to better handle catastrophes when they happen. If there is one common theme to the vast range of crises, it is that excessive debt accumulation, whether it is by the government, banks, corporations, or consumers, often poses greater systemic risks than it seems during a boom." Large-scale buildups of debt, particularly when debt is short term and needs to be constantly refinanced, pose systemic risks because it makes an economy vulnerable to a crisis of confidence. They go on to offer this chilling advice. "Debt-fueled booms all too often provide false affirmation of a government's policies, a financial institution's ability to make outsized profits or a country's living standard. Most of the booms end badly." Although debt is a crucial element to all economies, balancing the risk and opportunities of debt is always a challenge.[67]

When discussing corporate debt, it is interesting to examine the ideas of a previously little-known economist, Hyman Minsky, whose views on debt and the economy suddenly became very popular in 2007. Indeed, the "Minsky moment" had become a fashionable catch phrase on Wall Street at the time. Minsky claimed that capitalism was by its very nature unstable and prone to collapse. Instability originates in the very financial institutions that make capitalism possible. Paradoxically, the innovation and vitality of capitalism contain the potential for runaway expansion, powered by an investment boom. Minsky showed that as banks and other financial institutions became increasingly complex and interdependent, they could crash the entire system. The centerpiece of his argument was how debt accumulated, was distributed, and was valued.[68] At its core, Minsky's hypothesis was straightforward: When times are good, investors take on risk; the longer times stay good, the more risk they take on, until they've taken on too much. Eventually, they reach a point where the cash generated by their assets is no longer sufficient to pay off the mountains of debt they took on to acquire the assets. Losses on such speculative assets prompt lenders to call in their loans, which is likely to lead to a collapse of asset values. When the downturn forces investors to sell even their less-speculative investments to make good on their loans, this move causes markets to spiral lower. At this point, the Minsky moment has arrived.[69]

The private sector's accumulation of debt is a key mechanism that pushes an economy towards a crisis. The use of debt to supplement investment is known as **leverage**. Minsky grasped an essential truth about leverage: the greater the reliance on debt and leverage, the more fragile the financial system. Journalist Nomi Prins claimed, "It wasn't the subprime market collapse that wrecked the banks and the greater economy; it was all of the borrowing on top of the subprime loans that did the deed."[70]

As a result of the Gramm, Leach, Biley Act in 1999, the government removed the firewall separating investment banks and commercial banks. However, some investment banks preferred to remain insulated from commercial banks. But the problem was that investment banks couldn't compete with the money and leverage of the commercial banks, which had access to their customers' deposits as collateral. The solution for the investment banks was to raise their own leverage limits, so they could borrow more money for speculative activities, without having to post as much collateral to secure the transaction. But investment banks felt stymied by a Securities Exchange Commission (SEC) rule that had been set up in 1975 requiring broker-dealers to cap their debt-to-net capital ratio at 12 to 1. On April 28, 2004 the biggest investment banks – Lehman Brothers, Bear Stearns, Merrill Lynch, J.P. Morgan, and Goldman Sachs – got approval from the SEC to increase their official leverage from 12 to 1 to 30 to 1. The SEC even allowed the banks to increase their debt-to-net capital ratios, as in the case of Merrill Lynch, to as high as 40 to 1.[71] The result of this change was a bout of borrowing and debt that contributed to the crisis in 2008.

---

**Questions to Consider**

1. Why does excessive debt create instability in a financial system? Explain.
2. Would excessive debt create the same instability in a household? Explain.

---

## FATAL FLAW #6: DICEY FINANCIAL PRODUCTS

For years, the financial sector was the mechanism by which savers were joined with entrepreneurs who had need of their funds to invest in production. Since the 1980s, as a result of technological and global financial changes, there was a rapid globalization of speculative capital circulating around the world, honing in on financial instruments with the highest returns. This tremendous burst of speculative activity has made finance the most profitable sector of the global economy, but it was also a source of economic instability. The 1980s and 1990s witnessed the development of ever more sophisticated financial instruments, such as futures, swaps, options, and other derivatives, where profits came not from trading assets but from speculation on the expectations of the movement of the underlying assets. Would it go up or down? If you thought that the financial sector was all about providing and arranging financing for great businesses, such as Apple, Paramount Pictures, Microsoft, General Motors, home purchases, or basketball franchises, think again. Unfortunately, it is not as simple as that. These financial products are opaque, complicated and combined with other products they create layer upon layer of different products that financiers have chopped up, reconfigured, repackaged and sold to investors around the world. The rest of this section describes the different financial products the financial sector has concocted to make their exorbitant profits. It is a difficult section. I have tried to make it as understandable as possible without over-simplifying. If you don't understand every detail, that is fine. If you grasp the fact that these financial products were (and still are) so complex that it is virtually impossible to know what they are and the risk involved, then you are getting the point of this section.

Wall Street revived the securitization industry because it proved to be their big profit center. Their old-fashioned business – making loans and helping business get started and grow – was much less profitable. Internet competition had dampened the profits in stock brokering along with those in more conventional sorts of bond brokering. Thus, to stay afloat in the competitive world of finance and make the big bucks the securitization gravy train was the answer.[72]

Going back to fatal flaw #4, the section on the real estate and housing bubble, you will remember (hopefully) how the mortgage loans that were made during the housing bubble went through a process known as securitization. As a refresher, securitization is the process of converting illiquid assets like mortgages that are not easily or quickly converted into money, into liquid assets that can be easily and quickly converted into money and thus tradable on the open market. The now liquid securitized mortgages were sliced and diced, packaged and repackaged, rated by rating-agencies as supposedly good investments, and then sold to banks and investment funds around the world.

Securitization offered one big advantage – it diversified and shared risks. The investors who bought the securities might not even know where the houses were located that were packaged in their investment portfolio. With securitization, diversification was easy for investors; they could buy shares in bundles of mortgages. Financiers commonly assumed at the time that mortgages from different geographic regions would not experience housing downturns at the same time; thus, the risks were geographically spread out. But securitization did not account for all sorts of risk. An increase in interest rates would obviously pose problems throughout the country, not just in one geographic region. Also, information about the origination of the mortgage was obscure. The buyer of the security knew little about the borrower or about the bank or firm that had originated the mortgage. And because the originator of the loan didn't bear the short-term consequences of his/her lending mistakes, incentives for doing a good job at credit assessment of the borrower were removed.[73] Yet, lenders ignored these risks as the feeding trough of riches brought out the greedy impulse to make money anyway and anyhow.

Securitizing was not just in home mortgages, but also in commercial real estate mortgages, in consumer/credit card debt, and in car, student, and corporate loans. The resulting bonds securitized from these loans – asset-backed securities – proved popular, and securitization soon spread. By the time the crisis hit, financiers applied securitization to airplane leases, timber revenues, delinquent tax liens, radio tower revenues, boat loans, state and local government revenues, and even the royalties of rock bands.[74]

Financiers sold the securities as bonds. Bonds have been around for many years and are not new financial products. For governments and for many corporations, bonds are the single most important way to raise money. A **bond** is a debt security in which the authorized issuer owes the holders a debt and is obliged to pay interest and to repay the principal at a later date. A bond repays an agreed upon rate of interest until it matures, and all of these facets are fixed – the price of the bond, the rate of interest it pays, and the date when it matures. Around 2008, the total value of the global bond market was in the region of $50 trillion.[75] Bonds vary widely as to whether they are a risky or a safe form of investment. Bonds considered to be a safe investment carry a lower interest rate than high risk bonds that carry a higher rate of interest. Therefore, Wall Street was eager to put together the mortgage-backed securities into packages that returned a higher rate of interest than ordinary low-yielding bonds.[76]

Securitization of the hottest financial products in the field provided a textbook example of the risks generated by the new innovations. Investors buying a mortgage-backed security are, in effect, lending to homeowners, about whom they know nothing. They trust the bank that sells them the product to have checked it out, and the bank trusts the mortgage originator. However, the mortgage originators' focused on the quantity of mortgages originated, not the quality. They originated massive numbers of truly lousy mortgages. If the banks had taken just a cursory glance at the mortgages they would have seen the inherent risks. The fact is that banks didn't want to know. Their incentives were based on their ability to pass on the securities as fast as they could to unsuspecting investors.[77]

Since the demand for mortgage-backed securities was so strong, even the poor were prime borrowing prospects. By the mid-2000s, house lending had taken a turn; no longer was the motive to help place poor-but-reliable people into their own home, but instead they had become a predatory process driven by money. Mortgage lenders were frantically searching for people, anybody with a pulse, to sign up. An epidemic began of what came to be called "**predatory lending**." Mortgage lenders were doing everything they could to sign up borrowers for subprime mortgages. The financiers then created securitized debt that they sold to willing investors. Some of this happened in the

UK, Ireland, Spain and elsewhere, but the overwhelming bulk of predatory lending happened in the U.S.[78]

Bankers had gone into the "moving" business – taking mortgages from the mortgage originators, repackaging them, and moving them onto the books of pension funds and other investors. That was where the fees were the highest, as opposed to the "storage" business – originating mortgages and then holding on to them – which had been the traditional business model for banks and had low fees.[79] The bankers gave no thought as to how dangerous some of the financial instruments were to the rest of us.

Even though some in the media simplified the 2008 crisis as solely caused by the sub-prime mortgage debacle, it was not. If it was merely caused by sub-prime mortgage defaults, it would have been relatively easy to solve. The government could have bought and paid off every single sub-prime mortgage in the country and it would have only cost $1.4 trillion. This seems like an astronomical figure, but compared to the $13 plus trillion estimated to ultimately have been spent on the bailouts and guarantees, it was a manageable amount.[80] The actual cause of the catastrophic economic meltdown was the debt that was piled onto the sub-prime mortgages. Now that is hard to wrap our heads around. There was debt on top of debt? In order to understand this a little better, let's look at some of the Wall Street players and the financial products they concocted that contributed to the financial crisis of 2008.

1. **Hedge Funds** are a private pool of capital actively managed by an investment adviser. Hedge funds are only open to a limited number of investors who typically invest a minimum of about $250,000 to over $10 million. These investors can be institutions, such as pension funds, university endowments and foundations, sovereign wealth funds, or high net-worth individuals. In 2011, $1.917 trillion was invested in hedge funds around the world.[81] Hedge fund managers typically invest their own money in the fund they manage, which serves to align their interests with investors in the fund. They typically make 2 percent management fees based on the value of investments, plus performance fees.[82] Most hedge fund investment strategies aim to achieve a positive return on investment, whether markets are rising or falling. A standard hedge fund takes in money or assets and promises to use them to provide a handsome return for the investor through various bets – on housing, oil, weather, pork bellies, wheat futures, or whatever. Since hedge funds are not limited to buying securities, they can potentially profit in any market environment, including one with sharply declining prices, using complex selling strategies. Hedge funds may borrow money against their assets from commercial and investment banks to make even bigger speculative wagers. The thinking goes: the more you bet right, the more money you make.[83]

Because they move billions of dollars in and out of markets quickly, hedge funds have a significant impact on the day-to-day trading developments in the markets. Before the crisis, hedge funds were largely unregulated pools of investment capital. Regulations passed in the U.S and Europe after the 2008 credit crisis are intended to increase government oversight of hedge funds.[84]

2. **Derivatives** are a long standing feature of financial markets. A derivative is a security whose price is dependent upon or derived from one or more underlying asset. Fluctuations in the underlying asset determine the derivative's value. The most common underlying assets include stocks, bonds, currencies, interest rates, commodities, and market indexes. High leverage characterizes most derivatives. Traders use derivatives as an instrument to hedge or circumvent risk, but traders

also use them for speculative purposes.[85] Speculation on tulip derivatives was a feature of the Dutch tulip bulb bubble in 1637 (see chapter 8). One of the oldest derivatives is rice futures, which were traded on the Dojima Rice Exchange, located in Osaka, Japan, since the 18th century.

It's no coincidence that commodities markets first extensively developed derivatives. In 1864 in the United States, the Chicago Board of Trade (CBOT) listed the first ever standardized futures contracts. In 1919, traders reorganized the Chicago Butter and Egg Board, a spin-off of the CBOT, to enable member traders to allow futures trading. At their simplest, **futures trading** is where a farmer will agree to a price for his/her next harvest months in advance. The future price of the harvest is thus a derivative, which can itself be bought and sold. The name comes from the fact that a derivative's value derives from an underlying product, the farmer's crop in this case. For years, derivatives have existed as a useful trading tool. The futures contract assures farmers of a price for their harvest, long before the crops are in. They are immensely practical but in their basic essence not too complicated. They have been around for a long time.[86]

It quickly became obvious in Chicago and elsewhere that there was a huge potential market in the field of financial derivatives. But a major drawback was that no one could work out how to price them. The interacting factors of time, risk, interest rates, and price volatility were so complex that they defeated the best mathematicians, until Fischer Black and Myron Scholes calculated their ground-breaking formula in 1973. Coincidentally, it was one month after the Chicago Board Options Exchange had opened for business. The revolutionary aspect of their formula was an equation that calculated the price of financial derivatives based on the value of the underlying assets. It was a defining moment in applying mathematical formulas to market pricing. Within months, traders were using these new inventions, and the worldwide derivatives business took off like a rocket.

**THE CHICAGO BOARD OF TRADE BUILDING WAS CHICAGO'S TALLEST FROM 1930 UNTIL 1965.**

The total market in derivative products around the world is today counted in the hundreds of trillions of dollars. Nobody knows the exact figure, but the notional amount certainly exceeds the total value of the all the world's economic output, roughly $66 trillion, by a huge factor – perhaps tenfold. The **notional value** is the total value of a leveraged position's assets. For example, an investor buys 250 units of a Standard and Poors (S&P) 500 Index futures contract that is trading at $1,000 a unit. The single futures contract is similar to investing $250,000 (250 x $1,000). Therefore, $250,000 is the notional value underlying the futures contract. Even if the $250,000 is borrowed, which it often is, the notional value remains the same. Notional values can spiral far, far away from the underlying value of the real assets.[87]

Derivatives are a double-edged sword. On one hand, they can manage risk. If Southwest

Airlines is worried about the rising price of fuel, it can insure against that risk by buying oil on the futures market, locking in a price today for oil to be delivered in six months. Using derivatives Southwest can, in effect, take out an "insurance policy" against the risk that the price will go up. On the other hand, a derivative is a speculative bet. For example, the bet that the price of a stock will be greater than $10 next Monday is a derivative. A bet that the market value of a bet that a stock will be greater than $10 next Monday is a derivative based on a derivative. A bet that a Hollywood film will be a blockbuster is a derivative. There are an infinite number of such products that one could invent.[88] And, indeed, in the 2000s, the financial sector had a heyday in concocting speculative derivatives that were far removed from their supposed mission of helping businesses grow and prosper.

In recent years derivatives have grown into something altogether different from in the past. Some derivatives have gone from being a means of hedging risk to a purely speculative instrument. It is akin to making wagers and bets in Las Vegas. Yet, the activities in Las Vegas are pure and simple gambling – gamblers do not promote bets as safe financial investments for a secure retirement. But that is how Wall Street promoted many of the speculative derivatives: promises to investors – pension fund managers, for example – as safe investments, instead of speculative instruments with massive amounts of leverage and risk.

Banks had created complex financial products resting on top of the mortgages. Worse still, they had engaged in multi-billion dollar bets with each other and with others around the world. Derivatives were a tool well suited to this sort of deception. And they are everywhere, many of them in London. Traders buy and sell more than a $1 trillion worth of derivatives every day. Every single thing which can be traded through derivatives is traded. In the words of the legendary billionaire investor Warren Buffet, "The range of derivatives contracts is limited only by the imagination of man (or sometimes, so it seems, madmen). Say you want to write a contract speculating on the number of twins to be born in Nebraska in 2020. No problem – at a price, you will easily find an obliging counterparty." Buffet distains derivatives; he prefers to know what's going on in the companies he invests in, and derivatives make that effectively impossible. Buffet prophetically said in 2002, "The derivatives genie is now well out of the bottle, and these instruments will almost certainly multiply in variety and number until some event makes their toxicity clear. …The derivatives business continues to expand unchecked. Central banks and governments have so far found no effective way to control, or even monitor, the risks posed by these contracts."[89]

3. A **Collateralized Debt Obligation CDO** is a pool of debt that financiers add together and then sell as a set of bonds paying a range of interest rates. Those who issue the bonds pay interest and principal to the investors of the bonds. I first introduced CDOs when explaining the functions of Ginnie Mae. There are two streams of revenue, one from the fees to set up the deal and another from the debt and interest repayment. A now defunct investment bank created the first CDO in 1987. The CDO was basically made up of a bunch of what were

GAMBLING AT A PACHINKO PARLOR IN TOKYO, JAPAN.

called junk bonds, a bond rated 'BB' or lower because of its high default risk. **Junk bonds** were one of the notable "innovations" of the 1980s. These bonds allowed companies that previously banks would not consider sufficiently credit worthy to issue debt. This debt paid higher yields to reflect greater risk.[90] After the implosion of the junk bond market in the 1980s, the use of CDOs went dormant for nearly a decade. But the stuffing, slicing and dicing of any security that contained credit risk – the possibility that a person or a company might default on payments – into another security reemerged as a highly profitable business in the late 1990s. At this time, a second wave of security stuffing emerged, in which junk bonds and emerging market bonds provided the ingredients for the stuffing. The years from 2002 to 2006 saw a third wave of CDO stuffing using risky subprime mortgages. These CDOs were essentially a reincarnation of the lucrative financial gimmicks from the 1980s junk bond era.[91] Excessive leveraging of these dubious CDOs contributed to the financial crisis.

In essence, CDOs are fabricated assets, which mean they are created by adding a little bit of reality and a lot of fakery. CDOs are bonds whose value is backed by loans and promises. Although the CDO idea sounds absurd, we must remember that financial folks know how to deal with things that often don't really exist. So a CDO is just a natural extension of the abstractions inherent in finance.[92] Journalist Michael Lewis has concluded, that "it was impossible to get to the bottom of exactly what was inside a CDO – which meant that no investor could possibly know either. Far too many people were taking far too many financial statements on faith." Nevertheless, the CDO market climbed from nearly nothing in 1996 to $2 trillion by 2008.[93]

If the regular CDO market was not complicated enough, investment wizards began to design CDOs of CDOs, pools of pools of structured debt, chopped and sliced and then chopped and sliced again; the underlying assets beneath these so-called "ingenious financial instruments" were none other than people with shaky credit who were struggling to pay back their loans. The new CDOs of CDOs were known as CDO², or CDO squared.[94] It is a good exercise to try and think for a moment what actually makes up a typical CDO². Warning, this may scare you. Start with a thousand different individual loans – commercial mortgages, residential mortgages, auto loans, credit card receivables, small business loans, student loans, or corporate loans. Package these loans together into an asset-backed security (ABS). Take that ABS and combine it with 99 other ABSs so that you have a hundred of them. That's your CDO. Now take that CDO and combine it with another 99 different CDOs. Want to pour your retirement savings into this "investment"? Do the math; in theory, the purchaser of this CDO² is supposed to somehow get a handle on the health of ten million underlying loans. Is this going to happen? Of course not![95] But for Wall Street, the CDO scheme was a machine that turned lead into gold.

4. **Credit default swap** (CDS), a form of insurance, is another financial gimmick that will boggle your mind. The buyer of a credit default swap receives credit protection, whereas the seller of the swap guarantees the credit worthiness of the product. By doing this, the holder of the fixed income security transfers the risk of default to the seller of the swap. It gives the buyer of the CDS insurance against the risk of default on any given debt instrument, whether it be a corporate bond, an auto loan, or a subprime mortgage. Trade in credit default swaps is based on the likelihood that whatever it is they are insuring will default. The greater the chance investors believe that a default will occur, the higher the price of the CDS. The CDS market made sense before it spun out of control.[96]

Managing the risk of default by those issuing debt is fundamental to the world of finance. Therefore, the market for CDSs – which acted as a form of insurance for creditors against the risk of a firm to which they lent money going under – grew at an explosive rate.[98] In June 2008, the total estimated notional value of CDSs issued was $54 trillion (some estimates claim $60 trillion), close to the total GDP of the whole planet, and many times more valuable than the total number of all the stocks traded in the world.[99]

CDSs turned into complicated financial products dreamed up by Wall Street financial inventors. Another way to think about a CDS wasn't insurance at all, but an outright speculative bet against the market.[100] One of the companies that would learn the lesson that it did not appropriately gauge the risk of all the CDSs it was writing, costing the American taxpayers billions of dollars in bailout money, was a company called American International Group, better known as AIG (see chapter 8).

6. **Synthetic Collateralized Debt Obligation.** By 2005, Wall Street firms were still trying to meet investor demands for all the mortgage-related products they had created. But they were running out of ways to do it. CDOs fueled demand for mortgage-backed securities. Mortgage backed securities fueled demand for mortgages. The problem was that there simply weren't enough new mortgages to meet the world wide demand Wall Street had created for the mortgage backed CDOs. Since Wall Street had run out of real mortgages to package up and sell, they started to create imaginary ones. By the mid-2000s, Wall Street's financial schemers had churned out even more products in the CDO family. In addition to the now staid CDO and CDS, there was also the synthetic CDO, and its renegade sister, the synthetic CDS.[101]

A synthetic CDO is a complex financial security used to speculate that an obligation will not be paid. It is typically negotiated between two or more counterparties that have different viewpoints about what will ultimately happen with respect to the underlying reference securities. A **synthetic CDS** is a form of collateralized debt obligation (CDO) that invests in credit default swaps (CDSs) or other non-cash assets. Wall Street financers first created the CDS in the late 1990s as a way to earn even more hefty fees, but they did not widely use the instruments until the mid-2000s.[102] What is even more insane is that practically all of these financial inventions had as their foundation bor-

---

### CDS and General Electric

In its simplest form, a CDS is an insurance policy, typically on a corporate bond with semiannual premium payments and a fixed term. For example, an investor purchasing $100 million in General Electric (GE) bonds might worry that the company could default on its bonds. The investor decides it would be wise to purchase a type of insurance policy to insure that s/he doesn't lose the whole $100 million if the company defaults on its bonds. Therefore, the investor decides to pay $200,000 a year to buy a ten-year credit default swap on $100 million in GE bonds. In case the company, General Electric, does not default on its bonds, the most the investor could lose would be $2 million: $200,000 a year x 10 years. In the case the company does default on its bonds, the insurer of the credit default swap would then have to pay the investor $100 million. The most the investor who bought a CDS could make would be $100 million if GE defaulted on its debt any time in the next ten years and the bondholders received nothing. But the CDS insurer knows that GE is a good company, and the risk of default is slim. Therefore, the CDS insurer feels pretty secure that s/he will make $200,000 of easy money each year with little risk of losing the whole $100 million.[97] So far, sounds easy enough.

rowers with generally poor credit ratings, who were trying to pay back their mortgage loans, student debt, automobile payments, and credit cards. When I mentioned above that debt piled upon more debt piled upon more debt exacerbated the financial crisis, now you understand what that means. The only thing that slowed down this money-making engine was the shortage of borrowers of even more debt.[103]

## Insights: Financial Products

An apt metaphor for the financial products sold leading up to the climax of the crisis in 2008 is a house of cards. This means that the cards are not really something of true value – like a bushel of wheat or barrel of oil, or a small business on Main Street – and when the reality sets in that the house of cards has no value, then it collapses. Everyone who owns individual cards in the house of cards then tries to sell their cards, but, alas, since everyone knows that the cards are now worthless, no one will buy them. Those who made a profit bought the cards when the price was climbing and then sold their cards at a higher price before everyone knew they were worthless. The value of the cards was worthless, but the lucky investor who sold at the right time made a profit. Wall Street's financial games added no value to the world economy, but they did create a profit. A profit Wall Street quickly devoured and hungered for more.

One of the reasons for regulation is to ensure the stability of the financial system. The government was perfectly capable of regulating the financial markets, but because the dominant neoliberal attitude prevailed, regulating the industry was only half-hearted at best. In the deregulatory frenzy from the 1980s onward, even attempts to restrict the worst lending practices – such as predatory lending in the subprime market – were beaten back by well-paid financial lobbyists in cahoots with sympathetic politicians of both political parties. Subprime financial institutions created an array of subprime mortgages all designed to maximize the fees they generated. Good financial markets are supposed to reduce fees due to efficiency. But that is not what happened; bankers love fees and they strove to maximize, not minimize them.[104]

The euphoria of enormous wealth blinded the financial wizards of Wall Street; they deceived themselves and those who bought their products. When the market crashed, they, like the consumers of their products, were left holding billions of dollars' worth of toxic assets. The crash left banks holding on to their own foolish creations, with borrowed money at that. They couldn't tell, nor could their investors, what was on their own balance sheets.[105]

When the house of cards finally collapsed, the crisis had drastic effects at home and abroad. But the travails did not stop at the U.S. border. These securitized mortgages, many sold around the world, turned out to be toxic for banks and investment funds as far away as Norway, Bahrain, and China.[106] Warren Buffet aptly compared the new financial products to weapons of mass destruc-

**HOUSE OF CARDS**

tion – one because they are lethal, and second because no one knows how to track them down. The trouble with the securitization model was that it broke with the fundamental principles that a bank had to individually assess and monitor every loan. The new instruments made that impossible. The complex mathematical equations of valuation took over the role of assessing risk. The whole idea that a banker looks a borrower in the eye and makes a decision on whether s/he can be trusted seemed very old fashioned.[107]

**Questions to Consider**

1. What is your opinion about the financial products invented and sold by Wall Street prior to the crisis?

# FATAL FLAW #7: FINANCIAL SPECULATIVE MANIA

There has been an increasing disconnect between the productive economy of Main Street and the increasingly non-productive, speculative, yet profitable economy of Wall Street. Since the 1980s, there has been a political policy shift from the productive economy to favoring the speculative financial sector of Wall Street. If credit provides funding for some productive activity, such as transportation or medical research, it can be beneficial. But, as in all too many cases in the past 30 plus years, the extension of credit has not increased the productive economy; instead, it has been concentrated in disruptive speculative activity.[108] The last two decades saw the deregulation of financial markets and as a result a tremendous burst of speculative activity that made finance the most profitable sector of the global economy. So profitable was speculation that in addition to traditional activities like lending and dealing in equities and bonds, the 1980s and onward witnessed the development of ever more sophisticated financial instruments, such as futures, swaps, options, and derivatives, where profits came not from trading assets but from speculation on the underlying assets.[109]

Now here is something to ponder. According to economist Nomi Prins, a person in the financial sector once commented to her "that finance is one of the few disciplines based on the creation of absolutely nothing. It is based on the principle of continuously pushing nothing for something throughout the system as long as someone else is around to pay for it." Walden Bello agrees, "The problem with investing in financial sector operations is that it is equivalent to squeezing value out of already created value. It may create profit, yes, but it does not create new value – only industry, agriculture, trade, and services create new value."[110] In other words, the financial products created did not contribute to the real economy.

You may be wondering why Wall Street traders are so wealthy if they do not create value. It does seem strange that this can happen. But they generate huge fees on their wild investment schemes, and they create profit through speculation, not adding value. Investment operations become very volatile, and prices of stocks, bonds, and other forms of investment can depart very radically from their real value. For example, the stock of Internet startups in the 1990s kept on rising, driven mainly by upwardly spiraling financial valuations, then crashed. Profits depended on taking advantage of the upward price departures from the value of the commodities, then selling before the reality enforced a correction in the market – that is, when the asset crashed back to real values. In other words, to make a profit one has to sell an inflated asset in a bubble economy before that bubble pops.

To be fair, the financial sector has done a good job in some areas and has played a key role in the country's economic growth. Financial innovations in centuries past, such as insurance and commodity options, have proven their value. One area of positive innovation was in the procedure for making home loans. Many potential homeowners in the pre-World War II era had to save a whopping 50 percent to purchase a home. This deferred the dream of home ownership for all but a select few. More recently, the financial sector has provided funding for some of the start-up, venture capital firms on the West coast. They have also provided capital to many new entrepreneurial companies and community banks, credit unions, and local banks that supply consumers and small to medium-sized enterprises with the credit they need.[111] However, these examples distinguish between productive and speculative investments. Productive investments are financial resources which reinforce manufacturing production and services in a particular nation, while speculative investments normally entail fast profits in the stock market or derivatives trading. They do not provide a country with a sustainable basis for long term economic growth and are more volatile. Stiglitz points out, "In spite of the pride about 'financial sector innovations' in the bloated financial sector, it is not clear that most of the innovations actually contributed very much to increased productivity or to the success of the U.S. economy or the living standards of the vast majority of Americans."[112]

The number of speculative manias in the U.S. has had the function of absorbing investments that could have found profitable returns in the real economy. But investors made more money in speculative activity on Wall Street than they could in the real Main Street economy. Walden Bello states that the reason for stagnation in the real economy is overcapacity, in which too much world-wide competitive production drove down the price of goods and profit margins. Therefore, the smart money on Wall Street sought out greater returns in the speculative economy. This atmosphere of a speculative economy on Wall Street trickled down to Main Street consumers, who used the increased values in their home as an ATM. Their consumer buying was not only artificially propping up the U.S. economy but also holding up the world economy owing to the stimulus to global production triggered by American consumer spending. In the late 1990's, the attractiveness of finance relative to other sectors of the economy was illustrated by the fact that the volume of transactions

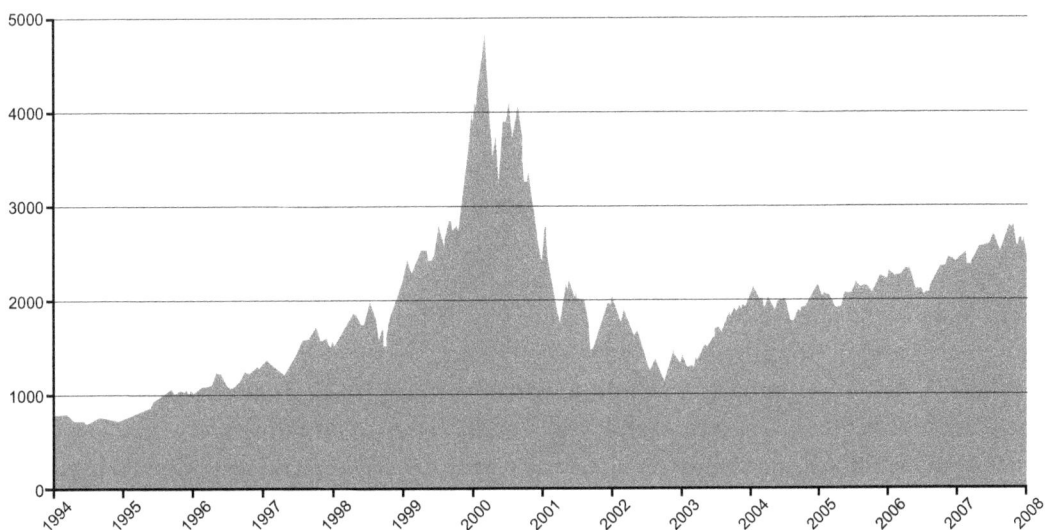

THE TECHNOLOGY-HEAVY NASDAQ COMPOSITE INDEX PEAKED AT 5,048 IN MARCH 2000,
REFLECTING THE HIGH POINT OF THE DOT-COM SPECULATIVE FEVER.

293

per day in foreign exchange markets came to over $1.2 trillion, which was equal to the value of trade in goods and services in an entire quarter.[113]

Since the profitability of the financial sector is dependent on speculative coups, it is not surprising that the finance sector lurches from one bubble to another. Because speculative mania drives finance driven capitalism, it has experienced about 100 financial crises since the deregulation and liberalization of capital markets in the 1980s.[114]

In the crisis of 2008, financial speculators outsmarted themselves by creating more and more complex financial contracts. This enabled investors to bet on the odds that the banks' own corporate borrowers would not be able to pay back their debt. However, Warren Buffet, a grand speculator himself, eliminated derivatives from his investment fund long before the recent crisis. He is the same Warren Buffet who called derivatives in 2003 "financial weapons of mass destruction" devised by "madmen" whom he defined as "geeks bearing formulas."[115]

# FATAL FLAW #8: MORAL HAZARD AND LACK OF TRANSPARENCY

Moral hazard and transparency are two similar concepts that I have included as flaw #8. The concept of **moral hazard** is simply someone's willingness to take risks – particularly excessive risks – that s/he would normally avoid, simply because s/he knows someone else will shoulder whatever negative consequences will follow. For example, someone who has auto theft insurance may be more willing to park his car in a place where it might be stolen, or neglect to buy an anti-theft device, than someone who lacks that insurance. The car owner knows the insurance company will cover the loss; the problem will fall on someone else's shoulders.

Moral hazard played a significant role in the economic crisis. Roubini explains, "In the securitization food chain, a mortgage broker who knowingly brought a liar loan to a bank got compensated for his efforts but bore no responsibility for what would happen as the mortgage moved down the line. Likewise, the trader who placed enormous bets on a CDO would be rewarded handsomely if he succeeded but was rarely punished if he failed."[116]

The market repeatedly mispriced and misjudged risk in the financial system. The market badly misjudged the risk of subprime mortgage defaults, and made an even worse mistake trusting the rating agencies and the investment banks when they repackaged the subprime mortgages with an AAA rating. The banks also badly misjudged the risk associated with their high degree of leverage that they thought was reasonable. Yet, the banks went ahead despite all the warnings with their risky decisions because of moral hazard. They believed that if troubles arose, the Federal Reserve and the U.S. Treasury Department would bail them out, and they were right.[117]

The story of the multi-billion dollar insurance firm American International Group (AIG), the largest underwriter of commercial and industrial insurance in the U.S., exemplifies the concept of moral hazard. At the height of its credit-default-writing frenzy in 2005-2006, AIG reigned as the single biggest player in the CDS market. It had a stellar AAA credit rating and a very low cost of borrowing money. But as the companies it insured started to collapse, AIG was left with paying out the premiums on its insurance policies. It did not have enough in reserve to do so. Thus, the federal government bailed out AIG because it had the entire economic system over a barrel.[118]

Financial markets lack transparency and are complex. **Transparency** is another word for information. Vast portions of global capital flow through secrecy havens like the Cayman Islands – a $2 trillion banking center in the Caribbean Sea. These are deliberately created loopholes in the global regulatory system to facilitate money laundering, tax and regulatory evasion, and other shadowy activities. Sheer complexity also played a significant role in the 2008 crisis. The financial products were so complex that no one fully understood the risk implications. Valuation of the complex products was done by computers running models that couldn't possibly include all of the pertinent information. In fact, some very important information was not included in the models, such as housing prices could fall. Financiers used the computer models to maximize the amount of money that they could make slicing and dicing mortgages into AAA tranches. Without such alchemy, the products would have gotten a straight F. [119]

The lack of transparency has cost society and the economy an enormous amount. The big banks don't like transparency. Stiglitz notes, "A fully transparent market would be highly competitive, and with intense competition, fees and profits would be driven down. The complexity thus allowed for higher fees, with the banks living off increased transaction costs."[120] With complexity and lack of transparency, banks have the power to exploit the uninformed, and they did so ruthlessly.

## FATAL FLAW # 9: DECEPTIVE RATING AGENCIES

There would have been no credit crisis and, therefore, no economic crisis if not for the involvement of the credit rating agencies. They were the oil that greased all the moving parts in the great machine Wall Street assembled to package and sell U.S. subprime mortgages around the world. Their supposed job was to protect investors when the machine went haywire. Instead, they protected the profits they were making.[121]

A **credit rating agency** (CRA) is a company that assigns credit ratings for issuers of certain types of debt. Debt issues with the highest credit ratings – AAA – from the agencies will incur the lowest interest rates. The credit rating agencies' analyses highly influence the investors' confidence in the borrowers' ability to meet their debt payment obligations. The credit rating agencies perform similar work as consumer credit bureaus, which calculate credit scores for individuals that may influence the interest rate at which they may borrow. Perhaps some of you know your credit score. If it is high, then perhaps you can borrow money at a lower interest rate than if you had a low score.

MCGRAW HILL, KNOWN TO EDUCATORS FOR ITS TEXTBOOKS, OWNS STANDARDS & POORS. ON NOVEMBER 26, 2012 MCGRAW-HILL AGREED TO SELL ITS EDUCATION DIVISION TO APOLLO GLOBAL MANAGEMENT FOR A REPORTED $2.5 BILLION.

The top three credit rating agencies dominate the business of deciding how safe or unsafe a particular piece of debt is. These companies are Standard & Poor's (42.2% market share), Moody's Investors Service (36.9%), and Fitch Ratings (17.9%). Standard & Poor's (S&P) is owned by the McGraw-Hill Company (they publish textbooks as well). Fimilac, a French company, owns Fitch. Moody's is the only public company of the three and boasts having Warren Buffet among its largest investors.[122]

Until the early 1970s, the rating agencies relied on investors to furnish the bulk of their revenues. They derived their income from publishing rating manuals and offering investment advisory services. But this changed when the agencies realized they could make more money with the issuer-pays model. Rating "structured products," such as CDOs, remained a small business for many years; the company paid little attention to the potential conflict of interest raised by the issuer-pays model that had become standard practice 30 years later. By then, structured products contributed to the bulk of profitability for the rating agencies.[123]

It should have been to no one's surprise that the rating agencies gave high ratings to mortgage-backed security bonds. In a clear case of conflict of interest, they depended on doing business with and being paid by the same institutions whose bonds they rated. The rating agencies failed to analyze the poor quality of the securities they were rating because of the way in which incentives were structured. The banks that originated the securities were paying the rating agencies to "objectively" rate their securities. Standard & Poor's and others might not have understood risk, but they did understand incentives. They had a clear incentive to satisfy those who were paying them. And cutthroat competition among the rating agencies just made matters worse; if one rating agency didn't give the grade that the investment bank wanted, they could turn to another.[124]

Increasingly, the ratings agencies had an interest in giving the customers what they wanted – and if a customer wanted an AAA rating for a CDO made up of subprime mortgages, there was a good chance they got it. They also garnered income from other, equally problematic, sources. Roubini explains, "A bank putting together a structured financial product would go to one of the ratings agencies and pay for advice on how to engineer that product to attract the best possible rating from the very agency the bank would ultimately pay to rate its securities….It was a bit like a professor's accepting a fee in exchange for telling students how to get an A on an exam."[125] They raked in fees as they told the investment houses how to get good ratings and then made still more money when they assigned the grades. Smart investment bankers soon figured out how to extract the highest mix of ratings from any set of securities.[126]

It is vitally important that ratings of financial products are accurate. Managers of pension funds, for example, have to be sure the securities they buy are safe, and the credit rating agencies play a vital role by certifying their safety. However, this was not the scenario that played out in the run-up to the financial crisis of 2008. Financial markets created an incentive structure which ensured that each of those in the chain of financial manipulation played its role in the grand deception with enthusiasm.[127] Moody's claimed that it "has no obligation to perform, and does not perform, due diligence." S&P claimed that "Any user of the information contained herein should not rely on any credit rating or other opinion contained herein in making any investment decision." With those disclaimers, what then is the purpose of a ratings agency?[128] I would answer that question: the purpose of the rating agencies was profit. At Moody's, profits quadrupled between 2000 and 2007, and it boasted the highest profit margin of any company in the S&P 500 for five of those years. Moody's operating margins during these years hovered slightly above 50 percent.[129] The credit rating business was indeed very lucrative.

## FATAL FLAW # 10: BLOATED COMPENSATION PLANS

The value of money is ephemeral. The financial world does not create anything beyond the temporary profits that it extracts. Wall Street doesn't produce anything of lasting value. Prins points out that the people in the industry get paid for creating an illusion of value that is based on some ill-defined notion or demand for a particular product, on assumptions, on internal evaluations, and on sheer spin. She continues, "On Wall Street pay is based on the deals that closed that year, never mind whether the long-term effects of those deals are disastrous. The bonus system, as a form of compensation, is gluttonous in the short term and careless in the long-term."[130] The more competitive and complex the financial industry became, the more firms had to find ways to extract money from increasingly complex securities and transactions they created. Plain-vanilla securities, as they were called, didn't return as much to investors or make as much for Wall Street bankers at year's end. Transactions are fleeting and revenues are booked up front, regardless of how transactions turn out in the end. It doesn't matter if a merger fails or succeeds; investment banks collect their fees nonetheless.[131]

Few people resent Bill Gates or the late Steve Jobs for making their wealth because they earned it by creating products and services that a vast number of people actually use and have a need for. An actor or actress might get paid millions for a film, but at least the film has lasting life and entertain-

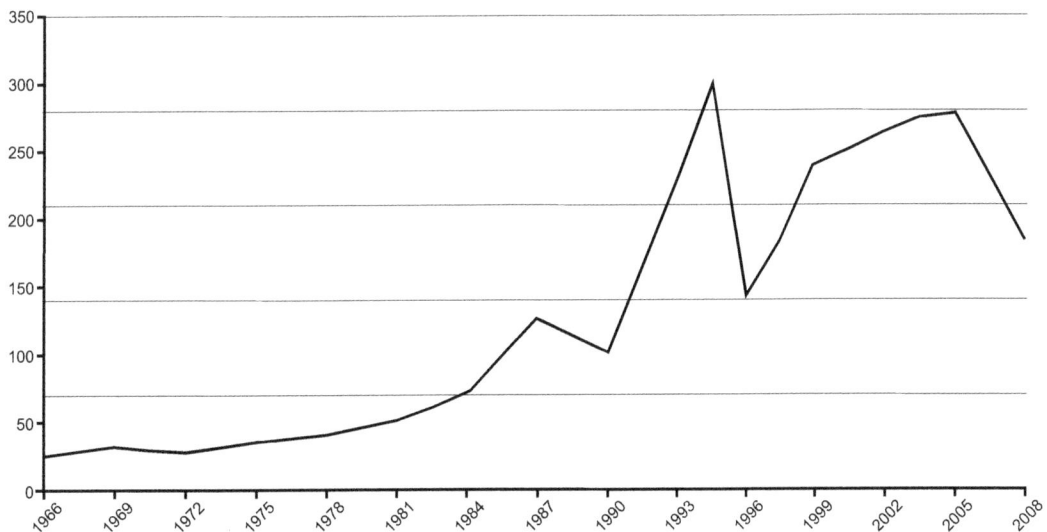

**RATIO OF AVERAGE COMPENSATION OF CEOS AND PRODUCTION WORKERS, 1965-2009.**
SOURCE: ECONOMIC POLICY INSTITUTE. 2011. BASED ON DATA FROM WALL STREET JOURNAL/MERCER, HAY GROUP 2010.

ment value. The same goes for an overpaid football or baseball player. At least s/he might produce a great moment that becomes part of the national culture. But for the most part, Wall Street financial products simply do not provide any immediate benefit to most of the country. Pushing money around and extracting huge profits are not activities that make Americans better, safer, or even more entertained.[132]

Those in the financial sector had more opportunity and stronger incentives to do mischief at other peoples' expense than the average worker. Rather than simply paying employees a salary, the traders and bankers who worked at investment banks, hedge funds, and other financial services firms were paid for their performance based on a system of annual bonuses related to income (fees) they helped to generate. While financial firms have over the years paid bonuses as a form of compensation, in the 2000s, the major investment banks – Goldman Sachs, Morgan Stanley, Merrill Lynch, Lehman Brothers, and Bear Stearns – paid ever more staggering sums. In 2005, the big five firms paid $25 billion in bonuses; in 2006, $36 billion, and in 2007, $38 billion. Even though the federal government bailed out these firms, they brazenly continued to pay bonuses.[133] Supporters of the bonus compensation system argue that this system provides strong incentives for executives to work hard for the betterment of the company. This argument is disingenuous because the executives found ways to get paid well, even when the firm floundered. Pay is high when performance is good and when it is poor. And the bonus system, which focused on short-term profits made over the course of a year, encouraged risk taking and excessive leverage on a widespread scale.[134]

Hedge fund managers have come under increasing scrutiny because of their outrageous compensation schemes. There were just 610 hedge funds with $39 billion in assets in 1990. By the end of 2006, there were 9,462 hedge funds with $1.5 trillion in assets under management. Remember, no government regulations govern hedge funds. Plus, those hedge funds can borrow or leverage substantial amounts of money against their assets. In addition, hedge fund head honchos make 20 percent of all returns and charge 20 percent fees simply for the privilege of taking investor money. In 2009, the 25 best-paid hedge-fund managers together earned $25.3 billion, an average of $1 billion each.[135]

In recent years, the financial services industry – and compensation within it – has undergone exorbitant and utterly unwarranted growth, driven by financial liberalization, financial innovation, elimination of capital controls, and the globalization of finance.[136] The financial crisis has not curbed these excesses. Compensation has continued to climb to all-time highs.

# CONCLUDING INSIGHTS:
# THE 10 FATAL FLAWS IN THE FINANCIAL SECTOR

As we have seen from the ten fatal flaws in the financial sector, the industry has been able to create its own financial Wall Street economy separate from the Main Street economy. The two economies operate on separate planes. But the Wall Street economy is the parasite that feeds on the Main Street economy; it would not be able to exist without it. To be fair, there are still many valuable actions that Wall Street performs. But as we have seen, the excesses have permeated the Wall Street economy so deeply that purging the glut will not be an easy chore. Wall Street will use their immense riches and political clout to resist every effort by politicians and the citizenry to pry open its treasure chest of financial tricks for full examination and reform. It will not be an easy task, but it must be done.

## Questions to Consider

1. How is Wall Street able to create their immense wealth?
2. In what ways does Main Street suffer from Wall Street's actions?
3. What can be done to stop this pattern of wealth flowing to Wall Street at the expense of Main Street?

**CHAPTER 8**

# The Financial Sector: Crisis and Its Aftermath

*"Ideas, knowledge, art, hospitality, travel – these are the things which should of their nature be international. But let goods be homespun whenever it is reasonably and conveniently possible; and above all, let finance be primarily national."*

*Economist, John Maynard Keynes*

# PATTERNS OF FINANCIAL CRISES

*"Contrary to conventional wisdom, crises are not black swans but white swans: the elements of boom and bust are remarkably predictable."*

*Nouriel Roubini*

Have you ever seen a black swan? Chances are the answer is no. They are rare in the Western hemisphere and breed mainly in the southeast and southwest regions of Australia. In the above quote economist Nouriel Roubini is using the metaphor of black and white swans that was developed in a book by Nassim Taleb called *The Black Swan: The Impact of the Highly Improbable*. The book focuses on the extreme impact of certain kinds of rare and unpredictable events (outliers) and the human tendency to find simplistic explanations for these events after they have occurred. Taleb claims that almost all consequential events in history come from the unexpected, yet humans later – in hindsight – convince themselves that these events are explainable.

Humans are caught off guard by or are slow to recognize rare and novel events. Taleb uses the examples of World War I, the 9/11 attacks, the personal computer and the Internet as black swan events. We tend not to anticipate a black swan event partly because built into the very nature of human experience is the tendency to extend existing knowledge and experience to future events and experiences. To exacerbate this natural inclination, much of our cultural

> ## Nassim Taleb's Criterion for Identifying a Black Swan Event
>
> * The event is a surprise (to the observer).
> * The event has a major impact.
> * After its first recording, the event is rationalized by hindsight, as if it could have been expected.

education, both formal and otherwise, is built upon historical knowledge. Taleb contends that banks and trading firms are very vulnerable to hazardous black swan events and are exposed to losses beyond those that are predicted by their financial models. In fact, many in the financial sector called the 2008 financial crisis a black swan event.[1]

Economist Nouriel Roubini, on the other hand, argues in his short quote above that the 2008 financial crisis was not a black swan event. It was a white swan event, which means that it is common and happens frequently. It is merely because we are short-sighted in our thinking and ignorant of the lessons of history, that we would label the 2008 crisis a black swan event. He sees financial disasters as proceeding along a predictable path following expected patterns that have proven through history to repeat under slightly different circumstances. Economists Carmen Reinhart and Kenneth Rogoff in their book *This Time is Different: Eight Centu-*

A BLACK SWAN, A MEMBER OF THE SPECIES CYGNUS ATRATUS, REMAINED UNDOCUMENTED IN THE WEST UNTIL THE 18TH CENTURY.

*ries of Financial Folly*, assembled historical data on financial crises, showing that while the details of financial crises change, the broader trajectory varies little from decade to decade, century to century.[2] Many bubbles, while fueled by concrete technological changes, gain force from shifts in the structure of finance. The desirable assets could be anything, but equities, housing, and real estate are the most common. As the assets' price shoots skyward, optimists zealously attempt to defend its overvaluation. When confronted with the evidence of previous downturns, they proclaim, according to Reinhart and Rogoff, "This time is different."[3]

You will find in the brief examination of several financial crises occurring through history that certain patterns emerge that are repeated in each of the crises.

# FINANCIAL CRISES

I have included in this section several different financial crises that have occurred in the past. There were many to choose from, each following the 10 basic patterns outlined below with slight variations. The first I have included is one of the most interesting and the earliest known financial crises: tulip mania.

## Tulip Mania

I have a deal for you. I have a beautiful tulip bulb that will cost you a mere year's salary! Are you interested? If you were transported back to early 17th century Netherlands, your answer might be yes. You may think that the Dutch seem like reasonable people. Could they be so foolish as to engage in such gambling? With the emergence of the Netherlands as the world's first capitalist dynamo in the 16th and 17th centuries, a new kind of crisis made its appearance: the asset bubble. In 1630, **tulip mania** gripped the country. This was a period in the Dutch Golden Age, during which time the contract prices for bulbs of the recently introduced tulip reached extraordinarily high levels and then suddenly collapsed. It is generally considered to be the first recorded speculative bubble. The term "tulip mania" is now sometimes used metaphorically to refer to any large economic bubble.

The Ottoman Empire introduced the tulip to Europe in the mid-16th century and it became very popular in the Netherlands. The flower rapidly became a coveted luxury item and a status symbol; a profusion of varieties followed. As the flowers grew in popularity, professional growers paid

---

### 10 Financial Crisis Patterns

1. A popular or valuable asset is in short supply while its demand is high.
2. Prices for the asset rise as demand increases.
3. Outsiders enter the market and buy coveted assets, seeking quick and high returns.
4. Over-investment in the desirable asset leads to a bubble.
5. When the tipping point is reached, where supply is greater than demand, the bubble bursts.
6. Panic selling ensues, there are more sellers than buyers, and asset prices swiftly decline.
7. Borrowers who bought the inflated asset are unable to repay their loans to lenders.
8. Either the government bails out the lender or their loans go into default.
9. If severe enough, the total economy collapses, resulting in a recession or depression.
10. Unless the government takes steps to curb abuses, the bubble can be repeated.

---

higher and higher prices for certain bulbs. By 1634, in part as a result of demand from the neigh-boring French, speculators began to enter the market. In 1636, the Dutch created a type of formal futures market where contracts to buy bulbs at the end of the season were bought and sold. The immense popularity of tulips caught the attention of the entire nation and people eagerly engaged in the tulip trade. By 1635, a sale of 40 bulbs for 100,000 florins (also known as Dutch guilders) was recorded. By way of comparison, a ton of butter cost around 100 florins, a skilled laborer might earn 150 florins a year, and "eight fat swine" cost 240 florins.[4] By 1636, in many Dutch towns and cities financial exchanges traded tulips. Some individuals suddenly grew rich. Every one imagined that the passion for tulips would last forever and that the wealthy from every part of the world would buy tulip bulbs from Holland at whatever prices they asked. They believed the riches of Europe would flow to their fair country; wealth would proliferate and the tulip trade would banish poverty forever. Nobles, citizens, farmers, mechanics, seamen, footmen, maidservants, even chimney sweepers and "old clotheswomen" dabbled in tulip speculation. At the peak of tulip mania in February 1637, some single tulip bulbs sold for more than 10 times the annual income of a skilled craftsman.[5]

People were purchasing bulbs at higher and higher prices, intending to re-sell them later for a nifty profit. However, such a scheme could not last unless someone was ultimately willing to pay the high prices. In February 1637, tulip traders could no longer find new buyers willing to pay increasingly inflated prices for their bulbs. As this realization set in, the demand for tulips collapsed, and prices plummeted – the speculative bubble burst. Some were left holding futures contracts to purchase tulips at prices now ten times greater than those on the open market, while others found themselves in possession of bulbs worth a fraction of the price they had paid for them. According to one account, the panicked tulip speculators sought help from the Dutch government that was unable to resolve the situation to the satisfaction of all parties. The mania finally ended with many individuals stuck with worthless tulip bulbs that they owned at the end of the crash – no court would enforce payment of a contract, since judges regarded the debts as gambling debts and thus not enforceable by law.[6]

A TULIP, KNOWN AS "THE VICEROY", DISPLAYED IN A 1637 DUTCH CATALOG. ITS BULB COST BETWEEN 3,000 AND 4,200 GUILDERS DEPENDING ON SIZE. A SKILLED CRAFTSMAN AT THE TIME EARNED ABOUT 300 GUILDERS A YEAR.

## The Roaring 1920s and the Stock Market Crash of 1929

*"Anyone who bought stocks in mid-1929 and held onto them saw most of his or her adult life pass by before getting back to even."*

*Richard M. Salsman*

The Roaring Twenties, the decade that led up to the stock market crash of October 1929, was a time of wealth and excess. A speculative boom had taken hold in the late 1920s during which thousands of Americans invested heavily in the stock market. In 1929, Charles Mitchell, president of the National City Bank (which would later become Citibank), had popularized the idea of selling stock and high yield bonds directly to smaller investors. The public loved the new innovation. But Mitchell and a small group of bankers, brokers, and speculators manipulated the stock market, grew wealthy and helped create the economic boom. Ironically, their successes made them folk heroes of the day.[7]

By August 1929, brokers were routinely lending small investors more than two-thirds of the face value of the stocks they were buying. Over $8.5 billion was out on loan, at the time it was more than the entire amount of currency circulating in the U.S. economy. The rising share prices encouraged more people to invest, hoping share prices would continue to go up. Speculation fueled an economic bubble. Investors who borrowed money to buy the stocks stood to lose large sums of money if the market turned down – or even failed to advance quickly enough. It was a crisis waiting to happen.

Just about everyone believed that the stock market was a no-risk, no-brainer investment, where everything went up. In 1929, while the market was rising seemingly without limits, there were few critics. Based on eight years of continued prosperity, presidents and economists alike confidently predicted that America would soon enter a time when there would be no more poverty, no more depressions – a "New Era" when everyone could be rich. Instead, it was the rich who became richer.[8] Many people poured all their savings into the stock market without learning about the system or the underlying companies they were investing in. With the flood of naïve investors into the market, it was ripe for manipulation and swindling. Investment bankers, brokers, traders, and sometimes owners banded together to manipulate stock prices. They did this by deviously acquiring large chunks of stock between them and then trading the stocks between each other for slightly more gains each time. When the public noticed the rising stock prices on the ticker tape, they decided it was an opportune time to buy. The market manipulators would then sell off their overpriced shares for a healthy profit. The deceived public was left holding stocks worth less than they paid for them. On and on the cycle went as fraudulent investors turned a profit by selling the manipulated, over-priced shares to someone who wanted to have a rising stock. During the speculative craze, a number of academics, including Roger Babson, were predicting a crash, but for every bit of cautionary advice there were four bullish academics guaranteeing the endless growth of the American stock market.[9]

The Stock Market Crash of 1929 was the most devastating stock market crash in U.S. history. The crash signaled the beginning of the 12-year Great Depression that greatly affected all Western industrialized countries. Despite the dangers of speculation, in the late 1920s many believed that the stock market would continue to rise indefinitely. Shortly before the crash, economist Irving Fisher famously proclaimed, "Stock prices have reached what looks like a permanently high plateau." The market had been on a six-year run that saw the Dow Jones Industrial Average increase in value fivefold, peaking at 381 points on September 3, 1929. A string of terrible days followed, with more than a 40 percent drop in the market at the end of October 1929. The optimism and financial gains of the great bull market were shaken on "Black Thursday," October 24, 1929, when share prices on the New York Stock Exchange (NYSE) abruptly lost 11 percent of their value at the opening bell on very heavy trading. On October 28, "Black Monday," more investors decided to get out of the market, and the slide continued with a record loss in the Dow for the day of 13 percent. The next day, the infamous "Black Tuesday," October 29, 1929, about 16 million shares were traded, and the Dow lost an additional 12 percent. The volume on stocks traded on that day was a record that was not broken for nearly 40 years. In fact, the market continued to decline until July 1932, when it bottomed out, down nearly 90 percent from its 1929 highs.[10]

The Wall Street Crash had a major impact on the U.S. and world economy. The fall in share prices of stocks on October 24 and 29, 1929, were practically instantaneous in all financial markets, except Japan. As the crisis spun out of control, the Federal Reserve stood idly by. Rather than pursuing an expansionary monetary policy, in which the Fed pumps more money into the economy, it tightened the economic reins, making a bad situation even worse. As a consequence, the money supply sharply contracted between 1929 and 1933, leading to a severe liquidity and credit crunch that turned a stock market bust into a banking crisis and eventually into a severe economic depression. The U.S. Treasury secretary Andrew Mellon believed that the financial panic would "purge the rottenness out of the system. High costs of living and high living will come down. People will work harder, live a more moral life." In addition, the U.S. raised protective tariffs with the passage of the infamous Smoot-Hawley Tariff, triggering a host of retaliatory tariffs across the world, which contributed to a breakdown of world trade.[11]

In the early 1930s, most of the economists believed that the economy was capable of regulating itself. Moreover, they assumed that full employment is the natural state of things and that when wages were too high, the economy would naturally contract. As unemployment rises, wages will start to fall and businesses will start to hire again, lured by the prospect of increased profits from low wages. The cycle then begins anew.[12] But this cycle did not begin anew. Instead, the most severe depression in modern history ensued. The roaring 1920s captured the unbounded optimism of the age; it was a time when the stock market epitomized the false promise of permanent prosperity. It did not last forever.

## The Dot-Com Bubble (1995-2000)

The boom and bust cycle, called the **dot-com bubble**, was a speculative bubble roughly covering the years 1995–2000. A new technology – the internet – was the craze in the 1990s that promised many positive applications. The

CROWD AT NEW YORK'S AMERICAN UNION BANK DURING A BANK RUN EARLY IN THE GREAT DEPRESSION.

period was marked by the founding and, in many cases, failure of a group of new Internet-based companies commonly referred to as dot-coms. Companies were seeing their stock prices shoot up if they simply added an "e" prefix to their name or a ".com" to the end. A combination of rapidly increasing stock prices, market confidence, individual speculation in stocks, and widely available venture capital created an atmosphere in which many investors overlooked traditional measurements of what constituted a successful business. Perhaps one of the most infamous dot-com companies was WorldCom, a long-distance telephone and internet-services provider that became notorious for using fraudulent accounting practices to increase their stock price. The company filed for bankruptcy in 2002, and former CEO Bernard Ebbers was convicted of fraud and conspiracy.

The disconnect between the real economy and the virtual economy of finance was evident in the dot-com bubble. With profits in the real economy stagnating, the smart money flocked to the financial sector. The workings of this virtual economy were exemplified by the rapid rise in the stock values of Internet firms which, like Amazon.com, still had to turn a profit. Never before had a U.S. economic expansion become so dependent upon the stock market's ascent. But stock prices could only proceed to a point before reality bit back and enforced a "correction."[13]

The peak of the bubble occurred on March 10, 2000, when stocks tumbled. The dot-com bubble fully burst in 2001, ultimately wiping out a whopping $5 trillion in market value of technology companies from March 2000, to October 2002.[14] When the bubble collapsed, only about 50 percent of new companies survived through 2004, but like the railroads in the 19th century, surviving meant a vast new communications infrastructure of coaxial cable lines, cell phone towers, and other tangible technological improvements.[15] The tragic events of 9/11 added to the stock market decline.

THE PETS.COM SOCK PUPPET WAS A CASUALTY OF THE DOT-COM BUBBLE. THE COMPANY WAS FOUNDED IN AUG. 1998, AND DEFUNCT IN NOV. 2000.

A long recession was avoided, but it was only by encouraging another bubble to form: the housing bubble.

## Japan's Asset Price Bubble (1980s onward)

Japan's economy was devastated during World War II. However, with American assistance and the hard-work of its citizens it launched a remarkable recovery to achieve the coveted status as the number 3 economy in the world today. After the war, Japanese industry competed in a low-tech world market, offering low prices and poor quality products. In the 1960s, American consumers sneeringly referred to Japanese-made products as "junk." However, it quickly moved into ever more sophisticated markets by honing its workers' skills and importing more advanced technology from around the world. By the 1980s, Japanese brand names such as Toyota and Sony had become famous for their high quality and reasonable prices. In the 1980s, America thought of Japan much as it does China today – as a rival for global economic dominance. Then, in 1990, the Japanese economy entered a decade of stagnation.

The growth of companies like Toyota and Sony was funded according to a model created by Finance Minister Hayato Ikeda in 1952. In this model, banks, rather than the stock exchange, were the main source of capital for industry. The British and American model of capitalism was built on the Dutch invention in the 17th century, the joint stock company. In this Western model, companies raise money through the sale of shares of stock on stock exchanges. Most large corporations are publicly listed on the stock exchange in order to access large pools of capital. Ikeda thought that this system focused too sharply on short-term profits to satisfy shareholders, rather than on long-term planning. He reasoned that the Japanese model of bank lending to corporations would solve these problems.[16]

The Japanese government played a role in directing Japan's banks to establish close, some say even cozy, relationships with their industrial borrowers, and freely lent to them for the long term. Banks used the funds from Japanese citizens, who were unsurpassed savers rather than consumers, for lending. The main purpose of the Japanese stock market was, instead of raising capital for enterprises, to allow industries and banks to hold shares in each other, which they believed made the system more stable.[17]

Despite Western skepticism, Ikeda's model seemed to be working. Japan ran trade surpluses year after year as it focused on export-led growth, much like China does today. By the 1980s, Japan was the world's largest creditor nation, a distinction once held by the U.S. This was achieved not just through industrial innovation and productivity but by the government's deliberate policy to keep the value of the yen low and Japanese exports competitive on the world market. The U.S., experiencing troublesome trade deficits, began to lean on Japan to raise the value of the yen in order to reduce its Japanese trade surplus. Japan finally agreed in 1985, when senior officials from the world's leading economies met at the Plaza Hotel in New York City to decide what to do. The following agreement, known as the **Plaza Accord**, directed the value of the Japanese currency to rise steadily against the dollar.[18]

As a result of the Plaza Accord, the spending power of Japanese companies in the U.S. and the rest of the world heated up. Since the yen was now worth more overseas, it sparked a wave of real-estate and other asset purchases abroad. Fearing the loss of competitiveness because a rising yen would lead to a drop in higher priced exports and an economic slump, the Bank of Japan repeatedly cut interest rates to stop the yen from appreciating further, a move that would also provide cheap credit to industry. It was at this point in Japan that a bubble in shares of stock and real estate started to inflate, driven by cheap and plentiful credit. In addition, in keeping with neoliberal principles, the U.S. pressured the Japanese to diversify and deregulate their financial sector. As a result Japanese banks, looking for new ways to make money, invested heavily in real estate, which they viewed as a fail-safe investment. They also began experimenting with sophisticated financial instruments, such as derivatives. At the same time, the banks continued to lend to their long-established clients without much due diligence regarding their credit worthiness or the prospect for returns.[19] This was unchartered water for Japanese banks, but since the days of Ikeda, the Japanese government had been active in directing the economy, and borrowers and lenders may have assumed that the government would never let the banks fail.[20]

Asset prices in Japan spiraled upward. By 1990, the value of all shares traded on Japanese stock exchanges was greater than that of those traded in the U.S., a country with an economy twice Japan's size. Real-estate prices soared as well. At the peak of Japan's real estate boom, the land beneath and surrounding Tokyo's Imperial Palace – several hundred acres in total – had by some estimates market value equivalent to all the real estate in California! Real estate in Tokyo was so valuable that it was selling by the square meter. Unbelievably, choice properties, such as in Tokyo's Ginza district, were fetching over 100 million yen (approximately $1 million) per square meter ($93,000 per square foot).[21] At the end of 1989, the Bank of Japan finally decided to pop the inflated bubble. It began to raise interest rates steadily from 2.5 percent to 6 percent in August 1990. The strategy worked. By October 1990, the Nikkei 225 Stock Exchange had fallen by nearly 50 percent from its peak and real-estate prices were in a tailspin, eventually falling 70 percent. As the economy slowed, Japanese companies that had invested heavily in real estate turned to their banks seeking short-term loans to ease their cash-flow woes. Fearing the potential bankruptcy of their clients, the banks lent freely, broadening their exposure to the sinking real-estate market. The banks were now being hit on all sides; 80 percent of the loans that they had made were backed by real-estate collateral that was declining in value. And much of their own reserve capital, which had always been kept to a minimum to encourage lending, was held as shares in other firms, which were declining in value as stock prices fell.[22]

Toxic assets were piling up in Japanese banks. Yet their managers refused to confront reality. Instead, bankers opted to wait until the crisis blew over and real-estate prices would rise again, effectively hiding the true extent of their losses. Bank managers hid revealing files from regulators, and they parked troubled assets in subsidiary companies where they were kept off the company's accounting balance sheet.[23]

Meanwhile, as worries about the reliability of the banks spread, depositors withdrew their money, putting it in postal savings banks (government banks) or under their futons. This only deepened

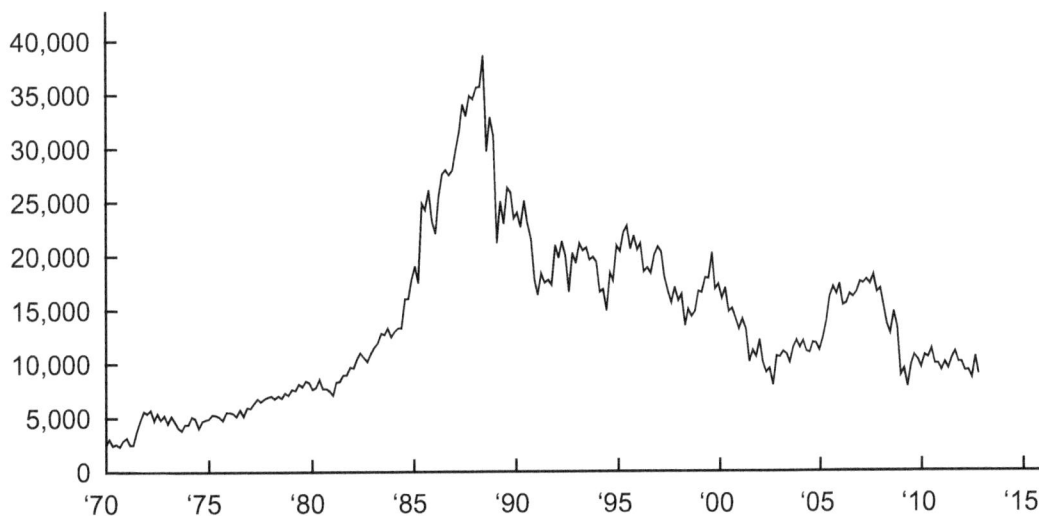

**THE NIKKEI 225, JAPAN'S STOCK MARKET INDEX, PEAKED ON DECEMBER 29, 1989 AT 39,957.
IT CLOSED ON MARCH 10, 2009 AT 7,054.**

the crisis in the banking system. The banks did not have the capital nor the government the determination to clean up the toxic assets. The result was a stalemate as banks continued to hide bad loans off their balance sheets and pay dividends, as if everything was normal.[24]

This denial could not last forever. The problem spread to larger mortgage lenders, saved only with a taxpayer-funded bailout. The government feared that letting them fail would lead to financial contagion spreading across the entire financial sector. Since Japan does not have a Federal Deposit Insurance Corporation (FDIC), as in the U.S., spooked savers continued to pull their money out of the banks.[25]

Unlike the U.S. in the 1930s, the Japanese economy did not melt down. It experienced stagnation, not depression. The bubble's deflation lasted for more than a decade with stock prices initially bottoming out in 2003, although they would descend even further during the global crisis in 2008. On March 10, 2009, the Japanese stock market Nikkei 225 stock index reached a 27-year low of 7054.98. The Japanese asset price bubble contributed to what the Japanese refer to as their "Lost Decade."[26] Today, as a result of a stagnate economy, many young people cannot find jobs or must resort to part-time work. Because of their reduced earnings, many share living space with their parents.

**The East Asian Financial Crisis of 1997-98**

Gripping much of East Asia beginning in July 1997, the **East Asian financial crisis** was a period in which financial institutions suddenly lost a large percentage of their asset values. The crisis raised fears of a worldwide economic meltdown due to financial contagion (spread). Eerily, the reasons for the crisis follow the patterns set out in other financial crises. It was during this time that the International Monetary Fund (IMF) and the U.S. Treasury Department targeted East Asia for market liberalization. They pushed for rapid financial and capital **market liberalization**, another name for opening up their internal markets to the inflow of money from other countries for investment, and banking deregulation. Market liberalization was a two-edged sword, but with one edge far sharper than the other. When markets were doing well, capital flowed in, and even though only a fraction went into productive investments, such as factories, growth was enhanced. But often the

good times got out of hand, and what followed was an onslaught of speculative money that quickly flowed in and out of a country, leaving economic havoc in its wake. This pattern has been repeated time and time again. The result was that developing countries lost far more as capital flowed out than they gained as capital flowed in. Events in South Korea in 1993, the Asian financial crisis of 1997, and later crises in Russia and Brazil, made it clear that something was terribly wrong.[27]

Global money traders are notoriously fickle. In the 1990s, East Asia was the next new investment destination. The economies of Thailand, Malaysia, Indonesia, Singapore, the Phil-

### Major Events of the Asian Financial Crisis of 1997-98

1. Financial liberalization at the urging of the IMF and the U.S. Treasury Department.
2. Entry of foreign funds seeking quick and high returns, mainly in real estate and the stock market.
3. Over-investment, leading to a bubble.
4. Panicky withdrawal of funds leading to a fall in stock and real estate prices.
5. Bailout of foreign speculators by the IMF.
6. Collapse of the real economy – recession throughout East Asia in 1998.

ippines, and South Korea were booming. But the East Asian countries had managed very high growth rates by violating the principles of neoliberalism. They followed a managed version of capitalism. It relied on close ties between local business and government, very low interest rates, high domestic savings, and a degree of consensual planning. The government closed the economy to foreign financial speculation.

The East Asian tigers, as these countries were called, were simply the best investment opportunities in the world in the late 1980s and early 1990s. They had a disciplined work force, low wages, pliable yet reliable governments, and a focus on producing goods destined for export, not domestic consumption. From 1985 to 1996, Thailand's economy grew at an average rate of over 9 percent per year, the highest economic growth rate of any country at the time. Inflation was kept reasonably low, within a range of 3.4 – 5.7 percent. They pegged the baht, their local currency, at 25 to the U.S. dollar.[28] International investment flooded into East Asia in the 1980s and 1990s because East Asia was a more profitable place to invest than anywhere else, and there was a mass of global wealth looking for a place to park itself. Rolling in foreign exchange yen from decades of trade surpluses, Japan, early on, was the biggest investor in the region. With an appreciating yen it was cheap for Japanese corporations to buy foreign currencies, or build subsidiaries in other Asian countries. The long-term Japanese strategy called for transferring manufacturing production abroad to take advantage of cheaper foreign labor. In short, the Japanese were rebuilding what they once called, prior to World War II, the "Japanese Asian Co-Prosperity Sphere."[29]

The U.S. Treasury Department and IMF pressured these East Asian countries to liberalize their economies and open them up to more foreign investment. Once these relatively small countries succumbed to neoliberal principles, their currencies became objects of speculation. Managed capitalism, which had served them well for years, was cast aside. In the late 1990s, traders and investors poured more money into the newly liberalized economies, creating a brief, artificial boom. Awash with money, Thailand, for example, went on a spending spree. Skyscrapers shot up in Bangkok, and so did real-estate prices. Private companies did the borrowing, not the government. According to optimistic investors, highly-leveraged borrowing in Thailand was not a problem.[30]

But the frenzied growth did not last forever. There was a problem with the storied Asian development model: it suffered from a problem known as the "**fallacy of composition**." The first Asian export-oriented economies, such as South Korea, competed with high-cost Western producers. Their low-cost labor, low taxes, and lax environmental laws allowed them to under price their competition and still make a tidy profit. But as more export-oriented countries entered the export game, increased competition meant a slice into high profit margins. As the East Asian exporting economies competed more and more with each other rather than with Western producers, regional recession be-

THE SUKHUMVIT AREA APPEARS AS A SEA OF HIGH-RISE BUILDINGS IN THIS IMAGE TAKEN FROM BAIYOKE TOWER II, THE TALLEST BUILDING IN BANGKOK. THAILAND WAS THE EPICENTER OF THE ASIAN FINANCIAL CRISIS.

came a greater likelihood. The export-game started to slow. Investments lost their luster and became less profitable than expected.[31]

In a matter of a few short weeks during the summer of 1997, the thriving countries of East Asia saw their economies overwhelmed by a financial tsunami. First Thailand and Indonesia, and then South Korea and Malaysia saw investors panic and then watched capital flee. Their currencies plummeted in value and their biggest companies wrestled with bankruptcy.[32] This caused a run against these countries' currencies. In the summer of 1997, Thailand's central bank could no longer defend its currency, the baht, and it abruptly plunged by about 25 percent. The "hot" speculative money that poured into the region for quick returns stopped; the so-called East Asian miracle had peaked. The money that quickly poured in, even more quickly poured out. Asian currency devaluations spread like wildfire to Malaysia, Indonesia, and the Philippines. The crisis spread to all the emerging markets. For example, Russia, which had lately started to receive large sums of international capital, defaulted on its debts.[33] Even the strong economy of South Korea was hit. In this country of tradition, ordinary citizens carried gifts of family gold to Korean banks to help the banks meet foreign payments and thereby avoid "shaming" the nation. A creditor's dream.[34]

The emerging-markets financial crisis of 1997 and 1998 countered the prevailing conventional wisdom of the IMF and U.S. Treasury Department that the quickest route to prosperity was for developing countries to open up their economies to inflows of international capital.[35] After being held up as models of successful development, these countries were suddenly denounced by the IMF and prominent economists everywhere for their lack of transparency, poor accounting standards and crony capitalism.[36] According to economist Walden Bello, "The IMF's performance during the Asian financial crisis of 1997, more than anything, torpedoed its credibility. The IMF helped bring about the crisis by pushing the Asian countries to eliminate capital controls and liberalize their financial sectors, promoting both the massive entry of speculative capital as well as its destabilizing exit at the slightest sign of crisis. It then pushed governments to cut expenditures on the theory that inflation was the problem, when it should have been pushing for greater government spending to counteract the collapse of the private sector."[37]

Reckless lending played a major part in the crisis, but the governments of the emerging markets were not entirely blameless. In Thailand, **crony capitalism**, based on murky political connections between government and business, had led to widespread misuse of money borrowed from abroad and lenders who thought the Thai government was guaranteeing loans extended to private companies.[38] All told, the crisis wiped out $7 trillion in investor wealth and contributed to the U.S. recession of 2001.[39]

The IMF's rescue plan imposed harsh conditions on the crisis-hit countries. It demanded that these countries enforce austerity plans and allow foreign investors to buy up their businesses at depressed stock prices. The billions of dollars of IMF rescue funds were not targeted to rescue the collapsing economies, but to compensate foreign financial institutions for their losses – a development that has become a textbook example of moral hazard. The other part of the story was that the IMF insisted that these countries repay their debts. The only way they could do so was to export like crazy. This route was opened to the Asian countries by the plunge in the value of their currencies, most significantly against the dollar. The result was that goods from the region became very cheap to American consumers, yielding a flood of imports to the United States and Europe.[40] Thailand paid off its IMF debt in 2003. Along with Brazil, Venezuela, Argentina, and Indonesia, it declared its "financial independence" from the IMF. Other countries likewise decided to stay away from IMF lending. This led to the IMF's budget crisis, for most of its income was from debt payments made by the bigger developing countries.[41]

## Questions to Consider
1. Identify the 10 patterns found in each of the financial crises described in the above section.
2. Could any of these financial crises been avoided? How.

# THE FINANCIAL CRISIS OF 2007-2008

### The Fall of Lehman Brothers

Monday morning broke on this beginning-of-fall day September 15, 2008, and like any other day throughout the United States, it seemed uneventful. But it was far from uneventful in the tiny enclave known as Wall Street, located at the southern tip of the island of Manhattan in the financial center of the world: New York City. In fact, the reverberations from the day's events would ripple throughout the world. Some insiders refer to it as the 9/11 of the financial world – the fall of the venerable 158 year old financial mainstay, Lehman Brothers. The firm was at the epicenter of the financial crisis gripping the nation. It had lost billions of dollars in the sub-prime mortgage crisis, which had sparked the plummeting of the financial markets that cost investors trillions of dollars in lost value. Its fall was swift.

Lehman Brothers started small and inconsequentially. In 1844, 23-year-old Henry Lehman, the son of a cattle merchant, immigrated to the United States from Bavaria, Germany. He settled in Montgomery, Alabama, where he opened a dry-goods store. Henry's two younger immigrant brothers, Emanuel and Mayer, joined him in the business. In 1850, the firm changed its name to "Lehman Brothers." Eventually the business started to trade the lucrative cotton commodity, and in 1858, opened a branch office in New York City. Soon after the end of the Civil War, the firm moved its headquarters to New York City, where it helped found the New York Cotton Exchange in 1870. Emmanuel Lehman became a member of the New York Stock Exchange in 1887. His son, Philip, expanded his father's investment bank business and became managing partner from 1901 until his retirement in 1925. Philip was one of the first financiers to recognize the potential of issuing stock as a way for new companies to raise capital.

Upon Philip's retirement, management of the company passed on to his son, Robert, who was the first to invite non-family members to become partners in the family firm. Under Robert's leadership, the bank concentrated on developing consumer industries with financing deals arranged in retailing, airlines, and the entertainment business. He guided his company through the perils of the stock-market crash of 1929 and the ensuing Great Depression of the 1930s. After World War II, he expanded the company's international operations and became one of the country's wealthiest people. After 44 years as patriarch of the firm, he died in 1969, leaving no member of the Lehman family actively involved with the partnership.

With no clear successor, the firm floundered in the early 1970s. To save the firm, the board of directors brought in Pete Peterson as CEO in 1973. Under his leadership, the firm returned to profitability through the turbulent 1970s and became the 4th largest investment bank at the time. Lewis Gluckman was promoted to co-CEO in the early 1980s amidst an inter-company conflict.

The dysfunctional company was then sold to Shearson/American Express in 1984. The company incorporated as Shearson Lehman Hutton in 1988, as a result of more mergers and reshuffling. During the 1980s and early 1990s, Shearson Lehman was aggressive in building its financial business. In 1994, management spun off Lehman Brothers in a successful initial public offering (IPO), in which investors eagerly bought up its shares.

Appointed CEO of Lehman Brothers in 1994, Richard S. Fuld had begun his career with the firm in 1969, the year Robert Lehman died. He stayed at the company until its bankruptcy. He began his career at Lehman's as a commercial paper trader and rose rapidly through the ranks. By 2008, at the time of Lehman's bankruptcy, Fuld had been with the company for almost 40 years and was the longest-tenured CEO on Wall Street. Lehman's performed quite well under Fuld's leadership. On December 17, 2005, when *International Financing Review* announced its 2005 Annual Awards – one of the securities industry's most prestigious awards – it had this to say: "Lehman Brothers is the most innovative [banking firm], …just doing things you won't see elsewhere."[42] Fuld also took in numerous honors for his management of the firm. In 2006, *Institutional Investor* magazine named Fuld America's top chief executive in the private sector. In March 2008, Fuld appeared in *Barron's* list of the 30 best CEOs and was dubbed "Mr. Wall Street." He received nearly half a billion dollars in total compensation from 1993 to 2007. By 2007, Fuld had turned a 1993 yearly loss of $102 million into a profit of $4.2 billion. But there was also a darker side to Fuld's personality. He was nicknamed the "Gorilla" on Wall Street for his competitive nature. *Condé Nast Portfolio* ranked Fuld number one on their Worst American CEOs of All Time list, stating he was "belligerent and unrepentant." Fuld's shadier, caustic personality traits emerged for full public viewing as the drama of Lehman's fall unfolded.

Almost overnight the successful investment bank and exemplary CEO turned from the darling of Wall Street to the whipping dog with the added humiliation of filing for the largest bankruptcy in U.S. history. In the years leading up to its bankruptcy in 2008, Lehman had borrowed significant amounts of money to fund its investing strategies, a process known as leveraging. A significant portion of this investing was in housing-related assets, making it vulnerable to even the slightest downturn in the housing market. Its risk-taking was reflected in its leverage ratios, which increased from approximately 24:1 in 2003 to 31:1 by 2007. The profits rolled in during the boom time, but its vulnerable position meant that just a 3 – 4 percent decline in the value of its assets would entirely eliminate its book value or equity, a very precarious financial position. Since investment banks such as Lehman were not subject to the same regulations as depository banks, their risk-taking was more excessive. In 2008, Lehman faced an unprecedented loss due to the escalating subprime mortgage crisis. Lehman's losses were apparently a result of having held on to those dicey subprime and other lower-rated mortgage tranches (categories). In the first half of 2008 alone, Lehman stock lost 73 percent of its value as the credit market continued to tighten. In

CEO DICK FULD, FORMER CHAIR OF BANKRUPT
LEHMAN BROTHERS, AFTER TESTIFYING BEFORE
CONGRESS ON OCTOBER 6. 2008

August 2008, Lehman reported that it intended to release 6 percent of its work force, 1,500 people, just ahead of its third-quarter report in September. Because of its dire financial predicament, feelers went out for a buyer of the firm. The state-controlled Korea Development Bank was one of its main suitors, but they never consummated the marriage. In September, investor confidence in the company continued to erode as Lehman's stock lost even more of its falling value. Treasury Secretary Hank Paulson, former CEO of rival investment bank Goldman Sachs, did not indicate that the U.S. government would come to the rescue of the ailing giant.

On September 13, 2008, Timothy F. Geithner, then president of the Federal Reserve Bank of New York and future Treasury Secretary under the Obama administration, called a meeting to discuss the future of Lehman, which included the possibility of an emergency liquidation of its assets. Leaders of major Wall Street banks and high-ranking government officials convened September 14 to try to prevent the bank's liquidation by buying up some of its toxic assets with the slim hope that Barclay's of London would purchase the good assets. Barclay's backed out at the 11th hour leaving bankruptcy the only option. Lehman Brothers filed for Chapter 11 bankruptcy protection on September 15, 2008.

The fall of Lehman Brothers alone did not cause the financial crisis, nor did just the sub-prime mortgage market. There was a lot more to it than simply a "few bad apple" bankers making unwise loans to foolish homeowners, who bought houses they couldn't afford. There is a lot more to the financial system than meets the eye. The financial crisis of 2008 is no exception.

## Finance: The Circulatory System

Finance is like the circulatory system in the human body and the banking system is the heart of the financial sector. Ideally, the banking system pumps the lifeblood of the economy – money – to the places where it is needed most. As the heart of the financial sector, the banking system suffered a heart attack in 2008, a massive one. This heart attack could have caused the death of the financial sector, and hence the death of the U.S. economy, but the U.S. government revived it on its deathbed. The government administered massive shocks to the dying heart, frantically trying to revive the comatose banking system. It was put on life support, infused with government loans and guarantees, paid for by the taxpayers. Slowly it began to revive. At the time of this writing, the government's revival of the banking system has perhaps saved the patient. But the whole circulatory system – the financial sector – has many plugged arteries that need tending. Will the patient return to its old ways of undisciplined living that caused its heart attack in the first place or has it changed its habits to a more sober and simple-living style that will unclog its arteries and prevent another heart attack that threatens the death of the whole economy?

Next, we will examine some of the highlights of what took place during the financial crisis of 2008. Not only will we look at the events but also a few of the prime players in the crisis, as well. Keep in mind the questions: "What is the prognosis for the heart attack patient? And is there a chance of recovery?"

## The Financial Crisis: Setting the Stage

In a period of less than 18 months, Wall Street had gone from celebrating its most profitable age to finding itself on the brink of ruin. Trillions of dollars vanished into thin air. Wall Street entirely reconfigured the financial landscape. The calamity would shatter some of the most cherished principles of capitalism. The idea that financial wizards had conjured up a new era of low-risk profits and that American-style financial engineering as the global gold standard was officially dead – at least for the moment.[43]

In 2007, at the peak of the economic bubble, the financial services sector had become a money-producing machine, ballooning to more than 40 percent of total corporate profits. Financial products – too complex to understand – were driving the nation's economy. The mortgage industry provided the loans that served as the raw material for Wall Street's elaborate creations, repackaging and then reselling securities as many times as necessary to generate fees and then selling them to an unsuspecting world.[44]

Financial titans were confident that they had invented a new financial model that could be successfully exported around the globe. "The whole world is moving to the American model of free enterprise and capital markets," proclaimed Sandy Weill, the CEO of Citigroup in 2007. He lamented, "Not having American financial institutions that really are at the fulcrum of how these countries are converting to a free-enterprise system would really be a shame." But the big brokerage firms had constructed their empires on a shaky foundation; they built it on a pile of enormous debt. Many Wall Street firms had unsustainable debt to capital ratios of 32 to 1 or more. This strategy worked spectacularly well for awhile – it always does in a bubble – validating the industry's complex models and generating record earnings pocketed by the financial elite.[45] When it failed, however, the catastrophic results of Wall Street's financial excesses trickled down to the 99 percent who suffered job losses and frozen lines of credit,.

Cheap and plentiful money issued by the Federal Reserve contributed to the Wall Street juggernaut that emerged after the collapse of the dot-com bubble and the post-9/11 downturn. The surplus savings in Asia, combined with unusually low U.S. interest rates, flooded the world with money. The subprime mortgage market, awash with liquidity, was a crowning example of cheap money run amok. At the height of the housing bubble, banks were eager to make home loans to nearly anyone who had a heart-beat and signed on the dotted line. Home prices skyrocketed. In the hottest real estate market in memory, ordinary people turned into speculators, flipping homes and tapping home equity lines of credit.[46]

The following is a story about how one mortgage company, Ameriquest, turned the staid and conservative field of mortgage lending into one in which money was as abundant as flies on a carcass and those involved as predatory as vultures searching for a fresh kill.

---

## Ameriquest: A Tale of a Shady Mortgage Business

It was the 2004 holiday season in Sacramento, California, Bob, a college student, was home for the holidays. One night, out on the town, he met a 26- year old young man – Slickdaddy G, who was a "larger-than-life personality type," Bob recalls. "He had perfectly highlighted blond hair, short and gelled, perfect white teeth, and perfectly bronzed skin." He also had his own limo driver and a seemingly endless supply of cash. Bob joined Slickdaddy G for a night of club hopping, picking up pretty girls and drinking Dom Perignon. The crew ended up at a penthouse apartment – it was just called "the P," as Bob recalls, and an "insane party" was taking place. "A DJ, and more girls, booze, and drugs than you can imagine," says Bob. "It was one

of the crazier experiences of my life." The next morning, Bob asked Slickdaddy G, "What do you do?" "Ameriquest," came his reply. "I'm in the mortgage business."[47]

The subprime bubble was as wild as anything ever seen in American business. Slickdaddy G told Bob that in one especially good month, he took home $125,000. In some places, like Ameriquest's Sacramento offices, drug usage was an open secret, former loan officers say, especially coke and meth so that the loan officers could sell 14 hours a day. And the money poured in. [48]

Ameriquest was the U.S. leader in subprime lending in 2003, having driven its volume to $39 billion, up from $4 billion in 2000. Minnesota assistant attorney general requested Ameriquest's files in 2003 and found that file after file listed the applicant's occupation as "antiques dealer." Borrowers told of signing a loan application and finding out at the closing that an entire financial record –tax forms and everything – had been fabricated for them. In 2007, Ameriquest was the object of major lawsuits filed by more than 20 state attorneys general during the bubble, while federal regulators and law enforcement agencies did nothing. As a reward for its large political contribution, in 2005 President Bush appointed Ameriquest's CEO ambassador to the Netherlands. Yet, even as the subprime bubble was collapsing , clueless Citigroup senior management purchased the dubious company in the summer of 2007, an event that contributed to the firm's receiving billions of dollars in taxpayer bailout money. [49]

---

### Questions to Consider

1. What is your reaction to the story about Ameriquest?
2. Were you surprised to learn about what was going on in one segment of the mortgage industry at the time?

---

## Events of the 2008 Financial Crisis

Along with a systemic failure of the financial sector, this drama is also a human one, a tale about the fallibility of people who thought they themselves were too big to fail. [50] By the spring of 2006, the financial system with its astonishing dependence on leverage – and its blind faith that asset prices would only continue to rise – was primed for a monumental collapse. Housing starts had leveled off, and home prices – which had doubled over the previous decade – stopped rising. Simply, the supply of new homes began to outstrip the demand, and a rise in interest rates made mortgages more expensive. The hundreds of unregulated nonbank mortgage lenders, who had been at the forefront of originating subprime mortgages, relied heavily on short-term financing from larger banks. Since subprime mortgage borrowers were defaulting at an accelerating rate, the larger banks refused to renew these lenders' lines of credit. The nonbank lenders began to fail.[51]

By the end of March 2007, the number of nonbank lenders that had collapsed soared to 50 or more. On April 2, the nation's second-largest subprime lender – New Century Financial – went bankrupt after its funding dried up. The government later charged it with a significant number of "improper and imprudent practices related to its loan originations, operations, accounting and financial reporting processes." At the same time, others who were in the business of originating mortgages – thousands of small-time mortgage brokers – went out of business. Most market commentators claimed that the problem was restricted to one small sector of the financial system. Roubini claims, "This too often happens as financial crises gather steam: the problem is widely seen as 'contained'."[52]

By late summer of 2007, the balance sheets of a range of financial institutions showed a distressful surprise: various financial institutions revealed that they held a dizzying array of toxic assets. Where might others lie? By the end of 2007, weighty uncertainty prevailed. Which banks had toxic assets buried off their balance sheets? The financial system lacked transparency, and much of its activity took place outside the gaze of regulated exchanges. As happens more often than not, crises wane before waxing anew; a period of calm may come before the storm of even the worse outbreaks of panic and disorder. This was that period of calm. But things were about to get worse.[53] The storm was gathering.

Hedge funds operate much as banks do, getting short-term investments from individuals and institutional investors, as well as short-term repurchase agreements, or repos from investment banks. Like conventional banks, hedge funds invest their short-term borrowings for the long term. Two hedge funds run by investment bank Bear Stearns sank billions of short-term loans into highly illiquid subprime collateralized debt obligations (CDOs). Bear Stearns, an investment bank founded in 1923, survived the Great Depression. Headquartered in New York City with offices worldwide, it employed 15,500 people at its peak. Its hedge funds had undergone explosive growth, which they spun into supposedly high-quality assets and rated AAA by the various rating agencies. Once demand dried up for these types of securities, their values plummeted. This meant that their value as collateral for borrowing also shrank. To make up for this difference, creditors started to ask Bear Stearns for more collateral to be posted, but at the same time investors were pulling out. The only way for the investment bank to come up with the money to post as collateral was to sell the declining assets at bargain-basement prices, which further decreased the value of the funds. In the end, the bank completely ran out of cash.[54]

Of the pre-crisis Big Five Investment Banks – Bear Stearns, Lehman Brothers, Goldman Sachs, JP Morgan, and Morgan Stanley – Bear Stearns, the weakest and most highly leveraged, was the first to fall.

In March 2008, the government orchestrated the sale of Bear Stearns to JPMorgan Chase for $10 per share, a price far below its pre-crisis 52-week high of $133.20 per share, but not as low as the $2 per share originally agreed upon. In January 2010, JPMorgan ceased using the august Bear Stearns name.[55]

In the spring of 2008, the crisis was gathering steam. The remnants of the shadow banking system collapsed, and even the conventional banking system came under assault. The securitization pipeline had all but shut down, not only for ordinary mortgages but for credit card loans, auto loans, and other consumer credit products as well. The economy was grinding to a standstill. There was a cry for the government to do something.

Even the federal government-sponsored entities (GSE), Fannie Mae and Freddie Mac, started to waver. Latecomers to the securitization club, they had leveraged themselves at the ratio of 40 to 1 by issuing debt that benefitted from the implicit backing of the U.S. Treasury Department. Their tried and true conservative lending principles of the past were cast aside, as they had used part of their purportedly risk-free debt to procure risky securities. Their investment portfolios were stuffed with toxic subprime mortgages and subprime securities.[56] Their troubles dated from 2004-2006, when the two GSEs purchased $434 billion in securities backed by subprime loans, further fueling the boom in subprime lending. In 2004 alone, they purchased $175 billion in subprime securities, accounting for 44 percent of the market and an increase of 116 percent from 2003, when they bought $81 billion. In 2005, Fannie Mae and Freddie Mac purchased $169 billion of subprime securities, accounting for 33 percent of the market, while in 2006, they scaled their purchases back to $90 billion. However, from 2007 onwards, as housing prices started to plummet, delinquencies and foreclosures began rising sharply. The GSEs recorded $14.9 billion in combined net losses in 2007, depleting their capital reserves and undermining their financial strength.[57] Concerns about their solvency grew.

On July 30, 2008, President George W. Bush signed a law that enabled the government to expand its regulatory authority over Fannie Mae and Freddie Mac and gave the U.S. Treasury the authority to advance funds for the purpose of stabilizing the two institutions. Stabilizing them didn't work. On September 7, 2008, government officials dismissed the chief executive officers and board of directors of Fannie Mae and Freddie Mac, and the companies were placed into the conservatorship of the Federal Housing Finance Agency (FHFA), with the government's commitment to keep both corporations solvent. The two companies needed to replenish their capital, which billions of dollars in mortgage losses had eroded. A **conservatorship** is essentially the equivalent of a Chapter 11 bankruptcy, with new leadership appointed to the bankrupt company. A conservatorship implies a more temporary control than **nationalization**, in which the government would more completely take over a private enterprise.

The intervention leading to the conservatorship of these two GSEs had become the largest in government history and was justified by the Treasury Department as a necessary step to prevent further damage to the financial sector. The Treasury Department committed to infuse as much as $100 billion into each GSE for a total of $200 billion to keep them both solvent and operating. In exchange, each GSE would issue $1 billion of senior preferred stock in the companies to the government. Together, the two GSEs have more than $5.2 trillion in outstanding mortgage backed securities (MBS).[58] In 2009, they held almost half of the estimated $12 trillion U.S. mortgage market.[59]

As Lehman Brothers and Merrill Lynch slid inescapably toward bankruptcy, Secretary of the Treasury Hank Paulson called a meeting of the city's financial elite to the office of the Federal Reserve in Lower Manhattan on Saturday, September 13, 2008. Paulson told the assembled bankers that the duty of dealing with the panic would rest with all of them. He prodded them relentlessly to figure out a way of either buying Lehman or organizing its orderly liquidation. After an all-night session, they reassembled the following morning with a deal to buy Lehman's toxic assets while Barclays of London bought the rest of the bank. However, British regulators scuttled the deal; Lehman would be forced to file for bankruptcy. At the government's beseeching, the venerable firm Merrill Lynch, fearful of sharing Lehman's looming bankruptcy fate, hastily accepted a purchase deal from Bank of America.[60]

FANNIE MAE HEADQUARTERS AT 3900 WISCONSIN AVENUE, NW IN WASHINGTON, D.C.

Lehman's bankruptcy on September 15, 2008, sent shock waves through the financial markets. Lehman's collapse did not cause the financial crisis, but it was a consequence of flawed lending practices and inadequate oversight by regulators. Whether Lehman Brothers had or had not been bailed out, the global economy was headed for difficulties.[61]

The following are 6 developments that occurred as a result of the financial crisis in the fall of 2008:

### 1. American International Group (AIG)

Lehman's bankruptcy shock waves hit the insurance giant AIG first. When Lehman declared bankruptcy, all the major ratings agencies downgraded AIG's credit rating. Its losses had been mounting for months, but the downgrade called into question the guarantees that the insurance company had conferred on half trillion dollars' worth of AAA-rated CDO tranches. Unable to survive on its own, AIG became a ward of the state with a handover of most of the firm's common stock to the government in exchange for an infusion of cash. In effect, it was not so much a government bailout of the company as it was a bailout of all the banks that had purchased insurance from AIG. It would have been perfectly appropriate, in a business sense, if the government had requested that the banks take a "**haircut**" – a slightly reduced price – on those tranches they had insured as a penalty for their unwise decision in trusting AIG to insure them against losses. But the government did not do so. Instead, the government paid 100 cents on the dollar – the full value – even though the market value of the tranches had fallen far below that price. By this time, any talk of holding the line against moral hazard had evaporated. Like the sheriff restoring order in the Wild West, the government was stepping in to rescue the banks from collapse.[62]

### 2. Money Market Funds

The parts of the financial system that had so far escaped the crisis were now in trouble. Money market funds were one of the first to fail. Even though money markets are part of the shadow banking system, the public considers them a safe investment with a nominal interest rate paid. Even though the FDIC does not insure most money market funds, there is the implied assurance that they will not depreciate. A dollar will be worth a dollar no matter what. The no-matter-what day arrived on September 16, 2008, just after the collapse of Lehman Brothers, when one of the most prominent money market funds, Reserve Primary Fund, "broke the buck." Because of its exposure to Lehman's toxic debt securities, the net asset value of their money market fund dipped below $1, meaning that a dollar invested with the fund was worth less than a dollar. This was almost unprecedented, and it sparked a run on the fund. Uncertainty surrounded the $4 trillion money market industry.[63] Since I had just resigned from my part-time position as a history instructor at the local community college to write educational books for the Center for Global Awareness, I had stashed my living expenses for two years in a money market fund. Along with millions of other people, I was worried. But the federal government stepped up to provide a blanket guarantee – the equivalent of deposit insurance – to all existing money market funds. They were safe, for the time being.

### 3. The Commercial Paper Market

Here is another financial term to mull over: the **commercial paper market**. Another part of shadow banking, this unnecessarily vague term describes what credit-worthy corporations do for their short-term borrowing needs, such as to meet regular operating expenses like payroll. Corporations can borrow billions of dollars for 30, 60, or 90 days, and when those debts come due, most corporations simply roll them over for another 30, 60, or 90 day term. The problem comes when no one wants to buy a company's commercial paper, and it is unable to roll over the debt. Money market funds are generally large buyers of commercial paper, and they had completely retreated from the market during the crisis. Because AIG was unable to borrow on the commercial paper market, it ran out of money. An overall lack of commercial paper resulted in the Fed's creation of the **Commercial Paper Funding Facility (CPFF)**. Under this act, the Fed could finance approximately $1.8 trillion worth of commercial paper.[64]

### 4. The Lender-of-Last-Resort: The Federal Reserve

Before the crisis of 2008 and the subsequent bailout of Wall Street, the Federal Reserve maintained $770 billion of safe Treasury bonds on its books, ready to step in as the national lender of last resort if need be. In an emergency, the Fed could loan financial institutions short-term money and, in return, these firms would post safe assets, such as Treasury bonds, as collateral. The better the collateral, the more favorable were the loan terms for the borrowing bank. It was a symbiotic relationship in which the Fed would receive interest payments on those Treasury bonds and hand a portion back to the Treasury Department. This low-risk practice was abruptly halted during the crisis. As the bailout unfolded, banks began to post all sorts of toxic, junk assets to the Fed as collateral, just to get it off their books, and in return they received low-cost loans.[65] It was a strategy dreamed up in Wall Street heaven.

For a few weeks during the fall of 2008, a **liquidity crisis** occurred as corporate borrowing and lending effectively collapsed. Perfectly solvent corporations were shut out of the commercial paper market as borrowing rates skyrocketed and blue-chip firms found themselves short of cash. In order to avoid further disaster, the Fed extended lender-of-last resort options to support nonfinancial corporations. Since other institutions were afraid to lend money, the Fed stepped in to do so. These interventions had little or no precedent in the history of central banking. This amounted to a massive expansion of government support of the financial system. But it was only the beginning.[66]

After the initial credit crunch, money from the Fed freely flowed to the banks at very low interest rates, sometimes even 0 percent. But despite the generous extension of cash to the banks, they continued to refuse to make longer-term loans to many businesses that needed credit to stay alive. Banks were getting no-interest loans from the Fed, but market rates for everyone else remained high. Financial institutions continued to stockpile cash in expectation of future losses on their toxic assets, or they sank it into the safest investments around: government debt. The banks could encounter very little risk and make a return. By borrowing money from the Fed at rates approaching zero, they took the borrowed money to buy ten-year or 30-year Treasury bonds paying 3 to 4 percent. This made economic sense to the banks and allowed them to steer clear of all the risky borrowers who were clamoring for loans. While this strategy was disastrous for the Main Street economy, it made sense from the standpoint of self-preservation for Wall Street.[67] As of this writing in 2012, Wall Street is still following this strategy.

### 5. The Federal Reserve's Quantitative Easing

By the fall of 2008, the belief that financial institutions should be allowed to fail outright without injections of government cash had evidently been thrown out the window. The Fed was lending lots of money and allowing the use of low-grade assets as collateral, but the credit market was still

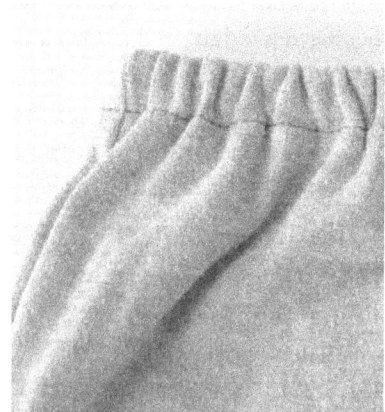

comatose.[68] The Fed would attack the problem of increasing the free flow of capital on multiple fronts; one of these fronts was an unconventional policy used by Central Banks called quantitative easing. When I heard the term quantitative easing, I immediately thought of the times when I may overeat and the waistband on my pants becomes too tight. If I had a really good elastic waistband on my pants, then an expanding elastic waistband could ease my quantitative overeating. End of my over-eating misery. In a way, that is what the Fed has done in the financial crisis. The overeating though was the wild gluttony exhibited by bankers, lenders, and home-buyers, which led to a situation where the Fed had to step in to ease the pain caused to the global economy. The Fed might not appreciate my waist band analogy though, so a slightly more technical definition is in order. **Quantitative easing** is used by Central Banks (the Fed) when interest rates are at or very near zero, and they cannot be lowered any further. In such a situation, the central bank may perform quantitative easing by purchasing a pre-determined number of bonds or other assets from financial institutions. The result of the purchase is that more money is pumped into the economy. The goal of this policy is to increase the money supply rather than to decrease the interest rate, which is already around 0 percent. This is often considered a "last resort" to stimulate the economy.[69]

Chairman of the Federal Reserve, Ben Bernanke, employed some highly unconventional measures in efforts to ease the crisis. The Fed started buying up long-term government debt: 10 and 30 year Treasury bonds. This act immediately injected massive amounts of liquidity into the markets because the Fed would pay for those bonds by creating money essentially out of thin air. As it purchased hundreds of billions of dollars' worth of bonds, cash flowed to the banks that sold them. As a result, the banks had even more cash and were more likely to lend it. An unintended consequence of this unorthodox remedy was that it sent a clear message to the financial markets that the Fed would try anything to prevent a financial crisis from spinning out of control. Although it was reassuring to the banks and general public, it created moral hazard on a grand scale. Sadly, the Fed's actions kept afloat both the insolvent and solvent banks; very few major banks and financial firms have declared chapter 11 bankruptcy. According to Roubini, "[They were] like the infamous zombie banks that became a symbol of Japan's Lost Decade, these firms must go bankrupt, and the sooner they do, the better."[70]

Another unintended consequence of the Fed's monetary policies is the Fed waded into the waters of the financial system and effectively subsidized its operations, potentially incurring losses that could ultimately be the taxpayers' responsibility. It basically granted many subsidies to the financial system in its time of need. When the time comes to sell the long-term debt the Fed has purchased from these zombie banks, they may end up having to unload these bonds at a substantial loss.[71] The Fed used a sleight of hand trick to take on trillions of dollars in useless toxic assets from the banks, giving cheap loans in return to the very banks that had created the financial crisis in the first place. While the Fed was pumping trillions into the economy, the general public was largely distracted by the fray taking place in Congress over the much less expensive $700 billion Treasury bailout package that would be known as TARP.[72]

## 6. The Troubled Asset Relief Program (TARP)

Let's review a moment – this can get confusing. In March 2008, the huge investment bank Bear Stearns was under significant financial duress and JP Morgan Chase acquired it. In September 2008, in the midst of the 2008 election, Lehman Brothers had declared bankruptcy. Fannie Mae and Freddie Mac, the two mortgage giants, were on federal life support. The federal government bailed out AIG, the country's largest insurer. At this point, Merrill Lynch, Morgan Stanley and Goldman Sachs, the three remaining independent investment banks, all faced runs that would quickly bankrupt them without government involvement. Bank of America quietly acquired Merrill Lynch, with some federal arm-twisting, for $50 billion. In the same month JP Morgan Chase absorbed the failing Washington Mutual Bank (WaMu) for $1.9 billion. In October 2008, Wells Fargo bought Wachovia in a $12.7 billion deal. Many other banks also faced insolvency, especially if they took big losses on their loans to other institutions that were about to go bankrupt.[73] The industry was more concentrated than ever, making the term TBTF even more relevant. This was a very uncertain time.

An important secretive meeting took place in mid-September between leading Wall Street executives and government officials – Treasury secretary Henry Paulson, Federal Reserve Board chairman Ben Bernanke, head of the New York Federal Reserve Bank Timothy Geithner, and chair of the Securities and Exchange Commission (SEC) Christopher Cox. The Wall Street bankers had billions of dollars of toxic assets on their books with no buyers, and they thought it would be great if the U.S. Treasury would buy them. Paulson essentially agreed. Over the weekend, Paulson put together a short three-page memo that he sent to the Senate Banking Committee on September 23, 2008, outlining his plans to have the Treasury purchase these toxic mortgage-backed assets right off the books of the banks that had made the bad bets in the first place.[74] The line coming out of the Treasury's office was that the economy would collapse if Congress did not immediately rescue the banks. They enlisted everyone that mattered in this massive public relations effort.

The **Troubled Asset Relief Program** (**TARP**) was a government program to purchase assets and equity from financial institutions with the intended purpose to strengthen the financial sector. President Bush signed the bill into law on October 3, 2008. The $700 billion TARP blank check and the more valuable loans and loan guarantees from the Fed and Federal Deposit Insurance Corporation (FDIC), enabled the financial sector to weather the crisis they had created. The TARP's $700 billion was the smallest part of the bailout. There was no Congressional furor about the trillions of dollars of Fed guarantees and loans. Wall Street was delighted with the government program to buy the bad assets. It was great for them to offload their junk to the government at inflated prices. The banks could have sold many of these assets on the open market at the time, but not at prices they would have liked.[75]

SECRETARY HENRY " HANK" PAULSON WAS NOMINATED BY PRESIDENT BUSH (LEFT) TO BE SECRETARY OF TREASURY. PAULSON GUIDED THE NATION THROUGH THE INITIAL STAGES OF THE FINANCIAL CRISIS.

### Insights: The 2008 Financial Crisis

The series of efforts to rescue the banking system were flawed, partly because those who were responsible for the mess, the advocates of deregulation, were put in charge of the repair. Economist Joseph Stiglitz states, "Not surprisingly, they all employed the same logic that had gotten the financial sector into trouble to get it out of it. The financial sector had engaged in highly leveraged, non-transparent transactions, many were placed off the official balance sheet. They believed they could create value by merely moving assets around and repackaging them.

The approach to getting the country out of the mess was based on the same principles. Toxic assets were shifted from banks to the government – but that didn't make them any less toxic."[76]

Pundits claimed that the subprime lending was necessary to extend the opportunity for home ownership to first-time home buyers. But the Center for Responsible Lending published numbers showing that between 1998 and 2006, only about 1.4 million first-time home buyers purchased their homes using subprime loans, representing about 9 percent of all sub-prime lending. The rest were refinancing or second home purchases. The Center also estimated that more than 2.4 million borrowers who had subprime loans lost their homes to foreclosure. By 2010, the homeownership rate had fallen to 66.9 percent, right where it had been before the housing bubble.[77]

One of the sore points in this financial crisis is the attitude exhibited by Wall Street financiers. They did not appear to be any sincere public repentance for the damage they inflicted on the global economy and many Americans. Perhaps comments by journalist Dan Schecter best summarize the attitude of many in the financial sector. "I went to a dinner party early in August [2011] and met a financial executive who worked at one of Wall Street's top investment firms. He acknowledged to me that the people shoveling out those sub-prime loans KNEW many of the borrowers couldn't afford to pay them back. They knew what misery they'd cause, but that didn't stop them. I asked: 'So, what happened to due diligence?' one of the market disciplines that these bankers are always preaching? He shrugged, indicating that there was so much to be made that normal safeguards and standards were pushed to the side or forgotten."[78]

---

### Questions to Consider

Nouriel Roubini's quote at the beginning of this chapter: *"Contrary to conventional wisdom, crises are not black swans but white swans: the elements of boom and bust are remarkably predictable."*

1. Do you think the financial crisis of 2007-2008 was a black swan or white swan event? Explain.

---

# THE AFTERMATH OF THE 2008 FINANCIAL CRISIS

### The New Normal: The 5 Rs

The financial crisis of 2008 was such a monumental global event that it is difficult to wrap our minds around the enormity of the consequences. We are still experiencing its aftermath. It is tricky to write about it because it is still in process. What are the problems that have not been resolved? What leaders are providing sensible solutions to the turmoil? Should we return to the type of economy that brought about the financial crisis, reform it, or institute a more conservative version? Should we stage a revolution and overthrow the existing economy and let the pieces fall where they may? Should we send out more petitions and hold more rallies, or should we rebuild the economy in a more equitable and sustainable way? These are just a few of the many questions that I am thinking about as I write this final section.

We are at a very critical juncture in our human history. Our planet is in crisis. Pressing economic needs have eclipsed the environmental issue for the past several years. Yet, the issue has not gone away. Our U.S. economy is built upon the foundation of a system devised over 150 years ago. Its apparatus is no longer sufficient for a complex nation such as the U.S., nor is it appropriate for the global community bursting at the seams with 7 billion plus people and critical environmental concerns. No wonder we, as a collective people, are confused, angry, and ready for real answers and solutions to the monumental problems we are facing. However, our political leaders, who we turn to for guidance, are as stymied as the rest of us. They have no idea which way to turn and are floundering about for coherent solutions. In fact, many are merely clinging to the past system that got us into such trouble in the first place. How can we sort out the workings of the global economy amidst such turmoil, indecision, stalemate, and fear? The shrillness of the debate masks the uncertainty people feel.

In researching the topic of the global economy and the financial sector over the last couple of years, I have come to the conclusion that Americans and others in the global community have responded in different ways to our current economic quandary. These responses, or movements, each view the economic system very differently. Since the teacher in me is always trying to simplify complex ideas, I have called these movements listed below the 5 Rs. I am listing the 5 Rs in what I consider a logical order. The rest of this chapter is devoted to explaining each of the 5 Rs.

---

## The 5 Rs: Movements in Response to the Economic Situation

1. **Revolution** – violently overthrow the whole system for a different system.
2. **Restore** – keep the same neoliberal system as before the crisis.
3. **Reaction** – keep the same neoliberal system as before the crisis except make it more conservative.
4. **Reform** – keep basically the same capitalist system but reform or regulate its excesses.
5. **Rebuild** – gradually work to build a new economic paradigm.

---

## #1. Revolution

When the economic and political structures of a country break down, as is happening in some countries in Europe, Africa, and the Middle East, then a country is ripe for a possible revolution. A **revolution** is an overthrow or repudiation and thorough replacement of an established government or political system by the people governed.[79] Revolution seemed a popular response to unstable governments and the desire for change in the tumultuous 19th and 20th centuries. Revolutionaries are eager to overthrow the government that they blame for all problems. But revolutionaries do not have a clear plan for what should follow once they topple the government in place. Revolutions result in more chaos, violence, and instability, rather than solving the issues leading to the revolution in the first. In my opinion, they are not a sensible way to bring about change.

DEMONSTRATORS IN THE PLAZA IN FRONT OF THE GREEK PARLIAMENT, MAY 25, 2011.

Greece has been in the news since 2010 for experiencing a breakdown in the rule of law. Greece is deeply in debt and struggling to avoid a debt default. No country is under more pressure to roll back spending than near-bankrupt Greece; a once booming nation is now saddled with 35 percent youth unemployment and facing the prospect of years of depressed growth. Buckling under a culture of tax evasion by elites and rampant public sector overspending, Greece received a $170 billion bailout from the International Monetary Fund (IMF) and European Union in 2010.[80] In some people's estimation, Greece is ripe for a revolution.

## #2. Restore

The tumultuous events that occurred in 2008 have settled down; we are no longer hearing the everyday headline news that another established financial firm has gone into bankruptcy court, has merged with another conglomerate, or has been taken over by the federal government. There is a desire by many to return to what they perceive as "normal," whatever that means anymore. I once lived in Normal, Illinois, home of Illinois State University where I taught history. When people asked where I was from, I would reply Normal, Illinois, always bracing for the tittering giggles that would follow. Although normal was poked fun at in the past, today many people crave for a return to what they think is normal. As far as the financial sector is concerned, it looks as though the days of normal are long past.

The unknown future poses some real risks and uncertainties. When people are faced with an unknown future or the safety of restoring what they knew in the past, many choose the safer alternative. Restoring the past is a powerful vision for many people at this point in time. Those in the political arena and in the financial sector are conducting their business as if the financial crisis was a mere blip on the financial radar screen, and by making a few tweaks and adjustments around the edges, business can basically go on as before. The financial sector is very profitable and financiers have every reason to try and prevent the reining in of their speculative activity through the regulatory process.

In 2012, Republican presidential candidate Mitt Romney had as one of his campaign slogans, "Restore America." Incumbent Democratic President Barack Obama did not run on his slogan of "Change in America," as he successfully did in 2008. Instead, his campaign too had an element of restore America. But what does it mean: restore America? It is another vague campaign term that means many different things to different people. As in Romney's case, economically he wished to restore the principles of neoliberalism and, in particular, the primacy of the financial sector from which he made his substantial fortune. For President Obama, he wished to have some reforms of the financial sector, but not enough to significantly curb its economic dominance. Romney's running mate, Republican Congressman Paul Ryan of Wisconsin, had no desire to restore America to what it was; his intention followed a more reactionary path, as outlined below.

Since we have already discussed in some depth in this book the policies of neoliberalism and economic globalization, I will not add to the information. Suffice it to say that many of the restorers in America have morphed into a reactionary movement, in which the neoliberal policies are even more conservative.

## #3. Reaction

**Reaction** is a movement that favors extreme conservatism or right wing political views. Reactionaries oppose political, economic, or social change or reforms and are considered to be at one end of a political spectrum whose opposite pole is radicalism or revolutionaries. I have included reaction as a third movement since many politicians and business leaders are moving even further to the right of the restore movement. They are advocating for more concentration of corporate power, smaller government, austerity programs to reduce the deficit, tax cuts – including capital gains – for the wealthy, vouchers for Medicare and schools, more deregulation, and increased privatization of public institutions such as schools, prisons, government services, the military, electricity, federal lands, and Social Security.

The following points are just 5 ways in which reactionaries are intent on instituting policies to favor a more conservative economy and government.

## 1. Reaction: Austerity

The austerity camp sees the threat of government default on the debt as a bigger problem than stagnation and unemployment and refuses to consider any more stimulus spending. Aside from cutting the military, they want to cut government spending through **austerity** measures targeted at social programs, especially education, Medicare, social security, infrastructure, and programs for the poor. For example, some, such as Paul Ryan, envision Medicare in the future to be organized according to a voucher system which restricts health care spending to a voucher amount. Despite high rates of unemployment, the austerity and anti-deficit forces, at the time of this writing in 2012, have the initiative in three key Western countries: in Britain, where the conservatives won on a platform of reducing the government; in Germany, where the image of spendthrift Greeks and Spaniards financed with loans from hardworking Germans became a powerful image, and in the United States, where Republicans have seized the austerity flag.[81]

The reduce-the-deficit slogan has gained ascendancy in the U.S. for a number of reasons. First of all, this call appeals to the anti-big government sentiments of many Americans. Second, Wall Street has opportunistically embraced anti-deficit calls to divert governmental efforts to enforce regulations. It proclaims, "Big government is the problem, not big banks." Third, the reemergence of neoliberal believers, who were temporarily discredited after the financial crisis, champion the idea that austerity measures would purge the excesses of a bloated government and lead to a healthier, leaner economy. Letting the economy heal itself is like letting the patient suffer. Fourth, the anti-spending, austerity measures are supported by the vocal Tea Party movement.[82]

A popular reactionary movement, the Tea Party, has gained force since the 2010 mid-term elections. It has been able to elect candidates to political office that support its cause. The party has several different slick websites, such as one that has a pop-up ad asking me to sign a petition that states "The Supreme Court Ruled against the American People. It's Time for the People to Take

**TEA PARTY PROTESTERS WALK TOWARDS THE UNITED STATES CAPITOL DURING THE TAXPAYER MARCH ON WASHINGTON, SEPTEMBER 12, 2009.**

Action." The party wants to repeal the Patient Protection and Affordable Care Act signed by President Obama on March 23, 2010, called Obamacare. I visited another well-designed website, which has an easy way to access local meetings and events.[83] Tea Party enthusiasts see government as the fundamental cause of all the problems. To them, the governmental bureaucracy is restricting our freedoms and limiting our entrepreneurial spirit with a socialist system that redistributes wealth through high taxes to those who are too lazy to put in a good day's work. Their solution to America's problems is to limit government, institute austerity measures, and follow the constitution in the way they think the Founding Fathers intended. I believe their motives are genuine; they see America adrift and they think they have targeted the problem. But, as the saying goes, "the devil is in the details." I found the platform was disturbingly abstract, with solutions that were too vague to understand but contained many words that resonate with Americans, such as liberty and freedom. Also, large corporations such as the Koch Brothers, heavily fund the party. If we dismantle government, as the Tea Partiers hope to do, then I worry about who is to stand between the elites and the powerless. Governments throughout world history have been the only ones able to fulfill this role; otherwise, the elites are able to entrench their power without any resistance.

## 2. Reaction: The Banks

The financial crisis and bailout led to further concentration of the financial sector. All of this has signaled a reactionary form of neoliberalism. The crisis gave stronger firms an opportunity to pick up weaker firms in a wave of mergers, such as the hastily arranged purchase of failing financial giants like Bear Stearns by Chase in March 2008. Policies during the crisis have made the banking system, stronger, more profitable and more politically influential. Since the crisis of 2008, the big six U.S. megabanks – Bank of America, Citigroup, J.P. Morgan Chase, Goldman Sachs Group, Wells Fargo, and Morgan Stanley – have staged a dramatic comeback. Profits, capital reserves, and stock prices are all up, executive compensation is exploding, while the banks have paid back government loans. But, according to journalist Rob Larson, "A closer look shows big-bank stability is just skin-deep, and opaque accounting rules hide a powder keg of bad debt and mounting funding issues." Smaller banks have had a different experience. Despite some TARP bailout crumbs, they have gone under in record numbers – 140 failed in 2009.[84]

Banks have staged a staunch resistance to reform. Banks were given money without being asked to change their compensation structures or make other reforms; they were simply allowed to go on as before. At the moment when Wall Street was on its knees, politicians avoided passing serious reforms. Instead, Wall Street was restored to its gargantuan status, thanks to taxpayer money and guarantees.[85] The financial sector has not faced any real regulatory scrutiny, and no system is in place to put them into insolvency should the need arise. Even worse, many of these institutions are starting to engage once more in **proprietary trading**, which occurs when a firm trades various financial instruments with the firm's own money as opposed to its customers' money, so as to make a profit for itself. These strategies, which are complicated bets on stocks, bonds, commodities, and derivatives driven by algorithms devised by the firm's traders, are considered more risky than other trading. Yet firms have resumed these practices.[86]

## 3. Reaction: The Federal Reserve

Through its actions the Federal Reserve is helping to make the financial sector even more concentrated then before the crisis. By lending at practically 0 percent interest, it has provided cheap funding for financial firms. The federal government doled out $13 trillion in guarantees and loans from the Fed, the Treasury department, and the FDIC, all going to Wall Street's biggest players. If the government wanted to get bailout assistance to consumers who really needed it, the government could have given it directly to them or at least directed it to smaller banks that were eager to give out or renegotiate loans. Despite all the bailouts, the same scenario is playing out in the financial sector: under-regulated financial institutions with a more concentrated playing field than ever, and the biggest players have even more control.[87]

## 4. Reaction: Housing and Consumption

America now faces a social tragedy alongside an economic one. Millions of poor Americans have lost or are losing their homes – by one estimate, 2.3 million in 2008 alone. In 2007, foreclosure actions stood at almost 1.3 million, while almost 3 million homeowners received at least one foreclosure filing during 2009, setting a new record for the number of people falling behind on their mortgage payments.[88] Lenders filed a record 3.8 million foreclosures in 2010, up 2 percent from 2009 and an increase of 23 percent from 2008.[89] Millions more are expected to go into foreclosure from 2011 onward, although by 2012 the numbers have leveled off.

The bad mortgage debt on banks' books has ceased to be primarily a subprime phenomenon of low-income loan recipients; over a third of new foreclosures in early 2011 were prime fixed-rate loans, as layoffs caused hardship for mortgage borrowers. The mortgage delinquency rate was hovering around 10 percent nationwide in late 2010, which included those behind on payments and those on the verge of eviction. The number of properties that were either delinquent or in foreclosure in November 2011 totaled 6.167 million. Meanwhile, the banks have allowed very few mortgage borrowers to modify their mortgages or reduce their principal. Just 8 percent of delinquent borrowers received any modification, while only 3 percent have received reductions in the principal they owe. Remarkably, the banks list the home mortgages still on their balance sheets at inflated values since they are for homes bought at the housing bubble peak, and government has not forced the banks to account for them at a reasonable value.[90] Hence, these toxic assets remain on the banks' books.

## 5. Reaction: Labor and Social Inequality

In much of the non-financial sector, workers have increased their productivity, but the gains have largely been transferred to greater corporate profits rather than rising wages. This means that labor produces more goods and services for less personal income. For example, the factory that Gen-

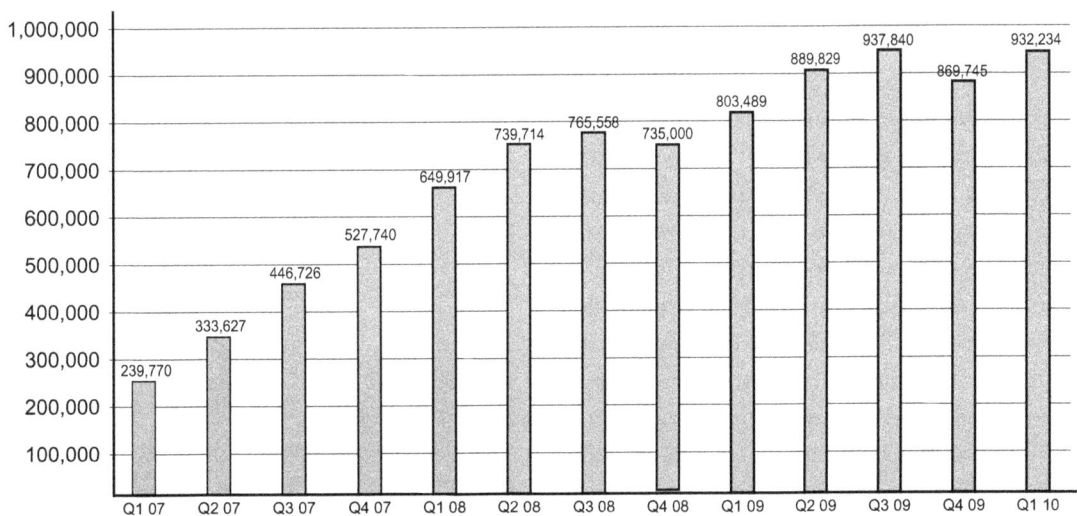

NUMBER OF U.S. RESIDENTIAL PROPERTIES SUBJECT TO FORECLOSURE ACTIONS BY QUARTER (2007–2010).

eral Motors (GM) reopened in Orion Township, Michigan, where, under a deal negotiated with the beleaguered United Auto Workers (UAW) union, 40 percent of the workers crawling through cars on the assembly line will be paid $15 an hour. That's about half the traditional UAW wage.[91] The continuation of depressing the pay of labor is part of the reactionary movement. To return unemployment to levels prior to the financial crisis will require sustained growth in excess of 3 percent.[92]

The country has suffered unemployment rates hovering around the range of 8 to 10 percent since the beginning of the financial crisis, with more than 25 million people unemployed, underemployed or who have given up looking for work altogether. The soaring unemployment caused tax revenues to tank, touching off fiscal crises in nearly every state. In reaction, governments dramatically cut spending and axed tens of thousands of teachers. Public school children all over the country were the ultimate losers, while the bankers who caused the crisis were the ultimate winners. For example, about 75 percent of the workforce, the average non-supervisory production worker in the U.S., has seen an 18 percent drop in real wages since the mid-1970s. Meanwhile, productivity has increased by more than 90 percent.[93] Yet, top hedge fund managers continue to pull in more than 26,000 times the pay of teachers. Are 25 hedge fund managers worth 658,000 teachers? Apparently they are, since that's what they netted in 2009. The government rescued hedge funds and banks, but more than 30 million Americans were left scrambling for full-time work.[94] It is easy to trace where the money from higher productivity went: into the hands of the few.

---

### Questions to Consider

1. Do you think the reactionary policies are the right approach to solving the global economic problems?
2. What are their benefits and drawbacks?

---

## #4. Reform

**Reform** is the fourth movement. It means to put or change into an improved form or condition. Reform is generally distinguished from revolution. The latter means radical change, whereas reform may be no more than fine tuning, or at most redressing serious wrongs without altering the fundamentals of the system. Reform seeks to improve the system as it stands, never to overthrow it wholesale.[95] Thus, generally, reformers do not want to overthrow the whole capitalist economic system but merely redress serious wrongs they see with neoliberalism, and usher in a more regulated or managed form of capitalism.

The big question for reformers in the 21st century is, "If there is a role for government in the global economy, what will that role be?" In the U.S. many in the neoliberal camp argue that the role of government is best when it governs least. Whenever the word reform surfaces, words like socialism, nationalization, communists, or do-gooders are hurdled like insults towards the would-be reformers. These words carry with them emotional baggage that makes clear thinking and sorting through solutions difficult. According to Stiglitz, "The financial crisis showed that financial markets do not automatically work well, and that markets are not self-

**GENERAL MOTORS (GM) AUTOMOBILE MANUFACTURING WORKERS.**

correcting. There is an important role for government."[96] If there is a reform effort to redo some of the un-doings of the neoliberal policies that have been enacted since the 1980s, clearly, government will need to take the lead.

Even though some in the Obama administration and other reformers are putting forth a reform agenda, they are still promoting economic growth as the path to economic prosperity. They see it as the way to exit from economic stagnation and high unemployment. Instead of neoliberalism though, many reformers are endorsing a more managed or regulated form of capitalism, which supports an important role for government rather than just relying on the "invisible hand" of the markets. However, most of those who are critics of neoliberal policies, such as Joseph Stiglitz, Paul Krugman, Robert Reich, and others whom I have cited in my sources, support economic growth as the way out of the current malaise with changes around the edges that they think will increase prosperity. These include a more equal tax system, targeted regulations, a stimulus to encourage consumer demand, and a curb on the excesses of neoliberalism.

In this section, I will highlight a few of the proposed and already passed reforms. However, those in the reactionary camp have waged a sizable backlash to stem the tide of reforms. In fact, the reforms that have been passed have endured repeated efforts to chip away at their intent. Although Obama's health care bill survived a 5-4 vote by the Supreme Court in the summer of 2012, initiatives continue to dilute or overturn the bill. The Dodd-Frank Wall Street Reform Bill is a case in point.

## 1. Reform: Stimulus

The reform camp thinks stagnation is a threat to the economy and suggests more **stimulus** (government spending) to counter it. The fear of burdening future generations with debt is odd to them, since they think the best way to benefit tomorrow's citizens is to ensure that they inherit a healthy economy. Reformers say government default is not a real threat for countries that borrow in currencies they control, like the U.S., since as a last option, debts can be repaid simply by having their central bank print more money.[97] They believe that reactionaries who want to impose austerity measures will not reduce the deficit but stymie growth and hurt the economy in the long run. According to economist Paul Krugman, the alternative to more aggressive deficit spending is "permanent stagnation and high unemployment."[98]

Government spending has what is called a **multiplier effect**. On average, the short-run multiplier for the U.S. economy is around 1.5. If the government spends a billion dollars now, GDP this year will go up by $1.5 billion. If stimulus money is invested in assets that increase the country's long-term productivity, the country will be in better shape in the long run as a result of a stimulus. However, not all spending has the same multiplier effect. Spending on foreign contractors working in Iraq has a low multiplier, because much of the consumption takes place outside the U.S.; so do tax cuts for the wealthy, who save much of what they receive. Unemployment benefits have a high multiplier, because those who find themselves suddenly short of income spend almost every dollar they receive.[99]

## 2. Reform: Break Up the TBTF Banks

America's major banks are too big to fail. The obvious solution is to break them up. Their competitive advantage arises from their monopolistic power and their hidden government subsidies and guarantees. Yet, when reforms are proposed to break them up or tax them or impose additional restrictions on them so that they would no longer be too big to fail, the financial sector lobbyists spring into action to prevent the government from enacting or implementing such reforms.[100] Wall Street lobbyists have spent over $700 million in the years after the financial crisis, as estimated by the Center for Responsive Politics.[101] According to Roubini, "A global system of smaller, more specialized financial institutions can more than meet the needs of even the largest, most sophisticated firms."[102]

### 3. Reform: The Financial Reform Bill

Signed into law by President Barack Obama on July 21, 2010, the **Dodd – Frank Wall Street Reform and Consumer Protection Act** is a federal statute instituting reform of the financial sector. This act was passed in response to the recession after the financial crisis. At 2,300 pages, the Act was intended to represent a significant reform of the American financial regulatory environment and the nation's financial services industry. As with most reforms, there are arguments on both sides of the political spectrum: on the one hand, critics contend the reforms were insufficient to prevent another financial crisis or future bail outs of financial institutions, and on the other hand, the financial sector argues that the reforms went too far and would unduly restrict the ability of banks and other financial institutions to make loans.

Those supporting financial reform see the act as putting an end to the potential abuses associated with having an oligopoly of banks controlling so much of the financial system. According to Roubini, "The reforms outlined go a long way toward increasing accountability and transparency in the financial system by reforming compensation, regulating securitization, bringing derivatives under public scrutiny, and putting the putative guardians of the system – rating agencies – on a very short leash." These reforms would also ensure that banks and other financial firms have enough capital and enough liquidity to weather a major financial crisis.[103]

Other critics question whether merely reimagining financial regulation is the way to prevent the next crisis. The bill arguably does nothing to slow the financialization of the U.S economy, which gobbles up more of the nation's economic activity than other economic sectors. Also, new regulations won't do anything to stop the financial sector from exerting its influence over Washington and the regulators themselves. During the 2000s, the regulated overpowered plenty of financial regulators. A Dodd-Frank critic, economist Walden Bello, adds "The measure did not have the minimum conditions for a reform with real teeth: the banning of derivatives, a Glass-Steagall provision preventing commercial banks from doubling as investment banks; the imposition of a financial transactions tax; and a strong lid on executive pay, bonuses, and stock options."[104]

Interestingly, even though the Congress passed and the president signed the Dodd-Frank Bill, the government has had difficulty in instituting and implementing its simplest and

PRESIDENT BARACK OBAMA MEETING WITH REP. BARNEY FRANK, SEN. DICK DURBIN, AND SEN. CHRIS DODD, IN THE GREEN ROOM AT THE WHITE HOUSE PRIOR TO A FINANCIAL REGULATORY REFORM ANNOUNCEMENT ON JUNE 17, 2009.

most obvious reforms, especially if those reforms happen to clash with powerful financial interests. The financial sector has called out its legions of lobbyists and lawyers to wage war against regulators over every line of the bill in the rulemaking process. You may be wondering how a financial lobby that represents a tiny minority of Americans, even one as large and powerful as the financial sector, could subvert a law passed by our duly-elected representatives. The manner in which they did so is instructive, since it is a blueprint followed by others who are out to obstruct the workings of government for their own self-serving agenda.

First, the financial sector made sure the law was not that sweeping in the first place. The main reason for the law was to make sure that the financial playground had some rules to play by, unlike the helter-skelter playground prior to the crisis. This meant moving swaps and other derivatives onto open exchanges, and making sure that federally insured banks that dabbled in those risky markets retained more capital to back up their bets. The law aimed to prevent another disaster like the demise of AIG and Lehmans. To restore the spirit of the Glass-Steagall Act, the so-called **Volcker Rule**, named after former Chair of the Federal Reserve Paul Volcker (1979-1987), would prevent federally insured banks from engaging in dangerous speculation, such as when customers' deposits are used to trade on the bank's own accounts to make a profit for itself. Dodd-Frank also envisioned a powerful new **Consumer Financial Protection Bureau** to represent the interests of the consumers against Wall Street and clean up the mortgage markets by ending predatory home-lending.[105] To the average person the law seemed reasonable enough. But before the law was even enacted, Wall Street lobbyists immediately got to work, whittling the final bill down to its barely-recognizable final version. All of the provisions were watered down, even the most obvious and necessary reform of all – breaking up the TBTF banks.[106]

Secondly, before the ink was even dry on the Dodd-Frank Bill, Wall Street started to initiate law suits against the bill. If the law is tied up in court for a long period of time, it undermines the law. And, if a law suit doesn't succeed, there is always the appeals court. As is the plan by those opposing reform, the cases could drag on for months, if not years.

Third, if you can't win, stall. Implementation is the key in any law passed; the Dodd-Frank Bill is no exception. However, the Securities and Exchange Commission has not gotten on board the implementation bandwagon. Delays by Congress in writing provisions of the law have turned into a stalling game that seems to know no limits. The deadline for implementation was July 21, 2012; two years after the bill was signed into law![107]

Fourth, don't fund the regulators. Congress controls the purse strings of the federal regulators who are charged with carrying out the Dodd-Frank Bill. Congress, doing the bidding of Wall Street, simply slashed the budget. They lobbied important lawmakers to rein in the regulators, and Congress complied. The regulators are then forced to compromise on enforcement in order to stave off budget cuts.

Fifth, pass lots of loopholes in the bill. Congress, with prodding from Wall Street, has embarked upon a campaign to write new laws designed to undercut the rules that the regulatory agencies had not even written yet. Are you confused yet? Well, if you are, then Wall Street has succeeded in making the matter so complex and confusing that it has its way. All of these loopholes are so oppressively dull and technical that it is not worth the time to go through them (even if I could understand them all). But they are so important that they affect many of us in our daily lives, such as getting a mortgage or a loan.

Thus, nearly two years after the Dodd-Frank legislation was passed, only 108 of 398 required regulations have been written, 148 deadlines have been missed (67 percent) and nearly two dozen Congressional bills have scrapped parts of the proposed law. The draft measures implementing the Volcker Rule are riddled with so many holes as to be almost meaningless. On the eve of the Great Depression in 1929, 250 banks controlled roughly half the nation's banking resources. Now, a mere six banks – Bank of America, J.P. Morgan Chase, Citigroup, Wells Fargo, Goldman Sachs Group, and Morgan Stanley[108] – control almost 74 percent of the nation's banking resources. As demonstrated time and again, corporations can undo the regulations affecting them.[109]

---

### Questions to Consider

1. How can reformers institute changes in the economy when confronted with such obstacles as described above?

---

## #5. Rebuild

The fifth response to the financial crisis is to rebuild the economy. By **rebuild** I mean developing an alternative economic structure that takes into consideration the environment, social and economic justice, and human well-being. It is not a revolution, where the whole existing economic structure is thrown out. But as journalist Naomi Klein states, "It's largely about changing the mix in a mixed economy. Markets are a big part of the rebuild economy, but not the only part."[110] Because communism failed so miserably and collapsed so ignominiously, many say that the best available economic system is neoliberal capitalism. But in the estimation of many it is failing also. It has not been ushered out on its deathbed, as was the case so dramatically with communism, but it is drawing its last breadth on the morgue's gurney, only kept alive with intravenous feeding from the government.

So here is the rub. Some people are promoting a rebuilding of a different economy, a mixed economy. But what is the mix in a mixed economy? A **mixed economy** is a diverse economy in which a mix of different economic sectors prevents the concentration of wealth and power and cushions the downturn in one economic sector from paralyzing the whole economy. It entails enacting the trust-busting provisions of the Sherman (1890) and Clayton (1914) Anti-Trust Laws to break up large corporations, such as TBTF banks, into smaller entities. The regulatory mechanisms of the government are shored up to guarantee corporations are in compliance with existing laws. It means government policy targets small businesses and small agriculture as favored sectors of the economy, instead of mega agri-business firms. Public ownership of certain large utilities is considered, to achieve efficiencies of scale and reasonable prices for consumers. Tax rates are more equitable and structured to encourage investment in companies and the creation of jobs rather than ostentatious consumption. And, most importantly, policies are geared to protect and preserve the environment.

The traditional reform strategies alone – as explained above – are no longer capable of bringing about solutions to ever more complex and pressing problems. Many possibilities have begun to take shape and move in a new direction. However, the rebuild strategy presents challenges to those advocating change. It is an evolutionary reconstructive strategy that is a form of change different not only from traditional reform, but different, too, from traditional theories of revolution. According to economist Gar Alperovitz, "The various efforts involve a sense of the importance of a long-term, evolutionary process that builds towards institutions (and ideas) that may offer ongoing ways to fundamentally alter economic and political relationships over time."[111]

I have organized this last section of the last chapter into five ways in which the rebuilding process can take place. I have tried to make the list positive, such as things that can actually be worked on, rather than a list of negative actions, such as "rein in big corporations," or "put an end to growth." When relying on these slogans exclusively for expressing frustrations with the economy, many fall into the trap of just passively signing another petition. Inspired individuals and groups can immediately implement some of these five actions. Although it takes more effort than changing light bulbs to energy-saving ones, it doesn't take monumental effort to start a community or school garden or buy fresh local produce at the farmer's market. This is not a definitive list but merely evolving suggestions on to build the road to a more sustainable, equitable, and life-affirming future.

---

### Rebuilding Actions

1. Emphasizing Small and Local
2. Challenging the Growth Model
3. Renewing Public Ownership
4. Healing our Planet
5. Creating Shared Values

---

### #1. Emphasizing Small and Local

When visionary writer E.F. Schumacher wrote *Small is Beautiful: Economics as if People Mattered* in 1973, he was expressing an idea that still has relevance today. Over 40 years ago, he was able to describe what is happening today: our economy, society, institutions, and way of life have become so complex that it is overwhelming our capacity to deal with it. One way to deal with this overpowering complexity is to simplify – simplify everything! This means emphasizing the local and small from business, electricity, health care, banking, housing, education, transportation, shopping to agriculture. Small, local, and diversified is the motto. There are different models for implementing this strategy; in this brief section I have highlighted two. Yet, there are many more possibilities emerging every day.

A **farmers market** is a collection of individual vendors – mostly farmers – who sell produce, fruits, meat products, and sometimes prepared foods and beverages. The local community benefits

**A FARMERS' MARKET**

from farmers markets because farmers sell directly to consumers, keeping dollars circulating in the locality instead of being siphoned off to large corporate conglomerates. Consumers can buy direct from the farmer/producer and enjoy fresh, seasonal food grown within a drivable distance from their homes. In addition, local, fresh food is much healthier than heavily processed foods.

The Bank of North Dakota (BND) is a state-owned financial institution based in Bismarck, North Dakota. At the time of this writing, it is the only state-owned bank in the nation. Although state agencies are required to place their funds in the bank, local governments are not required to do so. Another fourteen states are considering creating state banks, following the long-established North Dakota model. Since 2010, legislation exploring or creating such banks has been introduced in 17 states. This trend is likely to continue. [112]

## #2. Challenging the Consumer Growth Model

The economic concept of constant economic growth is so widespread, yet we are living on a finite planet where continued, unlimited growth is impossible. After all, we are exploring the last frontier for precious resources, such as oil, in inhospitable climes, such as the far Arctic and dangerous deep water drilling. Countries such as Saudi Arabia and China that cannot grow enough food for its population are snapping up valuable agricultural land in Africa. [113]

Can our environment survive in a system that requires exponential growth to continue? Klein asks, "Where is the imperative of growth coming from? What part of our economy is demanding growth year after year?" The dominant economic paradigm today is a particular brand of corporate capitalism in which shareholders who aren't involved in the business itself demand that their investments grow. She claims, "That part of our economy has to shrink, and that's terrifying people who are deeply invested in it. We have a mixed economy, but it's one in which large corporations are controlled by outside investors, and we won't change that mix until that influence is reduced." [114] For example, locally based businesses don't need to grow year after year. Business needs to provide enough revenue to pay salaries, expenses, and stash away enough for hard times. Below is a sampling of different business models that don't necessarily rely on growth and are locally based; they also are models in which the revenues are not siphoned off to distant shareholders and corporate owners. These models are not new; they have a long history in the U.S. and Europe, but the fixation on neoliberalism has overshadowed them in the last 30 plus years.

**Worker ownership** is where the workers have an equal equity stake in the company they are working for; they share common goals and adhere to common principles. Additionally, this model benefits from lower overhead costs and offers benefit plans, such as healthcare and pensions. [115] Interestingly, the United Steel Workers Union once dismissed this model in the past, but now the union has become a strong advocate of worker ownership and is actively developing new models. One established and successful model is based upon the Mondragón Cooperative Corporation in the Basque country of Spain. Groups of worker-owned cooperatives employ 85,000 people in fields ranging from sophisticated medical technology and the production of appliances to large supermarkets and a credit union. [116]

In the United States, a worker-owned initiative is in the economically hard-hit city of Cleveland, Ohio. The "Cleveland Model" involves an integrated array of worker-owned cooperative enterprises targeted at the $3 billion purchasing power of such large scale "anchor institutions" as the Cleveland Clinic, University Hospital, and Case Western Reserve University.

CLEVELAND, OHIO, CONSTRUCTION OF THE GREEN CITY GROWERS GREENHOUSE IN 2008. A WORKER-OWNED HYDROPONIC GREENHOUSE CAPABLE OF SUPPLYING THE AREA WITH FRESH PRODUCE.

The association of enterprises also includes a revolving fund so that profits made by the businesses help establish new ventures. The first of the worker-owned companies, Evergreen Cooperative Laundry, is a state-of-the-art commercial laundry that provides clean linens for area hospitals, nursing homes, and hotels. It uses energy-saving design for its building and uses much less water per pound of laundry than its competitors. It includes 50 worker-owners, pays above-market wages, provides health insurance, and is still able to compete successfully against other commercial laundries. Another enterprise, Ohio Cooperative Solar (OCS), provides weatherization services and installs, owns, and maintains solar panels. Each year, two to four new worker-owned ventures are planned for opening. A 20-acre land trust will own the land of the worker-owned businesses. Like the steelworkers, the Cleveland group has also drawn upon the experience of the Mondragón cooperative model.[117]

Comprising an emerging "fourth sector" of the economy, and different from the government, business, and non-profit sectors are "**social enterprises,**" which are organizations applying commercial strategies to maximize improvements in human and environmental well-being, rather than maximizing profits for external shareholders. These businesses support missions such as drug rehabilitation and training programs. Another 130 million Americans are members of urban food and housing co-ops, traditional agricultural cooperatives, and credit unions. There are other models as well. More than 4,500 not-for-profit community development corporations operate affordable housing and other community-building programs in the U.S. In many cities new "community land trusts," increasingly use nonprofit or municipal ownership to develop and maintain permanently affordable housing. I like this model because our non-profit organization, the Center for Global Awareness, is one of approximately 1.5 million non-profits providing more than 10 percent of the nation's employment.[118]

The democratized ownership forms – including thousands of co-ops, land trusts, social enterprises, and worker-owned companies – are essentially anchored in, and supportive of, the local economy. Unlike private corporations, worker-owned companies rarely move to another city. As Aperovitz explains, "The fate of those who own the company is intimately tied to the fate and health of the locality in which they both live and work. Virtually all the many other non-profit and related institutions based on democratized ownership principles are similarly place-anchored."[119]

### #3. Renewing Public Ownership

A case can be made to renew public ownership in certain industries. But to be clear, this does not mean public ownership of small, medium-sized or even large businesses nor the democratic enterprises described above. Even with this caveat, those advocating for public ownership would be labeled socialist, bent on destroying the fabric of America. But if looked at sanely, we would see that the U.S. has a mixed economy in which there already is public ownership. Most people would not want to see the Grand Canyon turned over to private land developers or mining interests; they would want the government to preserve and protect this national treasure for ourselves and generations to come.

The first step toward renewing public ownership is recognizing that it is not a radical departure from the past. For example, the Tennessee Valley Authority (TVA), a public enterprise, established in 1933, is one of the largest energy companies in the nation. In fact, local public utilities and cooperatives in the U.S supply more than 25 percent of its electricity. And the government owns timber, mineral, oil and other resources on public land covering almost 30 percent of the nation's territory. The government runs two of the most cost-effective health providers in the United States – Medicare and the Veterans Administration. The largest pension manager in the country is a public entity: the Social Security Administration. The US Postal Service, which employs 645,000 men and women, is another public enterprise that is generally regarded as well-run by most experts.[120]

Public enterprises do not spend large amounts on advertising to sell their products, they do not add a profit margin to their prices, nor do they pay exorbitant executive salaries. The government-run Medicare administrator made a base salary of approximately $170,000 in 2010 while, Stephen Hemsley, CEO of the privately-held United Health Group, made a base salary of $1.3 million and received $101.96 million in total compensation that same year. Thus, our private healthcare system costs the nation up to twice the share of GDP spent on equal or better care in many other countries – inefficiencies that waste perhaps a trillion dollars a year. Public enterprises do not force cities and states to pay millions in "incentives" to encourage businesses to locate in their locality, as private businesses often do. Often these private businesses take these incentives and then move on when they expire. Public enterprises do not spend huge amounts of money lobbying public officials, as do corporate interests. And public corporations are open to public scrutiny, while private corporations keep most of their activities secret.[121]

Many developed nations have found large-scale, publicly regulated companies beneficial in such key areas of large scale operations as energy, transportation, and banking. In energy, for example, worldwide publicly-owned corporations produce roughly 75 percent of all oil. Saudi Aramco, the national oil company of Saudi Arabia, was estimated to be worth $781 billion in 2005, making it the world's most valuable company, almost twice as wealthy as ExxonMobil, the largest private sector company.[122] In transportation, governments in France, Spain, Belgium, Germany, Italy, the Netherlands, Turkey and South Korea run high-speed rail systems. The public ownership of significant or controlling shares of airlines is common: France holds 16 percent of Air France-KLM; Sweden, Denmark and Norway hold a 50 percent stake in SAS; Israel, holds 35 percent of El Al; Singapore, holds 56 percent of Singapore Airlines, which is ranked as one of the world's best. In banking, there are more than 200 public and semi-public banks and 81 funding agencies, accounting for one-fifth of all bank assets in the European Union. Japan Post Bank is the world's biggest public bank and one of their largest employers. Brazil has more than 100 state-owned or state-controlled enterprises, including Petrobras, an oil company known for its deep-water oil explorations. Other countries, where public corporations exist side by side with private companies, have better and faster Internet service than the U.S.[123]

### #4. Healing our Planet

The fate of our planet hangs in a precarious position. The earth's atmosphere, which cannot safely absorb the amount of carbon we are pumping into it, is only one of a number of significant environmental crises facing all of us. We are also exploiting the oceans, freshwater supplies, the topsoil and biodiversity. Klein

PUMPING WATER FROM A WELL BEFORE THE CONSTRUCTION OF THE TVA.

explains that the much larger crises are "born of the central fiction on which our economic model is based: that nature is limitless, that we will always be able to find more of what we need, and that if something runs out it can be seamlessly replaced by another resource that we can endlessly extract." She continues, "The expansionist, extractive mindset, which has so long governed our relationship to nature, is what the climate crisis calls into question so fundamentally. The abundance of scientific research showing we have pushed nature beyond its limits does not just demand green products and market-based solutions; it demands a new civilizational paradigm, one grounded not in dominance over nature but in respect for natural cycles of renewal – and acutely sensitive to natural limits."[124] This is a tall order coming from a leading journalist and popular writer. Klein recognizes the essential arrangement of the neoliberal economic model: unrelenting expansion of consumer markets, exploitation of the environment as resources for these markets, and bringing the world and its people into its economic web. It is simply and clearly unsustainable. Therefore, it must be changed.

## #5. Changing to Shared Values

A society is shaped by the values and beliefs it extols and, in turn, how the society is structured shapes its values and beliefs. In this interacting dance, a society holistically forms such cultural traits as its economy, ways of living, technology, politics, religions, the way it treats the environment, and, thus, its worldview, or as Klein called it, a civilizational paradigm. Most of us were raised according to a modern worldview in which Enlightenment ideals of progress taught us that our ambitions could not be confined by nature's limits. This is true for the progressive left, as well as the neoliberal right. It means a re-evaluation of our values and attitudes, from the long cherished belief in rugged individu-alism and cut-throat competition to an ethic of more collective action, an ethic of sharing and cooperation. Climate change is a message from the earth, screaming to us all that many of our culture's most cherished ideas and values are no longer working. It is a wake-up call that we must heed.[125]

### Questions to Consider

1. What do you think about the rebuild ideas I presented in this short section? Do you think they are a viable alternative to neoliberalism? What others might you include?

CHINA'S LARGEST OPEN-PIT COAL MINE
IS LOCATED IN HAERWUSU IN THE INNER MONGOLIA
AUTONOMOUS REGION.

# CONCLUDING INSIGHTS: THE AFTERMATH OF THE 2008 FINANCIAL CRISIS

America will likely remain the world's largest economy for years to come. But it is not inevitable that the American standard of living will continue to increase as it did, for instance, in the years following World War II. The U.S. is no longer operating within the confines of a national economy, where policies and wages are played out primarily on a national stage. Now our standard of living and job opportunities compete with 7 billion people on the planet. Many Americans have been living in a fantasy world of easy credit, and that world is over. It won't and it shouldn't return. The country as a whole will face a drop in living standards. Not only was the country living beyond its means, but so were many families.[126] This is a stunning rebuke of what we thought life should be like in America. Each generation would have a better life than the previous generation, in a spiral of upward progression. These are intensely challenging revelations, shaking us to the very core.

This brings us back to the rebuilding movement described above. Rebuilding a more just, equitable and sustainable economy may be the most difficult and yet most important challenge we face as a human species. It involves changing the way we think, work, act, what we prize, and what we believe in. This profound and deep examination of who we are as a people and what type of economy and way of life we want to leave for the next generations is not an easy shift. We are deeply embedded in this way of life.

But change we must. We must heed the call of the planet. Either we change with planning and insight to a way of life of our choosing within nature's limits, or we will have changes forced upon us by an angry planet ravaged by our excesses. The choice is ours to make.

## Questions to Consider

1. What do you think are the choices we need to make?

**austerity** to cut government spending through austerity measures mainly targeted at social programs, especially education, Medicare, social security, infrastructure, and programs for the poor. (8)

**balancing feedback** limits, restricts, and impedes change and keeps the system stable. Commonly called negative feedback, it is neither good nor bad but means the system resists change. (1)

**Bank Holding Company Act** passed under President Eisenhower in 1956, the Federal Reserve Board of Governors had to approve establishing a bank holding company (BHC). Also, prohibited a BHC headquartered in one state from purchasing a bank in another state and it forbad banks from participating in most nonbanking activities. (3)

**bilateral trade** unlike free trade, it is trade that deals country-to-country. (5)

**bond** a debt security, the issuer owes the holders a debt and is obliged to pay interest and to repay the principal at a later date. (7)

**Bretton Woods** in July 1944 nearly 1,000 delegates from more than 40 countries gathered at the Mount Washington Hotel in the New Hampshire resort of Bretton Woods to finalize plans for a postwar monetary and financial order. (2)

**British East India Company** chartered in 1600 by England's Queen Elizabeth I. The company got monopoly trading privileges with India that were expanded into virtual rule of the sub-continent until its end in 1858. (2,3)

**bubble** the radical rise of prices of an asset far beyond real values. (7)

**capitalism** an economic system in which private parties make their goods and services available on a free market and seek to make a profit on their activities. Private parties, either individuals or companies, own the means of production — land, machinery, tools, equipment, buildings, workshops, and raw materials. Private parties decide what to produce. The free market is where businesses compete, and the forces of supply and demand determine the prices received for goods and services. Businesses may realize profits from their endeavors, reinvest profits gained, or suffer losses. (1)

**Chapter 11** under this section of NAFTA corporations have the right to sue governments for actions that may decrease the corporation's future profits. (3)

**classical economic order** the system of capitalism, from the mid-19th century to 1914, relied on flexible wages, laying off workers or lowering their wages during bust cycles. Supporters also advocated for minimal government involvement in the economy. Based on the gold standard. The business sector influenced political policy. (2)

**climate change** takes place when the climate is altered during two different periods of time, with changes in average weather conditions, as well as how much the weather varies around these averages. Humans contribute to climate change by releasing greenhouse gases and aerosols into the atmosphere. (6)

**Cochabamba Water Wars** a series of protests due to the privatization of the municipal water supply in Cochabamba, Bolivia in 2000. The protesters were successful in outlawing the privatization of their municipal water supply by foreign corporations. (5)

**collateralized debt obligation CDO** is a pool of debt that is added together and then sold as a set of bonds paying a range of interest rates. Those who issue the bonds pay interest and principal to the investors of the bonds. (7)

**colonialism** extension of a powerful country's control over a dependent, weaker country, territory, or people. (2)

**commercial banks** lend out the money deposited in them. Called the piggy banks. (7)

**Commercial Paper Funding Facility (CPFF)** under this act, the Fed could finance approximately $1.8 trillion worth of commercial paper, it was created in response to the financial crisis in fall 2008, when the commercial paper market froze up, causing the economy to grind to a halt. (8)

**commercial paper market** part of shadow banking, it is what credit-worthy corporations do for short-term borrowing, such as to meet expenses like payroll. Corporations can borrow billions of dollars for 30, 60, or 90 days, and when those debts come due, they simply roll over the debt for another 30, 60, or 90 day term. (8)

**commodification** comes from the word commodity, used here as the process of turning something with little or no economic value into a product or service that has a specific value or a higher monetary value. (4)

**Commodities Futures Modernization Act** of 2000 officially marked the deregulation of financial products known as over-the-counter derivatives, spearheaded by Senator Phil Gramm of Texas. (7)

**commons** shared areas that are collectively owned by the people. (3)

**Community Reinvestment Act** in 1977, designed to encourage banks and savings associations to help meet the needs of all borrowers, including those in low-and moderate-income neighborhoods. (7)

**comparative advantage** countries should specialize in goods they can produce efficiently rather than trying to be self-sufficient. In a free market economy, a country's comparative advantage is traded internationally. (5)

**conservatorship** is similar to a Chapter 11 bankruptcy, new leadership is appointed to the bankrupt company. A conservatorship implies a more temporary control than nationalization, in which the government more completely takes over the bankrupt enterprise. (8)

**consumer debt** is owed as a result of purchasing goods that are consumable and/or do not appreciate. (4)

**Consumer Financial Protection Bureau** represents the interests of the consumers against Wall Street, it cleans up the mortgage markets by ending predatory home-lending. (8)

**consumer society** consumerism and materialism are central aspects of the dominant culture, where goods and services are acquired not only to satisfy common needs but also to secure identity and meaning. (4)

**consumerism** is a social and economic order based on the creation and fostering of a desire to purchase goods or services in ever greater amounts. In economics, consumerism refers to policies emphasizing consumption. (4)

**conventional thinking** or traditional, linear or mechanistic thinking, people see simple sequences of cause and effect that are limited in time and space, which assumes that cause and effect occur within a close time frame. (1)

**core areas** are where intense modern developments in technology, military, society, politics, culture, and especially the economy have taken place. These areas are where wealth generation and accumulation are concentrated and also where rules for the system are devised and enforced. (1)

**Corn Laws** Britain, the taxes imposed in the early 1800s on imports of grain (corn). The tariffs increased the domestic price of grain. Farmers wanted to keep high tariffs on imported grain in order to protect their grain market, and rightly argued that repeal of the laws would doom British farming. (2)

**corporate raiders** during the 1980s, they bought up a company's stock when it was undervalued, thus, the company's assets were worth more than their stock. The raiders would then sell off the assets of the company to make a profit, but then the companies taken over were no longer operational. (4)

**corporation** is a formal business association with a publicly registered charter recognizing it as a separate legal entity having its own privileges, and liabilities distinct from those of its members. (2)

**cottage industries** flourished alongside the domestic economy and guild system during the Middle Ages in Europe. Textile merchants moved production to the countryside, in rural cottages, hence, cottage industries. (2)

**credit default swap** (CDS), a form of insurance, the buyer of a credit default swap receives credit protection, whereas the seller of the swap guarantees the credit worthiness of the product. By doing this, the risk of default is transferred from the holder of the fixed income security to the seller of the swap. (7)

**credit rating agency** (CRA) assigns credit ratings for issuers of certain types of debt. Debt issues with the highest credit ratings – triple A – from the agencies will have the lowest interest rates. The analysis of the CRA influences the investors' confidence in the borrowers' ability to meet their debt payment obligations. (7)

**crony capitalism** is based on shadowy political connections between government and business. (8)

**cyclical unemployment** is cause by recessions. An increase in demand can be a cure for cyclical unemployment. As demand increases, employers may increase output, and this may motivate them to start hiring again. (4)

**Dawes Act** in 1887 divided commonly held tribal lands in Oklahoma (US) into individually-owned parcels, while the remaining "surplus" lands were opened up for settlement and the railroads. (3)

**debt** something that is owed or that one is bound to pay to or perform for another. (7)

**deficit** an excess of expenditure over revenue. (3)

**delay in feedback** for example, we are not yet in a situation where the stresses on the earth have sent strong enough signals to force us to shrink our ecological footprint. Overshoot is possible because there are accumulated resource stocks that can be drawn down. (6)

**demand** means goods and services are wanted or needed by consumers, inadequate demand could lead to prolonged periods of high unemployment. (2)

**deregulation** removal or simplification of government rules that regulate the operation of market forces by eliminating or reducing government control of business, thereby moving toward a more free market. (3)

**derivative** is a security whose price is dependent upon or derived from one or more underlying asset. Fluctuations in the underlying asset determine the derivative's value. (7)

**desertification** expanding deserts that are mainly the consequence of deforested land and also overstocked and overgrazed grasslands. (6)

**devalue** currencies are worth less than they were before. (2)

**developmentalism** an economic theory which says the best way for the periphery countries to develop is through a strong and diverse internal market and to impose high tariffs on imported goods. Instead of going to foreign corporations in core countries, profits stay in national firms and thus circulate within the national economy. (2)

**Dispute Settlement Body (DSB)** judicial branch of the World Trade Organization. It has panels of corporate and trade lawyers and officials who preside in secret hearings as final judges of disputes among members. (5)

**Dodd – Frank Wall Street Reform and Consumer Protection Act** passed in 2010, it is a federal statute instituting reform of the financial sector. Passed in response to the recession after the financial crisis in 2008. (8)

**dot-com bubble** speculative bubble based on a new technology, the internet, covering the years 1995–2000. (8)

**East Asian financial crisis** beginning in 1997, financial institutions lost a large percentage of their asset values. The crisis raised fears of a worldwide economic meltdown due to financial contagion. (8)

**ecological footprint** calculates the amount of land required to supply needed resources, such as grain, food, water, and wood, and absorb the resulting wastes such as carbon dioxide and pollutants. (6)

**economic development** increases the standard of living in a nation's population through economic growth that requires a transition from a simple, low-income economy to a modern, high-income economy. (5)

**economic gap** governmental rules that tilt policies to favor those with more wealth than those with less, such as a low inheritance tax, low marginal tax rates that further the concentration of wealth. (6)

**economic globalization** refers to the increasing integration and expansion of the capitalist economy around the world. Trade, investment, business, capital, financial flows, production, management, markets, movement of labor (although somewhat restricted), information, competition, and technology are carried out across local and national boundaries on a world stage, subsuming many national and local economies into one integrated economic system. There is also a growing concentration of wealth and influence of multi-national corporations, huge financial institutions, and state-run enterprises. (1,5)

**economic growth** is the process by which wealth increases over time as new commodified value is added to goods and services in the economy. Growth is an essential component of the capitalist economic system, which must expand constantly to generate new wealth. (4)

**Efficient Market Theory** markets rather than government are able by their very nature to be more efficient and accurate in pricing and allocating resources. (3)

**elite democracy** elites manipulate the democratic process for their own self-interest and control. (4)

**enclosure** farms and the commons were converted to privately owned plots marked with clear boundaries and specific private ownership. (2)

**equity** the difference between the market value and unpaid mortgage balance on a home. (7)

**Export-Oriented Industrialization (EOI)** countries such as South Korea, Taiwan, Singapore, and Hong Kong pushed exporting manufactured goods to core countries. They turned to EOI in part because they had few natural resources to export to pay for necessary imports, and the only way to earn foreign currency was to export manufactures. They specialized in labor-intensive manufacturers for export. (2)

**external areas** are those that have not been incorporated into the core-and-periphery world system; they remain outside modern developments. (1)

**external costs** the cost(s) not paid for by the producer but which is (are) imposed on others. (4)

**externalities** external benefits or external costs. (4)

**factory** where numerous workers, sometimes hundreds, gather under one roof, paid a standard wage, divide tasks into individual parts, and work under the close supervision of the owner or manager. (2)

**fallacy of composition** export-oriented economies in East Asia competed with high-cost Western producers. They under priced their competition but made a profit. As more export-oriented countries entered the export game, increased competition meant a slice into high profit margins. As competition increased, they competed more against each other than with Western producers. Exports slowed and investments were less profitable. (8)

**Fannie Mae (Federal National Mortgage Association)** authorized in 1938 by Congress, the GSE bought mortgages from lenders, thereby freeing up capital in order that those lenders could extend more mortgages. (7)

**farmers market** individual vendors – mostly farmers – who sell produce, fruits, meat products, and sometimes prepared foods and beverages. The local community benefits because farmers sell directly to consumers, keeping dollars circulating in the locality instead of being siphoned off to large corporate conglomerates. (8)

**Federal Deposit Insurance Corporation** (FDIC), part of the 1933 Glass Steagall Act, it insures deposits in certain commercial banks. (7)

**Federal Reserve** (sometime called the Fed or central bank) central banking system of the U.S.. Created in 1913 under President Woodrow Wilson. It conducts the nation's monetary policy, supervises and regulates banking institutions, maintains the stability of the financial system and provides financial services. (3)

**feedback** when change occurs in one part of a system it ripples out to affect all the other parts. The new parts change, and the effect of this change ripples back to affect the original part. The original part then responds to the new influences, and the influences then come back or feed back to the original part in a modified way, making a loop, not a straight line. (1)

**Financial Services Modernization Act** or **Gramm-Leach-Bliley Act** of 1999, rescinded the Glass-Steagall Act of 1933, signed by President Bill Clinton. Allowed commercial banks, investment banks, securities firms, and insurance companies to consolidate, which was prohibited by the Glass-Steagall Act. (7)

**financialization** a sector of the economy specializing in creating financial products that have a certain value and can be traded in the market place, such as insurance, loans, real estate sales, stocks, bonds, derivatives, etc. (7)

**fine-tuning** the economy, the Fed's actions in raising or lowering interest rates. (7)

**fiscal austerity** raising taxes and reducing government spending. (5)

**fiscal policy** governmental decisions on spending and taxes. (7)

**float** when a nation's currency value is allowed to fluctuate according to the foreign exchange market. (2)

**Fordism** mass production assembly line invented by automobile manufacturer Henry Ford in the 1920s. (2)

**Freddie Mac (Federal Home Loan Mortgage Corp.)** 1970, expanded the secondary mortgage market. (7)

**free trade** elimination of import and export quotas and tariffs that are considered to be "barriers to trade." (3)

**full employment profit squeeze** described the 1960s when the cushion of unemployment benefits, resulted in a declining "cost of job-loss." Workers more confident in demanding higher wages since little fear of being fired because of a labor shortage. Management enforced a high pace of work to increase productivity and profits, but with a labor shortage their authority over their workers was weak, the rate of productivity growth declined. (2)

**fundamentalism** a strict belief in a set of basic principles (often religious), it is sometimes a reaction to supposed compromises with modern social, ideological and political life. (1)

**futures trading** for example, where a farmer will agree to a price for his/her next harvest months in advance. The future price of the harvest is thus a derivative, which can itself be sold. (7)

**General Agreement on Tariffs and Trade** (GATT) a result of the Bretton Woods convention, signed by 23 countries in 1948. Reduced and conformed tariff rates among the major industrialized countries, but mainly limited to manufactured goods. (5)

**Genuine Progress Indicator (GPI)** created by the organization Redefining Progress in 1995, measures the general economic and social well-being of all citizens. (6)

**Government National Mortgage Association (Ginnie Mae)** put together the first mortgage-backed securities. It bought mortgages on the secondary market, pooled the mortgages it had originated, issued them as bonds, and then sold these pools of bonds as a mortgage-backed security to investors on the open market. Rather than waiting 30 years to make back the proceeds from a mortgage. (7)

**Glass-Steagall Act** of 1933, part of the New Deal regulatory reforms in the U.S. that prohibited a single company from offering investment banking, commercial banking, and insurance services. (3)

**global warming** general shifts in climate but specifically any change in global average surface temperature. Some areas warm more than others, such as the North and South poles. Some areas will even become cooler. (6)

**Global Wave** transforming our human story as this new millennium dawns. In it are five conflicting worldviews, with contradictory ways of knowing and understanding the world. Most people identify with one or a combination of these worldviews: indigenous, modern, fundamentalist, globalized, and transformative. (1)

**globalization** complex, dominant, multi-dimensional phenomenon that interconnects worldwide economic, political, cultural, social, environmental, and technological forces that transcended national boundaries. Greatly intensifying since the 1980s, it reflects the many ways in which people are being drawn together not only by their own movements but also through the flow of goods, services, capital, labor, technology, ideas, and information. Globalization refers to the worldwide compression of space and time and reduction of the state in importance. In globalization the world becomes a single place that serves as a frame of reference for everyone, and it influences the way billions of people around the world conduct their everyday lives. (1)

**globalized worldview** differs from the modern worldview in that "time has speeded up," the pace of growth and development has intensified and spread to the farthest reaches of the earth. (1)

**gold standard** system of a standard currency followed by leading core countries of the time. A country's currency was equal to gold, interchangeable at a fixed rate with the money of any other gold standard country. (2)

**"golden straight-jacket"** a mandate that indebted nations must open their markets to development, inviting foreign corporations to enter their national economies, must sell their natural resources at world market prices. Must cut government funded social programs, which usually means medical care and education. Money from these efforts is used for repayment of the debt to the World Bank or IMF. (5)

**Gramm-Leach-Bliley Act** see **Financial Services Modernization Act**

**greenhouse gases** a natural system that regulates the temperature on earth, just as glass in a greenhouse keeps heat in. (6)

**Gross Domestic Product** (GDP) a measure of a country's overall, official economic output. It is the market value of all goods and services officially made within the borders of a country in a year. (4)

**Gross National Happiness** (GNH) in Bhutan, economic growth and modernization would not be allowed to jeopardize the peoples' quality of life, their traditional values or the environment, and all would have to benefit equally from development through education, health care and a voice in a democratic government. (6)

**guild** artisans had a common business or trade banded together to carefully control and regulate the production and distribution of their products. They restricted membership, regulated standards of quality and price, discouraged competition, and resisted technological innovations. Did not follow capitalist principles. (2)

**haircut** a slightly reduced price. (8)

**hedge funds** a private pool of capital managed by an investment adviser. Open only to a limited number of investors who typically invest a minimum range from about $250,000 to $10 million. (7)

**hegemony** the political, economic, ideological or cultural power exerted by a dominant group over other groups, regardless of the explicit consent of the latter. (6)

**holistic** all a society's cultural traits – political, economic, technological, cultural, religious, social, arts, values, attitudes, and environmental – reinforce and support each other. (1)

**home equity loans** homeowners refinance their mortgages and withdraw their excess equity in their homes. (7)

*Homo Economicus* or Economic Man, model that states human nature says humans are rational players. (3)

**hostile takeovers** corporate raiders buy up a company's undervalued stock, company's assets are worth more than their stock. Raiders sell off the company's assets for a profit. A company is then out of business. (4)

**imperialism** 1873-1914, different from colonialism in early modern era. It describes political and economic control by a greater power over a less powerful territory or country. During this era much of Asia, the Pacific islands, the Middle East, and sub-Saharan Africa were taken over by Great Britain and France, and to lesser extent the Netherlands, Belgium, Russia, Portugal, Spain, and Germany, the United States, Japan, and Australia. (2)

**import substitution industrialization (ISI)** 20th century trade and economic policy that aims for domestic production to replace goods that were previously imported in order to reduce foreign dependency. Adopted in many Latin American countries from the 1930s until the late 1980s, and in some Asian and African countries from the 1950s onward. (2)

**indigenous peoples** any ethnic group who share a similar ethnic identity and inhabit a geographic region with which they have the earliest known historical connection. (1)

**inequality** used in this book to mean the disparity between rich and poor. (6)

**Industrial Revolution** is the industrialization process, which moved rapidly from Britain, its place of origin, to neighboring countries. (2)

**industrialization** process of change from an economy based on home production of goods to one based on large-scale, mechanized factory production with a wage-based labor force. (2)

**infant industry argument** tariffs, quotas, and other regulations benefit new industries because this protection allows industries to grow until they achieve an economy of scale that enables them to compete on an equal basis with foreign competitors. (2,3)

**inflation** when price levels rise and the value of money drops. More money is needed than before to buy the same amount of goods and services. (7)

**illiquid assets** not easily or quickly converted into money, like mortgages. (7)

**Intellectual Property (IP)** creations of the mind for which property rights are recognized under the law. Owners are granted certain exclusive rights to intangible assets, such as musical, literary, and artistic works; discoveries and inventions; and words, phrases, symbols, and designs. (5)

**International Monetary Fund (IMF)** regulates an international monetary system based on convertible currencies, lends to countries experiencing temporary balance of payment problems, and to facilitate global trade, while leaving sovereign governments in charge of their own monetary, fiscal, and international investment policies. (5)

**investment banks** issue bonds and shares of stock, and other complex financial instruments; trade on capital markets, and put together mergers and acquisitions, called casino banks. (7)

**joint stock companies** granted a charter by the monarch for trade with their colonies. One individual was not required to raise all the capital for entrepreneurial activities, which lessened their possible losses from risky ventures. (2, 3)

**junk bonds** a bond rated 'BB' or lower because of its high default risk. These bonds allowed companies that would not previously have been considered sufficiently credit worthy to issue debt. (7)

**just price** in the Middle Ages, guilds did not seek to realize profits as much as to protect markets and preserve their members' livelihoods and security. They did not follow capitalist principles. (2)

**Keynes, John Maynard** (1883-1946) British economist who shaped the transition from laissez faire capitalism to the era of social democracy in the 1930s. His policies are referred to as Keynesian Economics. (1, 2)

**labor** productive activity, especially for the sake of economic gain. Body of persons engaged in such activity, especially those working for wages. This body of persons is considered as a separate class of people who are distinguished from management (employers, owners) and capital (those engaged in finance). (3)

**labor productivity** the amount a worker produces in a unit of time, usually per hour. (4)

**laissez faire capitalism** a French term that describes free trade, deregulated, unfettered capitalism. (2)

**lender of last resort** traditional banks are subject to government regulation and can, therefore, if need be, borrow from the Federal Reserve. (7)

**leverage** the use of debt to supplement investment. (7)

**leveraged buyouts** companies "go private" by buying up their own stock with borrowed funds to avoid the acquisitions of their corporation by another rival firm. (4)

**liberalism** emerged during the Enlightenment era, ideas include a representative government, division of government, individual rights and freedoms (speech and press), private property, scientific method, reason, individualism, freedom of religion or secularism, and later women's and gay rights and sexual freedoms. (1)

**liberalizing** national regulations are lessened and markets opened up to investors. (7)

**liquid assets** easily and quickly converted into money that were tradable on the open market. (7)

**liquidity** money. (7)

**liquidity crisis** when corporate borrowing and lending collapses, as it did during the financial crisis of 2008. Solvent corporations were shut out of the commercial paper market and found themselves short of cash. The Fed extended lender-of-last resort options to support nonfinancial corporations. (8)

**Long Depression** of 1873-1896 often referred to as the Great Depression before the 1930s depression, it contributed to great dissatisfaction with free trade and the gold standard by many people. (2)

**Main Street** considered the real economy, the part of the economy that produces real wealth, as opposed to the phantom wealth of the Wall Street economy. (7)

**managed capitalism** the government closely regulates the financial sector to prevent wild financial speculation and insures transparency of the system. Tariffs protect manufacturing jobs in the home country; therefore, wages and prices are set according to supply and demand at the national level rather than the global level. Services such as education, health care, the military, and prisons are government run and paid for through taxes. The state sometimes owns large service providers such as utilities, airlines and transportation networks or regulates them. Private enterprise is carefully regulated, with high tax brackets for the wealthiest individuals. Corporations pay a larger share of their profits in taxes than in the neoliberal model. Labor unions have a say in wages and other benefits, as long as their wages keep up with productivity. There is a more equal circulation of wealth than with neoliberalism, hence a vital middle and working class and less of a concentration of wealth in the hands of the elite and corporations. (1)

**marginal-productivity theory** rationalized that those with higher incomes would generate higher productivity and, thus, they would make greater contributions to society than their lower income fellow citizens. (4)

**market liberalization** opening up internal markets to the inflow of money from other countries for investment, and the deregulation of their banks. (8)

**Marshall Plan** (1947-1951) named for Secretary of State George Marshall, millions of dollars spent for rebuilding Europe after World War II. The plan was successful. (2)

**Marx, Karl** (1818-1883), critiqued capitalism, along with co-author Frederich Engels, proposed a socialist/communist alternative to capitalism in their short book, the *Communist Manifesto* in 1848. (1)

**materialism** approach to life and social well-being that elevates the material conditions of life over the spiritual and social dimensions. (4)

**mercantilism** based on the economic relationship between the "mother country," and its colonies. The colonial rulers strove to maintain a favorable balance of trade for their country by importing cheap raw materials from their colonies and exporting the more profitable manufactured goods that the mother country produced. (2)

**middle** between the core and periphery are middle countries or areas, or people in the middle, they form the middle class. (1)

**mixed economy** a diverse economy in which a mix of different economic sectors prevents the concentration of wealth and power and cushions the downturn in one economic sector from paralyzing the whole economy. (8)

**modern** applies to that which is near to or characteristic of the present in contrast to that of a former age or an age long past; hence the word sometimes has the connotation of up-to-date and, thus good, such as modern ideas. (1)

**modern worldview** traces its historical origins back more than 500 years to the expansion of Western European power and its influence and/or ultimate dominance around the world. The modern worldview has been especially powerful over the last two centuries and has today expanded to the farthest reaches of the world. (1)

**modernization** transformation from traditional to modern societies. Takes place with European colonization and their imposition and spread of European or modern values and ways of thinking on the rest of the world. This perspective says traditional societies benefit from modernization – economically, politically, culturally, socially, and psychologically, as they "progress" from backward, primitive, uneducated societies to modern, enlightened, educated societies.

**monetarism** Milton Friedman and others theorized that the central bank should expand the money supply at a constant rate every year, equal to the rate of GDP growth, and irrespective of business cycles. In contrast to Keynesian theory. (3)

**monetary policy**, the Federal Reserve influences the flow or availability of money and credit. (7)

**moral hazard** someone's willingness to take risks – particularly excessive risks – that s/he would normally avoid, simply because s/he knows someone else will shoulder whatever negative consequences will follow. (7)

**mortgage** a loan secured by real property through the use of a mortgage note. (4)

**mortgage-backed securities** the collateral backing the securities are home mortgages. (7)

**multinational corporations (MNCs)** corporations that have services in at least two countries. (5)

**multiplier effect** of a government stimulus infusion. On average, the short-run multiplier for the U.S. economy is around 1.5. If the government spends a billion dollars now, GDP this year will go up by $1.5 billion. (8)

**nationalization** the government completely takes over a private enterprise. (8)

**natural monopoly** exists when the minimum size to guarantee maximum economic efficiency is equal to the actual size of the market. (3)

**neoliberalism** modern politico-economic theory favoring free trade, privatization, minimal government intervention in business, and reduced public expenditure on social services, etc. (1)

**nonprofit sector** (quaternary) an organization that uses surplus revenues to achieve its goals rather than distributing them as profit or dividends. (7)

**North American Free Trade Agreement (NAFTA)** signed on January 1, 1994 by President Bill Clinton. Created a free trade bloc between the U.S., Canada, and Mexico, with the goal of eliminating tariffs and regulations on investments. (3)

**notional value** total value of a leveraged position's assets. (7)

**open field system** peasants farmed large tracks of land for elite landlords. They produced food for their own subsistence needs, and paid a required amount of the surplus as tribute to the landowner. (2,3)

**Organization for Economic Cooperation and Development (OECD)** formed in 1961, formalized the economic bond of core democratic countries. The system brought economic growth, low unemployment, and stable prices. (2)

**OPEC (Organization of Oil Producing Countries)** in 1961 the major oil producing nations – Iran, Iraq, Kuwait, Saudi Arabia, and Venezuela – formed a cartel to regulate the price of oil and production. (2)

**originate and distribute** investment banks bought pools of home mortgage bonds from loan originators, securitized into bonds, and then sold to investors. (7)

**originate and hold** the bank would lend money to a homeowner, then collect payments on the principal and interest. The bank that originated the mortgage held the mortgage. (7)

**outsourcing** contracting out a business function to an external provider, usually to a low-wage country. (6)

**overcapacity** or overproduction means there is a tendency for capitalist economies to build up tremendous productive capacity to produce goods and services that outruns the population's capacity to consume. (2)

**overdetermined** a term that has multiple meanings depending upon one's particular perspective. (1)

**overshoot** humans are taking more resources from the planet than can be replaced by natural processes in a year. (6)

**participatory democracy** attempts to check the abuses of elite democracy and corporate economic and political power with oversight of the whole process. (4)

**periphery areas** drawn into a dependent relationship with the core regions; commercial wealth is extracted from the periphery in the form of cheap raw materials produced with cheap labor – or, more recently, manufactured goods produced with cheap labor. The wealth is siphoned to core areas where it is concentrated or generates more wealth. (1)

**Plaza Accord** in 1985, the U.S. directed Japan to raise the value of the yen against the dollar to offset its huge trade imbalance with the Japanese. (8)

**poverty** state of being poor, not having enough money to take care of basic needs such as food, clothing, and housing. (6)

**predatory lending** mortgage lenders were doing everything they could to sign up borrowers for subprime mortgages. (7)

**primary industries (sector)** wealth creation that includes mining, agriculture, forestry, trapping animals, and fishing – changed natural resources into primary products. (1)

**private sector** businesses owned by individuals or corporations. (3)

**privatization** the sale of state-owned enterprises, goods and services to private investors. Transfer of assets or service delivery from the government to the private sector. (3)

**progressive tax rates** increase as the taxable base amount increases, which means those who have a higher income pay more of their total income in taxes. Federal income taxes are progressive. (4)

**proprietary trading** when a firm trades various financial instruments with the firm's own money as opposed to its customers' money, so as to make a profit for itself. (8)

**public sector** where ownership is collectively held by the government for the people. (3)

**quantitative easing** used by Central Banks (the Fed) when interest rates are at or very near zero, and cannot be lowered any further, the Fed may purchase a number of bonds or other assets from financial institutions, thus, money is pumped into the economy. The goal is to increase the money supply rather than to decrease the interest rate, which is already around 0 percent, often considered a "last resort" to stimulate the economy. (8)

**quaternary sector** of the economy is informational and intellectual activities, which include government, libraries, culture, scientific research and development, education, consultation, and information technology. (7)

**reaction** a movement that favors extreme conservatism or right wing political views. They oppose political, economic, or social change or reforms and are considered to be at one end of a political spectrum. (8)

**rebuild** developing an alternative economic structure that takes into consideration the environment, social and economic justice, and human well-being. (8)

**reform** change into an improved form or condition. Not radical change, reform may be no more than redressing serious wrongs without altering the fundamentals of the system. (8)

**regressive tax rates** decrease as amount subject to taxation increases, those who have a higher income pay less of their total income on taxed items. Social security and Medicare (FICA) taxes are regressive. (4)

**reinforcing feedback** changes in the whole system feed back to amplify the original change. Change goes through the system, producing more change in the same direction as the initial change. It drives a system in the way it is going. Also called positive feedback. (1)

**revolution** an overthrow or repudiation and thorough replacement of an established government or political system by the people governed. (8)

**Riegle-Neal Interstate Banking and Branching Efficiency Act** of 1994 overturned the Bank Holding Act of 1956 and allowed interstate mergers between adequately capitalized and managed banks. (3)

*Santa Clara County v. Southern Pacific Railroad* 1886, the Supreme court's reporter sympathetic to the railroad barons, secretly inserted into the Court Reporter's headnotes the ruling that the railroad corporations were persons in the same category as humans. It stood in subsequent cases. (3)

**secondary industries (sector)** manufacturing and construction – process raw materials into manufactured goods. (1)

**Securities Exchange Act** of 1934, part of the New Deal reforms in the U.S., a law regulating the trading of stocks and bonds. (3)

**securitization** illiquid assets – not easily or quickly converted into money, like mortgages – could be pooled into bonds and made into liquid assets – easily and quickly converted into money – that were tradable on the open market. (7)

**self-reliance** trust in one's own capabilities, judgment, or resources; independence, reliance on one's own efforts and abilities. It is the opposite of dependence. (4)

**service industries** serving the customer rather than transforming physical goods. Includes retail, police, government, insurance, tourism, banking, education, public utilities, entertainment, legal, medical, accounting, finance, etc. (1)

**services** intangible goods provided to businesses and final consumers. (1)

**shadow banks** organizations that lend money to people like traditional banks, which comes from depositors, while shadow banks money comes from investors, they are not regulated by the government. (7)

**sixth extinction** alarming extinction of species, it follows five previous known extinctions in the Ordovician, Devonian, Permian, Triassic and Cretaceous periods. (6)

**slums** densely populated, squalid, sections of the cities inhabited by poor people, worldwide, approximately 1 billion people live in slums. (6)

**Smith, Adam** (1723-1790), Englishman, wrote *The Wealth of Nations* in 1776, he opposed mercantilism and instead argued that a free market or free trade economy was better. (2)

**social democracy** alternative to laissez faire capitalism in Western democracies during the 1930s, where workers and farmers demanded and got economic planning, social security, and labor rights. (2)

**social enterprises** organizations applying commercial strategies to maximize improvements in human and environmental well-being, rather than maximizing profits for external shareholders. (8)

**social gap** individuals do not have equal access to governmental social programs. Includes voting rights, freedom of speech and assembly, security, quality education, health care, and other social protections. (6)

**socialism** collective or governmental ownership and administration of the means of production and distribution of goods and services. (1)

**socioeconomic gap** combining two concepts into one: the social gap and economic gap. (6)

**sovereign wealth funds** state-owned investment funds composed of financial assets and invest globally. (1)

**specialization** individuals and organizations focus on the limited range of production tasks and skills they perform best. Workers give up performing other tasks they are not as skilled, leaving those jobs to others. (5)

**spreads** difference in what interest is paid depositors and the interest banks charge borrowers for loans. (7)

**stagflation** combination of low economic growth and high unemployment ("stagnation") with high rates of high inflation, occurred in the 1970s. (2)

**state capitalism** the state plays the role of leading economic actor and uses markets primarily for political gain. Public wealth, public investment and public enterprise offer the surest path toward economic development. (1)

**stimulus** government spending to counter economic stagnation and/or recession. (8)

**Structural Adjust Policy (SAPs)** the IMF issues emergency loan packages tied to certain conditions such as how much debtor countries can spend on education, health care, and environmental protection and they must open their markets to outside investment and development. (5)

**structural unemployment** a mismatch between workers' skills and the skills employers are seeking. (4)

**Stolper-Samuelson theorem** effect of trade between a core and a periphery nation, the wages for unskilled labor force in core nation is lower because of global competition with the unskilled workers in a periphery nation. (5)

**suprime mortgage** a new market of riskier but more profitable home loans to less creditworthy borrowers. (7)

**subsidy** form of financial assistance paid to a business or particular economic sector. (4)

**supply and demand** relation between these two factors determines the price of a commodity, thought to be the driving force in a free market. As demand for an item increases, prices rise. (2)

**supply side economics** emphasizes the importance of tax cuts and business supports to encourage economic growth, with the belief they will use their tax savings to create new businesses and expand old businesses. (3)

**synthetic CDO** complex financial security used to speculate that an obligation will not be paid. Negotiated between counterparties that have different viewpoints about what will happen to the underlying security. (7)

**synthetic CDS** collateralized debt obligation (CDO), invests in credit default swaps (CDSs) or other assets. (7)

**system** something that maintains its existence and functions as a whole through the interaction of its parts. (1)

**systems thinking** a way of thinking in which the whole system is understood and recognized as interconnected, reoccurring patterns in the system and the interrelationships of these patterns are recognized. (1)

**tariffs** duties or customs imposed by government on exports or imports. (2, 3)

**Telecommunications Act** 1996, passed under President Clinton, amended the Communications Act of 1934, deregulated the broadcasting market, media cross-ownership was now allowed. (3)

**tertiary sector** the service industry. (7)

**trade deficit** when a country imports more than it exports, it accumulates a trade deficit. (2)

**Trade-Related Aspects of Intellectual Property Rights (TRIPS)** introduced intellectual property law into the international trading system for the first time, under the purview of the WTO that sets minimum standards. (5)

**transformative worldview** alternative to prevailing notions of cultural uniformity, corporate dominance, consumer-driven values, unchecked individualism, concentration of wealth and power, and environmental destruction. (1)

**transparency** another word for information. (7)

**Treaty of Detroit** 1950s, understanding between capital and labor, employers accepted that compensation would grow as productivity increased, continued until the crisis of the 1970s when labor compensation exceeded productivity. (4)

**Triangle Trade** 18th century, trade between Africa, Europe, and the Americas. European ships carried guns, knives, metal ware, manufactured items, beads, colored cloth, and liquor to the West African coast to be exchanged with African slaves, who were shipped to the Americas and exchanged for raw materials, such as sugar, tobacco, furs, precious metals, and raw cotton that were transported to Europe to be made into finished goods that started the trading network again. (2)

**Troubled Asset Relief Program (TARP)** a $700 billion government program to purchase assets and equity from financial institutions in the fall of 2008 with the intended purpose to strengthen the financial sector. (8)

**tulip mania** first financial crisis or speculative bubble in modern history, occurred in 17th century Netherlands. (8)

**underwater** meaning the value of homes has fallen so much it is now below the value of their original mortgage. (4)

**Volcker, Paul** Chairman of the Federal Reserve (1979-1987), he pushed short-term interest rates up to above 20%, stayed at these high levels for almost three years in order to break inflation. (2)

**Volcker Rule** named after former Fed chair Paul Volcker, it would prevent federally insured banks from engaging in speculation such as in proprietary trading when customers' deposits are used to trade on the bank's own accounts to make a profit for itself. (8)

**Wall Street** located in the financial district of lower Manhattan in New York City. A collective phrase to refer to the financial sector of the economy, the phantom economy, opposite of Main Street considered to be the real economy. (7)

**Washington Consensus** named for the three institutions that shaped global neoliberal policies, all located in downtown Washington D.C.: IMF, World Bank, and the U.S. Treasury. (5)

**welfare capitalism** 1930s, corporations in Western social democracies backed economic, social, and labor reforms. (2)

**well-being** a kind of contentment, happiness, or a state of life-satisfaction. (6)

**Western** ideas, often called liberalism, emerged during Enlightenment era or added later and partially include a representative government, individual rights and freedoms (speech and press), private property, scientific method, reason, individualism, freedom of religion or secularism, and later women's and gay rights. (1)

**Western U.S. Energy Crisis** of 2000 and 2001, in which California had a shortage of electricity caused by market manipulations and illegal shutdowns of pipelines by primarily the Enron corporation. (3)

**white man's burden** satirized by Rudyard Kipling's poem of the same name, this philosophy placed responsibility on Christians and Europeans to "civilize" those considered unfortunate enough to be non-Western. (2)

**worker ownership** where workers have an equal equity stake in the company they are working for; they share common goals and adhere to common principles. (8)

**World Bank** provides loans to developing countries for capital programs with the stated goal of reducing poverty. (5)

**World Trade Organization** (WTO) deals with regulation of trade between participating countries; it provides a framework for negotiating and formalizing trade agreements, and a dispute resolution process. (5)

**worldview** an overall perspective from which one sees and interprets the world, a set of simplifying suppositions about how the world works and what is seen and not seen. It is an internal collection of assumptions, held by an individual or a group that are firmly believed to be self-evident truths. (1)

# List of Commonly Used Acronyms

AAA     triple A rated securities, the best
ABS     asset-backed security
AIG     American International Group
AU     African Union
BP     British Petroleum
BRIC     countries Brazil, Russia, India, and China
CBO     Congressional Budget Office
CDO     collateralized debt obligation
CDS     credit default swap
CEO     Chief Executive Officer
CFTC     Commodity Futures Trading Commission
CPFF     Commercial Paper Funding Facility
CRA     credit rating agency
DRC     Democratic Republic of the Congo
DSB     Dispute Settlement Body
EOI     Export-Oriented Industrialization
EU     European Union
FDIC     Federal Deposit Insurance Corporation
FHFA     Federal Housing Finance Agency
GATT     General Agreement on Tariffs and Trade
GDP     Gross Domestic Product (or GNP Gross National Product)
GE     General Electric
GE     genetically engineered
GM     General Motors Corporation
GMO     genetically modified organisms
GNP     Gross National Happiness
GPI     Genuine Progress Indicator
GSE     Government Sponsored Entity
HDI     Human Development Index
IMF     International Monetary Fund
IP     Intellectual Property
ISI     Import Substitution Industrialization
LDC     Least Developed Countries
MBS     Mortgage Backed Securities
MNC     multinational corporation
OECD     Organization for Economic Cooperation and Development
OPEC     Organization of Oil Producing Countries
S & P     Standard & Poor's
SEC     Securities and Exchange Commission
SLABS     Student Loan Asset Backed Securities
TARP     Troubled Asset Relief Program
TBTF     too big to fail
TRIPS     Trade-Related Aspects of Intellectual Property Rights
TVA     Tennessee Valley Authority
UAW     United Auto Workers
UK     United Kingdom
U.S.     United States
WTO     World Trade Organization

# Index

## F

factory 61, 343
fallacy of composition 311, 343
Fannie Mae (Federal National Mortgage Association) 278, 343
farmers market 335, 344
fascism 23
Federal Deposit Insurance Corporation (FDIC) 269, 344, 352
Federal Reserve 274–277, 321–322, 328, 344
feedback 41–42, 344
financialization 30, 263, 344
Financial Services Modernization Act 272–273, 344
fine-tuning 344
fiscal austerity 189, 344
fiscal policy 275, 344
float 85, 344
Fordism 75, 344
Freddie Mac (Federal Home Loan Mortgage Corp.) 278, 344
free trade 22, 101–107, 190–196, 344
Friedman, Milton 96–100
full employment profit squeeze 87, 130, 344
fundamentalism 46–47, 344
futures trading 287, 344

## G

General Agreement on Tariffs and Trade (GATT) 82, 191–192, 344, 352
Genuine Progress Indicator (GPI) 246, 247, 344, 352
Glass-Steagall Act 113, 269, 344
globalization 21–22, 93, 176–215, 218–257, 344
globalized worldview 47, 48, 49, 50, 345
global warming 225, 344
Global Wave 43–45, 344
"golden straight-jacket" 188, 345
gold standard 65–67, 345
Government National Mortgage Association (Ginnie Mae) 279, 344
Gramm-Leach-Bliley Act *see Financial Services Modernization Act*
Great Depression 76–77, 129, 305–306
Great Recession 51
greenhouse gas 225–226, 345
Greenspan, Alan 98–100, 276–277
Gross Domestic Product (GDP) 140–142, 347, 352
Gross National Happiness (GNP) 252–253, 345, 352
guild 54–55, 345

## H

haircut 320, 345
Heckscher–Ohlin 208
hedge funds 286, 345
hegemony 210, 345
holistic 21, 37–38, 345,
home equity loans 281, 345
*Homo Economicus* 123, 345
hostile takeovers 151, 345
human rights 126

## I

illiquid assets 279, 346
immigration 64–65
imperialism 68–70, 211, 345
import substitution industrialization (ISI) 78–79, 83–84, 89–90, 345, 352
indigenous peoples 44–45, 345
individualism 131–133
industrial capitalism 59–73
industrialization 59–60, 345
Industrial Revolution 59, 61, 345
inequality 166–172, 233–245, 345
infant industry argument 102, 346
inflation 275, 346
infrastructure ?????
Intellectual Property (IP) 193, 346
International Monetary Fund (IMF) 184–185, 187–189, 346, 352
investment banks 269, 346

## J

joint stock companies 58, 124–125, 346
junk bonds 289, 346
just price 54, 346

## K

Keynes, John Maynard 26, 80–82, 346

## L

labor 63–65, 128–131, 162–166, 208–210, 329–330, 346
labor productivity 164, 346
laissez faire capitalism 346
left 35–36
Lehman 313–315
lender of last resort 271, 346
leverage 41, 283–284, 346

354

## About the Author

Dr. Denise R. Ames is an educator with over 30 years teaching experience at secondary schools, universities, a community college, adult educational programs, and professional development workshops. She took her bachelor's degree in history education from Southern Illinois University, and master's degree and doctorate in history education with a focus in world history from Illinois State University. Her teaching topics range from academic subjects such as world history, global issues, United States history, Western Civilization, world humanities, cultural studies, and global business issues, to secondary social studies classes, pedagogy, and current topics such as global issues, the global economy, and global education.

Dr. Ames is currently the founder and President of the Center for Global Awareness, a non-profit organization developing globally-focused books and educational resources for students and educators in grades 9 through college. She is dedicated to working with teachers, students, and the general public to foster a better understanding of the myriad of global issues we face, a teaching model for world history, and the effects of the global economy on ourselves, the global community, and the environment. She has presented numerous classes, workshops, and lectures on her holistic world history and the global economy locally, nationally, and internationally. She is the author of *Waves of Global Change: A Holistic World History* and its accompanying book for educators: *Waves of Global Change: An Educator's Handbook for Teaching a Holistic World History*. Along with this book, *The Global Economy: Connecting the Roots of a Holistic System*, is the forthcoming book *Financial Literacy: Wall Street and How it Works*. She is finishing her partially completed book for students and educators on human rights.

World cultures and history have been Dr. Ames' life-long interest and study. Her extensive travels, personal experiences, reflections, and scholarly research have all contributed to her common sense approach to the often overwhelming subjects she teaches. Her extensive travels have taken her throughout Europe, and she has visited several countries in the Middle East/Southwest Asia region, including Iran, Syria, Palestine, Israel, Turkey, and Lebanon. She has also traveled to Mexico, Brazil, Paraguay, and Argentina. She visited the former Soviet Union in 1989 and taught word history at the Vladimir Pedagogical Institute in 1998. She found in her two trips to China, in 1991 and 2011 that the country had changed dramatically.

Along with her professional interests and work in history, global issues, and education, Dr. Ames has owned her own small business for eight years, constructed and remodeled eight houses, and exhibited and trained Arabian horses. She has two adult children and their spouses, and one granddaughter. She particularly enjoys traveling, hiking, yoga, reading, biking, gardening, and visiting with family and friends. She and her husband Jim currently reside near the campus of the University of New Mexico in sunny Albuquerque, New Mexico.

www.ingramcontent.com/pod-product-compliance
Lightning Source LLC
Chambersburg PA
CBHW051204200326

41519CB00025B/6998